MW01040525

TOYOTA
CRESSIDA AND VAN
1983-90 REPAIR MANUAL

CHILTON'S

Covers all U.S. and Canadian models of Toyota Cressida and Van

by Dawn M. Hoch, S.A.E.

CHILTON *Automotive Books*

PUBLISHED BY **HAYNES NORTH AMERICA**, Inc.

Manufactured in USA
© 1997 Haynes North America, Inc.
ISBN 0-8019-9066-1
Library of Congress Catalog Card No. 97-67984
5678901234 9876543210

Haynes Publishing Group
Sparkford Nr Yeovil
Somerset BA22 7JJ England

Haynes North America, Inc
861 Lawrence Drive
Newbury Park
California 91320 USA

ABCDE
FGHIJ
K

7F1

Contents

Contents

DRIVE TRAIN

7

SUSPENSION AND STEERING

8

BRAKES

9

BODY

10

GLOSSARY

MASTER INDEX

SAFETY NOTICE

Proper service and repair procedures are vital to the safe, reliable operation of all motor vehicles, as well as the personal safety of those performing repairs. This manual outlines procedures for servicing and repairing vehicles using safe, effective methods. The procedures contain many NOTES, CAUTIONS and WARNINGS which should be followed, along with standard procedures to eliminate the possibility of personal injury or improper service which could damage the vehicle or compromise its safety.

It is important to note that repair procedures and techniques, tools and parts for servicing motor vehicles, as well as the skill and experience of the individual performing the work vary widely. It is not possible to anticipate all of the conceivable ways or conditions under which vehicles may be serviced, or to provide cautions as to all possible hazards that may result. Standard and accepted safety precautions and equipment should be used when handling toxic or flammable fluids, and safety goggles or other protection should be used during cutting, grinding, chiseling, prying, or any other process that can cause material removal or projectiles.

Some procedures require the use of tools specially designed for a specific purpose. Before substituting another tool or procedure, you must be completely satisfied that neither your personal safety, nor the performance of the vehicle will be endangered.

Although information in this manual is based on industry sources and is complete as possible at the time of publication, the possibility exists that some car manufacturers made later changes which could not be included here. While striving for total accuracy, the authors or publishers cannot assume responsibility for any errors, changes or omissions that may occur in the compilation of this data.

PART NUMBERS

Part numbers listed in this reference are not recommendations by Haynes North America, Inc. for any product brand name. They are references that can be used with interchange manuals and aftermarket supplier catalogs to locate each brand supplier's discrete part number.

SPECIAL TOOLS

Special tools are recommended by the vehicle manufacturer to perform their specific job. Use has been kept to a minimum, but where absolutely necessary, they are referred to in the text by the part number of the tool manufacturer. These tools can be purchased, under the appropriate part number, from your local dealer or regional distributor, or an equivalent tool can be purchased locally from a tool supplier or parts outlet. Before substituting any tool for the one recommended, read the SAFETY NOTICE at the top of this page.

ACKNOWLEDGMENTS

The publisher expresses appreciation to Toyota Motor Corporation for their generous assistance.

1

GENERAL INFORMATION AND MAINTENANCE

HOW TO USE THIS BOOK

Chilton's Total Car Care manual is intended to help you learn more about the inner workings of your vehicle while saving you money on its upkeep and operation.

The beginning of the book will likely be referred to the most, since that is where you will find information for maintenance and tune-up. The other sections deal with the more complex systems of your vehicle. Operating systems from engine through brakes are covered to the extent that the average do-it-yourselfer becomes mechanically involved. This book will not explain such things as rebuilding a differential for the simple reason that the expertise required and the investment in special tools make this task uneconomical. It will, however, give you detailed instructions to help you change your own brake pads and shoes, replace spark plugs, and perform many more jobs that can save you money, give you personal satisfaction and help you avoid expensive problems.

A secondary purpose of this book is a reference for owners who want to understand their vehicle and/or their mechanics better. In this case, no tools at all are required.

Where to Begin

Before removing any bolts, read through the entire procedure. This will give you the overall view of what tools and supplies will be required. There is nothing more frustrating than having to walk to the bus stop on Monday morning because you were short one bolt on Sunday afternoon. So read ahead and plan ahead. Each operation should be approached logically and all procedures thoroughly understood before attempting any work.

All sections contain adjustments, maintenance, removal and installation procedures, and in some cases, repair or overhaul procedures. When repair is not considered practical, we tell you how to remove the part and then how to install the new or rebuilt replacement. In this way, you at least save the labor costs. Backyard repair of some components is just not practical.

Avoiding Trouble

Many procedures in this book require you to "label and disconnect . . ." a group of lines, hoses or wires. Don't be lulled into thinking you can remember where everything goes—you won't. If you hook up vacuum or fuel lines incorrectly, the vehicle will run poorly, if at all. If you hook up electrical wiring incorrectly, you may instantly learn a very expensive lesson.

You don't need to know the official or engineering name for each hose or line. A piece of masking tape on the hose and a piece on its fitting will allow you to assign your own label such as the letter A or a short name. As long as you remember your own code, the lines can be reconnected by matching similar letters or names. Do remember that tape will dissolve in gasoline or other fluids; if a component is to be washed or cleaned, use another method of identification. A permanent felt-tipped marker can be very handy for marking metal parts. Remove any tape or paper labels after assembly.

Maintenance or Repair?

It's necessary to mention the difference between maintenance and repair. Maintenance includes routine inspections, adjustments, and replacement of parts which show signs of normal wear. Maintenance compensates for wear or deterioration. Repair implies that something has broken or is not working. A need for repair is often caused by lack of maintenance. Example: draining and refilling the automatic transmission fluid is maintenance recommended by the manufacturer at specific mileage intervals. Failure to do this can ruin the transmission/transaxle, requiring very expensive repairs. While no maintenance program can prevent items from breaking or wearing out, a general rule can be stated: MAINTENANCE IS CHEAPER THAN REPAIR.

Two basic mechanic's rules should be mentioned here. First, whenever the left side of the vehicle or engine is referred to, it is meant to specify the driver's side. Conversely, the right side of the vehicle means the passenger's side. Second, most screws and bolts are removed by turning counterclockwise, and tightened by turning clockwise.

Safety is always the most important rule. Constantly be aware of the dangers involved in working on an automobile and take the proper precautions. See the information in this section regarding SERVICING YOUR VEHICLE SAFELY and the SAFETY NOTICE on the acknowledgment page.

Avoiding the Most Common Mistakes

Pay attention to the instructions provided. There are 3 common mistakes in mechanical work:

1. **Incorrect order of assembly, disassembly or adjustment.** When taking something apart or putting it together, performing steps in the wrong order usually just costs you extra time; however, it CAN break something. Read the entire procedure before beginning disassembly. Perform everything in the order in which the instructions say you should, even if you can't immediately see a reason for it. When you're taking apart something that is very intricate, you might want to draw a picture of how it looks when assembled at one point in order to make sure you get everything back in its proper position. We will supply exploded views whenever possible. When making adjustments, perform them in the proper order; often, one adjustment affects another, and you cannot expect even satisfactory results unless each adjustment is made only when it cannot be changed by any other.

2. **Overtorquing (or undertorquing).** While it is more common for overtorquing to cause damage, undertorquing may allow a fastener to vibrate loose causing serious damage. Especially when dealing with aluminum parts, pay attention to torque specifications and utilize a torque wrench in assembly. If a torque figure is not available, remember that if you are using the right tool to perform the job, you will probably not have to strain yourself to get a fastener tight enough. The pitch of most threads is so slight that the tension you put on the wrench will be multiplied many times in actual force on what you are tightening. A good example of how critical torque is can be seen in the case of spark plug in-

stallation, especially where you are putting the plug into an aluminum cylinder head. Too little torque can fail to crush the gasket, causing leakage of combustion gases and consequent overheating of the plug and engine parts. Too much torque can damage the threads or distort the plug, changing the spark gap.

There are many commercial products available for ensuring that fasteners won't come loose, even if they are not torqued just right (a very common brand is Loctite®). If you're worried about getting something together tight enough to hold, but loose enough to avoid mechanical damage during assembly, one of these products might offer substantial insurance. Before choosing a threadlocking compound, read the label on the package and make sure the product is compatible with the materials, fluids, etc. involved.

3. **Crossthreading.** This occurs when a part such as a bolt is screwed into a nut or casting at the wrong angle and forced. Crossthreading is more likely to occur if access is difficult. It helps to clean and lubricate fasteners, then to start threading with the part to be installed positioned straight in. Then, start the bolt, spark plug, etc. with your fingers. If you encounter resistance, unscrew the part and start over again at a different angle until it can be inserted and turned several times without much effort. Keep in mind that many parts, especially spark plugs, have tapered threads, so that gentle turning will automatically bring the part you're threading to the proper angle, but only if you don't force it or resist a change in angle. Don't put a wrench on the part until it's been tightened a couple of turns by hand. If you suddenly encounter resistance, and the part has not seated fully, don't force it. Pull it back out to make sure it's clean and threading properly.

Always take your time and be patient; once you have some experience, working on your vehicle may well become an enjoyable hobby.

TOOLS AND EQUIPMENT

Naturally, without the proper tools and equipment it is impossible to properly service your vehicle. It would also be virtually impossible to catalog every tool that you would need to perform all of the operations in this book. Of course, It would be unwise for the amateur to rush out and buy an expensive set of tools on the theory that he/she may need one or more of them at some time.

The best approach is to proceed slowly, gathering a good quality set of those tools that are used most frequently. Don't be misled by the low cost of bargain tools. It is far better to spend a little more for better quality. Forged wrenches, 6 or 12-point sockets and fine tooth ratchets are by far preferable to their less expensive counterparts. As any good mechanic can tell you, there are few worse experiences than trying to work on a vehicle with bad tools. Your monetary savings will be far outweighed by frustration and mangled knuckles.

Begin accumulating those tools that are used most frequently: those associated with routine maintenance and tune-up. In addition to the normal assortment of screwdrivers and pliers, you should have the following tools:

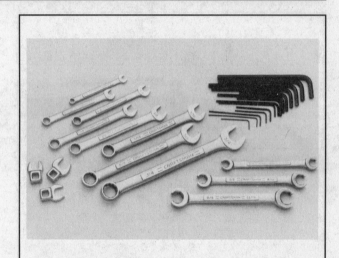

In addition to ratchets, a good set of wrenches and hex keys will be necessary

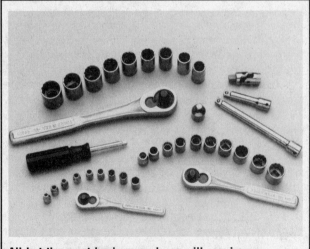

All but the most basic procedures will require an assortment of ratchets and sockets

A hydraulic floor jack and a set of jackstands are essential for lifting and supporting the vehicle

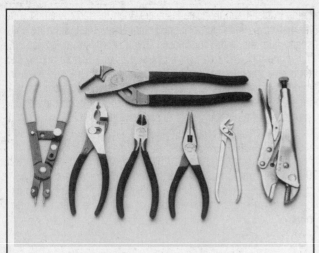

An assortment of pliers, grippers and cutters will be handy for old rusted parts and stripped bolt heads

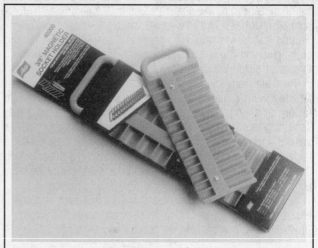

Tools from specialty manufacturers such as Lisle® are designed to make your job easier . . .

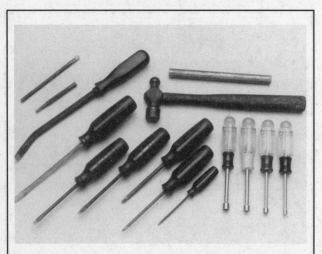

Various drivers, chisels and prybars are great tools to have in your toolbox

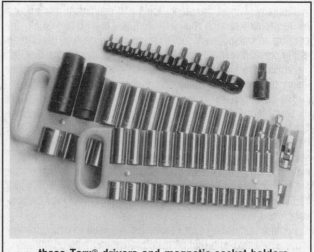

. . . these Torx® drivers and magnetic socket holders are just 2 examples of their handy products

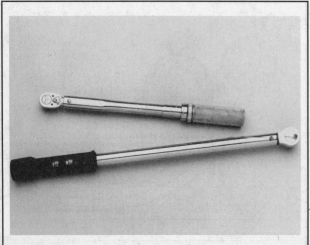

Many repairs will require the use of a torque wrench to assure the components are properly fastened

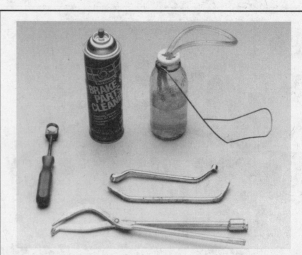

Although not always necessary, using specialized brake tools will save time

A few inexpensive lubrication tools will make maintenance easier

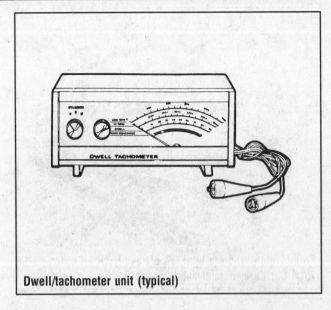

Dwell/tachometer unit (typical)

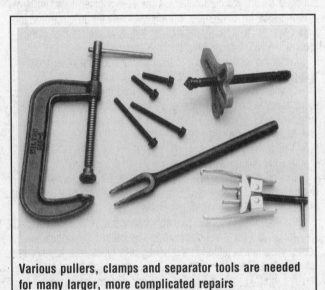

Various pullers, clamps and separator tools are needed for many larger, more complicated repairs

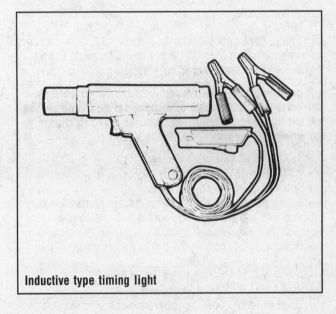

Inductive type timing light

A variety of tools and gauges should be used for spark plug gapping and installation

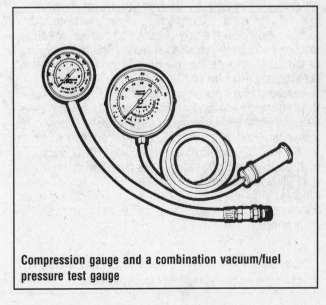

Compression gauge and a combination vacuum/fuel pressure test gauge

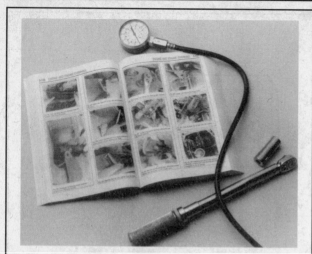

Proper information is vital, so always have a Chilton Total Car Care manual handy

• Wrenches/sockets and combination open end/box end wrenches in sizes from ⅛–¾ in. or 3mm–19mm (depending on whether your vehicle uses standard or metric fasteners) and a ¹³⁄₁₆ in. or ⅝ in. spark plug socket (depending on plug type).

➡**If possible, buy various length socket drive extensions. Universal-joint and wobble extensions can be extremely useful, but be careful when using them, as they can change the amount of torque applied to the socket.**

• Jackstands for support.
• Oil filter wrench.
• Spout or funnel for pouring fluids.
• Grease gun for chassis lubrication (unless your vehicle is not equipped with any grease fittings—for details, please refer to information on Fluids and Lubricants found later in this section).
• Hydrometer for checking the battery (unless equipped with a sealed, maintenance-free battery).
• A container for draining oil and other fluids.
• Rags for wiping up the inevitable mess.

In addition to the above items there are several others that are not absolutely necessary, but handy to have around. These include Oil Dry® (or an equivalent oil absorbent gravel—such as cat litter) and the usual supply of lubricants, antifreeze and fluids, although these can be purchased as needed. This is a basic list for routine maintenance, but only your personal needs and desire can accurately determine your list of tools.

After performing a few projects on the vehicle, you'll be amazed at the other tools and non-tools on your workbench. Some useful household items are: a large turkey baster or siphon, empty coffee cans and ice trays (to store parts), ball of twine, electrical tape for wiring, small rolls of colored tape for tagging lines or hoses, markers and pens, a note pad, golf tees (for plugging vacuum lines), metal coat hangers or a roll of mechanics's wire (to hold things out of the way), dental pick or similar long, pointed probe, a strong magnet, and a small mirror (to see into recesses and under manifolds).

A more advanced set of tools, suitable for tune-up work, can be drawn up easily. While the tools are slightly more sophisticated, they need not be outrageously expensive. There are several inexpensive tach/dwell meters on the market that are every bit as good for the average mechanic as a professional model. Just be sure that it goes to a least 1200–1500 rpm on the tach scale and that it works on 4, 6 and 8-cylinder engines. (If you own one or more vehicles with a diesel engine, a special tachometer is required since diesels don't use spark plug ignition systems). The key to these purchases is to make them with an eye towards adaptability and wide range. A basic list of tune-up tools could include:

• Tach/dwell meter.
• Spark plug wrench and gapping tool.
• Feeler gauges for valve or point adjustment. (Even if your vehicle does not use points or require valve adjustments, a feeler gauge is helpful for many repair/overhaul procedures).

A tachometer/dwell meter will ensure accurate tune-up work on vehicles without electronic ignition. The choice of a timing light should be made carefully. A light which works on the DC current supplied by the vehicle's battery is the best choice; it should have a xenon tube for brightness. On any vehicle with an electronic ignition system, a timing light with an inductive pickup that clamps around the No. 1 spark plug cable is preferred.

In addition to these basic tools, there are several other tools and gauges you may find useful. These include:

• Compression gauge. The screw-in type is slower to use, but eliminates the possibility of a faulty reading due to escaping pressure.
• Manifold vacuum gauge.
• 12V test light.
• A combination volt/ohmmeter
• Induction Ammeter. This is used for determining whether or not there is current in a wire. These are handy for use if a wire is broken somewhere in a wiring harness.

As a final note, you will probably find a torque wrench necessary for all but the most basic work. The beam type models are perfectly adequate, although the newer click types (breakaway) are easier to use. The click type torque wrenches tend to be more expensive. Also keep in mind that all types of torque wrenches should be periodically checked and/or recalibrated. You will have to decide for yourself which better fits your purpose.

Special Tools

Normally, the use of special factory tools is avoided for repair procedures, since these are not readily available for the do-it-yourself mechanic. When it is possible to perform the job with more commonly available tools, it will be pointed out, but occasionally, a special tool was designed to perform a specific function and should be used. Before substituting another tool, you should be convinced that neither your safety nor the performance of the vehicle will be compromised.

Special tools can usually be purchased from an automotive parts store or from your dealer. In some cases special tools may be available directly from the tool manufacturer.

SERVICING YOUR VEHICLE SAFELY

It is virtually impossible to anticipate all of the hazards involved with automotive maintenance and service, but care and common sense will prevent most accidents.

The rules of safety for mechanics range from "don't smoke around gasoline," to "use the proper tool(s) for the job." The trick to avoiding injuries is to develop safe work habits and to take every possible precaution.

Do's

• Do keep a fire extinguisher and first aid kit handy.
• Do wear safety glasses or goggles when cutting, drilling, grinding or prying, even if you have 20–20 vision. If you wear glasses for the sake of vision, wear safety goggles over your regular glasses.
• Do shield your eyes whenever you work around the battery. Batteries contain sulfuric acid. In case of contact with the eyes or

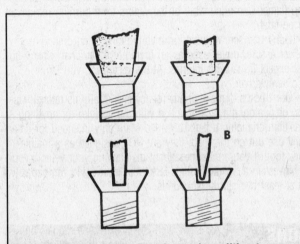

Screwdrivers should be kept in good condition to prevent injury or damage which could result if the blade slips from the screw

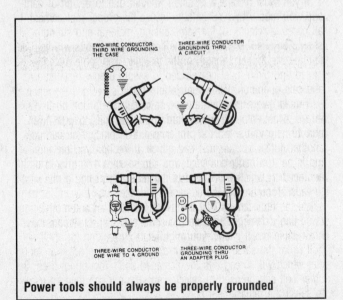

Power tools should always be properly grounded

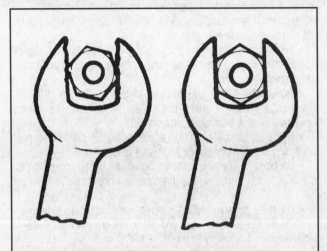

Using the correct size wrench will help prevent the possibility of rounding off a nut

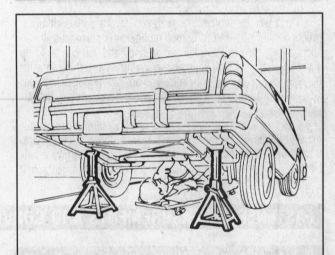

NEVER work under a vehicle unless it is supported using safety stands (jackstands)

skin, flush the area with water or a mixture of water and baking soda, then seek immediate medical attention.
• Do use safety stands (jackstands) for any undervehicle service. Jacks are for raising vehicles; jackstands are for making sure the vehicle stays raised until you want it to come down. Whenever the vehicle is raised, block the wheels remaining on the ground and set the parking brake.
• Do use adequate ventilation when working with any chemicals or hazardous materials. Like carbon monoxide, the asbestos dust resulting from some brake lining wear can be hazardous in sufficient quantities.
• Do disconnect the negative battery cable when working on the electrical system. The secondary ignition system contains EXTREMELY HIGH VOLTAGE. In some cases it can even exceed 50,000 volts.
• Do follow manufacturer's directions whenever working with potentially hazardous materials. Most chemicals and fluids are poisonous if taken internally.

• Do properly maintain your tools. Loose hammerheads, mushroomed punches and chisels, frayed or poorly grounded electrical cords, excessively worn screwdrivers, spread wrenches (open end), cracked sockets, slipping ratchets, or faulty droplight sockets can cause accidents.

• Likewise, keep your tools clean; a greasy wrench can slip off a bolt head, ruining the bolt and often harming your knuckles in the process.

• Do use the proper size and type of tool for the job at hand. Do select a wrench or socket that fits the nut or bolt. The wrench or socket should sit straight, not cocked.

• Do, when possible, pull on a wrench handle rather than push on it, and adjust your stance to prevent a fall.

• Do be sure that adjustable wrenches are tightly closed on the nut or bolt and pulled so that the force is on the side of the fixed jaw.

• Do strike squarely with a hammer; avoid glancing blows.

• Do set the parking brake and block the drive wheels if the work requires a running engine.

Don'ts

• Don't run the engine in a garage or anywhere else without proper ventilation—EVER! Carbon monoxide is poisonous; it takes a long time to leave the human body and you can build up a deadly supply of it in your system by simply breathing in a little every day. You may not realize you are slowly poisoning yourself. Always use power vents, windows, fans and/or open the garage door.

• Don't work around moving parts while wearing loose clothing. Short sleeves are much safer than long, loose sleeves. Hard-toed shoes with neoprene soles protect your toes and give a better grip on slippery surfaces. Jewelry such as watches, fancy belt buckles, beads or body adornment of any kind is not safe working around a vehicle. Long hair should be tied back under a hat or cap.

• Don't use pockets for toolboxes. A fall or bump can drive a screwdriver deep into your body. Even a rag hanging from your back pocket can wrap around a spinning shaft or fan.

• Don't smoke when working around gasoline, cleaning solvent or other flammable material.

• Don't smoke when working around the battery. When the battery is being charged, it gives off explosive hydrogen gas.

• Don't use gasoline to wash your hands; there are excellent soaps available. Gasoline contains dangerous additives which can enter the body through a cut or through your pores. Gasoline also removes all the natural oils from the skin so that bone dry hands will suck up oil and grease.

• Don't service the air conditioning system unless you are equipped with the necessary tools and training. When liquid or compressed gas refrigerant is released to atmospheric pressure it will absorb heat from whatever it contacts. This will chill or freeze anything it touches. Although refrigerant is normally non-toxic, R-12 becomes a deadly poisonous gas in the presence of an open flame. One good whiff of the vapors from burning refrigerant can be fatal.

• Don't use screwdrivers for anything other than driving screws! A screwdriver used as an prying tool can snap when you least expect it, causing injuries. At the very least, you'll ruin a good screwdriver.

• Don't use a bumper or emergency jack (that little ratchet, scissors, or pantograph jack supplied with the vehicle) for anything other than changing a flat! These jacks are only intended for emergency use out on the road; they are NOT designed as a maintenance tool. If you are serious about maintaining your vehicle yourself, invest in a hydraulic floor jack of at least a 1½ ton capacity, and at least two sturdy jackstands.

FASTENERS, MEASUREMENTS AND CONVERSIONS

Bolts, Nuts and Other Threaded Retainers

Although there are a great variety of fasteners found in the modern car or truck, the most commonly used retainer is the threaded fastener (nuts, bolts, screws, studs, etc). Most threaded retainers may be reused, provided that they are not damaged in use or during the repair. Some retainers (such as stretch bolts or torque prevailing nuts) are designed to deform when tightened or in use and should not be reinstalled.

Whenever possible, we will note any special retainers which should be replaced during a procedure. But you should always inspect the condition of a retainer when it is removed and replace any that show signs of damage. Check all threads for rust or corrosion which can increase the torque necessary to achieve the desired clamp load for which that fastener was originally selected. Additionally, be sure that the driver surface of the fastener has not been compromised by rounding or other damage. In some cases a driver surface may become only partially rounded, allowing the driver to catch in only one direction. In many of these occurrences, a fastener may be installed and tightened, but the driver would not be able to grip and loosen the fastener again. (This could lead to frustration down the line should that component ever need to be disassembled again).

If you must replace a fastener, whether due to design or damage, you must ALWAYS be sure to use the proper replacement. In all cases, a retainer of the same design, material and strength should be used. Markings on the heads of most bolts will help determine the proper strength of the fastener. The same material, thread and pitch must be selected to assure proper installation and safe operation of the vehicle afterwards.

Thread gauges are available to help measure a bolt or stud's thread. Most automotive and hardware stores keep gauges available to help you select the proper size. In a pinch, you can use another nut or bolt for a thread gauge. If the bolt you are replacing is not too badly damaged, you can select a match by finding another bolt which will thread in its place. If you find a nut which threads properly onto the damaged bolt, then use that nut to help select the replacement bolt. If however, the bolt you are replacing is so badly damaged (broken or drilled out) that its threads cannot be used as a gauge, you might start by looking for another bolt (from the same assembly or a similar location on your vehicle) which will thread into the damaged bolt's mounting. If so, the other bolt can be used to select a nut; the nut can then be used to select the replacement bolt.

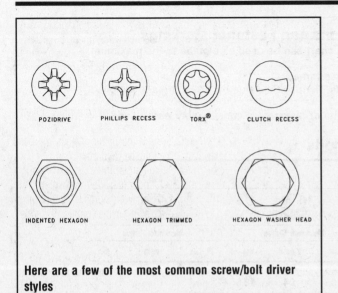

Here are a few of the most common screw/bolt driver styles

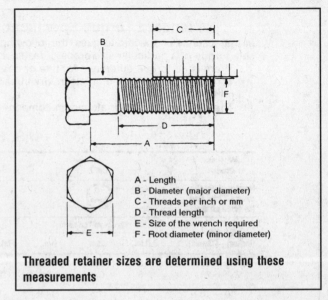

A - Length
B - Diameter (major diameter)
C - Threads per inch or mm
D - Thread length
E - Size of the wrench required
F - Root diameter (minor diameter)

Threaded retainer sizes are determined using these measurements

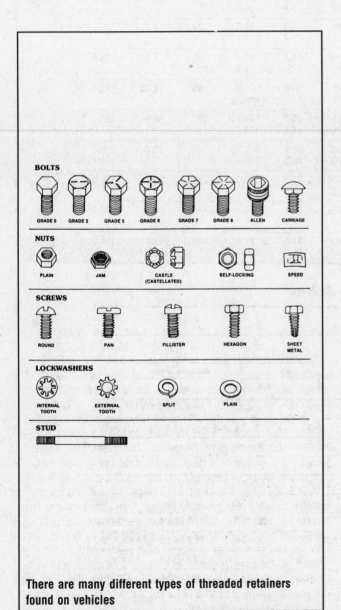

There are many different types of threaded retainers found on vehicles

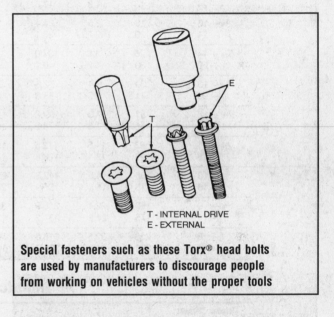

T - INTERNAL DRIVE
E - EXTERNAL

Special fasteners such as these Torx® head bolts are used by manufacturers to discourage people from working on vehicles without the proper tools

In all cases, be absolutely sure you have selected the proper replacement. Don't be shy, you can always ask the store clerk for help.

✳✳ WARNING

Be aware that when you find a bolt with damaged threads, you may also find the nut or drilled hole it was threaded into has also been damaged. If this is the case, you may have to drill and tap the hole, replace the nut or otherwise repair the threads. NEVER try to force a replacement bolt to fit into the damaged threads.

Torque

Torque is defined as the measurement of resistance to turning or rotating. It tends to twist a body about an axis of rotation. A common example of this would be tightening a threaded retainer such as a nut, bolt or screw. Measuring torque is one of the most

Standard Torque Specifications and Fastener Markings

In the absence of specific torques, the following chart can be used as a guide to the maximum safe torque of a particular size/grade of fastener.

- There is no torque difference for fine or coarse threads.
- Torque values are based on clean, dry threads. Reduce the value by 10% if threads are oiled prior to assembly.
- The torque required for aluminum components or fasteners is considerably less.

U.S. Bolts

SAE Grade Number	1 or 2			5			6 or 7		
Number of lines always 2 less than the grade number.									
Bolt Size (Inches)—(Thread)	Maximum Torque			Maximum Torque			Maximum Torque		
	Ft./Lbs.	Kgm	Nm	Ft./Lbs.	Kgm	Nm	Ft./Lbs.	Kgm	Nm
¼ — 20	5	0.7	6.8	8	1.1	10.8	10	1.4	13.5
— 28	6	0.8	8.1	10	1.4	13.6			
5/16 — 18	11	1.5	14.9	17	2.3	23.0	19	2.6	25.8
— 24	13	1.8	17.6	19	2.6	25.7			
⅜ — 16	18	2.5	24.4	31	4.3	42.0	34	4.7	46.0
— 24	20	2.75	27.1	35	4.8	47.5			
7/16 — 14	28	3.8	37.0	49	6.8	66.4	55	7.6	74.5
— 20	30	4.2	40.7	55	7.6	74.5			
½ — 13	39	5.4	52.8	75	10.4	101.7	85	11.75	115.2
— 20	41	5.7	55.6	85	11.7	115.2			
9/16 — 12	51	7.0	69.2	110	15.2	149.1	120	16.6	162.7
— 18	55	7.6	74.5	120	16.6	162.7			
⅝ — 11	83	11.5	112.5	150	20.7	203.3	167	23.0	226.5
— 18	95	13.1	128.8	170	23.5	230.5			
¾ — 10	105	14.5	142.3	270	37.3	366.0	280	38.7	379.6
— 16	115	15.9	155.9	295	40.8	400.0			
⅞ — 9	160	22.1	216.9	395	54.6	535.5	440	60.9	596.5
— 14	175	24.2	237.2	435	60.1	589.7			
1 — 8	236	32.5	318.6	590	81.6	799.9	660	91.3	894.8
— 14	250	34.6	338.9	660	91.3	849.8			

Metric Bolts

Relative Strength Marking	4.6, 4.8			8.8		
Bolt Markings						
Bolt Size Thread Size x Pitch (mm)	Maximum Torque			Maximum Torque		
	Ft./Lbs.	Kgm	Nm	Ft./Lbs.	Kgm	Nm
6 x 1.0	2–3	.2–.4	3–4	3–6	.4–.8	5–8
8 x 1.25	6–8	.8–1	8–12	9–14	1.2–1.9	13–19
10 x 1.25	12–17	1.5–2.3	16–23	20–29	2.7–4.0	27–39
12 x 1.25	21–32	2.9–4.4	29–43	35–53	4.8–7.3	47–72
14 x 1.5	35–52	4.8–7.1	48–70	57–85	7.8–11.7	77–110
16 x 1.5	51–77	7.0–10.6	67–100	90–120	12.4–16.5	130–160
18 x 1.5	74–110	10.2–15.1	100–150	130–170	17.9–23.4	180–230
20 x 1.5	110–140	15.1–19.3	150–190	190–240	26.2–46.9	160–320
22 x 1.5	150–190	22.0–26.2	200–260	250–320	34.5–44.1	340–430
24 x 1.5	190–240	26.2–46.9	260–320	310–410	42.7–56.5	420–550

Standard and metric bolt torque specifications based on bolt strengths—WARNING: use only as a guide common ways to help assure that a threaded retainer has been properly fastened.

When tightening a threaded fastener, torque is applied in three distinct areas, the head, the bearing surface and the clamp load. About 50 percent of the measured torque is used in overcoming bearing friction. This is the friction between the bearing surface of the bolt head, screw head or nut face and the base material or washer (the surface on which the fastener is rotating). Approximately 40 percent of the applied torque is used in overcoming thread friction. This leaves only about 10 percent of the applied torque to develop a useful clamp load (the force which holds a joint together). This means that friction can account for as much as 90 percent of the applied torque on a fastener.

TORQUE WRENCHES

In most applications, a torque wrench can be used to assure proper installation of a fastener. Torque wrenches come in various designs and most automotive supply stores will carry a variety to suit your needs. A torque wrench should be used any time we supply a specific torque value for a fastener. A torque wrench can also be used if you are following the general guidelines in the accompanying charts. Keep in mind that because there is no worldwide standardization of fasteners, the charts are a general guideline and should be used with caution. Again, the general rule of "if you are using the right tool for the job, you should not have to strain to tighten a fastener" applies here.

Beam Type

The beam type torque wrench is one of the most popular types. It consists of a pointer attached to the head that runs the length of the flexible beam (shaft) to a scale located near the handle. As the wrench is pulled, the beam bends and the pointer indicates the torque using the scale.

Click (Breakaway) Type

Another popular design of torque wrench is the click type. To use the click type wrench you pre-adjust it to a torque setting. Once the torque is reached, the wrench has a reflex signalling fea-

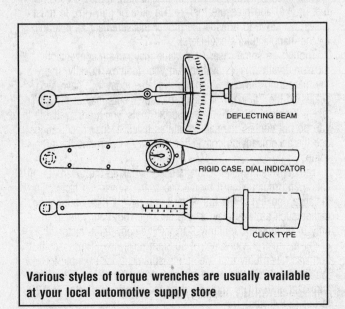

Various styles of torque wrenches are usually available at your local automotive supply store

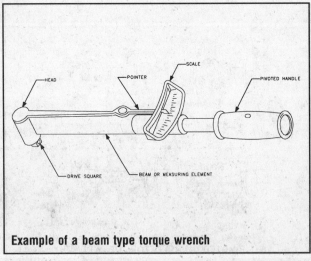

Example of a beam type torque wrench

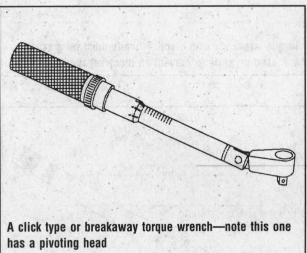

A click type or breakaway torque wrench—note this one has a pivoting head

ture that causes a momentary breakaway of the torque wrench body, sending an impulse to the operator's hand.

Pivot Head Type

Some torque wrenches (usually of the click type) may be equipped with a pivot head which can allow it to be used in areas of limited access. BUT, it must be used properly. To hold a pivot head wrench, grasp the handle lightly, and as you pull on the handle, it should be floated on the pivot point. If the handle comes in contact with the yoke extension during the process of pulling, there is a very good chance the torque readings will be inaccurate because this could alter the wrench loading point. The design of the handle is usually such as to make it inconvenient to deliberately misuse the wrench.

➡It should be mentioned that the use of any U-joint, wobble or extension will have an effect on the torque readings, no matter what type of wrench you are using. For the most accurate readings, install the socket directly on the wrench driver. If necessary, straight extensions (which hold a socket directly under the wrench driver) will have the least effect on the torque reading. Avoid any extension that alters the length of the wrench from the handle to the head/driving point (such as a crow's foot). U-joint or Wobble extensions can greatly affect the readings; avoid their use at all times.

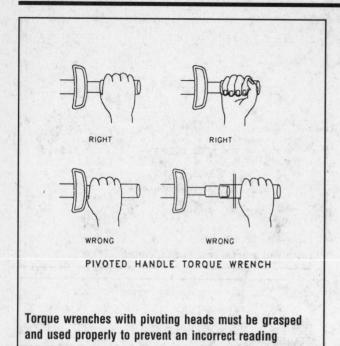

Torque wrenches with pivoting heads must be grasped and used properly to prevent an incorrect reading

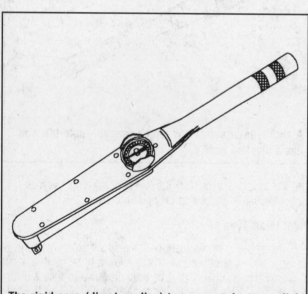

The rigid case (direct reading) torque wrench uses a dial indicator to show torque

Rigid Case (Direct Reading)

A rigid case or direct reading torque wrench is equipped with a dial indicator to show torque values. One advantage of these wrenches is that they can be held at any position on the wrench without affecting accuracy. These wrenches are often preferred because they tend to be compact, easy to read and have a great degree of accuracy.

TORQUE ANGLE METERS

Because the frictional characteristics of each fastener or threaded hole will vary, clamp loads which are based strictly on

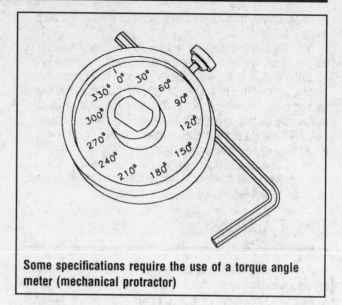

Some specifications require the use of a torque angle meter (mechanical protractor)

torque will vary as well. In most applications, this variance is not significant enough to cause worry. But, in certain applications, a manufacturer's engineers may determine that more precise clamp loads are necessary (such is the case with many aluminum cylinder heads). In these cases, a torque angle method of installation would be specified. When installing fasteners which are torque angle tightened, a predetermined seating torque and standard torque wrench are usually used first to remove any compliance from the joint. The fastener is then tightened the specified additional portion of a turn measured in degrees. A torque angle gauge (mechanical protractor) is used for these applications.

Standard and Metric Measurements

Throughout this manual, specifications are given to help you determine the condition of various components on your vehicle, or to assist you in their installation. Some of the most common measurements include length (in. or cm/mm), torque (ft. lbs., inch lbs. or Nm) and pressure (psi, in. Hg, kPa or mm Hg). In most cases, we strive to provide the proper measurement as determined by the manufacturer's engineers.

Though, in some cases, that value may not be conveniently measured with what is available in your toolbox. Luckily, many of the measuring devices which are available today will have two scales so the Standard or Metric measurements may easily be taken. If any of the various measuring tools which are available to you do not contain the same scale as listed in the specifications, use the accompanying conversion factors to determine the proper value.

The conversion factor chart is used by taking the given specification and multiplying it by the necessary conversion factor. For instance, looking at the first line, if you have a measurement in inches such as "free-play should be 2 in." but your ruler reads only in millimeters, multiply 2 in. by the conversion factor of 25.4 to get the metric equivalent of 50.8mm. Likewise, if the specification was given only in a Metric measurement, for example in Newton Meters (Nm), then look at the center column first. If the measurement is 100 Nm, multiply it by the conversion factor of 0.738 to get 73.8 ft. lbs.

CONVERSION FACTORS

LENGTH–DISTANCE

Inches (in.)	x 25.4	= Millimeters (mm)	x .0394	= Inches
Feet (ft.)	x .305	= Meters (m)	x 3.281	= Feet
Miles	x 1.609	= Kilometers (km)	x .0621	= Miles

VOLUME

Cubic Inches (in3)	x 16.387	= Cubic Centimeters	x .061	= in3
IMP Pints (IMP pt.)	x .568	= Liters (L)	x 1.76	= IMP pt.
IMP Quarts (IMP qt.)	x 1.137	= Liters (L)	x .88	= IMP qt.
IMP Gallons (IMP gal.)	x 4.546	= Liters (L)	x .22	= IMP gal.
IMP Quarts (IMP qt.)	x 1.201	= US Quarts (US qt.)	x .833	= IMP qt.
IMP Gallons (IMP gal.)	x 1.201	= US Gallons (US gal.)	x .833	= IMP gal.
Fl. Ounces	x 29.573	= Milliliters	x .034	= Ounces
US Pints (US pt.)	x .473	= Liters (L)	x 2.113	= Pints
US Quarts (US qt.)	x .946	= Liters (L)	x 1.057	= Quarts
US Gallons (US gal.)	x 3.785	= Liters (L)	x .264	= Gallons

MASS–WEIGHT

Ounces (oz.)	x 28.35	= Grams (g)	x .035	= Ounces
Pounds (lb.)	x .454	= Kilograms (kg)	x 2.205	= Pounds

PRESSURE

Pounds Per Sq. In. (psi)	x 6.895	= Kilopascals (kPa)	x .145	= psi
Inches of Mercury (Hg)	x .4912	= psi	x 2.036	= Hg
Inches of Mercury (Hg)	x 3.377	= Kilopascals (kPa)	x .2961	= Hg
Inches of Water (H_2O)	x .07355	= Inches of Mercury	x 13.783	= H_2O
Inches of Water (H_2O)	x .03613	= psi	x 27.684	= H_2O
Inches of Water (H_2O)	x .248	= Kilopascals (kPa)	x 4.026	= H_2O

TORQUE

Pounds–Force Inches (in–lb)	x .113	= Newton Meters (N·m)	x 8.85	= in–lb
Pounds–Force Feet (ft–lb)	x 1.356	= Newton Meters (N·m)	x .738	= ft–lb

VELOCITY

Miles Per Hour (MPH)	x 1.609	= Kilometers Per Hour (KPH)	x .621	= MPH

POWER

Horsepower (Hp)	x .745	= Kilowatts	x 1.34	= Horsepower

FUEL CONSUMPTION*

Miles Per Gallon IMP (MPG)	x .354	= Kilometers Per Liter (Km/L)
Kilometers Per Liter (Km/L)	x 2.352	= IMP MPG
Miles Per Gallon US (MPG)	x .425	= Kilometers Per Liter (Km/L)
Kilometers Per Liter (Km/L)	x 2.352	= US MPG

*It is common to covert from miles per gallon (mpg) to liters/100 kilometers (1/100 km), where mpg (IMP) x 1/100 km = 282 and mpg (US) x 1/100 km = 235.

TEMPERATURE

Degree Fahrenheit (°F) = (°C x 1.8) + 32

Degree Celsius (°C) = (°F – 32) x .56

Standard and metric conversion factors chart

HISTORY

In 1933, the Toyota Automatic Loom Works started an automobile division. Several models, mostly experimental, were produced between 1935 and 1937. Automobile production started on a large scale in 1937 when the Toyota Motor Co. Ltd. was founded. The name for the automobile company was changed from the family name, Toyoda, to Toyota, because a numerologist suggested that this would be a more auspicious name to use for this endeavor. It must have been; by 1947, Toyota had produced 100,000 vehicles. Today Toyota is Japan's largest producer of motor vehicles and ranks among the largest in world production.

It was not until the late 1950s, that Toyota began exporting cars to the United States. Public reception of the Toyopet was rather cool. The car was heavy and under-powered by U.S. standards. Several other models were exported, including the almost indestructible Land Cruiser. It was not until 1965, however, with the introduction of the Corona sedan, that Toyota enjoyed a real success on the U.S. market.

SERIAL NUMBER IDENTIFICATION

Vehicle

▶ **See Figures 1, 2, 3 and 4**

All models have the vehicle identification number (VIN) stamped on a plate which is attached to the left side of the instrument panel. This plate is visible through the windshield.

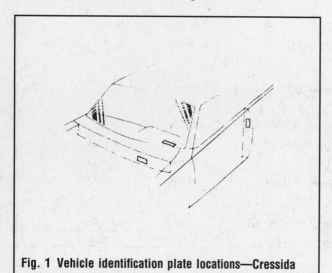

Fig. 1 Vehicle identification plate locations—Cressida

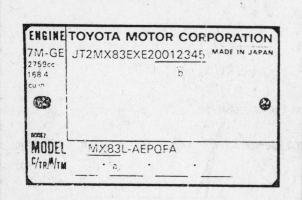

Fig. 2 The VIN plate has a series of numbers on it to identify the model—Cressida shown

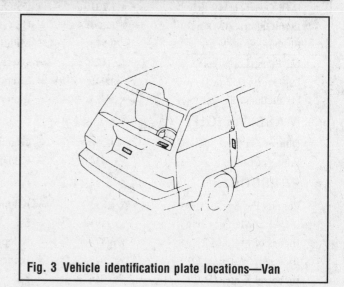

Fig. 3 Vehicle identification plate locations—Van

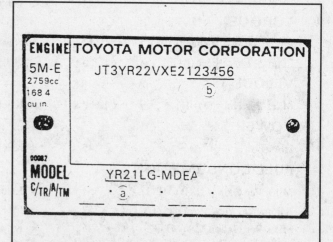

Fig. 4 The VIN plate has a series of numbers on it to identify the model—Van shown

The VIN is also stamped on a plate in the engine compartment which is usually located on the firewall and can be found on the driver's door post.

Beginning with 1981 models the serial number consists of seventeen symbols (letters and numbers).

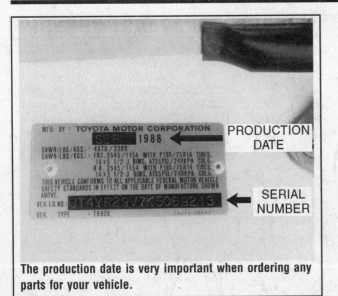

The production date is very important when ordering any parts for your vehicle.

Engine

♦ **See Figures 5, 6 and 7**

The engine serial number consists of an engine series identification number, followed by a six-digit production number. On the Cressida models, the engine number is usually stamped on the lower portion of the engine block and on the Van models the engine number is usually stamped on the upper portion of the engine block. Both numbers are on the passenger's side of the vehicle. The location of this serial number may vary at times from one year to another.

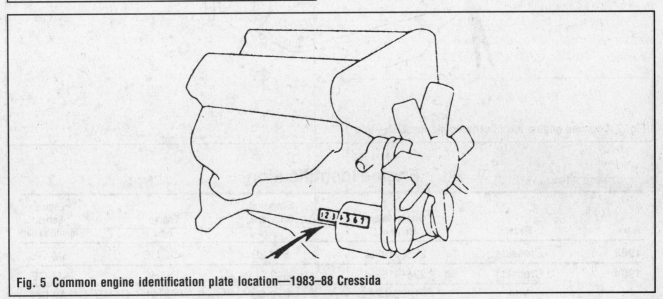

Fig. 5 Common engine identification plate location—1983–88 Cressida

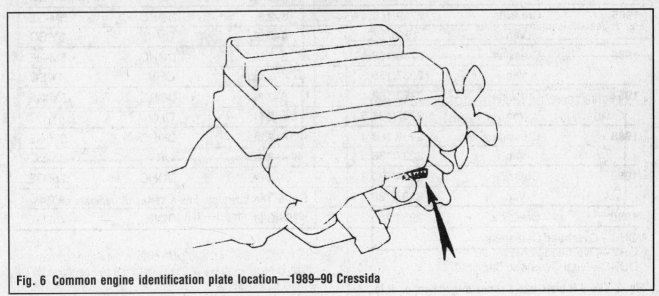

Fig. 6 Common engine identification plate location—1989–90 Cressida

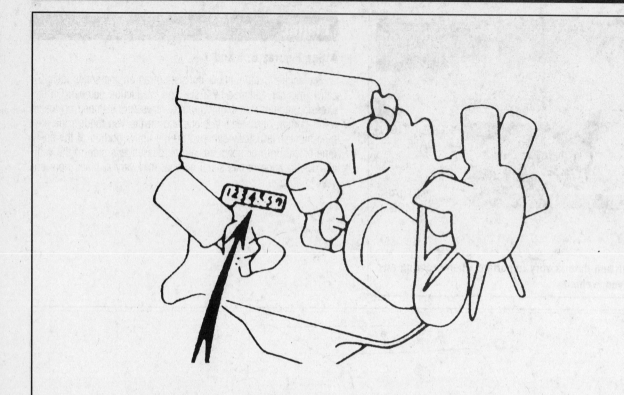

Fig. 7 Common engine identification plate location—Van

Engine Identification

Year	Model	Displacement (cc/cu in.)	Number of Cylinders/ Liters	Engine Type	Engine Series Identification
1983	Cressida	2759/168.4	6–2.8L	DOHC	5M-GE
1984	Cressida	2759/168.4	6–2.8L	DOHC	5M-GE
	Van	1998/122	4–2.0L	OHV	3Y-EC
1985	Cressida	2759/168.4	6–2.8L	DOHC	5M-GE
	Van	1998/122	4–2.0L	OHV	3Y-EC
1986	Cressida	2759/168.4	6–2.8L	DOHC	5M-GE
	Van	2237/136.5	4–2.2L	OHV	4Y-EC
1987	Cressida	2759/168.4	6–2.8L	DOHC	5M-GE
	Van	2237/136.5	4–2.2L	OHV	4Y-EC
1988	Cressida	2759/168.4	6–2.8L	DOHC	5M-GE
	Van	2237/136.5	4–2.2L	OHV	4Y-EC
1989	Cressida	2954/180.3	6–3.0L	DOHC	7M-GE
	Van	2237/136.5	4–2.2L	OHV	4Y-EC
1990	Cressida	2954/180.3	6–3.0L	DOHC	7M-GE

OHC—Overhead Camshaft
OHV—Overhead Valves
DOHC—Dual Overhead Camshaft

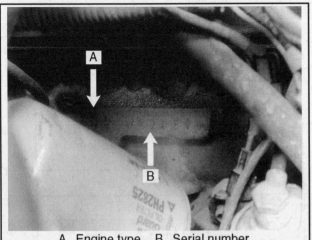

A. Engine type   B. Serial number
The engine type is stamped into the block along with an engine serial number

Model

♦ See Figures 8 thru 14

The model identification number is located on the VIN plate under the hood on Cressida models, and under the carpet on the passengers seat on Van models. The model number identifies exactly what type of vehicle you are driving. The model number identifies the transmission, fuel type, body style and grade level of the vehicle. This model number along with the VIN number is very useful when ordering parts for your vehicle.

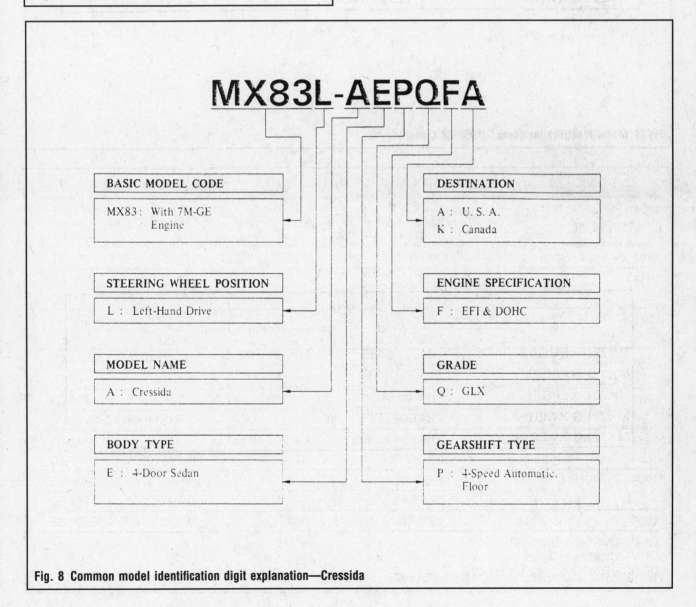

MX83L-AEPQFA

BASIC MODEL CODE

MX83: With 7M-GE
Engine

STEERING WHEEL POSITION

L : Left-Hand Drive

MODEL NAME

A : Cressida

BODY TYPE

E : 4-Door Sedan

DESTINATION

A : U.S.A.
K : Canada

ENGINE SPECIFICATION

F : EFI & DOHC

GRADE

Q : GLX

GEARSHIFT TYPE

P : 4-Speed Automatic,
Floor

Fig. 8 Common model identification digit explanation—Cressida

Model	Engine	Production Period	Characteristic Expression in Catalog Model Column			Model Name
MX63L-XEMMFA	5M-GE	8208—8407	SED	MTM	USA	Sedan
MX63L-XEPMFA	"	8208—8407	"	ATM	"	"
MX63L-XEPMFK	"	8208—8407	"	"	CND	"
MX62LG-XWPMFA	"	8208—8407	WG	"	USA	Station Wagon
MX62LG-XWPMFK	"	8208—8407	"	"	CND	" "

Fig. 9 Model identification codes—1983–84 Cressida

Model	Engine	Production Period	Characteristic Expression in Catalog Model Column			Model Name
MX73L-XEMGFA	5M-GE	8408—8708	SED	MTM	USA	Sedan
MX73L-XEPGFA	"	8408—8808	"	ATM	"	"
MX73L-XEPGFK	"	8408—8808	"	"	CND	"
MX72LG-XWPGFA	"	8411—8708	WG	"	USA	Station Wagon
MX72LG-XWPGFK	"	8411—8608	"	"	CND	"

Fig. 10 Model identification codes—1985–88 Cressida

Model	Engine	Production Period	Characteristic Expression in Catalog Model Column						Model Name
MX83L-AEPQFA	7M-GE	8808–9207	SED	ATM	4FC	GLX	TWC	USA	Sedan
'' -AEPQFK	''	8808–9207	''	''	''	''	''	CND	''

SED   Sedan
ATM   Automatic transmission
4FC   ATM, 4-speed floor shift
GLX   GLX type
TWC   Twin cam
USA   For United States of America
CND   For Canada
WG   Station wagon
MTM   Manual transmission

Fig. 11 Model identification codes—1989–90 Cressida

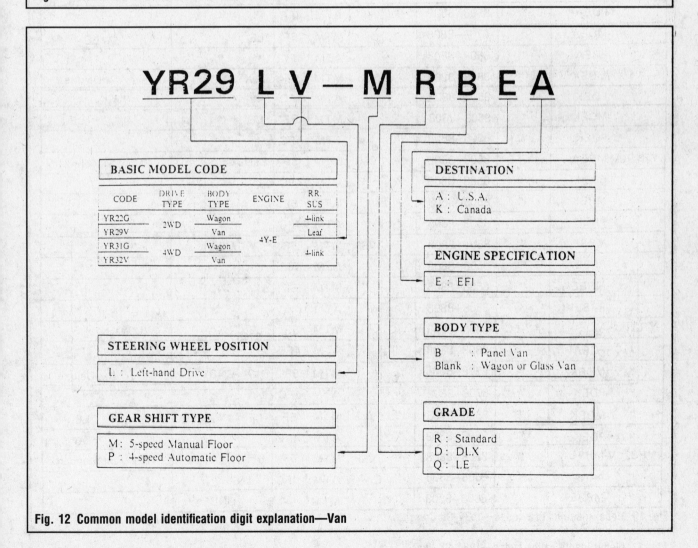

Fig. 12 Common model identification digit explanation—Van

Model	Engine	Production Period	Characteristic Expressions in Catalog Model Column						Model Name
YR21LG-MDEA	3Y-EC	8308–8508	WG		MTM	5F	DLX	USA	Wagon, Deluxe
" -PDEA	"	8308–8508	"		ATM	4FC	"	"	" , "
" -MQEA	"	8308–8508	"		MTM	5F	LE	"	" , LE
" -PQEA	"	8308–8508	"		ATM	4FC	"	"	" , "
" -MDEK	"	8308–8508	"		MTM	5F	DLX	CND	Wagon, Deluxe
" -PDEK	"	8308–8508	"		ATM	4FC	"	"	" , "
" -MQEK	"	8308–8508	"		MTM	5F	LE	"	" , LE
" -PQEK	"	8308–8508	"		ATM	4FC	"	"	" , "
YR27LV-MREA	3Y-EC	8402–8508	V	VSG	MTM	5F	STD	USA	Van, Standard
" -PREA	"	8402–8508	"	"	ATM	4FC	"	"	" , "
" -MREK	"	8311–8508	"	"	MTM	5F	STD	CND	" , "
" -PREK	"	8311–8508	"	"	ATM	4FC	"	"	" , "
YR22LG-MDEA	4Y-EC	8508–8808	WG		MTM	5F	DLX	USA	Wagon, Deluxe
" -PDEA	"	8508–8808	"		ATM	4FC	"	"	" , "
" -MQEA	"	8708–8808	"		MTM	5F	LE	"	" , LE
" -PQEA	"	8508–8808	"		ATM	4FC	"	"	" , "
" -MDEK	"	8608–8808	"		MTM	5F	DLX	CND	" , Deluxe
" -PDEK	"	8608–8808	"		ATM	4FC	"	"	" , "
" -MQEK	"	8508–8608	"		MTM	5F	LE	"	" , LE
" -PQEK	"	8508–8808	"		ATM	4FC	"	"	" , "
YR29LV-MREA	4Y-EC	8508–8808	V	VSG	MTM	5F	STD	USA	Van, Standard
" -PREA	"	8508–8808	"	"	ATM	4FC	"	"	" , "
" -MREK	"	8508–8608	"	"	MTM	5F		CND	" , "
" -PREK	"	8508–8608	"	"	ATM	4FC	"	"	" , "
" -MRBEA	"	8508–8808	"	VSP	MTM	5F	"	USA	" , "
" -PRBEA	"	8508–8808	"	"	ATM	4FC	"	"	" , "
" -MRBEK	"	8508–8808	"	"	MTM	5F		CND	" , "
" -PRBEK	"	8508–8808	"	"	ATM	4FC	"	"	" , "
YR31LG-MQEA	4Y-EC	8608–8808	WG		MTM	5F	LE	USA	4WD Wagon, LE
" -PQEA	"	8608–8808	"		ATM	4FC	"	"	" , " , "
" -MDEK	"	8708–8808	"		MTM	5F	DLX	CND	" , " , Deluxe
" -PDEK	"	8708–8808	"		ATM	4FC	"	"	" , " , "
" -MQEK	"	8608–8708	"		MTM	5F	LE	"	" , " , LE
" -PQEK	"	8608–8808	"		ATM	4FC	"	"	" , " , "
YR32LV-MRBEA	"	8608–8808	V	VSP	MTM	5F	STD	USA	4WD Van, Standard
" -PRBEA	"	8608–8808	"	"	ATM	4FC	"	"	" , " , "
" -MRBEK	"	8608–8808	"	"	MTM	5F	"	CND	" , " , "

Fig. 13 Model identification codes—1984–88 Van

Model	Engine	Production Period	Characteristic Expressions in Catalog Model Column						Model Name
YR29LV-MREA	4Y-EC	8808–9001	V	VSG	MTM	5F	STD	USA	Van, Standard
" -PREA	"	8808–9001	"	"	ATM	4FC	"	"	" , "
" -MRBEA	"	8808–9001	"	VSP	MTM	5F	"	"	" , "
" -PRBEA	"	8808–9001	"	"	ATM	4FC	"	"	" , "
" -MRBEK	"	8808–9001	"	"	MTM	5F	"	CND	" , "
" -PRBEK	"	8808–9001	"	"	ATM	4FC	"	"	" , "
YR32LV-PRBEA	4Y-EC	8808–9001	V	VSP	ATM	4FC	STD	USA	4WD Van, Standard
" -MRBEK	"	8808–9001	"	"	MTM	5F	"	CND	" " , "
YR22LG-MDEA	4Y-EC	8808–9001	WG		MTM	5F	DLX	USA	Wagon, Deluxe
" -PDEA	"	8808–9001	"		ATM	4FC	"	"	" , "
" -MQEA	"	8808–9001	"		MTM	5F	LE	"	" , LE
" -PQEA	"	8808–9001	"		ATM	4FC	"	"	" , "
" -MDEK	"	8808–9001	"		MTM	5F	DLX	CND	" , Deluxe
" -PDEK	"	8808–9001	"		ATM	4FC	"	"	" , "
" -PQEK	"	8808–9001	"		"	"	LE	"	" , "
YR31LG-MDEA	4Y-EC	8808–9001	WG		MTM	5F	DLX	USA	4WD Wagon, Deluxe
" -PDEA	"	8808–9001	"		ATM	4FC	"	"	" " , "
" -PQEA	"	8808–9001	"		"	"	LE	"	" " , LE
" -MDEK	"	8808–9001	"		MTM	5F	DLX	CND	" " , Deluxe
" -PDEK	"	8808–9001	"		ATM	4FC	"	"	" , "
" -PQEK	"	8808–9001	"		"	"	LE	"	" " , LE

WG	Wagon		STD	Standard type
V	Van		DLX	Deluxe type
VSG	Van, side glass		LE	LE type
VSP	Van, side panel			
MTM	Manual transmission		USA	For U.S.A.
5F	MTM, 5-speed floor shift		CND	For Canada
ATM	Automatic transmission			
4FC	ATM, 4-speed floor shift			

Fig. 14 Model identification codes—1989–90 Van

The model identification plate is located under the passengers seat carpet on the Van models

Transmission

The transmission can be identified by the identification number stamped on the tag that is attached to the side of the transmission.

Transfer Case

The transfer case can be identified by the identification number stamped on the tag that is attached to the side of the unit.

Vehicle Identification

Year	Model Type	Series Identification Number*
1983	Cressida Sedan	MX-63
	Cressida Wagon	MX-62
1984	Cressida Sedan	MX-63
	Cressida Wagon	MX-62
	Van	YR22,26
1985	Cressida Sedan	MX-73
	Cressida Wagon	MX-72
	Van DLX	YR-22V
	Van LE	YR-26V
	Van Cargo	YR-27V
1986	Cressida Sedan	MX-73
	Cressida Wagon	MX-72
	Van DLX	YR-22W
	Van LE	YR-26W
	Van Cargo	YR-29V
1987	Cressida Sedan	MX-73E
	Cressida Wagon	MX-72W
	Van DLX	YR-22W
	Van LE	YR-26W
	Van 4 × 4 LE	YR-36W
	Van Cargo (Window)	YR-29V
	Van Cargo (Panel)	YR-28V
	Van Cargo (Panel) 4 × 4	YR-34V
1988	Cressida Sedan	MX-73E
	Van LE	YR-26W
	Van 4 × 4 LE	YR-36W
	Van Cargo (Window)	YR-29V
	Van Cargo (Panel)	YR-28V
	Van Cargo (Panel) 4 × 4	YR-34V
1989	Cressida Sedan	MX-83E
	Van LE	YR-26W
	Van 4 × 4 LE	YR-32W
	Van Cargo (Window)	YR-29V
	Van Cargo (Panel)	YR-28V
	Van Cargo (Panel) 4 × 4	YR-34V
1990	Cressida Sedan	MX-83E

*The suffixes, E, V, W, MX etc., may not appear in the serial number; a typical Toyota serial number would look like this: MS55-132246.

ROUTINE MAINTENANCE

▶ See Figures 15, 16, 17 and 18

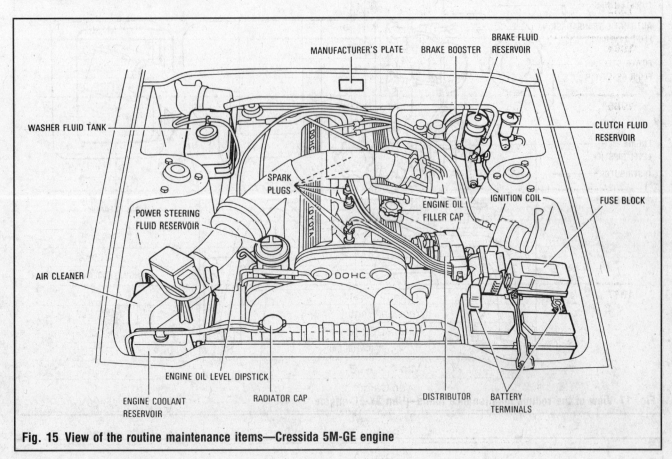

Fig. 15 View of the routine maintenance items—Cressida 5M-GE engine

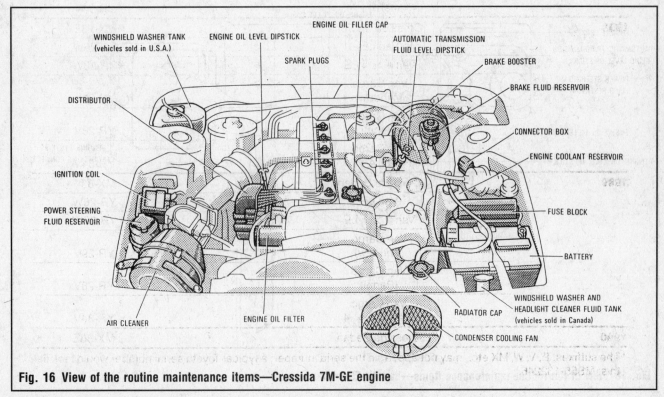

Fig. 16 View of the routine maintenance items—Cressida 7M-GE engine

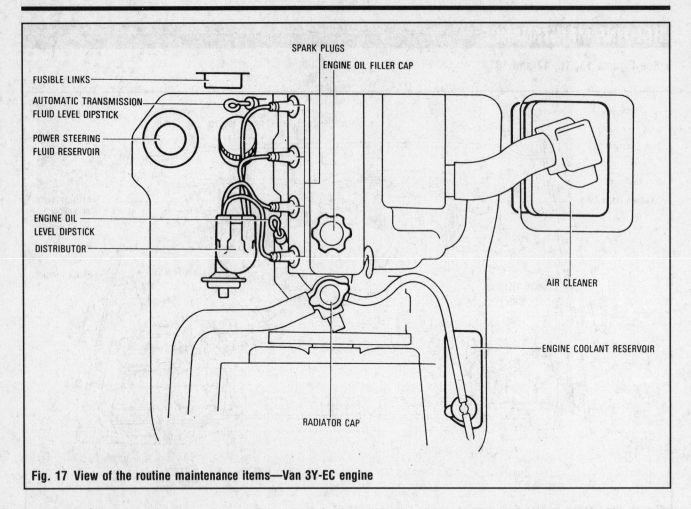

Fig. 17 View of the routine maintenance items—Van 3Y-EC engine

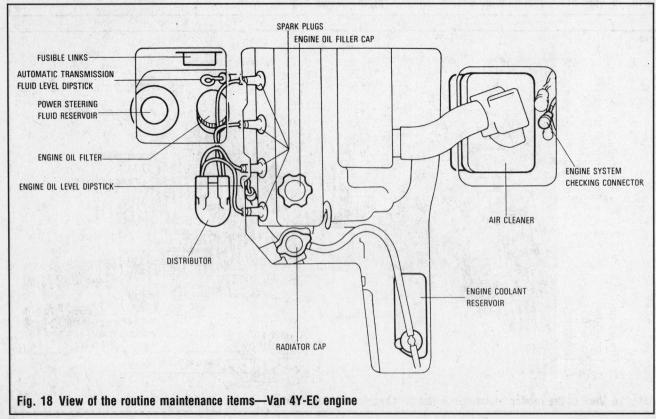

Fig. 18 View of the routine maintenance items—Van 4Y-EC engine

MAINTENANCE COMPONENT LOCATIONS - VAN

1. Drive belt
2. Radiator
3. Coolant reservior
4. Thermostat
5. Coolant system cap
6. Distributor cap
7. Oil filter
8. Automatic transmission dipstick
9. Engine oil dipstick
10. Engine oil filler cap
11. Air cleaner
12. Igniter
13. Spark plug wires
14. Radiator hose

Air Cleaner

The air cleaners used on Toyota vehicles are of the dry element, disposable type. They should never be washed or oiled.

Clean the element every 3,000 miles, or more often under dry, dusty conditions, by using low pressure compressed air. Blow from the inside toward the outside.

✲✲ CAUTION

Never use high air pressure to clean the element, as this will probably damage it.

Replace the element every 30,000 miles; or more often under dry, dusty conditions. Be sure to use the correct one; all Toyota elements are of the same type but they come in a variety of sizes.

REMOVAL & INSTALLATION

▶ **See Figures 19, 20, 21 and 22**

1. To remove the air cleaner element, pull the wire tab to release each clip on top of the housing and loosen the air inlet duct clamp. Lift off the top section. Set it aside carefully since the emission system hoses are attached to it on some models.

2. On the 1989–90 Cressida models, loosen the air inlet duct clamp, disconnect the air flow meter connector and remove the air filter element cover retainer bolt. Then release the clips and remove the air cleaner element.

3. Disconnect and tag these hoses first (if so equipped), to remove it entirely from the car. Lift the air cleaner element out for service or replacement.

4. Inspect the lower surface of the element. If it is dirty it should be replaced. If it is just moderately dusty, it may be cleaned by blowing a low volume of compressed air from the upper surface.

5. Installation is the reverse of removal.

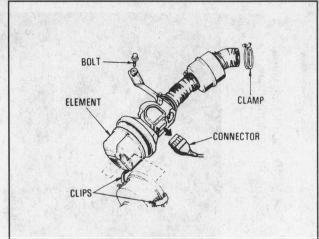

Fig. 20 Common air cleaner assembly—1989–90 Cressida

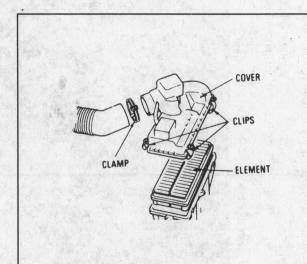

Fig. 21 Common air cleaner assembly—Van

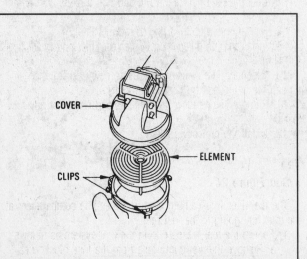

Fig. 19 Common air cleaner assembly—1983–88 Cressida

When removing the Van air cleaner, unclamp the filter cover . . .

. . . then lift the filter out of the housing

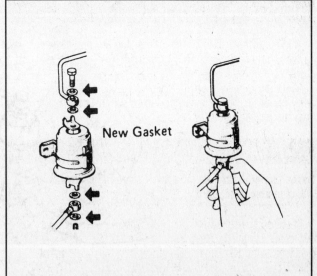

Fig. 23 When installing the fuel filter on the Cressida, make sure the gaskets are placed correctly

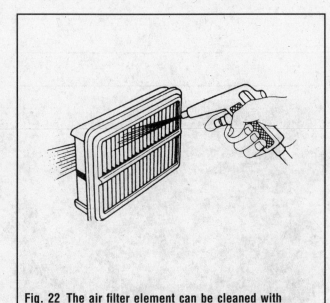

Fig. 22 The air filter element can be cleaned with compressed air

Fuel Filter

REMOVAL & INSTALLATION

Cressida

◆ See Figure 23

1. Relieve the fuel pressure from the fuel system as follows:
   a. Remove the fuel pump fuse from the fuse block, fuel pump relay or disconnect the harness connector at the tank while engine is running.
   b. It should run and then stall when the fuel in the lines is exhausted. When the engine stops, crank the starter for about three seconds to make sure all pressure in the fuel lines is released.

   c. Install the fuel pump fuse, relay or harness connector after repair is made.
2. Disconnect the negative battery cable. Unbolt the retaining screws and remove the protective shield for the fuel filter.
3. Place a pan under the delivery pipe to catch the dripping fuel and slowly loosen the union bolt or flare nut to bleed off the fuel pressure.
4. Drain the remaining fuel.
5. Disconnect and plug the inlet line.
6. Unbolt and remove the fuel filter.

To install:

➡ When tightening the fuel line bolts to the fuel filter, use a torque wrench. The tightening torque is very important, as under or over tightening may cause fuel leakage. Insure that there is no fuel line interference and that there is sufficient clearance between it and any other parts.

7. Coat the flare nut, union nut and bolt threads with engine oil.
8. Hand-tighten the inlet line to the fuel filter.
9. Install the fuel filter, then tighten the inlet bolt to 22 ft. lbs. (30 Nm).
10. Reconnect the delivery pipe using new gaskets, then tighten the union bolt to 22 ft. lbs. (30 Nm).
11. Run the engine for a few minutes and check for any fuel leaks.
12. Install the protective shield.

Van

◆ See Figure 24

The fuel filter is usually located in the engine compartment at the inlet line going to the fuel rail.

1. Relieve the fuel pressure from the fuel system as follows:
   a. Remove the fuel pump fuse from the fuse block, fuel pump relay or disconnect the harness connector at the tank while engine is running.

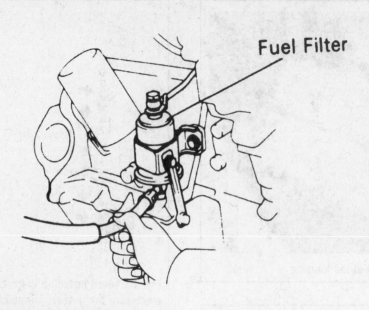

Fuel Filter

Fig. 24 The fuel filter on the Van is located near the oil filter

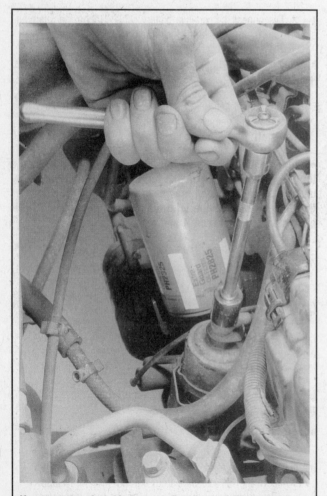

Use an extension when removing the fuel filter on the Van

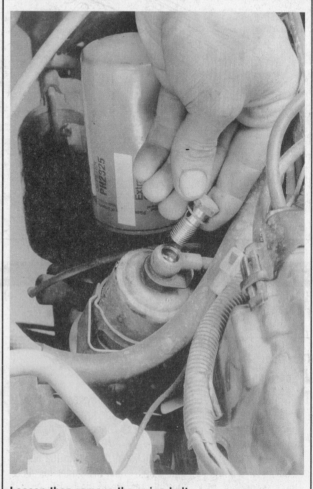

Loosen then remove the union bolt

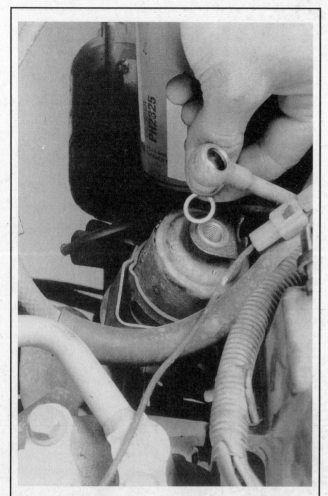

Set the union pipe aside and remove the O-ring gasket from the fuel filter

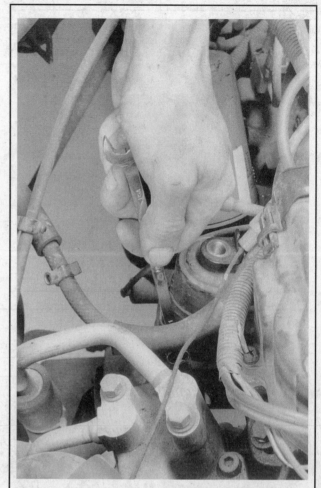

Remove the fuel filter bracket mounting bolts from the engine

    b. It should run and then stall when the fuel in the lines is exhausted. When the engine stops, crank the starter for about three seconds to make sure all pressure in the fuel lines is released.

    c. Install the fuel pump fuse, relay or harness connector after repair is made.

2. Disconnect the negative battery cable. Raise and support the vehicle safely.

3. Disconnect and plug the inlet and outlet lines from the filter.

4. Remove the fuel filter retaining bolts and bands and remove the filter.

5. Installation is the reverse of the removal procedure.

6. Use new O-rings and tighten the lines to 22 ft. lbs. (29 Nm).

7. Connect the negative battery cable. Run the engine and check for leaks.

Remove the rear fuel pipe from the filter . . .

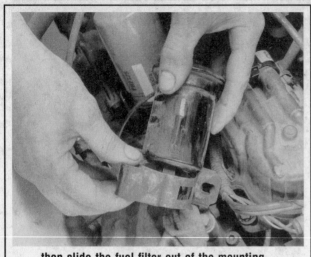

. . . then slide the fuel filter out of the mounting bracket

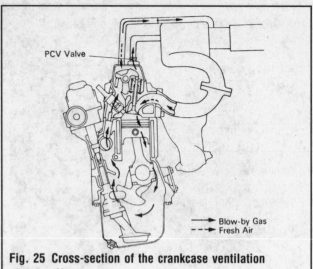

Fig. 25 Cross-section of the crankcase ventilation system—Van

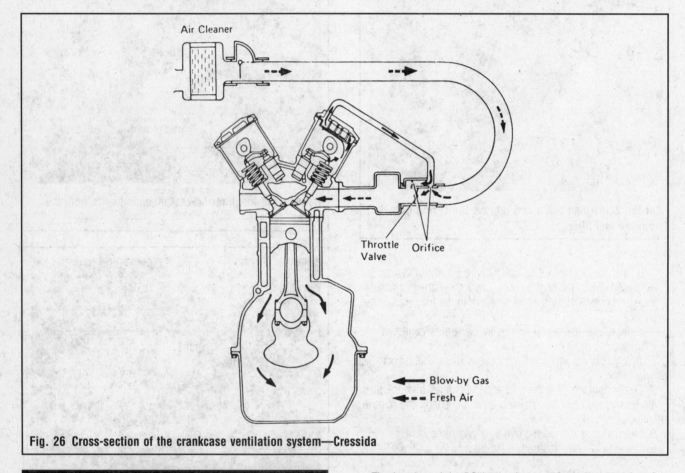

Fig. 26 Cross-section of the crankcase ventilation system—Cressida

PCV Valve

▶ **See Figures 25 and 26**

The only model to use a PCV valve is the Van. To reduce hydrocarbon emissions, crankcase blow-by gas is routed through the PCV valve to the intake manifold for combustion in the cylinders. On the Cressida models, to reduce hydrocarbons emissions, crankcase blow-by gas is routed through two metering orifices to the intake manifold for combustion in the cylinders.

The function of the PCV valve is to purge the crankcase of harmful vapors through a system using engine vacuum to draw fresh air through the crankcase. It reburns crankcase vapors, rather than exhausting. Proper operation of the PCV valve depends on a sealed engine.

Engine operating conditions that would indicate a malfunctioning PCV system are rough idle, oil present in the air cleaner, oil leaks or excessive oil sludging.

The simplest check for the PCV valve is to remove it from its rubber hose and shake it. If it rattles, it is functioning. If not, replace it. In any event, it should be replaced at the recommended interval whether it rattles or not. While your at it, check the PCV hoses for breaks or restrictions. As necessary, the hoses should also be replaced.

The positive crankcase vent valve (PCV) should be replaced every 30,000 miles or 24 months. (California models, every 60,000 miles).

REMOVAL & INSTALLATION

1. Pull the valve, with the hose still attached to the valve, from its rubber grommet.

2. Use a pair of pliers to release the hose clamp, remove the PCV valve from the hose.

To install:

3. Install the new valve into the hose, slide the clamp into position, and install the valve into the rubber grommet.

Evaporative Emission Canister

♦ See Figures 27, 28, 29 and 30

To prevent gasoline vapors from being vented into the atmosphere, an evaporative emission system captures the vapors and stores them in a charcoal filled canister.

The charcoal canister vacuum lines, fittings, and connections should be checked every 6,000 miles for clogging, pinching, looseness, etc. Clean or replace components as necessary. If the canister is clogged, it may be cleaned using low pressure compressed air, as shown.

The entire canister should be replaced every six years or 60,000 miles.

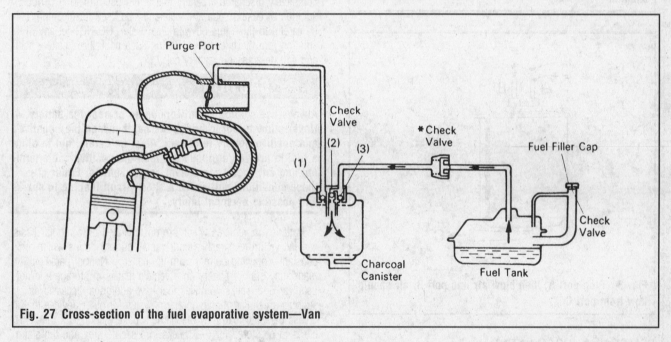

Fig. 27 Cross-section of the fuel evaporative system—Van

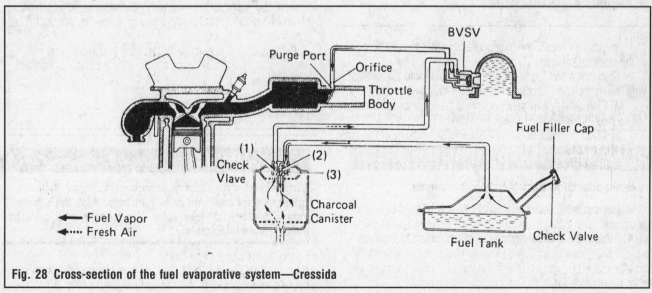

Fig. 28 Cross-section of the fuel evaporative system—Cressida

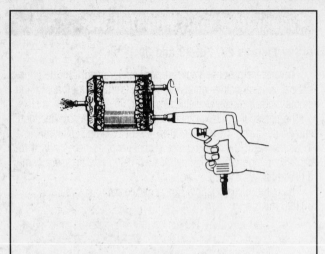

Fig. 29 Use compressed air to clean the charcoal canister

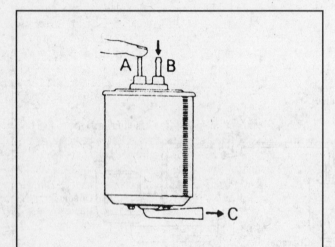

Fig. 30 Plug port A, then blow air into port B, air should flow from port C

REMOVAL & INSTALLATION

1. Remove all necessary components in order to gain access to the charcoal canister.

2. Disconnect and tag the vapor hoses going into the canister. With the vapor lines disconnected, inspect the canister as follows:

    a. Plug pipe A with your finger and blow compressed air (43 psi) through pipe B (fuel tank side).

    b. Check to see that air comes out of the bottom of the pipe without resistance.

    c. There should also be no activated charcoal coming out.

➡**Never attempt to wash the charcoal canister.**

3. Remove the canister retaining bolts and band, if so equipped.

4. Installation is the reverse order of the removal procedure.

Battery

GENERAL MAINTENANCE

All batteries, regardless of type, should be carefully secured by a battery hold-down device. If this is not done, the battery terminals or casing may crack from stress applied to the battery during vehicle operation. A battery which is not secured may allow acid to leak out, making it discharge faster; such leaking corrosive acid can also eat away components under the hood. A battery that is not sealed must be checked periodically for electrolyte level. You cannot add water to a sealed maintenance-free battery (though not all maintenance-free batteries are sealed), but a sealed battery must also be checked for proper electrolyte level as indicated by the color of the built-in hydrometer "eye."

Keep the top of the battery clean, as a film of dirt can help completely discharge a battery that is not used for long periods. A solution of baking soda and water may be used for cleaning, but be careful to flush this off with clear water. DO NOT let any of the solution into the filler holes. Baking soda neutralizes battery acid and will de-activate a battery cell.

✳✳ CAUTION

Always use caution when working on or near the battery. Never allow a tool to bridge the gap between the negative and positive battery terminals. Also, be careful not to allow a tool to provide a ground between the positive cable/terminal and any metal component on the vehicle. Either of these conditions will cause a short circuit leading to sparks and possible personal injury.

Batteries in vehicles which are not operated on a regular basis can fall victim to parasitic loads (small current drains which are constantly drawing current from the battery). Normal parasitic loads may drain a battery on a vehicle that is in storage and not used for 6–8 weeks. Vehicles that have additional accessories such as a cellular phone, an alarm system or other devices that increase parasitic load may discharge a battery sooner. If the vehicle is to be stored for 6–8 weeks in a secure area and the alarm system, if present, is not necessary, the negative battery cable should be disconnected at the onset of storage to protect the battery charge.

Remember that constantly discharging and recharging will shorten battery life. Take care not to allow a battery to be needlessly discharged.

BATTERY FLUID

✳✳ CAUTION

Battery electrolyte contains sulfuric acid. If you should splash any on your skin or in your eyes, flush the affected area with plenty of clear water. If it lands in your eyes, get medical help immediately.

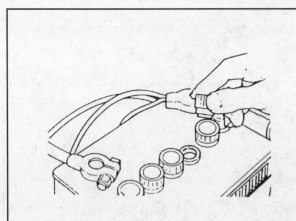

On non-maintenance free batteries, the level can be checked through the case on translucent batteries; the cell caps must be removed on other models

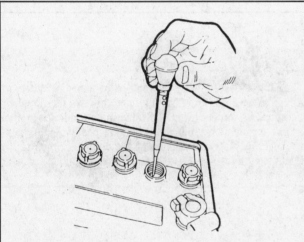

Check the specific gravity of the battery's electrolyte with a hydrometer

The fluid (sulfuric acid solution) contained in the battery cells will tell you many things about the condition of the battery. Because the cell plates must be kept submerged below the fluid level in order to operate, maintaining the fluid level is extremely important. And, because the specific gravity of the acid is an indication of electrical charge, testing the fluid can be an aid in determining if the battery must be replaced. A battery in a vehicle with a properly operating charging system should require little maintenance, but careful, periodic inspection should reveal problems before they leave you stranded.

Fluid Level

Check the battery electrolyte level at least once a month, or more often in hot weather or during periods of extended vehicle operation. On non-sealed batteries, the level can be checked either through the case on translucent batteries or by removing the cell caps on opaque-cased types. The electrolyte level in each cell should be kept filled to the split ring inside each cell, or the line marked on the outside of the case.

If the level is low, add only distilled water through the opening until the level is correct. Each cell is separate from the others, so each must be checked and filled individually. Distilled water should be used, because the chemicals and minerals found in most drinking water are harmful to the battery and could significantly shorten its life.

If water is added in freezing weather, the vehicle should be driven several miles to allow the water to mix with the electrolyte. Otherwise, the battery could freeze.

Although some maintenance-free batteries have removable cell caps for access to the electrolyte, the electrolyte condition and level on all sealed maintenance-free batteries must be checked using the built-in hydrometer "eye." The exact type of eye varies between battery manufacturers, but most apply a sticker to the battery itself explaining the possible readings. When in doubt, refer to the battery manufacturer's instructions to interpret battery condition using the built-in hydrometer.

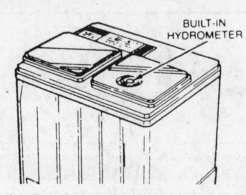

Location of indicator on sealed battery

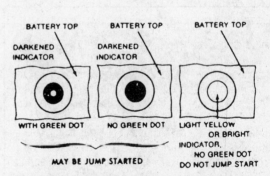

Check the appearance of the charge indicator on top of the battery before attempting a jump start; if it's not green or dark, do not jump start the car

A typical sealed (maintenance-free) battery with a built-in hydrometer—NOTE that the hydrometer eye may vary between battery manufacturers; always refer to the battery's label

➡Although the readings from built-in hydrometers found in sealed batteries may vary, a green eye usually indicates a properly charged battery with sufficient fluid level. A dark eye is normally an indicator of a battery with sufficient fluid, but one which may be low in charge. And a light or yellow eye is usually an indication that electrolyte supply has dropped below the necessary level for battery (and hydrometer) operation. In this last case, sealed batteries with an insufficient electrolyte level must usually be discarded.

Specific Gravity

As stated earlier, the specific gravity of a battery's electrolyte level can be used as an indication of battery charge. At least once a year, check the specific gravity of the battery. It should be between 1.20 and 1.26 on the gravity scale. Most auto supply stores carry a variety of inexpensive battery testing hydrometers. These can be used on any non-sealed battery to test the specific gravity in each cell.

The battery testing hydrometer has a squeeze bulb at one end and a nozzle at the other. Battery electrolyte is sucked into the hydrometer until the float is lifted from its seat. The specific gravity is then read by noting the position of the float. If gravity is low in one or more cells, the battery should be slowly charged and checked again to see if the gravity has come up. Generally, if after charging, the specific gravity between any two cells varies more than 50 points (0.50), the battery should be replaced as it can no longer produce sufficient voltage to guarantee proper operation.

On sealed batteries, the built-in hydrometer is the only way of checking specific gravity. Again, check with your battery's manufacturer for proper interpretation of its built-in hydrometer readings.

CABLES

Once a year (or as necessary), the battery terminals and the cable clamps should be cleaned. Loosen the clamps and remove the cables, negative cable first. On batteries with posts on top, the use of a puller specially made for this purpose is recommended. These are inexpensive and available in most auto parts stores. Side terminal battery cables are secured with a small bolt.

Clean the cable clamps and the battery terminal with a wire

The underside of this special battery tool has a wire brush to clean post terminals

Place the tool over the terminals and twist to clean the post

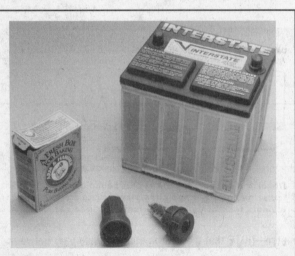
Maintenance is performed with household items and with special tools like this post cleaner

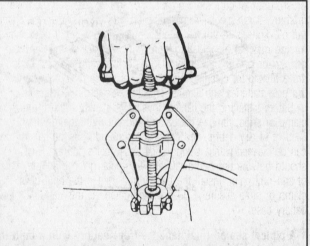
A special tool is available to pull the clamp from the post

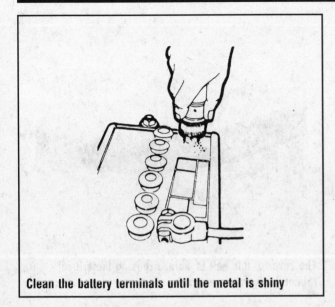

Clean the battery terminals until the metal is shiny

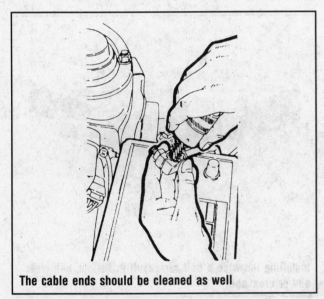

The cable ends should be cleaned as well

brush, until all corrosion, grease, etc., is removed and the metal is shiny. It is especially important to clean the inside of the clamp (an old knife is useful here) thoroughly, since a small deposit of foreign material or oxidation there will prevent a sound electrical connection and inhibit either starting or charging. Special tools are available for cleaning these parts, one type for conventional top post batteries and another type for side terminal batteries.

Before installing the cables, loosen the battery hold-down clamp or strap, remove the battery and check the battery tray. Clear it of any debris, and check it for soundness (the battery tray can be cleaned with a baking soda and water solution). Rust should be wire brushed away, and the metal given a couple coats of anti-rust paint. Install the battery and tighten the hold-down clamp or strap securely. Do not overtighten, as this can crack the battery case.

After the clamps and terminals are clean, reinstall the cables, negative cable last; DO NOT hammer the clamps onto post batteries. Tighten the clamps securely, but do not distort them. Give the clamps and terminals a thin external coating of grease after installation, to retard corrosion.

Check the cables at the same time that the terminals are cleaned. If the cable insulation is cracked or broken, or if the ends are frayed, the cable should be replaced with a new cable of the same length and gauge.

CHARGING

✳✳ CAUTION

The chemical reaction which takes place in all batteries generates explosive hydrogen gas. A spark can cause the battery to explode and splash acid. To avoid serious personal injury, be sure there is proper ventilation and take appropriate fire safety precautions when connecting, disconnecting, or charging a battery and when using jumper cables.

A battery should be charged at a slow rate to keep the plates inside from getting too hot. However, if some maintenance-free batteries are allowed to discharge until they are almost "dead," they may have to be charged at a high rate to bring them back to "life." Always follow the charger manufacturer's instructions on charging the battery.

REPLACEMENT

When it becomes necessary to replace the battery, select one with a rating equal to or greater than the battery originally installed. Deterioration and just plain aging of the battery cables, starter motor, and associated wires makes the battery's job harder in successive years. The slow increase in electrical resistance over time makes it prudent to install a new battery with a greater capacity than the old.

Belts

INSPECTION

Inspect the belts for signs of glazing or cracking. A glazed belt will be perfectly smooth from slippage, while a good belt will have a slight texture of fabric visible. Cracks will usually start at the inner edge of the belt and run outward. All worn or damaged drive belts should be replaced immediately. It is best to replace all drive belts at one time, as a preventive maintenance measure, during this service operation.

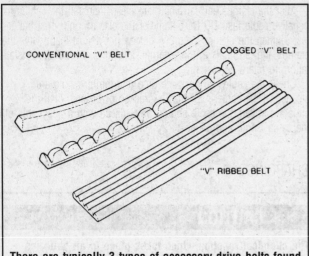

There are typically 3 types of accessory drive belts found on vehicles today

The cover of this belt is worn, exposing the critical reinforcing cords to excessive wear

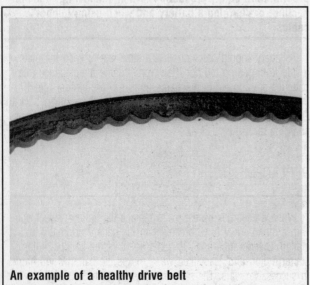

An example of a healthy drive belt

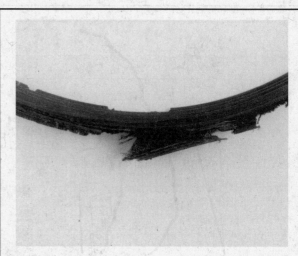

Installing too wide a belt can result in serious belt wear and/or breakage

Deep cracks in this belt will cause flex, building up heat that will eventually lead to belt failure

ADJUSTMENT

▶ **See Figure 31**

Toyota measures belt tension in pounds of force as determined by a belt tension tester. The Nippondenso and Burroughs testers are available through dealers or may be found at retail auto parts stores. The tester slips over a short section of the drive belt, and, when tightened, reads the deflection pressure on a dial. This is one of the most exact ways of setting tension and purchase of this tool or its equivalent is recommended.

Specifications for new belts are slightly higher than for used belts. A new belt is one which has not been run under tension for more than 5 minutes. Anything else is a used belt.

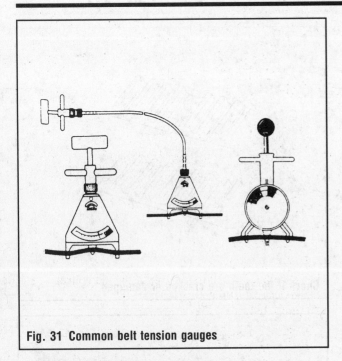

Fig. 31 Common belt tension gauges

REMOVAL & INSTALLATION

When buying replacement belts, remember that the fit is critical according to the length of the belt ("diameter"), the width of the belt, the depth of the belt and the angle or profile of the V shape. The belt shape should exactly match the shape of the pulley; belts that are not an exact match can cause noise, slippage and premature failure.

If a belt must be replaced, the driven unit must be loosened and moved to its extreme loosest position, generally by moving it toward the center of the motor. After removing the old belt, check the pulleys for dirt or build-up material which could affect belt contact. Carefully install the new belt, remembering that it is new and unused-it may appear to be just a little too small to fit over the pulley flanges.

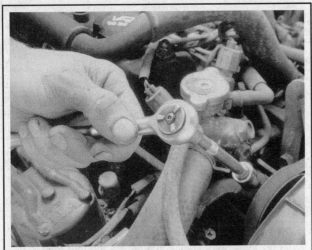

When removing a belt on the Van models, loosen the idler pulley adjuster bolt located on top . . .

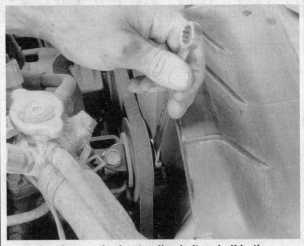

. . . then loosen the front pulley bolt and slide the pulley slightly to loosen the tension of the belt

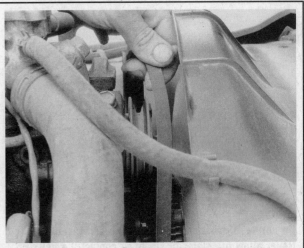

Remove the belt from the idler and around any other components

Fit the belt over the largest pulley (usually the crankshaft pulley at the bottom center of the motor) first, then work on the smaller one(s). Gentle pressure in the direction of rotation is helpful. Some belts run around a third or idler pulley, which acts as an additional pivot in the belt's path. It may be possible to loosen the idler pulley as well as the main component, making your job much easier. Depending on which belt(s) you are changing, it may be necessary to loosen or remove other interfering belts to get at the one(s) you want.

After the new belt is installed, draw tension on it by moving the driven unit away from the motor and tighten its mounting bolts. This is sometimes a three or four-handed job; you may find an assistant helpful. Make sure that all the bolts you loosened get re-tightened and that any other loosened belts also have the correct tension. A new belt can be expected to stretch a bit after installation so be prepared to re-adjust your new belt, if needed, within the first hundred miles/kilometers of use.

Timing Belts

INSPECTION

Toyota recommends that the timing belt be replaced on vehicles that are used in extensive idling or low speed driving for long distances. Police, taxi and door-to-door deliveries are commonly used in this manner. The timing belt should be replaced every 60,000 miles (96,000 km) in these cases. Toyota trucks do not have interference engines; where engine damage will occur if the belt snaps. If your vehicle has high mileage, you may want to consider replacing the belt to prevent the possibility of having it snap. Or if your engine is being overhauled, inspect the belt for wear and replace if needed. In the event the belt does snap while you are driving, turn the engine **OFF** immediately. Section 3 has removal and installation procedures available.

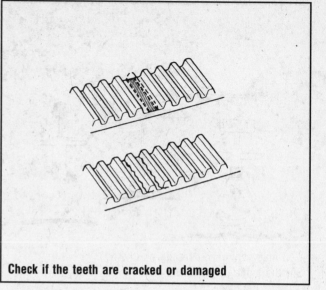

Check if the teeth are cracked or damaged

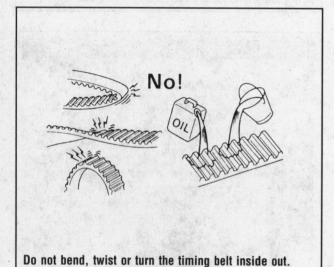

Do not bend, twist or turn the timing belt inside out. Never allow oil, water or steam to contact the belt

Inspect the timing belt for cracks, fraying, glazing or damage of any kind

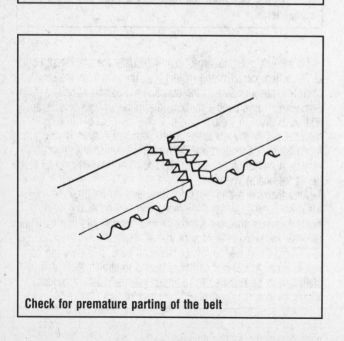

Check for premature parting of the belt

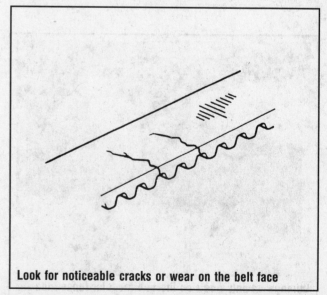

Look for noticeable cracks or wear on the belt face

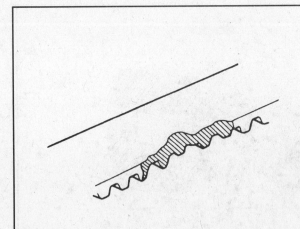

You may only have damage on one side of the belt; if so, the guide could be the culprit

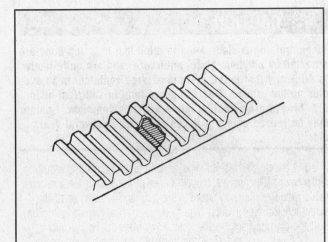

Foreign materials can get in between the teeth and cause damage

Damage on only one side of the timing belt may indicate a faulty guide

ALWAYS replace the timing belt at the interval specified by the manufacturer

Hoses

INSPECTION

Upper and lower radiator hoses along with the heater hoses should be checked for deterioration, leaks and loose hose clamps at least every 15,000 miles (24,000 km). It is also wise to check the hoses periodically in early spring and at the beginning of the fall or winter when you are performing other maintenance. A quick visual inspection could discover a weakened hose which might have left you stranded if it had remained unrepaired.

Whenever you are checking the hoses, make sure the engine and cooling system are cold. Visually inspect for cracking, rotting or collapsed hoses, and replace as necessary. Run your hand along the length of the hose. If a weak or swollen spot is noted when squeezing the hose wall, the hose should be replaced.

REMOVAL & INSTALLATION

1. Remove the radiator pressure cap.

✳✳ CAUTION

Never remove the pressure cap while the engine is running, or personal injury from scalding hot coolant or steam may result. If possible, wait until the engine has cooled to remove the pressure cap. If this is not possible, wrap a thick cloth around the pressure cap and turn it slowly to the stop. Step back while the pressure is released from the cooling system. When you are sure all the pressure has been released, use the cloth to turn and remove the cap.

2. Position a clean container under the radiator and/or engine draincock or plug, then open the drain and allow the cooling system to drain to an appropriate level. For some upper hoses, only a little coolant must be drained. To remove hoses positioned lower on the engine, such as a lower radiator hose, the entire cooling system must be emptied.

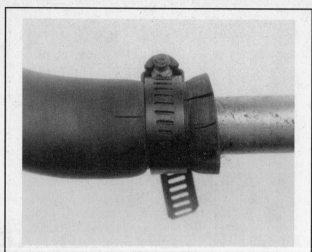

The cracks developing along this hose are a result of age-related hardening

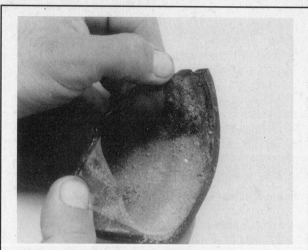

Hoses are likely to deteriorate from the inside if the cooling system is not periodically flushed

A hose clamp that is too tight can cause older hoses to separate and tear on either side of the clamp

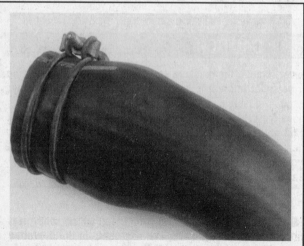

A soft spongy hose (identifiable by the swollen section) will eventually burst and should be replaced

✳✳ CAUTION

When draining coolant, keep in mind that cats and dogs are attracted by ethylene glycol antifreeze, and are quite likely to drink any that is left in an uncovered container or in puddles on the ground. This will prove fatal in sufficient quantity. Always drain coolant into a sealable container. Coolant may be reused unless it is contaminated or several years old.

3. Loosen the hose clamps at each end of the hose requiring replacement. Clamps are usually either of the spring tension type (which require pliers to squeeze the tabs and loosen) or of the screw tension type (which require screw or hex drivers to loosen). Pull the clamps back on the hose away from the connection.

4. Twist, pull and slide the hose off the fitting, taking care not to damage the neck of the component from which the hose is being removed.

→If the hose is stuck at the connection, do not try to insert a screwdriver or other sharp tool under the hose end in an effort to free it, as the connection and/or hose may become damaged. Heater connections especially may be easily damaged by such a procedure. If the hose is to be replaced, use a single-edged razor blade to make a slice along the portion of the hose which is stuck on the connection, perpendicular to the end of the hose. Do not cut deep so as to prevent damaging the connection. The hose can then be peeled from the connection and discarded.

5. Clean both hose mounting connections. Inspect the condition of the hose clamps and replace them, if necessary.

To install:

6. Dip the ends of the new hose into clean engine coolant to ease installation.

7. Slide the clamps over the replacement hose, then slide the hose ends over the connections into position.

8. Position and secure the clamps at least ¼ in. (6.35mm) from the ends of the hose. Make sure they are located beyond the raised bead of the connector.

9. Close the radiator or engine drains and properly refill the cooling system with the clean drained engine coolant or a suitable mixture of ethylene glycol coolant and water.

10. If available, install a pressure tester and check for leaks. If a pressure tester is not available, run the engine until normal operating temperature is reached (allowing the system to naturally pressurize), then check for leaks.

✳✳ CAUTION

If you are checking for leaks with the system at normal operating temperature, BE EXTREMELY CAREFUL not to touch any moving or hot engine parts. Once temperature has been reached, shut the engine OFF, and check for leaks around the hose fittings and connections which were removed earlier.

CV-Boots

INSPECTION

The CV (Constant Velocity) boots should be checked for damage each time the oil is changed and any other time the vehicle is raised for service. These boots keep water, grime, dirt and other damaging matter from entering the CV-joints. Any of these could cause early CV-joint failure which can be expensive to repair. Heavy grease thrown around the inside of the front wheel(s) and on the brake caliper/drum can be an indication of a torn boot. Thoroughly check the boots for missing clamps and tears. If the boot is damaged, it should be replaced immediately.

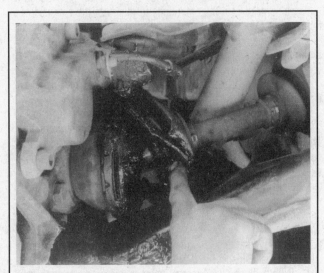

A torn boot should be replaced immediately

CV-boots must be inspected periodically for damage

Air Conditioning

➡Be sure to consult the laws in your area before servicing the air conditioning system. In most areas, it is illegal to perform repairs involving refrigerant unless the work is done by a certified technician. Also, it is quite likely that you will not be able to purchase refrigerant without proof of certification.

SAFETY PRECAUTIONS

There are two major hazards associated with air conditioning systems and they both relate to the refrigerant gas. First, the refrigerant gas (R-12) is an extremely cold substance. When exposed to air, it will instantly freeze any surface it comes in contact with, including your eyes. The other hazard relates to fire. Although normally non-toxic, the R-12 gas becomes highly poisonous in the presence of an open flame. One good whiff of the vapor formed by burning R-12 can be fatal. Keep all forms of fire (including cigarettes) well clear of the air conditioning system.

Because of the inherent dangers involved with working on air conditioning systems and R-12 refrigerant, these safety precautions must be strictly followed.

• Avoid contact with a charged refrigeration system, even when working on another part of the air conditioning system or vehicle. If a heavy tool comes into contact with a section of tubing or a heat exchanger, it can easily cause the relatively soft material to rupture.

• When it is necessary to apply force to a fitting which contains refrigerant, as when checking that all system couplings are securely tightened, use a wrench on both parts of the fitting involved, if possible. This will avoid putting torque on refrigerant tubing. (It is also advisable to use tube or line wrenches when tightening these flare nut fittings.)

➡R-12 refrigerant is a chlorofluorocarbon which, when released into the atmosphere, can contribute to the depletion of the ozone layer in the upper atmosphere. Ozone filters out harmful radiation from the sun.

• Do not attempt to discharge the system without the proper tools. Precise control is possible only when using the service gauges and a proper A/C refrigerant recovery station. Wear protective gloves when connecting or disconnecting service gauge hoses.

• Discharge the system only in a well ventilated area, as high concentrations of the gas which might accidentally escape can exclude oxygen and act as an anesthetic. When leak testing or soldering, this is particularly important, as toxic gas is formed when R-12 contacts any flame.

• Never start a system without first verifying that both service valves are properly installed, and that all fittings throughout the system are snugly connected.

• Avoid applying heat to any refrigerant line or storage vessel. Charging may be aided by using water heated to less than 125°F (50°C) to warm the refrigerant container. Never allow a refrigerant storage container to sit out in the sun, or near any other source of heat, such as a radiator or heater.

• Always wear goggles to protect your eyes when working on a system. If refrigerant contacts the eyes, it is advisable in all cases to consult a physician immediately.

• Frostbite from liquid refrigerant should be treated by first gradually warming the area with cool water, and then gently applying petroleum jelly. A physician should be consulted.

• Always keep refrigerant drum fittings capped when not in use. If the container is equipped with a safety cap to protect the valve, make sure the cap is in place when the can is not being used. Avoid sudden shock to the drum, which might occur from dropping it, or from banging a heavy tool against it. Never carry a drum in the passenger compartment of a vehicle.

• Always completely discharge the system into a suitable recovery unit before painting the vehicle (if the paint is to be baked on), or before welding anywhere near refrigerant lines.

• When servicing the system, minimize the time that any refrigerant line or fitting is open to the air in order to prevent moisture or dirt from entering the system. Contaminants such as moisture or dirt can damage internal system components. Always replace O-rings on lines or fittings which are disconnected. Prior to installation coat, but do not soak, replacement O-rings with suitable compressor oil.

GENERAL SERVICING PROCEDURES

➡️**It is recommended, and possibly required by law, that a qualified technician perform the following services.**

The most important aspect of air conditioning service is the maintenance of a pure and adequate charge of refrigerant in the system. A refrigeration system cannot function properly if a significant percentage of the charge is lost. Leaks are common because the severe vibration encountered underhood in an automobile can easily cause a sufficient cracking or loosening of the air conditioning fittings; allowing, the extreme operating pressures of the system to force refrigerant out.

The problem can be understood by considering what happens to the system as it is operated with a continuous leak. Because the expansion valve regulates the flow of refrigerant to the evaporator, the level of refrigerant there is fairly constant. The receiver/drier stores any excess refrigerant, and so a loss will first appear there as a reduction in the level of liquid. As this level nears the bottom of the vessel, some refrigerant vapor bubbles will begin to appear in the stream of liquid supplied to the expansion valve. This vapor decreases the capacity of the expansion valve very little as the valve opens to compensate for its presence. As the quantity of liquid in the condenser decreases, the operating pressure will drop there and throughout the high side of the system. As the R-12 continues to be expelled, the pressure available to force the liquid through the expansion valve will continue to decrease, and, eventually, the valve's orifice will prove to be too much of a restriction for adequate flow even with the needle fully withdrawn.

At this point, low side pressure will start to drop, and a severe reduction in cooling capacity, marked by freeze-up of the evaporator coil, will result. Eventually, the operating pressure of the evaporator will be lower than the pressure of the atmosphere surrounding it, and air will be drawn into the system wherever there are leaks in the low side.

Because all atmospheric air contains at least some moisture, water will enter the system and mix with the R-12 and the oil. Trace amounts of moisture will cause sludging of the oil, and corrosion of the system. Saturation and clogging of the filter/drier, and freezing of the expansion valve orifice will eventually result. As air fills the system to a greater and greater extent, it will interfere more and more with the normal flows of refrigerant and heat.

From this description, it should be obvious that much of the repairman's focus in on detecting leaks, repairing them, and then restoring the purity and quantity of the refrigerant charge. A list of general rules should be followed in addition to all safety precautions:

• Keep all tools as clean and dry as possible.

• Thoroughly purge the service gauges/hoses of air and moisture before connecting them to the system. Keep them capped when not in use.

• Thoroughly clean any refrigerant fitting before disconnecting it, in order to minimize the entrance of dirt into the system.

• Plan any operation that requires opening the system beforehand, in order to minimize the length of time it will be exposed to open air. Cap or seal the open ends to minimize the entrance of foreign material.

• When adding oil, pour it through an extremely clean and dry tube or funnel. Keep the oil capped whenever possible. Do not use oil that has not been kept tightly sealed.

• Use only R-12 refrigerant. Purchase refrigerant intended for use only in automatic air conditioning systems.

• Completely evacuate any system that has been opened for service, or that has leaked sufficiently to draw in moisture and air. This requires evacuating air and moisture with a good vacuum pump for at least one hour. If a system has been open for a considerable length of time it may be advisable to evacuate the system for up to 12 hours (overnight).

• Use a wrench on both halves of a fitting that is to be disconnected, so as to avoid placing torque on any of the refrigerant lines.

• When overhauling a compressor, pour some of the oil into a clean glass and inspect it. If there is evidence of dirt, metal particles, or both, flush all refrigerant components with clean refrigerant before evacuating and recharging the system. In addition, if metal particles are present, the compressor should be replaced.

• Schrader valves may leak only when under full operating pressure. Therefore, if leakage is suspected but cannot be located, operate the system with a full charge of refrigerant and look for leaks from all Schrader valves. Replace any faulty valves.

Additional Preventive Maintenance

USING THE SYSTEM

The easiest and most important preventive maintenance for your A/C system is to be sure that it is used on a regular basis. Running the system for five minutes each month (no matter what the season) will help assure that the seals and all internal components remain lubricated.

ANTIFREEZE

In order to prevent heater core freeze-up during A/C operation, it is necessary to maintain a proper antifreeze protection. Use a hand-held antifreeze tester (hydrometer) to periodically check the condition of the antifreeze in your engine's cooling system.

➡**Antifreeze should not be used longer than the manufacturer specifies.**

RADIATOR CAP

For efficient operation of an air conditioned vehicle's cooling system, the radiator cap should have a holding pressure which meets manufacturer's specifications. A cap which fails to hold these pressures should be replaced.

CONDENSER

Any obstruction of or damage to the condenser configuration will restrict the air flow which is essential to its efficient operation. It is therefore a good rule to keep this unit clean and in proper physical shape.

➡**Bug screens which are mounted in front of the condenser, (unless they are original equipment), are regarded as obstructions.**

CONDENSATION DRAIN TUBE

This single molded drain tube expels the condensation, which accumulates on the bottom of the evaporator housing, into the engine compartment. If this tube is obstructed, the air conditioning performance can be restricted and condensation buildup can spill over onto the vehicle's floor.

SYSTEM INSPECTION

➡**R-12 refrigerant is a chlorofluorocarbon which, when released into the atmosphere, can contribute to the depletion of the ozone layer in the upper atmosphere. Ozone filters out harmful radiation from the sun.**

The easiest and often most important check for the air conditioning system consists of a visual inspection of the system components. Visually inspect the air conditioning system for refrigerant leaks, damaged compressor clutch, compressor drive belt tension and condition, plugged evaporator drain tube, blocked condenser fins, disconnected or broken wires, blown fuses, corroded connections and poor insulation.

A refrigerant leak will usually appear as an oily residue at the leakage point in the system. The oily residue soon picks up dust or dirt particles from the surrounding air and appears greasy. Through time, this will build up and appear to be a heavy dirt impregnated grease. Most leaks are caused by damaged or missing O-ring seals at the component connections, damaged charging valve cores or missing service gauge port caps.

An antifreeze tester can be used to determine the freezing and boiling levels of the coolant

For a thorough visual and operational inspection, check the following:

1. Check the surface of the radiator and condenser for dirt, leaves or other material which might block air flow.
2. Check for kinks in hoses and lines. Check the system for leaks.
3. Make sure the drive belt is under the proper tension. When the air conditioning is operating, make sure the drive belt is free of noise or slippage.
4. Make sure the blower motor operates at all appropriate positions, then check for distribution of the air from all outlets with the blower on **HIGH.**

➡**Keep in mind that under conditions of high humidity, air discharged from the A/C vents may not feel as cold as expected, even if the system is working properly. This is because the vaporized moisture in humid air retains heat more effectively than does dry air, making the humid air more difficult to cool.**

5. Make sure the air passage selection lever is operating correctly. Start the engine and warm it to normal operating temperature, then make sure the hot/cold selection lever is operating correctly.

DISCHARGING, EVACUATING & CHARGING

Discharging, evacuating and charging the air conditioning system must be performed by a properly trained and certified mechanic in a facility equipped with refrigerant recovery/recycling equipment that meets SAE standards for the type of system to be serviced.

If you don't have access to the necessary equipment, we recommend that you take your vehicle to a reputable service station to have the work done. If you still wish to perform repairs on the vehicle, have them discharge the system, then take your vehicle home and perform the necessary work. When you are finished, return the vehicle to the station for evacuation and charging. Just be sure to cap ALL A/C system fittings immediately after opening them and keep them protected until the system is recharged.

Windshield Wipers

ELEMENT (REFILL) CARE & REPLACEMENT

▶ **See Figures 32 and 33**

For maximum effectiveness and longest element life, the windshield and wiper blades should be kept clean. Dirt, tree sap, road tar and so on will cause streaking, smearing and blade deterioration if left on the glass. It is advisable to wash the windshield carefully with a commercial glass cleaner at least once a month. Wipe off the rubber blades with the wet rag afterwards. Do not attempt to move wipers across the windshield by hand; damage to the motor and drive mechanism will result.

To inspect and/or replace the wiper blade elements, place the wiper switch in the **LOW** speed position and the ignition switch in the **ACC** position. When the wiper blades are approximately vertical on the windshield, turn the ignition switch to **OFF.**

Examine the wiper blade elements. If they are found to be cracked, broken or torn, they should be replaced immediately. Replacement intervals will vary with usage, although ozone deterioration usually limits element life to about one year. If the wiper pattern is smeared or streaked, or if the blade chatters across the glass, the elements should be replaced. It is easiest and most sensible to replace the elements in pairs.

If your vehicle is equipped with aftermarket blades, there are several different types of refills and your vehicle might have any kind. Aftermarket blades and arms rarely use the exact same type blade or refill as the original equipment. Here are some typical aftermarket blades; not all may be available for your vehicle:

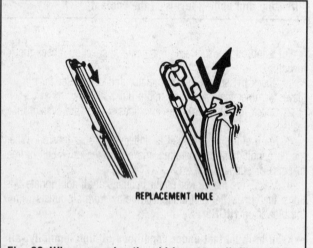

Fig. 32 When removing the old inserts, pull down then, slide it up and out

Bosch® wiper blade and fit kit

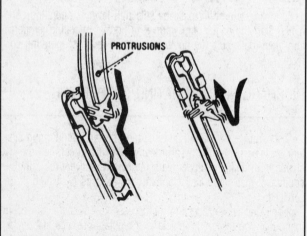
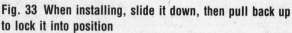

Fig. 33 When installing, slide it down, then pull back up to lock it into position

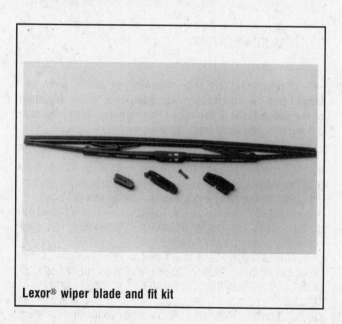

Lexor® wiper blade and fit kit

Pylon® wiper blade and adaptor

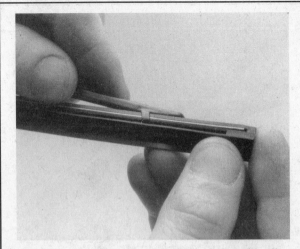

To remove and install a Lexor® wiper blade refill, slip out the old insert and slide in a new one

Trico® wiper blade and fit kit

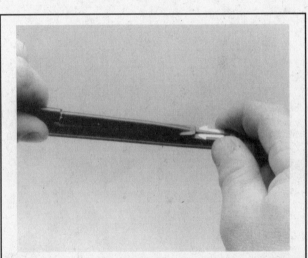

On Pylon® inserts, the clip at the end has to be removed prior to sliding the insert off

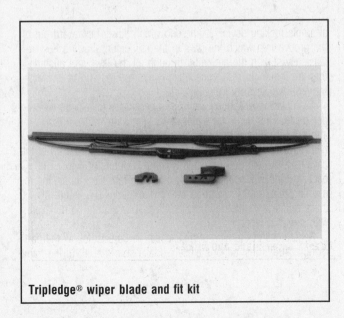

Tripledge® wiper blade and fit kit

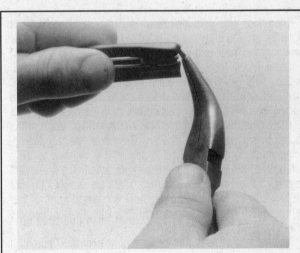

On Trico® wiper blades, the tab at the end of the blade must be turned up . . .

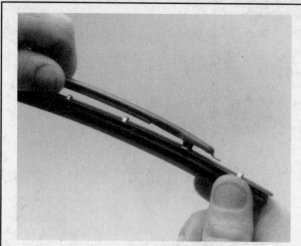

. . . then the insert can be removed. After installing the replacement insert, bend the tab back

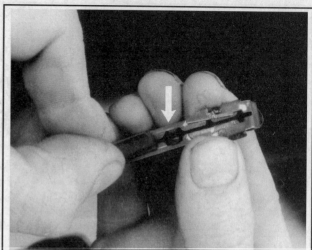

When removing a Toyota wiper insert, pull down on the insert from the top of the blade past the hole

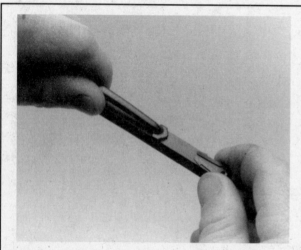

The Tripledge® wiper blade insert is removed and installed using a securing clip

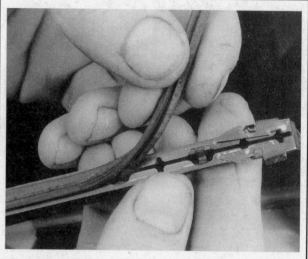

Now pull the wiper insert up and out of the large hole

The Anco® type uses a release button that is pushed down to allow the refill to slide out of the yoke jaws. The new refill slides back into the frame and locks in place.

Some Trico® refills are removed by locating where the metal backing strip or the refill is wider. Insert a small screwdriver blade between the frame and metal backing strip. Press down to release the refill from the retaining tab.

Other types of Trico® refills have two metal tabs which are unlocked by squeezing them together. The rubber filler can then be withdrawn from the frame jaws. A new refill is installed by inserting the refill into the front frame jaws and sliding it rearward to engage the remaining frame jaws. There are usually four jaws; be certain when installing that the refill is engaged in all of them. At the end of its travel, the tabs will lock into place on the front jaws of the wiper blade frame.

Another type of refill is made from polycarbonate. The refill has

a simple locking device at one end which flexes downward out of the groove into which the jaws of the holder fit, allowing easy release. By sliding the new refill through all the jaws and pushing through the slight resistance when it reaches the end of its travel, the refill will lock into position.

To replace the Tridon® refill, it is necessary to remove the wiper blade. This refill has a plastic backing strip with a notch about 1 in. (25mm) from the end. Hold the blade (frame) on a hard surface so that the frame is tightly bowed. Grip the tip of the backing strip and pull up while twisting counterclockwise. The backing strip will snap out of the retaining tab. Do this for the remaining tabs until the refill is free of the blade. The length of these refills is molded into the end and they should be replaced with identical types.

Regardless of the type of refill used, be sure to follow the part manufacturer's instructions closely. Make sure that all of the frame jaws are engaged as the refill is pushed into place and locked. If the metal blade holder and frame are allowed to touch the glass during wiper operation, the glass will be scratched.

INSERT REPLACEMENT

1. Cycle the wiper arm and blade assembly and stop at a position on the windshield where removal can be accomplished without difficulty.
2. To remove the blade: Pull the wiper arm out and away from the windshield. Grasp the wiper blade assembly and pull the top end of the rubber inward until the rubber blade is free of the end slot and you can see the replacement hole.
3. Pull the rubber blade out of the replacement hole.
4. To install a new rubber, insert the end with the small protrusions into the replacement hole, and work the rubber along the slot in the blade frame.
5. Once the rubber is in the frame slot, allow it to expand and fill in the end.

Tires and Wheels

Common sense and good driving habits will afford maximum tire life. Fast starts, sudden stops and hard cornering are hard on tires and will shorten their useful life span. Make sure that you don't overload the vehicle or run with incorrect pressure in the tires. Both of these practices will increase tread wear.

➡For optimum tire life, keep the tires properly inflated, rotate them often and have the wheel alignment checked periodically.

Inspect your tires frequently. Be especially careful to watch for bubbles in the tread or sidewall, deep cuts or underinflation. Replace any tires with bubbles in the sidewall. If cuts are so deep that they penetrate to the cords, discard the tire. Any cut in the sidewall of a radial tire renders it unsafe. Also look for uneven tread wear patterns that may indicate the front end is out of alignment or that the tires are out of balance.

TIRE ROTATION

Tires must be rotated periodically to equalize wear patterns that vary with a tire's position on the vehicle. Tires will also wear in an uneven way as the front steering/suspension system wears to the point where the alignment should be reset.

Rotating the tires will ensure maximum life for the tires as a set, so you will not have to discard a tire early due to wear on only part of the tread. Regular rotation is required to equalize wear.

When rotating "unidirectional tires," make sure that they always roll in the same direction. This means that a tire used on the left side of the vehicle must not be switched to the right side and vice-versa. Such tires should only be rotated front-to-rear or rear-to-front, while always remaining on the same side of the vehicle. These tires are marked on the sidewall as to the direction of rotation; observe the marks when reinstalling the tire(s).

Some styled or "mag" wheels may have different offsets front

Unidirectional tires are identifiable by sidewall arrows and/or the word "rotation"

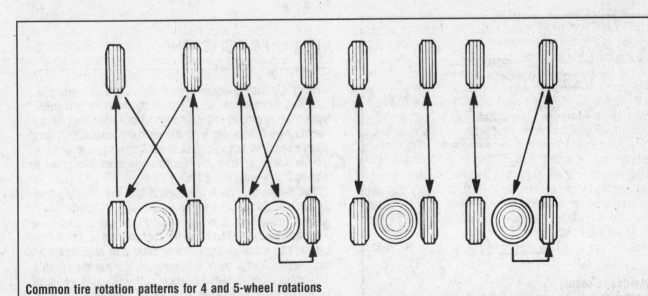

Common tire rotation patterns for 4 and 5-wheel rotations

to rear. In these cases, the rear wheels must not be used up front and vice-versa. Furthermore, if these wheels are equipped with uni-directional tires, they cannot be rotated unless the tire is re-mounted for the proper direction of rotation.

➡**The compact or space-saver spare is strictly for emergency use. It must never be included in the tire rotation or placed on the vehicle for everyday use.**

TIRE DESIGN

For maximum satisfaction, tires should be used in sets of four. Mixing of different types (radial, bias-belted, fiberglass belted) must be avoided. In most cases, the vehicle manufacturer has designated a type of tire on which the vehicle will perform best. Your first choice when replacing tires should be to use the same type of tire that the manufacturer recommends.

When radial tires are used, tire sizes and wheel diameters should be selected to maintain ground clearance and tire load capacity equivalent to the original specified tire. Radial tires should always be used in sets of four.

✳✳ CAUTION

Radial tires should never be used on only the front axle.

When selecting tires, pay attention to the original size as marked on the tire. Most tires are described using an industry size code sometimes referred to as P-Metric. This allows the exact identification of the tire specifications, regardless of the manufacturer. If selecting a different tire size or brand, remember to check the installed tire for any sign of interference with the body or suspension while the vehicle is stopping, turning sharply or heavily loaded.

Snow Tires

Good radial tires can produce a big advantage in slippery weather, but in snow, a street radial tire does not have sufficient tread to provide traction and control. The small grooves of a street tire quickly pack with snow and the tire behaves like a billiard ball on a marble floor. The more open, chunky tread of a snow tire will self-clean as the tire turns, providing much better grip on snowy surfaces.

To satisfy municipalities requiring snow tires during weather emergencies, most snow tires carry either an M + S designation after the tire size stamped on the sidewall, or the designation "all-season." In general, no change in tire size is necessary when buying snow tires.

Most manufacturers strongly recommend the use of 4 snow tires on their vehicles for reasons of stability. If snow tires are fitted only to the drive wheels, the opposite end of the vehicle may become very unstable when braking or turning on slippery surfaces. This instability can lead to unpleasant endings if the driver can't counteract the slide in time.

Note that snow tires, whether 2 or 4, will affect vehicle handling in all non-snow situations. The stiffer, heavier snow tires will noticeably change the turning and braking characteristics of the vehicle. Once the snow tires are installed, you must re-learn the behavior of the vehicle and drive accordingly.

➡**Consider buying extra wheels on which to mount the snow tires. Once done, the "snow wheels" can be installed and removed as needed. This eliminates the potential damage to tires or wheels from seasonal removal and installation. Even if your vehicle has styled wheels, see if inexpensive steel wheels are available. Although the look of the vehicle will change, the expensive wheels will be protected from salt, curb hits and pothole damage.**

TIRE STORAGE

If they are mounted on wheels, store the tires at proper inflation pressure. All tires should be kept in a cool, dry place. If they are stored in the garage or basement, do not let them stand on a concrete floor; set them on strips of wood, a mat or a large stack of newspaper. Keeping them away from direct moisture is of paramount importance. Tires should not be stored upright, but in a flat position.

INFLATION & INSPECTION

The importance of proper tire inflation cannot be overemphasized. A tire employs air as part of its structure. It is designed around the supporting strength of the air at a specified pressure. For this reason, improper inflation drastically reduces the tires's ability to perform as intended. A tire will lose some air in day-to-day use; having to add a few pounds of air periodically is not necessarily a sign of a leaking tire.

Two items should be a permanent fixture in every glove compartment: an accurate tire pressure gauge and a tread depth gauge. Check the tire pressure (including the spare) regularly with a pocket type gauge. Too often, the gauge on the end of the air hose at your corner garage is not accurate because it suffers too much abuse. Always check tire pressure when the tires are cold, as pressure increases with temperature. If you must move the vehicle to check the tire inflation, do not drive more than a mile be-

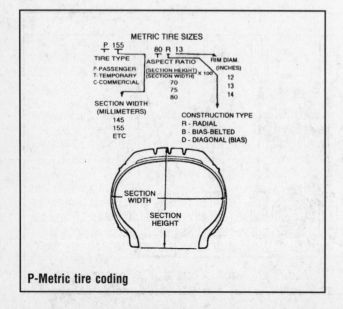

P-Metric tire coding

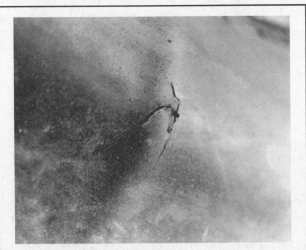

Tires should be checked frequently for any sign of puncture or damage

Tires with deep cuts, or cuts which show bulging should be replaced immediately

• DRIVE WHEEL HEAVY
  ACCELERATION
• OVERINFLATION

• HARD CORNERING
• UNDERINFLATION
• LACK OF ROTATION

Examples of inflation-related tire wear patterns

fore checking. A cold tire is generally one that has not been driven for more than three hours.

A plate or sticker is normally provided somewhere in the vehicle (door post, hood, tailgate or trunk lid) which shows the proper pressure for the tires. Never counteract excessive pressure build-up by bleeding off air pressure (letting some air out). This will cause the tire to run hotter and wear quicker.

✳✳ CAUTION

Never exceed the maximum tire pressure embossed on the tire! This is the pressure to be used when the tire is at maximum loading, but it is rarely the correct pressure for everyday driving. Consult the owner's manual or the tire pressure sticker for the correct tire pressure.

Once you've maintained the correct tire pressures for several weeks, you'll be familiar with the vehicle's braking and handling personality. Slight adjustments in tire pressures can fine-tune these characteristics, but never change the cold pressure specification by more than 2 psi. A slightly softer tire pressure will give a softer ride but also yield lower fuel mileage. A slightly harder tire will give crisper dry road handling but can cause skidding on wet surfaces. Unless you're fully attuned to the vehicle, stick to the recommended inflation pressures.

All tires made since 1968 have built-in tread wear indicator bars that show up as ½ in. (13mm) wide smooth bands across the tire when 1/16 in. (1.5mm) of tread remains. The appearance of tread wear indicators means that the tires should be replaced. In fact, many states have laws prohibiting the use of tires with less than this amount of tread.

You can check your own tread depth with an inexpensive gauge or by using a Lincoln head penny. Slip the Lincoln penny (with Lincoln's head upside-down) into several tread grooves. If you can see the top of Lincoln's head in 2 adjacent grooves, the tire has less than 1/16 in. (1.5mm) tread left and should be replaced. You can measure snow tires in the same manner by using the "tails" side of the Lincoln penny. If you can see the top of the Lincoln memorial, it's time to replace the snow tire(s).

CARE OF SPECIAL WHEELS

If you have invested money in magnesium, aluminum alloy or sport wheels, special precautions should be taken to make sure your investment is not wasted and that your special wheels look good for the life of the vehicle.

Special wheels are easily damaged and/or scratched. Occasionally check the rims for cracking, impact damage or air leaks. If any of these are found, replace the wheel. But in order to prevent this type of damage and the costly replacement of a special wheel, observe the following precautions:

• Use extra care not to damage the wheels during removal, installation, balancing, etc. After removal of the wheels from the vehicle, place them on a mat or other protective surface. If they are to be stored for any length of time, support them on strips of wood. Never store tires and wheels upright; the tread may develop flat spots.

• When driving, watch for hazards; it doesn't take much to crack a wheel.

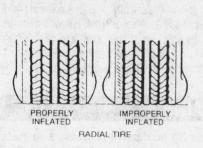

Radial tires have a characteristic sidewall bulge; don't try to measure pressure by looking at the tire. Use a quality air pressure gauge

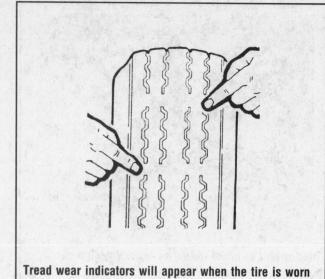

Tread wear indicators will appear when the tire is worn

CONDITION	RAPID WEAR AT SHOULDERS	RAPID WEAR AT CENTER	CRACKED TREADS	WEAR ON ONE SIDE	FEATHERED EDGE	BALD SPOTS	SCALLOPED WEAR
EFFECT							
CAUSE	UNDER-INFLATION OR LACK OF ROTATION	OVER-INFLATION OR LACK OF ROTATION	UNDER-INFLATION OR EXCESSIVE SPEED*	EXCESSIVE CAMBER	INCORRECT TOE	UNBALANCED WHEEL OR TIRE DEFECT *	LACK OF ROTATION OF TIRES OR WORN OR OUT-OF-ALIGNMENT SUSPENSION.
CORRECTION	ADJUST PRESSURE TO SPECIFICATIONS WHEN TIRES ARE COOL ROTATE TIRES			ADJUST CAMBER TO SPECIFICATIONS	ADJUST TOE-IN TO SPECIFICATIONS	DYNAMIC OR STATIC BALANCE WHEELS	ROTATE TIRES AND INSPECT SUSPENSION

*HAVE TIRE INSPECTED FOR FURTHER USE.

Common tire wear patterns and causes

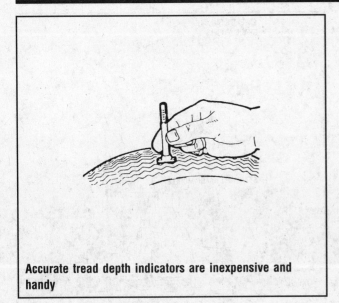

Accurate tread depth indicators are inexpensive and handy

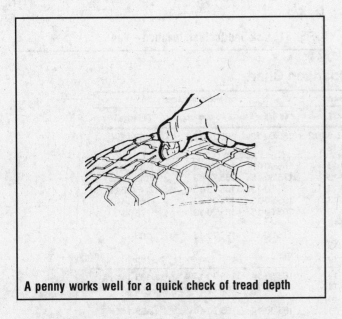

A penny works well for a quick check of tread depth

• When washing, use a mild soap or non-abrasive dish detergent (keeping in mind that detergent tends to remove wax). Avoid cleansers with abrasives or the use of hard brushes. There are many cleaners and polishes for special wheels.

• If possible, remove the wheels during the winter. Salt and sand used for snow removal can severely damage the finish of a wheel.

• Make certain the recommended lug nut torque is never exceeded or the wheel may crack. Never use snow chains on special wheels; severe scratching will occur.

SPARE TIRES

▶ **See Figures 34, 35, 36 and 37**

The spare tires for your vehicle are in the trunk of the Cressida sedans and under the rear of the Vans and Cressida wagons. On all Toyota models, in the trunk, you should have a lug nut wrench along with a jack and jack handle. These are required to change a

tire on all vehicles. On the Cressida sedan models, unscrew the spare tire screw and remove the tire and wheel assembly. On Cressida wagon and Van models, to get to the clamp bolt, the tailgate must be raised. The bolt is at the right side of the tailgate latch. The lugnut wrench can be used to loosen the bolt. To unlock the clamp bolt from the tire holder, lift the holder up slightly while pulling the clamp outward. The tire holder will now drop to the ground, now slide the tire out.

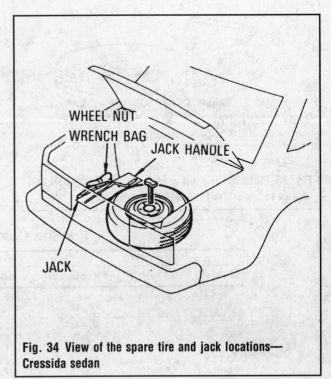

Fig. 34 View of the spare tire and jack locations— Cressida sedan

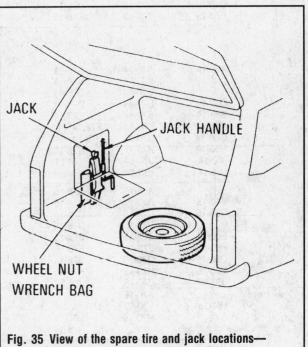

Fig. 35 View of the spare tire and jack locations— Cressida wagon

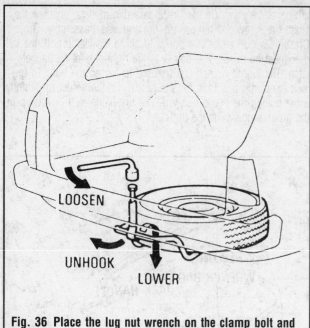

Fig. 36 Place the lug nut wrench on the clamp bolt and loosen to lower the tire—wagons and Vans

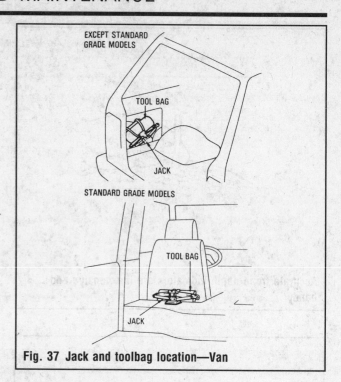

Fig. 37 Jack and toolbag location—Van

Tire Size Comparison Chart

| "Letter" sizes | | | Inch Sizes | Metric-inch Sizes | | |
"60 Series"	"70 Series"	"78 Series"	1965–77	"60 Series"	"70 Series"	"80 Series"
		Y78-12	5.50-12, 5.60-12 6.00-12	165/60-12	165/70-12	155-12
		W78-13	5.20-13	165/60-13	145/70-13	135-13
		Y78-13	5.60-13	175/60-13	155/70-13	145-13
			6.15-13	185/60-13	165/70-13	155-13, P155/80-13
A60-13	A70-13	A78-13	6.40-13	195/60-13	175/70-13	165-13
B60-13	B70-13	B78-13	6.70-13	205/60-13	185/70-13	175-13
			6.90-13			
C60-13	C70-13	C78-13	7.00-13	215/60-13	195/70-13	185-13
D60-13	D70-13	D78-13	7.25-13			
E60-13	E70-13	E78-13	7.75-13			195-13
			5.20-14	165/60-14	145/70-14	135-14
			5.60-14	175/60-14	155/70-14	145-14
			5.90-14			
A60-14	A70-14	A78-14	6.15-14	185/60-14	165/70-14	155-14
	B70-14	B78-14	6.45-14	195/60-14	175/70-14	165-14
	C70-14	C78-14	6.95-14	205/60-14	185/70-14	175-14
D60-14	D70-14	D78-14				
E60-14	E70-14	E78-14	7.35-14	215/60-14	195/70-14	185-14
F60-14	F70-14	F78-14, F83-14	7.75-14	225/60-14	200/70-14	195-14
G60-14	G70-14	G77-14, G78-14	8.25-14	235/60-14	205/70-14	205-14
H60-14	H70-14	H78-14	8.55-14	245/60-14	215/70-14	215-14
J60-14	J70-14	J78-14	8.85-14	255/60-14	225/70-14	225-14
L60-14	L70-14		9.15-14	265/60-14	235/70-14	
	A70-15	A78-15	5.60-15	185/60-15	165/70-15	155-15
B60-15	B70-15	B78-15	6.35-15	195/60-15	175/70-15	165-15
C60-15	C70-15	C78-15	6.85-15	205/60-15	185/70-15	175-15
	D70-15	D78-15				
E60-15	E70-15	E78-15	7.35-15	215/60-15	195/70-15	185-15
F60-15	F70-15	F78-15	7.75-15	225/60-15	205/70-15	195-15
G60-15	G70-15	G78-15	8.15-15/8.25-15	235/60-15	215/70-15	205-15
H60-15	H70-15	H78-15	8.45-15/8.55-15	245/60-15	225/70-15	215-15
J60-15	J70-15	J78-15	8.85-15/8.90-15	255/60-15	235/70-15	225-15
	K70-15		9.00-15	265/60-15	245/70-15	230-15
L60-15	L70-15	L78-15, L84-15	9.15-15			235-15
	M70-15	M78-15				255-15
		N78-15				

Note: Every size tire is not listed and many size comparisons are approximate, based on load ratings. Wider tires than those supplied new with the vehicle, should always be checked for clearance.

Troubleshooting Basic Tire Problems

Problem	Cause	Solution
The car's front end vibrates at high speeds and the steering wheel shakes	• Wheels out of balance • Front end needs aligning	• Have wheels balanced • Have front end alignment checked
The car pulls to one side while cruising	• Unequal tire pressure (car will usually pull to the low side) • Mismatched tires • Front end needs aligning	• Check/adjust tire pressure • Be sure tires are of the same type and size • Have front end alignment checked
Abnormal, excessive or uneven tire wear See "How to Read Tire Wear"	• Infrequent tire rotation • Improper tire pressure • Sudden stops/starts or high speed on curves	• Rotate tires more frequently to equalize wear • Check/adjust pressure • Correct driving habits
Tire squeals	• Improper tire pressure • Front end needs aligning	• Check/adjust tire pressure • Have front end alignment checked

FLUIDS AND LUBRICANTS

Fluid Disposal

Used fluids such as engine oil, transmission fluid, antifreeze and brake fluid are hazardous wastes and must be disposed of properly. Before draining fluids, consult with the authorities; in many areas, waste oil, etc. is being accepted as a part of recycling programs. A number of service stations and auto parts stores are also accepting waste fluids for recycling.

Be sure of the recycling center's policies before draining any fluids, as many will not accept different fluids that have been mixed together, such as oil and antifreeze.

Fuel and Engine Recommendations

FUEL

Unleaded gasoline having a Research Octane Number (RON) of 91, or an Antiknock Index of 87 is recommended for your car. Leaded gasoline will quickly interfere with the operation of the catalytic converter and just a few tankfuls of leaded gasoline will render the converter useless. This will cause the emission of much greater amounts of hydrocarbons and carbon monoxide from the exhaust system, void you warranty and cost a considerable amount of money for converter replacement.

Using a high quality unleaded gasoline will help maintain the driveability, fuel economy and emissions performance of your vehicle. A properly formulated gasoline will be comprised of well refined hydrocarbons and chemical additives and will perform the following.
• Minimize varnish, lacquer and other induction system deposits.
• Prevent gum formation or other deterioration.
• Protect the fuel tank and other fuel system components from corrosion or degradation.

• Provide the correct seasonally and geographically adjusted volatility. This will provide easy starting in the winter and avoid vapor lock in the summer. Avoid fuel system icing.

In addition, the fuel will be free of water debris and other impurities. Some driveability deterioration on multi-port electronically fuel injected vehicles can be traced to continuous use of certain gasolines which may have insufficient amounts of detergent additives to provide adequate deposit control protection.

OIL

Oil meeting API classification SG or SG/CC is recommended for use in your vehicle. Viscosity grades 10W-30 or 10W-40 are recommended on models before 1984 and 5W-30 or 15W-40 on models 1984 and later. See the viscosity to temperature chart in this section.

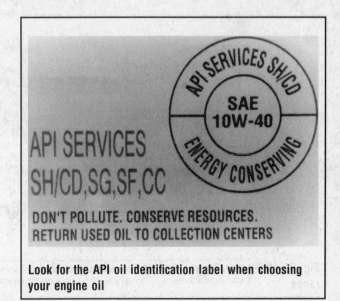

API SERVICES SH/CD, SG, SF, CC

API SERVICES SH/CD
SAE 10W-40
ENERGY CONSERVING

DON'T POLLUTE. CONSERVE RESOURCES. RETURN USED OIL TO COLLECTION CENTERS

Look for the API oil identification label when choosing your engine oil

Engine

OIL LEVEL CHECK

◆ **See Figure 38**

It is a good idea to check the engine oil each time or at least every other time you fill your gas tank. Check the oil level, if the red oil warning light comes on or if the oil pressure gauge shows an abnormally low reading.

It is preferable to check the oil level when the engine is cold or after the car has been standing for a while. Checking the oil immediately after the engine has been running will result in a false reading. Be sure that the car is on a level surface before checking the oil level.

1. Be sure your car is on level ground. Shut **OFF** the engine and wait for a few minutes to allow the oil to drain back into the oil pan.

2. Remove the engine oil dipstick and wipe clean with a rag.

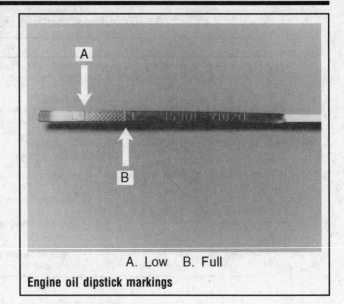

A. Low   B. Full

Engine oil dipstick markings

3. Reinsert the dipstick and push it down until it is fully seated in the tube.

4. Remove the stick and check the oil level shown. The oil level should be at the F mark (Full) or between the F and the L (Low) marks. Do not run the engine if the oil level is below the L. Add oil, as necessary. Use only oil which carries the API designation SH. Do not use unlabeled oil or a lower grade of oil which does not meet SH specifications.

5. If you wish, you may carefully fill the oil pan to the upper mark on the dipstick with less than a full quart. Do not, however, add a full quart when it would overfill the crankcase (level above the upper mark on the dipstick). The excess oil will generally be consumed at an excessive rate even if no damage to the engine seals occurs.

OIL & FILTER CHANGE

◆ **See Figures 39 thru 42a**

The manufacturer recommends changing the engine oil and oil filter every 8 months or 10,000 miles (16,000 km). However, it is recommended that the engine oil and oil filter be changed every 3 months or 3,000 miles (4,800 km). The engine oil and oil filter can be changed at 2,000 (3,200 km) or 2 month intervals if the driving conditions for your vehicle is done through severe dust and dirty conditions. Following these recommended intervals will help keep you car engine in good condition.

1. Make sure the engine is at normal operating temperature (this promotes complete draining of the old oil).

✳✳ CAUTION

The EPA warns that prolonged contact with used engine oil may cause a number of skin disorders, including cancer! You should make every effort to minimize your exposure to used engine oil. Protective gloves should be worn when changing the oil. Wash your hands and any other exposed skin areas as soon as possible after exposure to used engine oil. Soap and water, or waterless hand cleaner should be used.

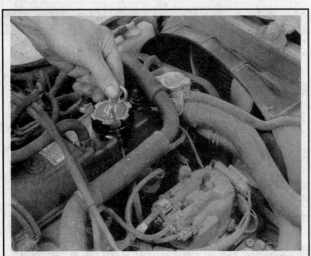

Lift the engine oil dipstick up and out of the tube in the engine—Van

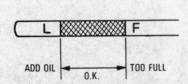

ADD OIL   O.K.   TOO FULL

Fig. 38 Make sure the engine oil level is in the correct range

Fig. 39 Remove the oil cap once the engine is warmed up

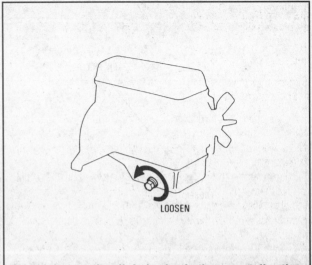

Fig. 40 Loosen the oil drain plug in the correct direction

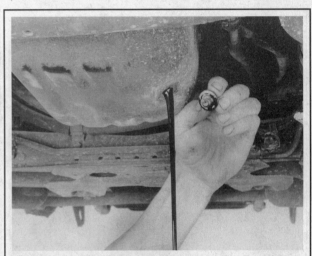

Remove the plug along with the gasket and allow the used engine oil to drain into a pan

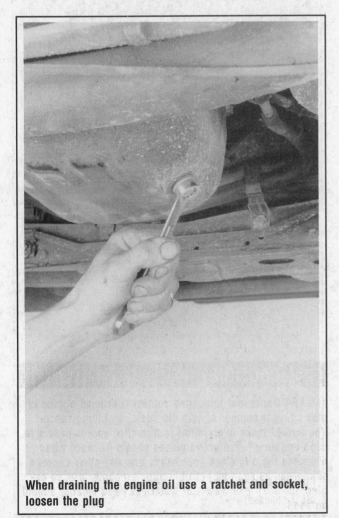

When draining the engine oil use a ratchet and socket, loosen the plug

Using a strap wrench, loosen the oil filter from the mounting base

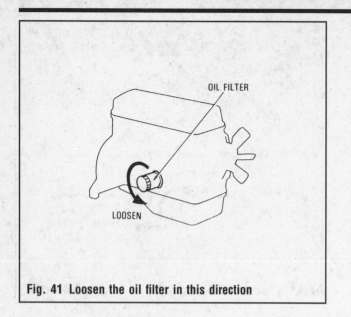

Fig. 41 Loosen the oil filter in this direction

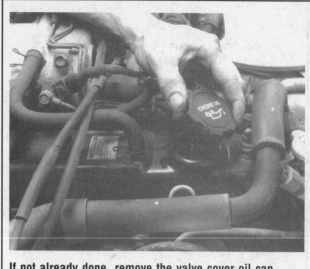

If not already done, remove the valve cover oil cap . . .

With your hands remove the oil filter

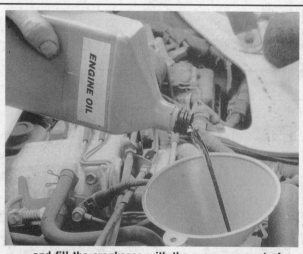

. . . and fill the crankcase with the proper amount of engine oil

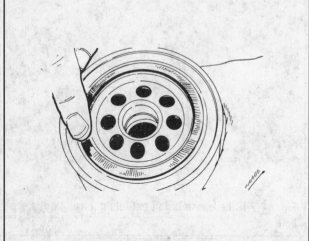

Fig. 41a Coat the new oil filter gasket with clean engine oil

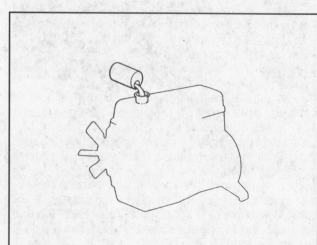

Fig. 42 Add oil, then check the level on the dipstick, top off if necessary

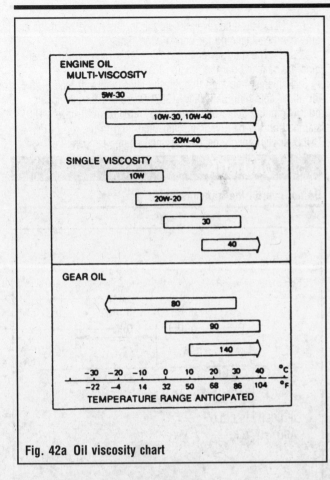

Fig. 42a Oil viscosity chart

2. Apply the parking brake and block the wheels or raise and support the car evenly on jackstands.

3. Place a drain pan of about a gallon and a half capacity under the engine oil pan drain plug. Use the proper size wrench, loosen and remove the plug. Allow all the old oil to drain. Wipe the pan and the drain plug with a clean rag. Inspect the drain plug gasket, replace if necessary.

4. Reinstall and tighten the drain plug. DO NOT OVER TIGHTEN!

5. Move the drain pan under the engine oil filter. Use a strap wrench and loosen the oil filter (do not remove), allow the oil to drain. Unscrew the filter the rest of the way by hand. Use a rag, if necessary, to keep from burning your fingers. When the filter comes loose from the engine, turn the mounting base upward to avoid spilling the remaining oil.

6. Wipe the engine filter mount clean with a rag. Coat the rubber gasket on the new oil filter with clean engine oil, applying it with a finger. Carefully start the filter onto the threaded engine mount. Turn the filter until it touches the engine mounting surface. Tighten the filter, by hand, ½ turn more or as recommended by the filter manufacturer.

7. Lower the vehicle to the ground. Refill the crankcase with four quarts of engine oil. Replace the filler cap and start the engine. Allow the engine to idle and check for oil leaks. Shut **OFF** the engine, wait for several minutes, then check the oil level with the dipstick. Add oil if necessary.

➡Store the used oil in a container made for that purpose until you can find a service station or garage that accepts used oil for recycling.

Manual Transmission

FLUID RECOMMENDATIONS

▸ **See Figures 43 and 44**

The oil in the manual transmission should be checked every 15,000 miles (24,000 km) or 12 months, whichever occurs first.

To check the oil level, remove the transmission filler plug. This is always the upper plug, the lower plug being the drain.

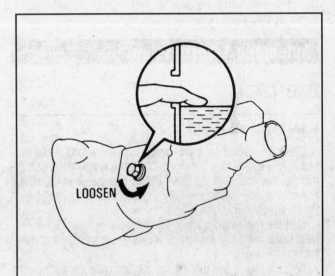

Fig. 43 Remove the manual transmission fill plug, then insert your finger to check the fluid level

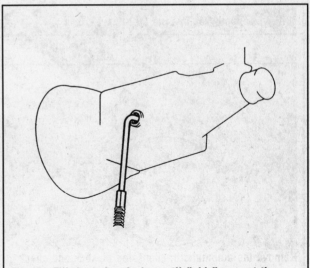

Fig. 44 Fill the transmission until fluid flows out the hole

The oil level should reach the bottom of the filler plug. If it is lower than this, add API grade multi-purpose gear oil GL-4 or GL-5 of the proper viscosity. Use SAE 75W-90 or 80W-90 oil in all models.

DRAIN & REFILL

Changing the fluid in a manual transmission is not necessary under normal operating conditions. However, the fluid levels should by checked at normal intervals. The only two ways to drain the oil from the transmission is by removing it and then turning the transmission on its side to drain or by using a suction pump and a tube, then use the pump to suck the transmission oil out. Then when refilling the transmission, the oil level should be even with the edge of the filler hole or within ¼ inch (6mm) of the hole.

Automatic Transmission

LEVEL CHECK

▶ **See Figure 45**

Check the level of the transmission fluid every 3,000 miles (4,800 km) and replace it every 15,000 (24,000 km) miles or 12 months. It is important that these figures be adhered to, in order to ensure a long transmission life. The procedures for checking the oil are given as follows:

Start the engine and allow to idle for a few minutes. Set the hand brake and apply the service brakes. Move the gear selector through all ranges.

With the engine still running, the parking brake on and the wheels blocked, place the selector in Neutral. Remove and clean the dipstick. Insert the dipstick fully, remove it and take a reading. The dipstick has two ranges.

1. COLD The fluid level should fall in this range when the engine has been running for only a short time.

2. HOT The fluid level should fall in this range when the engine has reached normal running temperatures.

3. Replenish the fluid through the filler tube with type F fluid for all models built until July, 1983; Dexron®II for all models built beginning July 1983. Models using Dexron®II have a DII stamped on the pan or drain plug. Add fluid to the top of the COLD or HOT range, depending upon engine temperature.

✳✳ CAUTION

Do not overfill the transmission!

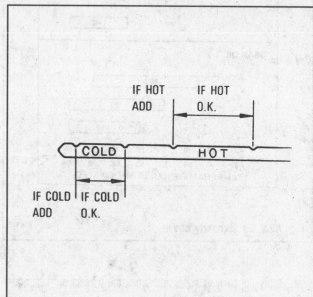

Fig. 45 Make sure the fluid level is between the correct marks

Remove the automatic transmission dipstick and check the fluid level

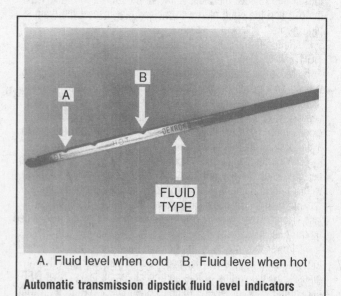

A. Fluid level when cold   B. Fluid level when hot

Automatic transmission dipstick fluid level indicators

When topping off the automatic transmission fluid, insert a funnel into the dipstick hole

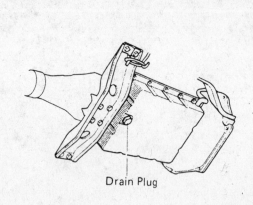

Fig. 45a The automatic drain plug is located on the bottom of the pan

6. Fill the transmission to the correct level. Remove the jackstands and lower the car to the ground.

Transfer Case

Changing the fluid in a transfer case is not necessary under normal operating conditions. The only way to drain the fluid from the transfer case is during the transfer case disassembly procedure. When reassembling the transfer case, add 1.3 oz. (38.4 mL) of API grade multipurpose gear oil GL-4 or GL-5 of the proper viscosity. Use SAE 75W-90 or 80W-90 oil in all models to refill the transfer case.

Differential

▶ **See Figures 46, 47 and 48**

The oil level in the differential should be checked every 15,000 miles (24,000) or 12 months, whichever comes first. The

DRAIN & REFILL

▶ **See Figure 45a**

When your vehicle is equipped with an automatic transmission and the region in which you live has severe cold weather, a multi-viscosity automatic transmission fluid should be used. Ask your auto parts retailer about the availability of MV Automatic Transmission Fluid.

Use of fluid other than specified could result in transmission malfunctions and/or failure.

1. Raise the car and safely support it on jackstands.
2. Place a suitable drain pan underneath the transmission oil pan. Loosen the oil pan mounting bolts and allow the fluid to drain until it reaches the level of the pan flange. Remove the attaching bolts, leaving one end attached so that the pan will tip and the rest of the fluid will drain.
3. Remove the oil pan. Thoroughly clean the pan. Remove the old gasket. Make sure that the gasket mounting surfaces are clean.
4. Remove the transmission filter screen retaining bolt. Remove the screen.
5. Install a new filter screen and O-ring. Place a new gasket on the pan and install the pan to the transmission.

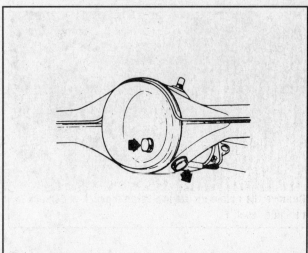

Fig. 46 The upper bolt is the fill plug, and the lower bolt is the drain plug

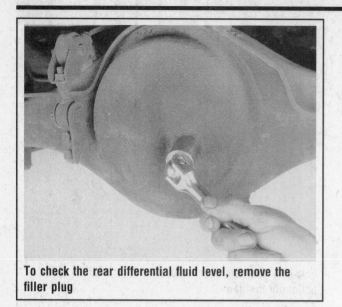

To check the rear differential fluid level, remove the filler plug

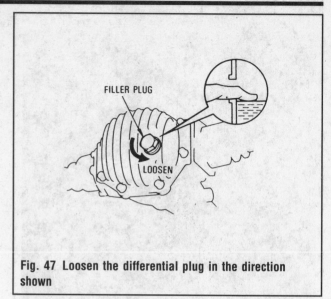

Fig. 47 Loosen the differential plug in the direction shown

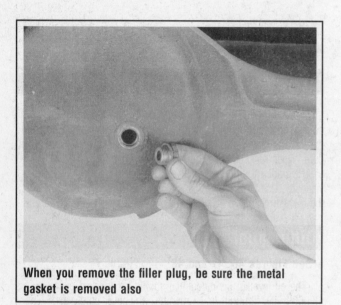

When you remove the filler plug, be sure the metal gasket is removed also

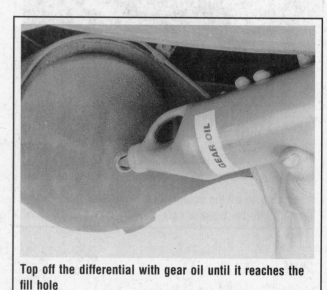

Top off the differential with gear oil until it reaches the fill hole

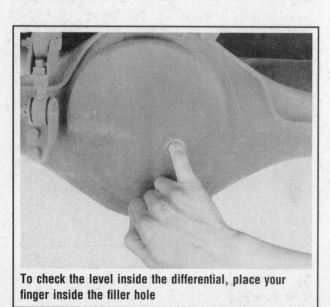

To check the level inside the differential, place your finger inside the filler hole

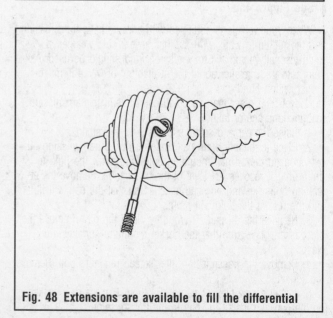

Fig. 48 Extensions are available to fill the differential

oil should be checked with the car on a level surface. Remove the oil filler and upper plug, located on the back of the differential.

➡**The bottom plug is the drain.**

The oil level should reach to the bottom edge of the filler hole. If low, replenish with API grade GL-4 or GL-5 gear oil of the proper viscosity. The viscosity is determined by the ambient temperature range. If the temperature averages above 10°F (−12°C), use SAE 90 gear oil. If the temperature averages below 10°F (−12°C), use SAE 80 oil. Always check for leaks when checking the oil level.

DRAIN & REFILL

1. Park the vehicle on a level surface. Set the parking brake.
2. Remove the filler (upper) plug. Place a container which is large enough to catch all of the differential oil, under the drain plug.

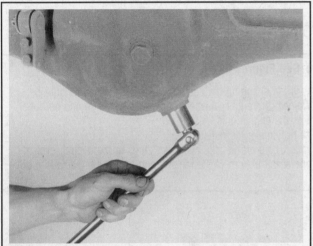

When draining the differential, remove the lower plug on the under side of the housing

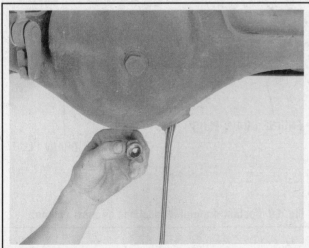

Allow all the gear oil to flow out of the differential, then install the drain plug using a new gasket

3. Remove the drain (lower) plug and gasket, if so equipped. Allow all of the oil to drain into the container.
4. Install the drain plug. Tighten it so that it will not leak, but do not over tighten.
5. Refill with the proper grade and viscosity of axle lubricant. Be sure that the level reaches the bottom of the filler plug.
6. Install the filler plug and check for leakage.

Cooling System

FLUID RECOMMENDATION

Whenever you add engine coolant use equal parts of water and premium cooling system ethylene-glycol type coolant (antifreeze) that meets Toyota specifications. Do not use alcohol or methanol antifreeze, or mix them with specified coolant.

➡**These vehicles have aluminum radiators and require a unique corrosion inhibited coolant formulation to avoid damage. Use only permanent type coolant that meets Toyota specifications. A coolant mixture of less than 40% engine coolant concentrate may result in engine corrosion and over-heating.**

The factory installed solution of cooling system fluid and water will protect your vehicle to −35°F (−37°C). Check the freezing protection rating of the coolant at least once a year, just before winter.

Maintain a protection rating consistent with the lowest temperature in which you operate your vehicle or at least −20°F (−29°C) to prevent engine damage as a result of freezing and to ensure proper engine operating temperature. Rust and corrosion inhibitors tend to deteriorate with time, changing the coolant every 4 years or 60,000 miles is recommended for proper protection of the cooling system.

➡**The Toyota Motor Corporation does not authorize the use of the recycled engine coolant nor do they sanction the use of any machines or devices that recycle engine coolant. Recycled engine coolant is not equivalent to the factory fill OEM coolant. The quality of the engine coolant degenerates with use. Recycling used engine coolant is very difficult to do without exposing the used coolant to additional foreign substances. Merely adding an additive to the coolant will not restore it. Always use new engine coolant that meets the Toyota coolant specifications for the engine being serviced.**

The disposal of all used engine coolant must always be done in accordance with all applicable Federal, State and Local laws and regulations.

LEVEL CHECK

◆ **See Figure 49**

Dealing with the cooling system can be a dangerous matter unless the proper precautions are observed. It is best to check the coolant level in the radiator when the engine is cold. This is done by removing the radiator cap, on models without an expansion tank, and seeing that the coolant is within 2 inch (50 mm) of the

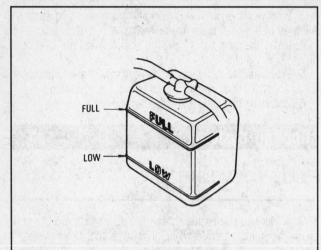

Fig. 49 The coolant reservoir specifies how much fluid is in the system

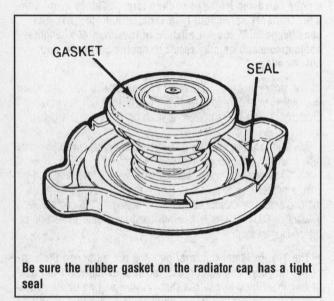

Be sure the rubber gasket on the radiator cap has a tight seal

➡ **Never add cold coolant to a hot engine unless the engine is running, to avoid cracking the engine block.**

The radiator hoses and clamps and the radiator cap should be checked at the same time as the coolant level. Hoses which are brittle, cracked, or swollen should be replaced. Clamps should be checked for tightness (screwdriver tight only. Do not allow the clamp to cut into the hose or crush the fitting). The radiator cap gasket should be checked for any obvious tears, cracks or swelling, or any signs of incorrect seating in the radiator neck.

The cooling fan motor is controlled by a temperature switch. The fan may come on and run when the engine is off. It will continue to run until the correct temperature is reached. Take care not to get your fingers, etc. caught in the fan blades.

Never remove the radiator cap under any circumstances when the engine is operating. Before removing the cap, switch **OFF** the engine and wait until it has cooled. Even then, use extreme care when removing the cap from a hot radiator. Wrap a thick cloth around the cap and turn it slowly to the first stop. Step back while the pressure is released from the cooling system. When you are sure all the pressure has been released, press down on the cap, still with a cloth, turn and remove it.

DRAIN & REFILL

▶ **See Figures 50 and 51**

When changing the coolant the cooling system should be drained, thoroughly flushed, and refilled. This should be done with the engine cold.

1. Remove the radiator cap.
2. There are usually two drain plugs in the cooling system; one at the bottom of the radiator and one at the rear of the driv-

bottom of the filler neck. On models with an expansion tank, if coolant visible above the MIN mark on the tank, the level is satisfactory. Always be certain that the filler caps on both the radiator and the reservoir are tightly closed.

In the event that the coolant level must be checked when the engine is warm on engines without the expansion tank, place a thick rag over the radiator cap and slowly turn the cap counterclockwise until it reaches the first detent. Allow all the hot steam to escape. This will allow the pressure in the system to drop gradually, preventing an explosion of hot coolant. When the hissing noise stops, remove the cap the rest of the way.

If the coolant level is low, add equal amounts of ethylene glycol based antifreeze and clean water. On models without an expansion tank, add coolant through the radiator filler neck. Fill the expansion tank to the MAX level on cars with that system.

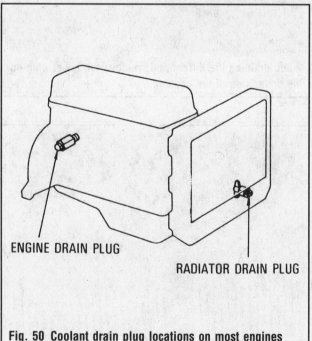

Fig. 50 Coolant drain plug locations on most engines

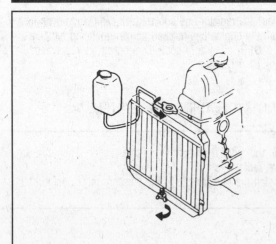

Fig. 51 Open the radiator cap and petcock to drain the cooling system

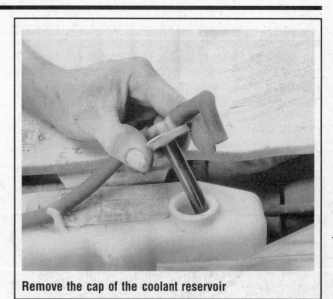

Remove the cap of the coolant reservoir

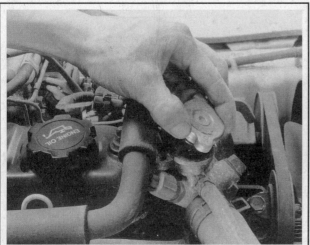

When topping off the coolant level in the radiator, remove the cap . . .

Fill the coolant reservoir tank half full with a 50/50 coolant water mixture

. . . then fill the system with the equal amounts of anti freeze and water—Van shown

er's side of the engine. Both should be loosened to allow the coolant to drain.

✳✳ CAUTION

When draining the coolant, keep in mind that cats and dogs are attracted by the ethylene glycol antifreeze, and are quite likely to drink any that is left in an uncovered container or in puddles on the ground. This will prove fatal in sufficient quantity. Always drain the coolant into a sealable container. Coolant should be reused unless it is contaminated or several years old.

3. Turn on the heater inside the car to its hottest position. This ensures that the heater core is flushed out completely. Flush out the system thoroughly by refilling it with clean water through the radiator opening as it escapes from the two drain cocks. Continue until the water running out is clear. Be sure to clean out the coolant recovery tank as well if your car has one.

4. If the system is badly contaminated with rust or scale, you

can use a commercial flushing solution to clear it out. Follow the manufacturer's instructions. Some causes of rust are air in the system, caused by a leaky radiator cap or an insufficiently filled or leaking system; failure to change the coolant regularly; use of excessively hard or soft water; and failure to use a proper mix of antifreeze and water.

5. When the system is clear, allow all the water to drain, then close the drain plugs. Fill the system through the radiator with a 50/50 mix of ethylene glycol type antifreeze and water.

6. Start the engine and top off the radiator with the antifreeze and water mixture. If your car has a coolant recovery tank, fill it half full with the coolant mix.

7. Replace the radiator and coolant tank caps, and check for leaks. When the engine has reached normal operating temperature, shut it **OFF,** allow it to cool, then top off the radiator or coolant tank as necessary.

FLUSHING & CLEANING THE SYSTEM

1. Drain the radiator as outlined in this section. Then add water until the radiator is full.
2. Reinstall the radiator cap to the pressure relief position by

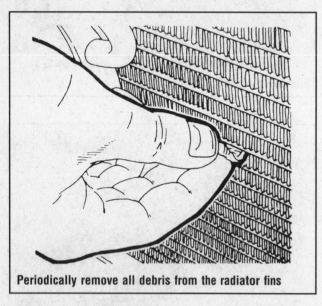

Periodically remove all debris from the radiator fins

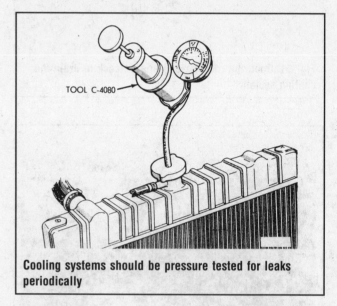

TOOL C-4080

Cooling systems should be pressure tested for leaks periodically

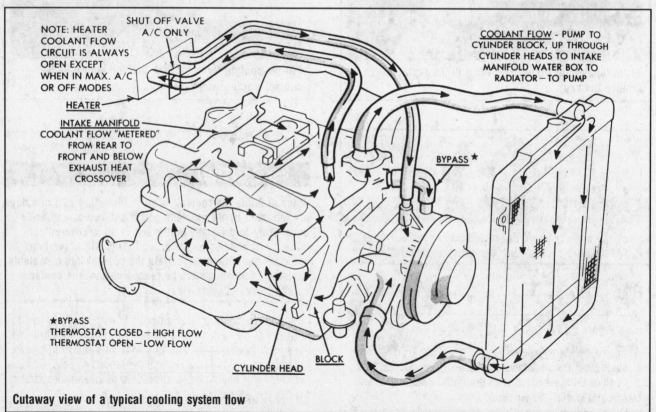

NOTE: HEATER COOLANT FLOW CIRCUIT IS ALWAYS OPEN EXCEPT WHEN IN MAX. A/C OR OFF MODES

SHUT OFF VALVE A/C ONLY

HEATER

INTAKE MANIFOLD COOLANT FLOW "METERED" FROM REAR TO FRONT AND BELOW EXHAUST HEAT CROSSOVER

COOLANT FLOW - PUMP TO CYLINDER BLOCK, UP THROUGH CYLINDER HEADS TO INTAKE MANIFOLD WATER BOX TO RADIATOR — TO PUMP

BYPASS ★

★BYPASS
THERMOSTAT CLOSED – HIGH FLOW
THERMOSTAT OPEN – LOW FLOW

CYLINDER HEAD

BLOCK

Cutaway view of a typical cooling system flow

installing the cap to the fully installed position and then backing off to the first stop.

3. Start and idle the engine until the upper radiator hose is warm.

4. Immediately shut **OFF** engine. Cautiously drain the water by opening the drain cock.

5. Repeat Steps 1–4 as many times as necessary until nearly clear water comes out of the radiator. Allow remaining water to drain and then close the petcock.

6. Disconnect the overflow hose from the radiator filler neck nipple.

7. Remove the coolant recovery reservoir from the fender apron and empty the fluid. Flush the reservoir with clean water, drain and install the reservoir and overflow hose and clamp to the radiator filler neck.

8. Refill the coolant system as outlined in this section.

➡**If the radiator has been removed, it is possible to back flush the system as follows:**

    a. Back flush the radiator, Ensure the radiator cap is in position. Turn the radiator upside down. Position a high pressure water in the bottom hose location and backflush. The radiator internal pressure must not exceed 20 psi.

    b. Remove the thermostat housing and thermostat. Back flush the engine by positioning a high pressure hose into the engine through the thermostat location and back flush the engine.

➡**If the radiator is showing signs of rust and wear, it may be a good idea to thoroughly clean and get the cooling fins free from debris, while the radiator is out of the vehicle. Then using a suitable high temperature rust proof engine paint, paint the radiator assembly.**

Brake and Clutch Master Cylinders

FLUID RECOMMENDATION

The brake and clutch (manual transmission) master cylinder reservoirs are made of a translucent plastic so that the fluid level can be checked without removing the cap. Check the fluid level frequently.

If the fluid is low, fill the reservoir with DOT 3 fluid, pouring so bubbles do not form in the reservoir. Use care not to spill any fluid on the car's paint, damage may result.

✳✳ CAUTION

Do not use a lower grade of brake fluid and never mix different types. Either could result in a brake system failure.

LEVEL CHECK

◆ **See Figure 52**

The brake master cylinder is located under the hood, on the left side firewall. Before removing the master cylinder reservoir cap, make sure the vehicle is resting on level ground and clean all the dirt away from the top of the master cylinder. Pry the retaining clip off to the side. Remove the master cylinder cover.

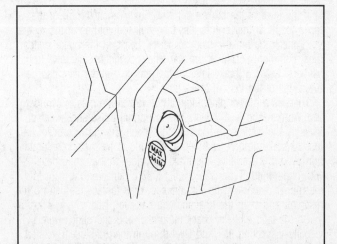

Fig. 52 The Van brake fluid reservoir is on the drivers side of the dash

Remove the cap to fill the brake fluid reservoir—Van

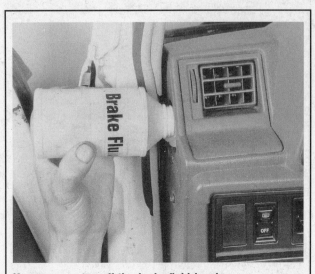

If necessary, top off the brake fluid level

If the level of the brake fluid is within ¼ inch (6mm) of the top it is OK. If the level is less than half the volume of the reservoir, check the brake system for leaks. Leaks in the brake system most commonly occur at the rear wheel cylinders, or at the front calipers. Leaks at brake lines or the master cylinder can also be the cause of the loss of brake fluid.

There is a rubber diaphragm at the top of the master cylinder cap. As the fluid level lowers due to normal brake shoe wear or leakage, the diaphragm takes up the space. This is to prevent the loss of brake fluid out the vented cap and to help stop contamination by dirt. After filling the master cylinder to the proper level with brake fluid (Type DOT 3), but before replacing the cap, fold the rubber diaphragm up into the cap, then replace the cap on the reservoir and snap the retaining clip back in place.

On the later models, check the brake fluid and clutch fluid by visually inspecting the fluid level through the translucent master cylinder reservoir. It should be between the **MIN** and the **MAX** level marks embossed on the side of the reservoir. If the level is found to be low, remove the reservoir cap and fill to the **MAX** level with DOT 3 brake fluid.

The level will decrease with accumulated mileage. This is a normal condition associated with a the wear of the disc brake linings. If the fluid is excessively low, it would be advisable to have the brake system checked.

➡**To avoid the possibility of brake failure that could result in property damage or personal injury, do not allow the master cylinder to run dry. Never reuse brake fluid that has been drained from the hydraulic system or fluid that has been allowed to stand in an open container for an extended period of time.**

Power Steering Reservoir

FLUID RECOMMENDATIONS

▶ **See Figures 52a and 52b**

Check the level of the power steering fluid periodically. The fluid level should fall within the crosshatched area of the gauge

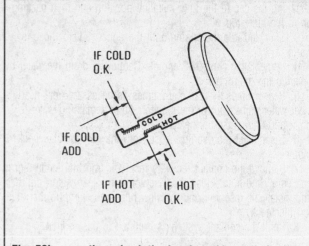

Fig. 52b . . . then check the level markings on the cap dipstick

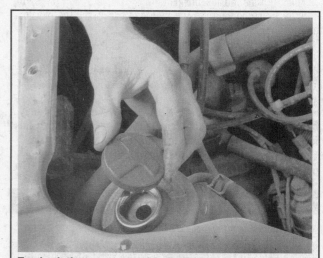

To check the power steering fluid level, remove the cap from the reservoir

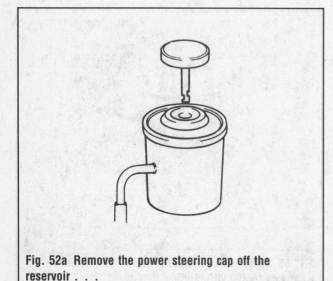

Fig. 52a Remove the power steering cap off the reservoir . . .

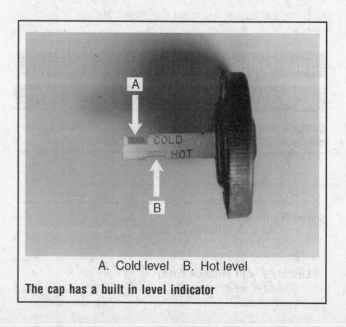

A. Cold level   B. Hot level

The cap has a built in level indicator

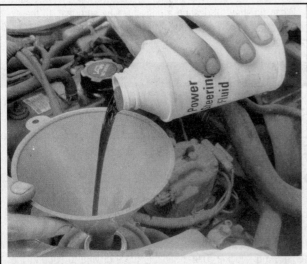

Top off the level using a funnel and power steering fluid

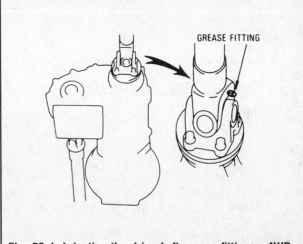

Fig. 53 Lubricating the driveshaft grease fittings—4WD Van shown

attached to the reservoir cap. If the fluid level is below this, add DEXRON® fluid. Remember to check for leaks.

Chassis Greasing

▶ **See Figures 53 thru 58**

The chassis lubrication for these models is limited to lubricating the front ball joints every 15,000 miles (24,000 km) or 12 months, whichever occurs first. To lubricate the ball joints, proceed as follows:

1. Remove the screw plug from the ball joint. Install a grease nipple.
2. Using a hand-operated grease gun, lubricate the ball joint with NGLI No. 1 molybdenum-disulphide lithium-based grease.

✳✳ WARNING

Do not use multipurpose or chassis grease.

3. Remove the nipple and reinstall the screw plug.
4. Repeat for the other ball joint(s).

Body Lubrication

There is no set period recommended by Toyota for body lubrication. However, it is a good idea to lubricate the following body points at least once a year, especially in the fall before cold weather.

Lubricate with engine oil:
  Door lock latches
  Door lock rollers
  Station wagon tailgate hinges
  Door, hood, and hinge pivots
Lubricate with silicone grease:
  Trunk lid latch and hinge
  Glove box door latch
Lubricate with silicone spray:
  All rubber weather stripping
  Hood stops

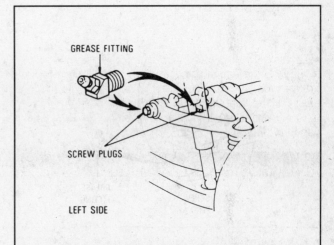

Fig. 54 Grease fitting locations on the control arms—left side Van

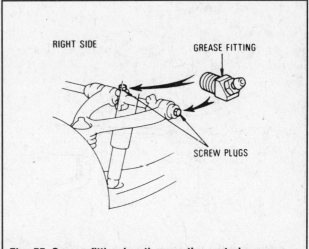

Fig. 55 Grease fitting locations on the control arms—right side Van

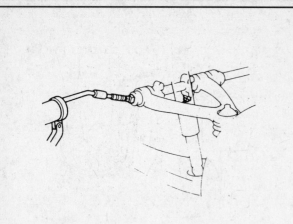

Fig. 56 Using a grease gun, pump the chassis grease into the fitting

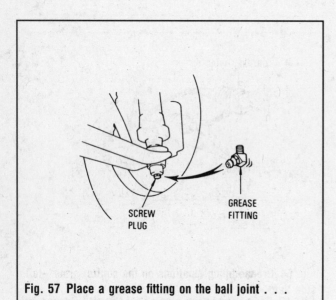

SCREW PLUG

GREASE FITTING

Fig. 57 Place a grease fitting on the ball joint . . .

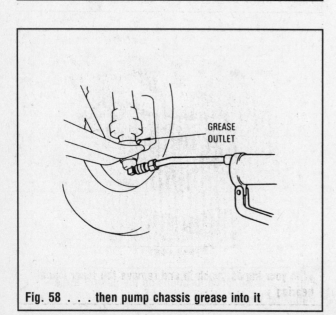

GREASE OUTLET

Fig. 58 . . . then pump chassis grease into it

When finished lubricating a body part, be sure that all the excess lubricant has been wiped off, especially in the areas of the car which may come in contact with clothing.

Wheel Bearings

REMOVAL, PACKING & INSTALLATION

Front Wheel Bearings
◆ **See Figures 59, 60, 61 and 62**

1. Remove the front wheel covers and loosen the lug nuts.
2. Raise and safely support the vehicle safely. Remove the front wheels.
3. Remove the brake caliper mounting bolts and caliper from the steering knuckle. Use a suitable piece of wire to support the brake caliper assembly. Do not disconnect the brake hose.
4. Remove the hub grease cap, cotter pin, lock cap, nut and axle hub.
5. Remove the hub and brake disc (rotor) together with the outer bearing and thrust washer. Be careful not to drop the outer bearing.
6. Remove the inner bearing and oil seal, by using a suitable tool to pry out the oil seal and remove the seal and inner bearing.
7. Inspect the spindle and bearings for wear and damage and replace as necessary.
8. If replacing the bearing outer races, use the following procedure.
   a. Using a brass drift and a hammer, drive out the bearing outer race.
   b. Using a suitable tool, carefully drive in a new bearing outer race.
9. Apply a high temperature multi-purpose grease in the palm of your hand. Pack grease into the bearing, continuing until the grease oozes out from the other side.
10. Do the same around the bearing circumference. Coat the inside of the hub and cap with multi-purpose grease.
11. Place the inner bearing into the hub and use a suitable seal driver to install the new seal, be sure to coat the new seal with the multi-purpose grease.
12. Place the axle hub on the spindle. Install the outer bearing and thrust washer.
13. Install and tighten the locknut to 22 ft. lbs.
14. Turn the hub right and left 2 or 3 times to allow the bearing to settle.
15. Loosen the locknut so that there is 0.020–0.039 inch (0.5–1.0 mm) play in the axial direction. Using the socket in your hand, tighten the nut as tight as possible.
16. Install lock cap, cotter pin and hub grease cap. If the cotter pin hole does not line-up, correct by tightening the nut by the smallest amount possible.
17. Install the brake caliper on the disc. Tighten the mounting bolts to 59–75 ft. lbs.

➡**Wheel bearings removal and installation on FWD cars, and rear axle bearings will be covered later in this manual.**

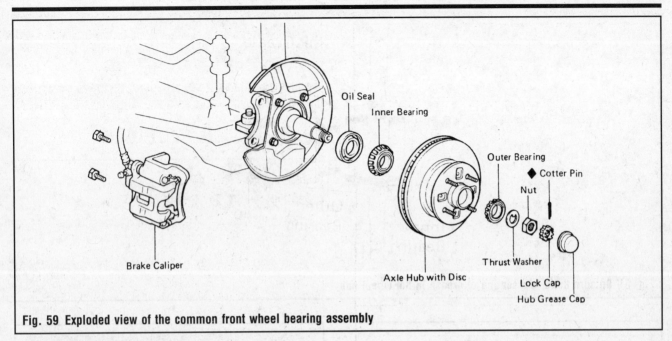

Fig. 59 Exploded view of the common front wheel bearing assembly

Use a seal removal tool to pry the oil seal from the hub and disc

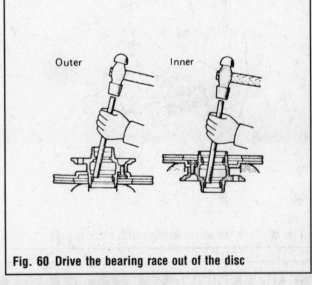

Fig. 60 Drive the bearing race out of the disc

Remove the old oil seal and discard it

With your hands, reach in and remove the inner wheel bearing

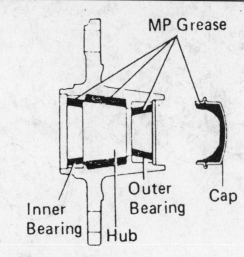

Fig. 61 Be sure there is a coating of grease in the wheel hub

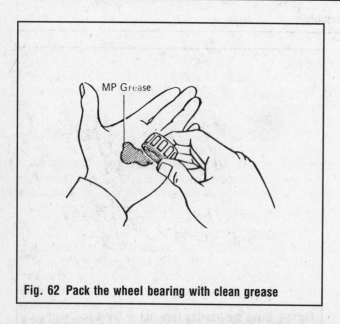

Fig. 62 Pack the wheel bearing with clean grease

Use a seal driver to seat the new seal

TRAILER TOWING

General Recommendations

Your vehicle was primarily designed to carry passengers and cargo. It is important to remember that towing a trailer will place additional loads on your vehicles engine, drivetrain, steering, braking and other systems. However, if you decide to tow a trailer, using the prior equipment is a must.

Local laws may require specific equipment such as trailer brakes or fender mounted mirrors. Check your local laws.

Trailer Weight

The weight of the trailer is the most important factor. A good weight-to-horsepower ratio is about 35:1, 35 lbs. of Gross Combined Weight (GCW) for every horsepower your engine develops. Multiply the engine's rated horsepower by 35 and subtract the weight of the vehicle passengers and luggage. The number remaining is the approximate ideal maximum weight you should tow, although a numerically higher axle ratio can help compensate for heavier weight.

Hitch (Tongue) Weight

Calculate the hitch weight in order to select a proper hitch. The weight of the hitch is usually 9–11% of the trailer gross weight and should be measured with the trailer loaded. Hitches fall into various categories: those that mount on the frame and rear bumper, the bolt-on type, or the weld-on distribution type used for larger trailers. Axle mounted or clamp-on bumper hitches should never be used.

Check the gross weight rating of your trailer. Tongue weight is usually figured as 10% of gross trailer weight. Therefore, a trailer

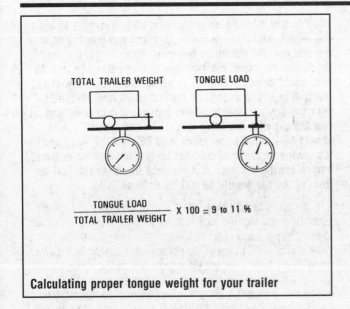

TONGUE LOAD

$$\frac{\text{TONGUE LOAD}}{\text{TOTAL TRAILER WEIGHT}} \times 100 = 9 \text{ to } 11 \%$$

Calculating proper tongue weight for your trailer

with a maximum gross weight of 2000 lbs. will have a maximum tongue weight of 200 lbs. Class I trailers fall into this category. Class II trailers are those with a gross weight rating of 2000–3000 lbs., while Class III trailers fall into the 3500–6000 lbs. category. Class IV trailers are those over 6000 lbs. and are for use with fifth wheel trucks, only.

When you've determined the hitch that you'll need, follow the manufacturer's installation instructions, exactly, especially when it comes to fastener torques. The hitch will subjected to a lot of stress and good hitches come with hardened bolts. Never substitute an inferior bolt for a hardened bolt.

Cooling

ENGINE

Overflow Tank

One of the most common, if not THE most common, problems associated with trailer towing is engine overheating. If you have a cooling system without an expansion tank, you'll definitely need to get an aftermarket expansion tank kit, preferably one with at least a 2 quart capacity. These kits are easily installed on the radiator's overflow hose, and come with a pressure cap designed for expansion tanks.

Flex Fan

Another helpful accessory for vehicles using a belt-driven radiator fan is a flex fan. These fans are large diameter units designed to provide more airflow at low speeds, by using fan blades that have deeply cupped surfaces. The blades then flex, or flatten out, at high speed, when less cooling air is needed. These fans are far lighter in weight than stock fans, requiring less horsepower to drive them. Also, they are far quieter than stock fans. If you do decide to replace your stock fan with a flex fan, note that if your vehicle has a fan clutch, a spacer will be needed between the flex fan and water pump hub.

Oil Cooler

Aftermarket engine oil coolers are helpful for prolonging engine oil life and reducing overall engine temperatures. Both of these factors increase engine life. While not absolutely necessary in towing Class I and some Class II trailers, they are recommended for heavier Class II and all Class III towing. Engine oil cooler systems usually consist of an adapter, screwed on in place of the oil filter, a remote filter mounting and a multi-tube, finned heat exchanger, which is mounted in front of the radiator or air conditioning condenser.

TRANSMISSION

An automatic transmission is usually recommended for trailer towing. Modern automatics have proven reliable and, of course, easy to operate, in trailer towing. The increased load of a trailer, however, causes an increase in the temperature of the automatic transmission fluid. Heat is the worst enemy of an automatic transmission. As the temperature of the fluid increases, the life of the fluid decreases.

It is essential, therefore, that you install an automatic transmission cooler. The cooler, which consists of a multi-tube, finned heat exchanger, is usually installed in front of the radiator or air conditioning compressor, and hooked in-line with the transmission cooler tank inlet line. Follow the cooler manufacturer's installation instructions.

Select a cooler of at least adequate capacity, based upon the combined gross weights of the vehicle and trailer.

Cooler manufacturers recommend that you use an aftermarket cooler in addition to, and not instead of, the present cooling tank in your radiator. If you do want to use it in place of the radiator cooling tank, get a cooler at least two sizes larger than normally necessary.

➡**A transmission cooler can, sometimes, cause slow or harsh shifting in the transmission during cold weather, until the fluid has a chance to come up to normal operating temperature. Some coolers can be purchased with or retrofitted with a temperature bypass valve which will allow fluid flow through the cooler only when the fluid has reached above a certain operating temperature.**

Handling A Trailer

Towing a trailer with ease and safety requires a certain amount of experience. It's a good idea to learn the feel of a trailer by practicing turning, stopping and backing in an open area such as an empty parking lot.

Towing

Always tow using the tie down tabs located under front and rear bumpers. The following precautions should be observed when towing the vehicle:

1. Always place the transmission in Neutral and release the parking brake.
2. Models equipped with automatic transmissions, may be

towed with the transmission in Neutral, but only for short distances at speeds below 20 mph (32 kmh). When towing a car with an automatic transmission, you may tow the car for up to 50 miles (80 km) and at speeds of up to 30 miles per hour (48 kmh).

3. If the rear axle is defective, the car must be towed with its rear wheels off the ground.

4. Always turn the steering column lock to ON and then return to ACC. This prevents the steering column from locking.

✳✳ WARNING

The steering column lock is not designed to hold the wheels straight while the car is being towed. Therefore, if the car is being towed with its front end down, place a dolly under the front wheels.

➡**Whenever you are towing another vehicle, or being towed, make sure the chain or strap is sufficiently long and strong. Attach the chain securely at a point on the frame, shipping tie-down slots are provided on the front and rear of you car and should be used. Never attach a chain or** strap to any steering or suspension part. Never try to start the vehicle when being towed, it might run into the back of the tow car. Do not allow too much slack in the tow line, the towed car could run over the line and damage to both cars could occur. If you car is being towed by a tow truck, the towing speed should be limited to 50 mph (80 kmh) with the driving wheels off the ground. If it is necessary to tow the car with the drive wheels on the ground, speed should be limited to no more then 35 mph (56 kmh) and the towing distance should not be greater than 50 miles (80 km). If towing distance is more than 50 miles (80 km) the front of the car should be put on dollies.

If the car is being towed with the front wheels on the ground, never allow the steering lock to keep the wheels straight, damage to the steering could occur. On vehicles equipped with the All Wheel Drive (AWD) system, do not tow your vehicle IN the AWD mode. If the AWD does not disengage, due to electrical or vacuum system failures, remove the driveshaft or use a dolly.

The rear bumper on some Van models may not be designed for trailer towing. A trailer hitch must not be installed to the rear bumper unless your vehicle bears a caution for trailer towing label on the driver's side sun visor.

JUMP STARTING A DEAD BATTERY

Whenever a vehicle is jump started, precautions must be followed in order to prevent the possibility of personal injury. Remember that batteries contain a small amount of explosive hydrogen gas which is a by-product of battery charging. Sparks should always be avoided when working around batteries, especially when attaching jumper cables. To minimize the possibility of accidental sparks, follow the procedure carefully.

✳✳ CAUTION

NEVER hook the batteries up in a series circuit or the entire electrical system will go up in smoke, including the starter!

Vehicles equipped with a diesel engine may utilize two 12 volt batteries. If so, the batteries are connected in a parallel circuit (positive terminal to positive terminal, negative terminal to negative terminal). Hooking the batteries up in parallel circuit increases battery cranking power without increasing total battery voltage output. Output remains at 12 volts. On the other hand, hooking two 12 volt batteries up in a series circuit (positive terminal to negative terminal, positive terminal to negative terminal) increases total battery output to 24 volts (12 volts plus 12 volts).

Jump Starting Precautions

• Be sure that both batteries are of the same voltage. Vehicles covered by this manual and most vehicles on the road today utilize a 12 volt charging system.

• Be sure that both batteries are of the same polarity (have the same terminal, in most cases NEGATIVE grounded).

• Be sure that the vehicles are not touching or a short could occur.

• On serviceable batteries, be sure the vent cap holes are not obstructed.

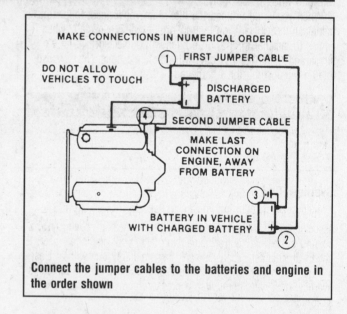

Connect the jumper cables to the batteries and engine in the order shown

• Do not smoke or allow sparks anywhere near the batteries.

• In cold weather, make sure the battery electrolyte is not frozen. This can occur more readily in a battery that has been in a state of discharge.

• Do not allow electrolyte to contact your skin or clothing.

Jump Starting Procedure

1. Make sure that the voltages of the 2 batteries are the same. Most batteries and charging systems are of the 12 volt variety.

2. Pull the jumping vehicle (with the good battery) into a posi-

tion so the jumper cables can reach the dead battery and that vehicle's engine. Make sure that the vehicles do NOT touch.

3. Place the transmissions/transaxles of both vehicles in **Neutral** (MT) or **P** (AT), as applicable, then firmly set their parking brakes.

➡**If necessary for safety reasons, the hazard lights on both vehicles may be operated throughout the entire procedure without significantly increasing the difficulty of jumping the dead battery.**

4. Turn all lights and accessories OFF on both vehicles. Make sure the ignition switches on both vehicles are turned to the **OFF** position.

5. Cover the battery cell caps with a rag, but do not cover the terminals.

6. Make sure the terminals on both batteries are clean and free of corrosion or proper electrical connection will be impeded. If necessary, clean the battery terminals before proceeding.

7. Identify the positive (+) and negative (−) terminals on both batteries.

8. Connect the first jumper cable to the positive (+) terminal of the dead battery, then connect the other end of that cable to the positive (+) terminal of the booster (good) battery.

9. Connect one end of the other jumper cable to the negative (−) terminal on the booster battery and the final cable clamp to an engine bolt head, alternator bracket or other solid, metallic point on the engine with the dead battery. Try to pick a ground on the engine that is positioned away from the battery in order to minimize the possibility of the 2 clamps touching should one loosen during the procedure. DO NOT connect this clamp to the negative (−) terminal of the bad battery.

✳✳ CAUTION

Be very careful to keep the jumper cables away from moving parts (cooling fan, belts, etc.) on both engines.

10. Check to make sure that the cables are routed away from any moving parts, then start the donor vehicle's engine. Run the engine at moderate speed for several minutes to allow the dead battery a chance to receive some initial charge.

11. With the donor vehicle's engine still running slightly above idle, try to start the vehicle with the dead battery. Crank the engine for no more than 10 seconds at a time and let the starter cool for at least 20 seconds between tries. If the vehicle does not start in 3 tries, it is likely that something else is also wrong or that the battery needs additional time to charge.

12. Once the vehicle is started, allow it to run at idle for a few seconds to make sure that it is operating properly.

13. Turn ON the headlights, heater blower and, if equipped, the rear defroster of both vehicles in order to reduce the severity of voltage spikes and subsequent risk of damage to the vehicles' electrical systems when the cables are disconnected. This step is especially important to any vehicle equipped with computer control modules.

14. Carefully disconnect the cables in the reverse order of connection. Start with the negative cable that is attached to the engine ground, then the negative cable on the donor battery. Disconnect the positive cable from the donor battery and finally, disconnect the positive cable from the formerly dead battery. Be careful when disconnecting the cables from the positive terminals not to allow the alligator clips to touch any metal on either vehicle or a short and sparks will occur.

JACKING

♦ **See Figure 63**

Your vehicle was supplied with a jack for emergency road repairs. This jack is fine for changing a flat tire or other short term procedures not requiring you to go beneath the vehicle. If it is used in an emergency situation, carefully follow the instructions provided either with the jack or in your owner's manual. Do not attempt to use the jack on any portions of the vehicle other than specified by the vehicle manufacturer. Always block the diagonally opposite wheel when using a jack.

A more convenient way of jacking is the use of a garage or floor jack.

Never place the jack under the radiator, engine or transmission components. Severe and expensive damage will result when the jack is raised. Additionally, never jack under the floorpan or bodywork; the metal will deform.

Whenever you plan to work under the vehicle, you must support it on jackstands or ramps. Never use cinder blocks or stacks of wood to support the vehicle, even if you're only going to be under it for a few minutes. Never crawl under the vehicle when it is supported only by the tire-changing jack or other floor jack.

➡**Always position a block of wood or small rubber pad on top of the jack or jackstand to protect the lifting point's finish when lifting or supporting the vehicle.**

Small hydraulic, screw, or scissors jacks are satisfactory for raising the vehicle. Drive-on trestles or ramps are also a handy and safe way to both raise and support the vehicle. Be careful though, some ramps may be too steep to drive your vehicle onto without scraping the front bottom panels. Never support the vehicle on any suspension member (unless specifically instructed to do so by a repair manual) or by an underbody panel.

Jacking Precautions

The following safety points cannot be overemphasized:
• Always block the opposite wheel or wheels to keep the vehicle from rolling off the jack.
• When raising the front of the vehicle, firmly apply the parking brake.
• When the drive wheels are to remain on the ground, leave the vehicle in gear to help prevent it from rolling.
• Always use jackstands to support the vehicle when you are working underneath. Place the stands beneath the vehicle's jacking brackets. Before climbing underneath, rock the vehicle a bit to make sure it is firmly supported.

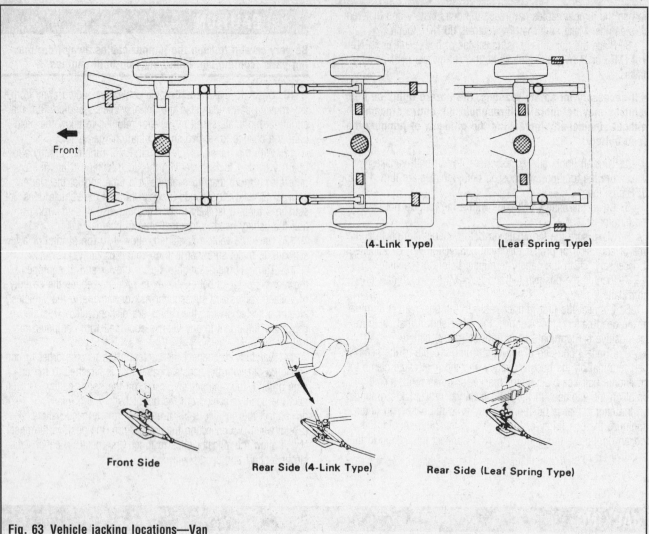

(4-Link Type)   (Leaf Spring Type)

Front Side   Rear Side (4-Link Type)   Rear Side (Leaf Spring Type)

Fig. 63 Vehicle jacking locations—Van

When jacking up the front of the vehicle place the floor jack under the center member—Van

After you have lifted the front end, use a jackstand for extra support—Van

When jacking up the rear of the vehicle, place the floor jack under the axle pumpkin housing

After you have lifted the rear end, use a jackstand for extra support

Maintenance Operations—Normal

A = Check and adjust as necessary; **I** = Inspect and correct or replace as necessary; **R** = Replace, change or lubricate.

SERVICE INTERVAL: (Use odometer reading or months, whichever comes first)		10	20	30	40	50	60
	x 1000 miles	10	20	30	40	50	60
	x 1000 km	16	32	48	64	80	96
	or Months	12	24	36	48	60	72
ENGINE COMPONENTS AND EMISSION CONTROL SYSTEMS							
1 Drive belts «See note 1.»		•	•	I	•	•	I
2 Engine oil and oil filter*		R	R	R	R	R	R
3 Engine coolant «See note 2.»		•	•	•	•	•	R
4 Exhaust pipes and mountings		•	•	I	•	•	I
5 Idle speed «See note 3.»		A	•	A	•	•	A
6 Air filter*		•	•	R	•	•	R
7 Fuel lines and connections		•	•	I	•	•	I
8 Fuel tank cap gasket		•	•	•	•	•	R
9 Spark plugs*		•	•	•	•	•	R
10 Charcoal canister (Calif. only)		•	•	•	•	•	I
11 Oxygen sensor* (except Calif.)		Replace at initial 80000 miles (128000 km).					
CHASSIS AND BODY							
12 Brake linings and drums		•	I	•	I	•	I
13 Brake pads and discs		•	I	•	I	•	I
14 Brake lines and hoses		•	I	•	I	•	I
15 Steering linkage		•	I	•	I	•	I
16 Steering gear box		•	I	•	I	•	I
17 Ball joints, dust covers and drive shaft boots (four-wheel drive models)		•	I	•	I	•	I
18 Ball joints and dust covers (two-wheel drive models)		•	I	•	I	•	I
19 Transmission, transfer and differential		•	I	•	I	•	I
20 Wheel bearing grease		•	•	•	R	•	•
21 Front suspension arm bushings grease (standard grade four-wheel drive models)		•	R	•	R	•	R
22 Propeller shaft grease (four-wheel drive models)		•	R	•	R	•	R
23 Bolts and nuts on chassis and body		•	I	•	I	•	I

Maintenance services indicated by ★ or * condition the Emission Control Systems Warranty. See *Owner's Guide* or *Warranty Booklet* for complete warranty information.

★ : For vehicles sold in California

* : For vehicles sold outside California

NOTE:
1. After 60000 miles (96000 km) or 72 months, inspect every 10000 miles (16000 km) or 12 months.
2. After 60000 miles (96000 km) or 72 months, replace every 30000 miles (48000 km) or 36 months.
3. After 60000 miles (96000 km) or 72 months, adjust every 30000 miles (48000 km) or 36 months.

Maintenance Operations—Severe

A = Check and adjust as necessary; **I** = Inspect and correct or replace as necessary; **R** = Replace. change or lubricate.

SERVICE INTERVAL: (Use odometer reading or months. whichever comes first.)	5 / 8 / 6	10 / 16 / 12	15 / 24 / 18	20 / 32 / 24	25 / 40 / 30	30 / 48 / 36	35 / 56 / 42	40 / 64 / 48	45 / 72 / 54	50 / 80 / 60	55 / 88 / 66	60 / 96 / 72
(x1000 miles / x1000 km / or Months)												

ENGINE COMPONENTS AND EMISSION CONTROL SYSTEMS

	5	10	15	20	25	30	35	40	45	50	55	60
1 Drive belts «See note 1.»									I			I
2 Engine oil and oil filter*	R	R	R	R	R	R	R	R	R	R	R	R
3 Engine coolant «See note 2.»												R
4 Exhaust pipes and mountings			I			I			I			I
5 Idle speed «See note 3.»		A				A						A
6 Air filter* «See note 4.»	I	I	I	I	I	R	I	I	I	I	I	R
7 Fuel lines and connections									I			I
8 Fuel tank cap gasket												R
9 Spark plugs*												R
10 Charcoal canister (Calif. only)												
11 Oxygen sensor* (except Calif.)	Replace at initial 80000 miles (128000 km).											

CHASSIS AND BODY

	5	10	15	20	25	30	35	40	45	50	55	60
12 Brake linings and drums			I		I		I		I		I	
13 Brake pads and discs			I		I		I		I		I	
14 Brake lines and hoses			I			I			I			I
15 Steering linkage			I			I			I			I
16 Steering gear box					I							I
17 Ball joints, dust covers and drive shaft boots (four-wheel drive models)			I			I			I			I
18 Ball joints and dust covers (two-wheel drive models)			I			I			I			I
19 Transmission, transfer and differential			R					R				R
20 Wheel bearing grease								R				
21 Front suspension arm bushings grease (standard grade four-wheel drive models)		R		R		R		R		R		R
22 Propeller shaft grease (four-wheel drive models)		R		R		R		R		R		R
23 Bolts and nuts on chassis and body «See note 5.»		I		I		I		I		I		I

Maintenance services indicated by ⚹ or * condition the Emission Control Systems Warranty. See *Owner's Guide* or *Warranty Booklet* for complete warranty information.

⚹:For vehicles sold in California
*:For vehicles sold outside California

NOTE:
1. After 60000 miles (96000 km) or 72 months, inspect every 10000 miles (16000 km) or 12 months.
2. After 60000 miles (96000 km) or 72 months, replace every 30000 miles (48000 km) or 36 months.
3. After 60000 miles (96000 km) or 72 months, adjust every 30000 miles (48000 km) or 36 months.
4. Applicable when you mainly operate your vehicle on dusty roads. If not, apply the normal condition schedule.
5. Applicable when you mainly operate your vehicle on rough and/or muddy roads. If not, apply the normal condition schedule.

Capacities

Year	Model	Crankcase Includes Filter (qts.)	Transmission (qts.) 4-sp	5-sp	Auto	Drive Axle (qts.)	Fuel Tank (gal.)	Cooling System w/Heater (qts.)
1983	Cressida	5.4	2.5	2.5	7.0 [1]	1.5	17.2 [2]	9.5
1984	Cressida	5.4	2.5	2.5	7.0 [1]	1.5	18.5	9.5
	Van	3.7	2.3	2.3	7.0 [1]	1.3	15.9	7.6 [3]
1985	Cressida	5.4	2.5	2.5	7.0 [1]	1.5	18.5	9.2
	Van	3.7	2.3	2.3	7.0 [1]	1.3	15.9	7.6 [3]
1986	Cressida	5.4	2.5	2.5	7.0 [1]	1.5	18.5 [4]	9.2
	Van	3.7	2.3	2.3	7.0 [1]	1.3	15.9	7.6 [3]
1987	Cressida	5.4	2.5	2.5	7.3 [1]	1.5	18.5	8.7
	Van	3.7	2.3e	2.3 [5]	7.0 [1]	1.5 [6]	15.9	8.3 [7]
1988	Cressida	5.2	—	—	7.3 [1]	1.3	18.5	8.6
	Van	3.7	2.3e	2.3 [5]	7.0 [1]	1.5 [6]	15.9	8.3 [7]
1989	Cressida	4.7	—	—	7.6 [1]	1.4	18.5	8.8
	Van	3.7	2.3e	2.3 [5]	7.0 [1]	1.5 [6]	15.9	8.3 [7]
1990	Cressida	4.7	—	—	7.6 [1]	1.4	18.5	8.8

[1] Total dry capacity converter, cooler and sump drained.
[2] 16.2 gallons on the Wagon models.
[3] 8.1 quarts if equipped with a rear heater.
[4] 18.2 gallons on Wagon models.
[5] 2.7 quarts on 4WD models.
[6] 2.0 quarts on 4WD models.
    1.3 quarts in the front differential
    1.3 quarts in the transfer case
[7] 8.9 quarts equipped with a rear heater
    7.4 quarts w/o rear heater—4WD
    7.9 quarts equipped with rear heater—4WD

ENGLISH TO METRIC CONVERSION: TORQUE

Torque is now expressed as either foot-pounds (ft./lbs.) or inch-pounds (in./lbs.). The metric measurement unit for torque is the Newton-meter (Nm). This unit—the Nm—will be used for all SI metric torque references, both the present ft. lbs. and in./lbs.

ft lbs	N-m	ft lbs	N-m	ft lbs	N-m	ft lbs	N-m
0.1	0.1	33	44.7	74	100.3	115	155.9
0.2	0.3	34	46.1	75	101.7	116	157.3
0.3	0.4	35	47.4	76	103.0	117	158.6
0.4	0.5	36	48.8	77	104.4	118	160.0
0.5	0.7	37	50.7	78	105.8	119	161.3
0.6	0.8	38	51.5	79	107.1	120	162.7
0.7	1.0	39	52.9	80	108.5	121	164.0
0.8	1.1	40	54.2	81	109.8	122	165.4
0.9	1.2	41	55.6	82	111.2	123	166.8
1	1.3	42	56.9	83	112.5	124	168.1
2	2.7	43	58.3	84	113.9	125	169.5
3	4.1	44	59.7	85	115.2	126	170.8
4	5.4	45	61.0	86	116.6	127	172.2
5	6.8	46	62.4	87	118.0	128	173.5
6	8.1	47	63.7	88	119.3	129	174.9
7	9.5	48	65.1	89	120.7	130	176.2
8	10.8	49	66.4	90	122.0	131	177.6
9	12.2	50	67.8	91	123.4	132	179.0
10	13.6	51	69.2	92	124.7	133	180.3
11	14.9	52	70.5	93	126.1	134	181.7
12	16.3	53	71.9	94	127.4	135	183.0
13	17.6	54	73.2	95	128.8	136	184.4
14	18.9	55	74.6	96	130.2	137	185.7
15	20.3	56	75.9	97	131.5	138	187.1
16	21.7	57	77.3	98	132.9	139	188.5
17	23.0	58	78.6	99	134.2	140	189.8
18	24.4	59	80.0	100	135.6	141	191.2
19	25.8	60	81.4	101	136.9	142	192.5
20	27.1	61	82.7	102	138.3	143	193.9
21	28.5	62	84.1	103	139.6	144	195.2
22	29.8	63	85.4	104	141.0	145	196.6
23	31.2	64	86.8	105	142.4	146	198.0
24	32.5	65	88.1	106	143.7	147	199.3
25	33.9	66	89.5	107	145.1	148	200.7
26	35.2	67	90.8	108	146.4	149	202.0
27	36.6	68	92.2	109	147.8	150	203.4
28	38.0	69	93.6	110	149.1	151	204.7
29	39.3	70	94.9	111	150.5	152	206.1
30	40.7	71	96.3	112	151.8	153	207.4
31	42.0	72	97.6	113	153.2	154	208.8
32	43.4	73	99.0	114	154.6	155	210.2

ENGLISH TO METRIC CONVERSION: LIQUID CAPACITY

Liquid or fluid capacity is presently expressed as pints, quarts or gallons, or a combination of all of these. In the metric system the liter (l) will become the basic unit. Fractions of a liter would be expressed as deciliters, centiliters, or most frequently (and commonly) as milliliters.

To convert pints (pts.) to liters (l): multiply the number of pints by .47
To convert liters (l) to pints (pts.): multiply the number of liters by 2.1
To convert quarts (qts.) to liters (l): multiply the number of quarts by .95

To convert liters (l) to quarts (qts.): multiply the number of liters by 1.06
To convert gallons (gals.) to liters (l): multiply the number of gallons by 3.8
To convert liters (l) to gallons (gals.): multiply the number of liters by .26

gals	liters	qts	liters	pts	liters
0.1	0.38	0.1	0.10	0.1	0.05
0.2	0.76	0.2	0.19	0.2	0.10
0.3	1.1	0.3	0.28	0.3	0.14
0.4	1.5	0.4	0.38	0.4	0.19
0.5	1.9	0.5	0.47	0.5	0.24
0.6	2.3	0.6	0.57	0.6	0.28
0.7	2.6	0.7	0.66	0.7	0.33
0.8	3.0	0.8	0.76	0.8	0.38
0.9	3.4	0.9	0.85	0.9	0.43
1	3.8	1	1.0	1	0.5
2	7.6	2	1.9	2	1.0
3	11.4	3	2.8	3	1.4
4	15.1	4	3.8	4	1.9
5	18.9	5	4.7	5	2.4
6	22.7	6	5.7	6	2.8
7	26.5	7	6.6	7	3.3
8	30.3	8	7.6	8	3.8
9	34.1	9	8.5	9	4.3
10	37.8	10	9.5	10	4.7
11	41.6	11	10.4	11	5.2
12	45.4	12	11.4	12	5.7
13	49.2	13	12.3	13	6.2
14	53.0	14	13.2	14	6.6
15	56.8	15	14.2	15	7.1
16	60.6	16	15.1	16	7.6
17	64.3	17	16.1	17	8.0
18	68.1	18	17.0	18	8.5
19	71.9	19	18.0	19	9.0
20	75.7	20	18.9	20	9.5
21	79.5	21	19.9	21	9.9
22	83.2	22	20.8	22	10.4
23	87.0	23	21.8	23	10.9
24	90.8	24	22.7	24	11.4
25	94.6	25	23.6	25	11.8
26	98.4	26	24.6	26	12.3
27	102.2	27	25.5	27	12.8
28	106.0	28	26.5	28	13.2
29	110.0	29	27.4	29	13.7
30	113.5	30	28.4	30	14.2

2

ENGINE PERFORMANCE AND TUNE-UP

TUNE-UP PROCEDURES

In order to extract the full measure of performance and economy from your engine it is essential that it be properly tuned at regular intervals. A regular tune-up will keep your car's engine running smoothly and will prevent the annoying minor breakdowns and poor performance associated with an untuned engine.

A complete tune-up should be performed every 60,000 miles (96,500 km) or 12 months, whichever comes first. This interval should be halved if the car is operated under severe conditions, such as trailer towing, prolonged idling, continual stop and start driving, or if starting or running problems are noticed. It is assumed that the routine maintenance described in Chapter 1 has been kept up, as this will have a decided effect on the results of a tune-up. All of the applicable steps of a tune-up should be followed in order, as the result is a cumulative one.

If the specifications on the tune-up sticker in the engine compartment disagree with the Tune-Up Specifications chart in this chapter, the figures on the sticker must be used. The sticker often reflects changes made during the production run.

Spark Plugs

A typical spark plug consists of a metal shell surrounding a ceramic insulator. A metal electrode extends downward through the center of the insulator and protrudes a small distance. Located at the end of the plug and attached to the side of the outer metal shell is the side electrode. The side electrode bends in at a 90° angle so that its tip is just past and parallel to the tip of the center electrode. The distance between these two electrodes (measured in thousandths of an inch or hundredths of a millimeter) is called the spark plug gap.

The spark plug does not produce a spark but instead provides a gap across which the current can arc. The coil produces anywhere from 20,000 to 50,000 volts (depending on the type and application) which travels through the wires to the spark plugs. The current passes along the center electrode and jumps the gap to the side electrode, and in doing so, ignites the air/fuel mixture in the combustion chamber.

SPARK PLUG HEAT RANGE

Spark plug heat range is the ability of the plug to dissipate heat. The longer the insulator (or the farther it extends into the engine), the hotter the plug will operate; the shorter the insulator (the closer the electrode is to the block's cooling passages) the cooler it will operate. A plug that absorbs little heat and remains too cool will quickly accumulate deposits of oil and carbon since it is not hot enough to burn them off. This leads to plug fouling and consequently to misfiring. A plug that absorbs too much heat will have no deposits but, due to the excessive heat, the electrodes will burn away quickly and might possibly lead to preignition or other ignition problems. Preignition takes place when plug tips get so hot that they glow sufficiently to ignite the air/fuel mixture before the actual spark occurs. This early ignition will usually cause a pinging during low speeds and heavy loads.

The general rule of thumb for choosing the correct heat range when picking a spark plug is: if most of your driving is long distance, high speed travel, use a colder plug; if most of your driv-

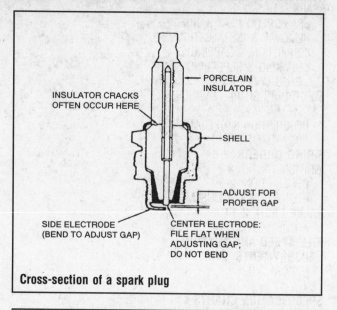

Cross-section of a spark plug

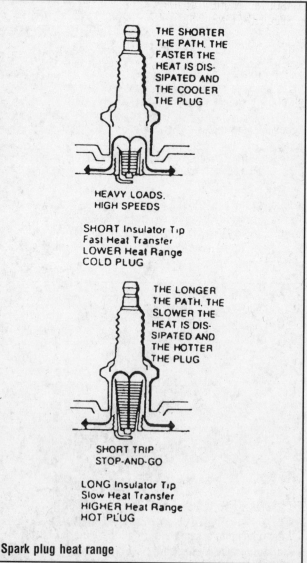

Spark plug heat range

ing is stop and go, use a hotter plug. Original equipment plugs are generally a good compromise between the 2 styles and most people never have the need to change their plugs from the factory-recommended heat range.

REMOVAL & INSTALLATION

A set of spark plugs usually requires replacement after about 20,000–30,000 miles (32,000–48,000 km), depending on your style of driving. In normal operation plug gap increases about 0.001 in. (0.025mm) for every 2500 miles (4000 km). As the gap increases, the plug's voltage requirement also increases. It requires a greater voltage to jump the wider gap and about two to three times as much voltage to fire the plug at high speeds than at idle. The improved air/fuel ratio control of modern fuel injection combined with the higher voltage output of modern ignition systems will often allow an engine to run significantly longer on a set of standard spark plugs, but keep in mind that efficiency will drop as the gap widdens (along with fuel economy and power).

When you're removing spark plugs, work on one at a time. Don't start by removing the plug wires all at once, because, unless you number them, they may become mixed up. Take a minute before you begin and number the wires with tape.

1. Disconnect the negative battery cable, and if the vehicle has been run recently, allow the engine to thoroughly cool.

2. Carefully twist the spark plug wire boot to loosen it, then pull upward and remove the boot from the plug. Be sure to pull on the boot and not on the wire, otherwise the connector located inside the boot may become separated.

3. Using compressed air, blow any water or debris from the spark plug well to assure that no harmful contaminants are allowed to enter the combustion chamber when the spark plug is removed. If compressed air is not available, use a rag or a brush to clean the area.

➡️Remove the spark plugs when the engine is cold, if possible, to prevent damage to the threads. If removal of the plugs is difficult, apply a few drops of penetrating oil or silicone spray to the area around the base of the plug, and allow it a few minutes to work.

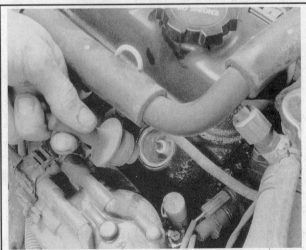

When changing a spark plug, pull the wire out of the spark plug tube by the boot

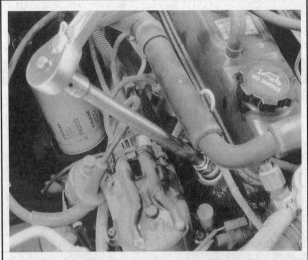

An extension may be necessary to remove the spark plug

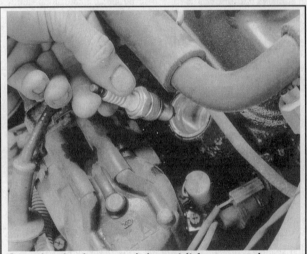

Once the plug is removed, inspect it for wear and replace as needed

4. Using a spark plug socket that is equipped with a rubber insert to properly hold the plug, turn the spark plug counterclockwise to loosen and remove the spark plug from the bore.

✳✳ WARNING

Be sure not to use a flexible extension on the socket. Use of a flexible extension may allow a shear force to be applied to the plug. A shear force could break the plug off in the cylinder head, leading to costly and frustrating repairs.

To install:

5. Inspect the spark plug boot for tears or damage. If a damaged boot is found, the spark plug wire must be replaced.

6. Using a wire feeler gauge, check and adjust the spark plug gap. When using a gauge, the proper size should pass between the electrodes with a slight drag. The next larger size should not be able to pass while the next smaller size should pass freely.

7. Carefully thread the plug into the bore by hand. If resistance is felt before the plug is almost completely threaded, back the plug out and begin threading again. In small, hard to reach areas,

an old spark plug wire and boot could be used as a threading tool. The boot will hold the plug while you twist the end of the wire and the wire is supple enough to twist before it would allow the plug to crossthread.

✳✳ WARNING

Do not use the spark plug socket to thread the plugs. Always carefully thread the plug by hand or using an old plug wire to prevent the possibility of crossthreading and damaging the cylinder head bore.

8. Carefully tighten the spark plug. If the plug you are installing is equipped with a crush washer, seat the plug, then tighten about ¼ turn to crush the washer. If you are installing a tapered seat plug, tighten the plug to specifications provided by the vehicle or plug manufacturer.

9. Apply a small amount of silicone dielectric compound to the end of the spark plug lead or inside the spark plug boot to prevent sticking, then install the boot to the spark plug and push until it clicks into place. The click may be felt or heard, then gently pull back on the boot to assure proper contact.

INSPECTION & GAPPING

Check the plugs for deposits and wear. If they are not going to be replaced, clean the plugs thoroughly. Remember that any kind of deposit will decrease the efficiency of the plug. Plugs can be cleaned on a spark plug cleaning machine, which can sometimes be found in service stations, or you can do an acceptable job of cleaning with a stiff brush. If the plugs are cleaned, the electrodes must be filed flat. Use an ignition points file, not an emery board or the like, which will leave deposits. The electrodes must be filed perfectly flat with sharp edges; rounded edges reduce the spark plug voltage by as much as 50%.

Check spark plug gap before installation. The ground electrode (the L-shaped one connected to the body of the plug) must be parallel to the center electrode and the specified size wire gauge (please refer to the Tune-Up Specifications chart for details) must pass between the electrodes with a slight drag.

A normally worn spark plug should have light tan or gray deposits on the firing tip

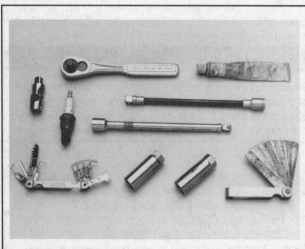

A variety of tools and gauges are needed for spark plug service

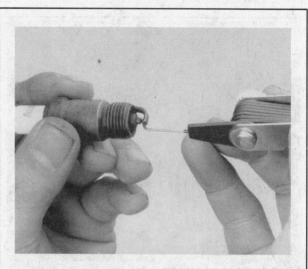

Checking the spark plug gap with a feeler gauge

A carbon fouled plug, identified by soft, sooty, black deposits, may indicate an improperly tuned vehicle. Check the air cleaner, ignition components and engine control system

A physically damaged spark plug may be evidence of severe detonation in that cylinder. Watch that cylinder carefully between services, as a continued detonation will not only damage the plug, but could also damage the engine

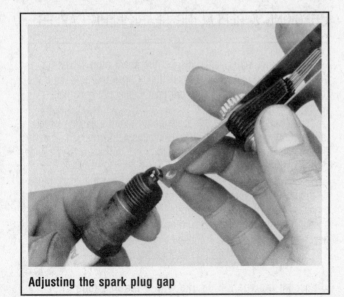

Adjusting the spark plug gap

If the standard plug is in good condition, the electrode may be filed flat—CAUTION: do not file platinum plugs

An oil fouled spark plug indicates an engine with worn piston rings and/or bad valve seals allowing excessive oil to enter the chamber

This spark plug has been left in the engine too long, as evidenced by the extreme gap—Plugs with such an extreme gap can cause misfiring and stumbling accompanied by a noticeable lack of power

➡**NEVER adjust the gap on a used platinum type spark plug.**

Always check the gap on new plugs as they are not always set correctly at the factory. Do not use a flat feeler gauge when measuring the gap on a used plug, because the reading may be inaccurate. A round-wire type gapping tool is the best way to check the gap. The correct gauge should pass through the electrode gap with a slight drag. If you're in doubt, try one size smaller and one larger. The smaller gauge should go through easily, while the larger one shouldn't go through at all. Wire gapping tools usually have a bending tool attached. Use that to adjust the side electrode until the proper distance is obtained. Absolutely never attempt to bend the center electrode. Also, be careful not to bend the side electrode too far or too often as it may weaken and break off within the engine, requiring removal of the cylinder head to retrieve it.

CHECKING & REPLACING SPARK PLUG CABLES

At every tune-up, visually inspect the spark plug cables for burns, cuts, or breaks in the insulation. Check the boots and the nipples on the distributor cap and coil. Replace any damaged wiring.

Your car is equipped with a electronic ignition system which utilizes 8mm wires to conduct the hotter spark produced. The boots on these wires are designed to cover the spark plug cavities on the cylinder head.

Inspect the wires without removing them from the spark plugs, distributor cap or primary. Look for visible damage such as cuts, pinches, cracks or torn boots. Replace any wires that show damage. If the boot is damaged, it may be replaced by itself. It is not necessary to replace the complete wire just for the boot.

A bridged or almost bridged spark plug, identified by a build-up between the electrodes caused by excessive carbon or oil build-up on the plug

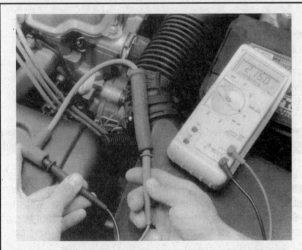

Checking individual plug wire resistance with a digital ohmmeter

To replace the wire, grasp and twist the boot back and forth while pulling away from the spark plug. Use a special pliers if available.

➡**Always coat the terminals of any wire removed or replaced with a thin layer of dielectric compound.**

When installing a wire be sure it is firmly mounted over or on the plug, distributor cap connector or primary terminal.

Every 36,000 miles (58,000 km) or 12 months, the resistance of the wires should be checked with an ohmmeter. Wires with excessive resistance will cause misfiring, and may make the engine difficult to start in damp weather. Generally, the useful life of the cables is 60,000 miles (96,500 km).

To check resistance, remove the spark plug cable from the engine (be sure to measure the resistance without disconnecting the spark plug wire from the distributor cap) and using a suitable ohmmeter, check the resistance of the spark plug cable. If the resistance is greater than 25,000Ω, replace the spark plug cable. Thus, if the cables on your car are longer than the factory originals, resistance will be higher, quite possibly outside these limits.

When installing new cables, replace them one at a time to avoid mixups. Start by replacing the longest one first. Install the boot firmly over the spark plug. Route the wire over the same path as the original. Insert the nipple firmly into the tower on the cap or the coil.

Electronic Spark Advance System

DESCRIPTION & OPERATION

The electronic spark advance system is one of the ignition system used on the Cressida and Van models. The ECU is programmed with data for the optimum ignition timing under any and all operating conditions. Using data provided by sensors which monitor various engine functions (rpm, intake air volume, engine temperature, etc.) the microcomputer (ECU) triggers the spark at precisely the right instant. The Van models also incorporate the Integrated Ignition Assembly (IIA). This system houses all of it components inside the distributor and is controlled by the ECU the same as the ESA system.

ADJUSTMENTS

The following procedure is to be used to adjust the air gap between the signal rotor and the pick-up coil projection that are located inside the distributor.

1983–88 Cressida
◗ **See Figure 1**

1. Using a feeler gauge, measure the air gap between the signal rotor and the signal generators (pick-up coils) projection.

2. The air gap should be 0.2–0.4mm (0.008–0.016 in.). If not within specification, replace the distributor assembly.

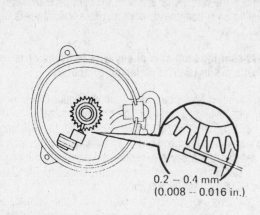

Fig. 1 Inspecting the pick-up coil air gap on the 1983–88 Cressida

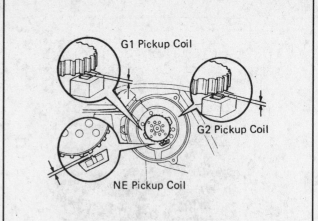

Fig. 2 Inspecting the pick-up coil air gap on the 1989–90 Cressida

1989–90 Cressida

▶ **See Figure 2**

1. Remove the distributor cap, rotor, and dust shield.
2. Turn the engine over (you may use a socket wrench on the front pulley bolt to do this) until the projection on the pickup coil is directly opposite the signal rotor tooth.
3. Get a non-ferrous (paper, brass, or plastic) set of feeler gauges and measure the gap between the signal rotor and the pick-up coil projection. DO NOT USE AN ORDINARY METAL FEELER GAUGE! The gauge should just touch either side of the gap, the permissible range is 0.2–0.4mm 0.008–0.016 in.).
4. If the gap is either too wide or too narrow, the distributor assembly (unfortunately) must be replaced.
5. If the gap is within specifications, place the dust shield, rotor and distributor cap back in their proper installed position.

Van

▶ **See Figure 3**

1. Remove the distributor cap, rotor, and dust shield.
2. Turn the engine over (you may use a socket wrench on the front pulley bolt to do this) until the projection on the pickup coil is directly opposite the signal rotor tooth.
3. Get a non-ferrous (paper, brass, or plastic) set of feeler gauges and measure the gap between the signal rotor and the pick-up coil projection. DO NOT USE AN ORDINARY METAL FEELER GAUGE! The gauge should just touch either side of the

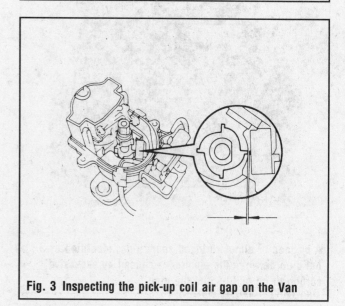

Fig. 3 Inspecting the pick-up coil air gap on the Van

gap, the permissible range is 0.2–0.4mm (0.008–0.016 in.) on the 1984–85 models and 0.2mm (0.008 in.) on the 1986–90 models.
4. If the gap is either too wide or too narrow, replace the pick-up coil, governor shaft and housing assembly.
5. If the gap is within specifications, place the dust shield, rotor and distributor cap back in their proper installed position.

FIRING ORDERS

▶ **See Figures 4, 5, 6 and 7**

➡**To avoid confusion, remove and tag the spark plug wires one at a time, for replacement.**

If a distributor is not keyed for installation with only one orientation, it could have been removed previously and rewired. The resultant wiring would hold the correct firing order, but could change the relative placement of the plug towers in relation to the engine. For this reason it is imperative that you label all wires before disconnecting any of them. Also, before removal, compare the current wiring with the accompanying illustrations. If the current wiring does not match, make notes in your book to reflect how your engine is wired.

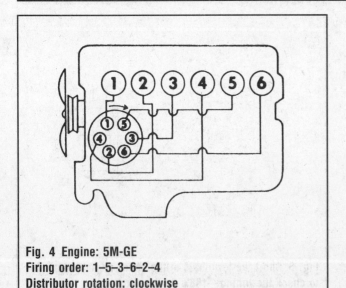

Fig. 4 Engine: 5M-GE
Firing order: 1–5–3–6–2–4
Distributor rotation: clockwise

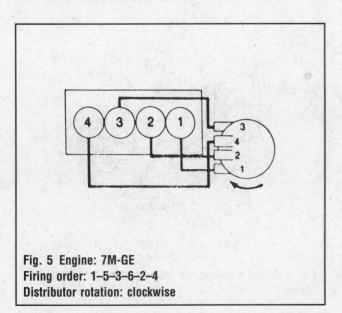

Fig. 5 Engine: 7M-GE
Firing order: 1–5–3–6–2–4
Distributor rotation: clockwise

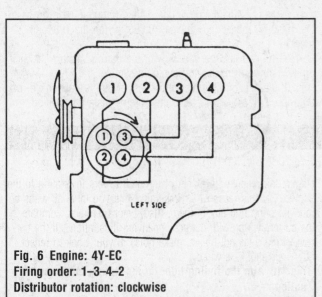

LEFT SIDE

Fig. 6 Engine: 4Y-EC
Firing order: 1–3–4–2
Distributor rotation: clockwise

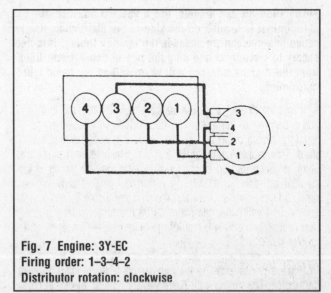

Fig. 7 Engine: 3Y-EC
Firing order: 1–3–4–2
Distributor rotation: clockwise

Ignition Timing

DESCRIPTION

Ignition timing is the measurement in degrees of crankshaft rotation of the instant the spark plugs in the cylinders fire, in relation to the location of the piston, while the piston is on its compression stroke.

Ignition timing is adjusted by loosening the distributor locking device and turning the distributor in the engine.

Ideally, the air/fuel mixture in the cylinder will be ignited (by the spark plug) and just beginning its rapid expansion as the piston passes top dead center (TDC) of the compression stroke. If this happens, the piston will be beginning the power stroke just as the compressed (by the movement of the piston) and ignited (by the spark plug) air/fuel mixture starts to expand. The expansion of the air/fuel mixture will then force the piston down on the power stroke and turn the crankshaft.

It takes a fraction of a second for the spark from the plug to completely ignite the mixture in the cylinder. Because of this, the spark plug must fire before the piston reaches TDC, if the mixture is to be completely ignited as the piston passes TDC. This measurement is given in degrees of top dead center (BTDC). If the ignition timing setting for your engine is seven degrees (7°) BTDC, this means that the spark plug must fire at a time when the piston for that cylinder is 7° before top dead center of the compression stroke. However, this only holds true while your engine is at idle speed.

As you accelerate from idle, the speed of your engine (rpm) increases. The increase in rpm means that the pistons are now traveling up and down much faster. Because of this, the spark plugs will have to fire even sooner it the mixture is to be completely ignited as the piston passes TDC. To accomplish this, the distributor incorporates means to advance the timing of the spark as engine speed increases.

The distributor in your Toyota has two means of advancing the ignition timing. One is called centrifugal advance and is actuated by weights in the distributor. The other advance system is controlled by that on board computer in your vehicle.

➡The 1984–85 Van models, use a vacuum advance diaphragm that is located on the side of the distributor. Because this mechanism changes the ignition timing, it is necessary to disconnect and plug the one or two vacuum lines from the vacuum advance unit when setting the basic ignition timing.

If ignition timing is set too far advanced (BTDC), the ignition and expansion of the air/fuel mixture in the cylinder will try to force the piston down the cylinder while it is still traveling upward. This causes engine ping, a sound which resembles marbles being dropped into an empty tin can. If the ignition timing is too far retarded (after, or ATDC), the piston will have already started down on the power stroke when the air/fuel mixture ignites and expands. This will cause the piston to be forced down only a portion of its travel and will result in poor engine performance and lack of power.

Ignition timing adjustment is checked with a timing light. This instrument is connected to the number one (No. 1) spark plug of the engine. The timing light flashes every time an electrical current is sent from the distributor, through the No. 1 spark plug wire, to the spark plug. The crankshaft pulley and the front cover of the engine are marked with a timing pointer and a timing scale. When the timing pointer is aligned with the 0 mark on the timing scale, the piston in No. 1 cylinder is at TDC of its compression stroke. With the engine running, and the timing light aimed at the timing pointer and timing scale, the stroboscopic flashes from the timing light will allow you to check the ignition timing setting of the engine. The timing light flashes every time the spark plug in the No. 1 cylinder of the engine fires. Since the flash from the timing light makes the crankshaft pulley seem stationary for a moment, you will be able to read the exact position of the piston in the No. 1 cylinder on the timing scale on the front of the engine.

INSPECTION & ADJUSTMENT

1983–88 Cressida
◆ See Figures 8, 9, 10 and 11

1. Warm up the engine. Connect a tachometer and check the engine idle speed to be sure that it is within the specification given in the Tune-Up Specifications chart at the beginning of the chapter.

➡As some tachometers are not compatible with this ignition system, we recommend that you confirm the compatibility of your tachometer before using. Never allow the ignition coil terminals to touch ground as it could result in damage to the igniter and/or the ignition coil. Do not disconnect the battery cables while the engine is running. Make sure that the igniter is properly grounded to the body. When a tachometer is connected to the vehicle, always connect the positive terminal of the tachometer to the engine service connector located under in the engine compartment.

2. If the timing marks are difficult to see, clean them off using a suitable solvent and use a dab of paint or chalk to make them more visible.

3. Using a suitable piece of jumper wire short the terminals of the check engine connector (T and E_1), located in the engine compartment.

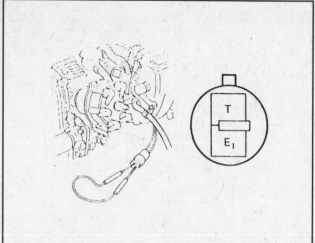
Fig. 8 Short the terminals of the check engine connector to check the timing—1983–84 Cressida

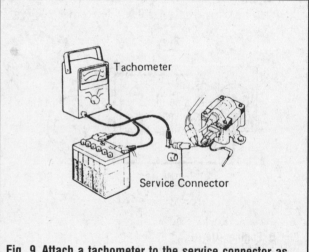
Fig. 9 Attach a tachometer to the service connector as shown

Fig. 10 Aim the timing light on the timing marks on the pulley

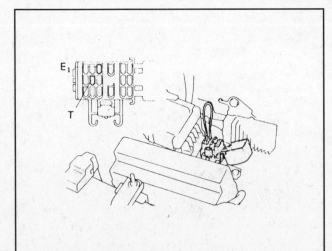

Fig. 11 Short these two terminals of the check engine connector on 1985–88 Cressida models

4. Connect a timing light according to the manufacturer's instructions. If the timing light being used is a non-inductive type light that has three wires, one (usually blue or green) must be installed with an adapter between the No. 1 spark plug lead and the spark plug. The other leads are connected to the positive (+) battery terminal (usually a red lead) and the other to the negative (−) battery terminal (usually a black lead).

5. If the timing light is an inductive type light, connect the inductive clamp around the number one spark plug wire and the other 2 cables to the positive and negative post of the battery.

6. Be sure that the timing light wires are clear of the fan and start the engine.

❊❊ CAUTION

Keep fingers, clothes, tools, hair, and leads clear of the spinning engine fan. Be sure that you are running the engine in a well ventilated area.

7. Allow the engine to run at the specified idle speed with the gearshift in Neutral with manual transmission and Drive (D) with automatic transmission.

❊❊ CAUTION

Be sure that the parking brake is set and that the front wheels are blocked to prevent the car from rolling forward, especially when Drive is selected with an automatic.

8. Point the timing marks at the timing marks that are on the engine. With the engine at idle, the timing should be at 10° before top dead center (BTDC).

9. If the timing is not at the specification, loosen the pinch bolt at the base of the distributor just enough so that the distributor can be turned. Turn the distributor to advance or retard the timing as required. Once the proper marks are seen to align with the timing light, timing is correct.

10. Stop the engine and tighten the pinch bolt. Start the engine and recheck timing and the idle speed, adjust as necessary.

Stop the engine. Disconnect the tachometer, jumper wire and timing light.

1989–90 Cressida
▶ See Figures 12, 13 and 14

1. Warm up the engine. Connect a tachometer and check the engine idle speed to be sure that it is within the specification given in the Tune-Up Specifications chart at the beginning of the chapter.

➡**As some tachometers are not compatible with this ignition system, we recommend that you confirm the compatibility of your tachometer before using. Never allow the ignition coil terminals to touch ground as it could result in damage to the igniter and/or the ignition coil. Do not disconnect the battery cables while the engine is running. Make sure that the igniter is properly grounded to the body. When a tachometer is connected to the vehicle, always connect the positive terminal of the tachometer to the ignition (IG) terminal of the engine service connector located under in the engine compartment.**

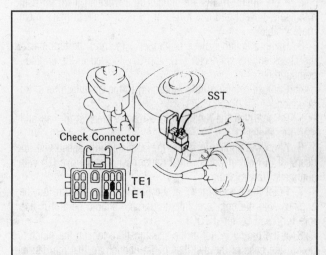

Fig. 12 Short these terminals of the check engine connector located on the strut tower—1989–90 Cressida

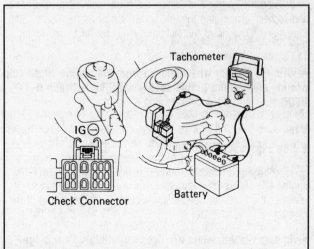

Fig. 13 Attaching a tachometer to the service connector—1989–90 Cressida

Fig. 14 Aim the timing light on the timing marks—1989–90 Cressida shown

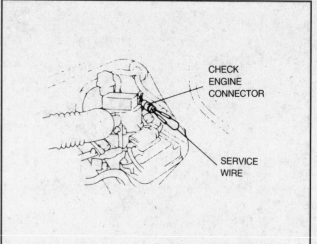

Fig. 15 Shorting the terminals of the check engine connector—3Y-EC and 4Y-EC engines

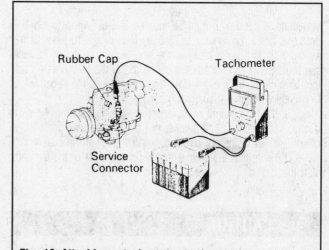

Fig. 16 Attaching a tachometer to the service connector—Van

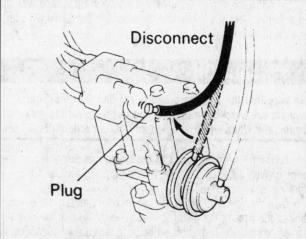

Fig. 17 Disconnect the vacuum line at the advance unit and plug it—1984–85 Van

2. If the timing marks are difficult to see, clean them off using a suitable solvent and use a dab of paint or chalk to make them more visible.

3. Using a suitable piece of jumper wire short the terminals of the check engine connector (TE₁ and E₁), located in the engine compartment.

4. Connect a timing light according to the manufacturer's instructions.

5. Be sure that the timing light wires are clear of the fan and start the engine.

6. Allow the engine to run at the specified idle speed with the gearshift in Neutral with manual transmission and Drive (D) with automatic transmission.

7. Point the timing marks at the timing marks that are on the engine. With the engine at idle, the timing should be at 10° before top dead center (BTDC).

8. If the timing is not at the specification, loosen the pinch bolt at the base of the distributor just enough so that the distributor can be turned. Turn the distributor to advance or retard the timing as required. Once the proper marks are seen to align with the timing light, timing is correct.

9. Stop the engine and tighten the pinch bolt. Start the engine and recheck timing and the idle speed, adjust as necessary. Stop the engine. Disconnect the tachometer, jumper wire and timing light.

➡**With the jumper wire removed from the engine check connector, the ignition timing advance will be between 9–11° BTDC.**

Van

▶ **See Figures 15 thru 19**

1. Warm up the engine. Connect a tachometer and check the engine idle speed to be sure that it is within the specification given in the Tune-Up Specifications chart at the beginning of the chapter.

➡**As some tachometers are not compatible with this ignition system, we recommend that you confirm the compatibility of your tachometer before using. Never allow the igni-**

The timing mark location on the 4Y-EC Van engine

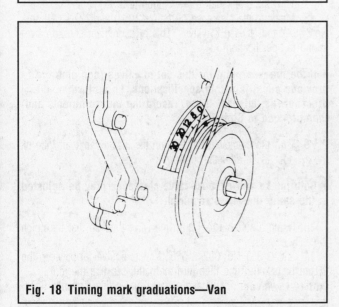

Fig. 18 Timing mark graduations—Van

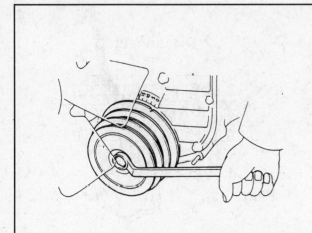

Fig. 19 Using a wrench, set the No. 1 cylinder to TDC of the compression stroke

tion coil terminals to touch ground as it could result in damage to the igniter and/or the ignition coil. Do not disconnect the battery cables while the engine is running. Make sure that the igniter is properly grounded to the body. When a tachometer is connected to the vehicle, always connect the positive terminal of the tachometer to the engine service connector located on or near the distributor assembly in the engine compartment.

2. If the timing marks are difficult to see, clean them off using a suitable solvent and use a dab of paint or chalk to make them more visible.

3. On the 1984–85 Van models, disconnect and plug the vacuum lines at the vacuum advance unit on the side of the distributor. On the 1986–89 van models, use a suitable piece of jumper wire to short the terminals of the check engine connector, located in the engine compartment.

4. Connect a timing light according to the manufacturer's instructions.

5. Be sure that the timing light wires are clear of the fan and start the engine.

❊❊ CAUTION

Keep fingers, clothes, tools, hair, and leads clear of the spinning engine fan. Be sure that you are running the engine in a well ventilated area.

6. Allow the engine to run at the specified idle speed with the gearshift in Neutral with manual transmission and Drive (D) with automatic transmission.

❊❊ CAUTION

Be sure that the parking brake is set and that the front wheels are blocked to prevent the car from rolling forward, especially when Drive is selected with an automatic.

7. Point the timing marks at the timing marks that are on the engine. With the engine at idle, the timing should be at:
• 1984–85 models, 8° before top dead center (BTDC) at idle
• 1986–89 models, 12° before top dead center (BTDC) at idle

8. If the timing is not at the specification, loosen the pinch bolt at the base of the distributor just enough so that the distributor can be turned. Turn the distributor to advance or retard the timing as required. Once the proper marks are seen to align with the timing light, timing is correct.

9. Stop the engine and tighten the pinch bolt. Start the engine and recheck timing and the idle speed, adjust as necessary. Stop the engine. Disconnect the tachometer, jumper wire and timing light. Reconnect the vacuum lines on the advance diaphragm.

VALVE LASH

All the Toyota models being covered in this manual, except for the 1989–90 Cressida are equipped with hydraulic lash adjusters in the valve train. These adjusters maintain a zero lash clearance between the rocker arm and the valve stem, no adjustment is possible or necessary.

ADJUSTMENT

Cressida

7M-GE ENGINE

▶ See Figures 20 thru 25

1. Disconnect the negative battery cable.
2. Remove the cylinder head covers as follows:
   a. Remove the air cleaner hose along with air connector pipe.
   b. Remove the PCV orifice pipe and hoses.
   c. Disconnect and remove the accelerator link.
   d. Remove the air intake connector, vacuum transmitting pipe and brackets.
   e. Disconnect and tag the spark plug cables.
   f. Remove the cylinder head cover retaining bolts and remove the cylinder head covers.
3. Use a wrench and turn the crankshaft until the notch in the pulley aligns with the timing mark **0** of the No. 1 timing belt cover. This will insure that engine is at TDC.

➡Check that the valve lifters on the No. 1 cylinder are loose and those on No. 6 cylinder are tight. If not, turn the crankshaft 1 complete revolution (360°) and then realign the marks.

4. Using a flat feeler gauge check the clearance between the camshaft lobe and the valve lifter on the No.1 (IN) and NO.4 (IN) and No.1 (EX) and NO.4 (EX) valves. This measurement should correspond to specification.

- Intake: 0.15–0.25mm (0.006–0.010 in.)
- Exhaust: 0.20–0.30mm (0.008–0.012 in.)

➡If the measurement is within specifications, go on to the next step. If not, record the measurement taken for each individual valve.

5. Turn the crankshaft ⅔ revolution (240°).
6. Measure the clearance of the No.3 (IN) and NO.5 (IN) and No.3 (EX) and NO.6 (EX) valves. This measurement should correspond to specification.

➡Hint; check that the valve lifters on the number 3 cylinder are loose. If the measurement is within specifications, go on to the next step. If not, record the measurement taken for each individual valve.

7. Turn the crankshaft ⅔ revolution (240°).
8. Measure the clearance of the No.2 (IN) and NO.6 (IN) and No.2 (EX) and NO.4 (EX) valves. This measurement should correspond to specification.

➡If the measurement for this set of valves (and also the previous ones) is within specifications, go no further, the procedure is finished. If not, record the measurements and then proceed to Step 8.

9. Turn the crankshaft to position the intake camshaft lobe of the cylinder to be adjusted, upward.

➡Both intake and exhaust valve clearance may be adjusted at the same time if so required.

10. Using a suitable tool, turn the valve lifter so that the notch is easily accessible.
11. Install SST No. 09248-55010 or its equivalent between the 2 camshafts lobes and then turn the handle so that the tool presses down both (intake and exhaust) valve lifters evenly. For

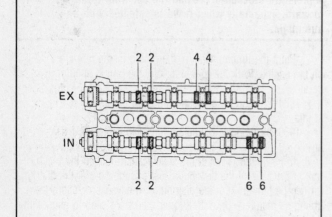

Fig. 20 Adjusting the No. 2 (IN), No. 6 (IN), No. 2 (EX) and No. 6 (EX) valves

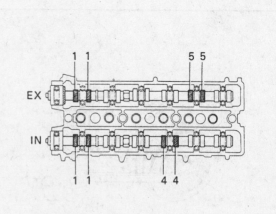

Fig. 21 Adjusting the No. 1 (IN), No. 4 (IN), No. 1 (EX) and No. 5 (EX) valves

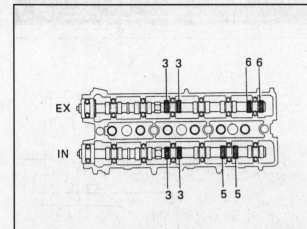

Fig. 22 Adjusting the No. 3 (IN), No. 5 (IN), No. 3 (EX) and No. 6 (EX) valves

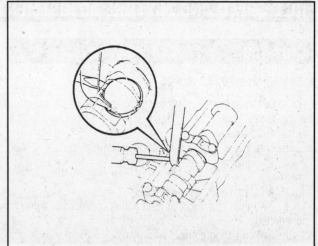

Fig. 24 A small pry tool and magnet can be used to remove the adjusting shim

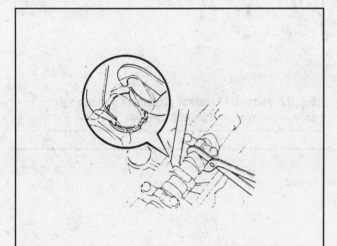

Fig. 23 A special tool is used to remove the adjusting shims

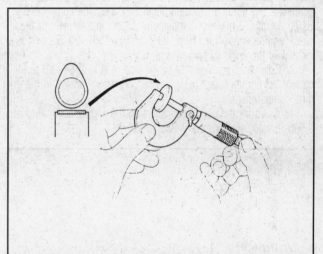

Fig. 25 Using a micrometer, measure the adjusting shim to determine its thickness

easy removal of the shim, when positioning the tool in between the 2 camshaft lobes, set it on the lifter so there is space enough to be able to remove the shim.

12. Using a suitable tool and a magnet, remove the valve shims.

13. Measure the thickness of the old shim with a micrometer. Using this measurement and the clearance of the ones made earlier (from Step 4, 6 or 8), determine what size replacement shim will be required in order to bring the valve clearance into specification. A good guide to use when determining shim thickness is as follows:

    a. T—Thickness of the old shim.
    b. A—Measured valve clearance.
    c. N—Thickness of the new shim.
    d. Intake: $N = T + (A - 0.20mm)$ example.
    e. Exhaust: $N = T + (A - 0.25mm)$ example.

➡Replacement shims are available in 17 sizes, in increments of 0.05mm, from 2.00mm to 3.300mm.

14. Install the new valve adjusting shim onto the valve lifter. Using the special shim installer tool (SST-09248-55010) press down the valve lifter and remove the tool and then recheck the valve clearance.

15. Install the cylinder head covers (using new gaskets) and install the retaining bolts. Tighten the bolts to 22 inch lbs.

16. Install the spark plug cables.

17. Install the air intake connector, vacuum transmitting pipe and brackets.

18. Install the accelerator link.

19. Install the PCV orifice pipe and hoses.

20. Install the air cleaner hose along with air connector pipe.

IDLE SPEED AND MIXTURE ADJUSTMENTS

Cressida

♦ **See Figures 26, 27 and 28**

1. Make sure the following conditions prevail before adjusting the idle speed:

   a. Air cleaner installed.

   b. Engine has reached normal operating temperature.

   c. All pipes and hoses of the air intake system are connected.

   d. All accessories are switched off.

   e. Electronic fuel injection (EFI) wiring connections tightly connected.

   f. Ignition timing correct.

   g. Transmission in Neutral, parking brake set and wheels blocked.

2. Connect a suitable tachometer to the engine, always connect the positive terminal of the tachometer to the engine service connector (IG terminal) located under in the engine compartment. Using a suitable piece of jumper wire short the terminals of the check engine connector (1983–88 T and E_1 1989–90 TE_1 and E_1), located in the engine compartment.

3. Connect a voltmeter to the Vf and E_1 (Vf_1 1989–90) terminals of the engine (diagnosis) service connector, located in the engine compartment.

4. Warm up the oxygen sensor with the engine at running at 2,500 rpm for approximately 2 minutes.

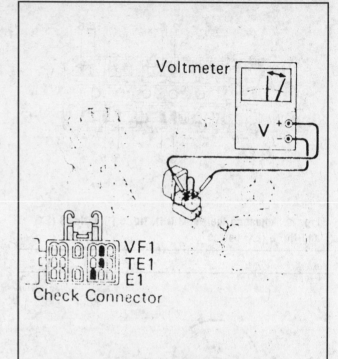

Fig. 27 Voltmeter terminal placement on the engine service connector—1989–90 Cressida

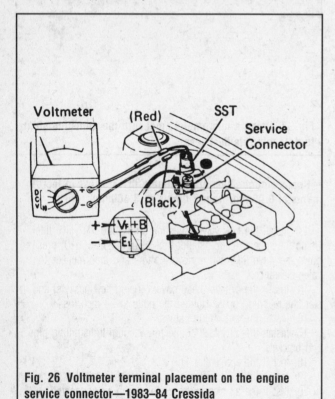

Fig. 26 Voltmeter terminal placement on the engine service connector—1983–84 Cressida

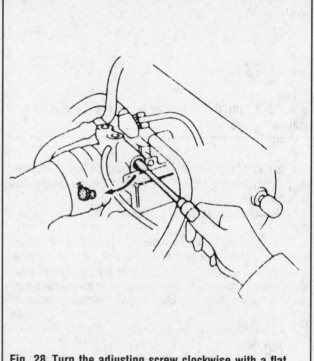

Fig. 28 Turn the adjusting screw clockwise with a flat bladed tool—Cressida shown

5. Maintain the engine speed at 2,500 rpm.

6. Check that the needle on the voltmeter fluctuates 8 times or more in 10 seconds. If not, inspect the EFI system and replace the oxygen sensor, if necessary.

7. With the engine idling, check that the idle RPM is within specifications:
- A/C switch **ON**—900 rpm in Neutral and 750 rpm in Drive.
- A/C switch **OFF**—650 rpm in Neutral and 600 rpm in Drive (1983–88).
- A/C switch **OFF**—750 rpm in Neutral and 700 rpm in Drive (1989–90).

8. With the engine idling, check that the Vf voltage is 2.5 plus or minus 1.25 volts. If not, check the intake system for a vacuum leak. If there is no vacuum leak in the intake manifold, investigate other areas.

9. If the idle speed is out of specifications, remove the rubber plug from the side of the throttle body exposing the idle adjustment screw.

10. Adjust the idle speed to obtain the specified rpm and reinstall the rubber plug.

➡**Always make sure that the idle speed control valve (ISC) is operating properly before making any idle speed adjustments. To see if the ISC valve is working properly, confirm that there is a clicking sound heard from it immediately after stopping the engine.**

Van

1. Make sure the following conditions prevail before adjusting the idle speed:
   a. Air cleaner installed.
   b. Engine has reached normal operating temperature.
   c. All pipes and hoses of the air intake system are connected.
   d. All accessories are switched off.
   e. Electronic fuel injection (EFI) wiring connections tightly attached.
   f. Ignition timing correct.
   g. Transmission in Neutral, parking brake set and wheels blocked.

2. Connect a tachometer and check the engine idle speed to be sure that it is within the specification given in the Tune-Up Specifications chart at the beginning of the chapter. Disconnect the vacuum switch valve (VSV), if so equipped.

➡**As some tachometers are not compatible with this ignition system, we recommend that you confirm the compatibility of your tachometer before using. Never allow the ignition coil terminals to touch ground as it could result in damage to the igniter and/or the ignition coil. Do not disconnect the battery cables while the engine is running. Make sure that the igniter is properly grounded to the body. When a tachometer is connected to the vehicle, always connect the positive terminal of the tachometer to the engine service connector located on or near the distributor assembly in the engine compartment.**

3. Run the engine at 2,500 rpm for 2 minutes.

4. Let the engine return to idle and set the idle speed for MT to 700 rpm or 750 rpm for AT, using the idle speed adjusting screw.

5. Remove the tachometer.

Gasoline Engine Tune-Up Specifications

Year	Engine Liters	Spark Plug Type ④	Gap (in.)	Ignition Timing (deg.) Man. Trans.	Auto. Trans.	Idle Speed RPM* Man. Trans.	Auto. Trans.	Valve Clearance In.	Exh.	Fuel Pump Pressure (psi)
1983	2.8L	BPR5EP-11	0.043	10B ①	10B ①	650	650	HYD.	HYD.	36–38
1984	2.8L	BPR5EP-11	0.043	10B ①	10B ①	650	650	HYD.	HYD.	36–38
	2.0L	BPR5EP-11	0.043	8B ②	8B ②	700	750	HYD.	HYD.	33–38
1985	2.8L	BPR5EP-11	0.043	10B ①	10B ①	650	650	HYD.	HYD.	36–38
	2.0L	BPR5EP-11	0.043	8B ②	8B ②	700	750	HYD.	HYD.	33–38
1986	2.8L	BPR5EP-11	0.043	10B ①	10B ①	650	650	HYD.	HYD.	36–38
	2.2L	BPR5EP-11	0.043	12B ①	12B ①	700	750	HYD.	HYD.	33–38
1987	2.8L	BPR5EP-11	0.043	10B ①	10B ①	650	600	HYD.	HYD.	36–38
	2.2L	BPR5EP-11	0.043	12B ①	12B ①	700	750	HYD.	HYD.	33–38
1988	2.8L	BPR5EP-11	0.043	10B ①	10B ①	—	650	HYD.	HYD.	36–38
	2.2L	BPR5EP-11	0.043	12B ①	12B ①	700	750	HYD.	HYD.	33–38
1989	3.0L	BCPR5EP-11	0.043	10B ③	10B ③	—	700	0.006 0.010	0.008 0.012	33–37
	2.2L	BPR5EP-11	0.043	12B ①	12B ①	700	750	HYD.	HYD.	33–38
1990	3.0L	BCPR5EP-11	0.043	10B ③	10B ③	—	700	0.006 0.010	0.008 0.012	33–37

Note: The underhood specifications sticker often reflects changes made in production. Sticker figures must be used if they disagree with those in the chart above.
① With a jumper wire between terminal T (it may be marked T1 on some models) and E1.
② With the vacuum advance unit disconnected.
③ With a jumper wire between terminals TE1 and E1.
HYD.—Hydraulic valve lifters used, there should be no need for adjustment.
*—On the Cressida models, the idle speed rpm when the air conditioning is on must be 750 rpm for vehicles equipped with automatic transmissions and 900 rpm for models equipped with manual transmissions.

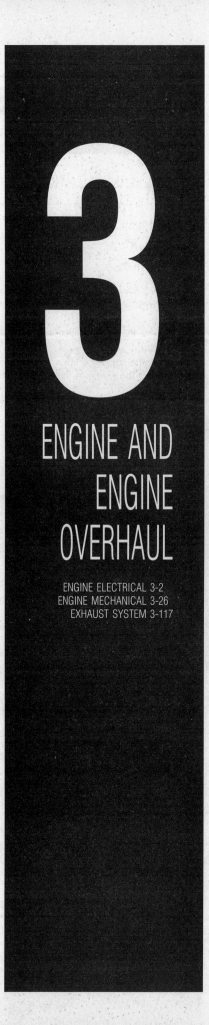

3

ENGINE AND ENGINE OVERHAUL

ENGINE ELECTRICAL

Ignition Coil

REMOVAL & INSTALLATION

Integrated Ignition Assembly (IIA)

1984–85 VAN

▶ **See Figure 1**

1. Disconnect the negative battery cable.
2. Remove the nuts and disconnect the wires from the terminals on the coil.
3. Remove the retaining screws and remove the coil.
To install:
4. Install the coil.
5. Connect the wiring to the coil and be careful of the routing of the wires.
6. Reconnect the battery.

Integrated Ignition Assembly With Electronic Spark Advance (IIA/ESA)

1986–89 VAN

▶ **See Figure 1a**

This system houses all of its components inside the distributor, including the ignition coil. The ECU is programmed with data for the optimum ignition timing under any and all operating conditions. Using data provided by sensors which monitor various engine functions (rpm, intake air volume, engine temperature, etc.), the microcomputer (ECU) triggers the spark at precisely the right instant. The electronic spark advance system is also used on Cressida, but without IIA.

1. Disconnect the negative battery cable. Remove the right seat.
2. Remove the engine service hole cover.
3. Remove the number one spark plug. Place a finger over the spark plug hole and rotate the crankshaft clockwise to Top Dead Center (TDC). When there is pressure felt on the finger at

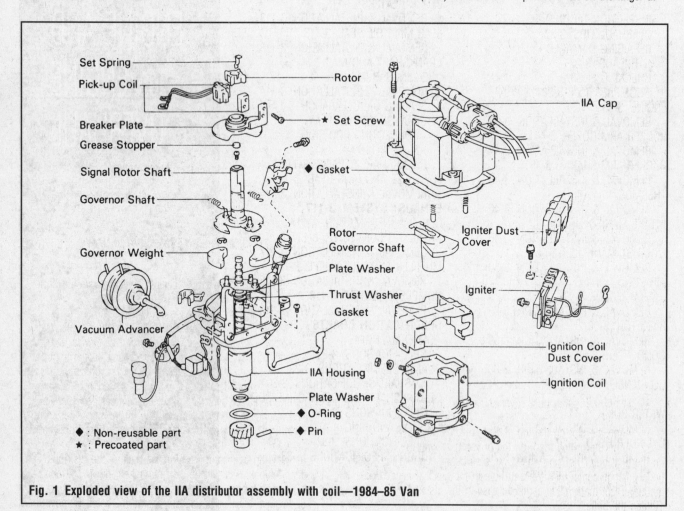

Fig. 1 Exploded view of the IIA distributor assembly with coil—1984–85 Van

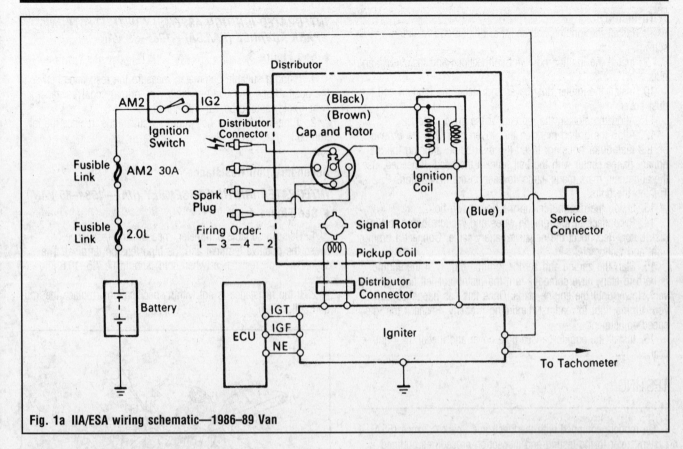

Fig. 1a IIA/ESA wiring schematic—1986–89 Van

the spark plug hole, this will be TDC of the compression stroke on number one cylinder. If not, repeat the procedure. Make sure the timing marks are set at 0. Install the number one spark plug.

4. Disconnect and tag (if necessary) all ignition wires from the distributor. Do not remove the high tension wire from the distributor cap.

5. Make an alignment mark on the base of the distributor and the engine block. Remove the distributor hold-down bolt and remove the distributor.

6. Remove the distributor cap, gasket and rotor. Remove the igniter dust cover and remove the ignition coil dust cover.

7. Remove the nuts and disconnect the wires from the terminals of the ignition coil. Remove the four ignition coil retaining screws and remove the ignition coil.

To install:

8. Install the ignition coil and the ignition coil retaining screws.

9. Install the ignition coil wire connections and their retaining nuts.

10. Install the igniter dust cover and install the ignition coil dust cover.

11. Align the slot on the top end of the drive rotor.

12. Align the drilled mark on the driven gear with the groove on the distributor housing. Insert the distributor, aligning the stationary flange center with the bolt hole in the head. If needed, use the alignment mark made earlier to ease in the installation. Tighten the bolts.

13. Install the IIA distributor and the hold-down bolt.

14. Reconnect all the ignition wires and vacuum hoses to the IIA distributor. Reconnect the negative battery cable. Connect a timing light and tachometer.

15. Start the engine and set the ignition timing. If the engine is hard to start, have someone turn the distributor left and right very slowly until the engine starts. Once this has happened, use your timing light to readjust the timing properly. Recheck the idle speed adjustment.

16. Install the engine service hole cover and install the right seat.

Electronic Spark Advance (ESA) Without IIA

CRESSIDA

1. Disconnect the negative battery cable. Remove the right seat.

2. Remove the engine service hole cover.

3. Remove the number one spark plug. Place a finger over the spark plug hole and rotate the crankshaft clockwise to Top Dead Center (TDC). When there is pressure felt on the finger at the spark plug hole, this will be TDC of the compression stroke on number one cylinder. If not, repeat the procedure. Make sure the timing marks are set at 0. Install the number one spark plug.

4. Disconnect and tag (if necessary) all ignition wires from the distributor. Do not remove the high tension wire from the distributor cap.

5. Make an alignment mark on the base of the distributor and the engine block. Remove the distributor hold-down bolt and remove the distributor.

6. Remove the distributor cap, gasket and rotor. Remove the igniter dust cover and remove the ignition coil dust cover.

7. Remove the nuts and disconnect the wires from the terminals of the ignition coil. Remove the four ignition coil retaining screws and remove the ignition coil.

To install:

8. Install the ignition coil and the ignition coil retaining screws.

9. Install the ignition coil wire connections and their retaining nuts.

10. Install the igniter dust cover and install the ignition coil dust cover.

11. Align the slot on the top end of the drive motor.

12. Align the drilled mark on the driven gear with the groove on the distributor housing. Insert the distributor, aligning the stationary flange center with the bolt hole in the head. If needed, use the alignment mark made earlier to ease in the installation. Tighten the bolts.

13. Install the distributor and the hold-down bolt.

14. Reconnect all the ignition wires and vacuum hoses to the distributor. Reconnect the negative battery cable. Connect a timing light and tachometer.

15. Start the engine and set the ignition timing. If the engine is hard to start, have someone turn the distributor left and right very slowly until the engine starts. Once this has happened, use your timing light to readjust the timing properly. Recheck the idle speed adjustment.

16. Install the engine service hole cover and install the right seat.

TESTING

On models equipped with the Electronic Spark Advance (ESA) system, refer to the testing and inspection procedures outlined later in this section.

Primary Coil Resistance

INTEGRATED IGNITION ASSEMBLY (IIA)—1984–85 VAN
▶ **See Figure 2**

1. Using a suitable ohmmeter, measure the resistance between the positive and negative terminals. The primary coil resistance (when cold) should be 0.3–0.5 ohms.

2. If the resistance is not within specifications, replace the ignition coil.

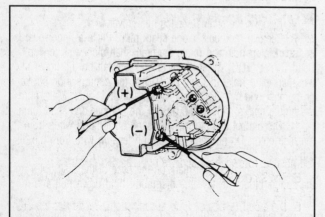

Fig. 2 Connect an ohmmeter across the coils positive and negative terminals to measure primary resistance— IIA distributor

INTEGRATED IGNITION ASSEMBLY WITH ELECTRONIC SPARK ADVANCE (IIA/ESA)—1986–89 VAN
▶ **See Figure 3**

1. Using a suitable ohmmeter, measure the resistance between the positive and negative terminals. The primary coil resistance (when cold) should be 1.2–1.5 ohms.

2. If the resistance is not within specifications, replace the ignition coil.

Secondary Coil Resistance

INTEGRATED IGNITION ASSEMBLY (IIA)—1984–85 VAN
▶ **See Figure 4**

1. Using a suitable ohmmeter, measure the resistance between the positive terminal and the high tension terminal. The secondary coil resistance (when cold) should be 7.5–10.5 kilo ohms.

2. If the resistance is not within specifications, replace the ignition coil.

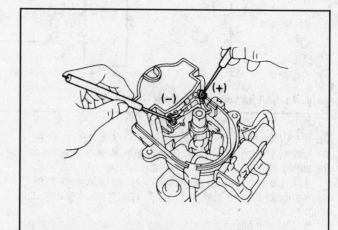

Fig. 3 Primary coil resistance between the positive and negative terminals should be 1.2–1.5 ohms when cold— IIA/ESA distributor

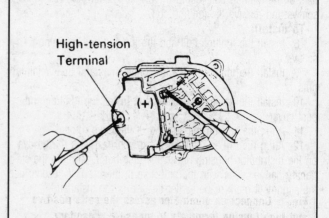

Fig. 4 Connect an ohmmeter across the coils positive and high tension terminals to measure secondary resistance—IIA distributor

INTEGRATED IGNITION ASSEMBLY WITH ELECTRONIC SPARK ADVANCE (IIA/ESA)—1986–89 VAN

▶ See Figure 5

1. Using a suitable ohmmeter, measure the resistance between the positive terminal and the high tension terminal. The secondary coil resistance (when cold) should be 7.5–10.5 kilo ohms.

2. If the resistance is not within specifications, replace the ignition coil.

Signal Generator (Pick-Up Coil) Resistance

INTEGRATED IGNITION ASSEMBLY (IIA)—1984–85 VAN

1. Using a suitable ohmmeter, check the resistance of the signal generator.

2. The signal generator resistance should be 140–180 ohms.

3. If the resistance is not correct, replace the signal generator with the distributor housing assembly.

INTEGRATED IGNITION ASSEMBLY WITH ELECTRONIC SPARK ADVANCE (IIA/ESA)—1986–89 VAN

▶ See Figure 6

1. Using a suitable ohmmeter, check the resistance of the pickup coil.

2. The pickup coil resistance should be 140–180 ohms.

3. If the resistance is not correct, replace the pickup coil with the distributor housing assembly.

ELECTRONIC SPARK ADVANCE (ESA)—1989–90 CRESSIDA

▶ See Figure 7

1. Using a suitable ohmmeter, check the resistance of the pickup coil at the pickup coil connector.

2. The resistance should be 140–180 ohms at all terminals of the connector except between terminals NE and G; between these 2 terminals the resistance should be 180–220 ohms.

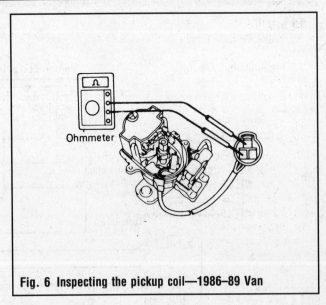

Fig. 6 Inspecting the pickup coil—1986–89 Van

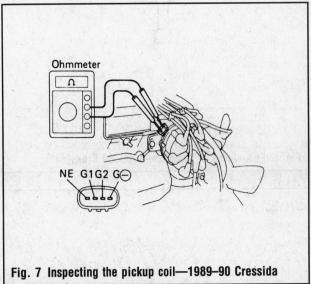

Fig. 7 Inspecting the pickup coil—1989–90 Cressida

Ignition Coil With Igniter Resistance

ELECTRONIC SPARK ADVANCE (ESA)—1983–88 CRESSIDA

▶ See Figures 8 and 9

1. Disconnect the high tension wire.

2. Using a suitable ohmmeter, measure the resistance between the positive (brown side) and negative (black side) terminals.

3. The primary resistance with the coil cold should be 0.4–0.5 ohms.

4. Using the same ohmmeter, measure the resistance between the positive (brown side) and the high tension terminals.

5. The secondary coil resistance with the coil cold should be 8.5–11.5 kilo ohms.

6. If the coil resistance is to specifications, reconnect the high tension wire.

7. If the coil resistance is not to specifications, replace the coil.

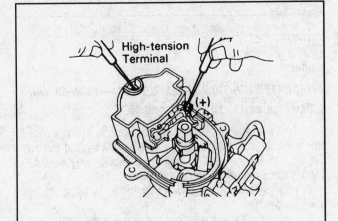

Fig. 5 Connect an ohmmeter across the coils positive and high tension terminals to measure secondary resistance—IIA/ESA distributor

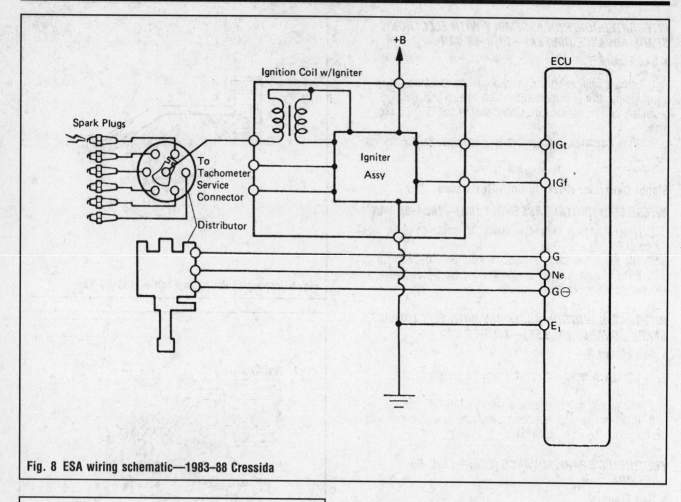

Fig. 8 ESA wiring schematic—1983–88 Cressida

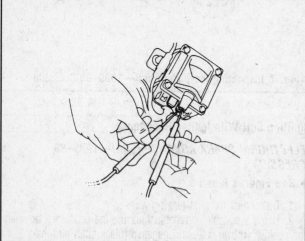

Fig. 9 Inspecting the secondary coil resistance—1983–88 Cressida

ELECTRONIC SPARK ADVANCE (ESA)—1989–90 CRESSIDA

▶ **See Figure 10**

1. Disconnect the high tension wire.
2. Using the suitable ohmmeter, measure the resistance between the positive and negative terminals.

3. The primary resistance with the coil cold should be 0.24–0.30 ohms.
4. Using the same ohmmeter, measure the resistance between the positive and the high tension terminals.
5. The secondary coil resistance with the coil cold should be 9.2–12.5 kilo ohms.
6. If the coil resistance is to specifications, reconnect the high tension wire.
7. If the coil resistance is not to specifications, replace the coil.

Igniter

INTEGRATED IGNITION ASSEMBLY (IIA)—1984–85 VAN

▶ **See Figures 11, 12, 13, 14 and 15**

1. Turn the ignition switch to the **ON** position. Using a suitable voltmeter, connect the positive probe to the ignition coil positive terminal and the negative probe to a suitable body ground. The voltage should be approximately 12 volts.
2. Inspect the power transistor in the igniter by using the following procedure:
   a. Connect the voltmeter positive probe to the ignition coil negative terminal and the negative probe to the body ground. The voltmeter should read approximately 12 volts.
   b. Using a dry cell (1.5V) battery, connect the positive terminal of the battery to the pink wire terminal and the negative terminal to the white wire terminal.

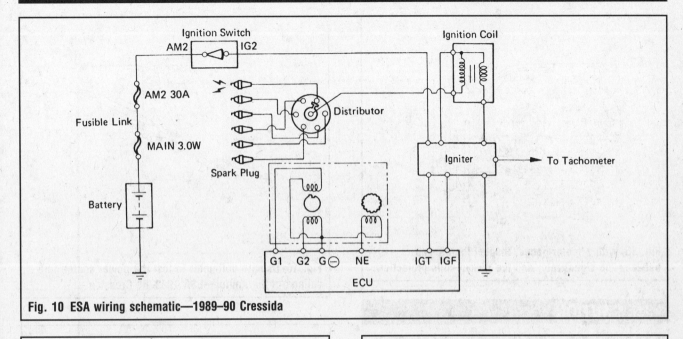

Fig. 10 ESA wiring schematic—1989–90 Cressida

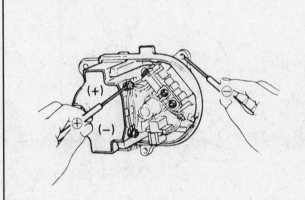

Fig. 11 Connect the (+) probe to the coils (+) terminal and the (-) probe to ground to inspect power source line voltage

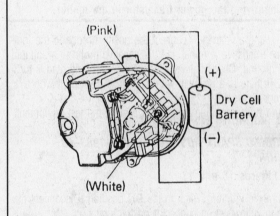

Fig. 13 Connect the batterys positive terminal to the power transistors pink post and the batterys negative terminal to the transistors white post—IIA distributor

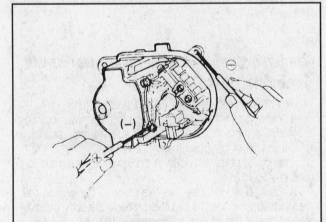

Fig. 12 Connect the (+) probe to the coils (-) terminal and the (-) probe to ground to inspect power transistor voltage

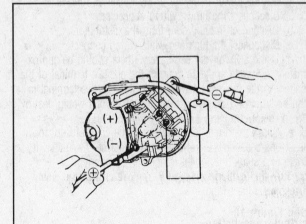

Fig. 14 If the igniter reading is not 0–3 volts, replace the igniter—IIA distributor

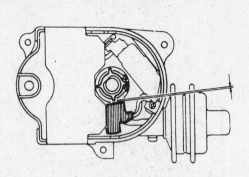

Fig. 15 With a feeler gauge, inspect the air gap between the signal rotor and the pickup coils projection

❈❈ CAUTION

Do not apply battery voltage for more than five seconds to avoid destroying the power transistor in the igniter.

    c. Using a voltmeter, connect the positive probe to the ignition coil negative terminal and the negative probe to a suitable body ground. Check the voltage reading; it should read 0 to 3 volts. If there is a problem with the igniter, replace it with a new one.

3. Turn off the ignition switch and remove the test equipment.

ELECTRONIC SPARK ADVANCE (ESA)—1983–88 CRESSIDA

▶ **See Figures 16 and 17**

1. Turn the ignition switch to the **ON** position. Disconnect the brown and yellow wiring connector on the igniter.

2. Using a suitable voltmeter, connect the positive probe to the brown connector on the wire harness side and the negative probe to the body ground.

3. The voltage should be approximately 12 volts.

4. Check the power transistor in the igniter as follows:

    a. Disconnect the brown wiring connector.

    b. Disconnect the coil cord from the distributor.

    c. Disconnect the pink and white wiring connector.

    d. Using a 3 volt dry cell battery (there should be approximately 2–5 volts applied), connect the positive terminal of the battery to the pink wire terminal and the negative terminal to the body ground. Applying more than five volts would destroy the diodes.

    e. Check that there is a spark from the coil cord tip, for at least one second. If there is no spark, replace the igniter. If there is a spark, the igniter is operating properly.

5. Turn the ignition switch **OFF**, remove all test equipment and reconnect the wiring.

Distributor Inspection

INTEGRATED IGNITION ASSEMBLY (IIA)—1984–85 VAN

1. Inspect the air gap, by using a feeler gauge. Measure the gap between the signal rotor and the pick-up coil

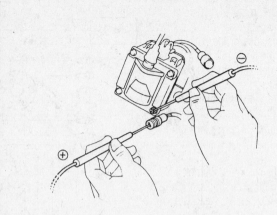

Fig. 16 Using a voltmeter to test the power source line voltage of the igniter—ESA 1983–88 Cressida

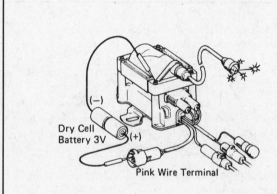

Dry Cell Battery 3V

(−) (+)

Pink Wire Terminal

Fig. 17 Apply 2–5 volts, then connect the positive (+) terminal of the battery to the pink wire and the batterys negative (-) terminal to ground—ESA

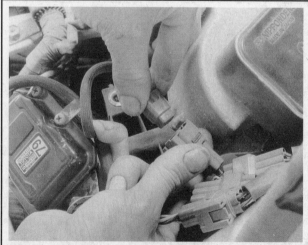

When testing the igniter, make sure you unplug the correct colored wires

projection. The air gap should be 0.008–0.016 in. (0.20–0.40mm).

2. Inspect the pick-up coil by using an ohmmeter to check the resistance of the pick-up coil. The pick-up coil resistance should be 140–180 ohms. If the resistance is not correct, replace the pick-up coil with the distributor housing assembly.

3. Inspect the vacuum advance (if so equipped) by disconnecting the vacuum hose and connecting a vacuum pump to the diaphragms. Apply a vacuum and check that the vacuum advance moves freely. If the advance unit does not respond to the vacuum, replace it.

4. Inspect the governor advance by turning the rotor shaft counterclockwise, release it and check that the rotor returns slightly clockwise. Check that the rotor shaft is not excessively loose.

INTEGRATED IGNITION ASSEMBLY WITH ELECTRONIC SPARK ADVANCE (IIA/ESA)—1986–89 VAN

▶ See Figure 18

1. Remove the distributor cap, rotor, and dust shield.

2. Turn the engine over (you may use a socket wrench on the front pulley bolt to do this) until the projection on the pickup coil is directly opposite the signal rotor tooth.

3. Get a non-ferrous (paper, brass, or plastic) set of feeler gauges and measure the gap between the signal rotor and the pick-up coil projection. DO NOT USE AN ORDINARY METAL FEELER GAUGE! The gauge should just touch either side of the gap; the permissible range is 0.008 in. (0.2mm).

4. If the gap is either too wide or too narrow, replace the pick-up coil, governor shaft and housing assembly.

5. If the gap is within specifications, place the dust shield, rotor and distributor cap back in their proper installed position.

ELECTRONIC SPARK ADVANCE (ESA) IGNITION SYSTEM—1983–88 CRESSIDA

▶ See Figures 19 and 20

1. Check for cracks, carbon tracks, burnt or corroded terminals.

2. Check the distributor center contact for wear. If a problem is found with any component, replace the component.

3. Using a suitable ohmmeter, check the two pickup coils as follows:

   a. Measure the resistance between the top center terminal (white wire) and the lower right terminal (yellow wire). The resistance should be 140–180 ohms.

   b. Measure the resistance between the top center terminal (white wire) and the lower left terminal (red wire). The resistance should be 140–180 ohms.

4. If the resistance is not correct, replace the distributor assembly.

5. Using a suitable feeler gauge, measure the air gap between the signal rotor and the signal generators' (pick-up coils') projection. The air gap should be 0.008–0.016 in. (0.2–0.4mm). If not within specifications, replace the distributor assembly.

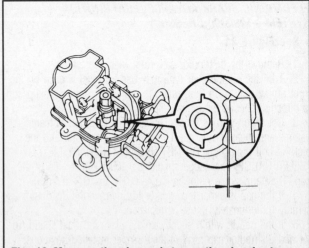

Fig. 18 Measure the air gap between the signal rotor and pickup coils projection—1986–89 Van

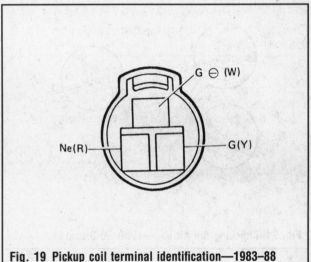

Fig. 19 Pickup coil terminal identification—1983–88 Cressida

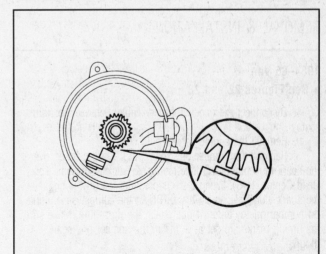

Fig. 20 Check the air gap between the signal rotor and pickup coils projection—1983–88 Cressida

ELECTRONIC SPARK ADVANCE (ESA) IGNITION SYSTEM—1989–90 CRESSIDA

▶ **See Figure 21**

1. Remove the distributor cap, rotor, and dust shield.

2. Turn the engine over (you may use a socket wrench on the front pulley bolt to do this) until the projection on the pickup coil is directly opposite the signal rotor tooth.

3. Get a non-ferrous (paper, brass, or plastic) set of feeler gauges and measure the gap between the signal rotor and the pick-up coil projection. DO NOT USE AN ORDINARY METAL FEELER GAUGE! The gauge should just touch either side of the gap. The permissible range is 0.008–0.016 in. (0.2–0.4mm).

4. If the gap is either too wide or too narrow, the distributor assembly (unfortunately) must be replaced.

5. If the gap is within specifications, place the dust shield, rotor and distributor cap back in their proper installed positions.

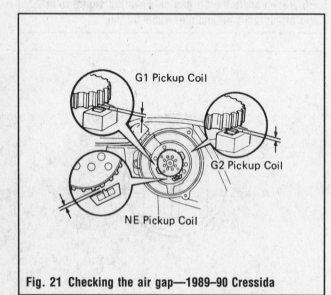

Fig. 21 Checking the air gap—1989–90 Cressida

Distributor

REMOVAL & INSTALLATION

1984–85 Van

▶ **See Figures 22 and 23**

1. Disconnect the negative battery cable. Remove the right seat.

2. Remove the engine service hole cover.

3. Remove the number one spark plug. Place a finger over the spark plug hole and rotate the crankshaft clockwise to Top Dead Center (TDC). When there is pressure felt on the finger at the spark plug hole, this will be TDC of the compression stroke on number one cylinder. If not, repeat the procedure. Make sure the timing marks are set at 0. Install the number one spark plug.

4. Disconnect and tag (if necessary) all ignition wires and vacuum hoses from the IIA distributor. Do not remove the high tension wire from the distributor cap.

5. Make an alignment mark on the base of the distributor and the engine block. Remove the IIA distributor hold-down bolt and remove the distributor.

6. Remove the IIA distributor cap, gasket and rotor. Remove the igniter dust cover and remove the ignition coil dust cover.

7. Remove the ignition coil by removing the nuts and disconnecting the wires from the terminals of the ignition coil. Remove the four ignition coil retaining screws and remove the coil.

8. Remove the IIA wire with the condenser. Remove the igniter screws and nuts and disconnect the wires from the terminals of the igniter. Remove the two igniter retaining screws and remove the igniter.

To install:

9. Install the igniter assembly along with the igniter.

10. Install the igniter screws and nuts and reconnect the wires to the terminals of the igniter.

11. Install the IIA wire with the condenser.

12. Install the ignition coil and the ignition coil retaining screws.

13. Install the ignition coil wire connections and their retaining nuts.

14. Install the igniter dust cover and install the ignition coil dust cover.

15. Align the slot on the top end of the drive rotor.

16. Align the drilled mark on the driven gear with the groove on the distributor housing. Insert the distributor, aligning the stationary flange center with the bolt hole in the head. If needed, use the alignment mark made earlier to ease in the installation. Tighten the bolts.

17. Install the IIA distributor and the hold-down bolt.

18. Reconnect all the ignition wires and vacuum hoses to the IIA distributor. Reconnect the negative battery cable. Connect a timing light and tachometer.

19. Start the engine and set the ignition timing. If the engine is hard to start, have someone turn the distributor left and right very slowly until the engine starts. Once this has happened, use your timing light to readjust the timing properly. Recheck the idle speed adjustment.

20. Install the engine service hole cover and install the right seat.

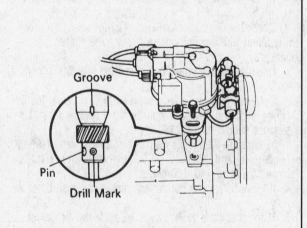

Fig. 22 Align the drilled mark on the driven gear with the groove on the distributor housing

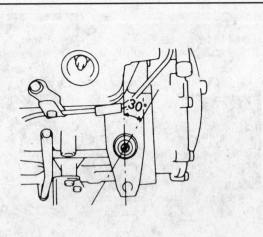

Fig. 23 Position the slot on the top end of the drive gear before installation

1986–89 Van
▶ See Figure 24

　　1. Disconnect the negative battery cable. Remove the right seat.
　　2. Remove the engine service hole cover.
　　3. Remove the number one spark plug. Place a finger over the spark plug hole and rotate the crankshaft clockwise to Top Dead Center (TDC). When there is pressure felt on the finger at the spark plug hole, this will be TDC of the compression stroke on number one cylinder. If not, repeat the procedure. Make sure the timing marks are set at 0. Install the number one spark plug.
　　4. Disconnect and tag (if necessary) all ignition wires from the distributor. Do not remove the high tension wire from the distributor cap.
　　5. Make an alignment mark on the base of the distributor and the engine block. Remove the distributor hold-down bolt and remove the distributor.

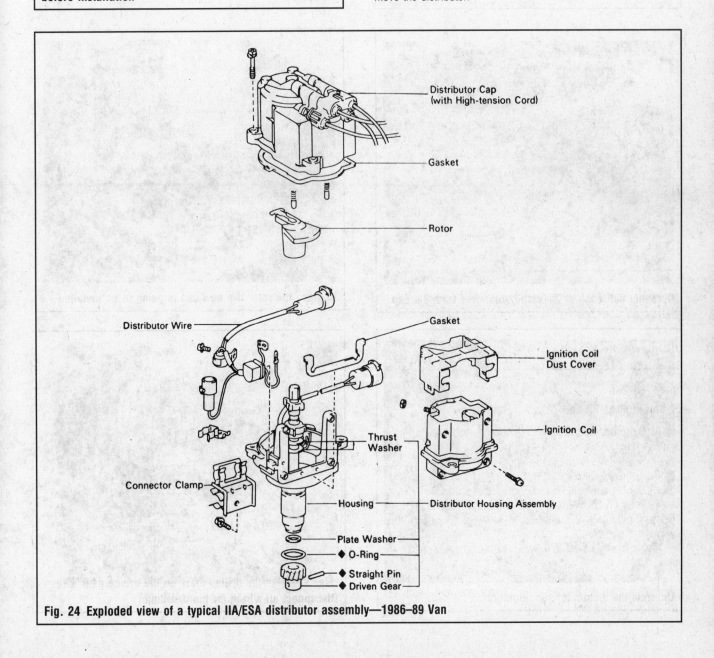

Fig. 24 Exploded view of a typical IIA/ESA distributor assembly—1986–89 Van

Remove the ignition wires dust cap from the distributor on IIA/ESA models

. . . and lift the cap off the distributor—IIA/ESA distributor

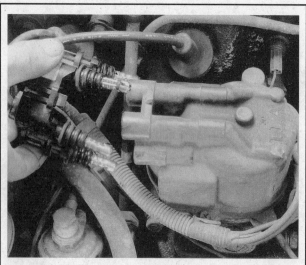

Carefully pull each of the distributor wires from the cap

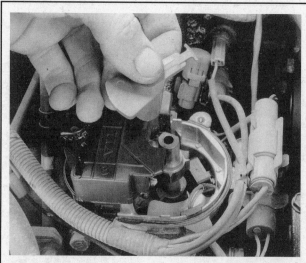

Replace the rotor if a new cap is going to be installed

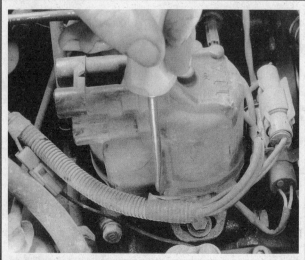

Unscrew the distributor cap retainers . . .

Disconnect all wiring for the distributor

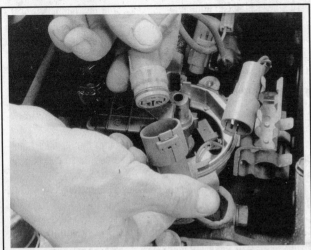

There may be more than one wire leading to the distributor

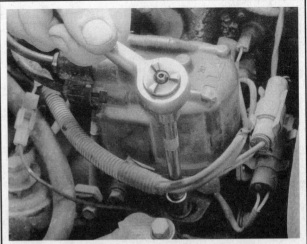

Once all of the distributor components have been assembled, tighten the mounting bolts

To install:

6. Align the slot on the top end of the drive rotor.

7. Align the drilled mark on the driven gear with the groove on the distributor housing. Insert the distributor, aligning the stationary flange center with the bolt hole in the head. If needed, use the alignment mark made earlier to ease in the installation. Tighten the bolts.

8. Install the IIA distributor and the hold-down bolt.

9. Reconnect all the ignition wires and vacuum hoses to the IIA distributor. Reconnect the negative battery cable. Connect a timing light and tachometer.

10. Start the engine and set the ignition timing. If the engine is hard to start, have some one turn the distributor left and right very slowly until the engine starts. Once this has happened, use your timing light to readjust the timing properly. Recheck the idle speed adjustment.

11. Install the engine service hole cover and install the right seat.

1983–88 Cressida

▶ See Figures 25 and 26

1. Disconnect the negative battery cable.

2. Remove the number one spark plug. Place a finger over the spark plug hole and rotate the crankshaft clockwise to Top Dead Center (TDC). When there is pressure felt on the finger at the spark plug hole, this will be TDC of the compression stroke on number one cylinder. If not, repeat the procedure. Make sure the timing marks are set at 0. Install the number one spark plug.

3. Disconnect and tag (if necessary) all ignition wires from the ESA distributor. Do not remove the high tension wire from the distributor cap.

4. Make an alignment mark on the base of the distributor and the engine block. Remove the ESA distributor hold-down bolt and remove the distributor assembly with O-ring.

To install:

5. Remove the oil filler cap. Make sure that the match hole on the No. 2 journal of the camshaft housing is aligned with that of the camshaft. If not, turn the crankshaft one full turn.

Unbolt the distributor and lift the unit out of the engine—IIA/ESA distributor

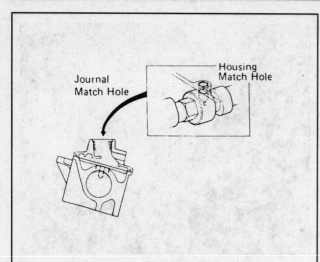

Fig. 25 Align the match holes in the No. 2 journal and the camshaft housing—1983–88 Cressida

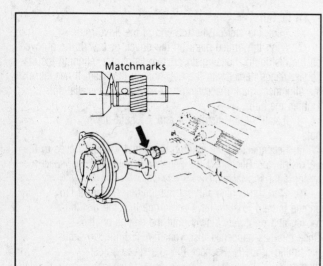

Fig. 26 Insert the distributor assembly with the matchmarks lined up—1983–88 Cressida

6. Install a new O-ring to the distributor. Always use a new O-ring when installing the distributor.

7. Align the matchmark of the distributor (the drill mark on the spiral gear) with that of the distributor housing.

8. Insert the distributor, aligning the center of the flange with that of the bolt hole of the cylinder head.

9. Align the rotor tooth with the signal generator (pick-up coil).

10. Temporarily install the distributor set bolt.

11. Install the cap and wires, connect the distributor connectors and install the oil filler cap.

12. Reconnect the negative battery cable. Connect a timing light and tachometer.

13. Start the engine and set the ignition timing. If the engine is hard to start, have someone turn the distributor left and right very slowly until the engine starts. Once this has happened, use your timing light to readjust the timing properly. Recheck the idle speed adjustment.

1989–90 Cressida
▶ See Figures 27, 28, 29 and 30

1. Disconnect the negative battery cable. Remove the water proof cover off of the distributor assembly.

2. Remove the oil filler cap. Look through the oil filler hole and turn the crankshaft clockwise until the cam nose can be seen.

3. Turn the crankshaft counterclockwise approximately 120 degrees.

4. Turn the crankshaft again approximately 10–40 degrees clockwise so that the timing belt cover TDC mark and the crankshaft pulley TDC mark are aligned.

5. Disconnect and tag (if necessary) all ignition wires from the ESA distributor. Do not remove the high tension wire from the distributor cap.

6. Make an alignment mark on the base of the distributor and the engine block. Remove the ESA distributor hold-down bolt and remove the distributor assembly with O-ring.

To install:

7. Install a new O-ring to the distributor. Always use a new O-ring when installing the distributor.

8. Align the groove of the distributor housing with the protrusion of the driven gear.

9. Insert the distributor, aligning the center of the flange with that of the bolt hole of the cylinder head.

10. Temporarily install the distributor set bolt.

11. Install the cap and wires, connect the distributor connectors and install the oil filler cap.

12. Reconnect the negative battery cable. Connect a timing light and tachometer.

13. Start the engine and set the ignition timing. If the engine is hard to start, have someone turn the distributor left and right very slowly until the engine starts. Once this has happened, use your timing light to readjust the timing properly. Recheck the idle speed adjustment.

Alternator

ALTERNATOR PRECAUTIONS

Several precautions must be observed with alternator equipped vehicles to avoid damage to the unit.

• If the battery is removed for any reason, make sure it is reconnected with the correct polarity. Reversing the battery connections may result in damage to the one-way rectifiers.

• When utilizing a booster battery as a starting aid, always connect the positive to positive terminals and the negative terminal from the booster battery to a good engine ground on the vehicle being started.

• Never use a fast charger as a booster to start vehicles.

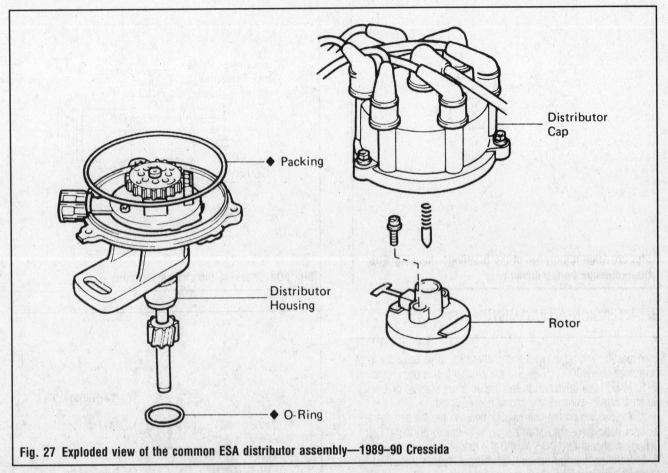

Fig. 27 Exploded view of the common ESA distributor assembly—1989–90 Cressida

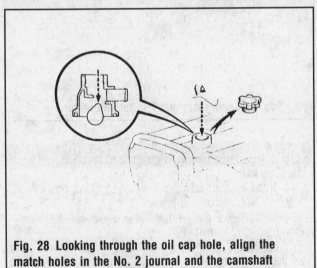

Fig. 28 Looking through the oil cap hole, align the match holes in the No. 2 journal and the camshaft housing—1989–90 Cressida

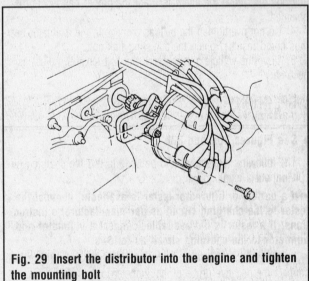

Fig. 29 Insert the distributor into the engine and tighten the mounting bolt

• Disconnect the battery cables when charging the battery with a fast charger.
• Never attempt to polarize the alternator.
• Do not use test lamps of more than 12 volts when checking diode continuity.
• Do not short across or ground any of the alternator terminals.
• The polarity of the battery, alternator and regulator must be matched and considered before making any electrical connections within the system.
• Never separate the alternator on an open circuit. Make sure all connections within the circuit are clean and tight.
• Disconnect the battery ground terminal when performing any service on electrical components.
• Disconnect the battery if arc welding is to be done on the vehicle.

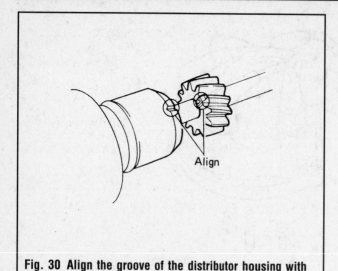

Fig. 30 Align the groove of the distributor housing with the protrusion on the driven gear

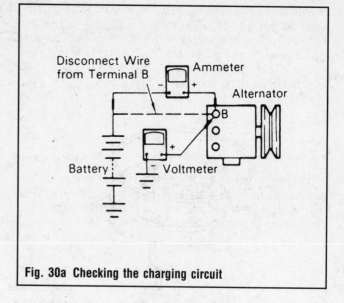

Fig. 30a Checking the charging circuit

BELT TENSION ADJUSTMENT

Inspection and adjustment to the alternator drive belt should be performed every 3000 miles or if the alternator has been removed.

1. Inspect the drive belt to see that it is not cracked or worn. Be sure that its surfaces are free of grease or oil.

2. Push down on the belt halfway between the fan and the alternator pulleys (or crankshaft pulley) with thumb pressure. Belt deflection should be 3/8–1/2 in. (10–12 mm).

3. If the belt tension requires adjustment, loosen the adjusting link bolt and move the alternator until the proper belt tension is obtained.

4. Do not overtighten the belt, as damage to the alternator bearings could result. Tighten the adjusting link bolt.

5. Drive the vehicle and re-check the belt tension. Adjust as necessary.

INSPECTION

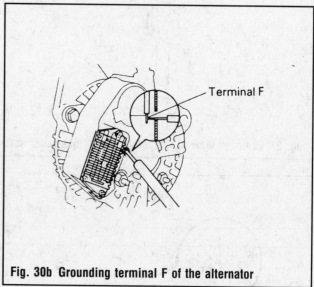

Fig. 30b Grounding terminal F of the alternator

▶ **See Figures 30a and 30b**

The following inspection is to be used to test the charging circuit without a load.

➡ **If a battery or alternator tester is available, connect the tester to the charging circuit as per manufacturer's instructions. If a tester is not available, connect a voltmeter and ammeter to the charging circuit as follows:**

1. Disconnect the wire from terminal **B** of the alternator and connect the negative probe of the ammeter to it.

2. Connect the test probe from the positive terminal of the ammeter to terminal **B** of the alternator.

3. Connect the positive probe of the voltmeter to terminal **B** of the alternator.

4. Ground the negative probe of the voltmeter.

5. Check the charging system as follows:

   a. With the engine running at 2000 rpm, the reading on the ammeter and voltmeter should be 10 amps or less and 13.5–15.1 volts at 77°F (25°C).

   b. If the voltage reading is greater than specified, replace the IC regulator.

   c. If the voltage reading is less than specified, check the IC regulator and alternator as follows:

6. With terminal **F** grounded, start the engine and check the voltage reading of terminal **B**.

7. If the voltage reading is greater than the standard voltage, replace the IC regulator.

8. If the voltage reading is less than the standard voltage, check the alternator.

9. To check the charging circuit with a load, use the following test.

   a. With the engine running at 2,000 rpm turn on the high beam headlights and place the heater fan control on HI.

   b. Check the reading on the ammeter. The standard amperage reading is 30 amp or more.

   c. If the ammeter reading is less than 30 amps, repair or replace the alternator as necessary.

➡With the battery fully charged, the indications will sometimes be less than 30 amps. If an IC regulator is found to be faulty, it is recommended that the alternator be replaced with a new one or a rebuilt one, due to the complexity involved with disassembling the alternator in order to gain access to the regulator and then to reassemble the unit.

REMOVAL & INSTALLATION

♦ **See Figures 31, 32, and 33**

➡On some vehicles, the alternator is mounted very low on the engine. On these vehicles it may be necessary to remove the gravel shield and work from underneath the vehicle in order to gain access to the alternator.

1. Disconnect the negative battery cable.
2. Remove the air cleaner, if necessary, to gain access to the alternator.
3. Remove the power steering or air conditioning drive belts, as required.
4. Unfasten the bolts which attach the adjusting link to the alternator. Remove the alternator drive belt.
5. Unfasten and tag the alternator attaching bolt and then withdraw the alternator from its bracket.
6. Installation is the reverse of the removal procedure. After installing the alternator, adjust the belt tension.

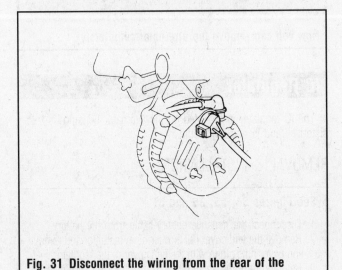

Fig. 31 Disconnect the wiring from the rear of the alternator

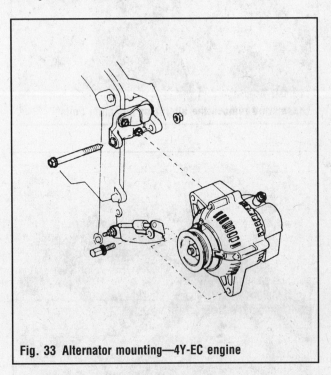

Fig. 33 Alternator mounting—4Y-EC engine

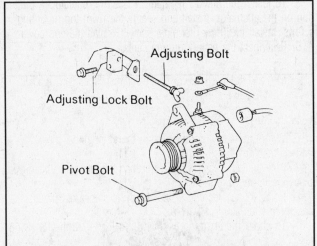

Fig. 32 Loosen the alternators adjusting lock, pivot and adjusting bolts—1989–90 Cressida shown

When removing the alternator, first remove its drive belt and any belts that are in the way—Van shown

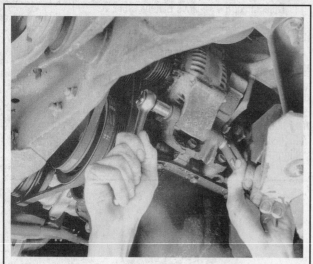

Loosen and remove the alternator mounting bolts

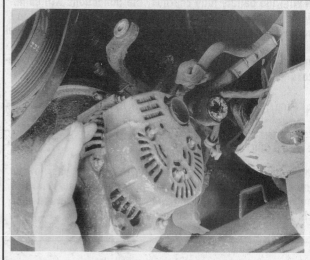

Now you can remove the alternator completely

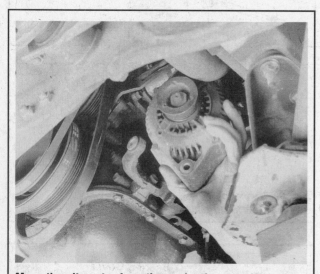

Move the alternator from the engine far enough so . . .

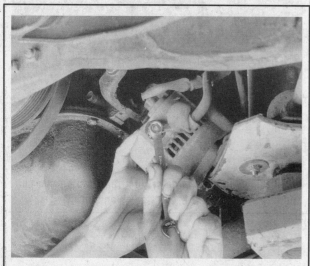

. . . you can separate the wiring from the alternator

IC Regulator

The IC regulator is mounted on the alternator housing, is transistorized and is non-adjustable.

REMOVAL & INSTALLATION

▶ **See Figures 34, 35, 36 and 37**

1. Disconnect the negative battery cable from the battery.
2. Remove the end cover nut and terminal insulator and remove the 3 end cover nuts along with the end cover of the regulator.
3. Remove the three screws that go through the terminals.
4. Remove the (two) top mounting screws that mount the regulator to the alternator. Remove the regulator.
5. To install the new IC regulator. Place the regulator in position on the alternator. Install and secure the (two) top mounting screws. Install the (three) terminal screws. Install the end cover.
6. Reconnect the battery ground cable.

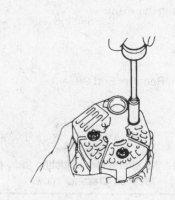

Fig. 34 Remove the alternators rear end cover to access the regulator

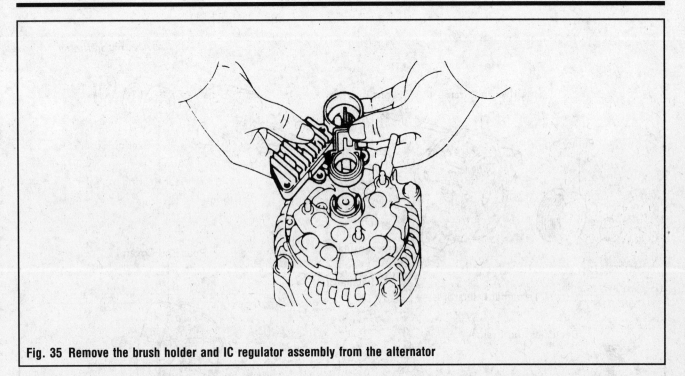

Fig. 35 Remove the brush holder and IC regulator assembly from the alternator

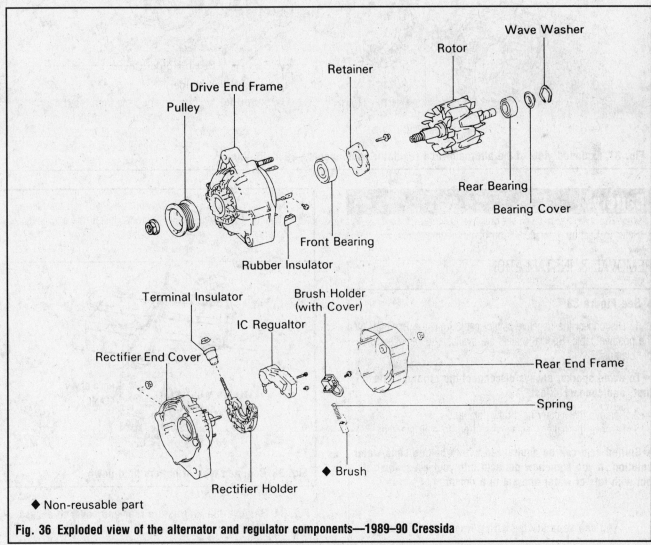

Fig. 36 Exploded view of the alternator and regulator components—1989–90 Cressida

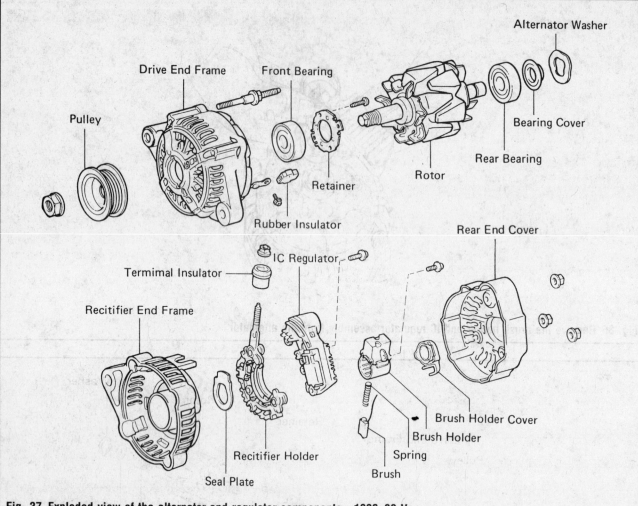

Fig. 37 Exploded view of the alternator and regulator components—1986–89 Van

Battery

Refer to Section 1 for details on battery maintenance.

REMOVAL & INSTALLATION

▶ See Figure 38

1. Disconnect the negative battery cable from the terminal, then the positive cable. Special pullers are available to remove the cable clamps.

➡**To avoid sparks, always disconnect the ground cable first, and connect it last.**

2. Remove the battery hold-down clamp.
3. Remove the battery, being careful not to spill the acid.

➡**Spilled acid can be neutralized with a baking soda/water solution. If you somehow get acid into your eyes, flush it out with lots of water and get to a doctor.**

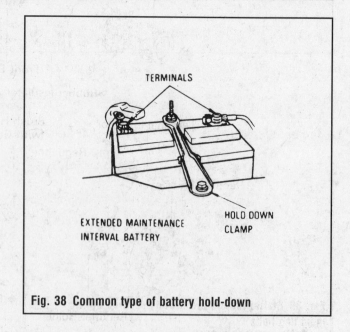

Fig. 38 Common type of battery hold-down

4. Clean the battery posts thoroughly before reinstalling, or when installing a new battery.

5. Clean the cable clamps, using a wire brush, both inside and out.

6. Install the battery and the hold-down clamp or strap. Connect the positive, then the negative cable. Do not hammer them in place. The terminals should be coated lightly (externally) with grease to prevent corrosion. There are also felt washers impregnated with an anti-corrosion substance which are slipped over the battery posts before installing the cables. These are available in auto parts stores.

✳✳ WARNING

Make absolutely sure that the battery is connected properly before you turn on the ignition switch. Reversed polarity can burn out your alternator and regulator within a matter of seconds.

Starter

REMOVAL & INSTALLATION

◆ **See Figure 39**

1. Disconnect the negative (ground) cable from the battery.

2. Disconnect the wires/cables connected to the starter motor.

3. On some models it may be necessary to remove the air cleaner, splash shields or linkage that is in the way of easy access to the starter motor.

4. Loosen and remove the starter motor mounting nuts/bolts while supporting the motor.

5. Remove the starter motor.

6. Installation is in the reverse order of removal.

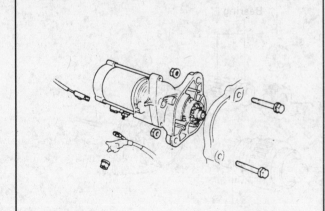

Fig. 39 Starter motors are usually secured by two mounting bolts

When unbolting the starter, it may be easier to use an extension on the wrench

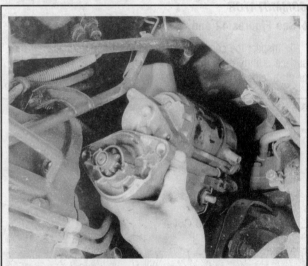

Lower the starter from the engine

OVERHAUL

◆ **See Figure 40**

Disassembly

➡**The starter must be removed from the vehicle in order to perform this operation.**

1. Disconnect the field coil lead from the solenoid terminal.

2. Remove the 2 through bolts. Pull out the field frame with the armature from the solenoid switch assembly.

3. Remove the O-ring. Remove the 2 screws that retain the starter housing, clutch assembly and gears.

4. Using a magnet, remove the steel ball from the clutch shaft hole.

5. Remove the 2 screws and end cover from the field frame. Remove the O-rings from the field frame and screws.

6. Using a suitable tool, hold the spring back and disconnect the brush from the brush holder. Disconnect the 4 brushes and remove the brush holder.

7. Remove the armature from the field frame.

Inspection

ARMATURE COIL

◆ **See Figure 41**

1. To inspect the commutator for an open circuit do the following:

    a. Using an ohmmeter, check that there is continuity between the segments of the commutator.

    b. If there is no continuity between any segment, replace the armature.

2. To inspect the commutator for a proper ground, do the following:

    a. Using an ohmmeter, check that there is no continuity between the commutator and the armature coil core.

    b. If there is continuity, replace the armature.

COMMUTATOR

◆ **See Figures 42 and 43**

1. Inspect the commutator for dirty and burnt surfaces. If the surface is dirty or burnt, correct it with sandpaper (No. 400 grit) or on a lathe.

2. Inspect the commutator diameter by using vernier calipers to measure it.

    a. The standard diameter is 30mm.

    b. The minimum diameter is 29mm.

3. If the diameter is less than minimum, replace the armature.

4. Check that the undercut depth is clean and free of any foreign materials. Smooth out the edge:

    a. Standard undercut depth is 0.6mm.

    b. Minimum undercut depth is 0.2mm.

5. If the undercut depth is less than minimum, correct it with the use of a hacksaw blade.

FIELD COIL (FRAME)

◆ **See Figure 44**

1. Inspect the field coil for an open circuit as follows:

    a. Using an ohmmeter, check that there is continuity between the lead wire and field coil brush lead.

    b. If there is no continuity, replace the field frame.

2. Inspect the field coil for ground as follows:

    a. Using an ohmmeter, check that there is no continuity between the field coil end and field frame.

    b. If there is continuity, repair or replace the field frame.

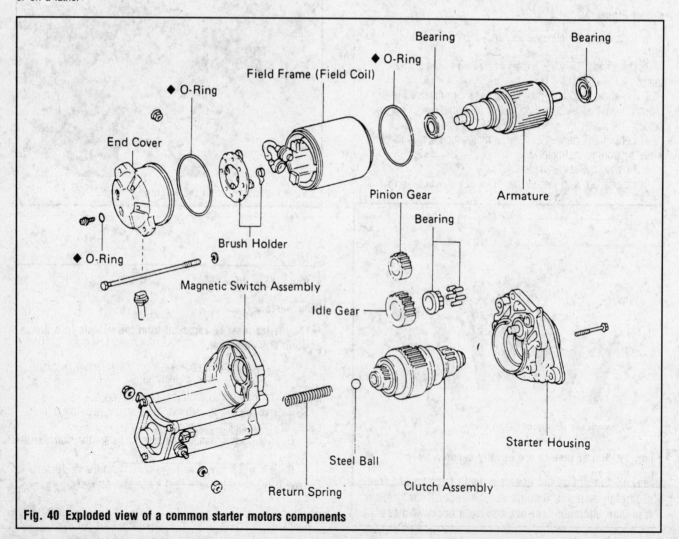

Fig. 40 Exploded view of a common starter motors components

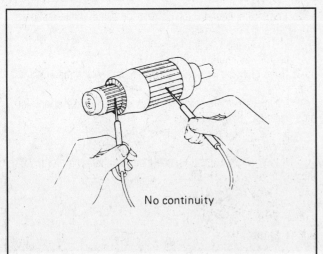

Fig. 41 Check the continuity of the starter motors armature coil

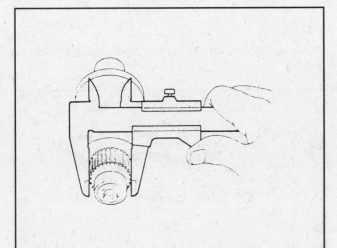

Fig. 42 Using a vernier caliper, measure the commutator diameter

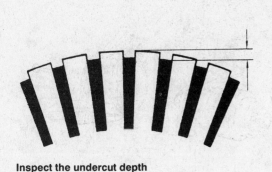

Inspect the undercut depth

Fig. 43 Check that the undercut depth is clean and free of foreign material. Smooth out the edge. If the depth is less than minimum, correct it using a hacksaw blade

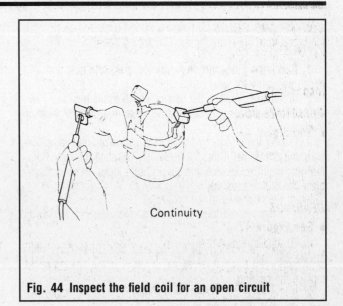

Fig. 44 Inspect the field coil for an open circuit

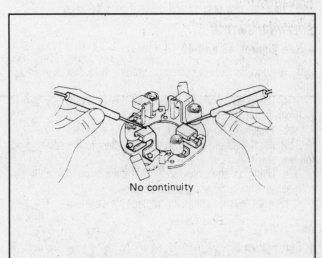

Fig. 45 Using an ohmmeter, make sure there is no continuity between the starter brush holders

BRUSHES
▶ **See Figure 45**

1. Using vernier calipers, measure the brush length:
   a. Standard length is 15.5mm.
   b. Minimum length is 10.0mm.
2. If the brush length is less than minimum, replace the brush holder and field frame.
3. Check the brush springs for weakness and replace as necessary.
4. Inspect the brush holder insulation as follows:
   a. Using an ohmmeter check that there is no continuity between the positive and the negative brush holders.
   b. If there is no continuity, repair or replace the brush holder.

CLUTCH AND GEARS
▶ See Figure 46

1. Check the gear teeth on the pinion gear, idle gear and clutch assembly for wear or damage.
2. If damaged, replace the gear or clutch assembly.
3. If damaged also check the drive plate ring gear for wear or damage.
4. Inspect the clutch, by rotating the clutch pinion gear clockwise and check that it turns it freely. Try to rotate the clutch pinion gear counterclockwise and check that it locks. If, necessary replace the clutch assembly.

BEARINGS
▶ See Figure 47

1. Inspect the bearings by turning each bearing by hand while applying inward force. If resistance is felt or is the bearing sticks, replace the bearing.
2. If it is necessary to remove the bearing, use a suitable bearing puller and remove the bearing.
3. Take the new bearing and press it onto the shaft.

SOLENOID SWITCH
▶ See Figures 48 and 49

1. Perform the pull-in coil open circuit test to the solenoid as follows:
  a. Using an ohmmeter, check that there is continuity between terminals 50 and C.
  b. If there is no continuity, replace the solenoid.
2. Perform the hold-in coil open circuit test to the solenoid as follows:
  a. Using an ohmmeter, check that there is no continuity between terminals 50 and the solenoid body.
  b. If there is no continuity, replace the solenoid.

Assembly
▶ See Figure 50

1. Apply high temperature grease to lubricate the bearings and then install the armature assembly into the field frame.
2. Place the brush holder on the armature. Using a suitable

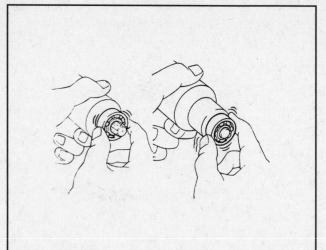

Fig. 47 Spin the bearings of the starter to check for resistance

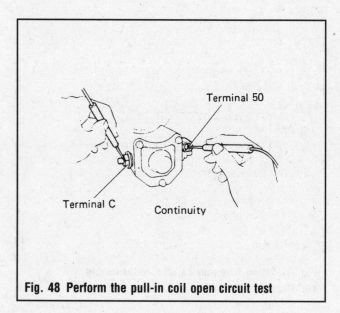

Fig. 48 Perform the pull-in coil open circuit test

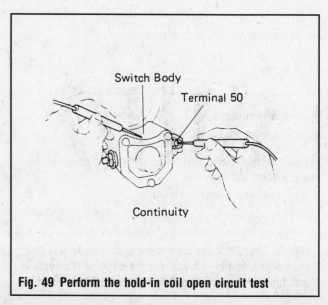

Fig. 49 Perform the hold-in coil open circuit test

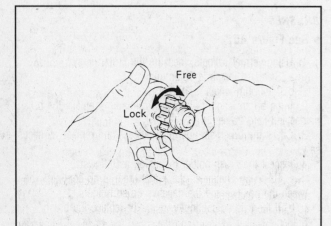

Fig. 46 Rotate the starter pinion gear clockwise to check for freedom of movement; the gear should lock up when you turn it counterclockwise

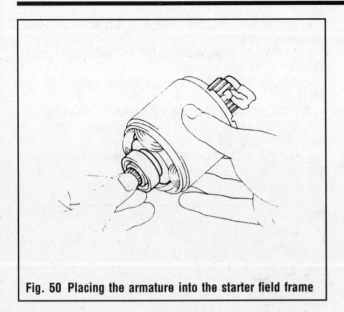

Fig. 50 Placing the armature into the starter field frame

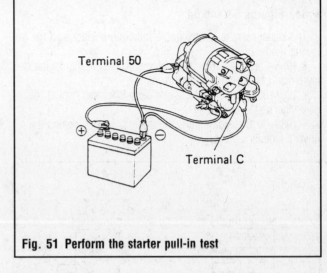

Fig. 51 Perform the starter pull-in test

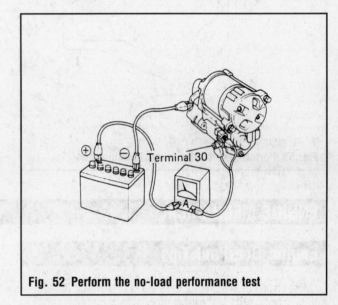

Fig. 52 Perform the no-load performance test

tool, hold the brush spring back and install the brush into the brush holder. Install all 4 brushes. Make sure to check that the positive lead wires are not grounded.

3. Place a new O-ring in position on the field frame. Install the new O-rings to the end cover mount screws.

4. Install the end cover to the field frame with the 2 screws.

5. Apply grease to the steel ball. Insert the steel ball in the clutch shaft holes.

6. Apply grease to the return spring, clutch assembly, idle gear and bearing.

7. Insert the return spring into the solenoid switch hole. Please the following parts in position on the starter housing:

    a. Clutch assembly.

    b. Pinion gear.

    c. Idle gear.

    d. Bearing.

8. Assemble the starter housing and solenoid switch assembly and install the 2 screws.

9. Place a new O-ring in position on the field frame. Align the protrusion of the field frame with the cut-out of the solenoid switch assembly.

10. Install the 2 through bolts. Connect the lead wire to the solenoid switch terminal C and install the nut.

TESTING

Starter Performance
▶ See Figures 51 and 52

➡These tests must be performed within 3–5 seconds to avoid burning out the coil.

1. Perform the pull-in test as follows:

    a. Disconnect field coil lead wire from the terminal C.

    b. Connect the battery to the solenoid as shown in the illustration.

    c. Check that the clutch pinion gear moves outward. If the clutch pinion gear does not move, replace the solenoid assembly.

2. Perform the hold-in test as follows:

    a. While the starter is connected to the battery as done in the pull-in test. With the clutch gear out, disconnect the negative lead from terminal C. Check that the pinion remains out.

    b. If the clutch pinion returns inward, replace the solenoid assembly.

3. Inspect the clutch pinion gear return as follows:

    a. Disconnect the negative battery cable from the switch body. Check that the clutch pinion gear returns inward.

    b. If the clutch pinion gear does not return, replace the solenoid switch assembly.

4. Perform a no-load performance test as follows:

    a. Connect a ammeter and battery to the starter as shown in the illustration.

    b. Check that the starter rotates smoothly and steadily with the pinion gear moving out. Check that the ammeter reads 90 amps or less at 11.5 volts.

Starter Relay

▶ **See Figures 53 and 54**

The starter relay is located in the following positions on the following models.

• 1986 Cressida—the starter relay is located in the engine relay block, of the engine compartment.

• 1987–88 Cressida—the starter relay is located behind the passenger's side kick panel.

• 1989–90 Cressida—the starter relay is located behind the driver's side kick panel.

• 1986–89 Van—the starter relay is located on the left side of the engine compartment.

1. To check the relay continuity, use an ohmmeter and check for continuity between terminals **1** and **3**.

2. Check that there is no continuity between terminals **2** and **4**.

3. If the continuity is not as specified, replace the relay.

4. Inspect the relay operation by applying battery voltage across terminals **1** and **3**.

5. Using an ohmmeter, check that there is continuity between terminals **2** and **4**.

6. If operation is not as specified, replace the relay.

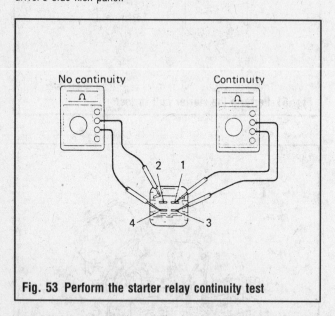

Fig. 53 Perform the starter relay continuity test

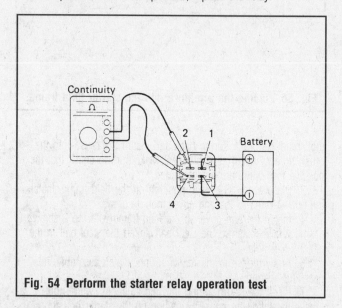

Fig. 54 Perform the starter relay operation test

ENGINE MECHANICAL

Engine Overhaul Tips

Most engine overhaul procedures are fairly standard. In addition to specific parts replacement procedures and specifications for your individual engine, this section is also a guide to acceptable rebuilding procedures. Examples of standard rebuilding practice are given and should be used along with specific details concerning your particular engine.

Competent and accurate machine shop services will ensure maximum performance, reliability and engine life. In most instances it is more profitable for the do-it-yourself mechanic to remove, clean and inspect the component, buy the necessary parts and deliver these to a shop for actual machine work.

On the other hand, much of the rebuilding work (crankshaft, block, bearings, piston rods, and other components) is well within the scope of the do-it-yourself mechanic's tools and abilities. You will have to decide for yourself the depth of involvement you desire in an engine repair or rebuild.

TOOLS

The tools required for an engine overhaul or parts replacement will depend on the depth of your involvement. With a few excep-

tions, they will be the tools found in a mechanic's tool kit (see Section 1 of this manual). More in-depth work will require some or all of the following:

• A dial indicator (reading in thousandths) mounted on a universal base
• Micrometers and telescope gauges
• Jaw and screw-type pullers
• Scraper
• Valve spring compressor
• Ring groove cleaner
• Piston ring expander and compressor
• Ridge reamer
• Cylinder hone or glaze breaker
• Plastigage®
• Engine stand

The use of most of these tools is illustrated in this chapter. Many can be rented for a one-time use from a local parts jobber or tool supply house specializing in automotive work.

Occasionally, the use of special tools is called for. See the information on Special Tools and the Safety Notice in the front of this book before substituting another tool.

INSPECTION TECHNIQUES

Procedures and specifications are given in this chapter for inspecting, cleaning and assessing the wear limits of most major components. Other procedures such as Magnaflux® and Zyglo® can be used to locate material flaws and stress cracks. Magnaflux® is a magnetic process applicable only to ferrous materials. The Zyglo® process coats the material with a fluorescent dye penetrant and can be used on any material.

Checking for suspected surface cracks can be more readily made using spot check dye. The dye is sprayed onto the suspected area, wiped off and the area sprayed with a developer. Cracks will show up brightly.

OVERHAUL TIPS

Aluminum has become extremely popular for use in engines, due to its low weight. Observe the following precautions when handling aluminum parts:
• Never hot tank aluminum parts (the caustic hot tank solution will eat the aluminum.
• Remove all aluminum parts (identification tag, etc.) from engine parts prior to the tanking.
• Always coat threads lightly with engine oil or anti-seize compounds before installation, to prevent seizure.
• Never overtorque bolts or spark plugs especially in aluminum threads.

Stripped threads in any component can be repaired using any of several commercial repair kits (Heli-Coil®, Microdot®, Keenserts®, etc.).

When assembling the engine, any parts that will be exposed to frictional contact must be prelubed to provide lubrication at initial start-up. Any product specifically formulated for this purpose can be used, but engine oil is not recommended as a prelube in most cases.

When semi-permanent (locked, but removable) installation of bolts or nuts is desired, threads should be cleaned and coated with Loctite® or another similar, commercial non-hardening sealant.

REPAIRING DAMAGED THREADS

Several methods of repairing damaged threads are available. Heli-Coil® (shown here), Keenserts® and Microdot® are among the most widely used. All involve basically the same principle—drilling out stripped threads, tapping the hole and installing a prewound insert—making welding, plugging and oversize fasteners unnecessary.

Two types of thread repair inserts are usually supplied: a standard type for most inch coarse, inch fine, metric course and metric fine thread sizes and a spark lug type to fit most spark plug port sizes. Consult the individual tool manufacturer's catalog to determine exact applications. Typical thread repair kits will contain a selection of prewound threaded inserts, a tap (corresponding to the outside diameter threads of the insert) and an installation tool. Spark plug inserts usually differ because they require a tap

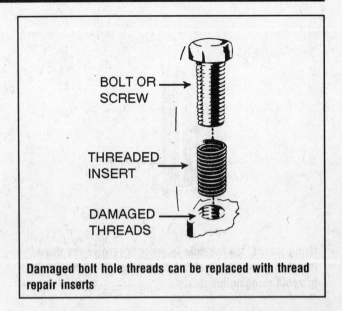

Damaged bolt hole threads can be replaced with thread repair inserts

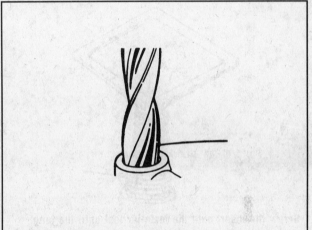

Drill out the damaged threads with the specified size bit. Be sure to drill completely through the hole or to the bottom of a blind hole

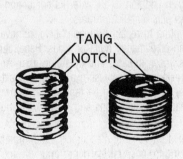

Standard thread repair insert (left), and spark plug thread insert

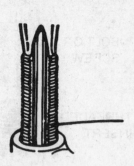

Using the kit, tap the hole in order to receive the thread insert. Keep the tap well oiled and back it out frequently to avoid clogging the threads

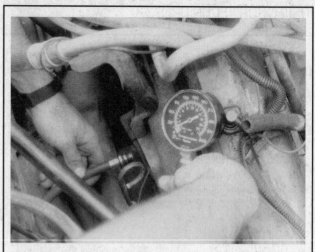

A screw-in type compression gauge is more accurate and easier to use without an assistant

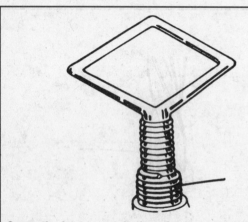

Screw the insert onto the installer tool until the tang engages the slot. Thread the insert into the hole until it is ¼–½ turn below the top surface, then remove the tool and break off the tang using a punch

equipped with pilot threads and a combined reamer/tap section. Most manufacturers also supply blister-packed thread repair inserts separately in addition to a master kit containing a variety of taps and inserts plus installation tools.

Before attempting to repair a threaded hole, remove any snapped, broken or damaged bolts or studs. Penetrating oil can be used to free frozen threads. The offending item can usually be removed with locking pliers or using a screw/stud extractor. After the hole is clear, the thread can be repaired, as shown in the series of accompanying illustrations and in the kit manufacturer's instructions.

CHECKING ENGINE COMPRESSION

A noticeable lack of engine power, excessive oil consumption and/or poor fuel mileage measured over an extended period are all indicators of internal engine war. Worn piston rings, scored or worn cylinder bores, blown head gaskets, sticking or burnt valves and worn valve seats are all possible culprits here. A check

of each cylinder's compression will help you locate the problems.

As mentioned in the Tools and Equipment section of Section 1, a screw-in type compression gauge is more accurate than the type you simply hold against the spark plug hole, although it takes slightly longer to use. It's worth it to obtain a more accurate reading. Follow the procedures below.

1. Warm up the engine to normal operating temperature.
2. Remove all spark plugs.
3. Disconnect the high tension lead from the ignition coil.
4. Disconnect all fuel injector electrical connections.
5. Screw the compression gauge into the No. 1 spark plug hole until the fitting is snug.

➡️Be careful not to crossthread the plug hole. On aluminum cylinder heads use extra care, as the threads in these heads are easily ruined.

6. Have an assistant depress the accelerator pedal fully. Then, while you read the compression gauge, ask the assistant to crank the engine two or three times in short bursts using the ignition switch.
7. Read the compression gauge at the end of each series of cranks, and record the highest of these readings. Repeat this procedure for each of the engine's cylinders. Maximum compression should be 175–185 psi. A cylinder's compression pressure is usually acceptable if it is not less than 80% of maximum. The difference between each cylinder should be no more than 12–14 psi.
8. If a cylinder is unusually low, pour a tablespoon of clean engine oil into the cylinder through the spark plug hole and repeat the compression test. If the compression comes up after adding the oil, it appears that the cylinder's piston rings or bore are damaged or worn. If the pressure remains low, the valves may not be seating properly (a valve job is needed), or the head gasket may be blown near that cylinder. If compression in any two adjacent cylinders is low, and if the addition of oil doesn't help the compression, there is leakage past the head gasket. Oil and coolant water in the combustion chamber can result from this problem. There may be evidence of water droplets on the engine dipstick when a head gasket has blown.

General Engine Specifications

Years	Engine Liters	Fuel Sys. Type	SAE net Horsepower @ rpm	SAE net Torque ft. lb. @ rpm	Bore × Stroke (in.)	Comp. Ratio	Oil Press. (Psi) @ 3000 rpm
1983	2.8L	EFI	156 @ 5200	165 @ 4500	3.27 × 3.35	9.2:1	36–71
1984	2.8L	EFI	156 @ 5200	165 @ 4500	3.27 × 3.35	9.2:1	36–71
	2.0L	EFI	90 @ 4400	120 @ 3000	3.58 × 3.40	9.0:1	36–71
1985	2.8L	EFI	156 @ 5200	165 @ 4500	3.27 × 3.35	9.2:1	36–71
	2.0L	EFI	90 @ 4400	120 @ 3000	3.58 × 3.40	9.0:1	36–71
1986	2.8L	EFI	156 @ 5200	165 @ 4500	3.27 × 3.35	9.2:1	36–71
	2.2L	EFI	101 @ 4400	132 @ 3000	3.58 × 3.40	8.8:1	36–71
1987	2.8L	EFI	156 @ 5200	165 @ 4500	3.27 × 3.35	9.2:1	36–71
	2.2L	EFI	101 @ 4400	133 @ 3000	3.38 × 3.58	8.8:1	36–71
1988	2.8L	EFI	156 @ 5200	165 @ 4500	3.27 × 3.35	9.2:1	36–71
	2.2L	EFI	101 @ 4400	133 @ 3000	3.38 × 3.58	8.8:1	36–71
1989	3.0L	EFI	190 @ 5600	185 @ 4400	3.27 × 3.35	9.2:1	36–71
	2.2L	EFI	101 @ 4400	133 @ 3000	3.38 × 3.58	8.8:1	36–71
1990	3.0L	EFI	190 @ 5600	185 @ 4400	3.27 × 3.35	9.2:1	36–71

EFI—Electronic Fuel Injection

Valve Specifications

Year	Engine Liter	Seat Angle (deg)	Face Angle (deg)	Spring Test Pressure (lbs. @ in.)	Spring Installed Height (in.)	Stem Clearance (in.) Intake	Stem Clearance (in.) Exhaust	Stem Diameter (in.) Intake	Stem Diameter (in.) Exhaust
1983	2.8L	45.5	45.5	①	②	0.0010–0.0024	0.0012–0.0026	0.3138–0.3144	0.3136–0.3142
1984	2.8L	45.5	45.5	①	②	0.0010–0.0024	0.0012–0.0026	0.3138–0.3144	0.3136–0.3142
	2.0L	45.5	45.5	63.0	1.598	0.0010–0.0024	0.0012–0.0026	0.3138–0.3144	0.3136–0.3142
1985	2.8L	45	44.5	①	②	0.0010–0.0024	0.0015–0.0027	0.3138–0.3144	0.3136–0.3142
	2.0L	45	44.5	63.5–77.6	1.598	0.0010–0.0024	0.0012–0.0026	0.3138–0.3144	0.3136–0.3142
1986	2.8L	45	44.5	①	②	0.0010–0.0024	0.0012–0.0026	0.3138–0.3144	0.3136–0.3142
	2.2L	45	44.5	63.5–77.6	1.598	0.0010–0.0024	0.0012–0.0026	0.3138–0.3144	0.3136–0.3142
1987	2.8L	45	44.5	①	②	0.0010–0.0024	0.0012–0.0026	0.3138–0.3144	0.3136–0.3142
	2.2L	45	44.5	63.5–77.6	1.598	0.0010–0.0024	0.0012–0.0026	0.3138–0.3144	0.3136–0.3142
1988	2.8L	45	44.5	①	②	0.0010–0.0024	0.0012–0.0026	0.3138–0.3144	0.3136–0.3142
	2.2L	45	44.5	63.5–78.7	1.598	0.0010–0.0024	0.0012–0.0026	0.3138–0.3144	0.3136–0.3142
1989	3.0L	45	44.5	35	1.378	0.0010–0.0024	0.0012–0.0026	0.2350–0.2356	0.2348–0.2354
	2.2L	45	44.5	63.5–78.7	1.598	0.0010–0.0024	0.0012–0.0026	0.3138–0.3144	0.3136–0.3142
1990	3.0L	45	44.5	35	1.378	0.0010–0.0024	0.0012–0.0026	0.2350–0.2356	0.2348–0.2354

① Intake—76.5–84.4
   Exhaust—73.4–80.9
② Intake—1.575
   Exhaust—1.693

Camshaft Specifications

All Specifications in inches

Year	Engine Liter	Journal Diameter							Bearing Clearance	End Play
		1	2	3	4	5	6	7		
1983	2.8L	1.4944–1.4951	1.6913–1.6919	1.7110–1.7116	1.7307–1.7313	1.7504–1.7510	1.7770–1.7707	1.7897–1.7904	0.0010–0.0026	0.0018–0.0060
1984	2.8L	1.4944–1.4951	1.6913–1.6919	1.7110–1.7116	1.7307–1.7313	1.7504–1.7510	1.7770–1.7707	1.7897–1.7904	0.0010–0.0026	0.0018–0.0060
	2.0L	1.8291–1.8297	1.8192–1.8199	1.8094–1.8100	1.7996–1.8002	1.7897–1.7904	—	—	0.0010–0.0032	0.0028–0.0087
1985	2.8L	1.4944–1.4951	1.6913–1.6919	1.7110–1.7116	1.7307–1.7313	1.7504–1.7510	1.7770–1.7707	1.7807–1.7904	0.0010–0.0026	0.0020–0.0098
	2.0L	1.8291–1.8297	1.8192–1.8199	1.8094–1.8100	1.7996–1.8002	1.7897–1.7904	—	—	0.0010–0.0032	0.0028–0.0087
1986	2.8L	1.4944–1.4951	1.6913–1.6919	1.7110–1.7116	1.7307–1.7313	1.7504–1.7510	1.7770–1.7707	1.7897–1.7904	0.0010–0.0026	0.0020–0.0098
	2.2L	1.8291–1.8297	1.8192–1.8199	1.8094–1.8100	1.7996–1.8002	1.7897–1.7904	—	—	0.0010–0.0032	0.0028–0.0087
1987	2.8L	1.4944–1.4951	1.6913–1.6919	1.7110–1.7116	1.7307–1.7313	1.7504–1.7510	1.7770–1.7707	1.7897–1.7904	0.0010–0.0026	0.0020–0.0098
	2.2L	1.8291–1.8297	1.8192–1.8199	1.8094–1.8100	1.7996–1.8002	1.7897–1.7904	—	—	0.0010–0.0032	0.0028–0.0087
1988	2.8L	1.4944–1.4951	1.6913–1.6919	1.7110–1.7116	1.7307–1.7313	1.7504–1.7510	1.7770–1.7707	1.7897–1.7904	0.0010–0.0026	0.0020–0.0098
	2.2L	1.8291–1.8297	1.8192–1.8199	1.8094–1.8100	1.7996–1.8002	1.7897–1.7904	—	—	0.0010–0.0032	0.0028–0.0087
1989	3.0L	1.0610–1.0616	1.0586–1.0620	1.0586–1.0620	1.0586–1.0620	1.0586–1.0620	1.0586–1.0620	1.0586–1.0620	0.0014–0.0028	0.0031–0.0075
	2.2L	1.8291–1.8297	1.8192–1.8199	1.8094–1.8100	1.7996–1.8002	1.7897–1.7904	—	—	0.0010–0.0032	0.0028–0.0087
1990	3.0L	1.0610–1.0616	1.0586–1.0620	1.0586–1.0620	1.0586–1.0620	1.0586–1.0620	1.0586–1.0620	1.0586–1.0620	0.0014–0.0028	0.0031–0.0075

Crankshaft and Connecting Rod Specifications

All Specifications in inches

Year	Engine Liter	Crankshaft				Connecting Rod		
		Main Bearing Journal Dia.	Main Bearing Oil Clearance	Shaft End Play	Thrust On Number	Journal Diameter	Oil Clearance	Side Clearance
1983	2.8L	2.3617–2.3627	0.0013–0.0023	0.0020–0.0098	4	2.0463–2.0472	0.0008–0.0021	0.006–0.012
1984	2.8L	2.3617–2.3627	0.0013–0.0023	0.0020–0.0098	4	2.0463–2.0472	0.0008–0.0021	0.006–0.012
	2.0L	2.2829–2.2835	0.0008–0.0020	0.0008–0.0087	3	1.8892–1.8898	0.0008–0.0020	0.0030–0.0037
1985	2.8L	2.3617–2.3627	0.0013–0.0023	0.0020–0.0098	4	2.0463–2.0472	0.0008–0.0021	0.0020–0.0028
	2.0L	2.2829–2.2835	0.0008–0.0020	0.0008–0.0087	3	1.8892–1.8898	0.0008–0.0020	0.0030–0.0037
1986	2.8L	2.3617–2.3627	0.0013–0.0023	0.0020–0.0098	4	2.0463–2.0472	0.0008–0.0021	0.0024–0.0031
	2.2L	2.2829–2.2835	0.0008–0.0020	0.0008–0.0087	3	1.8892–1.8898	0.0008–0.0020	0.0026–0.0033
1987	2.8L	2.3625–2.3627 ①	0.0013–0.0023	0.0020–0.0098	4	2.0470–2.0472 ②	0.0008–0.0021	0.0024–0.0031
	2.2L	2.2829–2.2835	0.0008–0.0020	0.0008–0.0087	3	1.8892–1.8898	0.0008–0.0020	0.0026–0.0033
1988	2.8L	2.3625–2.3627 ①	0.0012–0.0048	0.0020–0.0098	4	2.0470–2.0472 ②	0.0008–0.0021	0.0024–0.0031
	2.2L	2.2829–2.2835	0.0008–0.0020	0.0008–0.0087	3	1.8892–1.8898	0.0008–0.0020	0.0020–0.0028
1989	3.0L	2.3625–2.3627 ①	0.0012–0.0019	0.0020–0.0098	4	2.0470–2.0472 ②	0.0008–0.0021	0.0024–0.0031
	2.2L	2.2829–2.2835	0.0008–0.0020	0.0008–0.0087	3	1.8892–1.8898	0.0008–0.0020	0.0020–0.0028
1990	3.0L	2.3625–2.3627 ①	0.0012–0.0019	0.0020–0.0098	4	2.0470–2.0472 ②	0.0008–0.0021	0.0024–0.0031

① No. 1 Journal: 2.3622–2.3624
 No. 2 Journal: 2.3620–2.3622
② No. 1 Journal: 2.0466–2.0469
 No. 2 Journal: 2.0463–2.0466

Piston and Ring Specifications

All Specifications in inches

Year	Engine Liter	Ring Gap			Ring Side Clearance			Piston Clearance
		#1 Compr.	#2 Compr.	Oil Control	#1 Compr.	#2 Compr.	Oil Control	
1983	2.8L	0.0083–0.0146	0.0067–0.0209	0.0079–0.0276	0.0012–0.0028	0.0008–0.0024	Snug	0.0020–0.0028
1984	2.8L	0.0114–0.0185	0.0098–0.0216	0.0067–0.0334	0.0012–0.0028	0.0008–0.0024	Snug	0.0020–0.0028
	2.0L	0.0087–0.0185	0.0059–0.0165	0.0079–0.0323	0.0012–0.0028	0.0012–0.0028	0.0012–0.0028	0.0030–0.0037
1985	2.8L	0.0091–0.0161	0.0098–0.0217	0.0067–0.0335	0.0012–0.0028	0.0008–0.0024	Snug	0.0020–0.0028
	2.0L	0.0087–0.0185	0.0059–0.0165	0.0079–0.0323	0.0012–0.0028	0.0012–0.0028	0.0012–0.0028	0.0030–0.0037
1986	2.8L	0.0114–0.0185	0.0098–0.0217	0.0067–0.0335	0.0012–0.0028	0.0008–0.0024	Snug	0.0024–0.0031
	2.2L	0.0091–0.0189	0.0063–0.0173	0.0051–0.0185	0.0012–0.0028	0.0012–0.0028	0.0012–0.0028	0.0026–0.0033
1987	2.8L	0.0091–0.0150	0.0098–0.0209	0.0040–0.0201	0.0012–0.0028	0.0008–0.0024	Snug	0.0024–0.0031
	2.2L	0.0091–0.0189	0.0063–0.0173	0.0051–0.0185	0.0012–0.0028	0.0012–0.0028	0.0012–0.0028	0.0026–0.0033
1988	2.8L	0.0091–0.0150	0.0098–0.0209	0.0040–0.0201	0.0012–0.0028	0.0008–0.0024	Snug	0.0024–0.0031
	2.2L	0.0091–0.0201	0.0158–0.0264	0.0051–0.0197	0.0012–0.0028	0.0012–0.0028	0.0012–0.0028	0.0020–0.0028
1989	3.0L	0.0091–0.0150	0.0098–0.0209	0.0039–0.0157	0.0012–0.0028	0.0008–0.0024	Snug	0.0020–0.0028
	2.2L	0.0091–0.0201	0.0158–0.0264	0.0051–0.0197	0.0012–0.0028	0.0012–0.0028	0.0012–0.0028	0.0020–0.0028
1990	3.0L	0.0091–0.0150	0.0098–0.0209	0.0039–0.0157	0.0012–0.0028	0.0008–0.0024	Snug	0.0020–0.0028

Torque Specifications

All specifications given in ft. lbs.

Year	Engine Liter	Cyl. Head	Conn. Rod	Main Bearing	Crankshaft Damper	Flywheel	Manifold	
							Intake	Exhaust
1983	2.8L	58 ①	33	75	108	54	16	29
1984	2.8L	58 ①	33	75	160	54	16	29
	2.0L	65 14mm 14 12mm	36	58	80	61	36 ②	36
1985	2.8L	58 ①	33	75	160	54	16	29
	2.0L	65 14mm 14 12mm	36	58	80	61	36 ②	36
1986	2.8L	58 ①	33	75	159	54	16	29
	2.0L	65 14mm 14 12mm	36	58	116	61	36 ②	29
1987	2.8L	58 ①	33	75	195	54	13	29
	2.2L	65 14mm 14 12mm	36	58	116	61	36 ②	46
1988	2.8L	58 ①	33	75	195	54	13	29
	2.2L	65 14mm 14 12mm	36	58	116	61	36 ②	46
1989	3.0L	58 ①	47	75	195	54	13	29
	2.2L	65 14mm 14 12mm	36	58	116	61	36 ②	46
1990	3.0L	58 ①	47	75	195	54	13	29

① See head removal and installation procedure for instructions.
② This engine uses a combination manifold; the air intake manifold bolts are torqued to 9 ft. lbs.

Engine

REMOVAL & INSTALLATION

▶ **See Figures 55, 56 and 56a**

5M-GE Engine

1. Disconnect the negative battery cable.
2. Remove the battery.
3. Remove the hood.
4. Remove the air cleaner assembly.
5. Remove the fan shroud.
6. Drain the cooling system.
7. Disconnect the upper and lower radiator hoses.
8. If equipped with automatic transmission, disconnect and plug the oil lines from the oil cooler.
9. Detach the hose which runs to the thermal expansion tank and remove the expansion tank from its mounting bracket.
10. Remove the radiator.
11. If equipped with automatic transmission, remove the throttle cable bracket from the cylinder head. Remove the accelerator and actuator cable bracket from the cylinder head.
12. Tag and disconnect the cylinder head ground cable, the oxygen sensor wire, the oil pressure sending unit, alternator wires, the high tension coil wire, the water temperature sending, the thermo switch wires, the starter wires, the ECT connectors, the solenoid resistor wire connector and the knock sensor wire.
13. Tag and disconnect the brake booster vacuum hose from the air intake chamber, along with the EGR valve vacuum hose. Disconnect the actuator vacuum hose from the air intake chamber, if equipped with cruise control. Disconnect the heater bypass hoses from the engine.
14. Remove the glove box, and remove the ECU computer module. Disconnect the 3 connectors, and pull out the EFI wiring harness from the engine compartment side of the firewall.
15. Remove the 4 shroud and 4 fluid coupling screws, and the shroud and coupling as a unit.
16. Remove the engine undercover protector.
17. Disconnect the coolant reservoir hose. Remove the radiator and the coolant expansion tank.
18. Remove the air conditioning compressor drive belt, and remove the compressor mounting bolts. Without disconnecting the refrigerant hoses, lay the compressor to one side and secure it.
19. Disconnect the power steering pump drive belt and remove the pump stay. Unbolt the pump and lay it aside without disconnecting the fluid hoses.
20. Remove the engine mounting bolts from each side of the engine. Remove the engine ground cable.

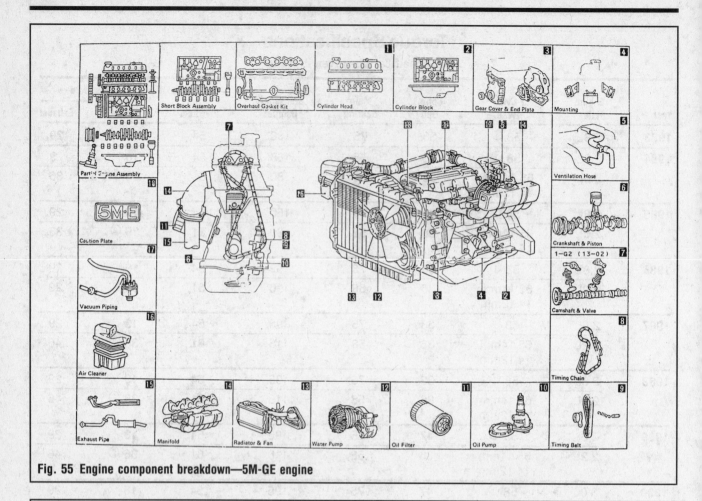

Fig. 55 Engine component breakdown—5M-GE engine

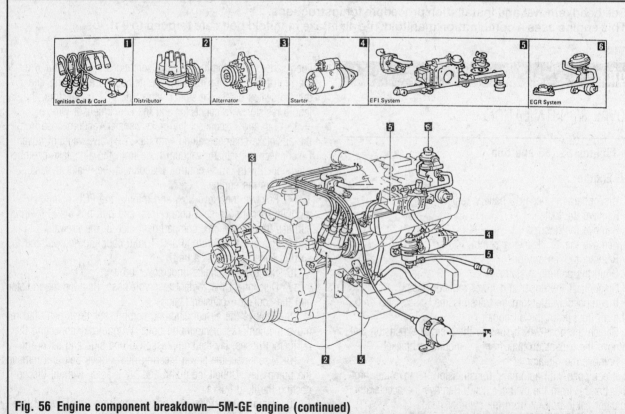

Fig. 56 Engine component breakdown—5M-GE engine (continued)

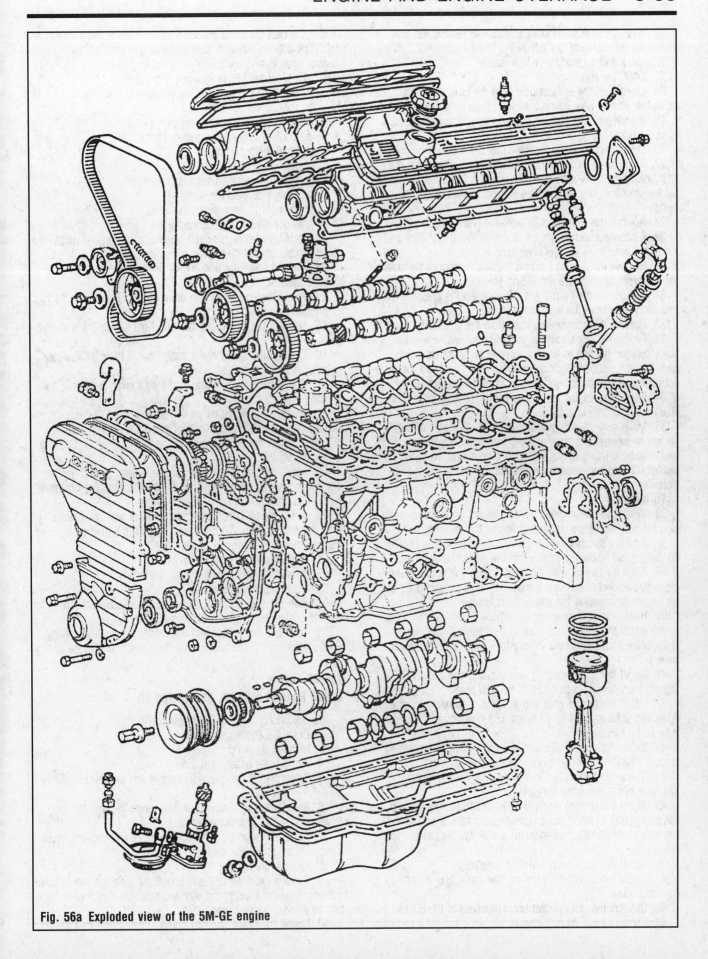

Fig. 56a Exploded view of the 5M-GE engine

21. If equipped with manual transmission, remove the shift lever from the inside of the vehicle.

22. Raise and support the vehicle safely.

23. Drain the engine oil.

24. Disconnect the exhaust pipe from the exhaust manifold. Remove the exhaust pipe clamp from the transmission housing.

25. If equipped with manual transmission, remove the clutch slave cylinder.

26. Disconnect the speedometer cable at the transmission.

27. If equipped with automatic transmission, disconnect the shift linkage from the shift lever. On vehicles equipped with manual transmission, disconnect the wire from the back-up light switch.

28. Remove the stiffener plate from the ground cable.

29. Disconnect and plug the fuel line from the fuel filter and the return hose from the fuel hose support.

30. Remove the 2 bolts from the top and bottom of the steering universal, and remove the sliding yoke.

31. Disconnect the tie rod ends. Disconnect the pressure line mounting bolts from the front crossmember.

32. Remove the intermediate shaft from the driveshaft.

33. Position a jack under the transmission, with a wooden block between the two to prevent damage to the transmission case. Place a wooden block between the cowl panel and the cylinder head rear end to prevent damage to the heater hoses.

34. Unbolt the engine rear support member from the frame, along with the ground cable.

35. Make sure all wiring is disconnected, all hoses disconnected, and everything clear of the engine and transmission. Connect a suitable lifting device to the lift brackets on the engine, and carefully lift the engine and transmission up and out of the vehicle.

To install:

36. Install the transmission housing mount bolts and exhaust pipe bracket. Install the starter and tighten the retaining bolts.

37. Attach a suitable engine hoist chain to the lifting bracket on the engine. Lower the engine into the engine compartment.

38. Align the engine with the transmission and engine mounting supports. Install the engine mounting bolts on each side of the engine and remove the engine hoist chain.

39. Raise and safely support the vehicle.

40. Install the engine rear support member with the ground strap to the body. Install the intermediate shaft to the propeller shaft.

41. Install the power steering gear housing and 2 brackets. Tighten the retaining bolts to 56 ft. lbs. (76 Nm).

42. Install the tie rod ends and install a new cotter pin after tightening the castle nut to 43 ft. lbs. (59 Nm). Install the sliding yoke and 2 lockbolts.

43. Connect the battery ground strap to the engine mounting bracket. Install the stiffener plate with the ground strap.

44. Connect the main fuel line to the fuel filter. Connect the fuel hose to the fuel hose support.

45. Install the coolant reservoir tank. Install the radiator and 2 mounting bolts. Connect the coolant receiver tube, the 2 oil cooler lines (automatic transmission) and install the radiator lower hose.

46. Install the fan shroud and fluid coupling.

47. Install the air cleaner case, air flow meter and air intake connector pipe.

48. Connect the fuel injection wiring harness to the ECU.

49. Connect the 2 heater hoses to the block and cylinder head.

50. Connect the brake booster vacuum hose to the intake manifold. The actuator vacuum hose to the intake manifold (with cruise control system) and the EGR valve vacuum hose.

51. Connect the following wires and cables:
   a. Ground strap to the cylinder head.
   b. Oxygen sensor wire.
   c. Oil pressure sending unit wire.
   d. Cooling temperature sensor connector.
   e. Spark plug cables.
   f. Distributor connector.
   g. Water temperature sending unit wire.
   h. Temperature switch wire.
   i. Solenoid resistor wire connector.
   j. Knock sensor wire connector.

52. Install the accelerator and actuator cable bracket. Install the throttle cable bracket (automatic transmission only).

53. Close the radiator and engine drain valves and refill the coolant system.

54. Put in the engine oil pan drain plug and refill with fresh clean motor oil.

55. Connect the wire to the back-up light switch (manual transmission only).

56. Connect the speedometer cable. Install the clutch release cylinder (manual transmission only).

57. Connect the shift linkage to the shift lever (automatic transmission only).

58. Position a new gasket on the exhaust pipe. Connect the exhaust pipe and install a new nuts. Tighten the nuts to 46 ft. lbs. (62 Nm). Install the exhaust pipe clamp to transmission housing. Lower the vehicle.

59. Install the power steering pump and stay bracket. Install the power steering pump pulley with the drive belt. Pry on the alternator to obtain the specified belt tension.

60. Install the air conditioning compressor with the bracket onto the engine block. Turn the adjusting on the idler pulley until the specified belt tension is obtained.

61. Install the engine under cover.

62. Install the washer tank. Install the battery.

63. Install the hood assembly.

64. Start the engine. Make all necessary adjustments, check for oil and coolant leaks and repair as necessary.

65. Road test the vehicle and make sure it operates properly. Shut off the engine and recheck the fluid levels, add as necessary.

7M-GE Engine

◆ **See Figures 56b, 57, 58, 59 and 60**

1. Disconnect the negative battery cable.

2. Drain the cooling system.

3. Remove the hood.

4. Remove the battery and tray.

5. Disconnect the accelerator, throttle and cruise control cables.

6. Remove the air cleaner assembly complete with the air flow meter, hoses and connector pipe.

7. Tag and disconnect all electrical wires and vacuum hoses necessary to remove the engine.

8. Remove the radiator.

9. Remove the drive belt and unbolt the air conditioning compressor. Position it out of the way and suspend it with wire. Do not disconnect the refrigerant lines.

10. Unbolt the power steering pump. Position it out of the way

and suspend it with wire. Do not disconnect the hydraulic lines.

11. Remove the windshield washer fluid reservoir.

12. Remove the glove box and disconnect the 6 connectors from the main wiring harness and then pull the main wiring harness through the firewall and into the engine compartment.

13. Disconnect the heater hoses.

14. Raise the vehicle and support it safely.

15. Remove the engine under cover and drain the oil.

16. Disconnect the exhaust pipe at the manifold.

17. Disconnect the driveshaft at the transmission flange and position it out of the way.

18. Disconnect the speedometer cable and the transmission linkage.

19. Disconnect the starter lead and the ground lines at the stiffener plate and left side engine mount.

20. Disconnect and plug the fuel lines.

21. Remove the front wheels and then disconnect the power steering rack. Leave the hydraulic lines attached and lay the rack aside.

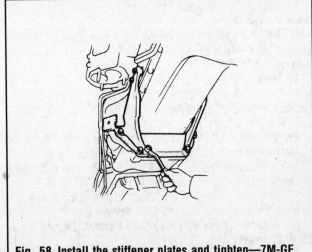

Fig. 58 Install the stiffener plates and tighten—7M-GE engine

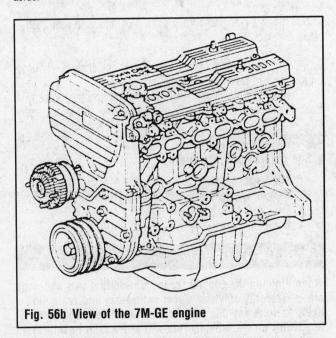

Fig. 56b View of the 7M-GE engine

Fig. 59 Place the rear support member into position and tighten—7M-GE engine

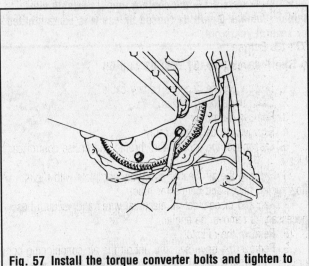

Fig. 57 Install the torque converter bolts and tighten to 47 ft. lbs. (64 Nm)

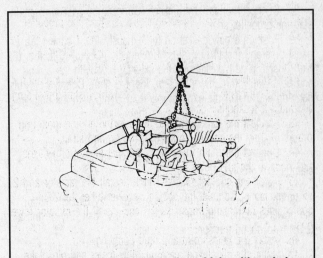

Fig. 60 Lower the engine into the vehicle with a chain and hoist

22. Loosen the 8 bolts and the ground strap and then remove the rear engine support.

23. Lower the vehicle and remove the 4 engine mount-to-suspension bolts. Attach an engine hoist to the 2 engine hangers and then slowly and vehicle fully lift the engine out of the vehicle.

To install:

24. Before installing the transmission, check for proper torque converter installation as follows:

   a. Using calipers (or a suitable measuring device) and a straight edge, measure from the installed surface of the torque converter to the front surface of the transmission housing.

   b. The correct distance 26.4mm. If the distance is less than standard, check for improper installation.

25. Assemble the engine and transmission with the four retaining bolts and torque them to 47 ft. lbs. (64 Nm).

26. Install the starter with the 2 bolts and nuts. Connect the electrical harness.

27. Attach the electrical connectors at the automatic transmission.

28. Clamp the throttle cable.

29. Install the torque converter mount bolts. Be sure to install the gray bolt first and then the other bolts. Tighten the bolts evenly to 30 ft. lbs. (41 Nm).

30. Install the oil cooler lines at the automatic transmission.

31. Install the engine rear end plate, stiffener plates and exhaust pipe stay bracket with the eight bolts.

32. Attach a suitable engine hoist chain to the lifting bracket on the engine. Lower the engine into the engine compartment. Place a suitable jack under the transmission.

➡**Be sure to put a wooden block between the jack and the transmission pan to prevent damage.**

33. Align the bolt holes of the engine mounting and suspension member. Install the 4 bolts and remove the chain hoist.

34. Raise and support the vehicle safely. Install the engine rear support member with the ground and strap along with the eight bolts.

35. Install the power steering gear housing.

36. Install the front wheel assemblies.

37. Install the fuel hoses. Connect the starter cable, ground strap to stiffener plate and the ground strap to the left-hand engine mounting.

38. Connect manual shift linkage. Connect the speedometer. Install the propeller shaft.

39. Position a new gasket on the exhaust pipe. Connect the exhaust pipe and install new nuts. Tighten the nuts to 46 ft. lbs. (62 Nm). Install a new gasket and the exhaust pipe with the 2 nuts and bolts and torque them to 32 ft. lbs. (43 Nm). Connect the rubber ring and install the exhaust manifold clamp with the bolt. Install the engine under cover. Lower the vehicle.

40. Connect the heater hoses.

41. Push in the engine wire harness through the cowl panel. Connect the 6 connectors. Install the glove box. Install the 2 clamps and ground strap.

42. Install the washer tank.

43. Install the power steering pump and stay bracket. Install the power steering pump pulley with the drive belt. Pry on the alternator to obtain the specified belt tension.

44. Install the air conditioning compressor with the bracket onto the engine block. Turn the adjusting on the idler pulley until the specified belt tension is obtained.

45. Install the radiator assembly.

46. Connect the following wire, connectors and vacuum hoses:

   a. Connect the connector to the fuse and relay block.
   b. Alternator connector and wire.
   c. The air conditioning connector.
   d. Check connector.
   e. The igniter connector.
   f. Spark plug cables.
   g. The brake booster vacuum hose.
   h. The cruise control vacuum hose.
   i. The charcoal canister vacuum hose.

47. Install the air cleaner assembly with the air flow meter, air cleaner hoses and air intake connector pipe with the three bolts and connect the hose.

48. Connect the air hose and connect the air flow meter connection.

49. Connect the accelerator cable, cruise control cable and throttle cable.

50. Install the battery tray and battery.

51. Close the radiator and engine drain valves and refill the coolant system.

52. Put in the engine oil pan drain plug and refill with fresh clean motor oil.

53. Install the hood assembly.

54. Start the engine. Make all necessary adjustments, check for oil and coolant leaks and repair as necessary.

55. Road test the vehicle and make sure it operates properly. Shut off the engine and recheck the fluid levels, add as necessary.

3Y-EC Engine

▸ **See Figures 60a, 61 and 62**

1. Disconnect the battery.
2. Remove the right front seat.
3. Remove the engine cover.
4. Drain the coolant.

❋❋ CAUTION

When draining the coolant, keep in mind that cats and dogs are attracted by ethylene glycol antifreeze, and are quite likely to drink any that is left in an uncovered container or in puddles on the ground. This will prove fatal in sufficient quantity. Always drain the coolant into a sealable container. Coolant should be reused unless it is contaminated or several years old.

5. Disconnect the following hoses:
• Radiator inlet hoses.
• Radiator breather hose.
• Reservoir tank hose.
• Heater outlet hose.
• Radiator outlet hose.
• Brake booster hose.
• Fuel inlet hose.
• Fuel outlet hose.
• Charcoal canister hose.

6. Disconnect and tag all vacuum hoses attached to various engine parts.

7. Disconnect the following wire connectors:
• The alternator connector and B terminal.
• The air flow meter connector.
• The solenoid resistor connector.

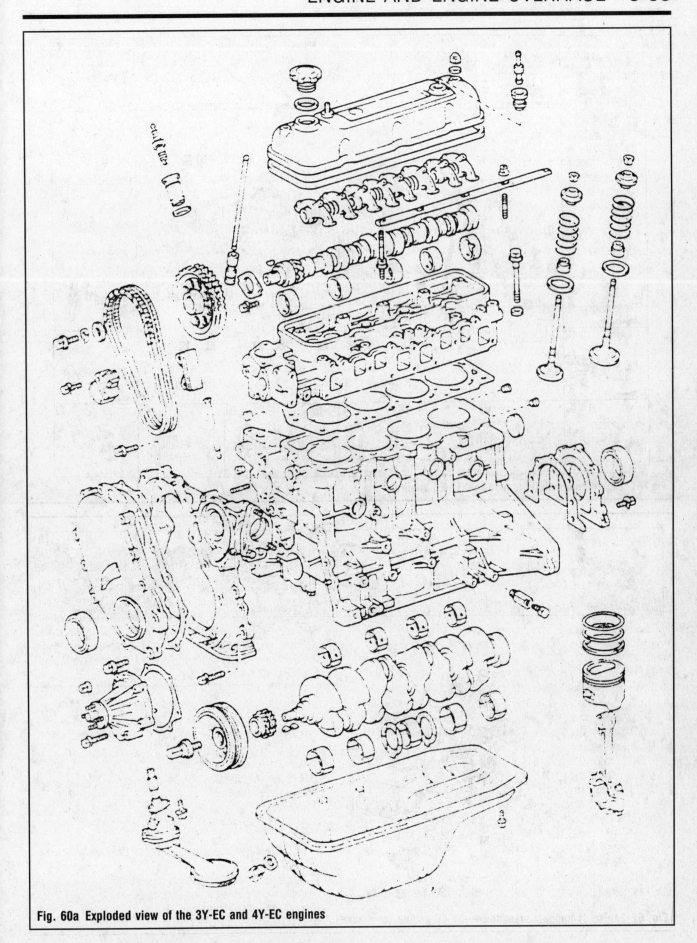

Fig. 60a Exploded view of the 3Y-EC and 4Y-EC engines

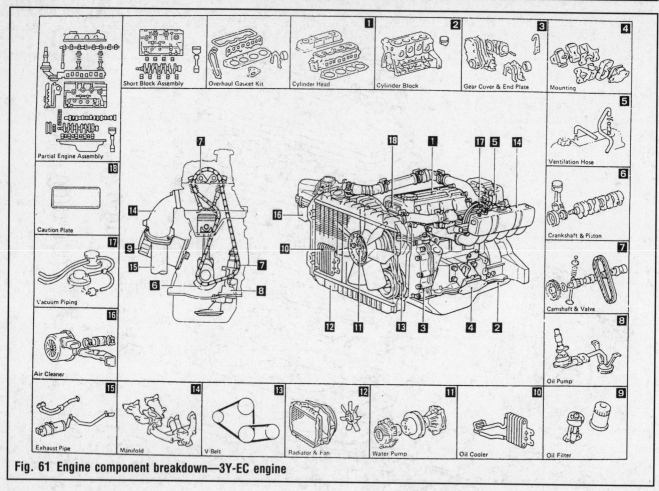

Fig. 61 Engine component breakdown—3Y-EC engine

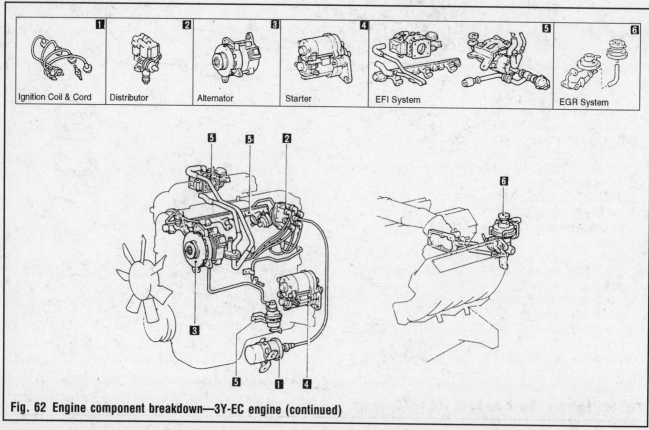

Fig. 62 Engine component breakdown—3Y-EC engine (continued)

- Water temperature sending unit connector.
- The oil pressure switch connector.
- The integrated ignition assembly connector.
- The air conditioning compressor connector, if so equipped.
- The air conditioning idle up solenoid connector, if so equipped.
- The vacuum switching valve, if so equipped.
- The coolant temperature switch.

8. Disconnect and tag all cables attached to various engine parts.

9. Remove the air cleaner.

10. Unbolt the power steering pump and secure it out of the way.

11. Remove the fan shroud.

12. Remove the fan and fan clutch. Do not lay the fan on its side. If you do, the fluid will leak out and the fan clutch will be permanently ruined.

13. Unbolt the air conditioning compressor and secure it out of the way.

14. Raise the vehicle about 39 in. (1 meter) off the floor and support it securely.

15. Drain the engine oil.

16. Disconnect the driveshaft.

17. Disconnect the remove the exhaust system.

18. Remove the transmission control cable.

19. Remove the clutch release starter.

20. Remove the starter.

21. Remove the speedometer cable.

22. Disconnect all remaining hoses and cable from the transmission.

23. Remove the engine tensioner cable.

24. Remove the engine underpan.

25. Remove the strut bar.

26. Place an engine jack under the engine and take up the weight. Unbolt and remove the engine mounts and lower the engine from the vehicle.

To install:

27. Install the engine mounting member to the engine. Raise the engine with the transmission and install the mounting member bolts and nuts. Torque them to 58 ft. lbs. (78 Nm).

28. Install the bracket with the engine rear mounting to the body. Tighten the bolts to 14–22 ft. lbs. (19–30 Nm).

29. Install the strut bar.

30. Install the 2 oil cooler lines at the automatic transmission.

31. Install the engine under cover. Connect the engine ground cable to the engine mounting.

32. Connect the heater outlet hose and the rear heater hoses, if so equipped.

33. Connect the heater air mix damper cable to the damper, if so equipped.

34. Connect the mode selector cable to the damper. Move the control lever back and fourth and check for stiffness and binding through full range of operation.

35. Connect the speedometer cable and ground cable. Connect the back-up light switch connector.

36. Install the starter with its 2 bolts. Connect the 2 wires to the starter.

37. Install the front exhaust pipe. Install the transmission control selector and shift cable.

38. Install the clutch release cylinder. Install the driveshaft.

39. Lower the vehicle.

40. Install the compressor and tighten the 4 bolts. Install the drive belt and adjust the drive belt to obtain the proper tension.

41. Connect the ECU connectors. Install the cover and the seat belt retractor. Install the center pillar garnish.

42. Install the fluid coupling with the fan assembly. Adjust the drive belt tension. Install the radiator assembly, if removed.

43. Install the fan shroud assembly. Connect the following wires:

- The alternator connector and B terminal.
- The air flow meter connector.
- The solenoid resistor connector.
- Water temperature sending unit connector.
- The oil pressure switch connector.
- The integrated ignition assembly connector.
- The air conditioning compressor connector, if so equipped.
- The air conditioning idle up solenoid connector, if so equipped.
- The vacuum switching valve, if so equipped.
- The coolant temperature switch.

44. Connect the accelerator cable to the throttle body.

45. Install the power steering pump assembly. Install the drive belt and adjust the belt tension.

46. Connect the following hoses:

- Radiator inlet hoses.
- Radiator breather hose.
- Reservoir tank hose.
- Heater outlet hose.
- Radiator outlet hose.
- Brake booster hose.
- Fuel inlet hose.
- Fuel outlet hose.
- Charcoal canister hose.

47. Refill the coolant system with the proper coolant mixture.

48. Refill the engine with clean fresh engine oil.

49. Connect the negative battery cable. Start the engine and check for any leaks, repair as necessary.

50. Make all necessary adjustments, such as idle speed and ignition timing.

51. Install the engine service hole cover. Install the right seat and then road test the vehicle to check that the vehicle is operating properly.

52. Shut down the engine and recheck the fluid levels once the engine has cooled down.

4Y-EC Engine

▶ **See Figures 60a, 63, 64, 65, 66 and 67**

1. Disconnect the battery.
2. Remove the right front seat.
3. Remove the engine service hole cover.
4. Drain the coolant.
5. Disconnect the following hoses:
- Radiator inlet hoses
- Radiator breather hose
- Reservoir tank hose
- Heater outlet hose
- Radiator outlet hose
- Brake booster hose
- Fuel inlet hose
- Fuel outlet hose
- Charcoal canister hose

6. Disconnect and tag all vacuum hoses attached to various engine parts.

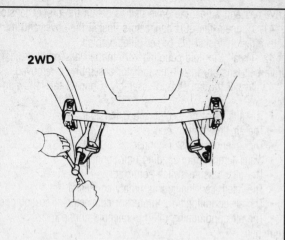

Fig. 63 Installing the front engine mounting member to the body—2WD Van

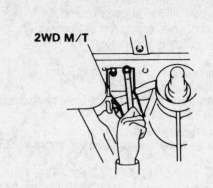

Fig. 66 Installing the rear mounting bracket—2WD Van with MT and 4WD Van

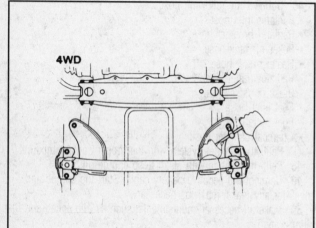

Fig. 64 Installing the front engine mounting member to the body—4WD Van

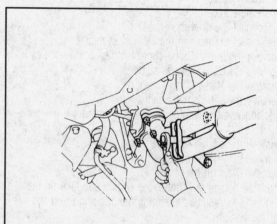

Fig. 67 Connect the exhaust pipes to the manifold; be sure to use a new gasket

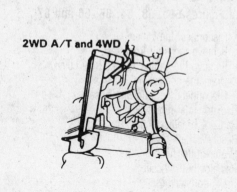

Fig. 65 Installing the rear mounting bracket—2WD Van with AT and 4WD Van

7. Disconnect the following wire connectors:
• The alternator connector and B terminal
• The air flow meter connector
• The solenoid resistor connector
• Water temperature sending unit connector
• The oil pressure switch connector
• The ignition connectors at the distributor
• The air conditioning compressor connector, if so equipped
• The air conditioning idle up solenoid connector, if so equipped
• The vacuum switching valve, if so equipped
• The coolant temperature switch

8. Disconnect and tag all cables attached to various engine parts.

9. Remove the air cleaner hose.

10. Unbolt the power steering pump and secure it out of the way.

11. Disconnect the accelerator cable and the throttle cable from the throttle linkage.

12. Remove the fan shroud. Remove the fan and fan clutch. Do not lay the fan on its side. If you do, the fluid will leak out and the fan clutch will be permanently ruined. Remove the radiator assembly.

13. Remove the center pillar garnish. Remove the seat belt retractor and ECU cover and disconnect the ECU wire connectors.

14. Loosen the air conditioning compressor drive belt adjusting bolts and remove the drive belt. Unbolt the air conditioning compressor and secure it out of the way.

15. Raise the vehicle about 4 feet off the floor and support it securely.

16. Drain the engine oil.

17. Disconnect the driveshaft.

18. Disconnect the transmission control cables. Remove the clutch release cylinder.

19. Disconnect the wire connectors at the starter, remove the 2 starter bolts and remove the starter assembly.

20. Disconnect the speedometer cable. Disconnect the back-up light connector.

21. On the 4-wheel drive models, disconnect the transfer case indicator switch connector.

22. Disconnect the heater mode selector cable from the air damper and disconnect the air mix damper cable from the damper, if so equipped.

23. Disconnect the heater hoses, including the rear heater hoses if equipped with a rear heater system.

24. Disconnect the ground strap from the engine mounting. Remove the engine under cover. Disconnect the connector on the oil level sensor.

25. Disconnect the oil cooler lines on models equipped with automatic transmissions.

26. On 2-wheel drive models, remove the strut bar.

27. On 4-wheel drive models, remove the stabilizer bar.

28. Support the engine and transmission with an engine hoist and jacks.

29. On 2-wheel drive models with manual transmissions, remove the bolts holding the engine rear mounting bracket to the body.

30. On 2-wheel drive models equipped with automatic transmissions and 4-wheel drive models, remove the through bolts holding the engine mounting insulator to the transmission.

31. Remove the bolts and nuts holding the engine front member to the body.

32. On 4-wheel drive models, remove the bolts, nuts and front suspension rear crossmember.

33. Lower the engine and transmission. Remove the engine mounting member from the engine. Separate the engine and transmission.

To install:

34. Assemble the engine and the transmission assembly. Install the assembly in to the engine compartment.

35. Install the engine front member to the engine and tighten the bolts 29 ft. lbs. (39 Nm). Raise the engine and install the tighten the bolts and nuts holding the engine front mounting mem ber to the body. The torque should be 65 ft. lbs. (88 Nm).

36. On 4-wheel drive models, install the front suspension rear crossmember with the bolts and nuts, torque them to 70 ft. lbs. (95 Nm).

37. On 2-wheel drive models with manual transmission, install the bolts holding the engine rear mounting bracket to the body. Tighten the nut to 9 ft. lbs. (13 Nm).

38. On 2-wheel drive models equipped with automatic transmissions and 4-wheel drive models, install the bolt and nut holding the engine rear mounting insulator to the body. Tighten the nut to 36 ft. lbs. (49 Nm).

39. On the 2-wheel drive models, install the strut bar.

40. On the 4-wheel drive install the stabilizer bar assembly.

41. Install the oil cooler lines on the automatic transmission models.

42. Connect the connector of the oil level sensor.

43. Install the engine under cover. Connect the engine ground strap to the engine mounting.

44. Connect the heater outlet hose and the rear heater hoses, if so equipped.

45. Connect the heater air mix damper cable to the damper, if so equipped.

46. Connect the mode selector cable to the damper. Move the control lever back and fourth and check for stiffness and binding through full range of operation.

47. Connect the speedometer cable and ground cable. Connect the back-up light switch connector. On the 4-wheel drive models, connect the transfer indicator switch connector.

48. Install the starter with its 2 bolts. Connect the 2 wires to the starter.

49. Install the front exhaust pipe. Install the transmission control selector and shift cable.

50. Install the clutch release cylinder. Install the driveshaft.

51. Lower the vehicle.

52. Install the compressor and tighten the 4 bolts. Install the drive belt and adjust the drive belt to obtain the proper tension.

53. Connect the ECU connectors. Install the cover and the seat belt retractor. Install the center pillar garnish.

54. Install the fluid coupling with the fan assembly. Adjust the drive belt tension. Install the radiator assembly.

55. Install the fan shroud assembly. Connect the following wires:
   • The alternator connector and B terminal
   • The air flow meter connector
   • The solenoid resistor connector
   • Water temperature sending unit connector
   • The oil pressure switch connector
   • The integrated ignition assembly connector
   • The air conditioning compressor connector, if so equipped
   • The air conditioning idle up solenoid connector, if so equipped
   • The vacuum switching valve, if so equipped
   • The coolant temperature switch

56. Connect the accelerator cable and the throttle cable to the throttle body.

57. Install the power steering pump assembly. Install the drive belt and adjust the belt tension.

58. Connect the following hoses:
   • Radiator inlet hoses
   • Radiator breather hose
   • Reservoir tank hose
   • Heater outlet hose
   • Radiator outlet hose

• Brake booster hose
• Fuel inlet hose
• Fuel outlet hose
• Charcoal canister hose

59. Refill the coolant system with the proper coolant mixture.

60. Refill the engine with clean fresh engine oil.

61. Connect the negative battery cable. Start the engine and check for any leaks, repair as necessary.

62. Make all necessary adjustments, such as idle speed and ignition timing.

63. Install the engine service hole cover. Install the right seat and then road test the vehicle to check that the vehicle is operating properly.

64. Shut down the engine and recheck the fluid levels once the engine has cooled down.

Rocker Arm Cover

REMOVAL & INSTALLATION

Cressida

▶ **See Figures 68 and 69**

1. Disconnect the negative battery cable.
2. Remove the air cleaner hose along with air connector pipe.
3. Remove the PCV orifice pipe and hoses.
4. Disconnect and remove the accelerator link.
5. Remove the air intake connector, vacuum transmitting pipe and brackets.
6. Disconnect and tag the spark plug cables.
7. Remove the cylinder head cover retaining bolts and remove the cylinder head covers.

To install:

8. Install the cylinder head covers (using new gaskets) and install the retaining bolts. Tighten the bolts to 22 inch lbs.
9. Install the spark plug cables.
10. Install the air intake connector, vacuum transmitting pipe and brackets.
11. Install the accelerator link.

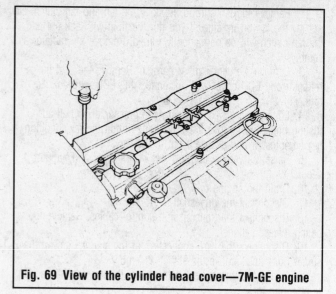

Fig. 69 View of the cylinder head cover—7M-GE engine

12. Install the PCV orifice pipe and hoses.
13. Install the air cleaner hose along with air connector pipe.
14. Reconnect the negative battery cable.

Van

1. Disconnect the battery.
2. Remove the right front seat.
3. Remove the engine service hole cover.
4. Remove the air cleaner hose and air cleaner assembly.
5. Disconnect and tag all cables and wires attached to various engine parts in order to gain access to the rocker arm cover and its retaining bolts.
6. Remove the cap nuts and seal washers that retain the rocker arm cover to the cylinder head and remove the rocker arm cover along with the old gasket.

To install:

7. Using a new gasket, install the rocker arm cover. Tighten the bolts to 13 ft. lbs. (18 Nm).
8. To complete this procedure, installation is the reverse order of the removal.

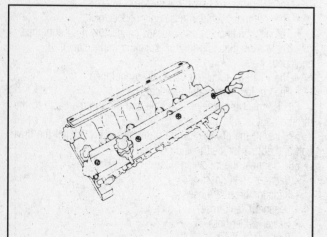

Fig. 68 The cylinder head cover mounting bolts go through the top of the cover as shown—5M-GE engine

When removing the valve cover, the air cleaner hose and assembly must be taken off

The valve cover is retained with nuts on top of the cover

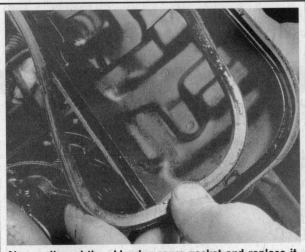
Lift the valve cover off the cylinder head

Rocker Arm/Shafts

REMOVAL & INSTALLATION

➡The 7M-GE engine does not utilize rocker arm shafts. The valves are activated directly by the camshaft.

5M-GE Engine

◆ **See Figure 70**

1. Disconnect the negative battery cable.
2. Remove the air cleaner hose along with air connector pipe.
3. Remove the PCV orifice pipe and hoses.
4. Disconnect and remove the accelerator link.
5. Remove the air intake connector, vacuum transmitting pipe and brackets.
6. Disconnect and tag the spark plug cables.
7. Remove the cylinder head cover retaining bolts and remove the cylinder head covers.
8. Remove the rocker arms and lash adjusters from the cylinder head being sure to keep them in their proper order. If it is necessary to remove the camshaft housings in order to gain access to the rocker arms, use the following procedure to remove the camshaft housing.

   a. Remove the No. 1 and No. 2 camshaft housings by removing the nuts on the front side and the bolts on the rear side.

   b. Loosen each camshaft housing nut and bolt a little at a time so as not to warp the housing.

To install:

9. Install the lash adjusters and rocker arms in their proper order. If the camshaft housings were removed, use the following procedure to install them.

   a. Place new gaskets over the dowels on the cylinder head.

   b. Position the camshaft housings over the dowels on the cylinder head.

   c. Install and tighten the housing nuts and bolts gradually in three passes until the final torque of 16 ft. lbs. (22 Nm) has been reached.

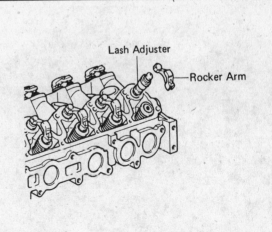
Fig. 70 Install the lash adjuster, then place the rocker arm on top—5M-GE engine

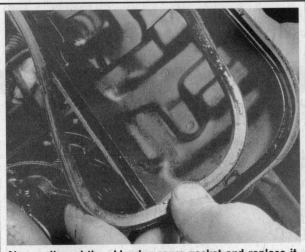
Always discard the old valve cover gasket and replace it with a new one

10. Install the cylinder head covers (using new gaskets) and install the retaining bolts. Tighten the bolts to 22 inch lbs.

11. Install the spark plug cables.

12. Install the air intake connector, vacuum transmitting pipe and brackets.

13. Install the accelerator link.

14. Install the PCV orifice pipe and hoses.

15. Install the air cleaner hose along with air connector pipe.

16. Install the cylinder head covers (using new gaskets) and install the retaining bolts. Tighten the bolts to 22 inch lbs.

17. Install the spark plug cables.

18. Install the air intake connector, vacuum transmitting pipe and brackets.

19. Install the accelerator link.

20. Install the PCV orifice pipe and hoses.

21. Install the air cleaner hose along with air connector pipe.

22. Reconnect the negative battery cable.

3Y-EC and 4Y-EC Engines

▶ **See Figure 71**

1. Disconnect the battery.
2. Remove the right front seat.

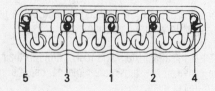

Fig. 71 Rocker arm shaft assembly tightening sequence—3Y-EC and 4Y-EC engines

Lift the rocker arm assembly out of the cylinder head as a unit—4Y-EC engine

3. Remove the engine service hole cover.

4. Remove the air cleaner hose and air cleaner assembly.

5. Disconnect and tag all cables and wires attached to various engine parts in order to gain access to the rocker arm cover and its retaining bolts.

6. Remove the cap nuts and seal washers that retain the rocker arm cover to the cylinder head and remove the rocker arm cover along with the old gasket.

7. Uniformly loosen and remove the 3 bolts and 2 nuts in several passes. Then remove the rocker arm assembly from the cylinder head.

To install:

8. Make sure the pushrods are installed in the correct position.

9. Hold the pushrods in place and install the rocker arm shaft assembly.

10. Uniformly tighten the 3 bolts and 2 nuts in several passes until a final torque of 17 ft. lbs. (24 Nm) is obtained.

11. Using a new gasket, install the rocker arm cover. Tighten the bolts to 13 ft. lbs. (18 Nm).

12. To complete this procedure, installation is the reverse order of the removal procedure.

Thermostat

REMOVAL & INSTALLATION

▶ **See Figures 72, 73, 74 and 75**

1. Disconnect the negative battery cable.
2. Drain the coolant into a suitable container.
3. Disconnect the radiator outlet hose from the water inlet.
4. Remove the retaining bolts from the thermostat housing.
5. Remove the thermostat housing and the thermostat.

To install:

6. Install a new gasket to the thermostat housing and place the thermostat with the jiggle valve upward into the engine block.

7. Install the thermostat housing along with the retaining bolts.

8. Reconnect the radiator outlet hose to the thermostat housing.

9. Refill the cooling system and reconnect the negative battery cable. Start the engine and check for leaks and proper operation of the thermostat. Repair any leaks as necessary.

Intake Manifold

REMOVAL & INSTALLATION

5M-GE Engine

▶ **See Figure 76 (p.48)**

1. Disconnect the negative battery cable. Drain the engine coolant. Relieve the fuel pressure from the fuel injection system.

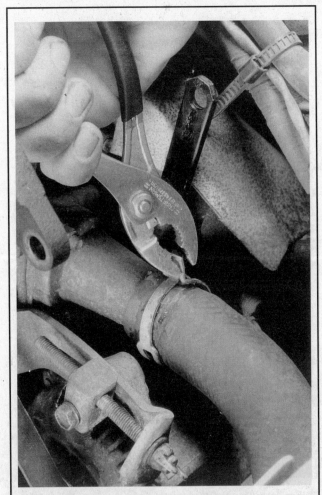

Remove the radiator hose clamp at the thermostat housing—4Y-EC engine

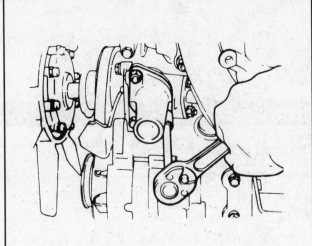

Fig. 72 Remove the upper radiator hose, then unbolt the thermostat housing—Van

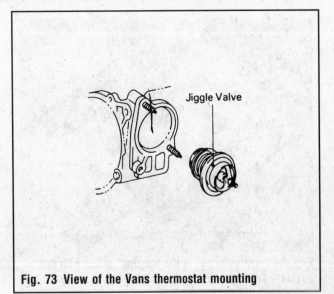

Fig. 73 View of the Vans thermostat mounting

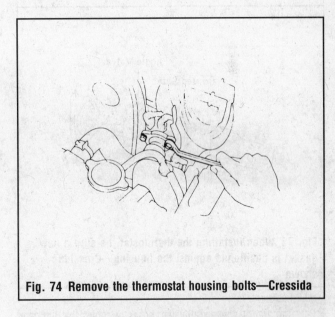

Fig. 74 Remove the thermostat housing bolts—Cressida

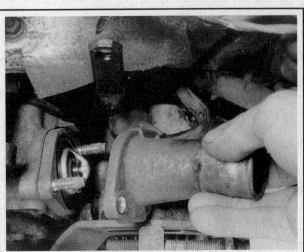

Separate the housing from the thermostat; be careful not to drop the housing, as it is fragile

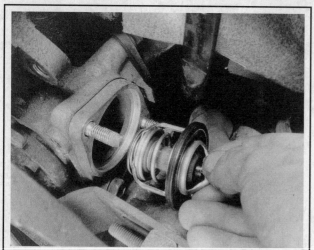

Pull the thermostat out of the housing, along with the gasket—4Y-EC engine

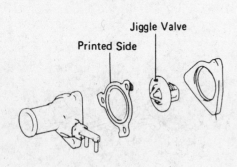

Printed Side

Jiggle Valve

Fig. 75 When installing the thermostat, be sure a new gasket is positioned against the housing—Cressida shown

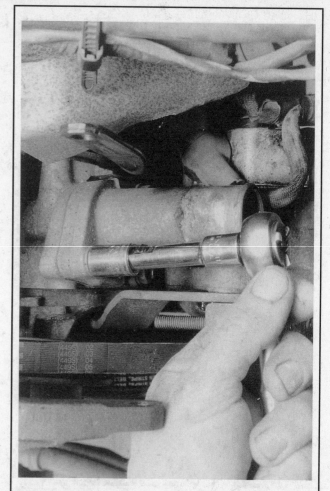

When installing the thermostat housing, do not tighten it too much, as it could easily break

2. Tag and disconnect all wires, hoses or cables that interfere with intake manifold removal.

3. Remove the air intake chamber.

4. Disconnect and move the wiring away from the fuel delivery and injector pipe.

5. Remove the fuel injector and delivery pipe.

6. Remove the fuel pressure regulator, which is mounted on the center of the intake manifold.

7. Remove the EGR valve from the rear of the manifold.

8. Disconnect the radiator hoses, heater hoses, and vacuum lines from the intake manifold.

9. Remove the distributor cap and position it out of the way.

10. Remove the intake manifold retaining bolts. Remove the intake manifold and gasket from the engine.

To install:

11. Install the intake manifold gasket along with the intake manifold. Install the intake manifold retaining bolts and torque to specification.

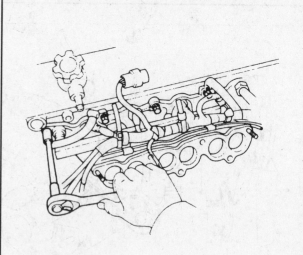

Fig. 76 Loosen and remove all of the intake manifold bolts—5M-GE engine

12. Install the distributor cap assembly.

13. Reconnect the radiator hoses, heater hoses, and vacuum lines going to the intake manifold.

14. Install the EGR valve to the rear of the manifold.

15. Install the fuel pressure regulator, which is mounted on the center of the intake manifold.

16. Install the fuel injector and delivery pipe.

17. Reconnect and put back in place the wiring to the fuel delivery and injector pipe.

18. Install the air intake chamber.

19. Reconnect all wires, hoses or cables that had interfered with the intake manifold removal.

20. Refill the coolant system. Reconnect the negative battery cable.

21. Start the engine check for any vacuum leaks at the intake manifold.

7M-GE Engine
♦ See Figure 77

1. Disconnect the negative battery cable. Drain the engine coolant. Relieve the fuel pressure from the fuel injection system.

2. Remove the air cleaner assembly.

3. Tag and disconnect all wires, hoses or cables that interfere with intake manifold removal.

4. Remove the necessary components in order to gain access to the intake manifold retaining bolts.

5. Remove the air intake connector along with the air intake chamber assembly.

6. Remove the fuel delivery pipe with the injectors still attached.

7. Remove the intake manifold retaining bolts. Remove the intake manifold from the vehicle.

To install:

8. Install the intake manifold gasket along with the intake manifold. Install the intake manifold retaining bolts and torque to specification.

9. Install the fuel delivery pipe along with the fuel injectors.

10. Install the air intake connector along with the air intake chamber assembly.

11. Install all the components that were removed in order to gain access to the intake manifold retaining bolts.

12. Reconnect and put back in place the wiring to the fuel delivery and injector pipe.

13. Reconnect all wires, hoses or cables that had interfered with the intake manifold removal.

14. Install the air cleaner assembly.

15. Reconnect all wires, hoses or cables that had interfered with the intake manifold removal.

16. Refill the coolant system. Reconnect the negative battery cable.

17. Start the engine check for any vacuum leaks at the intake manifold.

3Y-EC and 4Y-EC Engines
➡**Refer to the exhaust manifold procedure for intake manifold removal illustrations.**

1. Relieve the fuel pressure from the fuel injection system. Disconnect the negative battery cable and remove the right-hand seat and engine service hole cover.

2. Drain the engine coolant into a suitable container.

3. Remove the air cleaner to the throttle body hose.

4. Remove the accelerator cable with the bracket from the throttle body.

5. Disconnect the air valve, throttle position sensor and oxygen sensor wiring.

6. Disconnect the PCV hose from the air intake chamber, the water bypass hoses from the throttle body, the booster vacuum hose and the charcoal canister hose, then label and disconnect the emission control cable.

7. Remove the throttle body from the air intake chamber, the EGR tube union nut from the exhaust manifold, the EGR valve from the air intake chamber.

8. Disconnect the cold start injector tube, water bypass hoses and the pressure regulator hose from the intake manifold.

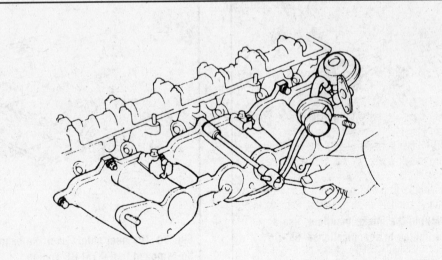

Fig. 77 Intake manifold mounting—7M-GE engine

9. Remove the air intake chamber brackets and the air intake chamber with the air valve from the intake manifold.

10. Remove the wire clamp bolt from the fuel injector rail, then, the fuel injector rail from the fuel injectors.

11. Remove the exhaust manifold to intake manifold bracket, the exhaust manifold to engine bracket, the exhaust pipe from the exhaust manifold, the fuel inlet and outlet tubes union nut from the fuel rail.

12. Remove the spark plug wires, the spark plugs and the tubes.

13. Remove the retaining nuts, then the intake manifold.

To install:

14. Clean the gasket mounting surfaces.

15. Installation is the reverse order of the removal procedure, except for the following.

   a. Install new gaskets.

   b. Tighten the manifold to cylinder head nuts to 36 ft. lbs. (49 Nm).

   c. Tighten the air intake chamber to intake manifold bolts to 9 ft. lbs.

   d. Tighten the throttle body bolts to 9 ft. lbs. (12 Nm).

   e. Refill the cooling system. Start the engine and allow it to reach normal operating temperature and check for leaks. Repair as necessary.

Exhaust Manifold

REMOVAL & INSTALLATION

5M-GE Engine

▶ See Figure 78

1. Disconnect the negative battery cable. Raise the vehicle and support safely. Remove the right-hand gravel shield from underneath the vehicle.

2. Remove the throttle body.

3. Remove the exhaust pipe support stay. Unbolt the exhaust pipe from the exhaust manifold flange.

4. Disconnect the oxygen sensor connector.

5. Remove the manifold retaining nuts. Remove the exhaust manifold from the vehicle.

To install:

6. Install the exhaust manifold gasket along with the exhaust manifold. Install the exhaust manifold retaining bolts and torque to specification.

7. Reconnect the oxygen sensor connector.

8. Install the exhaust pipe support stay. Install the exhaust pipe to the exhaust manifold flange.

9. Install the throttle body.

10. Install the right-hand gravel shield underneath the vehicle. Lower the vehicle and install the negative battery cable.

11. Start the engine check for any exhaust leaks at the manifold.

7M-GE Engine

▶ See Figure 79

1. Disconnect the negative battery cable. Remove the exhaust manifold heat insulator shield assembly, if equipped.

2. Remove the necessary components in order to gain access to the exhaust manifold retaining bolts.

3. Disconnect the exhaust manifold bolts at the exhaust pipe. It may be necessary to raise and support the vehicle safely before removing these bolts.

4. Remove the exhaust manifold retaining bolts. Remove the exhaust manifold from the vehicle.

To install:

5. Install the exhaust manifold gasket along with the exhaust manifold. Install the exhaust manifold retaining bolts and torque to specification.

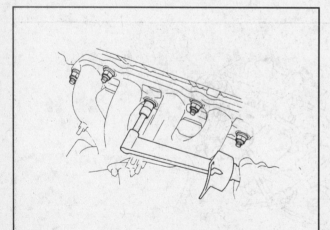

Fig. 78 When installing the intake manifold, use a torque wrench and tighten to specifications—5M-GE engine

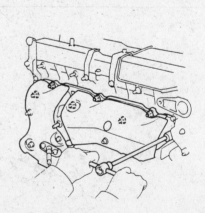

Fig. 79 The heat shield over the exhaust manifold must be removed first—7M-GE engine

6. Install all the components that had been removed in order to gain access to the exhaust manifold.

7. Install the exhaust manifold heat shield and negative battery cable.

8. Start the engine check for any exhaust leaks at the manifold.

3Y-EC and 4Y-EC Engines

♦ See Figure 80

1. Relieve the fuel pressure from the fuel injection system. Disconnect the negative battery cable and remove the right-hand seat and engine service hole cover.

2. Drain the engine coolant into a suitable container.

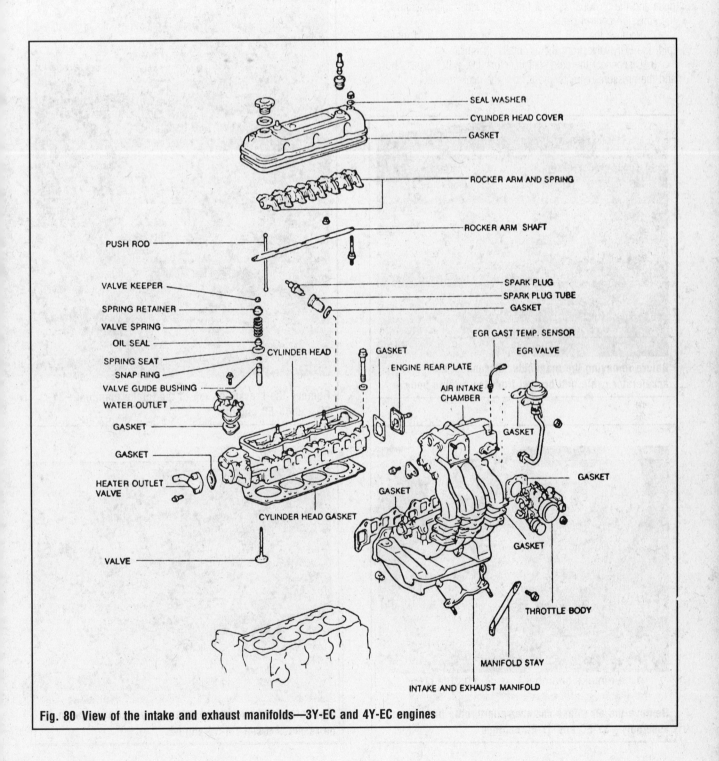

Fig. 80 View of the intake and exhaust manifolds—3Y-EC and 4Y-EC engines

3. Remove the air cleaner to the throttle body hose.

4. Remove the accelerator cable with the bracket from the throttle body.

5. Disconnect the air valve, throttle position sensor connector and the oxygen sensor wiring.

6. Disconnect the PCV hose from the air intake chamber, the water bypass hoses from the throttle body, the booster vacuum hose and the charcoal canister hose, then label and disconnect the emission control cable.

7. Remove the EGR tube union nut from the exhaust manifold, the EGR valve from the air intake chamber.

8. Disconnect the cold start injector tube, water bypass hoses and the pressure regulator hose from the intake manifold.

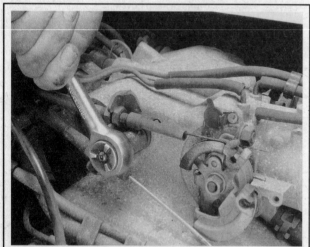

Before removing the manifolds, disconnect the accelerator cable and bracket from the throttle body

Remove the bracket on top of the intake manifold—3Y-EC and 4Y-EC engines

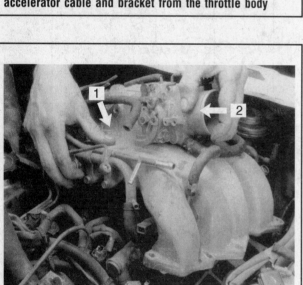

1. Air intake chamber   2. Throttle body

Remove the air intake chamber and throttle body as an assembly—3Y-EC and 4Y-EC engines

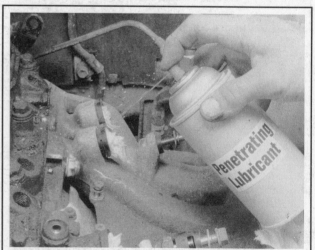

Spray the intake manifold nuts with penetrating oil to ease nut removal

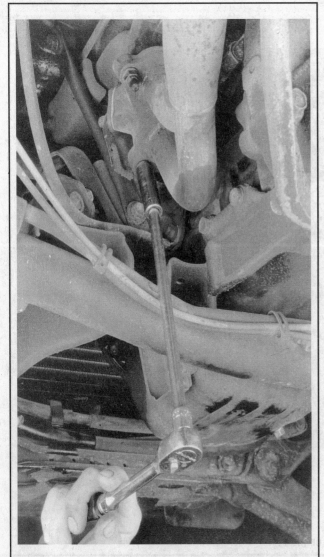

Remove the exhaust manifold down pipe mounting nuts

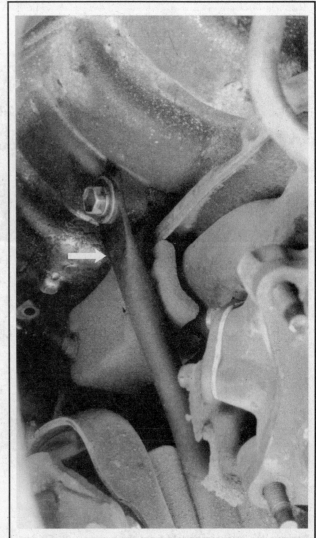

Unbolt the manifold stay bracket from the engine—3Y-EC and 4Y-EC engines

9. Remove the air intake chamber brackets and the air intake chamber with the air valve from the intake manifold.

10. Remove the wire clamp bolt from the fuel injector rail, then, the fuel injector rail from the fuel injectors.

11. Remove the exhaust manifold to intake manifold bracket, the exhaust manifold to engine bracket, the fuel inlet and outlet tubes union nut from the fuel rail.

12. Remove the spark plug wires, the spark plugs and the tubes.

13. Remove the retaining nuts, then the intake manifold.

14. Unbolt and remove the exhaust manifold heat shields.

15. Separate the exhaust manifold from the head pipe and discard the gasket.

16. Pull the exhaust manifold off the engine and discard the gasket.

To install:

17. Clean the gasket mounting surfaces.

18. Installation is the reverse order of the removal procedure, except for the following.

 a. Install new gaskets.

 b. Tighten the manifold to cylinder head nuts to 36 ft. lbs. (49 Nm).

 c. Tighten the air intake chamber to intake manifold bolts to 9 ft. lbs.

 d. Tighten the throttle body bolts to 9 ft. lbs. (12 Nm).

 e. Refill the cooling system. Start the engine and allow it to reach normal operating temperature and check for leaks. Repair as necessary.

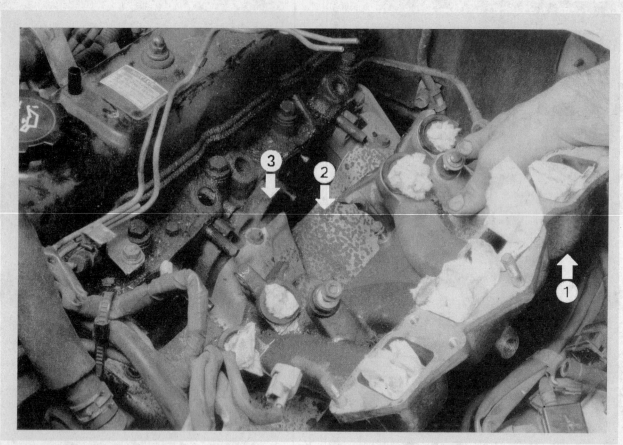

1. Intake manifold
2. Exhaust manifold heat shield
3. Exhaust manifold

Remove the intake manifold from the engine—3Y-EC and 4Y-EC engines

Unbolt the exhaust manifold heat shields

First remove the small shield from on top of the large heat shield . . .

. . . then remove the large exhaust manifold heat shield—3Y-EC and 4Y-EC engines

Dont forget to remove and discard the old exhaust manifold-to-head pipe gasket

Separate the exhaust manifold from the engine . . .

. . . then remove and discard the gasket

Air Conditioning Compressor

✳✳ CAUTION

Please refer to Section 1 before discharging the compressor or disconnecting air conditioning lines. Damage to the air conditioning system or personal injury could result. Consult your local laws concerning refrigerant discharge and recycling. In many areas it may be illegal for anyone but a certified technician to service the A/C system. Always use an approved recovery station when discharging the air conditioning.

REMOVAL & INSTALLATION

◆ See Figures 81 and 82

➡Be sure to take notice of the location of the compressor for it may be easier to remove the compressor from underneath the vehicle. If the compressor has to be removed from underneath the vehicle, be sure to raise and support the vehicle safely on suitable jackstands.

1. Run the engine at idle with the air conditioning on for 10 minutes, then shut off the engine.
2. Disconnect the battery cables and remove the battery (Cressida only), if necessary.
3. Disconnect the air conditioning clutch lead wire from the wiring harness. Discharge the refrigerant from the air conditioning system. Be sure to cap the open fitting immediately to keep the moisture out of the system.
4. Loosen the air conditioning drive belt and remove it from the compressor.
5. Remove the air conditioning compressor mounting bolts and remove the compressor.
   To install:
6. Install the compressor with the mounting bolts. Tighten the mounting bolts to 20 ft. lbs. (27 Nm).

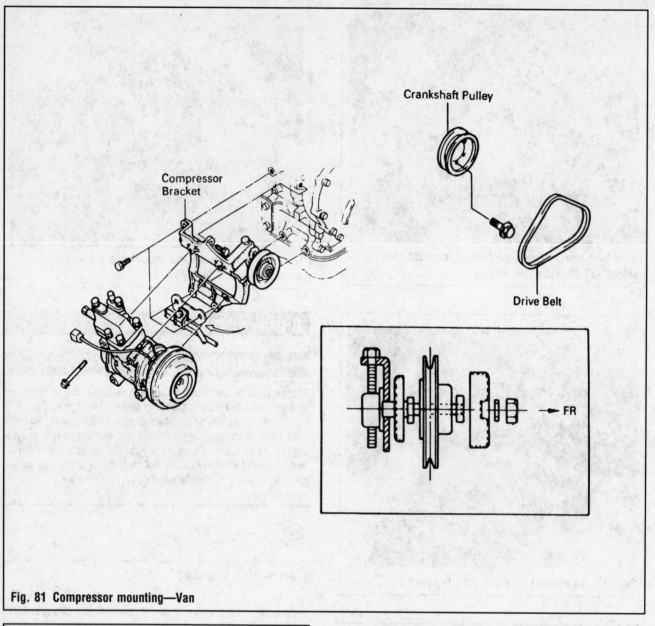

Fig. 81 Compressor mounting—Van

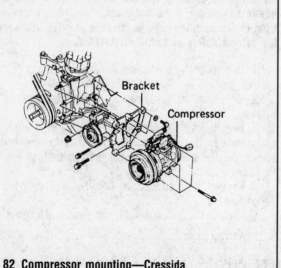

Fig. 82 Compressor mounting—Cressida

7. Install the drive belt and adjust it to obtain the proper tension.

8. Connect the 2 flexible hoses to the service valves on the compressor (if removed). Tighten the discharge and suction lines to 18 ft. lbs. (20–24 Nm).

9. Connect the clutch lead wire to the wiring harness.

10. Install the battery and connect the battery cables. Evacuate and recharge the air conditioning refrigeration system.

Radiator

REMOVAL & INSTALLATION

Cressida

▶ **See Figure 83**

1. Drain the coolant into a suitable drain pan.
2. Disconnect the 2 radiator hoses.

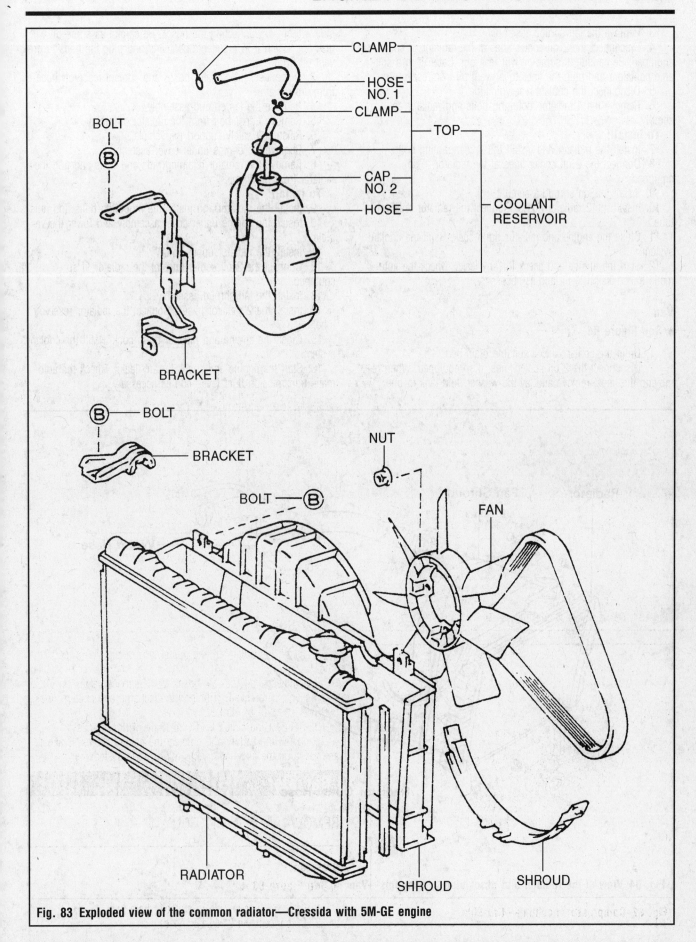

Fig. 83 Exploded view of the common radiator—Cressida with 5M-GE engine

3. Remove the fan shroud assembly.

4. Disconnect the 2 oil cooler lines at the radiator, if so equipped. Be careful as some oil will leak out. Catch it in a suitable container and plug the lines to prevent oil from escaping.

5. Disconnect the coolant reservoir tube.

6. Remove the 4 radiator mounting bolts and radiator assembly.

To install:

7. Install the radiator and install the four mounting bolts.

8. Connect the 2 oil cooler lines at the radiator, if so equipped.

9. Install the fan shroud assembly.

10. Install the 2 radiator hoses. Connect the radiator reservoir tube.

11. Close the engine and radiator drain cock. Refill the coolant system.

12. Start the engine and check for any leaks. Check the automatic transmission level, add as necessary.

Van

▶ **See Figure 84**

1. Drain the coolant into a suitable drain pan.

2. Disconnect the 2 oil cooler lines, if so equipped. When removing the lines, remove and lay the washer fluid tank to one side without disconnecting the hoses. Be careful as some oil will leak out. Catch it in a suitable container and plug the lines to prevent oil from escaping.

3. Disconnect the radiator hoses and coolant reservoir hose from the radiator.

4. Remove the fan shroud assembly.

5. Remove upper bolt from the radiator assembly.

6. Raise and safely support the vehicle.

7. Remove the engine under cover assembly.

8. Remove the radiator retaining nuts and bolts and pull the radiator from the frame.

To install:

9. Install the radiator and install the mounting bolts and nuts.

10. Install the engine under cover assembly and lower the vehicle.

11. Install the radiator upper bolt.

12. Connect the 2 oil cooler lines at the radiator, if so equipped.

13. Install the fan shroud assembly.

14. Install the 2 radiator hoses. Connect the radiator reservoir tube.

15. Close the engine and radiator drain cock. Refill the coolant system.

16. Start the engine and check for any leaks. Check the automatic transmission fluid level, add as necessary.

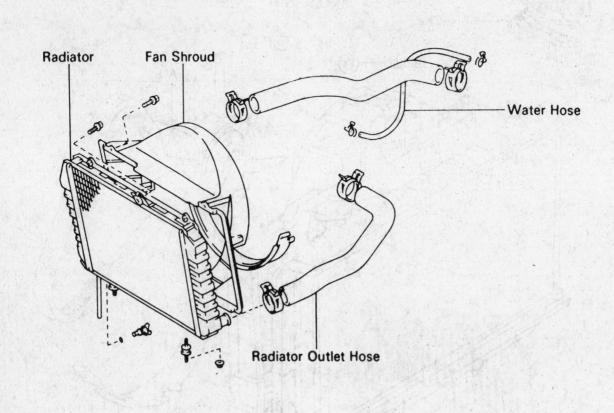

Fig. 84 View of the radiator and associated components—Van

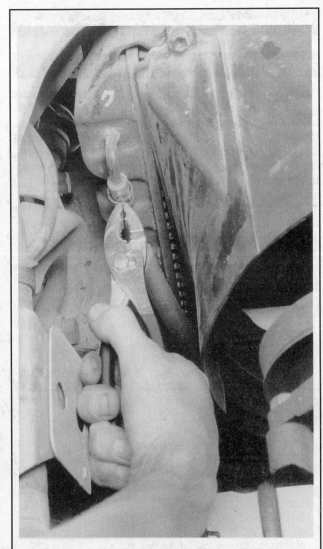

Use a pair of pliers to remove the hose clamps on the coolant hoses attached to the radiator . . .

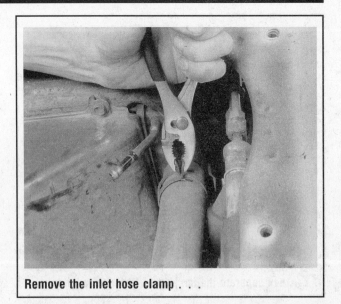

Remove the inlet hose clamp . . .

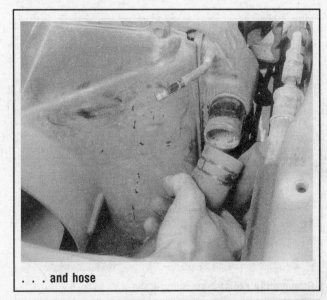

. . . and hose

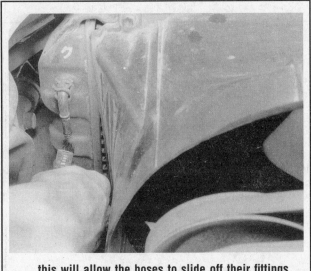

. . . this will allow the hoses to slide off their fittings

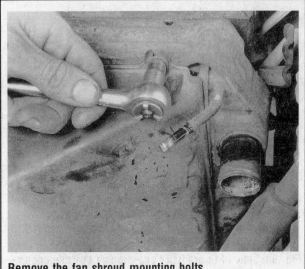

Remove the fan shroud mounting bolts . . .

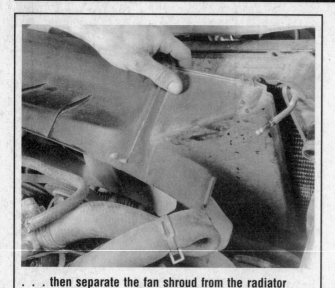
. . . then separate the fan shroud from the radiator

Remove the radiator mounting bolts . . .

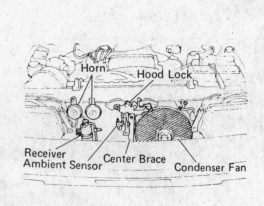
Fig. 85 View of the components which must be removed to access the condenser—Cressida

Condenser

✳✳ CAUTION

Please refer to Section 1 before discharging the compressor or disconnecting air conditioning lines. Damage to the air conditioning system or personal injury could result. Consult your local laws concerning refrigerant discharge and recycling. In many areas it may be illegal for anyone but a certified technician to service the A/C system. Always use an approved recovery station when discharging the air conditioning.

REMOVAL & INSTALLATION

Cressida

◆ **See Figure 85**

1. Run the engine at idle with the air conditioning on for 10 minutes.
2. Disconnect the battery cables.
3. Discharge the refrigerant from the air conditioning system. Be sure to cap the open fitting immediately to keep the moisture out of the system.
4. Remove the following parts:
   a. The front grille.
   b. The hood lock and center brace.
   c. The horn assembly.
   d. The bumper assembly.
   e. The oil cooler assembly, the oil cooler lines do not have to be removed.
5. Disconnect the liquid line and discharge line from the condenser outlet fitting. Be sure to cap the open fitting immediately to keep the moisture out of the system.
6. Remove the 4 condenser mounting bolts and remove the condenser.

. . . and pull the radiator from the engine compartment

To install:

7. Install the condenser along with the 4 retaining bolts and tighten the bolts securely. If the condenser was replaced, add compressor oil to the compressor 1.4–1.7 fluid ounces.

8. Reconnect the liquid iine and discharge line to the condenser outlet fitting.

9. Reconnect the following parts.

• The oil cooler assembly, the oil cooler lines do not have to be removed.

  • The bumper assembly.

  • The horn assembly.

  • The hood lock and center brace.

  • The front grille.

10. Install the battery cables. Evacuate and recharge the air conditioning refrigeration system. Check for leaks and repair as necessary.

Van

2-WHEEL DRIVE MODELS

▶ **See Figure 86**

1. Run the engine at idle with the air conditioning on for 10 minutes.

2. Disconnect the battery cables.

3. Discharge the refrigerant from the air conditioning system. Be sure to cap the open fitting immediately to keep the moisture out of the system.

4. Remove the fan shroud assembly.

5. Remove the radiator mounting bolts.

6. Disconnect the discharge hose from the condenser inlet fitting.

7. Disconnect the liquid line hose from the condenser outlet fitting.

8. Remove the front condenser housing retaining bolts and remove the front condenser.

9. To remove the rear condenser use the following procedure.

10. Disconnect the liquid line from the sight glass.

11. Disconnect the 3 discharge lines from the condenser inlet fitting and discharge tube.

12. Disconnect the pressure switch lead wire.

13. Remove the 4 retaining bolts for the rear condenser and remove the rear condenser.

To install:

14. Install the rear condenser along with the 4 retaining bolts and tighten the bolts securely. If the condenser was replaced, add compressor oil to the compressor 1.4–1.7 fluid ounces.

15. Reconnect the pressure switch lead wire.

16. Reconnect the 3 discharge lines to the condenser inlet fitting and discharge tube.

17. Reconnect the liquid line to the sight glass.

18. To install the front condenser use the following procedure.

a. Install the front condenser along with the 4 retaining bolts and tighten the bolts securely. If the condenser was replaced, add compressor oil to the compressor 1.4–1.7 fluid ounces.

b. Reconnect the liquid line hose to the condenser outlet fitting.

c. Reconnect the discharge hose to the condenser inlet fitting.

d. Install the radiator mounting bolts.

19. Install the battery cables. Evacuate and recharge the air conditioning refrigeration system. Check for leaks and repair as necessary.

4-WHEEL DRIVE MODELS

▶ **See Figure 87**

·1. Run the engine at idle with the air conditioning on for 10 minutes.

2. Disconnect the battery cables.

3. Discharge the refrigerant from the air conditioning system. Be sure to cap the open fitting immediately to keep the moisture out of the system.

4. Disconnect the discharge hose from the condenser inlet fitting.

5. Disconnect the liquid line hose from the condenser outlet fitting.

6. Disconnect the condenser fan motor connector.

7. Remove the condenser retaining bolts and remove the front condenser.

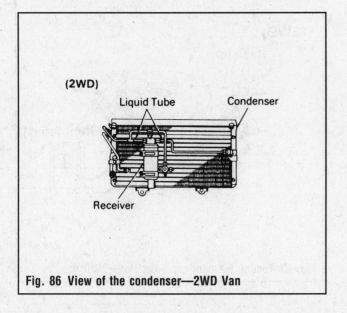

Fig. 86 View of the condenser—2WD Van

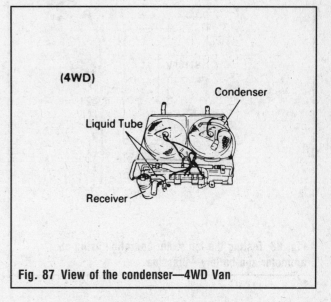

Fig. 87 View of the condenser—4WD Van

To install:

8. Install the condenser along with the 4 retaining bolts and tighten the bolts securely. If the condenser was replaced, add compressor oil to the compressor 1.4–1.7 fluid ounces.

9. Reconnect the condenser fan motor lead wire.

10. Reconnect the liquid line hose to the condenser outlet fitting.

11. Reconnect the discharge hose to the condenser inlet fitting.

12. Install the battery cables. Evacuate and recharge the air conditioning refrigeration system. Check for leaks and repair as necessary.

Condenser Fan Motor

TESTING

Cressida

1989–90 MODELS

▶ **See Figures 88 and 89**

1. Disconnect negative battery cable.
2. Disconnect fusible link.
3. Using an ohmmeter, check for continuity of the fusible link. If there is no continuity, replace the fusible link.
4. Reconnect the fusible link.
5. Disconnect the connector at the fan motor.
6. Using the fan motor wiring harness, apply battery voltage (12 volts) to the fan motor connector.
7. Confirm the smooth rotation of the motor.
8. If the motor does not turn or moves to slowly, replace it.
9. Connect the connector of the fan motor. Reconnect the negative battery cable.

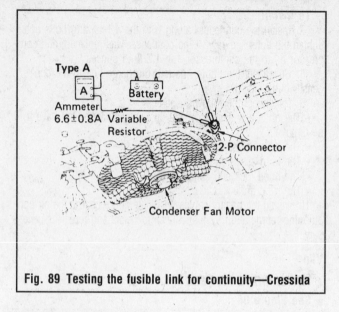

Fig. 89 Testing the fusible link for continuity—Cressida

2-Wheel Drive Van

1987–90 MODELS

▶ **See Figures 90 and 91**

1. Disconnect negative battery cable.
2. Using an ohmmeter, measure the resistance of the resistor. If the resistance is not as specified, replace the resistor. Standard resistance is 0.9–0.10 kΩ at 68°F (20°C).
3. Disconnect the connector at the fan motor.
4. Using the fan motor wiring harness, apply battery voltage (12 volts) to the fan motor connector.
5. Confirm the smooth rotation of the motor.
6. If the motor does not turn or moves to slowly, replace it.
7. Connect the connector of the fan motor. Reconnect the negative battery cable.

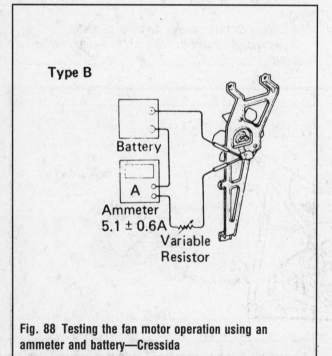

Fig. 88 Testing the fan motor operation using an ammeter and battery—Cressida

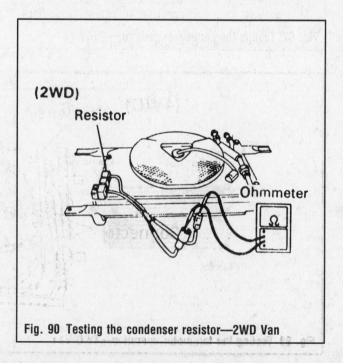

Fig. 90 Testing the condenser resistor—2WD Van

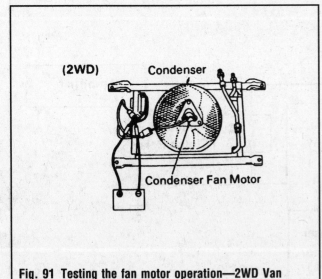

Fig. 91 Testing the fan motor operation—2WD Van

4-Wheel Drive Van

1987–90 MODELS

◗ **See Figures 92, 93 and 94**

1. Disconnect negative battery cable.
2. Using an ohmmeter, measure the resistance of the resistor between terminals B and B1 and D and d1. If the resistance is not as specified, replace the resistor. Standard resistance is 0.24–0.30Ω at 68°F (20°C).
3. Disconnect the connector at the fan motor.
4. Using the fan motor wiring harness, apply battery voltage (12 volts) to the fan motor connector.
5. Confirm the smooth rotation of the motor.
6. If the motor does not turn or moves to slowly, replace it.
7. Connect the connector of the fan motor. Reconnect the negative battery cable.

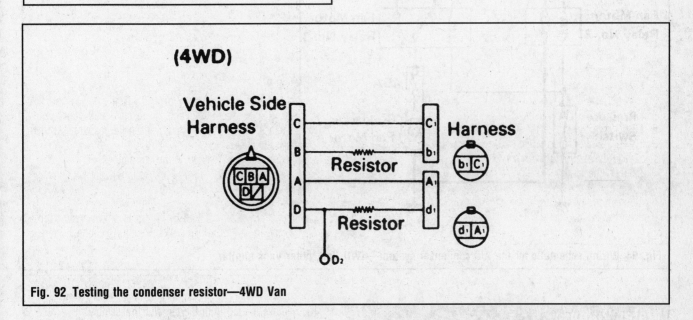

Fig. 92 Testing the condenser resistor—4WD Van

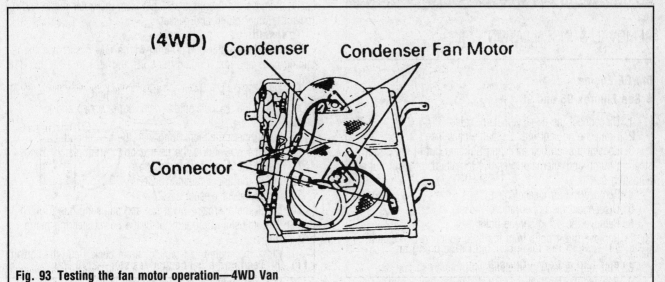

Fig. 93 Testing the fan motor operation—4WD Van

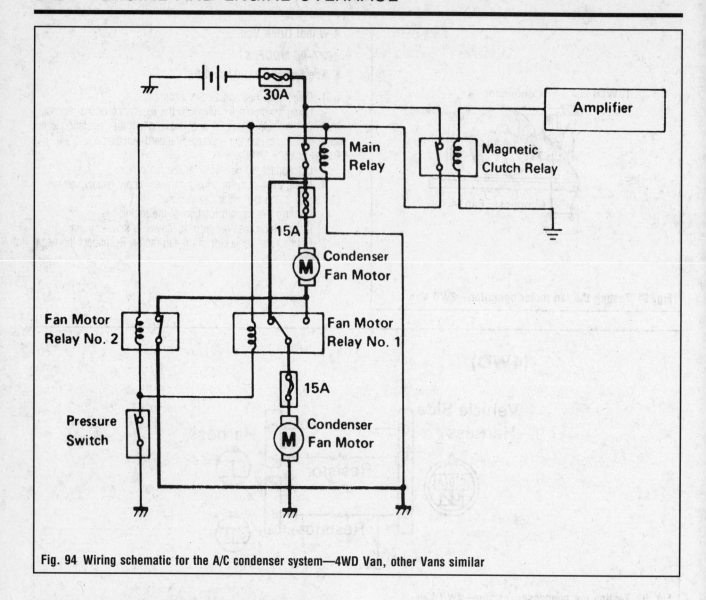

Fig. 94 Wiring schematic for the A/C condenser system—4WD Van, other Vans similar

Water Pump

REMOVAL & INSTALLATION

5M-GE Engine

♦ **See Figures 95 and 96**

1. Disconnect the negative battery cable.
2. Drain the coolant into a suitable container.
3. Loosen the fan belt adjusting bolt and nut of the power steering pump and alternator. Remove the alternator pivot nut and adjusting bar.
4. Remove the air cleaner case.
5. Disconnect the upper radiator hose.
6. Remove the 4 fan shroud bolts.
7. Remove the 4 bolts from the fluid coupling (fan clutch) flange.
8. Pull out the fan clutch along with the fan shroud.
9. Remove the fan belt guide, water pump pulley and fan belts.

10. Remove the fan from the fan clutch assembly.
11. Remove the 8 bolts and 1 nut from the water pump and remove the water pump and gasket.

To install:

12. Install the water pump along with a new gasket and the retaining bolts and nut. Tighten the bolts and nuts to 13 ft. lbs. (18 Nm).
13. Install the fan to the fan clutch assembly.
14. Install the fan belt guide, water pump pulley and fan belts.
15. Install the fan clutch along with the fan shroud.
16. Install the 4 bolt to the fluid coupling (fan clutch) flange.
17. Install the 4 fan shroud bolts.
18. Install the upper radiator hose.
19. Install the air cleaner case.
20. Install the alternator pivot nut and adjusting bar. Tighten the fan belt adjusting bolt and nut of the power steering pump and alternator.
21. Close the engine and radiator drain cock. Refill the coolant system.
22. Start the engine and check for any leaks.

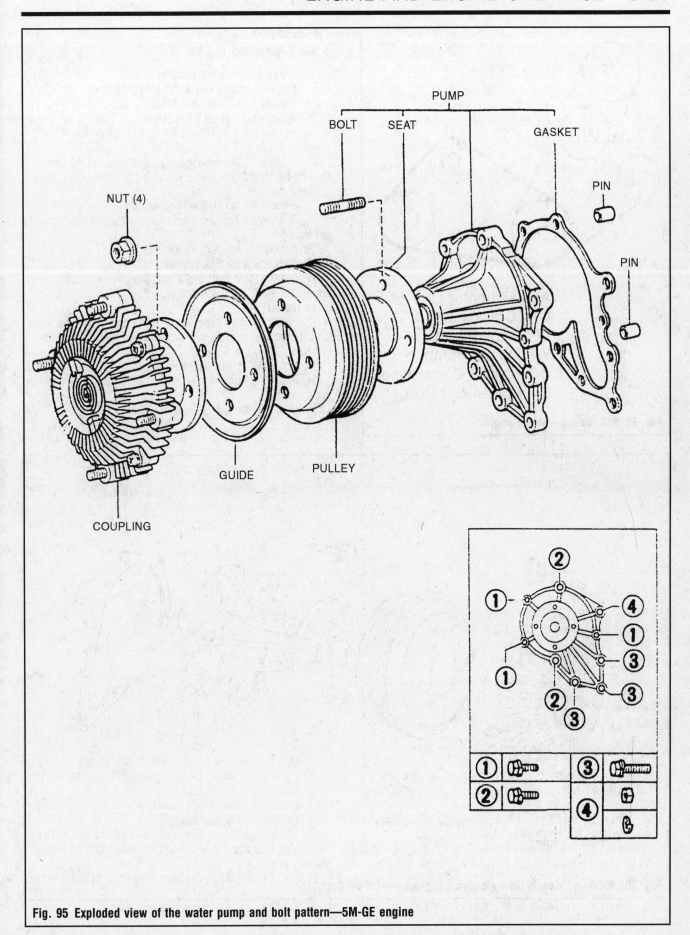

Fig. 95 Exploded view of the water pump and bolt pattern—5M-GE engine

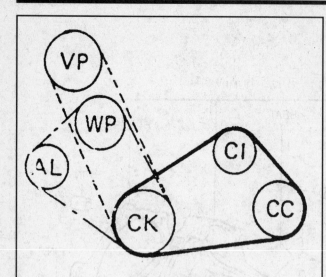

AL: Alternator
CK: Crankshaft
VP: Vane Pump
WP: Water Pump
CC: Cooler Compressor
CI: Cooler Idler Pulley

Fig. 96 Belt routing—5M-GE engine

7M-GE Engine
◆ **See Figures 96a and 97**

1. Disconnect the negative battery cable.
2. Drain the coolant into a suitable container.
3. Remove the radiator inlet hose.
4. Remove the number 2 fan shroud.
5. Remove the 4 bolts from the fluid coupling (fan clutch) flange.
6. Loosen the fan belt adjusting bolt and nut of the power steering pump and alternator. Remove the alternator pivot nut and adjusting bar.
7. Remove the fan shroud mounting nuts.
8. Remove the four bolts, fan clutch, water pump pulley and fan shroud.
9. Remove the fan from the fan clutch.
10. Remove the air pipe assembly.
11. Remove the 8 bolts and 2 nuts from the water pump and remove the water pump and gasket.

To install:
12. Install the water pump along with a new gasket and the retaining bolts and nuts. Tighten the bolts and nuts to 13 ft. lbs. (18 N.m).
13. Install the air pipe assembly.
14. Install the four bolts, fan clutch, water pump pulley and fan shroud.
15. Install the fan shroud mounting nuts.

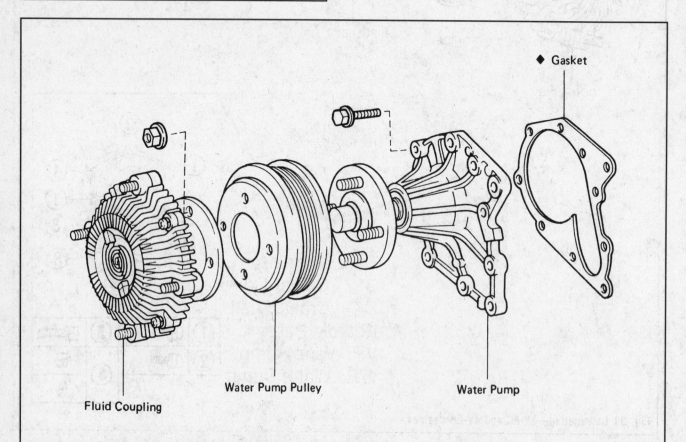

◆ Gasket

Fluid Coupling

Water Pump Pulley

Water Pump

Fig. 96a Exploded view of the water pump assembly—7M-GE Cressida

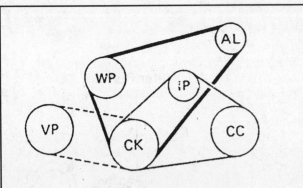

IP: Idle Pulley
VP: Vane Pump
WP: Water Pump
AL: Alternator
CK: Crankshaft
CC: Cooler Compressor

Fig. 97 Belt routing—7M-GE engine

16. Install the alternator pivot nut and adjusting bar. Tighten the drive belt adjusting bolt and nut.

17. Install the 4 bolts to the fluid coupling (fan clutch) flange.

18. Install the number 2 fan shroud.

19. Install the radiator inlet hose.

20. Close the engine and radiator drain cock. Refill the coolant system.

21. Start the engine and check for any leaks.

3Y-EC and 4Y-EC Engines
▶ **See Figures 98 and 99**

1. Disconnect the negative battery cable.

2. Drain the coolant into a suitable container.

3. Remove the 4 nuts holding the fan clutch to the pulley and remove the fan and fan clutch assembly along with the water pump pulley.

4. Remove the bolt and disconnect the drive belt adjusting bar from the water pump.

5. Remove the nuts and bolts retaining the water pump to the engine block, remove the water pump and gasket.

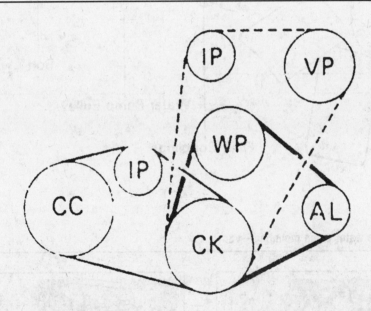

AL : Alternator
CC : Cooler Compressor
CK : Crank Shaft
IP: Idle Pulley
VP: Vane Pump
WP: Water Pump

Fig. 98 Belt routing—3Y-EC and 4Y-EC engines

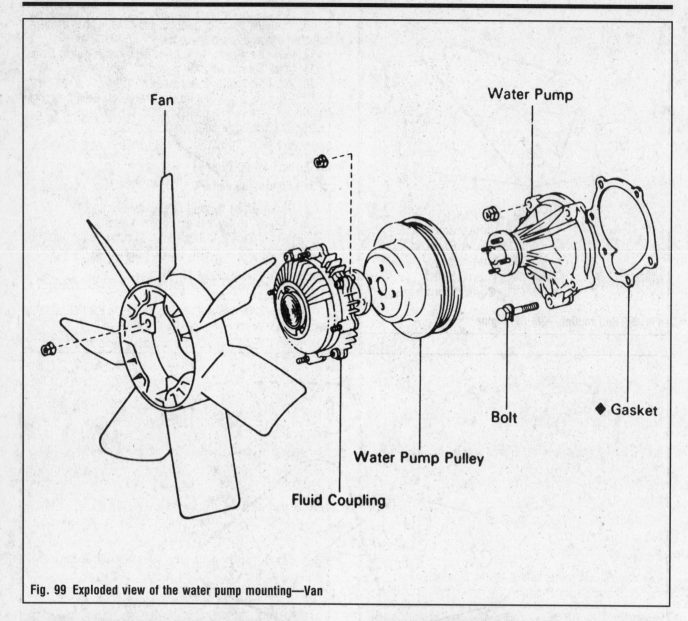

Fan

Water Pump

Water Pump Pulley

Fluid Coupling

Bolt

◆ Gasket

Fig. 99 Exploded view of the water pump mounting—Van

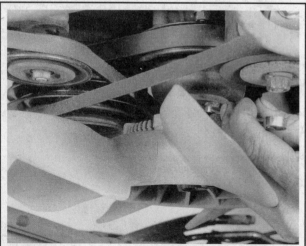

Remove the mounting nuts retaining the fan clutch and blade assembly to the pulley

Pull the fan clutch/blade assembly off the water pump studs

The water pump pulley slides off the studs also

Remove the water pump nuts and bolts retaining it to the block—3Y-EC and 4Y-EC engines

Separate the water pump from the block and remove any old gasket material

Unbolt and remove the drive belt adjusting bar from in front of the water pump

To install:

6. Install the water pump along with a new gasket and the retaining bolts and nuts. Tighten the bolts and nuts to 13 ft. lbs. (18 Nm).

7. Install the bolt and reconnect the drive belt adjusting bar to the water pump. Tighten the belt adjusting bar bolt to 29 ft. lbs. (39 Nm).

8. Install the water pump pulley and fan clutch along with the fan assembly. Install the 4 bolts that retain the fan clutch to the water pump pulley.

9. Close the engine and radiator drain cock. Refill the coolant system.

10. Start the engine and check for any leaks.

Cylinder Head

REMOVAL & INSTALLATION

5M-GE Engine

◆ **See Figures 100 thru 105**

1. Rotate the engine so as to bring the number one cylinder up to top dead center of its compression stroke. Disconnect the negative battery cable.

2. Remove the air cleaner assembly.

3. Drain the cooling system.

4. Disconnect the exhaust pipe from the exhaust manifold.

5. Remove the throttle cable bracket from the cylinder head if equipped with automatic transmission, and remove the accelerator and actuator cable bracket.

6. Tag and disconnect the cylinder head ground cable, the oxygen sensor wire, the distributor connector, oil pressure sending unit, alternator wires, the high tension coil wire, the water temperature sending, the thermo switch wires, the starter wires, the ECT connectors, the solenoid resistor wire connector and the knock sensor wire.

7. Tag and disconnect the brake booster vacuum hose from the air intake chamber, along with the EGR valve vacuum hose. Disconnect the actuator vacuum hose from the air intake chamber, if equipped with cruise control. Disconnect the heater bypass hoses from the engine.

8. Disconnect the upper radiator hose from the thermostat housing, and disconnect the 2 heater hoses.

9. Disconnect the No. 1 air hose from the air intake connector. Remove the 2 clamp bolts, loosen the throttle body hose

clamp and remove the air intake connector and the connector pipe.

10. Disconnect the No.1 water by-pass hose from the idle speed control valve. Disconnect the No.2 water by-pass hose from the throttle body.

11. Tag and disconnect all emission control hoses from the throttle body and air intake chamber, the 2 PCV hoses from the cam cover and the fuel hose from the fuel hose support.

12. Remove the air intake chamber stay and the vacuum pipe and ground cable. Remove the bolt that attaches the spark plug wire clip, leaving the wires attached to the clip.

13. Make an alignment mark on the distributor base and the engine block. Remove the distributor from the cylinder head with the cap and wires attached, by removing the distributor holding bolt.

14. Remove the spark plugs. Disconnect and tag the following connections:
- Cold start injector wire
- Water temperature sensor wire
- Start injection time switch wire
- Water temperature sending unit wire
- Throttle position sensor wire connector
- Idle speed control valve wire connectors

15. Disconnect the cold start injector fuel hose from the delivery pipe.

16. Loosen the nut of the EGR pipe, remove the 5 bolts and 2 nuts that retain the air intake chamber and remove the chamber and gasket.

17. Remove the glove box and remove the ECU module. Disconnect the 3 connectors and pull the ECU wire harness out through the engine side of the firewall.

18. Remove the pulsation damper and the No. 1 fuel pipe. Remove the water outlet housing by first loosening the clamp and

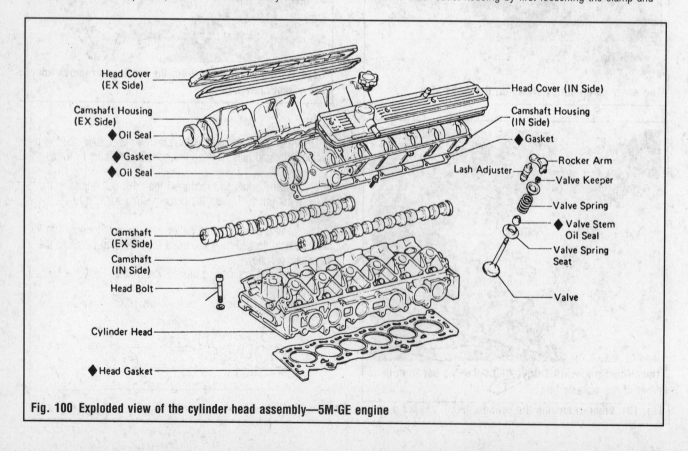

Fig. 100 Exploded view of the cylinder head assembly—5M-GE engine

ENGINE OVERHAUL GASKET KIT

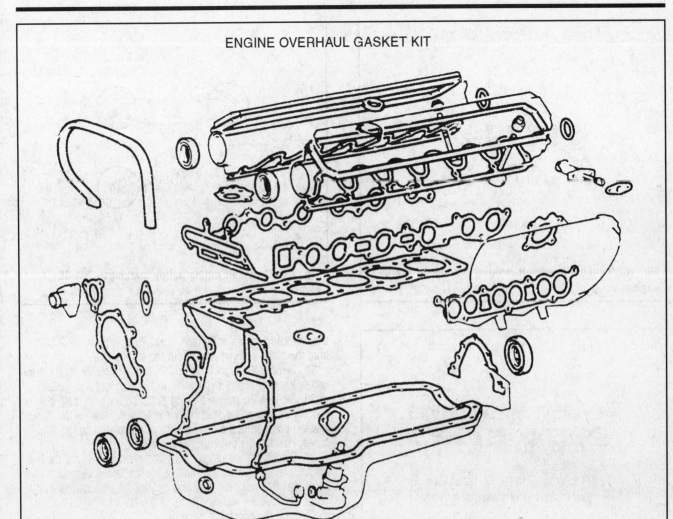

CYLINDER HEAD SET

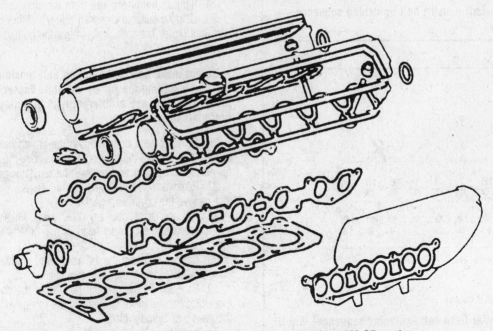

Fig. 101 When removing the cylinder head, always purchase a new gasket kit—5M-GE engine

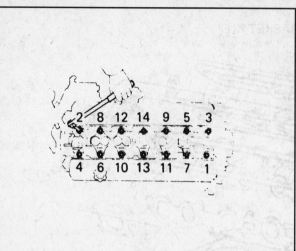

Fig. 102 Cylinder head bolt removal sequence—5M-GE engine

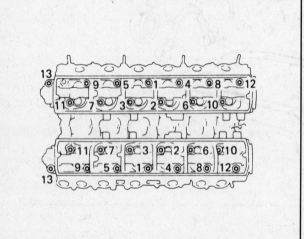

Fig. 103 Camshaft housing bolt tightening sequence—5M-GE engine

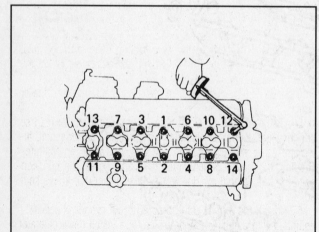

Fig. 104 Cylinder head bolt tightening sequence—5M-GE engine

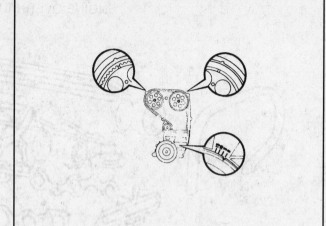

Fig. 105 Camshaft timing pulley markings—5M-GE engine

disconnecting the water by pass hose. Then remove the 2 bolts from the outlet and remove it from the engine.

19. Remove the eight bolts and 2 nuts holding the intake manifold to the engine and remove the intake manifold and gasket.

20. Remove the power steering pump pulley with drive belt and remove the power steering pump bracket. Remove the power steering pump from the bracket without disconnecting the fluid hoses. Position the pump out of the way.

21. Disconnect the oxygen sensor connector. Remove the heat insulator retaining nuts and remove the insulators. Remove the exhaust manifold retaining nuts and remove the exhaust manifold.

22. Remove the retaining bolts of the No.3 timing belt cover and remove the cover and gasket.

23. Loosen the idler pulley set bolt and shift the idler pulley towards the alternator side. Finger-tighten the set bolt and then relieve the timing belt tension.

24. Remove the timing belt from the camshaft timing pulleys.

25. Using a suitable camshaft pulley holding tool, remove the camshaft pulley set bolts and remove the pulleys along with the match pin.

➡**Do not make use of the timing belt tension when removing and installing the pulley set bolt. The exhaust and intake sides each use a different type of pulley and they are not interchangeable.**

26. Remove the 2 bolts holding the timing belt cover stay bracket and remove the stay bracket. Remove the 3 bolts from the oil pressure regulator and remove the regulator and gasket.

27. Remove the No.2 timing belt cover retaining bolts and nuts and remove the cover with gasket.

28. Tag and disconnect any other wires, linkage and/or hoses still attached to the cylinder head or may interfere with its removal.

29. Carefully remove the 14 head bolts gradually in two or three passes and in the proper sequence.

30. Carefully lift the cylinder head from the dowels on the cylinder block and remove it. Remove the old gasket material from the head and cylinder block.

To install:

31. Install the EGR cooler.

32. Install a small bead of a suitable high temperature silicone sealer to the 4 corners of the cylinder head and engine block mating surface.

33. Place a new cylinder head gasket over the dowel pins on the cylinder block.

34. Position the cylinder head over the dowel pins. Once the cylinder head is seated properly over the gasket and engine block, install the cylinder head bolts. Tighten the head bolts gradually in 3 passes working from the middle out, to obtain a final torque of 58 ft. lbs. (78 Nm).

35. Install the No.2 timing belt cover and gasket and tighten the bolts and nuts to 9 ft. lbs. (13 Nm).

36. Install the oil pressure regulator along with a new gasket onto the cylinder head.

37. Install the timing belt cover stay bracket and bolts.

38. Install the camshaft timing pulleys and timing belt as follows:

a. Make sure that the match hole on the No. 2 journal of the camshaft housing is aligned with that of the camshaft.

b. If not aligned properly, temporarily install the camshaft timing pulley and insert the match pin into the pin hole. Then align the match holes by turning the camshaft timing pulley.

c. Install the camshaft timing pulleys with the guide facing the direction as indicated. The exhaust side will be with the pulley guide facing the No. 2 timing belt cover. The intake side will be with the pulley guide facing the front side.

d. Align the matchmarks of the No.2 timing belt cover with those of the camshaft timing pulleys and of the crankshaft pulley. Be sure that the No. 1 cylinder is set to top dead center on its compression stroke, which it should be if the engine has not been disturbed.

e. Install the timing belt with the belt having the proper tension between the crankshaft timing pulley and the camshaft timing pulley on the exhaust side.

f. Loosen the idler pulley set bolt and stretch the timing belt. Tighten the idler pulley set bolt to 36 ft. lbs. (49 Nm). Be sure that the timing belt tension is applied evenly throughout the belt.

g. There are 3 pin holes on the camshaft and timing pulleys. Select the one overlapped hole and insert the pin into it.

➡**If there is no overlapping hole, find one that is nearly overlapped and rotate the crankshaft slightly to overlap it and insert the pin.**

h. The crankshaft pulley angle can be adjusted approximately 3° by changing the pin hole to the next one.

i. Using a suitable camshaft pulley holding tool, install the camshaft pulley set bolts and torque them to 50 ft. lbs. (69 Nm).

✸✸ WARNING

Do not disturb the timing belt tension when tightening the camshaft pulley bolt.

j. Loosen the idler pulley set bolt. Turn the crankshaft clockwise 2 times and retighten the idler pulley set bolt.

k. Install the No. 3 timing belt cover and gasket along with the retaining bolts.

39. Position a new exhaust manifold gasket onto the cylinder head. Install the exhaust manifold with retaining nuts and tighten the nuts to 29 ft. lbs. (39 Nm).

40. Install the heat insulators.

41. Install the power steering pump and stay bracket. Install the power steering pump pulley with the drive belt. Adjust the belt to obtain the proper tension. Tighten the idler pulley nut and adjusting bolt.

42. Position a new intake manifold gasket onto the cylinder head. Install the intake manifold with retaining nuts and tighten the nuts to 13 ft. lbs. (18 Nm). Connect the EFI wiring harness to the ECU.

43. Install the water outlet housing with the 2 bolts. Connect the water by-pass hose and tighten the clamp.

44. Finger-tighten the pulsation damper and union bolt with a new gaskets on the fuel pipe. Tighten the fuel pipe, being careful not to bend it.

45. Position a new air intake chamber gasket onto the intake manifold. Install the air chamber with the retaining bolts and nuts. Tighten the nut of the EGR valve connecting pipe.

46. Install a new gasket on the cold start injector fuel hose delivery pipe and install the fuel hose, another gasket and the union bolt to the delivery pipe.

47. Install the following connectors:
- Cold start injector wire
- Water temperature sensor wire
- Start injection time switch wire
- Water temperature sending unit wire
- Throttle position sensor wire connector
- Idle speed control valve wire connectors

48. Using the alignment mark made earlier on the distributor and being sure the No. 1 cylinder is set up at top dead center of its compression stroke. Install the distributor assembly.

49. Install the spark plugs, spark plug wire clips with bolt and the spark plug wires.

50. Install the air intake chamber stay bracket, vacuum pipe and ground cable with 3 bolts.

51. Reconnect all emission control hoses to the throttle body and air intake chamber, the 2 PCV hoses to the cam cover and the fuel hose to the fuel hose support.

52. Reconnect the No. 1 water by-pass hose to the idle speed control valve. Reconnect the No. 2 water bypass hose to the throttle body.

53. Reconnect the No. 1 air hose to the air intake connector. Install the 2 clamp bolts, tighten the throttle body hose clamp and install the air intake connector and the connector pipe.

54. Install the 2 heater hoses and install the radiator upper hose.

55. Reconnect the brake booster vacuum hose to the air intake chamber, along with the EGR valve vacuum hose. Reconnect the actuator vacuum hose to the air intake chamber, if equipped with cruise control. Reconnect the heater bypass hoses to the engine.

56. Reconnect the cylinder head ground cable, the oxygen sensor wire, the distributor connector, oil pressure sending unit, alternator wires, the high tension coil wire, the water temperature sending, the thermo switch wires, the starter wires, the ECT connectors, the solenoid resistor wire connector and the knock sensor wire.

57. Install the throttle cable bracket to the cylinder head if equipped with automatic transmission, and install the accelerator and actuator cable bracket.

58. Reconnect the exhaust pipe to the exhaust manifold.

59. Close the engine block and radiator draincocks and refill the cooling system.

60. Reconnect the negative battery cable. Start the engine. If the engine is hard to start it may be necessary to have someone turn the base of the distributor left or right to get close to the base timing marks and allowing the engine to start.

61. Perform all engine adjustments. Road test the vehicle and then make all final adjustments. Be sure to also check for any leaks and refill as necessary.

7M-GE Engine

▶ **See Figures 106 thru 111**

1. Rotate the engine so as to bring up the No. 1 cylinder to top dead center of its compression stroke. Disconnect the negative battery cable. Drain the cooling system.

2. Raise and support the vehicle safely. Disconnect the ex-

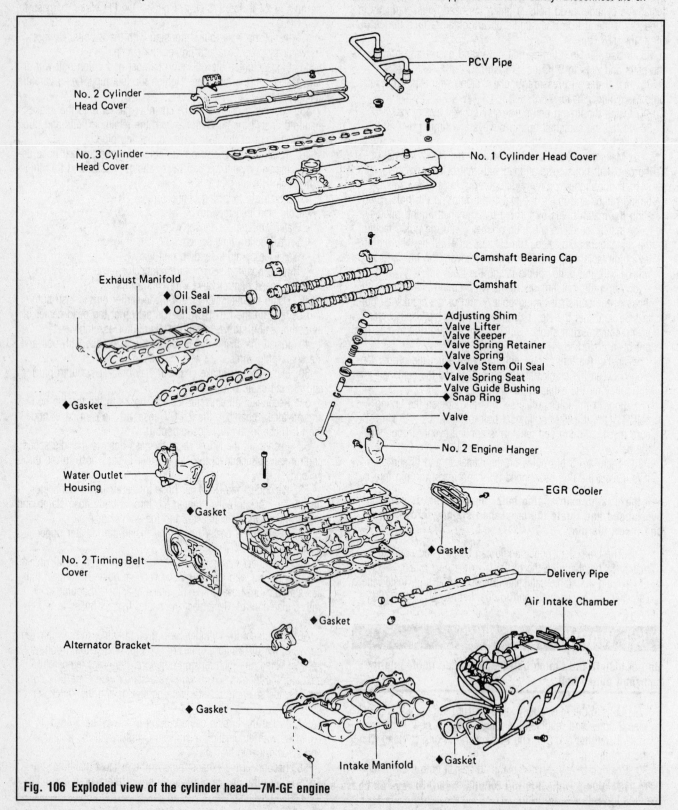

Fig. 106 Exploded view of the cylinder head—7M-GE engine

ENGINE OVERHAUL GASKET KIT

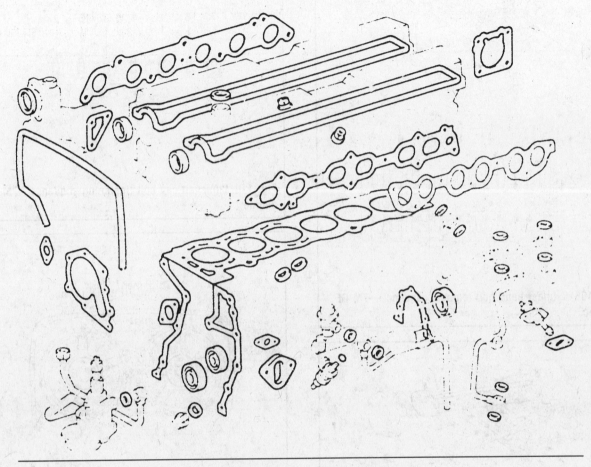

CYLINDER HEAD GASKET KIT

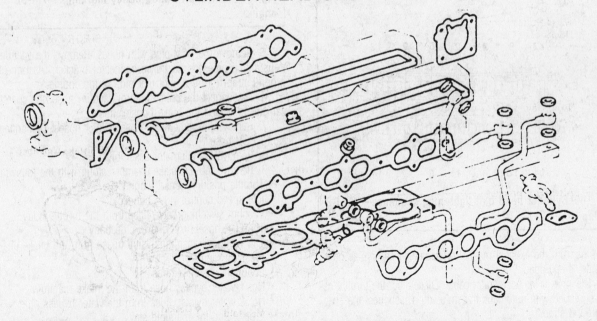

Fig. 107 When removing the cylinder head, always purchase a new gasket kit—7M-GE engine

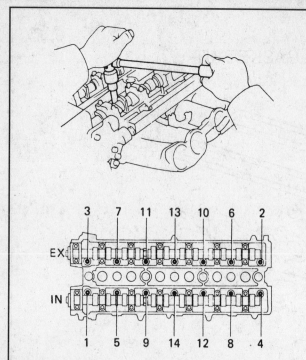

Fig. 108 Cylinder head bolt removal sequence—7M-GE engine

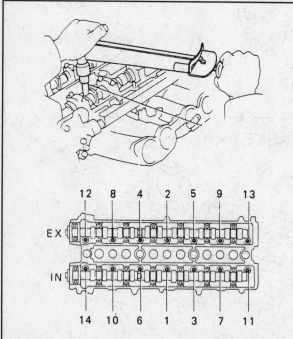

Fig. 109 Cylinder head bolt tightening sequence—7M-GE engine

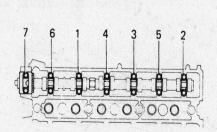

Fig. 110 Camshaft cap bolt tightening sequence—7M-GE engine

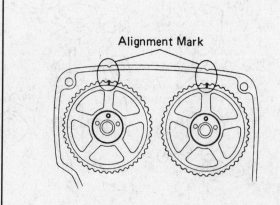

Fig. 111 Camshaft timing pulley markings—7M-GE engine

haust pipe from the exhaust manifold. Disconnect the cruise control cable, if equipped.

3. Disconnect the accelerator cable. Disconnect the throttle cable, if equipped with automatic transmission. Disconnect the engine ground strap.

4. Remove the No. 1 air cleaner hose along with the intake air pipe assembly and air intake connector.

5. Remove the PCV pipe with hoses. Remove the vacuum transmitting pipe and air intake connector bracket. Disconnect the ground strap from the right rear side of the engine.

6. Disconnect the cruise control vacuum hose, the charcoal canister hose and the brake booster hose.

7. Remove the radiator and heater inlet hoses. Disconnect the No. 3 PCV hose.

8. Remove the alternator assembly.

9. Remove the air intake chamber along with the following:
• Throttle position sensor connector
• Idle speed control valve connector
• Vacuum switching valve hose from the throttle body
• The EGR hoses from the throttle body
• The vacuum transmitting pipe hoses from the intake chamber
• Pressure regulator hose
• Pollution system air hose
• No. 1 water bypass hose from the intake manifold
• No. 3 water bypass hose from the water bypass pipe
• 2 bolts and the manifold stay
• Cold start injector tube assembly

10. Remove the mount bolts for the EGR pipe.

11. Remove the EGR vacuum modulator from the bracket.

12. Disconnect the engine wire harness from the clamps of the air intake chamber.

13. Remove the bolt holding the vacuum transmitting pipe to the No. 2 fuel pipe stay bracket.

14. Remove the vacuum transmitting pipes and air intake chamber retaining nuts and bolts. Remove this assembly along with the gasket from the engine.

15. Disconnect the cold start injector connector.

16. Disconnect the following wiring connectors:
- The oxygen sensor connector
- The oil pressure sender gauge connector
- Water temperature sensor connector
- Water temperature sender gauge connector
- Cold start injector time switch connector
- Distributor connector
- Igniter connector
- Noise filter connector
- Injector connectors
- Vacuum switching valve connector
- Knock sensor connector
- EGR gas temperature sensor connector (if so equipped)
- The ground strap from the intake manifold
- Starter connector
- Transmission connector
- Air conditioning compressor connector
- Check engine connector
- Relay block connector

17. Disconnect the engine wire from each clamp.

18. Remove the No. 1 fuel pipe.

19. Disconnect the fuel hose from the No. 2 fuel pipe. Remove the bolt, union bolt and No. 2 fuel pipe and gaskets.

20. Make an alignment mark on the distributor base and the engine block. Remove the distributor from the cylinder head with the cap and wires attached, by removing the distributor holding bolt.

21. Remove the engine oil dipstick.

22. Remove the exhaust manifold retaining nuts and remove the manifold along with the gasket.

23. Remove the union bolts, unions along with the No. 4 water bypass hose and gaskets. Disconnect the No. 6 water bypass hose from the water bypass pipe.

24. Remove the water outlet retaining bolt and nuts and remove the water outlet along with the gasket.

25. Remove the cylinder head cover retaining bolts and remove the cylinder head covers. Remove the center cylinder head cover and gasket.

26. Remove the spark plugs.

27. Remove the timing belt and camshaft timing pulleys as follows:

a. Remove the 4 bolts from the fluid coupling (fan clutch) flange.

b. Loosen the fan belt adjusting bolt and nut of the power steering pump.

c. Remove the fan shroud mounting nuts.

d. Remove the four bolts, fan clutch, water pump pulley and fan shroud.

e. Remove the power steering pump belt.

f. Remove the No. 3 timing cover retaining bolts and nuts. Remove the cover and gasket.

g. Turn the crankshaft pulley and align its groove with the 0 mark on the No. 1 timing belt cover. If the engine has not been disturbed, the engine should still be in this position.

h. Check that the alignment marks on the camshaft timing pulleys and the No. 2 timing belt cover are aligned. If not, turn the crankshaft pulley one complete revolution.

i. Loosen the mount bolt of the idler pulley and shift it to the left as far as it can go. Temporarily tighten the mount bolt thus relieving the tension on the timing belt.

j. Remove the timing belt from the camshaft timing pulley. Be sure to support the belt so that the meshing of the crankshaft timing pulley and timing belt do not shift. Be careful not to drop anything inside of the timing belt cover. Do not allow the belt to come in contact with oil, water or dust.

➡ **If reusing the timing belt, please mark the direction of rotation before removing it. But a word to the wise, if you are this far into the cylinder head repair of your vehicle, it would be wise to replace the timing belt at this time, so as to avoid this situation in the near future.**

k. Using a suitable camshaft pulley holding tool, remove the camshaft pulley set bolts and remove the pulleys along with the match pin. Do not make use of the timing belt tensioner when removing and installing the pulley set bolt.

28. Tag and disconnect any other wires, linkage and/or hoses still attached to the cylinder head or may interfere with its removal.

29. Carefully remove the head bolts gradually in two or three passes and in the proper sequence.

30. Carefully lift the cylinder head from the dowels on the cylinder block and remove it. Remove the old gasket material from the head and cylinder block.

To install:

31. Install a small bead of a suitable high temperature silicone sealer to the corners of the cylinder head and engine block mating surface.

32. Place a new cylinder head gasket over the dowel pins on the cylinder block.

33. Position the cylinder head over the dowel pins. Connect the No. 5 water bypass hose to the union. Apply a light coat of engine oil on the threads and under the cylinder head bolts.

34. Once the cylinder head is seated properly over the gasket and engine block, install the cylinder head bolts. Tighten the head bolts gradually in 3 passes working from the middle out, to obtain a final torque of 58 ft. lbs. (78 Nm).

35. Install the camshaft timing pulleys and timing belt as follows:

a. Turn the crankshaft pulley and align its groove with the 0 mark on the No. 1 timing belt cover. If the engine has not been disturbed, the engine should still be in this position.

b. Align the alignment marks on the camshaft timing pulleys and the No. 2 timing belt cover. Install the timing pulley.

c. Install the straight pin into the hole.

d. When replacing the camshaft or the camshaft timing pulley, always align the center holes of the camshaft and timing pulleys and insert the straight pin. When reusing the camshaft or camshaft timing pulleys, check that the straight pin hole position is in the same position it was at disassembly, insert the straight pin. Install the plate washer and pulley bolt.

e. Using a suitable camshaft pulley holding tool, check the pin hole position, hold the pulley and tighten the pulley bolts to 36 ft. lbs. (49 Nm).

f. Check that the matchmarks on the camshaft timing pulley are aligned with those on the No. 2 timing belt cover.

g. Install the timing belt to the intake camshaft timing pulley, the exhaust camshaft timing pulley and the idler pulley.

h. Loosen the idler pulley mount bolt until the pulley is moved slightly by the spring tension. Tighten the idler pulley mount bolt to 36 ft. lbs. (49 Nm).

i. Check that the timing belt tension is equal all the way through. Turn the crankshaft pulley 2 revolutions clockwise from TDC to TDC.

j. Check that the alignment marks on the camshaft timing pulleys are aligned with those on the No. 2 timing belt cover.

k. If the marks do not align, remove the belt and install it again.

l. Install the No. 3 timing cover gasket, cover and retaining bolts.

m. Install the power steering pump belt.

n. Install the four bolts, fan clutch, water pump pulley and fan shroud.

o. Install the fan shroud mounting nuts.

p. Tighten the fan belt adjusting bolt and nut of the power steering pump.

q. Install the 4 bolts to the fluid coupling (fan clutch) flange.

36. Install the spark plugs.

37. Install the cylinder head cover gaskets, covers and retaining bolts.

38. Install the water outlet housing gasket, housing, retaining bolt and nuts.

39. Install the union bolts, unions along with the No. 4 water bypass hose and gaskets. Reconnect the No. 6 water bypass hose to the water bypass pipe.

40. Install the exhaust manifold gasket, manifold and retaining nuts. Tighten the nuts to 29 ft. lbs. (39 Nm).

41. Install the engine oil dipstick.

42. Using the alignment mark made earlier on the distributor base and the engine block, be sure the No. 1 cylinder is still at top dead center of its compression stroke. Install the distributor to the cylinder head with the cap and wires attached, install the distributor holding bolt.

43. Reconnect the fuel hose to the No. 2 fuel pipe. Install the bolt, union bolt and No. 2 fuel pipe and gaskets. Tighten the union bolt to 18 ft. lbs. (25 Nm).

44. Install the No. 1 fuel pipe. Tighten the union bolt to 29 ft. lbs. (25 Nm) and the fuel pipe to 22 ft. lbs. (29 Nm).

45. Reconnect the engine wire to each clamp.

46. Reconnect the following wiring connectors:
- The oxygen sensor connector
- The oil pressure sender gauge connector
- Water temperature sensor connector
- Water temperature sender gauge connector
- Cold start injector time switch connector
- Distributor connector
- Igniter connector
- Noise filter connector
- Injector connectors
- Vacuum switching valve connector
- Knock sensor connector
- EGR gas temperature sensor connector (if so equipped)
- The ground strap from the intake manifold
- Starter connector
- Transmission connector

- Air conditioning compressor connector
- Check engine connector
- Relay block connector

47. Reconnect the cold start injector connector.

48. Install the vacuum transmitting pipes and air intake chamber along with a new gasket and the retaining nuts and bolts.

49. Install the bolt holding the vacuum transmitting pipe to the No. 2 fuel pipe stay bracket.

50. Reconnect the engine wire harness to the clamps of the air intake chamber.

51. Install the EGR vacuum modulator to the bracket.

52. Install the mount bolts for the EGR pipe.

53. Install the air intake chamber along with the following:
- Throttle position sensor connector
- Idle speed control valve connector
- Vacuum switching valve hose from the throttle body
- The EGR hoses from the throttle body
- The vacuum transmitting pipe hoses from the intake chamber
- Pressure regulator hose
- Pollution system air hose
- No. 1 water bypass hose from the intake manifold
- No. 3 water bypass hose from the water bypass pipe
- 2 bolts and the manifold stay
- Cold start injector tube assembly

54. Install the alternator assembly.

55. Install the radiator and heater inlet hoses. Reconnect the No. 3 PCV hose.

56. Reconnect the cruise control vacuum hose, the charcoal canister hose and the brake booster hose.

57. Install the PCV pipe with hoses. Install the vacuum transmitting pipe and air intake connector bracket. Reconnect the ground strap to the right rear side of the engine.

58. Install the No. 1 air cleaner hose along with the intake air pipe assembly and air intake connector.

59. Reconnect the accelerator cable. Reconnect the throttle cable, if equipped with automatic transmission. Reconnect the engine ground strap.

60. Reconnect the exhaust pipe to the exhaust manifold. Reconnect the cruise control cable, if equipped. Lower the vehicle.

61. Close the engine block and radiator draincocks and refill the cooling system.

62. Reconnect the negative battery cable. Start the engine. If the engine is hard to start it may be necessary to have someone turn the base of the distributor left or right to get close to the base timing marks and allowing the engine to start.

63. Perform all engine adjustments. Road test the vehicle and then make all final adjustments. Be sure to also check for any leaks and refill as necessary.

3Y-EC and 4Y-EC Engines
▶ See Figure 112, 113, 114, 115 and 116

1. Disconnect the negative battery cable.
2. Remove the right front seat.
3. Remove the engine service hole cover.
4. Drain the coolant.
5. Disconnect the following hoses:
- Radiator inlet hoses
- Radiator breather hose
- Reservoir tank hose
- Heater outlet hose
- Radiator outlet hose

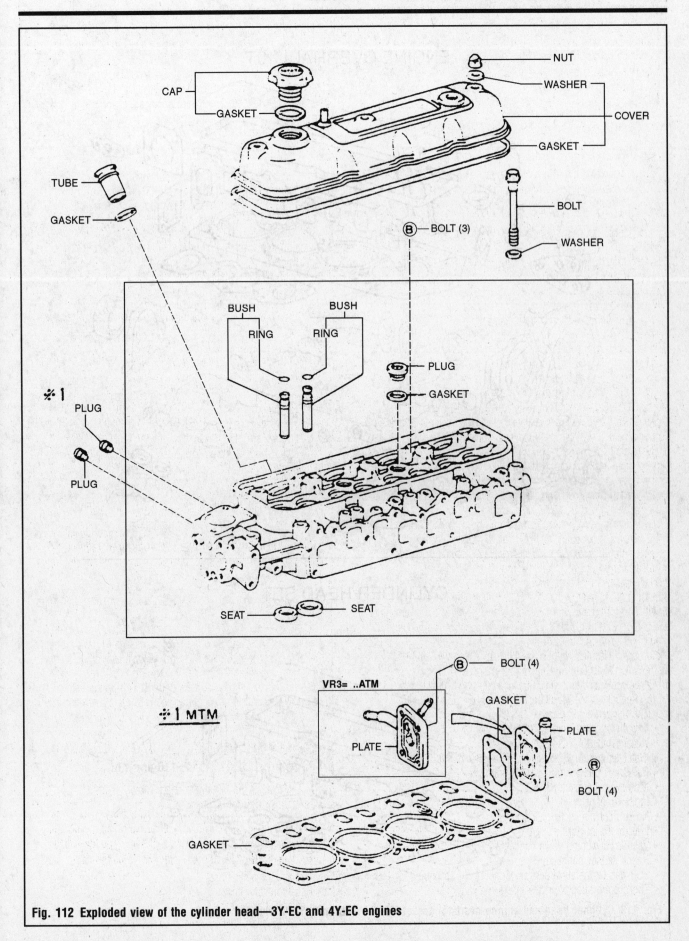

Fig. 112 Exploded view of the cylinder head—3Y-EC and 4Y-EC engines

ENGINE OVERHAUL KIT

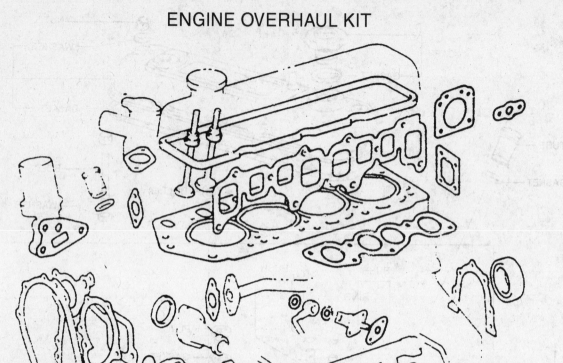

CYLINDER HEAD SET

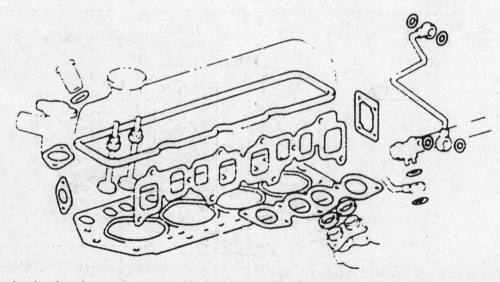

Fig. 113 Cylinder head and engine overhaul gasket kits—3Y-EC and 4Y-EC engines

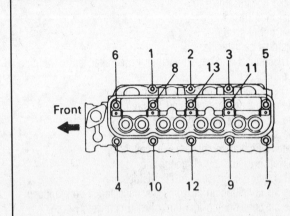

Fig. 114 Cylinder head bolt removal sequence—3Y-EC and 4Y-EC engines

Remove the rocker arm shaft assembly from the cylinder head—3Y-EC and 4Y-EC engines

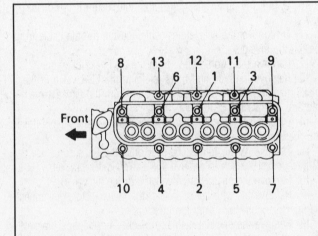

Fig. 115 Cylinder head bolt tightening sequence— 3Y-EC and 4Y-EC engines

When removing the pushrods, place them in a marked cardboard sheet to keep them in order

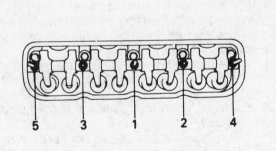

Fig. 116 Rocker shaft bolt tightening sequence— 3Y-EC and 4Y-EC engines

Uniformly loosen and remove the cylinder head bolts

Lift the cylinder head and intake/exhaust manifold assembly off the block

Before installing the cylinder head on the block, clean and scrape the mating surfaces

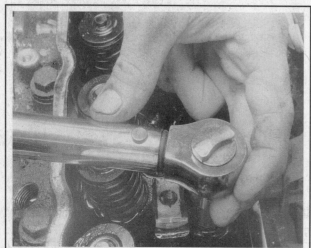

When installing the cylinder head, uniformly tighten the cylinder head bolts in the proper sequence

• Brake booster hose
• Fuel inlet hose
• Fuel outlet hose
• Charcoal canister hose

6. Disconnect and tag all vacuum hoses attached to various engine parts.

7. Disconnect the following wire connectors:
• The alternator connector and B terminal
• The air flow meter connector
• The solenoid resistor connector
• Water temperature sending unit connector
• The oil pressure switch connector
• The ignition connectors at the distributor
• The air conditioning compressor connector, if so equipped
• The air conditioning idle up solenoid connector, if so equipped
• The vacuum switching valve, if so equipped
• The coolant temperature switch

8. Disconnect and tag all cables attached to various engine parts.

9. Remove the air cleaner hose.

10. Unbolt the power steering pump and secure it out of the way.

11. Disconnect the accelerator cable and the throttle cable from the throttle linkage.

12. Remove the throttle body from the air intake chamber.

13. Remove the nuts and bolts retaining the EGR valve to the intake manifold. Disconnect the union nut from the exhaust manifold and remove the EGR valve.

14. Disconnect the cold start injector pipe, water by-pass hose and pressure regulator hose.

15. Remove the air intake chamber brackets. Be sure to use a 12 mm socket wrench to remove the rear chamber bracket.

16. Remove the air intake chamber with the air valve.

17. Remove the wire clamp bolt of the fuel injector, disconnect the injector connectors from the injectors.

18. Remove the exhaust manifold bracket, heater pipe bracket, fuel inlet pipe union bolt from the fuel filter and the fuel outlet hose.

19. Remove the spark plugs and spark plug tubes.

20. Remove the cylinder head cover retaining bolts, cover and gasket.

21. Uniformly loosen and remove the 3 bolts and 2 nuts holding the rocker arm assembly in the cylinder head.

22. Remove the pushrods and keep them in their proper order.

23. Uniformly loosen and remove the cylinder head bolts. Lift the cylinder head manifold assembly from the dowels in the block and place it on 2 wooden blocks on a suitable work bench.

To install:

24. Install a small bead of a suitable high temperature silicone sealer to the corners of the cylinder head and engine block mating surface.

25. Place a new cylinder head gasket over the dowel pins on the cylinder block.

26. Position the cylinder head over the dowel pins. Apply a light coat of engine oil on the threads and under the cylinder head bolts.

27. Once the cylinder head is seated properly over the gasket and engine block, install the cylinder head bolts. Tighten the head bolts gradually in 3 passes working from the middle out, to obtain a final torque of 65 ft. lbs. for the 14mm bolts and 14 ft. lbs. for the 12mm bolts.

28. Make sure the pushrods are installed in the correct position.

29. Hold the pushrods in place and install the rocker arm shaft assembly.

30. Uniformly tighten the 3 bolts and 2 nuts in several passes until a final torque of 17 ft. lbs. (24 Nm) is obtained.

31. Using a new gasket, install the rocker arm cover. Tighten the bolts to 13 ft. lbs. (18 Nm).

32. Install the cylinder head cover gaskets, cover and retaining bolts.

33. Install the spark plugs and spark plug tubes.

34. Install the exhaust manifold bracket, heater pipe bracket, fuel inlet pipe union bolt from the fuel filter and the fuel outlet hose.

35. Install the wire clamp bolt to the fuel injector, reconnect the injector connectors to the injectors.

36. Install the air intake chamber with the air valve.

37. Install the air intake chamber brackets. Be sure to use a 12mm socket wrench to install the rear chamber bracket.

38. Reconnect the cold start injector pipe, water bypass hose and pressure regulator hose.

39. Install the EGR valve along with the nuts and bolts retaining the EGR valve to the intake manifold. Reconnect the union nut from the exhaust manifold.

40. Install the throttle body to the air intake chamber.

41. Reconnect the accelerator cable and the throttle cable to the throttle linkage.

42. Install the power steering pump assembly.

43. Reconnect all cables attached to various engine parts.

44. Reconnect the following wire connectors:
• The alternator connector and B terminal
• The air flow meter connector
• The solenoid resistor connector
• Water temperature sending unit connector
• The oil pressure switch connector
• The ignition connectors at the distributor
• The air conditioning compressor connector, if so equipped
• The air conditioning idle up solenoid connector, if so equipped
• The vacuum switching valve, if so equipped
• The coolant temperature switch

45. Reconnect all vacuum hoses attached to various engine parts.

46. Reconnect the following hoses:
• Radiator inlet hoses
• Radiator breather hose
• Reservoir tank hose
• Heater outlet hose
• Radiator outlet hose
• Brake booster hose
• Fuel inlet hose
• Fuel outlet hose
• Charcoal canister hose

47. Install the air cleaner assembly.

48. Refill the coolant system.

49. Install the engine service hole cover.

50. Install the right front seat.

51. Reconnect the negative battery cable.

52. Start the engine. Perform all engine adjustments. Road test the vehicle and then make all final adjustments. Be sure to also check for any leaks and refill fluids as necessary.

CLEANING & INSPECTING

➡Unless you are very familiar with engine rebuilding, it would be less time consuming and more cost efficient to send your old cylinder head out and have it rebuilt by a professional machine shop. Most machine shops guarantee their work and, that way, if there is a problem with the cylinder head rebuild, you can always take it back to be corrected at no extra cost to yourself.

1. With the cylinder head removed from the car engine (see Cylinder Head Removal and Installation). Place the head on a workbench and remove any manifolds that are may be still connected. Remove all rocker arm retaining parts and the rocker arms, if still installed or the camshaft (see Camshaft Removal).

2. Turn the cylinder head over so that the mounting surface is facing up and support evenly on wooden blocks.

When removing nuts, bolts and other parts, place them in a tray or other container

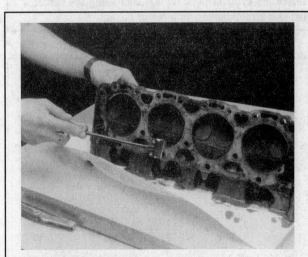

Use a gasket scraper to remove the bulk of the old head gasket from the mating surface

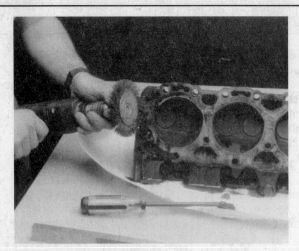

An electric drill equipped with a wire wheel will expedite complete gasket removal

Check the cylinder head for warpage along the center using a straightedge and a feeler gauge

Be sure to check for warpage across the cylinder head at both diagonals

> ## ✳✳ WARNING
>
> **If an aluminum cylinder head, exercise care when cleaning.**

3. Use a scraper and remove all of the gasket material stuck to the head mounting surface. Mount a wire carbon removal brush in an electric drill and clean away the carbon on the valves and head combustion chambers.

4. Use a suitable dye penetrant, check the combustion chamber, intake and exhaust ports, head surfaces and the top of the head for cracks. If cracked, replace the cylinder head.

> ## ✳✳ WARNING
>
> **When scraping or decarbonizing the cylinder head, take care not to damage or nick the gasket mounting surface.**

5. Number the valve heads with a permanent felt-tip marker for cylinder location.

RESURFACING

If the cylinder head is warped, resurfacing by a machine shop is required. Place a straightedge across the gasket surface of the head. Using feeler gauges, determine the clearance at the center and along the length between the head and straightedge. Measure clearance at the center and along the lengths of both diagonals. If warpage exceeds the following specifications, the cylinder head must be resurfaced.

- Maximum cylinder head warpage: 0.10mm
- Maximum intake manifold surface warpage: 0.10mm
- Maximum exhaust manifold surface warpage:
     5M-GE engine—0.10mm
     7M-GE engine—0.8mm
- Maximum camshaft housing surface warpage: 0.10mm
- Maximum cylinder head (block side) warpage:
     3Y-EC and 4Y-EC engines—0.15mm

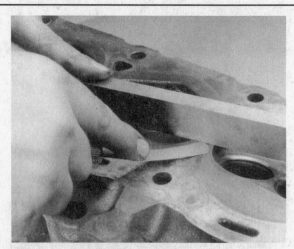

Check the cylinder head for flatness across the head surface

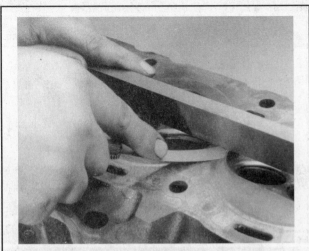
Checks should be made both straight across the cylinder head and at both diagonals

A small magnet will help in removal of the valve keepers

Valves and Springs

REMOVAL & INSTALLATION

1. On the 5M-GE engine, remove the individual rocker arms and valve lash adjusters from the cylinder head. Arrange the rocker arms and lash adjusters in the order in which they were removed.

2. On the 7M-GE engine, remove the camshaft bearing cap bolts in several passes. Remove the camshaft bearing caps, oil seal and camshaft. Remove the valve lifters and shims. Arrange the valve lifters and shims in the order in which they were removed.

3. Block the head on its side, or install a pair of head-holding brackets made especially for valve removal.

4. Use a socket slightly larger than the valve stem and keepers, place the socket over the valve stem and gently hit the socket with a plastic hammer to break loose any varnish buildup.

Be careful not to lose the valve keepers

Use a valve spring compressor tool to relieve spring tension from the valve caps

Once the spring has been removed, the O-ring may be removed from the valve stem

A magnet may be helpful in removing the valve keepers

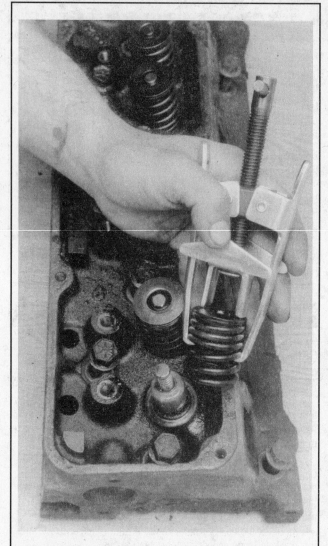

Remove the spring from the valve stem in order to access the seal

5. Remove the valve keepers, retainer, spring shield and valve spring using a valve spring compressor (the locking C-clamp type is the easiest kind to use).

6. Put the parts in a separate container numbered for the cylinder being worked on. Do not mix them with other parts removed.

7. Remove and discard the valve stem oil seal, a new seal will be used at assembly time.

8. Remove the valve from the cylinder head and place, in order, through numbered holes punched in a stiff piece of cardboard or wooden valve holding stick.

9. Use an electric drill and rotary wire brush to clean the intake and exhaust valve ports, combustion chamber and valve seats. In some cases, the carbon will need to be chipped away. Use a blunt pointed drift for carbon chipping, be careful around the valve seat areas.

10. Use a wire valve guide cleaning brush and safe solvent to clean the valve guides.

11. Clean the valves with a revolving wire brush. Heavy carbon deposits may be removed with the blunt drift.

➡**When using a wire brush to clean carbon on the valve ports, valves etc., be sure that the deposits are actually removed, rather than burnished.**

12. Wash and clean all valve spring, keepers, retaining caps etc., in safe solvent.

13. Clean the head with a brush and some safe solvent and wipe dry.

14. Check the head for cracks. Cracks in the cylinder head usually start around an exhaust valve seat because it is the hottest part of the combustion chamber. If a crack is suspected but cannot be detected visually have the area checked with dye penetrate or other method by the machine shop.

15. After all cylinder head parts are reasonably clean check the valve stem-to-guide clearance. If a dial indicator is not on hand, a visual inspection can give you a fairly good idea if the guide, valve stem or both are worn.

16. Insert the valve into the guide until slightly away from the valve seat. Wiggle the valve sideways. A small amount of wobble is normal, excessive wobble means a worn guide or valve stem. If

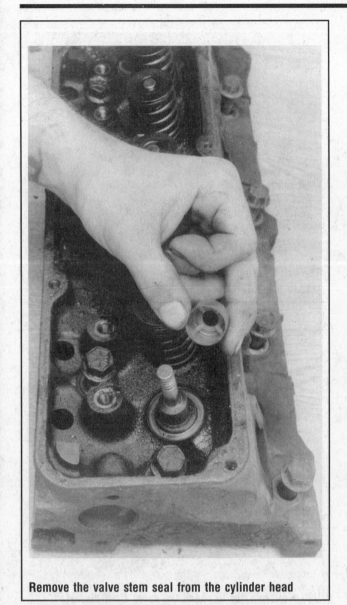

Remove the valve stem seal from the cylinder head

A wire wheel may be used to clean the combustion chambers of carbon deposits

A dial gauge may be used to check valve stem-to-guide clearance

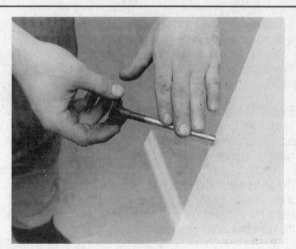

Invert the cylinder head and withdraw the valve from the cylinder head bore

Valve stems may be rolled on a flat surface to check for bends

With the valve spring out of the way, the valve stem seals may now be replaced

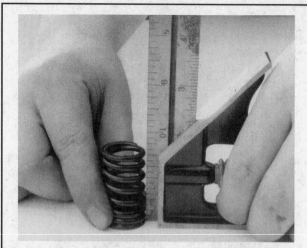

The valve spring should be straight up and down when placed like this

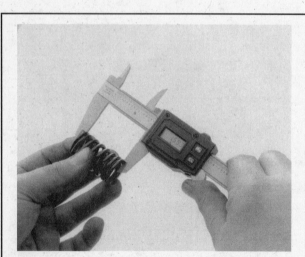

Use a caliper gauge to check the valve spring free-length

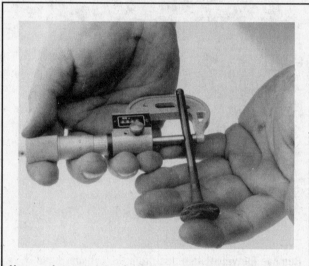

Use a micrometer to check the valve stem diameter

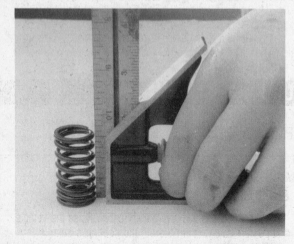

Check the valve spring for squareness on a flat surface; a carpenter's square can be used

a dial indicator is on hand, mount the indicator so that the stem of the valve is at 90° to the valve stem, as close to the valve guide as possible. Move the valve off the seat, and measure the valve guide-to-stem clearance by rocking the stem back and forth to actuate the dial indicator. Measure the valve stem using a micrometer and compare to specifications to determine whether stem or guide wear is causing excessive clearance.

17. The valve guide, if worn, must be repaired before the valve seats can be resurfaced. Some manufacturers supply valves with oversize stems to fit valve guides that are reamed to oversize for repair. The machine shop will be able to handle the guide reaming for you. In some cases, if the guide is not too badly worn, knurling may be all that is required.

18. Reface, or have the valves and valve seats refaced. The valve seats should be a true 45° angle. Remove only enough material to clean up any pits or grooves. Be sure the valve seat is not too wide or narrow. Use a 60° or a 45° grinding wheel to remove material from the bottom of the seat for raising and a 30° or a 45° grinding wheel to remove material from the top of the seat to narrow.

19. After all valve and valve seats have been machined, check the remaining valve train parts (springs, retainers, keepers, etc.) for wear. Check the valve springs for straightness and tension.

20. Hand lap the valve and valve seat with an abrasive compound. After hand lapping, clean the valve and valve seat.

21. Insert the valves into the cylinder head valve guides. Make sure that the valves are installed in the correct order.

22. Install the valve spring seats and new seals. Install the springs and spring retainers on the valves.

23. Block the head on its side, or install a pair of head-holding brackets made especially for valve removal. Using a valve spring compressor tool, compress the valve springs and place 2 keepers around the valve stem. Tap the valve stem lightly to assure the proper fit.

24. On the 7M-GE engine, install the camshaft, oil seal, bearing caps and bearing cap bolts in several passes to obtain a final torque of 14 ft. lbs. (20 Nm). Install the valve lifters and shims. In the same order in which they were removed.

25. On the 5M-GE engine, install the individual rocker arms and valve lash adjusters to the cylinder head. In the same order in which they were removed.

26. Reassemble the head in the reverse order of disassembly using new valve guide seals and lubricating the valve stems. Check the valve spring installed height, shim or replace as necessary.

Valve Guides

REPLACEMENT

◆ **See Figures 117, 118 and 119**

1. Heat the cylinder head to 176–212°F (80–100°C), evenly, before beginning the replacement procedure.

2. Use a brass rod to break the valve guide off above its snapring. (See the illustration).

3. Drive out the valve guide, toward the combustion chamber.

4. Heat the cylinder head to 176–212°F (80–100°C), evenly, before beginning the replacement procedure.

5. Install a snapring on the new valve guide. Apply liquid

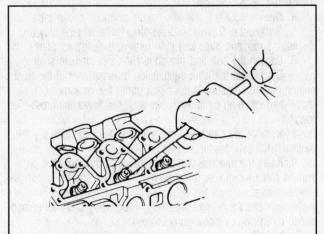

Fig. 117 Breaking off the valve guide with a hammer and brass rod

Fig. 118 Drive out the valve guide, toward the combustion chamber

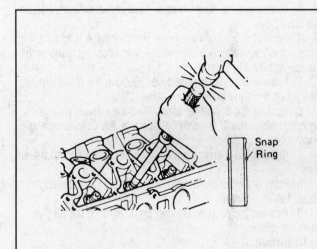

Fig. 119 Drive in the valve guide until the snapring contacts the cylinder head

sealer. Drive in the valve guide until the snapring contacts the head. Use the tool previously described.

6. Measure the guide bore. If the stem-to-guide clearance is below specification, ream it out, using a valve guide reamer.

Oil Pan

REMOVAL & INSTALLATION

5M-GE Engine
◆ **See Figure 120**

1. Disconnect the negative battery cable. Raise the vehicle and support it safely. Drain the oil and cooling system.

2. Remove the air cleaner assembly. Mark any disconnected lines and/or hoses for easy reassembly. Remove the oil level gauge.

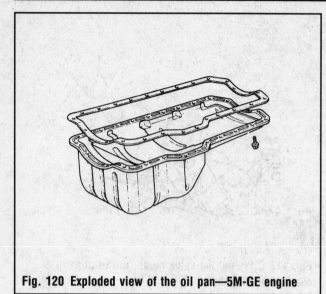

Fig. 120 Exploded view of the oil pan—5M-GE engine

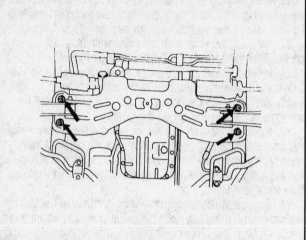

Fig. 121 Unbolt and remove the front suspension crossmember prior to oil pan removal—7M-GE engine

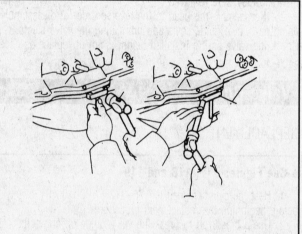

Fig. 122 If the oil pan is hard to remove once the bolts are removed, pry or tap the pan slightly to loosen

3. Disconnect the upper radiator hose at the radiator. Loosen the drive belts.

4. Remove the fan shroud bolts. Remove the 4 fluid coupling flange attaching nuts, then remove the fluid coupling along with the fan and the fan shroud.

5. Remove the engine undercover. Remove the exhaust pipe clamp bolt from the exhaust pipe stay.

6. Remove the 2 stiffener plates from the exhaust pipe. If equipped with manual transmission, remove the clutch housing undercover.

7. Remove the 4 engine mount bolts from each side of the engine.

8. Place a jack under the transmission and raise the engine about 1¾ in. (45mm).

9. Remove the oil pan retaining bolts. Remove the oil pan from the engine.

To install:

10. Apply a suitable silicone sealer to the new oil pan gasket.

11. Install the oil pan over the block, install the retaining bolts and tighten the bolts to 57–82 inch lbs. (5–10 Nm). Lower the engine and install the 4 motor mount nuts.

12. Install the flywheel housing under cover.

13. Install the exhaust pipe clamp bolt to the pipe stay bracket.

14. Install the 2 stiffener plates. Install the engine undercover assembly.

15. Install the fan shroud together with the fluid coupling (fan clutch) to the engine compartment. Install the fan clutch on the pulley with the 4 nuts. Install the 4 fan shroud bolts.

16. Install the drive belt and adjust the fan belt to obtain the proper tension.

17. Connect the upper radiator hose. Install the air connector pipe with the air cleaner hoses.

18. Refill the coolant system and the engine oil.

19. Start the engine and check for leaks.

7M-GE Engine

▶ **See Figures 121 and 122**

1. Disconnect the negative battery cable and drain the cooling system.

2. Raise the vehicle and support it with safety stands. Remove the engine under cover and drain the oil.

3. Disconnect the front exhaust pipe at the manifold and at the main tube and remove it.

4. Disconnect the automatic transmission oil cooler pipe.

5. Remove the 9 bolts, ground strap, exhaust pipe stay and the engine rear end plate and then remove the stiffener plates.

6. Loosen the bolt and disconnect the intermediate shaft.

7. Disconnect the front suspension crossmember at the front engine mounts. Position a floor jack under the crossmember, remove the remaining mounting bolts and then lower the crossmember.

8. Remove the pan retaining bolts and then carefully pry the pan from the cylinder block.

9. Raise the transmission housing with a suitable jack, be sure to place a block of wood between the jack and the transmission housing.

10. Remove the oil pan assembly. Thoroughly clean all components to remove all loose gasket material.

To install:

11. Apply a suitable silicone sealer to the new oil pan gasket.

12. Install the oil pan over the block, install the retaining bolts and tighten the bolts to 9 ft. lbs. (13 Nm).

13. Install the front suspension member to the body and tighten the bolts to 94 ft. lbs. (127 Nm).

14. Install the 4 bolts holding the engine mounting to suspension member. Tighten the bolts 27 ft. lbs. (37 Nm).

15. Connect the intermediate shaft with the retaining bolt. Tighten the bolt to 26 ft. lbs. 35 Nm).

16. Install the engine rear end plate, stiffener plates, ground strap and exhaust pipe stay bracket.

17. Install the oil cooler pipe at the automatic transmission.

18. Install the exhaust pipe along with a new gasket and the retaining nuts. Tighten the nuts to 46 ft. lbs. (62 Nm). Connect the exhaust pipe with the 2 bolts and nuts and torque them to 32 ft. lbs. (43 Nm). Install exhaust manifold clamp with bolt. Connect the rubber ring.

19. Install the engine under cover and lower the vehicle.

20. Fill the engine with the proper amount of engine oil.

21. Start the engine and check for leaks. Shut the engine off and recheck the oil level, add as necessary.

3Y-EC and 4Y-EC Engines

1. Raise and support the vehicle safely.
2. Drain the engine oil.
3. Remove the right and left stiffener plates.
4. Disconnect the connector of the oil sensor, if necessary remove the oil level sensor.
5. Remove the oil pan retaining bolts. Insert a suitable tool between the engine block and the oil pan, and pry the oil pan loose from the engine block. Be careful not to damage the oil pan flange. Thoroughly clean all components to remove all loose gasket material.

To install:

6. Apply a suitable silicone sealer to the new oil pan gasket.
7. Install the oil pan over the block, install the retaining bolts and tighten the bolts to 9 ft. lbs. (13 Nm).
8. Install a new gasket along with the oil level sensor with the 4 bolts. Tighten the bolts 48 inch lbs. (5 Nm). Install the protector of the oil level sensor with the 2 bolts. Be careful not to drop the oil level sensor when installing it.
9. Connect the connector of the oil level sensor.
10. Install the right and left stiffener plates. Lower the vehicle.
11. Refill the engine with the proper amount of engine oil.
12. Start the engine and check for leaks. Shut the engine off and recheck the oil level, add as necessary.

Oil Pump

REMOVAL & INSTALLATION

5M-GE Engine

1. Disconnect the negative battery cable. Raise the vehicle and support it safely. Drain the oil and cooling system.
2. Remove the air cleaner assembly. Mark any disconnected lines and/or hoses for easy reassembly. Remove the oil level gauge.
3. Disconnect the upper radiator hose at the radiator. Loosen the drive belts.
4. Remove the fan shroud bolts. Remove the 4 fluid coupling flange attaching nuts, then remove the fluid coupling along with the fan and the fan shroud.

5. Remove the engine undercover. Remove the exhaust pipe clamp bolt from the exhaust pipe stay.

6. Remove the 2 stiffener plates from the exhaust pipe. If equipped with manual transmission, remove the clutch housing undercover.

7. Remove the 4 engine mount bolts from each side of the engine.

8. Place a jack under the transmission and raise the engine about 1¾ in. (45mm).

9. Remove the oil pan retaining bolts. Remove the oil pan from the engine.

10. Remove the oil pump union bolt and nut and disconnect the oil pump outlet.

11. Remove the oil pump mounting bolt and remove the oil pump.

To install:

12. Install the oil pump and mounting bolt. Tighten the bolt to 15–17 ft. lbs. (20–23 Nm). It may be a good idea to prime the pump with clean engine oil before installing it onto the engine.

13. Install the oil pipe with gasket, lock washer and union nut. Tighten the oil pipe union bolt 22–28 ft. lbs. (30–39 Nm) and the union nut to 26–32 ft. lbs. (35–44 Nm).

14. Apply a suitable silicone sealer to the new oil pan gasket.

15. Install the oil pan over the block, install the retaining bolts and tighten the bolts to 57–82 inch lbs. (5–10 Nm). Lower the engine and install the 4 motor mount nuts.

16. Install the flywheel housing under cover.

17. Install the exhaust pipe clamp bolt to the pipe stay bracket.

18. Install the 2 stiffener plates. Install the engine undercover assembly.

19. Install the fan shroud together with the fluid coupling (fan clutch) to the engine compartment. Install the fan clutch on the pulley with the 4 nuts. Install the 4 fan shroud bolts.

20. Install the drive belt and adjust the fan belt to obtain the proper tension.

21. Connect the upper radiator hose. Install the air connector pipe with the air cleaner hoses.

22. Refill the coolant system and the engine oil.

23. Start the engine and check for leaks, repair as necessary.

7M-GE Engine

◆ See Figure 123

1. Disconnect the negative battery cable and drain the cooling system.

2. Raise the vehicle and support it with safety stands. Remove the engine under cover and drain the oil.

3. Disconnect the front exhaust pipe at the manifold and at the main tube and remove it.

4. Disconnect the automatic transmission oil cooler pipe.

5. Remove the 9 bolts, ground strap, exhaust pipe stay and the engine rear end plate and then remove the stiffener plates.

6. Loosen the bolt and disconnect the intermediate shaft.

7. Disconnect the front suspension crossmember at the front engine mounts. Position a floor jack under the crossmember, remove the remaining mounting bolts and then lower the crossmember.

8. Attach an engine hoist to the engine. Disconnect the engine mounts and raise the engine approximately 2 inches.

9. Remove the pan retaining bolts and then carefully pry the pan from the cylinder block.

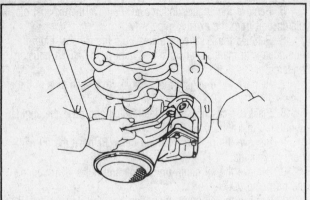

Fig. 123 With the oil pan removed, unbolt the oil pump from the engine

10. Raise the transmission housing with a suitable jack, be sure to place a block of wood between the jack and the transmission housing.

11. Remove the oil pan assembly. Thoroughly clean all components to remove all loose gasket material.

12. Unstake the lock washer on the oil pump outlet pump. Loosen the union nut. Remove the union bolt, lock washer, oil pump outlet pipe and gasket.

13. Remove the oil pump retaining bolt and remove the oil pump.

To install:

14. Install the oil pump with the retaining bolt. Tighten the retaining bolt to 16 ft. lbs. (22 Nm).

15. Install the oil pump outlet pipe with a new lock washer, gasket, the union bolt and nut. Tighten the union bolt and nut to 25 ft. lbs. (34 Nm). Stake the lock washer.

16. Apply a suitable silicone sealer to the new oil pan gasket.

17. Install the oil pan over the block, install the retaining bolts and tighten the bolts to 9 ft. lbs. (13 Nm).

18. Install the front suspension member to the body and tighten the bolts to 94 ft. lbs. (127 Nm).

19. Install the 4 bolts holding the engine mounting to suspension member. Tighten the bolts 27 ft. lbs. (37 Nm).

20. Connect the intermediate shaft with the retaining bolt. Tighten the bolt to 26 ft. lbs. 35 Nm).

21. Install the engine rear end plate, stiffener plates, ground strap and exhaust pipe stay bracket.

22. Install the oil cooler pipe at the automatic transmission.

23. Install the exhaust pipe along with a new gasket and the retaining nuts. Tighten the nuts to 46 ft. lbs. (62 Nm). Connect the exhaust pipe with the 2 bolts and nuts and torque them to 32 ft. lbs. (43 Nm). Install exhaust manifold clamp with bolt. Connect the rubber ring.

24. Install the engine under cover and lower the vehicle.

25. Fill the engine with the proper amount of engine oil.

26. Start the engine and check for leaks. Shut the engine off and recheck the oil level, add as necessary.

3Y-EC and 4Y-EC Engines

1. Raise and support the vehicle safely.
2. Drain the engine oil.
3. Remove the right and left stiffener plates.
4. Disconnect the connector of the oil sensor, if necessary remove the oil level sensor.

5. Remove the oil pan retaining bolts. Insert a suitable tool between the engine block and the oil pan, and pry the oil pan loose from the engine block. Be careful not to damage the oil pan flange. Thoroughly clean all components to remove all loose gasket material.

6. Remove the oil pump retaining bolt and remove the pump.

To install:

7. To install the oil pump, align the governor shaft protrusion of the integrated ignition assembly with the drive rotor slot of the oil pump. Install the oil pump and retaining bolt. Tighten the retaining bolt to 13 ft. lbs. (18 Nm).

8. Apply a suitable silicone sealer to the new oil pan gasket. Install the oil pan over the block, install the retaining bolts and tighten the bolts to 9 ft. lbs. (13 Nm).

9. Install a new gasket along with the oil level sensor with the 4 bolts. Tighten the bolts 48 inch lbs. (5 Nm). Install the protector of the oil level sensor with the 2 bolts. Be careful not to drop the oil level sensor when installing it.

10. Connect the connector of the oil level sensor.

11. Install the right and left stiffener plates. Lower the vehicle.

12. Refill the engine with the proper amount of engine oil.

13. Start the engine and check for leaks. Shut the engine off and recheck the oil level, add as necessary.

Timing Chain and Sprockets, Cover and Seal

REMOVAL & INSTALLATION

3Y-EC and 4Y-EC Engines

▶ **See Figures 124 thru 130**

1. Disconnect the negative battery cable.
2. Remove the right front seat.
3. Remove the engine service hole cover.
4. Drain the coolant.
5. Disconnect the radiator inlet hoses, radiator breather hose, reservoir tank hose and remove the radiator assembly.
6. Remove the fan assembly along with the water pump, if needed, as previously outlined.
7. Remove the distributor assembly as previously outlined.
8. Remove the cold start injector.
9. Remove the crankshaft pulley bolt and, using a suitable pulley puller, remove the crankshaft pulley.
10. Remove the timing chain cover retaining bolts and pry off the timing chain cover.
11. Remove the 2 timing chain tensioner bolts and remove the chain tensioner.
12. Using a suitable camshaft gear holding tool, remove the camshaft sprocket bolt.
13. Using a suitable puller, uniformly remove the camshaft sprocket together with the crankshaft sprocket and chain.
14. Remove the timing chain cover seal as follows:
    a. Using a suitable punch and hammer, tap out the old oil seal from the cover.
    b. Using a suitable seal driver and hammer, drive in a new oil seal until the surface is flush with the edge of the timing chain cover.
    c. Apply some high temperature multipurpose grease to the lip of the oil seal.

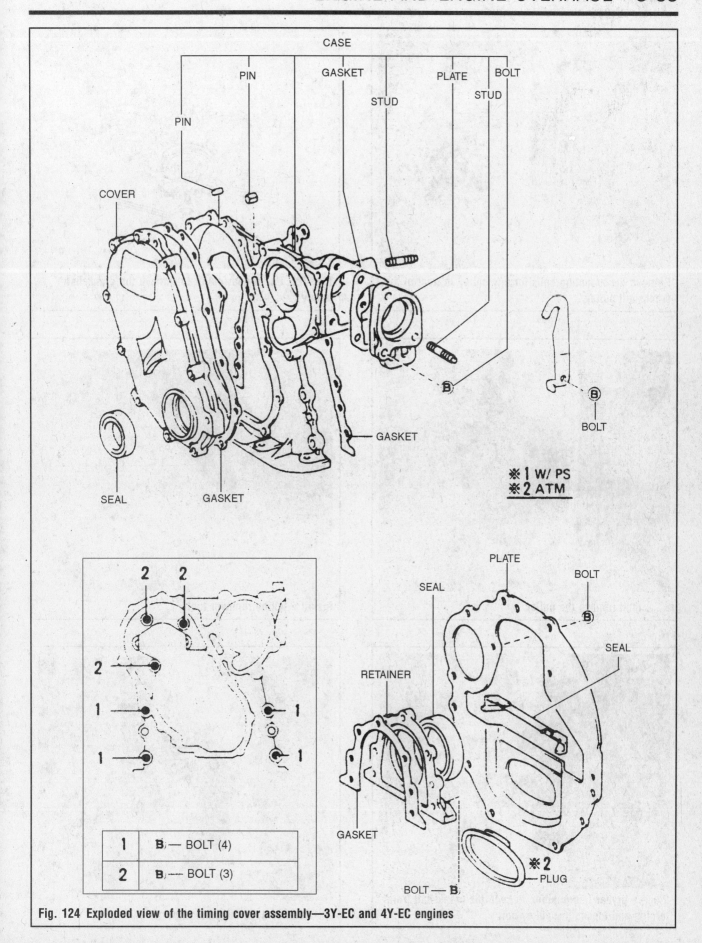

Fig. 124 Exploded view of the timing cover assembly—3Y-EC and 4Y-EC engines

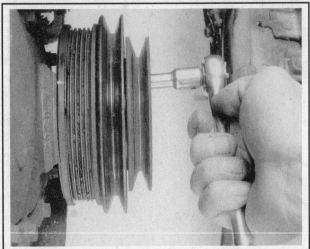

Remove the mounting bolts for any pulley in front of the crankshaft pulley . . .

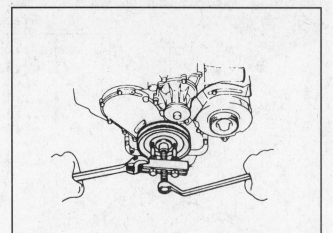

Fig. 125 Use a gear puller to remove the crankshaft pulley

. . . then remove the pulley

Install a pulley remover tool . . .

Place a prybar into position to keep the crankshaft from turning and loosen the pulley bolt

. . . and remove the crankshaft pulley

Loosen and remove the timing chain cover bolts

Place a mark on the timing chain and camshaft sprocket to aid in alignment for installation

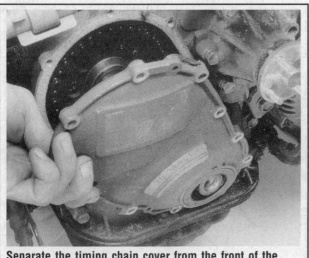

Separate the timing chain cover from the front of the engine—3Y-EC and 4Y-EC engines

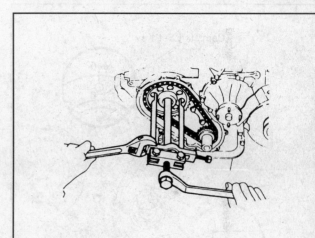

Fig. 127 Using a puller, remove the camshaft sprocket—3Y-EC and 4Y-EC engines

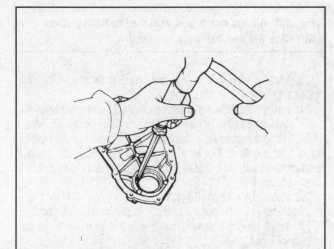

Fig. 126 A hammer and seal driver are required to pop the seal out of the timing cover

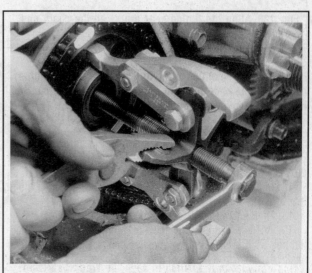

Place a gear remover tool on the camshaft sprocket

Remove the camshaft and crankshaft sprockets along with the timing chain as an assembly

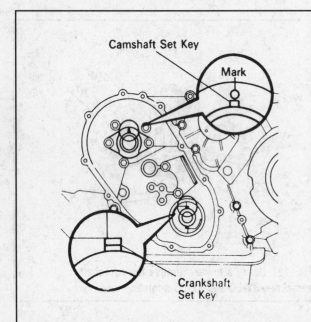

Fig. 128 Align the timing gear marks on the chain and sprocket—3Y-EC and 4Y-EC engines

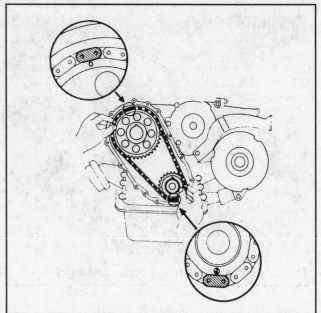

Fig. 129 Install the timing chain and sprockets as an assembly to the front of the engine—3Y-EC and 4Y-EC engines

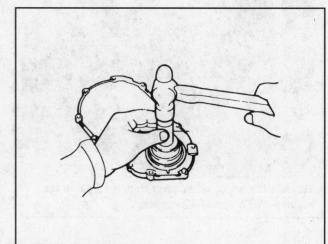

Fig. 130 Always use a new seal for the timing cover when the old one has been removed

➥If the timing chain cover is still attached to the engine, use a suitable seal puller to remove the seal and use the rest of the above procedure to finish the job.

To install:

15. Set the key of the crankshaft sprocket facing upward.

16. Align the set key of the camshaft sprocket with the mark on the thrust plate.

17. Install the sprocket onto the timing chain. Align the timing marks of the timing chain and sprocket.

18. Uniformly install the chain together with the sprockets.

19. Apply a light coat of engine oil on the threads and under the bolt head of the camshaft sprocket bolt. Using a suitable camshaft gear holding tool, install the camshaft sprocket bolt. Tighten it to 67 ft. lbs. (90 Nm).

20. Install the chain tensioner with the 2 bolts and tighten the bolts to 13 ft. lbs. (18 Nm).

21. Install a new timing chain cover gasket and install the chain cover and bolts. Tighten the bolts to 52 inch lbs. (6 Nm).

22. Using a plastic-faced hammer, tap in the crankshaft pulley. Apply a light coat of engine oil on the threads and under the bolt head of the pulley bolt. Install the bolt and tighten the bolt to specifications.

23. Install the cold start injector.

24. Install the distributor assembly as previously outlined.

25. Install the fan assembly along with the water pump as previously outlined.

26. Install the radiator assembly and reconnect the radiator inlet hoses, radiator breather hose and reservoir tank hose.

27. Refill the coolant system.

28. Reconnect the negative battery cable. Connect a timing light and tachometer.

29. Start the engine and set the ignition timing. If the engine is hard to start, have some one turn the distributor left and right very slowly until the engine starts. Once this has happened, use your timing light to readjust the timing properly. Recheck the idle speed adjustment. Check for leaks and add coolant as necessary.

30. Install the engine service hole cover and install the right seat.

Timing Belt, Pulleys, Cover and Seal

REMOVAL & INSTALLATION

5M-GE Engine

▶ **See Figures 131 thru 141**

1. Disconnect the negative battery cable.
2. Remove the air cleaner assembly.

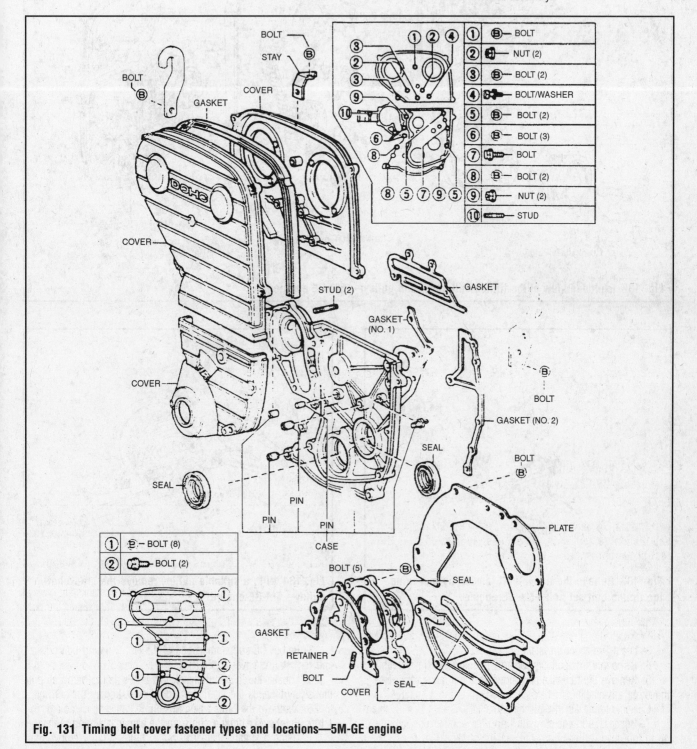

Fig. 131 Timing belt cover fastener types and locations—5M-GE engine

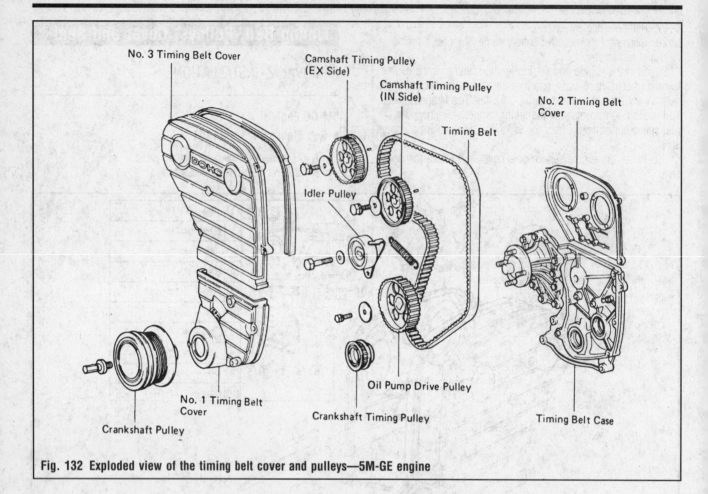

No. 3 Timing Belt Cover

Camshaft Timing Pulley
(EX Side)

Camshaft Timing Pulley
(IN Side)

No. 2 Timing Belt
Cover

Timing Belt

Idler Pulley

DOHC

Oil Pump Drive Pulley

No. 1 Timing Belt
Cover

Crankshaft Timing Pulley

Timing Belt Case

Crankshaft Pulley

Fig. 132 Exploded view of the timing belt cover and pulleys—5M-GE engine

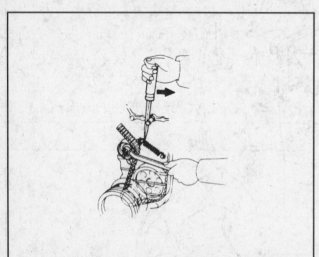

Fig. 133 Relieve the timing belt tension by loosening the timing belt set bolt—5M-GE engine

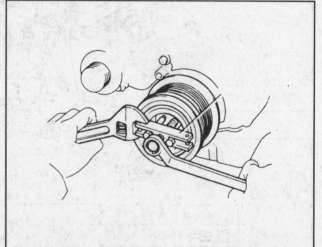

Fig. 134 With a suitable puller, remove the crankshaft pulley—5M-GE engine

3. Drain the cooling system.

4. Remove the upper radiator hose. Loosen the drive belts.

5. Remove the fan assembly along with the fan shroud. Remove the drive belts.

6. Remove the air intake connector.

7. Rotate the engine so as to bring the number one cylinder up to top dead center of its compression stroke.

8. Remove the retaining bolts of the No. 3 timing belt cover and remove the cover and gasket.

9. Loosen the idler pulley set bolt of the timing belt and shift the pulley towards the alternator side. Finger-tighten the set bolt and then relieve the timing belt tension.

10. Remove the timing belt from the camshaft timing pulleys.

11. Using a suitable camshaft pulley holding tool, remove the

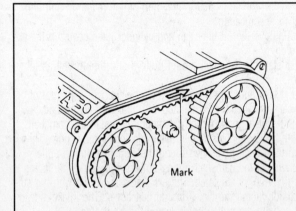

Fig. 135 Note the direction of rotation on the timing belt, and be sure to install the belt in that same direction

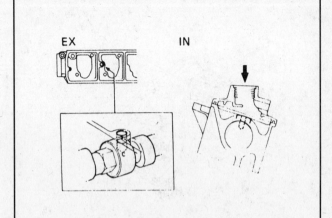

Fig. 138 Check the match hole on the No. 2 journal of the camshaft housing, and align it with that of the camshaft—5M-GE engine

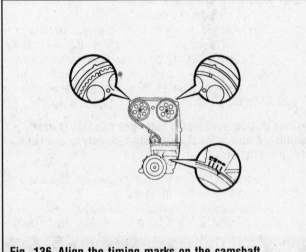

Fig. 136 Align the timing marks on the camshaft pulleys—5M-GE engine

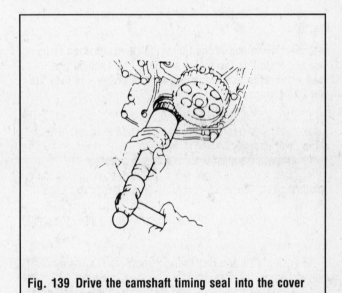

Fig. 139 Drive the camshaft timing seal into the cover

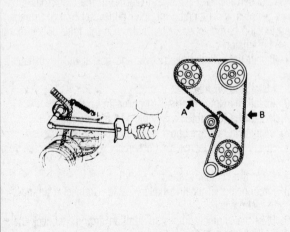

Fig. 137 Installing the timing belt—5M-GE engine

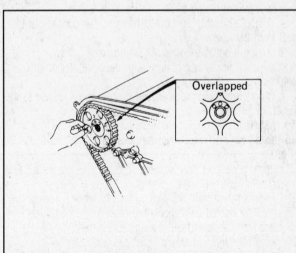

Fig. 140 The 3 pin hole locations on the camshaft and timing pulleys—5M-GE engine

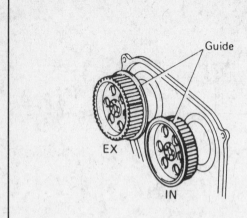

Fig. 141 Camshaft timing pulley guide locations—5M-GE engines

camshaft pulley set bolts and remove the pulleys along with the match pin.

➡**Do not make use of the timing belt tension when removing and installing the pulley set bolt. The exhaust and intake sides each use a different type of pulley and they are not interchangeable.**

12. Using a suitable crankshaft pulley holding tool, remove the crankshaft pulley retaining bolt. Using a suitable puller, remove the crankshaft pulley.

13. Remove the bracket of the cooler compressor.

14. Take a piece of chalk and mark the direction of rotation on the timing belt. Be sure to install the timing belt in this same direction.

15. Remove the No. 1 timing belt cover and remove the timing belt.

16. Remove the idler pulley and tension spring.

17. Using a suitable gear puller, remove the crankshaft timing pulley. Remove the seal behind the pulley at this time.

18. Using a suitable tool, hold the oil pump drive shaft gear still and remove the retaining bolt. Remove the gear.

19. Remove the timing chain cover seal as follows:

a. Using a suitable punch and hammer, tap out the old oil seal from the cover.

b. Using a suitable seal driver and hammer, drive in a new oil seal until the surface is flush with the edge of the timing chain cover.

c. Apply some high temperature multi-purpose grease to the lip of the oil seal.

To install:

20. Install the oil pump drive gear and tighten the 16 ft. lbs. (22 Nm).

21. Using a suitable seal installer, install a new crankshaft timing gear seal. Install the gear.

22. Temporarily install the idler pulley and tension spring.

23. If using the old belt, check the rotation direction chalk mark placed on the timing belt during disassembly.

24. Install the timing belt on the crankshaft pulley.

25. Install the No. 1 timing belt cover (lower cover).

26. Install the bracket of the cooler compressor.

27. Install the crankshaft pulley and pulley retaining bolt and tighten to specification.

28. Remove the oil filler cap and cylinder head cover on the exhaust side.

29. Install the camshaft timing pulleys and timing belt as follows:

a. Make sure that the match hole on the No. 2 journal of the camshaft housing is aligned with that of the camshaft.

b. If not aligned properly, temporarily install the camshaft timing pulley and insert the match pin into the pin hole. Then align the match holes by turning the camshaft timing pulley.

c. Install the camshaft timing pulleys with the guide facing the direction as indicated. The exhaust side will be with the pulley guide facing the No. 2 timing belt cover. The intake side will be with the pulley guide facing the front side.

d. Align the matchmarks of the No. 2 timing belt cover with those of the camshaft timing pulleys and of the crankshaft pulley. Be sure that the No. 1 cylinder is set to top dead center on its compression stroke, which it should be if the engine has not been disturbed.

e. Install the timing belt with the belt having the proper tension between the crankshaft timing pulley and the camshaft timing pulley on the exhaust side.

f. Loosen the idler pulley set bolt and stretch the timing belt. Tighten the idler pulley set bolt to 36 ft. lbs. (49 Nm). Be sure that the timing belt tension is applied evenly throughout the belt.

g. There are 3 pin holes on the camshaft and timing pulleys. Select the one overlapped hole and insert the pin into it.

➡**If there is no overlapping hole, find one that is nearly overlapped and rotate the crankshaft slightly to overlap it and insert the pin.**

h. The crankshaft pulley angle can be adjusted approximately 3° by changing the pin hole to the next one.

i. Using a suitable camshaft pulley holding tool, install the camshaft pulley set bolts and torque them to 50 ft. lbs. (69 Nm).

✳✳ WARNING

Do not disturb the timing belt tension when tightening the camshaft pulley bolt.

j. Loosen the idler pulley set bolt. Turn the crankshaft clockwise 2 times and retighten the idler pulley set bolt. If timing belt tension is too loose or too tight, use the idler pulley to adjust the tension.

31. Install the cylinder head cover and gasket on the exhaust side.

32. Install the oil filler cap.

33. Install the No. 3 timing belt cover and gasket.

34. Install the fan clutch assembly and fan shroud.

35. Install the radiator upper hose. Install the drive belts.

36. Install the air cleaner case assembly with the air intake connector.

37. Refill the coolant system.

38. Reconnect the negative battery cable. Connect a timing light and tachometer.

39. Start the engine and set the ignition timing. Recheck the idle speed adjustment. Check for leaks and add coolant as necessary.

7M-GE Engine

♦ **See Figures 142, 143 and 144**

1. Disconnect the negative battery cable.
2. Remove the air cleaner assembly.
3. Drain the cooling system.
4. Remove the radiator hoses and remove the radiator as previously outlined.
5. Disconnect and tag the spark plug wires and remove the spark plugs.
6. Remove the water outlet retaining bolts and remove the water outlet.
7. Remove the air conditioning compressor belt.
8. Remove the timing belt and camshaft timing pulleys as follows:

   a. Remove the 4 bolts from the fluid coupling (fan clutch) flange.

   b. Loosen the fan belt adjusting bolt and nut of the power steering pump.

   c. Remove the fan shroud mounting nuts.

   d. Remove the four bolts, fan clutch, water pump pulley and fan shroud.

   e. Remove the power steering pump belt.

   f. Remove the No. 3 timing cover retaining bolts and nuts. Remove the cover and gasket.

   g. Turn the crankshaft pulley an align its groove with the 0 mark on the No. 1 timing belt cover. If the engine has not been disturbed, the engine should still be in this position.

   h. Check that the alignment marks on the camshaft timing pulleys and the No. 2 timing belt cover are aligned. If not, turn the crankshaft pulley one complete revolution.

   i. Loosen the mount bolt of the idler pulley and shift it to the left as far as it can go. Temporarily tighten the mount bolt thus relieving the tension on the timing belt.

   j. Remove the timing belt from the camshaft timing pulley. Be sure to support the belt so that the meshing of the crankshaft timing pulley and timing belt do not shift. Be careful not to drop anything inside of the timing belt cover. Do not allow the belt to come in contact with oil, water or dust.

➡ **If reusing the timing belt, please mark the direction of rotation before removing it.**

   k. Using a suitable camshaft pulley holding tool, remove the camshaft pulley set bolts and remove the pulleys along with the match pin. Do not make use of the timing belt tension when removing and installing the pulley set bolt.

9. Using a suitable crankshaft pulley holding tool, remove the crankshaft pulley retaining bolt. Using a suitable pulley puller, remove the crankshaft pulley.
10. Remove the pollution system air pipe assembly.
11. Remove the lower timing belt cover retaining bolts and nuts, air conditioning idler pulley bracket, compressor bracket and the lower timing belt cover.
12. Remove the timing belt. Remove the idler pulley and tension spring.
13. Using a suitable gear puller, remove the crankshaft timing pulley. Remove the seal behind the gear at this time.
14. Using a suitable tool, hold the oil pump drive shaft gear still and remove the retaining bolt. Remove the gear.
15. Remove the timing belt cover seal as follows:

    a. Using a suitable punch and hammer, tap out the old oil seal from the cover.

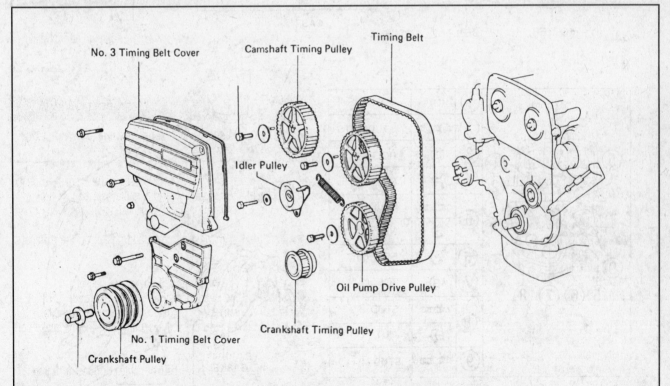

Fig. 142 Exploded view of the timing belt cover, pulleys and timing belt—7M-GE engine

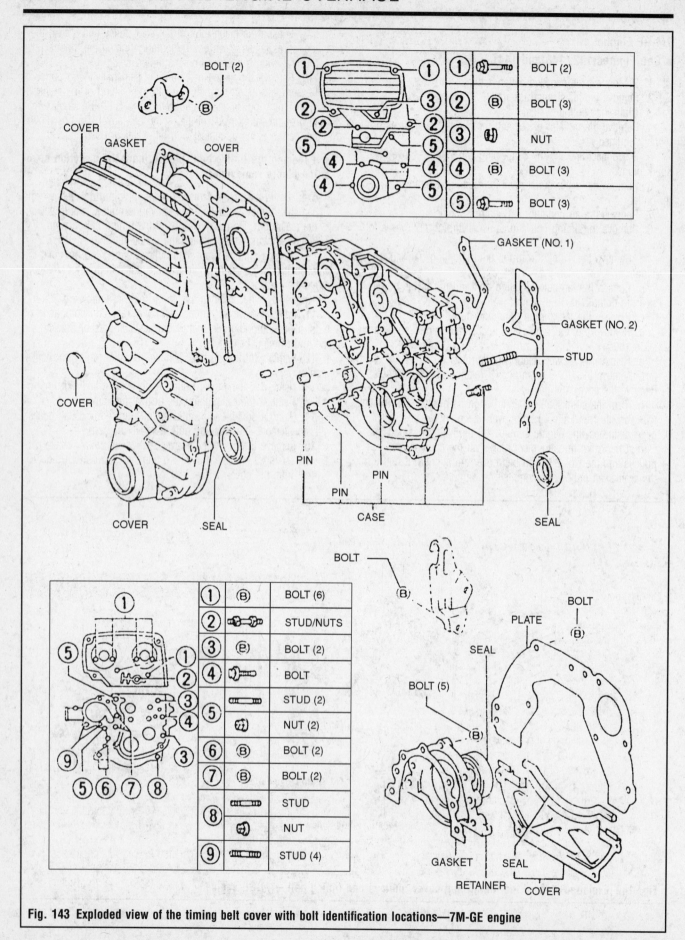

Fig. 143 Exploded view of the timing belt cover with bolt identification locations—7M-GE engine

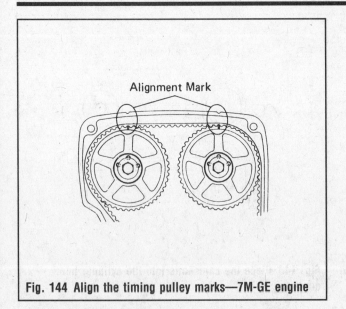

Fig. 144 Align the timing pulley marks—7M-GE engine

b. Using a suitable seal driver and hammer, drive in a new oil seal until the surface is flush with the edge of the timing belt cover.

c. Apply some high temperature multi-purpose grease to the lip of the oil seal.

To install:

16. Install the oil pump drive gear and tighten the 16 ft. lbs. (22 Nm).

17. Using a suitable seal installer, install a new crankshaft timing gear seal. Install the gear.

18. Temporarily install the idler pulley and tension spring.

19. If using the old belt, check the rotation direction chalk mark placed on the timing belt during disassembly.

20. Install the timing belt on the crankshaft pulley.

21. Install the lower timing belt cover, air conditioning idler pulley bracket, compressor bracket and the lower timing belt cover retaining bolts and nuts. Install the pollution system air pipe assembly.

22. Install the crankshaft pulley and pulley retaining bolt and torque to specification.

23. Turn the crankshaft pulley and align its groove with the 0 mark on the lower timing belt cover.

24. Install the camshaft timing pulleys and timing belt as follows:

a. Turn the crankshaft pulley and align its groove with the 0 mark on the No. 1 timing belt cover. If the engine has not been disturbed, the engine should still be in this position.

b. Align the alignment marks on the camshaft timing pulleys and the No. 2 timing belt cover. Install the timing pulley.

c. Install the straight pin into the hole.

d. When replacing the camshaft or the camshaft timing pulley. Always align the center holes of the camshaft and timing pulleys and insert the straight pin. When reusing the camshaft or camshaft timing pulleys, check that the straight pin hole position is in the same position it was at disassembly, insert the straight pin. Install the plate washer and pulley bolt.

e. Using a suitable camshaft pulley holding tool, hold the pulley and tighten the pulley bolts to 36 ft. lbs. (49 Nm).

f. Check that the matchmarks on the camshaft timing pulley are aligned with those on the No. 2 timing belt cover.

g. Install the timing belt to the intake camshaft timing pulley, the exhaust camshaft timing pulley and the idler pulley.

h. Loosen the idler pulley mount bolt until the pulley is moved slightly by the spring tension. Tighten the idler pulley mount bolt to 36 ft. lbs. (49 Nm).

i. Check that the timing belt tension is equal all the way through. Turn the crankshaft pulley 2 revolutions clockwise from TDC to TDC.

j. Check that the alignment marks on the camshaft timing pulleys are aligned with those on the No. 2 timing belt cover.

k. If the marks do not align, remove the belt and install it again.

l. Install the No. 3 timing cover gasket, cover and retaining bolts.

m. Install the power steering pump belt.

n. Install the four bolts, fan clutch, water pump pulley and fan shroud.

o. Install the fan shroud mounting nuts.

p. Tighten the fan belt adjusting bolt and nut of the power steering pump.

q. Install the 4 bolts to the fluid coupling (fan clutch) flange.

35. Install the air conditioning drive belt.

36. Install the thermostat and water outlet along with it retaining bolts.

37. Install the spark plugs and spark plug wires.

38. Install the radiator assembly along with the radiator hoses.

39. Install the drive belts and adjust as necessary.

40. Install the air cleaner case assembly with the air intake connector.

41. Refill the coolant system.

42. Reconnect the negative battery cable. Connect a timing light and tachometer.

43. Start the engine and set the ignition timing. Recheck the idle speed adjustment. Check for leaks and add coolant as necessary.

Camshaft

REMOVAL & INSTALLATION

5M-GE Engine

1. Remove the cylinder head assembly as previously outlined in this section.

2. Remove the cylinder head covers.

3. Remove the No. 1 and No. 2 camshaft housing retaining nuts and remove the housings along with the camshafts.

4. Remove the camshaft housing rear covers by removing the retaining bolts.

5. Squirt clean oil down around the cam journals in the housing, to lubricate the lobes, oil seals and bearings as the cam is removed. Begin to pull the camshaft out of the back of the housing slowly, turning it as you pull. Remove the cam completely.

6. Replace the camshaft housing oil seal as follows:

a. If the camshaft is removed from the camshaft housing, use a suitable prytool and pry out the oil seal from the housing.

b. Install a new seal into the housing using a suitable seal driver tool. Apply a high temperature multi-purpose grease to the oil seal.

c. If the camshaft housing is installed on the cylinder head, using a suitable tool cut off the edge of the oil seal lips.

d. Use a suitable pry tool and pry out the oil seal from the housing. So as not to damage the camshaft, be sure to put some tape around the end of the prytool.

e. Install a new seal into the housing using a suitable seal driver tool. Apply a high temperature multi-purpose grease to the oil seal.

To install:

7. Lubricate the entire camshaft with clean oil. Insert the cam into the housing from the back, and slowly turn it as you push it into the housing. Install new O-rings and the housing end covers.

8. Install new camshaft housing gaskets over the dowel pins in the cylinder head. Position the camshaft housing including the camshafts over the dowels on the cylinder head.

9. Install and tighten the housing nuts and bolts gradually in 3 passes. Tighten the nuts and bolts to 16 ft. lbs. (22 Nm).

10. Install the cylinder head covers.

11. Install the cylinder head assembly as previously outlined in this section.

7M-GE Engine

▶ **See Figure 145 thru 150**

1. Remove the cylinder head assembly as previously outlined in this section.

2. Uniformly loosen and remove the bearing cap bolts in several passes.

3. Remove the camshaft bearing caps, oil seal and camshaft.

To install:

4. Apply a high temperature multi-purpose grease to the lip of the new oil seal. Install the seal onto the camshaft.

5. Apply engine oil to all the bearing journals.

6. Place the camshafts on the cylinder head. The exhaust camshaft has a distributor drive gear.

7. Apply a suitable sealer to the No. 1 bearing caps. Install the No. 1 bearing cap immediately after applying the sealant.

8. Place the bearing caps on each journal with the front marks pointing toward the front and in numerical order from the front side.

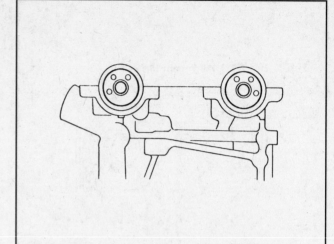

Fig. 146 Place the camshafts into the cylinder head correctly

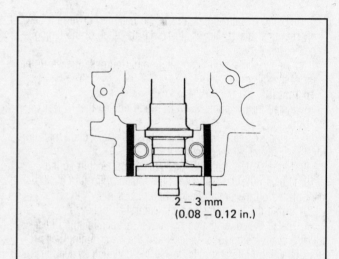

Fig. 147 Apply sealer to the No. 1 bearing cap—7M-GE engine

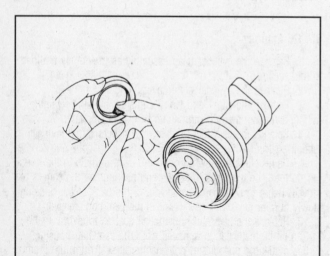

Fig. 145 Apply multi-purpose grease on the new camshaft seals—7M-GE engine

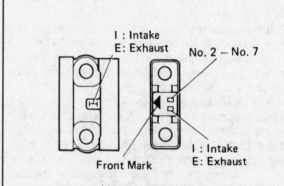

Fig. 148 Place the bearing caps with their front marks pointing toward the front, and in numerical order—7M-GE engine

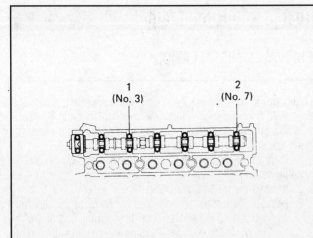

Fig. 149 Uniformly tighten No. 3 and No. 7 bearing caps—7M-GE engine

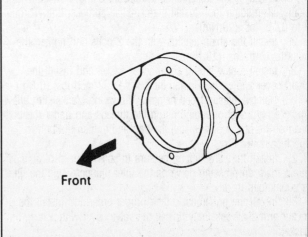

Fig. 151 Install the thrust plate with the front facing as shown—3Y-EC and 4Y-EC engines

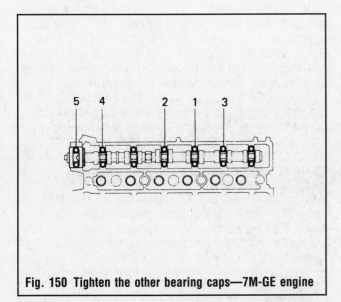

Fig. 150 Tighten the other bearing caps—7M-GE engine

9. Temporarily install the bearing cap retaining bolts and tighten them in several passes.
10. Using a suitable seal driver, tap in the camshaft oil seal.
11. Uniformly tighten the No. 3 and No. 7 bearing cap bolts in several passes to obtain a final torque of 14 ft. lbs. (20 Nm).
12. Uniformly tighten the other bearing cap retaining bolts in several passes until a final torque of 14 ft. lbs. (20 Nm) is obtained.
13. Install the cylinder head assembly as previously outlined in this section.

3Y-EC and 4Y-EC Engines
♦ See Figure 151

1. Disconnect the negative battery cable.
2. Remove the right front seat.
3. Remove the engine service hole cover.
4. Drain the coolant.
5. Disconnect the radiator inlet hoses, radiator breather hose, reservoir tank hose and remove the radiator assembly.

6. Remove the fan assembly along with the water pump as previously outlined.
7. Remove the distributor assembly as previously outlined.
8. Remove the cold start injector.
9. Remove the valve cover and gasket. Remove the rocker shaft assembly and pushrods. Be sure to keep them in their proper order.
10. Remove the 8 valve lifters with a magnet or suitable lifter removal tool.
11. Remove the crankshaft pulley bolt and using a suitable pulley puller, remove the crankshaft pulley.
12. Remove the timing chain cover retaining bolts and pry off the timing chain cover.
13. Remove the 2 timing chain tensioner bolts and remove the chain tensioner.
14. Using a suitable camshaft gear holding tool, remove the camshaft sprocket bolt.
15. Using a suitable puller, uniformly remove the camshaft sprocket together with the crankshaft sprocket and chain.
16. Remove the vibration damper retaining bolts and remove the damper.
17. Remove the camshaft thrust plate retaining bolts and remove the thrust plate.
18. Squirt clean oil down around the cam journals in the housing, to lubricate the lobes, oil seals and bearings as the cam is removed. Begin to pull the camshaft out of the cylinder head slowly, turning it as you pull. Remove the cam completely.
To install:
19. Lubricate the entire camshaft with clean oil. Insert the cam into the engine block and slowly turn it as you push it into the block. Install the thrust plate with the 2 retaining bolts and torque them to 13 ft. lbs. (18 Nm).
20. Install the vibration damper and retaining bolts. Tighten the bolts to 13 ft. lbs. (18 Nm).
21. Set the key of the crankshaft sprocket facing upward.
22. Align the set key of the camshaft sprocket with the mark on the thrust plate.
23. Install the sprocket onto the timing chain. Align the timing marks of the timing chain and sprocket.
24. Uniformly install the chain together with the sprockets.
25. Apply a light coat of engine oil on the threads and under

the bolt head of the camshaft sprocket bolt. Using a suitable camshaft gear holding tool, install the camshaft sprocket bolt. Torque it to 67 ft. lbs. (90 Nm).

26. Install the chain tension with the 2 bolts and tighten the bolts to 13 ft. lbs. (18 Nm).

27. Install a new timing chain cover gasket and install the chain cover and bolts. Tighten the bolts to 52 inch lbs. (6 Nm).

28. Using a plastic-faced hammer, tap in the crankshaft pulley. Apply a light coat of engine oil on the threads and under the bolt head of the pulley bolt. Install the bolt and tighten the bolt to specifications.

29. Install the valve lifters (be sure to soak them in oil and pump them up pressing down on the lifter plunger while the lifter is submerged in oil).

30. Install the pushrods in their proper order and install the rocker arm shaft assembly. Install the valve cover with a new gasket.

31. Install the cold start injector.

32. Install the distributor assembly as previously outlined.

33. Install the fan assembly along with the water pump as previously outlined.

34. Install the radiator assembly and reconnect the radiator inlet hoses, radiator breather hose and reservoir tank hose.

35. Refill the coolant system.

36. Reconnect the negative battery cable. Connect a timing light and tachometer.

37. Start the engine and set the ignition timing. If the engine is hard to start, have some one turn the distributor left and right very slowly until the engine starts. Once this has happened, use your timing light to readjust the timing properly. Recheck the idle speed adjustment. Check for leaks and add coolant as necessary.

38. Install the engine service hole cover and install the right seat.

CAMSHAFT INSPECTION

Prior to removal of the camshaft, measure the end-play with a feeler gauge. Refer to the Specifications Chart, if the end-play is beyond specs, it may be necessary to replace the cylinder head or camshaft.

Measure the bearing oil clearance by placing a piece of Plastigage® on each bearing journal. Replace the bearing caps and tighten the bolts to 13–16 ft. lbs.

➡**Do not turn the camshaft.**

Remove the caps and measure each piece of Plastigage®. If the clearance is greater than the values on the Specifications Chart, replace the bearings, head or cam, depending on which engine you are working on.

Place the camshaft in V-block supports and measure its runout at the center bearing journal with a dial indicator. If the runout exceeds specs, replace the cam.

Use a micrometer and measure the bearing journals and the cam lobe heights. If the bearing journals are not within specs, or the lobes differ greatly in size from wear, replace the camshaft.

Pistons and Connecting Rods

REMOVAL & INSTALLATION

Although, in most cases, the pistons and connecting rods can be removed from the engine (after the cylinder head and oil pan are removed) while the engine is still in the car, it is far easier to remove the engine from the car.

1. Remove the cylinder head as outlined in the appropriate preceding section.

2. Remove the oil pan and pump.

3. Because the top piston ring does not travel to the very top of the cylinder bore, a ridge is built up between the end of the travel and the top of the cylinder. Pushing the piston and connecting rod assembly past the ridge is difficult and may cause damage to the piston. If new rings are installed and the ridge has not been removed, ring breakage and piston damage can occur when the ridge is encountered at engine speed.

4. Turn the crankshaft to position the piston at the bottom of the cylinder bore. Cover the top of the piston with a rag. Install a ridge reamer in the bore and follow the manufacturer's instructions to remove the ridge. Use caution. Avoid cutting too deeply or into the ring travel area. Remove the rag and cuttings from the top of the piston. Remove the ridge from all cylinders.

5. Check the edges of the connecting rod and bearing cap for numbers or matchmarks, if none are present mark the rod and cap numerically and in sequence from front to back of engine. The numbers or marks not only tell from which cylinder the piston came from but also ensures that the rod caps are installed in the correct matching position.

6. Turn the engine until the connecting rod to be serviced is at the bottom of travel. Unbolt the connecting rod caps. Mark the caps with the number of the cylinder from which they were removed. Place two pieces of rubber hose over the rod cap bolts and push the piston and rod assembly up through the top of the cylinder bore.

Place rubber hose over the connecting rod studs to protect the crank and bores from damage

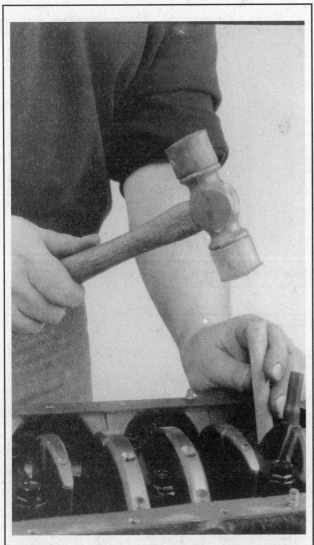

Carefully tap the piston out of the bore using a wooden dowel

Clean the piston grooves using a ring groove cleaner

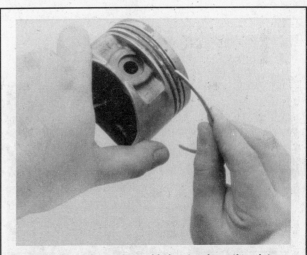

You can use a piece of an old ring to clean the piston grooves, BUT be careful, the ring is sharp

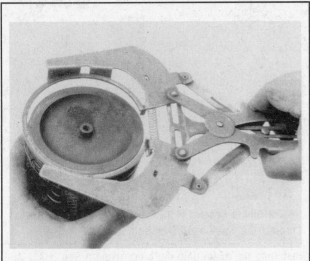

Use a ring expander tool to remove the piston rings

Measure the piston's outer diameter using a micrometer

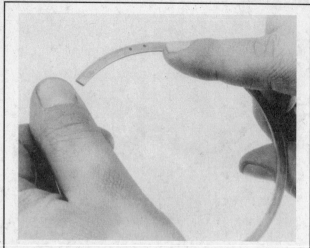

Most rings are marked to show which side should face upward

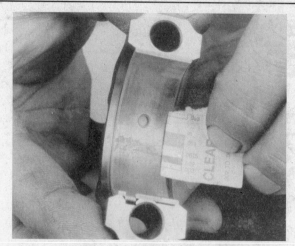

After the cap is removed again, use the scale supplied with the gauge material to check clearances

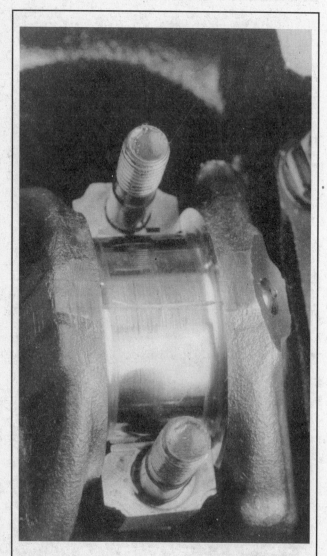

Apply a strip of gauging material to the bearing journal, then install and torque the cap

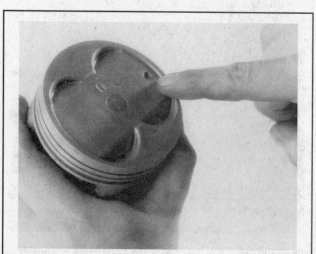

Most pistons are marked to indicate positioning in the engine (usually a mark means the side facing front)

Installing the piston into the block using a ring compressor and the handle of a hammer

7. Mark the pistons and connecting rods with the numbers of the cylinders from which they were removed.

To install:

8. Apply a light coating of engine oil to the pistons, rings, and wrist pins.

9. Examine the piston to ensure that it has been assembled with its parts positioned correctly. (See the illustrations.) Be sure that the ring gaps are not pointed toward the thrust face of the piston and that they do not overlap.

10. Install the pistons, using a ring compressor, into the cylinder bore. Be sure that the appropriate marks on the piston are facing the front of the cylinder.

➡ **It is important that the pistons, rods, bearings, etc., be returned to the same cylinder bore from which they were removed.**

11. Clean the rod journal, the connecting rod end and the bearing cap after removing the old bearing inserts. Install the new inserts in the rod and bearing cap, lubricate them with oil. Position the rod over the crankshaft journal and install the rod cap. Make sure the cap and rod numbers match, tighten the rod nuts to specifications.

➡ **Be sure that the mating marks on the connecting rods and rod bearing caps are aligned.**

12. The rest of the removal procedure is performed in the reverse order of installation.

CLEANING AND INSPECTION

1. Use a piston ring expander and remove the rings from the piston.

2. Clean the ring grooves using an appropriate cleaning tool, exercise care to avoid cutting too deeply.

3. Clean all varnish and carbon from the piston with a safe

A solid hone can also be used to cross-hatch the cylinder bore

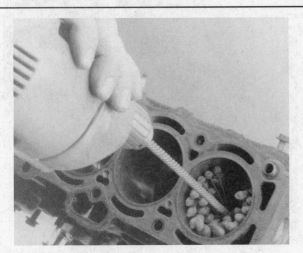

Using a ball type cylinder hone is an easy way to hone the cylinder bore

As with a ball hone, work the hone carefully up and down the bore to achieve the desired results

A properly cross-hatched cylinder bore

solvent. Do not use a wire brush or caustic solution on the pistons.

4. Inspect the pistons for scuffing, scoring, cracks, pitting or excessive ring groove wear. If wear is evident, the piston must be replaced.

5. Have the piston and connecting rod assembly checked by a machine shop for correct alignment, piston pin wear and piston diameter. If the piston has collapsed, it will have to be replaced or knurled to restore original diameter. Connecting rod bushing replacement, piston pin fitting and piston changing can be handled by the machine shop.

CYLINDER BORE

Check the cylinder bore for wear using a telescope gauge and a micrometer, measure the cylinder bore diameter perpendicular to the piston pin at a point 2½ in. (63.5mm) below the top of the engine block. Measure the piston skirt perpendicular to the piston

A telescoping gauge may be used to measure the cylinder bore diameter

pin. The difference between the two measurements is the piston clearance. If the clearance is within specifications, finish honing or glaze breaking is all that is required. If clearance is excessive a slightly oversize piston may be required. If greatly oversize, the engine will have to be bored and 0.010 in. (0.25mm) or larger oversized pistons installed.

FITTING AND POSITIONING PISTON RINGS

1. Take the new piston rings and compress them, one at a time into the cylinder that they will be used in. Press the ring about 1 in. (25mm) below the top of the cylinder block using an inverted piston.

2. Use a feeler gauge and measure the distance between the ends of the ring. This is called measuring the ring end-gap. Compare the reading to the one called for in the specifications table. File the ends of the ring with a fine file to obtain necessary clearance.

Checking the ring-to-ring groove clearance

✳✳ WARNING

If inadequate ring end-gap is utilized, ring breakage will result.

3. Inspect the ring grooves on the piston for excessive wear or taper. If necessary have the grooves recut for use with a standard ring and spacer. The machine shop can handle the job for you.

4. Check the ring grooves by rolling the new piston ring around the groove to check for burrs or carbon deposits. If any are found, remove with a fine file. Hold the ring in the groove and measure side clearance with a feeler gauge. If clearance is excessive, spacer(s) will have to be added.

➡**Always add spacers above the piston ring.**

5. Install the ring on the piston, lower oil ring first. Use a ring installing tool on the compression rings. Consult the instruction sheet that comes with the rings to be sure they are installed with the correct side up. A mark on the ring usually faces upward.

6. When installing oil rings, first, install the expanding ring in the groove. Hold the ends of the ring butted together (they must not overlap) and install the bottom rail (scraper) with the end about 1 in. (25mm) away from the butted end of the control ring. Install the top rail about (1 in.) 25mm away from the butted end of the control but on the opposite side from the lower rail.

7. Install the two compression rings.

8. Install the rings in their proper order, install a ring compressor and insert the piston and rod assembly into the engine.

PISTON PIN REPLACEMENT

▶ **See Figures 152 thru 157**

1. Using a suitable pair of snapring pliers or equivalent, remove the snaprings from the side of the piston.

2. Gradually heat the pistons to approximately 140°F (60°C).

3. Place the piston upside down in a suitable holding fixture and using a plastic mallet and a brass drift, drive out the piston pin and remove the connecting rod.

4. Be sure to arrange the piston pins, rings, connecting rods

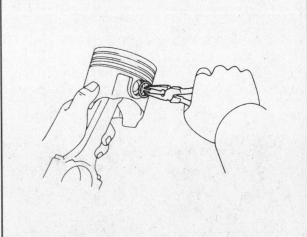

Fig. 153 Use a pair of snapring pliers to remove the wrist pins snapring

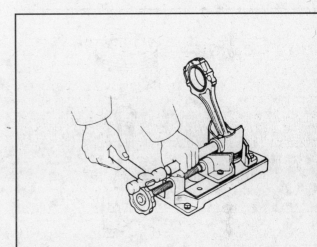

Fig. 154 With the piston in a vise, tap the pin out of the piston

Fig. 152 Heat up the pistons to remove the wrist pin

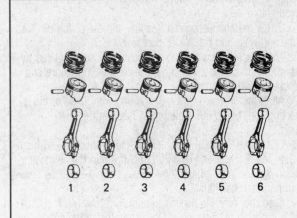

Fig. 155 Keep all of the connecting rods and pistons in order

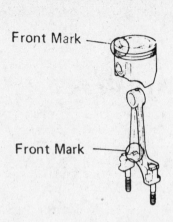

Fig. 156 When assembling the pistons and rods, be sure they are aligned correctly—5M-GE and 7M-GE engines

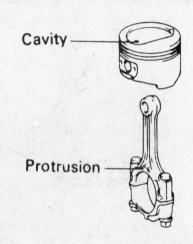

Fig. 157 When assembling the pistons and rods, be sure they are aligned correctly—3Y-EC and 4Y-EC engines

and bearings in the correct order. The pistons and pins are a matched set.

5. Check the connecting rod bushing and the piston pin for damage and wear and replace as necessary.

6. To replace the connecting rod bushing, use a suitable hydraulic press, place the connecting rod in a holding fixture and press out the old bushing.

7. Align the oil holes of a new bushing with those of the connecting rod. Using the same press, press in the new bushing.

8. Check the fit of the piston pin in the connecting rod bushing. Coat the pin with engine oil and push it into the connecting rod bushing with your thumb. If the pin is to tight it will be necessary to hone the new bushing.

9. Gradually heat the pistons to approximately 140°F (60°C). Install a snapring to one side of the piston. Install the connecting rod into the piston and push in a new piston pin with your thumb. If the pin can be installed at a lower temperature, replace the piston.

10. Install a snapring to the other side of the piston.

Freeze Plugs

REMOVAL & INSTALLATION

1. Raise and safely support the vehicle, as required.

✳✳ CAUTION

When draining coolant, keep in mind that cats and dogs are attracted by ethylene glycol antifreeze, and are quite likely to drink any that is left in an uncovered container or in puddles on the ground. This will prove fatal in sufficient quantity. Always drain coolant into a sealable container. Coolant may be reused unless it is contaminated or several years old.

2. Drain the cooling system. If the freeze plug is located in the cylinder block, it will be necessary to remove the drain plug from the side of the block to make sure all coolant is drained.

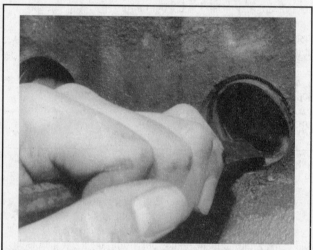

Using a punch and hammer, the freeze plug can be loosened in the block

Once the freeze plug has been loosened, it can be removed from the block

3. Drill a ½ in. (13mm) hole in the center of the plug. Remove the plug with a slide hammer or pry it out with a prybar.

➡️**Be careful to stop drilling as soon as the bit breaks through the plug to prevent damaging the engine.**

4. Clean all dirt and corrosion from the freeze plug bore. Check the freeze plug bore for damage that would interfere with sealing. If the bore is damaged, the bore will have to be machined for an oversize plug.

To install:

5. Coat the plug bore and the freeze plug sealing surface with water proof sealer.

6. Install cup-type freeze plugs with the flanged edge outward. The plug must be driven in with a tool that does not contact the flange of the plug. If an improper tool is used, the plug sealing edge will be damaged and leakage will result.

7. Expansion-type freeze plugs are installed with the flanged edge inward. The plug must be driven in with a tool that does not contact the crowned portion of the plug. If an improper tool is used, the plug and/or plug bore will be damaged.

8. Replace any drain plugs that were removed and lower the vehicle.

9. Fill the cooling system, start the engine and check for leaks.

Block Heaters

REMOVAL & INSTALLATION

Factory block heaters are not installed on Toyota vehicles any more. If an aftermarket one has been installed, the following procedure should be useful. There are two basic types, one for oil and one for coolant. The oil heater usually just slips into the dipstick tube or replaces the oil drain plug. The following procedure is for the coolant type.

1. Remove the negative battery cable.
2. Drain the cooling system.

✳✳ CAUTION

When draining coolant, keep in mind that cats and dogs are attracted by ethylene glycol antifreeze, and are quite likely to drink any that is left in an uncovered container or in puddles on the ground. This will prove fatal in sufficient quantity. Always drain coolant into a sealable container. Coolant may be reused unless it is contaminated or several years old.

3. Remove the block heater in the same way as the freeze plugs. Some heater units have a bolt that must be loosened or a V-clamp that must be unsecured to remove the heating element.

4. Disconnect the heater wire and remove the heater element.

5. Coat the new heater with sealant and reinstall into the engine.

6. Fill the engine with a coolant and water mixture.

7. Start the engine, check for leaks and top off the coolant.

Rear Main Oil Seal

REMOVAL & INSTALLATION

◆ **See Figures 158, 159, 160 and 161**

➡️**Unless you are very familiar with working on cars and removing engines and transmissions, the removal and installation of this seal is a very complex procedure and could be very costly if any mistakes are made. It may be in your best interest to leave this one in the hands of a factory authorized dealer.**

1. Remove the transmission as detailed in Section 7 of this manual.

2. On vehicles equipped with manual transmissions, remove the clutch cover assembly and flywheel. See Section 7 also.

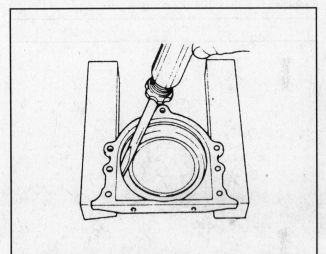

Fig. 158 The rear main seal can be removed either with its retaining plate off the engine . . .

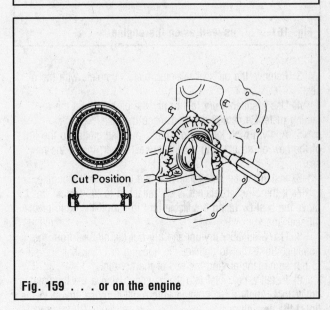

Cut Position

Fig. 159 . . . or on the engine

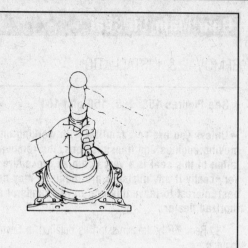

Fig. 160 Use a seal driver when the retainer is off the engine . . .

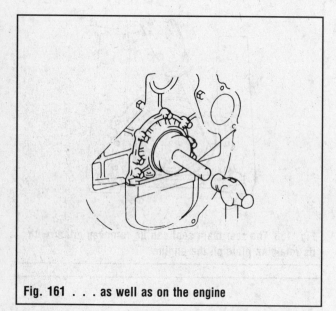

Fig. 161 . . . as well as on the engine

3. Remove the oil seal retaining plate, complete with the oil seal.

4. Use a suitable pry tool to pry the oil seal from the retaining plate. Be careful not to damage the plate.

5. Apply a high temperature multi-purpose grease to the lip of the new oil seal. Using a suitable seal driver, install the new seal.

6. Install the oil seal retaining plate back onto the engine.

7. If the oil seal retainer is still attached to the engine, remove the seal by using a suitable tool to cut off the edge of the oil seal lips.

8. Use a suitable prytool and pry out the oil seal from the housing. So as not to damage the housing or crankshaft, be sure to put some tape around the end of the pry tool.

9. Install a new seal into the housing using a suitable seal driver tool. Apply a high temperature multi-purpose grease to the lip of the new oil seal.

10. Install the clutch assembly and flywheel. Reinstall the transmission assembly.

Crankshaft and Main Bearings

REMOVAL & INSTALLATION

▶ **See Figures 162 and 163**

1. For in car service, remove the oil pan, spark plugs and front cover if necessary. The main bearings may be replaced while the engine is still in the car by rolling them out and in.

➡ **Check the edges of the main bearing cap for numbers or matchmarks, if none are present mark the caps numerically and in sequence from front to back of engine. The numbers or marks not only tell from which journal the cap came, but also ensures that the caps are installed in the correct matching position.**

2. Turn the engine until the main bearing cap to be serviced is at the bottom of travel. Remove the bearing cap bolts and remove the cap.

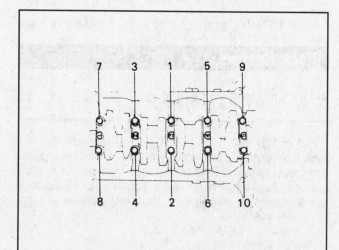

Fig. 162 Main bearing bolt tightening sequence—3Y-EC and 4Y-EC engines

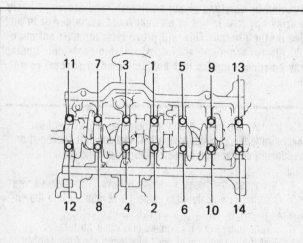

Fig. 163 Main bearing bolt tightening sequence—5M-GE and 7M-GE engines

3. Special roll out pins are available from automotive parts houses or can be fabricated from a cotter pin. The roll out pin fits in the oil hole of the main bearing journal. When the crankshaft is rotated opposite the direction of the bearing lock tab, the pin engages the end of the bearing and rolls out the insert.

4. Remove main bearing cap and roll out upper bearing insert. Remove insert from main bearing cap. Clean the inside of the bearing cap and crankshaft journal.

5. Lubricate and roll upper insert into position, make sure the lock tab is anchored and the insert is not cocked. Install the lower bearing insert into the cap, lubricate and install on the engine. Make sure the main bearing cap is installed facing in the correct direction and torque to specifications.

6. With the engine out of the car, remove the intake manifold, cylinder heads, front cover, timing gears and/or chain, oil pan, oil pump and flywheel.

7. Remove the piston and rod assemblies. Remove the main bearing caps after marking them for position and direction.

8. Remove the crankshaft, bearing inserts and rear main oil seal. Clean the engine block and cap bearing saddles. Clean the crankshaft and inspect for wear. Check the bearing journals with a micrometer for out-of-round condition and to determine what size rod and main bearing inserts to install.

9. Install the main bearing upper inserts and rear main oil seal half into the engine block.

10. Lubricate the bearing inserts and the crankshaft journals. Slowly and carefully lower the crankshaft into position.

11. Install the bearing inserts and rear main seal into the bearing caps, install the caps working from the middle out. Torque cap bolts to specifications in stages, rotate the crankshaft after each torque state.

➡ **On the 5M-GE and 7M-GE engines, install the thrust washers on the number 4 bearing cap with the oil grooves facing outward. On the 3Y-EC and the 4Y-EC engines install the thrust washers on the number 3 bearing cap with the oil grooves facing outward.**

12. Remove bearing caps, one at a time and check the oil clearance with Plastigage®. Reinstall if clearance is within specifications. Check the crankshaft end-play, if within specifications install connecting rod and piston assemblies with new rod bearing inserts. Check connecting rod bearing oil clearance and side play, if correct assemble the rest of the engine.

BEARING OIL CLEARANCE

Remove cap from the bearing to be checked. Using a clean, dry rag, thoroughly clean all oil from crankshaft journal and bearing insert.

➡ **Plastigage® is soluble in oil, therefore, oil on the journal or bearing could result in erroneous readings.**

Place a piece of Plastigage® along the full width of the bearing insert, reinstall cap, and torque to specifications.

➡ **Specifications are given earlier in this section.**

Remove bearing cap, and determine bearing clearance by comparing width of Plastigage® to the scale on Plastigage® envelope. Journal taper is determined by comparing width of the bearing insert, reinstall cap, and torque to specifications.

The notch on the the side of the bearing cap matches the groove on the bearing insert

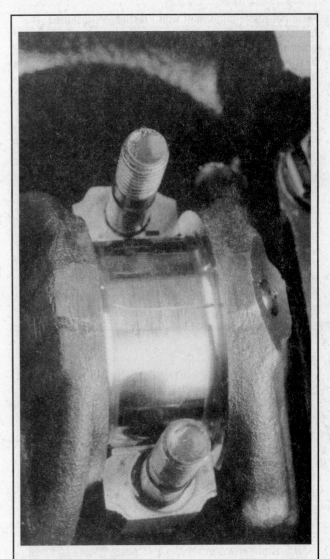

Apply a strip of gauging material to the bearing journal, then install and torque the cap

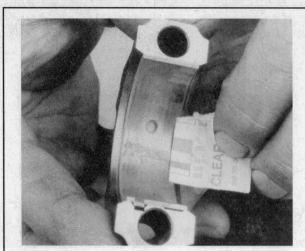

After the cap is removed again, use the scale supplied with the gauge material to check clearances

Carefully pry the shaft back and forth while reading the dial gauge for play

➡ Do not rotate crankshaft with Plastigage® installed. If bearing insert and journal appear intact, and are within tolerances, no further main bearing service is required. If bearing or journal appear defective, cause of failure should be determined before replacement.

CRANKSHAFT END-PLAY/CONNECTING ROD SIDE PLAY

Place a prybar between a main bearing cap and crankshaft casting taking care not to damage any journals. Pry backward and forward, measure the distance between the thrust bearing and crankshaft with a feeler gauge. Compare reading with specifications. If too great a clearance is determined, a main bearing with a larger thrust surface or crank machining may be required. Check with an automotive machine shop for their advice.

Connecting rod clearance between the rod and crank throw casting can be checked with a feeler gauge. Pry the rod carefully on one side as far as possible and measure the distance on the other side of the rod.

A dial gauge may be used to check crankshaft end-play

CRANKSHAFT REPAIRS

If a journal is damaged on the crankshaft, repair is possible by having the crankshaft machined to a standard undersize.

In most cases, however, since the engine must be removed from the car and disassembled, some thought should be given to replacing the damaged crankshaft with a reground shaft kit. A reground crankshaft kit contains the necessary main and rod bearings for installation. The shaft has been ground and polished to undersize specifications and will usually hold up well if installed correctly.

Flywheel and Ring Gear

REMOVAL & INSTALLATION

1. Disconnect the negative battery cable.
2. Remove the transaxle and clutch assemblies. Remove the rear cover plate, if so equipped.
3. Install a suitable flywheel holding tool and remove the flywheel retaining bolts. Remove the flywheel.
   To install:
4. Inspect the flywheel for cracks, heat checks or other damage that would make it unfit for further service. On the vehicles equipped with manual transmissions, check the machine surface of the flywheel to see if it is scored or worn. If the flywheel run-out is more than 0.008 in. (0.2mm), replace the flywheel with a new one.
5. Install the flywheel and using a suitable flywheel holding tool, tighten the flywheel retaining bolts to specifications.
6. Install the clutch and transaxle assemblies. Rear cover plate, if so equipped. Adjust the clutch as necessary.
7. Reconnect the negative battery. Start the engine and check for proper starter gear to flywheel meshing.

➡ The ring gear is welded to the base of the flywheel assembly and therefore this assembly must be replaced as a unit.

EXHAUST SYSTEM

General Information

→Safety glasses should be worn at all times when working on or near the exhaust system. Older exhaust systems will almost always be covered with loose rust particles which will shower you when disturbed. These particles are more than a nuisance and could injure your eye.

Whenever working on the exhaust system always keep the following in mind:

• Check the complete exhaust system for open seams, holes loose connections, or other deterioration which could permit exhaust fumes to seep into the passenger compartment.

• The exhaust system is usually supported by free-hanging rubber mountings which permit some movement of the exhaust system, but does not permit transfer of noise and vibration into the passenger compartment. Do not replace the rubber mounts with solid ones.

• Before removing any component of the exhaust system, ALWAYS squirt a liquid rust dissolving agent onto the fasteners for ease of removal. A lot of knuckle skin will be saved by following this rule. It may even be wise to spray the fasteners and allow them to sit overnight.

✳✳ CAUTION

Allow the exhaust system to cool sufficiently before spraying a solvent exhaust fasteners. Some solvents are highly flammable and could ignite when sprayed on hot exhaust components.

• Annoying rattles and noise vibrations in the exhaust system are usually caused by misalignment of the parts. When aligning the system, leave all bolts and nuts loose until all parts are properly aligned, then tighten, working from front to rear.

• When installing exhaust system parts, make sure there is enough clearance between the hot exhaust parts and pipes and hoses that would be adversely affected by excessive heat. Also make sure there is adequate clearance from the floor pan to avoid possible overheating of the floor.

In addition to its pipes and hangers, the chief components of an exhaust system are the catalytic converter and muffler.

The converter contains 2 separate ceramic honeycombs coated with different catalytic material. The front catalyst is coated with a rhodium/platinum catalyst designed to control oxides of nitrogen (NOx), unburned hydrocarbons (HC) and carbon monoxide (CO). This is therefore called a three-way catalytic converter (TWC). The rear catalyst is coated with platinum/palladium and is called a conventional oxidation catalyst (COC).

The TWC converter operates on the exhaust gases as they arrive from the engine. As the gases flow from the TWC to the COC converter, they mix with the air in the secondary air system into the mixing chamber between the two ceramic honeycombs. This air is required for optimum operating conditions for the oxidation of the HC and CO on the COC converter. Air is diverted upstream of the TWC during cold start to provide faster catalyst light off and better HC/CO control.

The factory-installed exhaust system usually uses a one-piece muffler system. This means that the whole system, except for the converter and exhaust manifold, is welded into place. This in turn usually means that once the muffler goes, the whole system has to be replaced. The converter assembly is a bolt-on catalyst installed at the rear of the flex joint and between the inlet pipe and muffler.

Inspect inlet pipes, outlet pipes and mufflers for cracked joints, broken welds and corrosion damage that would result in a leaking exhaust system. It is normal for a certain amount of moisture and staining to be present around the muffler seams. The presence of soot, light surface rust or moisture does not indicate a faulty muffler. Inspect the clamps, brackets and insulators for cracks and stripped or badly corroded bolt threads. When flat joints are loosened and/or disconnected to replace a shield pipe or muffler, replace the bolts and flange nuts if there is reasonable doubt that its service life is limited.

The exhaust system, including heat shields, must be free of leaks, binding, grounding and excessive vibrations. These conditions are usually caused by loose or broken flange bolts, shields, brackets or pipes. If any of these conditions exist, check the exhaust system components and alignment. Align or replace as necessary. Brush shields are positioned on the underside of the catalytic converter and should be free from bends which would bring any part of the shield in contact with the catalytic converter or muffler. The shield should also be clear of any combustible material, such as dried grass or leaves.

→The operating temperature of the exhaust system is very high. Never attempt to service any part of the system until it has cooled. Be especially careful when working around the catalytic converter. The temperature of the converter rises to a high level after only a few minutes of operation.

Catalytic Converter

REMOVAL & INSTALLATION

▶ See Figures 164, 165 and 166

✳✳ CAUTION

Do NOT perform exhaust repairs with the engine or exhaust hot. Allow the system to cool completely before attempting any work. Exhaust systems are noted for sharp edges, flaking metal and rusted bolts. Gloves and eye protection are required. A healthy supply of penetrating oil and rags is highly recommended.

1. Raise and safely support the vehicle on jackstands.
2. Remove the heat shield.
3. Some models have rubber O-ring supports that may be in the way of removal; if so equipped, detach them, ensuring there is another support for the converter once removed.
4. On some models, you will need to remove the oxygen sensor. Unbolt the oxygen sensor and remove it. Protect the tip of the sensor from damage and do not place it on or near any petroleum based solvents. This includes putting it on a greasy rag.
5. Remove the bolts at the front and rear of the converter.

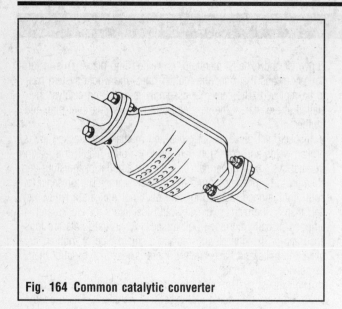

Fig. 164 Common catalytic converter

pipe to the muffler. All Toyota exhaust components bolt together with gaskets at the joints; no welding is involved.

1. Elevate and firmly support the rear of the vehicle.
2. On some models, you will need to remove the oxygen sensor. Unbolt the oxygen sensor and remove it. Protect the tip of the sensor from damage and do not place it on or near any petroleum based solvents. This includes putting it on a greasy rag.
3. Unfasten the nuts holding the muffler and/or tailpipe to the adjacent pipes.
4. Remove or disconnect the clamps and supports holding the pipe at either end. Leave the supports closest to the center in place until last.
5. Remove the last supports or hangers and lower the unit to the ground. At NO TIME should the muffler be allowed to hang partially supported; the leverage can break the next component in line.

➡**If the muffler or tailpipe is being replaced due to rust or corrosion, adjacent pipes should be checked for the same condition. The pieces tend to age at about the same rate.**

To install:
6. Check the rubber supports that hang the exhaust, they have a tendency to stretch and crack with age; replace if necessary.
7. Lift the new unit into place and loosely attach the hangers or supports to hold it in place. Allow some play to adjust the muffler.
8. Using new gaskets, connect each end to the adjoining pipe. Tighten the joint bolts and nuts to 29–32 ft. lbs. (39–43 Nm).

➡**ALWAYS use a new gasket at each pipe joint whenever the joint is disassembled. Use new nuts and bolts to hold the joint properly. These two low-cost items will serve to prevent future leaks as the system ages.**

9. Tighten the supports and hangers. Make certain the rubber hangers are securely attached to their mounts.

Complete System

REMOVAL & INSTALLATION

♦ **See Figures 165 and 166**

✴✴ CAUTION

Do NOT perform exhaust repairs with the engine or exhaust hot. Allow the system to cool completely before attempting any work. Exhaust systems are noted for sharp edges, flaking metal and rusted bolts. Gloves and eye protection are required. A healthy supply of penetrating oil and rags is highly recommended.

If the entire exhaust system is to be replaced, it is much easier to remove the system as a unit than to remove each individual piece. Disconnect the first pipe at the manifold joint and work towards the rear, removing brackets and hangers as you go. Separate the rear pipe at the catalytic converter. Remove any retaining brackets and O-rings from the center of the exhaust system and back. Then, slide the rear section of the exhaust system out from

➡**Always support the pipe running to the manifold, either by the normal clamps/hangers or by using string, stiff wire, etc. If left loose, the pipe can develop enough leverage to crack the manifold.**

6. Remove the converter and gaskets.
To install:
7. Check the rubber supports that suspend the exhaust, they have a tendency to stretch and crack with age; replace if necessary.
8. Using new gaskets, attach the converter to the exhaust pipes. Tighten the bolts to 29–32 ft. lbs. (39–43 Nm).

➡**ALWAYS use a new gasket at each pipe joint whenever the joint is disassembled. Use new nuts and bolts to hold the joint properly. These two low-cost items will serve to prevent future leaks as the system ages.**

9. On models with the oxygen sensor in the catalyst, tighten the nuts to 14 ft. lbs. (20 Nm). Don't forget to connect the wire harness.

Muffler and/or Tailpipe

REMOVAL & INSTALLATION

♦ **See Figures 165 and 166**

✴✴ CAUTION

Do NOT perform exhaust repairs with the engine or exhaust hot. Allow the system to cool completely before attempting any work. Exhaust systems are noted for sharp edges, flaking metal and rusted bolts. Gloves and eye protection are required. A healthy supply of penetrating oil and rags is highly recommended.

The muffler and tailpipe on Cressidas and Vans is one piece and should be replaced as a unit. The muffler includes a lead-in the back of the vehicle. Once removed from the vehicle, you can detach the catalytic converter from the system, as it is usually good enough to reuse.

The new system can then be bolted up on the workbench and easily checked for proper tightness and gasket integrity. When in-stalling the new assembly, suspend it from the flexible hangers first, then attach the fixed (solid) brackets. Check the clearance to the body and suspension and install the manifold joint bolts, tight-ening them correctly.

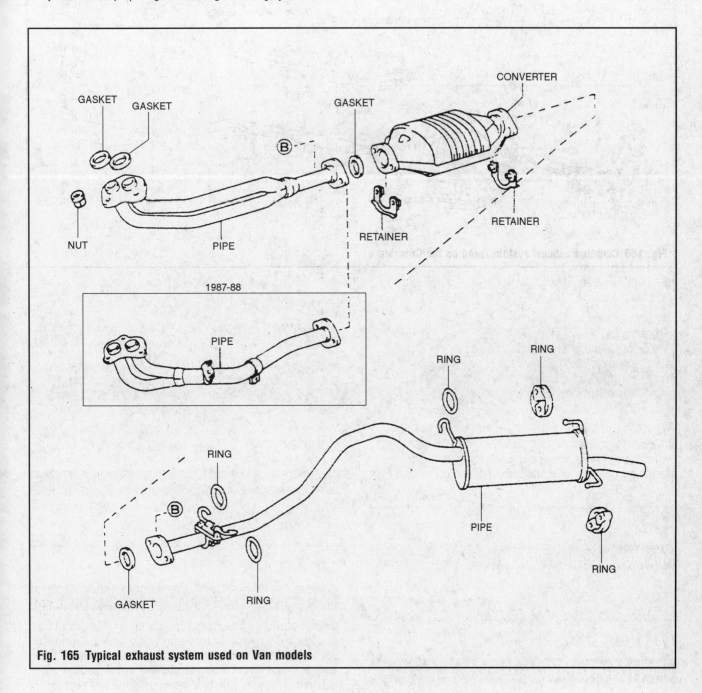

Fig. 165 Typical exhaust system used on Van models

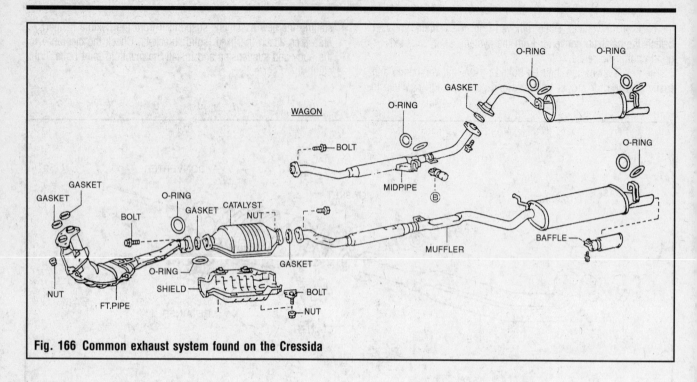

Fig. 166 Common exhaust system found on the Cressida

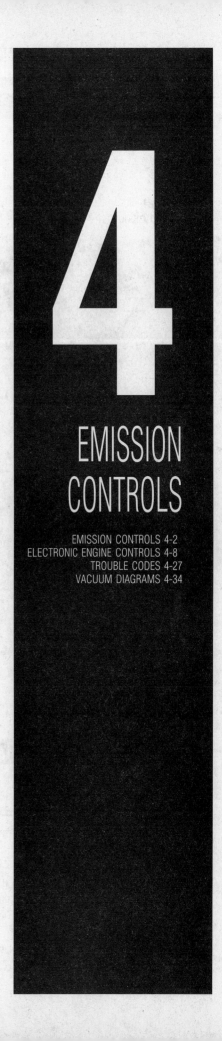

4

EMISSION CONTROLS

EMISSION CONTROLS

EMISSION COMPONENT LOCATIONS - VAN

1. Air flow meter
2. Vacuum modulator
3. EGR valve
4. Throttle position sensor
5. Bi-metal vacuum switching valve
6. PCV orifice
7. Emission label

Crankcase Ventilation System

OPERATION

▶ **See Figure 1**

A positive crankcase ventilation system is used on all Toyota engines sold in the United States. Blow-by gases are routed from the crankcase to the intake manifold, where they are combined with the air/fuel charge and burned in the combustion process. On fuel injected engines, a pair of fixed orifices in the PCV line regulates the blow-by flow.

SERVICE

Every 30,000 miles, the PCV system should be checked for tight hose connections, leaks, cracks or deterioration. Any hoses found to be leaking should be replaced. To check the PCV valve operation, remove the valve from the valve cover and blow through both ends. When blowing from the intake manifold side, very little air should pass through the valve. When blowing from the crankcase (valve cover) side, air should pass through freely. If the valve fails either of these tests, it should be replaced. Do not attempt to clean the PCV valve. Simply clean the calibrated orifices with solvent and blow dry with compressed air.

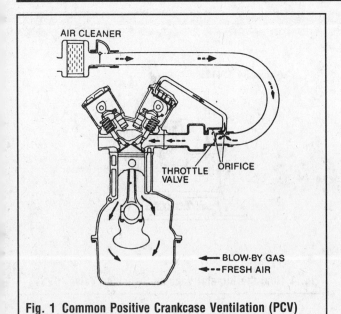

Fig. 1 Common Positive Crankcase Ventilation (PCV) system air flow

manifold for combustion in the engine. A fuel filler cap with a check valve allows air to enter the fuel tank as the fuel is used to prevent a vacuum build up and equalize the pressure, but does not allow fuel vapors to escape to the atmosphere. When the engine coolant temperature reaches 129°F (54°C), the vacuum switching valve opens to allow vapors trapped in the charcoal canister to enter the intake manifold, where they are drawn into the combustion chambers and burned with the fuel charge.

SERVICE

The EVAP system should be checked for proper operation every 60,000 miles. Check all hose and connections for leaks or deterioration and remove the charcoal canister to inspect for cracks or damage. Check for a clogged filter or frozen check valve by blowing low pressure compressed air into the tank and check that air flows freely to the canister port. Blow into the charcoal canis-

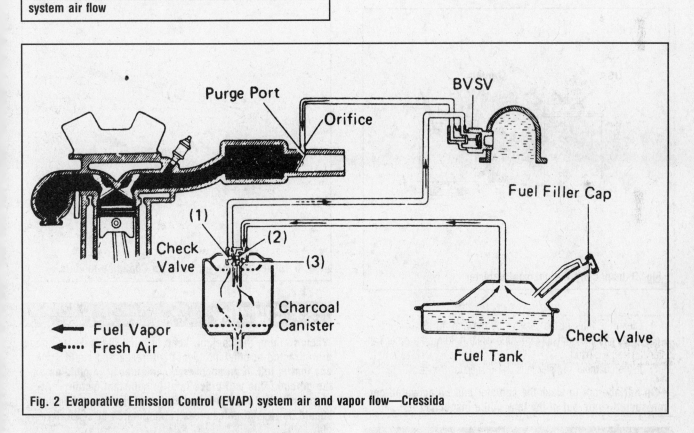

Fig. 2 Evaporative Emission Control (EVAP) system air and vapor flow—Cressida

Evaporative Emission Control (EVAP) System

OPERATION

♦ **See Figure 2**

To reduce hydrocarbon (HC) emissions, evaporated fuel from the fuel tank is routed through the charcoal canister to the intake

ter purge pipe and make sure no air flows from the tank connection or from the fresh air inlet at the bottom of the canister. If it does, replace the canister. Clean the pipe while holding the purge connection closed. Do not attempt to wash the canister in any way.

Check the Bi-metal Vacuum Switching Valve (BVSV) operation by allowing the engine to cool completely and blowing through the valve. When cold, the valve should be closed (no air should pass). Start and warm up the engine, then blow through the valve again. Air should now pass freely (switch open). Any results other than these, replace the BVSV.

The thermo switch is tested by allowing the engine to cool completely and checking for continuity across the thermo switch terminals. Start and warm up the engine and check that the thermo switch is open (no continuity) at normal operating temperature. If not, replace the thermo switch.

Charcoal Canister

TESTING

◆ **See Figure 3**

1. Remove the charcoal canister from the vehicle. Visually inspect charcoal canister case for cracks or damage.
2. Using a low pressure compressed air, blow into the tank pipe and check that air flows without resistance from the other pipes.
3. Blow compressed air into the purge pipe and check that air does not flow from the other pipes.

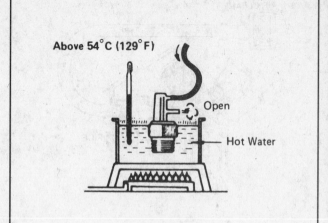

Fig. 4 Heat the Bimetal Vacuum Switching Valve (BVSV)

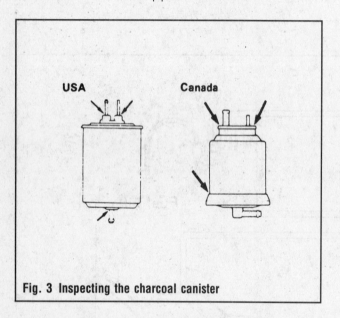

Fig. 3 Inspecting the charcoal canister

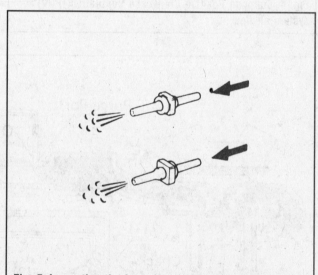

Fig. 5 Inspecting the jet valve on Canadian models

4. Clean the filter in the canister by blowing 43 psi of compressed air into the canister tank pipe while holding the other canister tank pipe closed.
5. If the charcoal canister fails the inspection replace it.

➡ **Do not attempt to wash the canister and no activated carbon should come out of the tank while inspecting it.**

Bimetal Vacuum Switching Valve (BVSV)

TESTING

◆ **See Figures 4 and 5**

1. Drain the coolant from the radiator into a suitable container. Remove the BVSV.

✳✳ CAUTION

When draining the coolant, keep in mind that cats and dogs are attracted to ethylene glycol antifreeze and could drink any that is left in an uncovered container or in puddles on the ground. This will prove fatal in sufficient quantity. Always drain the coolant into a sealable container. Coolant should be reused unless it is contaminated or several years old.

2. Cool the BVSV to below 95°F (35°C) with cool water. Blow air into a hose that is connected to the BVSV and check that the BVSV is closed.
3. Heat the BVSV to above 129°F (54°C) with hot water. Blow air into a hose that is connected to the BVSV and check that the BVSV is open.
4. If the BVSV fails the inspection replace it. Apply a liquid sealer to the threads of the BVSV and reinstall it on the engine. Refill the radiator with coolant.

➡The Canadian models use a jet valve, it can be checked by blowing air into it from each side to see if it is clogged.

Dashpot (DP) System

OPERATION

On fuel injected models, a dashpot system performs the same function as the throttle positioner that is used on a carbureted model. When decelerating, the dashpot opens the throttle valve slightly to lean out the temporarily rich fuel mixture and reduce the amount of HC and CO emissions. The system consists of the dashpot and a vacuum transducer valve with an air filter.

TESTING

◆ **See Figures 6, 7 and 8**

1. Start the engine and warm it up so as to let the engine reach normal operating temperature.
2. Check the idle speed and adjust as necessary.
3. Maintain a engine speed of 3000 rpm.
4. Pinch the vacuum hose between the dash pot and the vacuum transducer valve. (On the Van models, plug the hole in the back of the vacuum transducer valve).
5. Release the throttle valve.
6. Check the dashpot setting. The dash pot setting should be 2000 rpm.
7. If not at specified speed, adjust the dashpot adjusting bolt or stopper screw.
8. Inspect the vacuum transducer valve as follows:
   a. Set the dashpot speed in the same manner as described above.
   b. Release the pinched vacuum hose or the plugged hole (which ever the case may be) and check that the engine returns to idle speed in approximately 1 minute.
   c. If no problem is found in the inspection the system is in proper working order, otherwise inspect each component.

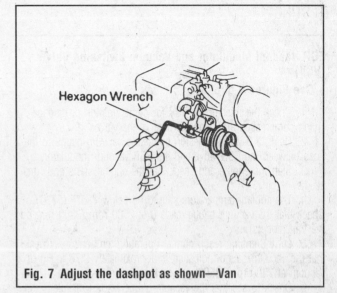

Fig. 7 Adjust the dashpot as shown—Van

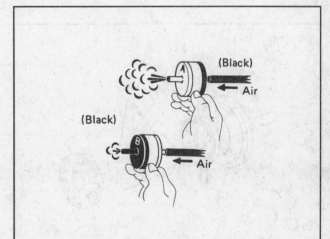

Fig. 8 To test the vacuum transducer valve, blow air into either side and check for absence of air discharge

9. Check the vacuum transducer valve by blowing air into each side.
10. Check that the air flows without resistance from one side. The other side the air should flow without restriction.

Exhaust Gas Recirculation (EGR) System

OPERATION

The EGR system recirculates part of the exhaust gas to lower the combustion chamber temperatures and reduce NOx emissions. The EGR system should be checked for proper operation every 60,000 miles. Check the filters on the vacuum modulator for contamination or damage and replace as necessary. Clean the filters with compressed air.

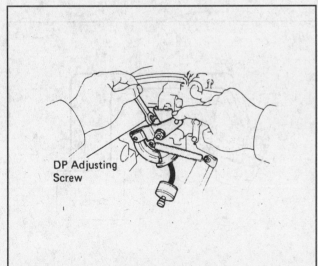

Fig. 6 Adjusting the dashpot adjusting screw—Cressida

TESTING

EGR Vacuum Modulator and Vacuum Switching Valve (VSV)

♦ **See Figures 9 thru 13**

1. Check the filter of the VSV for contamination of damage. Using compressed air, clean the filter of the valve.

2. Using a 3-way connector, connect a vacuum gauge to the hose between the EGR valve and the EGR vacuum modulator.

3. Start the engine and check that the engine starts and runs at idle.

4. The coolant temperature should be below 135°F (57°C). Check that the vacuum gauge reads 0 at 2500 rpm (3500 rpm on the Van models).

5. Let the engine reach normal operating temperature. Check that the vacuum gauge indication is approximately 2.76 in.Hg of vacuum at 2500 rpm (3500 rpm on the Van models).

6. Check to see that the vacuum gauge reads 0 at idle.

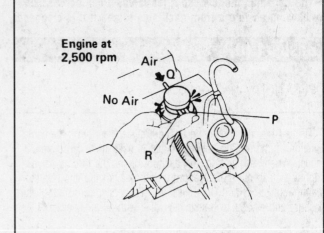

Fig. 11 Inspecting the EGR vacuum modulator valve— Cressida

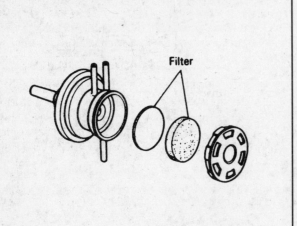

Fig. 9 Exploded view of the EGR vacuum modulator valve

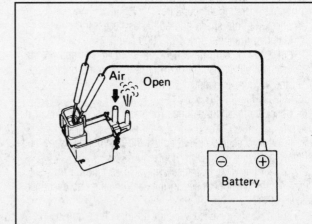

Fig. 12 To test the vacuum switching valve operation, apply battery voltage to the valve terminals—Cressida

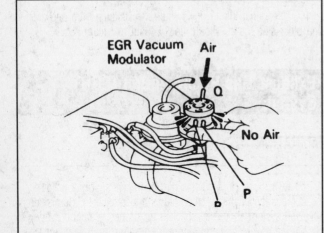

Fig. 10 To test the EGR modulator valve, apply air to the Q port while closing the R and P ports—Van

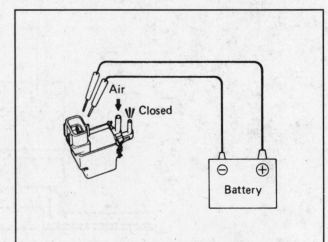

Fig. 13 When the power is removed from the vacuum switching valve, the valve should open—Cressida

7. On the 1983–88 Cressida models, use the following procedure:

a. Disconnect the vacuum hoses from ports P, Q and R of the EGR vacuum modulator. Plug off ports P and R.

b. Blow compressed air into port Q. Check that the air passes through to the air filter side freely.

c. Start the engine and maintain a speed of 2,500 rpm. Repeat the above test. Check that there is a strong resistance to air flow.

d. If the vacuum modulator fails the inspection, replace it with a new one. Reconnect the vacuum hoses to the proper location.

8. On the 1989–90 Cressida and Van Models, use the following procedure.

a. Disconnect the vacuum hose from the EGR valve and tee a vacuum gauge inline.

b. Start the engine and make sure it idles smoothly. With the engine cold—below 135°F (57°C)—the vacuum gauge should read zero at 2500 rpm (3500 on the Van models).

c. Allow the engine to reach normal operating temperature and check that the vacuum gauge now indicates about 3 in. Hg at 2500 rpm (3500 rpm on the Van models). On Van models, the vacuum gauge should read zero at 5000 rpm.

d. Disconnect the vacuum hose from the "R" port of the vacuum modulator, then connect the port directly to the intake manifold using another hose. The vacuum gauge should read high vacuum at 2500 rpm (3500 rpm on the Van models).

➡The engine should misfire slightly as a large amount of EGR gas enters the engine.

e. If so, the EGR system is working properly. Disconnect the vacuum gauge and restore all disconnected vacuum hoses to their proper connections.

9. On all models, inspect the EGR modulator valve operation by disconnecting the hoses from ports P, Q and R. Plug ports P and R, then blow air into port Q and check that air passes freely. Start the engine and hold the engine speed at 2500 rpm. Repeat

the test and check that there is now a strong resistance to air flow. If not, replace the EGR vacuum modulator and retest. If so, restore the vacuum hoses to their proper connections.

10. Check the vacuum switching valve (VSV) operation by applying battery voltage to the terminals and blowing through the valve. On Cressida models, the VSV should be open (air passes through) when energized and closed (no air passage) when power is removed. On The Van models, air should pass between the two vacuum ports when the VSV is energized, and from the back port to the air filter when power is removed. Any results other than these, replace the VSV and retest.

Bimetal Vacuum Switching Valve (EGR System)
▶ See Figure 14

1. Drain the coolant from the radiator into a suitable container. Remove the BVSV.

✳✳ CAUTION

When draining engine coolant, keep in mind that cats and dogs are attracted to ethylene glycol antifreeze and could drink any that is left in an uncovered container or in puddles on the ground. This will prove fatal in sufficient quantity. Always drain coolant into a sealable container. Coolant should be reused unless it is contaminated or is several years old.

2. Cool the BVSV to below 104°F (40°C) with cool water. Blow air into a hose that is connected to the BVSV and check that the BVSV is closed.

3. Heat the BVSV to above 129°F (54°C) with hot water. Blow air into a hose that is connected to the BVSV and check that the BVSV is open.

4. If the BVSV fails the inspection replace it. Apply a liquid sealer to the threads of the BVSV and reinstall it on the engine. Refill the radiator with coolant.

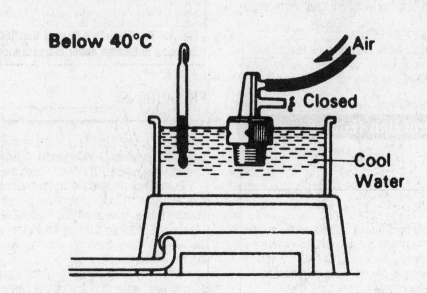

Fig. 14 Place the Bimetal Vacuum Switching Valve (BVSV) into cold water and check to see when it opens

ELECTRONIC ENGINE CONTROLS

General Information

The engine is equipped with a Toyota Computer Control System (TCSS) which centrally controls the electronic fuel injection, electronic spark advance and the exhaust gas recirculation valve. The systems can be diagnosed by means of an Electronic Control Unit (ECU) which employs a microcomputer. The ECU and the TCCS control the following functions:

1. Electronic Fuel Injection (EFI). The ECU receives signals from the various sensors indicating changing engine operations conditions such as:

- Intake air volume
- Intake air temperature
- Coolant Temperature sensor
- Engine rpm
- Acceleration/deceleration
- Exhaust oxygen content

These signals are utilized by the ECU to determine the injection duration necessary for an optimum air/fuel ratio.

2. The Electronic Spark Advance (ESA) is programmed with data for optimum ignition timing during any and all operating conditions. Using the data provided by sensors which monitor various engine functions (rpm, intake air volume, coolant temperature, etc.), the microcomputer (ECU) triggers the spark at precisely the right moment.

3. Idle Speed Control (ISC) is programmed with specific engine speed values to respond to different engine conditions (coolant temperature, air conditioner on/off, etc.). Sensors transmit signals to the ECU which controls the flow of air through the bypass of the throttle valve and adjusts the idle speed to the specified value.

4. Exhaust Gas Recirculation (EGR) detects the coolant temperature and controls the EGR operations accordingly.

5. Electronic Controlled Transmission (ECT—automatic transmission only). A serial signal is transmitted to the ECT computer to prevent shift up to third or overdrive during cold engine operation.

6. Diagnostics, which are outlined below.

7. Fail-safe function. In the event of a computer malfunction, a backup circuit will take over to provide minimal driveability. Simultaneously, the "CHECK ENGINE" warning light is activated.

Electronic Control Unit (ECU)

OPERATION

♦ **See Figures 15 and 16**

The ECU receives signals from various sensors on the engine. It will then process this information and calculate the correct air/fuel mixture under all operating conditions. The ECU is a very fragile and expensive component. Always follow the precautions when servicing the electronic control system.

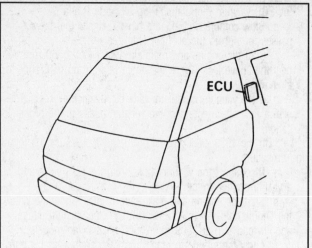

Fig. 15 The Electronic Control Unit (ECU) on the Van is located in the drivers side pillar

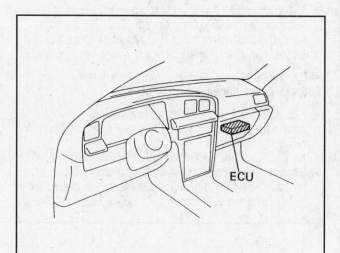

Fig. 16 The Electronic Control Unit (ECU) on the Cressida is located under the passenger's side dash

PRECAUTIONS

- Do not permit parts to receive a severe impact during removal or installation. Always handle all fuel injection parts with care, especially the ECU. DO NOT open the ECU cover!

- Before removing the fuel injected wiring connectors, terminals, etc., first disconnect the power by either disconnecting the negative battery cable or turning the ignition switch **OFF**.

- Do not be careless during troubleshooting as there are numerous amounts of tasnsistor circuits; even a slight terminal contact can induce troubles.

- When inspecting during rainy days, take extra caution not to allow entry of water in or on the unit. When washing the engine compartment, prevent water from getting on the fuel injection parts and wiring connectors.

ECU Connectors Voltage
▶ **See Figures 17, 18, 19, 20, and 21**

The EFI circuit can be checked by measuring the resistance and the voltage at the wiring connectors of the ECU. The following list should be followed before making the ECU inspection:

1. Perform all voltage measurements with the connectors attached.
2. Verify that the battery voltage is 11 volts or more when the ignition switch is turned **OFF.**
3. The testing probes must not make contact with the ECU Ox and Vf terminals.
4. Remove the glove box, turn the ignition switch to the **ON** position and measure the voltage at each terminal.

No.	Terminals	Condition		STD Voltage
1	BAT – E_1	—		
	+B – E_1	Ignition S/W ON		10 – 14
	IG S/W – E_1			
	M-REL – E_1			
2	IDL – E_1	Ignition S/W ON	Throttle valve open	4 – 6
	PSW – E_1		Throttle valve fully closed	4 – 6
3	Vc – E_2	Ignition S/W ON	—	4 – 6
	Vs – E_2		Measuring plate fully closed	4 – 5
			Measuring plate fully open	0.02 – 0.08
			Idling	2 – 4
			3,000 rpm	0.3 – 1.0
	THA – E_2	IG S/W ON	Intake air temperature 20°C (68°F)	1 – 2
4	THW – E_1	IG S/W ON	Coolant temperature 80°C (176°F)	0.1 – 0.5
5	STA – E_1	Ignition switch ST position		6 – 12
6	No.10 No.20 – E_1	Ignition switch ON		9 – 14
7	IGt – E_1	Idling		0.7 – 1.0
8	ISC_1 ~ ISC_4 – E_1	Ignition switch ON		9 – 14
		2–3 secs, after engine off		9 – 14

Fig. 17 Voltage specifications at the ECU connectors—1983–84 Cressida

Fig. 19 Voltage specifications at the ECU connectors—1989–90 Cressida

No.	Terminals	Condition	STD Voltage
1	BATT – E1		10 – 14
	IG SW – E1	Ignition SW ON	10 – 14
	M-REL – E1		
	+B (+B1) – E1		
2	IDL – E2	Throttle valve open	4 – 6
	VC – E2	Ignition SW ON / —	4 – 6
	VTA – E2	Throttle valve fully closed	0.1 – 1.0
		Throttle valve fully open	3.2 – 4.2
3	VC – E2	Ignition SW ON / —	4 – 6
	VS – E2	Measuring plate fully closed	3.7 – 4.3
		Measuring plate fully open	0.2 – 0.5
		Idling	2.3 – 2.8
		3,000 rpm	1.0 – 2.0
4	No.10 – E01	Ignition SW ON	10 – 14
	No.20 – E02		
	No.10		
5	THA – E2	Ignition SW ON / Intake air temperature 20°C (68°F)	1 – 3
6	THW – E2	Ignition SW ON / Coolant temperature 80°C (176°F)	0.1 – 1.0
7	STA – E1	Cranking	6 – 14
8	IGT – E1	Idling	0.7 – 1.0
9	ISC1 ~ ISC4 – E1	Ignition SW ON	9 – 14
10	W – E1	No trouble ("CHECK" engine warning light off) and engine running	8 – 14
11	A/C – E1	Air conditioning ON	10 – 14

ECU Terminals

* California specification vehicles only

Fig. 18 Voltage specifications at the ECU connectors—1985–88 Cressida

No.	Terminals	Condition	STD Voltage
1	BAT – E1	—	10 – 14
	+B – E1	Ignition S/W ON	
	IG S/W – E1		
	M-REL – E1		
2	IDL – E22	Throttle valve open	4 – 6
	Vc – E22	Ignition S/W ON / —	4 – 6
	VTA – E22	Throttle valve fully closed	0.1 – 1.0
		Throttle valve fully opened	4 – 5
3	Vc – E2	Ignition S/W ON / —	4 – 6
	Vs – E2	Measuring plate fully closed	4 – 5
		Measuring plate fully open	0.02 – 0.08
		Idling	2 – 4
		3,000 rpm	0.3 – 1.0
4	THA – E2	IG S/W ON / Intake air temperature 20°C (68°F)	1 – 2
5	THW – E2	IG S/W ON / Coolant temperature 80°C (176°F)	0.1 – 0.5
6	STA – E1	Ignition S/W ST position	6 – 12
7	No.10 / No.20 – E1	Ignition S/W ON	9 – 14
	IGt – E1	Cranking or idling	0.7 – 1.0
8	ISC1 ~ ISC4 – E1	Ignition S/W ON	9 – 14
		2 – 3 secs, after engine off	9 – 14

No.	Terminals	Voltage (V)	Condition
1	$+B - E_1$	10 - 14	Ignition switch ON
2	$BAT - E_1$	10 - 14	-
3	$IDL - E_1$ $Psw - E_1$ $TL - E_1$	8 - 14 8 - 14 8 - 14	Throttle valve fully closed (IG s/w ON) Throttle valve fully open (IG s/w ON)
4	$IG - E_1$	above 3	Cranking or engine running
5	$STA - E_1$	6 - 12	Cranking
6	$No.10 - E_1$ $No.20 - E_1$	9 - 14 9 - 14	Ignition switch ON Ignition switch ON
7	$W - E_1$	8 - 14	No trouble ("CHECK" engine warning light off) and engine running
8	$V_C - E_2$ $V_S - E_2$	4 - 9 0.5 - 2.5 5 - 8 2.5 - 5.5	 Measuring plate fully closed (IG s/w ON) Measuring plate fully open (IG s/w ON) Idling
9	$THA - E_2$	2 - 6	Intake air temperature 20°C (68°F)
10	$THW - E_2$	0.5 - 2.5	Coolant temperature 80°C (176°F)
11	$A/C - E_1$	8 - 14	Air conditioning ON

ECU Connectors

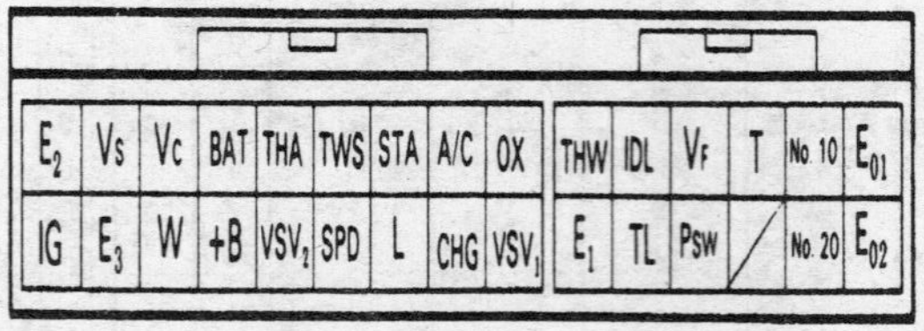

Fig. 20 Voltage specifications at the ECU connectors—1984–85 Van

No.	Terminals	STD voltage	Condition	
1	+B +B1 – E1	10 – 14	Ignition switch ON	
2	BATT – E1	10 – 14	—	
3	IDL – E1	8 – 14	Ignition switch ON	Throttle valve open
	PSW – E1	8 – 14		Throttle valve fully closed
4	IGT – E1	0.7 – 1.0	Idling	
5	STA – E1	6 – 12	Cranking	
6	No. 10 – E01 No. 20 – E02	9 – 14	Ignition switch ON	
7	W – E1	8 – 14	No trouble ("CHECK" engine warning light off) and engine running	
8	VC – E2	6 – 10	Ignition switch ON	—
	VS – E2	0.5 – 2.5		Measuring plate fully closed
		5 – 10		Measuring plate fully open
		2 – 8	—	
9	THA – E2	1 – 3	Ignition switch ON	Intake air temperature 20°C (68°F)
10	THW – E2	0.1 – 1.0	Ignition switch ON	Coolant temperature 80°C (176°F)
11	A/C – E1	8 – 14	Ignition switch ON	A/C ON

ECU Terminals

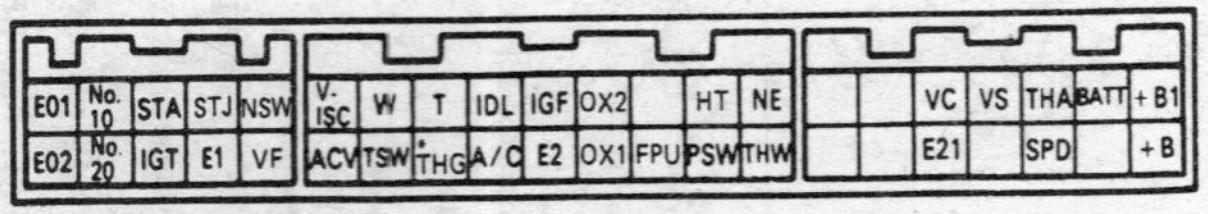

* California vehicles only

Fig. 21 Voltage specifications at the ECU connectors—1986–89 Van

ECU Connectors Resistance
▶ **See Figure 22, 23, 24, 25 and 26**

Be sure not to touch the ECU terminals. The tester probe should be inserted into the wiring connector from the wiring side.

1. Remove the glove box. Unplug the wiring connectors from the ECU.
2. Measure the resistance between each terminal of the wiring connector.

REMOVAL & INSTALLATION

1. Disconnect the negative battery cable.
2. Locate the ECU and release the lock, then pull out the connector. Pull on the connectors only!
3. Unbolt the ECU from its mounting area.
To install:
4. Mount the ECU on the vehicle in the proper location.
5. Fully insert the connector, then check that it is locked.

Oxygen Sensor

➡**During handling of the oxygen sensor, do not hit the end of the sensor. The sensor can be easily damaged by impact or rough handling. Additionally, do not allow the sensor to come in contact with water or petroleum products.**

OPERATION

The exhaust oxygen sensor or O2S, is mounted in the exhaust stream where it monitors oxygen content in the exhaust gas. The oxygen content in the exhaust is a measure of the air/fuel mixture going into the engine. The oxygen in the exhaust reacts with the oxygen sensor to produce a voltage which is read by the ECU.

TESTING

Testing With a Voltmeter

CRESSIDA

1. Make sure the following conditions prevail before checking the oxygen sensor:
   a. Air cleaner installed.
   b. Engine has reached normal operating temperature.
   c. All pipes and hoses of the air intake system are connected.
   d. All accessories are switched off.
   e. Electronic fuel injection (EFI) wiring connections tightly connected.
   f. Ignition timing correct.
   g. Transmission in Neutral, parking brake set and wheels blocked.
2. Connect a suitable tachometer to the engine, always connect the positive terminal of the tachometer to the engine service connector (IG terminal) located under in the engine compartment. Using a suitable piece of jumper wire short the terminals of the check engine connector (1983–88 T and E1 1989–90 TE1 and E1), located in the engine compartment.
3. Connect a voltmeter to the Vf and E1 (Vf1 1989–90) terminals of the engine (diagnosis) service connector, located in the engine compartment.
4. Warm up the oxygen sensor with the engine at running at 2500 rpm for approximately 2 minutes.

Terminals	Condition	Resistance (Ω)
IDL — E22	Throttle valve open	∞
	Throttle valve fully closed	0 — 100Ω
VTA — E22	Throttle valve fully opened	3,300 — 10,000
	Throttle valve fully closed	200 — 800
Vc — E22	Disconnect air flow meter connector	3,000 — 7,000
	Disconnect throttle position sensor connector	200 — 400
Vs — E2	Measuring plate fully closed	20 — 400
	Measuring plate fully opened	20 — 1,000
THA — E2	Intake air temperature 20°C (68°F)	2,000 — 3,000
G — G⊖	—	140 — 180
Ne — G⊖	—	140 — 180
ISC1, ISC2 ISC3, ISC4 — +B	—	10 — 30

Fig. 22 Resistance specifications at the ECU connectors—1985–88 Cressida

Resistances at ECU Wiring Connectors

Terminals	Condition	Resistance
TL – IDL	0	(Throttle valve fully closed)
TL – IDL	∞	(Throttle valve fully open)
TL – Psw	∞	(Throttle valve fully closed)
TL – Psw	0	(Throttle valve fully open)
IDL, TL, P_{sw} – Ground	∞	
THW – E_2	200 – 400 Ω	(Coolant temp. 80°C or 176°F)
THA – E_2	2.2 – 2.7 kΩ	(Intake air temp. 20°C or 68°F)
THW, THA – Ground	∞	
+B – E_2	200 – 400 Ω	
VC – E_2	100 – 300 Ω	
VS – E_2	20 – 400 Ω	(Measuring plate fully closed)
VS – E_2	20 – 1,000 Ω	(Measuring plate fully open)
E_1, E_{01}, E_{02} – Ground	0	

ECU Connectors

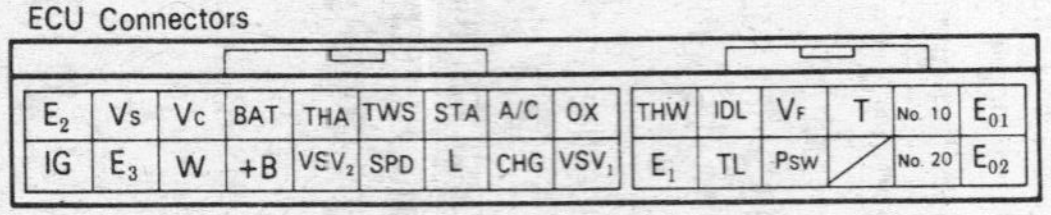

Fig. 24 Resistance specifications at the ECU connectors—1983–85 Van

Resistance at ECU Wiring Connectors

Terminals	Condition	Resistance (Ω)
IDL – E1	Throttle valve open	∞
	Throttle valve fully closed	0
PSW – E1	Throttle valve open	0
	Throttle valve fully closed	∞
+B – E2		200 – 400
VC – E2		100 – 300
VS – E2	Measuring plate fully closed	20 – 400
	Measuring plate fully open	20 – 1,000
THA – E2	Intake air temperature 20°C (68°F)	2,000 – 3,000
THW – E2	Coolant temperature 80°C (176°F)	200 – 400

ECU Terminals

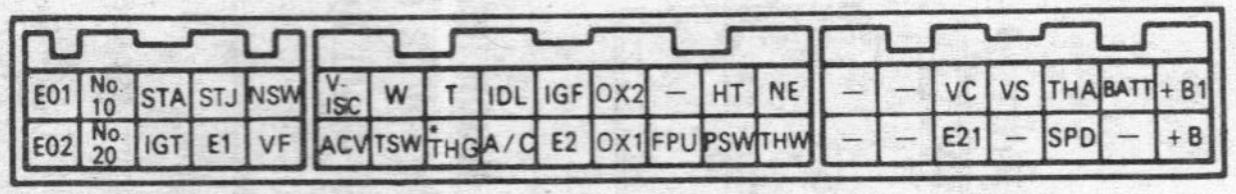

* California vehicles only

Fig. 25 Resistance specifications at the ECU connectors—1986–89 Van

Resistance of ECU Wiring Connectors

Terminals	Condition	Resistance (Ω)
IDL – E2	Throttle valve open	∞
	Throttle valve fully closed	2,300 or less
VTA – E2	Throttle valve open	3,500 – 10,300
	Throttle valve fully closed	300 – 6,300
VC – E2		200 – 400
VS – E2	Measuring plate fully closed	200 – 600
	Measuring plate fully open	20 – 1,200
THA – E2	Intake air temperature 20°C (68°F)	2,000 – 3,000
THW – E2	Coolant temperature 80°C (176°F)	200 – 400
G1, G2 – G(–)		140 – 180
NE – G(–)		180 – 220
ISC1, ISC2 – +B		
ISC3, ISC4		10 – 30

ECU Terminals

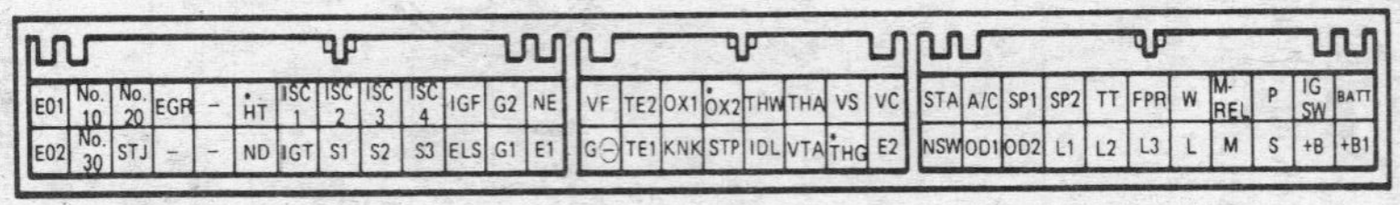

* California specification vehicles only

Fig. 23 Resistance specifications at the ECU connectors—1989–90 Cressida

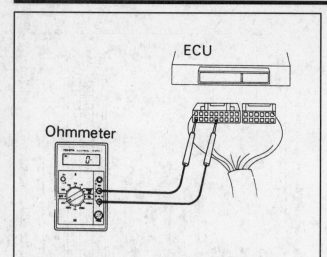

Fig. 26 When testing the resistance of the ECU, the test probe should be carefully inserted into the wiring connector from the wiring side. Do not damage the connector

5. Maintain the engine speed at 2500 rpm.
6. Check that the needle on the voltmeter fluctuates 8 times or more in 10 seconds. If not, inspect the EFI system and replace the oxygen sensor, if necessary.

VAN

▶ **See Figure 27**

1. With the engine at normal operating temperature, connect a voltmeter to the service connector located in the engine compartment. Using the service connector test wire lead (SST 09842-14010 or equivalent), connect the positive (+) probe to the red wire lead and the negative (−) probe to the black wire.
2. Raise the engine speed to 2500 rpm for about 120 seconds.
3. Maintain the engine speed at 2500 rpm and check that the needle of the voltmeter fluctuates 8 times or more in 10 seconds within 0–7 volts.

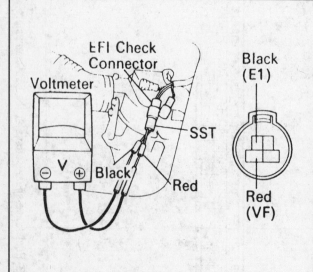

Fig. 27 To test the oxygen sensor, connect a voltmeter as shown—Van

→ **If this test is positive, the oxygen sensor is functioning properly. If not, inspect the other parts, hose connections and wiring of the air bleed system. If no problem is found, replace the oxygen sensor.**

Using an EFI Tester

1. Install EFI tester SST 09991-00100 or equivalent to the EFI service connector and oxygen sensor check connector EFI.
2. Start the engine and let it run until it reaches normal operating temperature. Connect a tachometer to the engine. On models with electronic ignition, attach the tachometer to the negative (−) side of the ignition coil, not to the distributor primary lead. Damage to the ignition control unit will result from improper connections.
3. Race the engine at 2,500 rpm for approximately 90 seconds. Then maintain a steady engine speed at 2,500 rpm.
4. Check that the oxygen sensor indicator light blinks 8 times or more in 10 seconds. If it does not, inspect the EFI system and replace the oxygen sensor if necessary.
5. Stop the engine and remove all test equipment. Install the rubber caps to the EFI service connector and the oxygen sensor check connector.

REMOVAL & INSTALLATION

1. Disconnect the negative battery cable.
2. Ensure that the engine and exhaust pipes are cold. Locate the oxygen sensor. Some sensors are on the front pipe, others are on the catalyst, you may have more than one.
3. Spray a lubricant on the studs to ease removal.
4. Disconnect the negative battery cable and disconnect the oxygen sensor wiring.
5. Remove the oxygen sensor retaining nuts.
6. Remove the oxygen sensor and gasket.
To install:
7. Install the oxygen sensor with a new gasket.
8. Apply a coating of anti-seize to the studs. Install the nuts and tighten to 14 ft. lbs. (20 Nm).
9. Connect the oxygen sensor wiring.
10. Connect the negative battery cable.

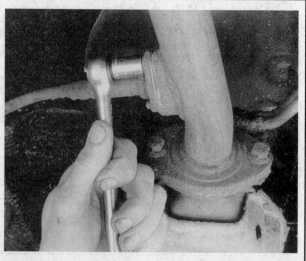

Loosen and remove the nuts securing the oxygen sensor

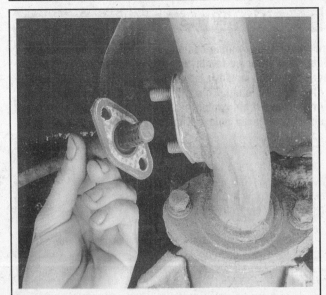

Pull the sensor from the exhaust pipe. Be sure to replace the gasket

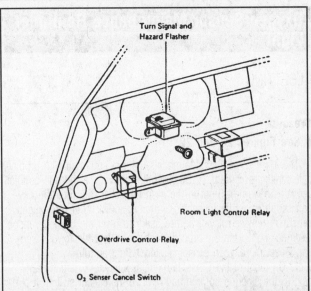

Fig. 29 Location of a common oxygen sensor cancel switch. Press it to reset the light

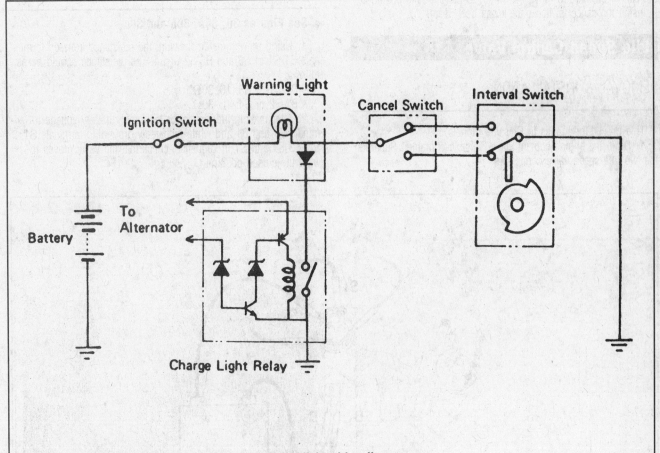

Fig. 28 Common oxygen sensor maintenance reminder light wiring diagram

Oxygen Sensor Maintenance Reminder Light

RESETTING

Cressida

▶ **See Figures 28 and 29**

There are some Cressida models that are equipped with an oxygen sensor reset light. At 30,000 mile intervals, a mileage counter activates a warning light in the dash panel. At this time the oxygen sensor must be inspected and/or replaced. After the oxygen sensor is replaced it will be necessary to reset the oxygen sensor reminder light. Use the procedure above to test the oxygen sensor. Reset the oxygen sensor reminder light as follows:

1. On most of the Cressida models, remove the small panel next to the steering column and remove the cancel switch. It should be noted, that this cancel switch has also been found to be taped to the main wiring harness located up above the left-hand side kick panel.

2. Once the cancel switch has been found, pry open the tab on the cancel switch and move the switch to the opposite position. Reinstall the cancel switch once it has been reset.

Idle Speed Control Valve

REMOVAL & INSTALLATION

This procedure applies to Cressida models only.

1. Drain the engine coolant into a suitable container. Separate the two idle speed valve connectors.

✳✳ CAUTION

When draining engine coolant, keep in mind that cats and dogs are attracted to ethylene glycol antifreeze and could drink any that is left in an uncovered container or in puddles on the ground. This will prove fatal in sufficient quantity. Always drain coolant into a sealable container. Coolant should be reused unless it is contaminated or is several years old.

2. Disconnect the two water by pass hoses and the vacuum hoses from the idle speed control valve body.

3. Remove the two idle speed control valve retaining bolts and remove the valve from the vehicle.

To install:

4. Install the valve onto the vehicle and install two idle speed control valve retaining bolts.

5. Reconnect the two water by pass hoses and the vacuum hoses to the idle speed control valve body.

6. Attach the two idle speed valve connectors and refill the engine coolant.

TESTING

▶ **See Figures 30, 30a, 30b and 30c**

1. Using an ohmmeter, measure the resistance between terminals B1-S1 or S3 and B2-S2 or S4. The resistance should be as follows:

- B1-S1 or S3: 10–30Ω
- B2-S2 or S4: 10–30Ω

2. After making the resistance test, apply battery voltage to terminals B1 and B1 and while repeatedly grounding terminals S1, S2, S3 S4 and S1 in sequence, check that the valve moves toward the closed position.

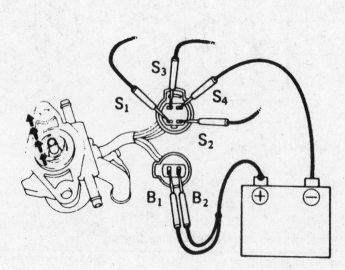

Fig. 30 To test the idle speed control valve, measure the resistance with an ohmmeter between the terminals

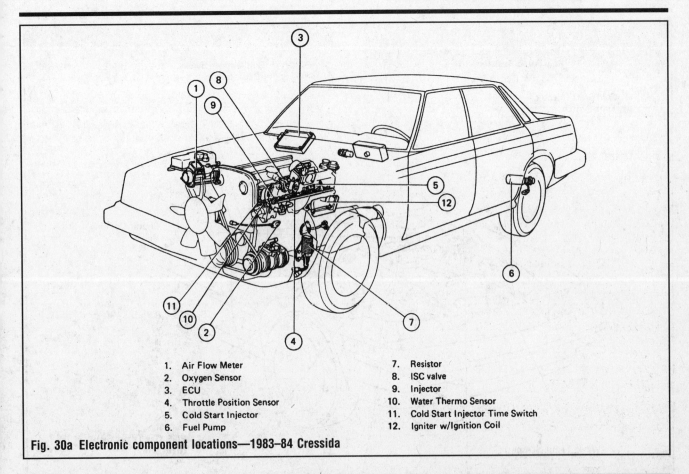

1. Air Flow Meter
2. Oxygen Sensor
3. ECU
4. Throttle Position Sensor
5. Cold Start Injector
6. Fuel Pump

7. Resistor
8. ISC valve
9. Injector
10. Water Thermo Sensor
11. Cold Start Injector Time Switch
12. Igniter w/Ignition Coil

Fig. 30a Electronic component locations—1983–84 Cressida

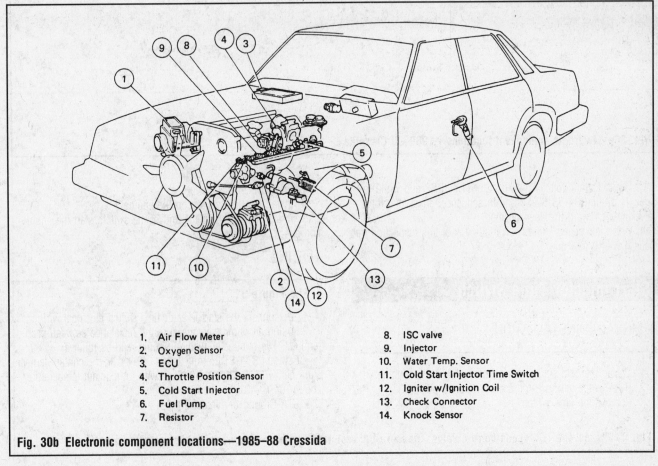

1. Air Flow Meter
2. Oxygen Sensor
3. ECU
4. Throttle Position Sensor
5. Cold Start Injector
6. Fuel Pump
7. Resistor

8. ISC valve
9. Injector
10. Water Temp. Sensor
11. Cold Start Injector Time Switch
12. Igniter w/Ignition Coil
13. Check Connector
14. Knock Sensor

Fig. 30b Electronic component locations—1985–88 Cressida

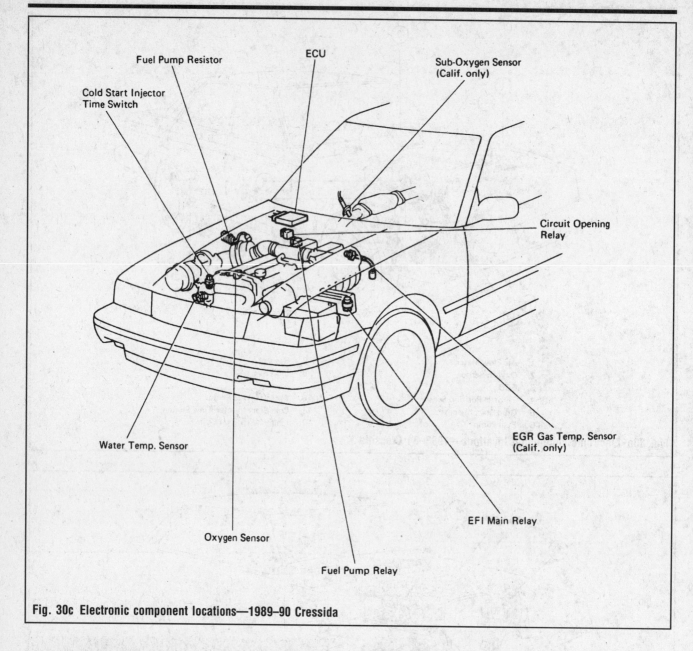

Fig. 30c Electronic component locations—1989–90 Cressida

3. Apply battery voltage to terminals B1 and B2 and while repeatedly ground S4-S3-S2-S1 and in sequence, check that the valve moves toward the open position.

4. If the idle speed control valve fails any of this inspection, replace it with a new one.

Start Injector Time Switch

REMOVAL & INSTALLATION

1. Locate the cold start injector time switch on the engine.
2. Remove the wiring harness leading to the switch.
3. Remove the time switch.

To install:

4. Install the time switch on the engine.
5. Attach the wiring to the end of the switch, start the engine and check operation.

TESTING

◆ **See Figure 31**

1. Disconnect the start injector time switch electrical wiring.
2. Using an ohmmeter, measure the resistance between each terminal. The ohmmeter reading should read as follows:
• Between STA-STJ terminals: 24–40Ω with the coolant temperature below 86°F (30°C); 40–60Ω with the coolant temperature above 104°F (40°C)
• STA-Ground terminals: 20–80Ω

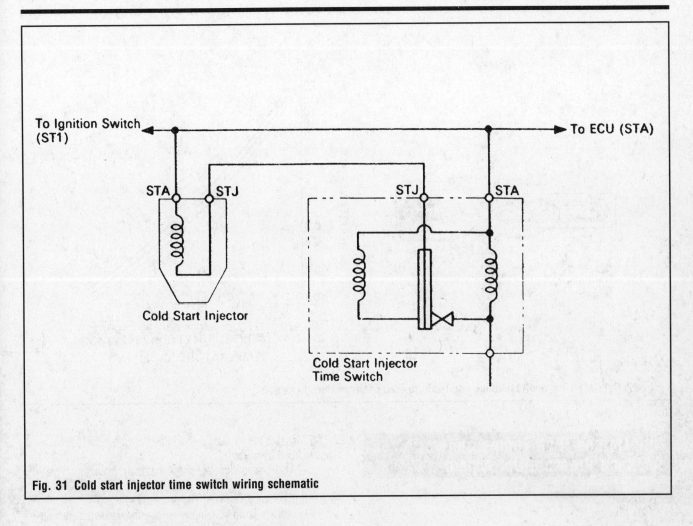

To Ignition Switch (ST1)

To ECU (STA)

STA   STJ

STJ   STA

Cold Start Injector

Cold Start Injector
Time Switch

Fig. 31 Cold start injector time switch wiring schematic

COLD START INJECTOR TIME SWITCH TEST

Terminals	Resistance (Ω)	Coolant temp.
STA – STJ	20 – 40	below 35°C (95°F)
	40 – 60	above 35°C (95°F)
STA – Ground	20 – 80	–

Water Thermo Sensor

REMOVAL & INSTALLATION

1. Locate the water thermo switch on the engine.
2. Remove the wiring harness leading to the switch.
3. Remove the water thermo switch.
To install:
4. Install the water thermo switch on the engine.
5. Attach the wiring to the end of the switch, start the engine and check operation.

TESTING

◗ **See Figure 32**

1. Disconnect the electrical wiring to the water thermo sensor.
2. Using an ohmmeter, measure the resistance between both charts. Refer to the water thermo sensor resistance chart.

Fuel Cut RPM

TESTING

1. Start the engine and let it run until it reaches normal operating temperature.
2. Separate the throttle position sensor connector from the throttle position sensor.
3. Short circuit terminals E1 (E2 on some models) and IDL on the wire connector side. Gradually raise the engine rpm and check that there is fluctuation between the fuel cut and fuel return points. The fuel cut rpm should be 1,800 rpm and the fuel return points 1,200 rpm; on the Van models the fuel cut rpm 2200 rpm and the fuel return point is 1800 rpm.

➡**The vehicle should be stopped.**

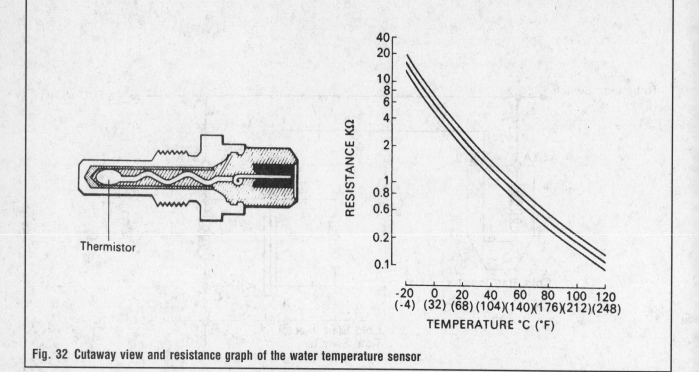

Fig. 32 Cutaway view and resistance graph of the water temperature sensor

Idle-Up and High Temperature A/C Line Pressure Up System

TESTING

▶ **See Figures 33 thru 37b**

This procedure applies to Van models only.

1. Drain the engine coolant into a suitable container. Separate the idle-up temperature switch connectors.

✳✳ CAUTION

When draining engine coolant, keep in mind that cats and dogs are attracted to ethylene glycol antifreeze and could drink any that is left in an uncovered container or in puddles on the ground. This will prove fatal in sufficient quantity. Always drain coolant into a sealable container. Coolant should be reused unless it is contaminated or is several years old.

2. Unscrew the switch from the engine.
3. Place the switch in a suitable container filled with water, then gradually heat the water.
4. Using an ohmmeter, check that there is no continuity between the terminal and body when the temperature is below 217°F (103°C).
5. Check that there is continuity between the terminal and the body when the temperature is above 230°F (110°C).
6. If the operation is not as specified, replace the switch.

7. Inspect the vacuum switching valve of the system for an open circuit as follows:
   a. Using an ohmmeter, check that there is continuity between the terminals.
   b. The resistance cold should be 37–44Ω.
   c. If there is no continuity, replace the vacuum switching valve.
8. Inspect the vacuum switching valve of the system for a ground as follows:
   a. Using an ohmmeter, check that there is no continuity between each terminal and the body.
   b. If there is continuity, replace the vacuum switching valve.
9. Inspect the vacuum switching valve operation:
   Check the Vacuum Switching Valve (VSV) operation by applying battery voltage to the terminals and blowing through the valve. The VSV should be open (air passes through) when energized and closed (no air passage) when power is removed.
10. Inspect the idle speed control vacuum switching valve of the system for an open circuit as follows:
    a. Using an ohmmeter, check that there is continuity between the terminals. The resistance cold should be 37–44Ω.
    b. If there is no continuity, replace the vacuum switching valve.
11. Inspect the idle speed control vacuum switching valve of the system for a ground as follows:
    a. Using an ohmmeter, check that there is no continuity between each terminal and the body.
    b. If there is continuity, replace the vacuum switching valve.
12. Inspect the idle speed control vacuum switching valve operation:
    Check the Vacuum Switching Valve (VSV) operation by applying battery voltage to the terminals and blowing through the valve. The VSV should be open (air passes through) when energized and closed (no air passage) when power is removed.

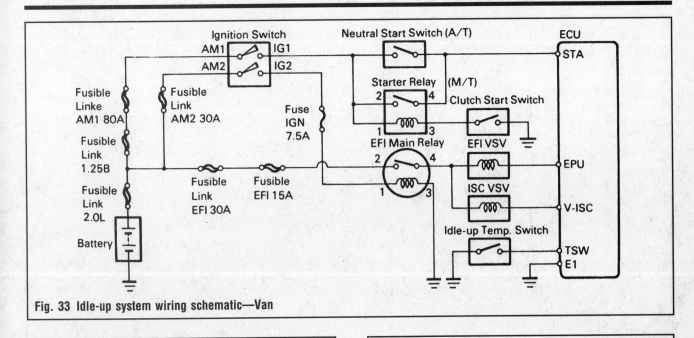

Fig. 33 Idle-up system wiring schematic—Van

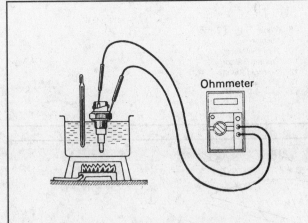

Fig. 34 Place the idle-up temperature switch into a canister of water and test the continuity with a ohmmeter

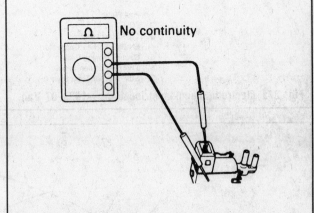

Fig. 36 Using an ohmmeter, make sure there is no continuity between each terminal and the body of the VSV

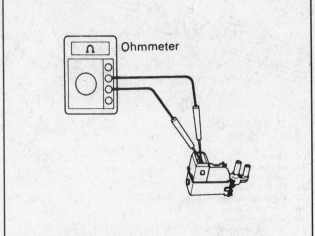

Fig. 35 Check the VSV system for an open circuit as shown—Van

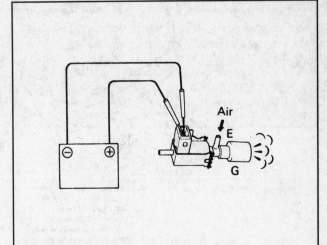

Fig. 37 Check the VSV operation by applying battery voltage and inserting air to the valve

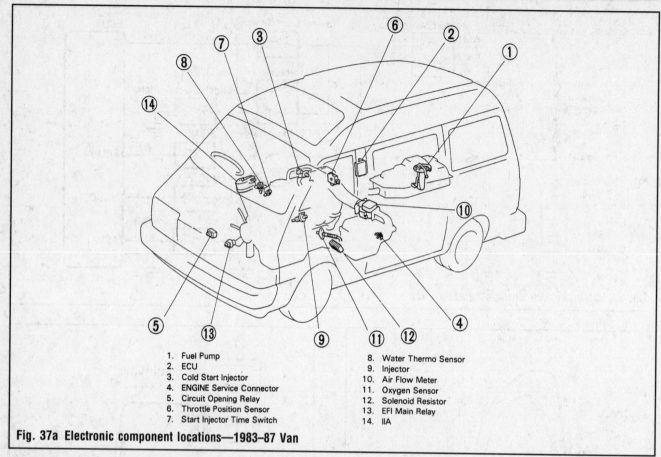

1. Fuel Pump
2. ECU
3. Cold Start Injector
4. ENGINE Service Connector
5. Circuit Opening Relay
6. Throttle Position Sensor
7. Start Injector Time Switch

8. Water Thermo Sensor
9. Injector
10. Air Flow Meter
11. Oxygen Sensor
12. Solenoid Resistor
13. EFI Main Relay
14. IIA

Fig. 37a Electronic component locations—1983–87 Van

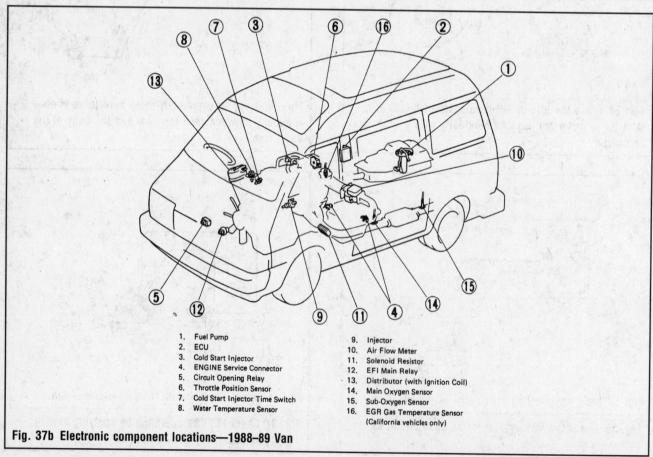

1. Fuel Pump
2. ECU
3. Cold Start Injector
4. ENGINE Service Connector
5. Circuit Opening Relay
6. Throttle Position Sensor
7. Cold Start Injector Time Switch
8. Water Temperature Sensor

9. Injector
10. Air Flow Meter
11. Solenoid Resistor
12. EFI Main Relay
13. Distributor (with Ignition Coil)
14. Main Oxygen Sensor
15. Sub-Oxygen Sensor
16. EGR Gas Temperature Sensor
    (California vehicles only)

Fig. 37b Electronic component locations—1988–89 Van

EFI Main Relay

REMOVAL & INSTALLATION

Locate the EFI relay in the fuse block. Pull the relay out of the fuse block, test and replace if necessary.

TESTING

Cressida

▸ **See Figures 38, 39 and 40**

1. Turn the ignition to the **ON** position.
2. At this time an operation noise will occur from the relay.

3. Remove the EFI main relay from the relay block.
4. Using an ohmmeter, measure the resistance between each terminal.
5. The resistance should be as follows:
- Between terminals 1 and 2: 40–60Ω
- Between terminals 3 and 4: infinity (∞)

Van

▸ **See Figures 41 and 42**

1. Using an ohmmeter, check that there is continuity between terminals 1 and 3.
2. Check that there is no continuity between terminals 2 and 4.
3. If continuity is not as specified, replace the relay.
4. Next, apply battery voltage across terminals 1 and 3.
5. Using an ohmmeter, check that there is continuity between terminals 2 and 4.
6. If operation is not as specified, replace the relay.

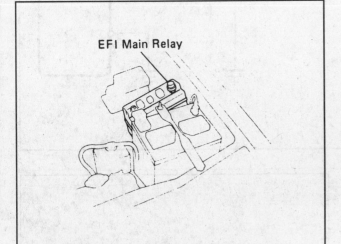

Fig. 38 The main relay is located in the fuse block under the hood near the battery on Cressida models

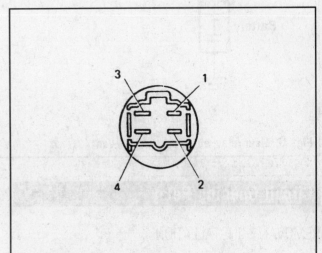

Fig. 40 Measure the resistance of the main relay between the terminals—Cressida

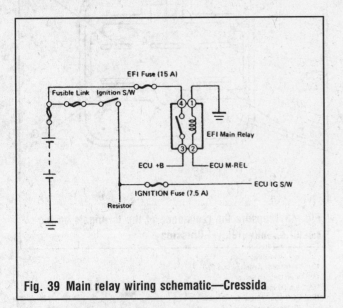

Fig. 39 Main relay wiring schematic—Cressida

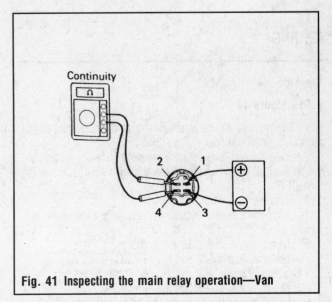

Fig. 41 Inspecting the main relay operation—Van

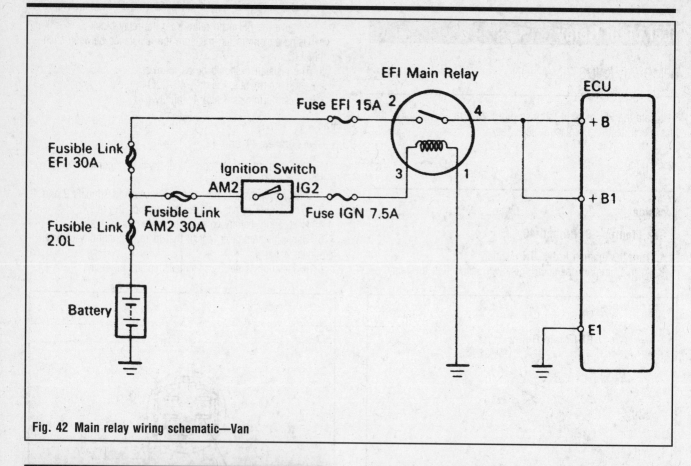

Fig. 42 Main relay wiring schematic—Van

Circuit Opening Relay

REMOVAL & INSTALLATION

Locate the relay in the fuse block. Pull the relay out of the fuse block, test and replace if necessary.

TESTING

Cressida

♦ **See Figure 43**

1. Remove the left kick panel. This relay is located next to the number 1 junction block.
2. Using a voltmeter, check the voltmeter indicates voltage at the Fp terminal during engine cranking and running. Turn the engine **OFF.**
3. Disconnect the wiring.
4. Using a ohmmeter, measure the resistance between the terminal.
5. The resistance should be as follows:
• Between terminals STA and E1: 17–25Ω
• Between terminals +B and Fc: 88–112Ω
• Between terminals +B and Fp: infinity (∞)
6. If resistance is not as specified, replace the relay.

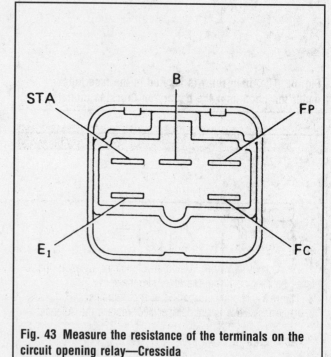

Fig. 43 Measure the resistance of the terminals on the circuit opening relay—Cressida

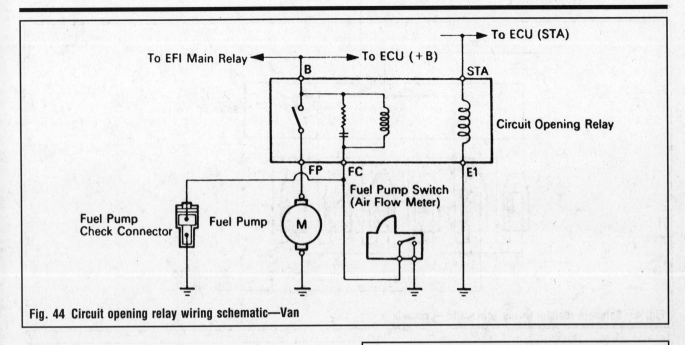

Fig. 44 Circuit opening relay wiring schematic—Van

Van

▶ **See Figures 44 and 45**

1. Disconnect the wiring.
2. Using an ohmmeter, check the continuity between the terminals.
3. The continuity should be as follows:
• Between terminals STA and E1: continuity
• Between terminals B and Fc: continuity
• Between terminals B and Fp: no continuity.
4. If continuity is not as specified, replace the relay.
5. Apply battery voltage across terminals STA and E1.
6. There should be continuity between terminals B and Fp.
7. Apply battery voltage across terminals B and Fc.
8. There should be continuity between terminals B and Fp.
9. If operation is not as specified, replace the relay.

Solenoid Resistor

TESTING

Cressida

▶ **See Figures 46, 47, 48 and 49**

1. Disconnect the wiring. Using an ohmmeter, measure the resistance between +B and the other terminals.
2. The resistance should be 2Ω at each terminal.
3. If the resistance is not as specified, replace the solenoid.

Van

1. Disconnect the wiring. Using an ohmmeter, measure the resistance between +B and the other terminals.
2. The resistance should be 2–3Ω at each terminal.
3. If the resistance is not as specified, replace the solenoid.

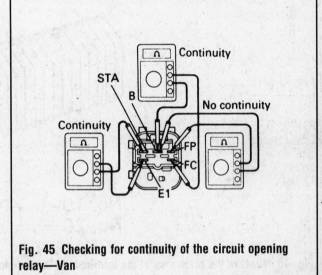

Fig. 45 Checking for continuity of the circuit opening relay—Van

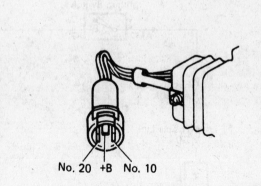

Fig. 46 Measure the resistance of the terminals in the solenoid resistor harness—Cressida

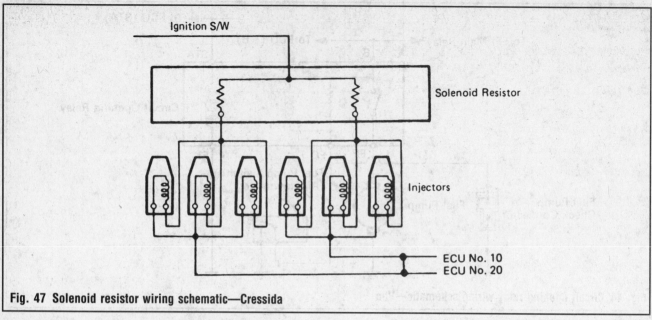

Fig. 47 Solenoid resistor wiring schematic—Cressida

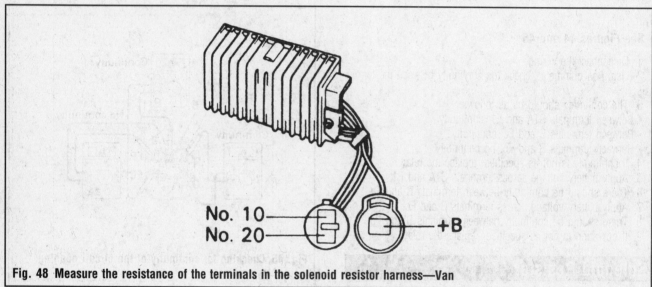

Fig. 48 Measure the resistance of the terminals in the solenoid resistor harness—Van

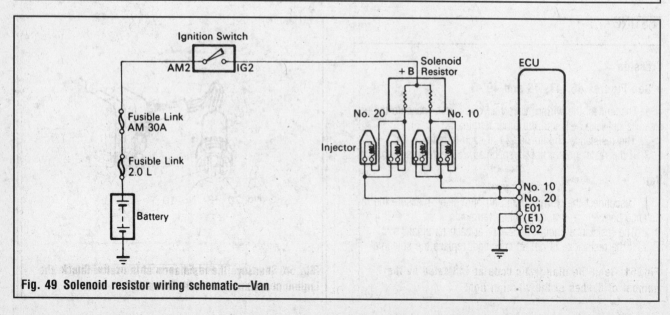

Fig. 49 Solenoid resistor wiring schematic—Van

TROUBLE CODES

General Information

▶ **See Figures 50 thru 56**

The ECU contains a built in self-diagnosis system which is tied into the trouble code system that is incorporated into the engine signal network. The trouble codes are detected and are exposed by a "CHECK ENGINE" warning light on the instrument panel, which flashes code numbers 12, 13, 14, 21, 22, 23, 24, 25, 26, 27, 31, 32, 41, 42, 43, 51, 52, 53 and 71. The CHECK ENGINE light on the instrument panel informs the driver that a malfunction has been detected. The light goes out automatically when the malfunction has been cleared.

➡ **The 1984–87 Van used malfunction code numbers 1 through 11.**

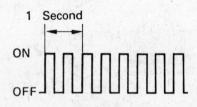

Fig. 52 For a normal system operation, the light will alternately blink ON and OFF 2 times per second

Fig. 50 The CHECK ENGINE warning lamp will light when the ignition is in the ON position

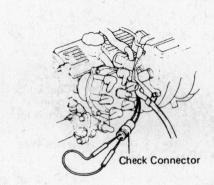

Fig. 53 Shorting the Check Engine connector—1983–84 Cressida

Fig. 51 Read the diagnostic code as indicated by the number of flashes of the warning light

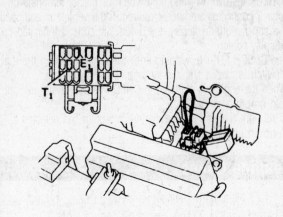

Fig. 54 Shorting T1 and E1 terminals on the Check Engine connector—1985–88 Cressida

Fig. 55 Shorting TE1 and E1 terminals on the Check Engine connector—1989–90 Cressida

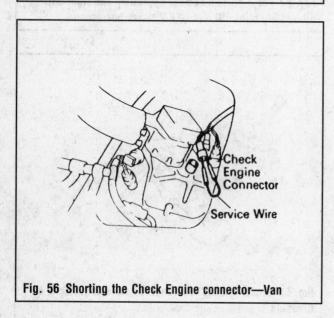

Fig. 56 Shorting the Check Engine connector—Van

The diagnostic code can be read by the number of blinks of the CHECK ENGINE warning light when the proper terminals of the check connector are short-circuited. If the vehicle is equipped with a super monitor display, the diagnostic code is indicated on the display screen.

The CHECK ENGINE warning light will come on when the ignition switch is placed **ON** and the engine is not running.

When the engine is started, the CHECK ENGINE warning light should go out.

If the light remains on, the diagnosis system has detected a malfunction in the system.

Reading Codes

1. The battery voltage should be above 11 volts. Throttle valve fully closed (throttle position sensor IDL points closed).
2. Place the transmission in **"P"** of **"N"** range. Turn the A/C switch OFF. Start the engine and let it run to reach its normal operating temperature.

WITHOUT SUPER MONITOR DISPLAY

♦ **See Figures 57 and 58**

1. Turn the ignition switch to the **ON** position. Do not start the engine. Use a suitable jumper wire and short the terminals of the check engine connector. Also on the 1989–90 Cressida use a suitable jumper wire and short terminals TE2 and E1 of the Toyota Diagnostic Communication Link (TDCL) located under the left-hand side of the instrument panel. When the engine is ready to go into diagnostic output mode, short terminals TE1 and E1, this is to be done on the 1989–90 Cressida only.

2. Read the diagnostic code as indicated by the number of flashes of the CHECK ENGINE warning light.

3. If the system is operating normally (no malfunction), the light will blink once every 0.25 seconds.

4. In the event of a malfunction, the light will blink once every 0.5 seconds. The first number of blinks will equal the first digit of a two digit diagnostic code. After a 1.5 second pause, the second

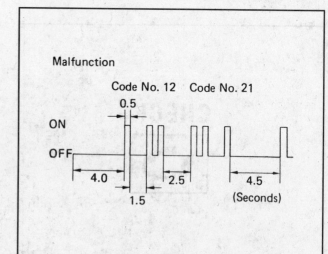

Fig. 57 In the event of malfunction code, the light will blink in a code sequence as shown

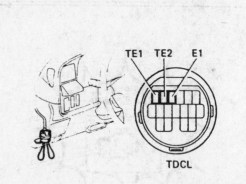

Fig. 58 Use a jumper wire to short terminals TE2 and E1 of the Toyota Diagnostic Communication Link (TDCL)—1989–90 Cressida

number of blinks will equal the second number of a 2 digit diagnostic code. If there are two or more codes, there will be a 2.5 second pause between each.

➡In event of a number of trouble codes, indication will begin from the smaller value and continue to the larger in order.

5. After the diagnosis check, remove the jumper wire from the check connector.

WITH SUPER MONITOR DISPLAY

▶ **See Figures 59, 60, 61 and 62**

1. Turn the ignition switch to the **ON** position. Do not start the engine. .

2. Simultaneously push and hold in the SELECT and INPUT M keys for at least three seconds. The letters DIAG will appear on the screen.

3. After a short pause, hold the SET key in for at least three seconds. If the system is normal (no malfunctions), ENG-OK will appear on the screen.

4. If there is a malfunction, the code number representing that malfunction will appear on the screen. In the event of two or more numbers, there will be a three second pause between each (Example ENG-42).

5. After confirmation of the diagnostic code, either turn **OFF** the ignition switch or push the super monitor display key on so the time appears.

Clearing Codes

▶ **See Figures 63, 64, 65, 66 and 67**

1. After repairing the trouble area, the diagnostic code that is retained in the ECU memory must be canceled out by removing the EFI (15A or 20A) fuse for thirty seconds or more, depending on the ambient temperature (the lower temperature, the longer the fuse must be left out with the ignition switch **OFF.**

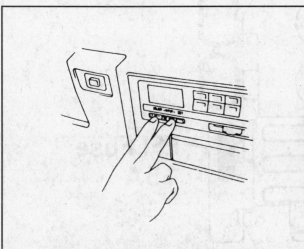

Fig. 59 Simultaneously push and hold the SELECT and INPUT M keys on the super monitor display . . .

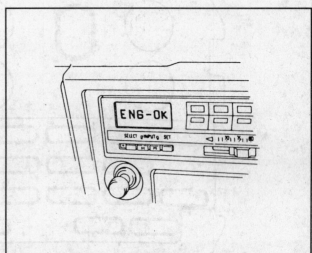

Fig. 61 If no malfunction code is found, the super monitor will state OK on the screen

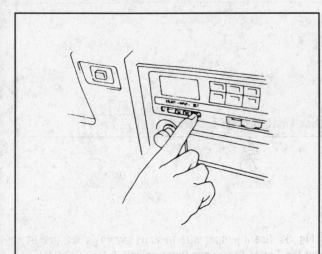

Fig. 60 . . . after a short pause, hold the SET key in for three seconds to check for malfunction codes

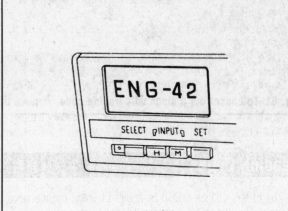

Fig. 62 A code will display on the super monitor ir a malfunction is found in the system

→Cancellation can also be done by removing the battery negative terminal, but keep in mind when removing the negative battery cable, the other memory systems (radio, ETR, clock, etc.) will also be canceled out.

If the diagnostic code is not canceled out, it will be retained by the ECU and appear along with a new code in event of future trouble. If it is necessary to work on engine components requiring re-moval of the battery terminal, a check must first be made to see if a diagnostic code is detected.

2. After cancellation, perform a road test, if necessary, confirm that a normal code is now read on the CHECK ENGINE warning light or super monitor display.

3. If the same diagnostic code is still indicated, it indicates that the trouble area has not been repaired thoroughly.

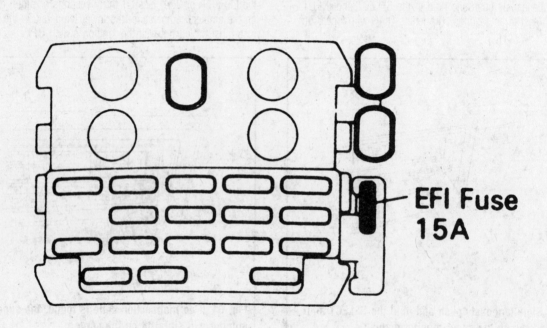

Fig. 63 To cancel out a diagnostic trouble code, remove the EFI fuse for 10 seconds or more

Code No.	Number of Check engine blinks	System	Diagnosis	Trouble area
—		Normal	This appears when none of the other codes are identified.	—
11		ECU (+B)	Momentary interruption in power supply to ECU.	• Ignition switch circuit • Ignition switch • Main relay circuit • Main relay • ECU
12		RPM Signal	No "NE" or "G" signal to ECU within 2 seconds after engine has been cranked.	• Distributor circuit • Distributor • Starter signal circuit • ECU
13		RPM Signal	No "NE" signal to ECU when engine speed is above 1,000 rpm.	• Distributor circuit • Distributor • ECU
14		Ignition Singal	No "IGF" signal to ECU 6 — 8 times in succession.	• Igniter and ignition coil circuit • Igniter and ignition coil • ECU
16		ECT Control Signal	ECT control program faulty.	• ECU
21		Oxygen Sensor Singal	Deterioration of the oxygen sensor.	• Oxygen sensor circuit • Oxygen sensor • ECU
22		Water Temp. Sensor Signal	Open or short circuit in water temp. sensor signal (THW).	• Water temp. sensor circuit • Water temp. sensor • ECU
24		Intake Air Temp. Sensor Singal	Open or short circuit in intake air temp. sensor signal (THA).	• Intake air temp. sensor circuit • Intake air temp. sensor • ECU
25		Air-Fuel Ratio Lean Malfunction	• When air-fuel ratio feedback correction value is not renewed for a certain period of time. • When air-fuel ratio feedback compensation value or adaptive control value feedback frequency is abnormally high during idle switch on and feedback condition.	• Injector circuit • Injector • Fuel line pressure • Air flow meter • Air intake system • Oxygen sensor circuit • Oxygen sensor • Ignition system • Water temp. sensor • ECU
26		Air-Fuel Ratio Rich Malfunction	• When marked variation is detected in engine revolutions for each cylinder during idle switch on and feedback condition.	• Oxygen sensor circuit • Oxygen sensor • Injector circuit • Injector • Fuel line pressure • Air flow meter • Cold start injector • Water temp. sensor • ECU

Fig. 65 Diagnostic malfunction codes—1989–90 Cressida

Code No.	System	Diagnosis	Trouble Area
	Normal	This appears when none of the other codes (11 thru 53) are identified.	
11	ECU (+ B)	Wire severence, however slight, in + B (ECU).	1. Main relay circuit 2. Main relay 3. ECU
12	RPM Signal	No Ne, G signal to ECU within several seconds after engine is cranked.	1. Distributor circuit 2. Distributor 3. Starter signal circuit 4. ECU
13	RPM Signal	No Ne signal to ECU within several seconds after engine reaches 1,000 rpm.	Same as 12, above.
14	Ignition Signal	No signal from igniter six times in succession.	1. Igniter circuit (+ B, IGt, IGf) 2. Igniter 3. ECU
21	Oxygen Sensor Signal	Oxygen sensor gives a lean signal for several seconds even when coolant temperature is above 50°C (122°F) and engine is running under high load conditions above 1,500 rpm.	1. Oxygen sensor circuit 2. Oxygen sensor 3. ECU
22	Water Temp. Sensor Signal	Open or short circuit in coolant temp. sensor signal.	1. Water temp. sensor circuit 2. Water temp. sensor 3. ECU
23	Intake Air Temp. Sensor Signal	Open or short circuit in intake air temp. sensor.	1. Intake air temp. sensor circuit 2. Intake air temp. sensor 3. ECU
31	Air Flow Meter Signal	Open circuit in Vc signal or Vs and E2 short circuited when idle points are closed.	1. Air flow meter circuit 2. Air flow meter 3. ECU
32	Air Flow Meter Signal	Open circuit in E2 or Vc and Vs short circuited.	Same as 31, above.
41	Throttle Position Sensor Signal	Open or short circuit in throttle position sensor signal.	1. Throttle position sensor circuit 2. Throttle position sensor 3. ECU
42	Vehile Speed Sensor Signal	Signal informing ECU that vehicle speed is 2.0 km/h or less has been input ECU for 5 seconds with engine running at 2,500 rpm or more and shift lever is in other than N or P range.	1. Vehicle speed sensor circuit 2. Vehicle speed sensor 3. Torque converter slipping 4. ECU
43	Starter Signal (+ B)	No STA signal to ECU when engine is running over 800 rpm.	1. Main relay circuit 2. IG switch circuit (starter) 3. IG switch 4. ECU
51	Switch Signal	Neutral start switch OFF or air conditioner switch ON during diagnostic check.	1. Neutral start S/W 2. Air con. S/W 3. ECU
52	Knock Sensor Signal	Open or short circuit in knock sensor.	1. Knock sensor circuit 2. Knock sensor 3. ECU
53	Knock Control Part (ECU)	Faulty ECU.	ECU

Fig. 64 Diagnostic malfunction codes—1983–88 Cressida

DIAGNOSTIC CODES

Fig. 66 Diagnostic malfunction codes—Van

Code No.	Number of Check engine blinks	System	Diagnosis	Trouble area
—	(blink pattern)	Normal	This appears when none of the other codes are identified.	—
12	(blink pattern)	RPM Signal	No "NE" signal to ECU within 2 seconds after engine has been cranked.	• Distributor circuit • Distributor • Stater signal circuit • Igniter circuit • ECU
13	(blink pattern)	RPM Signal	No "NE" signal to ECU when engine speed is above 1,500 rpm	• Distributor circuit • Distributor • Igniter circuit • ECU
14	(blink pattern)	Ignition Signal	No "IGF" signal to ECU 4-5 times in succession.	• Igniter and ignition coil circuit • Igniter and ignition coil • ECU
21	(blink pattern)	Oxygen Sensor Signal	Detection of oxygen sensor detrioration.	• Oxygen sensor circuit • Oxygen sensor • ECU
22	(blink pattern)	Oxygen Sensor Heater Signal	Open or short circuit in oxygen sensor heater signal.	• Oxygen sensor heater circuit • Oxygen sensor heater • ECU
23	(blink pattern)	Water Temp. Sensor Signal	Open or short circuit in water temp. sensor signal.	• Water temp. sensor circuit • Water temp. sensor • ECU
24	(blink pattern)	Intake Air Temp. Sensor Signal	Open or short circuit in intake air temp. sensor signal.	• Intake air temp sensor circuit • Intake air temp. sensor • ECU
25	(blink pattern)	Air-fuel Ratio Lean Malfunction	(1) When air-fuel ratio feedback compensation value or adaptive control value continues at the upper (lean) or lower (rich) limit renewed for a certain period of time. (2) When air-fuel ratio feedback compensation value or adaptive control value feedback frequency is abnormally high during feedback condition.	• Injector circuit • Injector • Fuel line pressure • Air flow meter • Air intake system • Oxygen sensor circuit • Ignition system • ECU
26	(blink pattern)	Air-fuel Ratio Rich Malfunction	NOTE: For condition (2), since neither a lean (Code No. 25) nor a rich (Code No. 26) diagnosis displayed consecutively.	• Injector circuit • Injector • Fuel line pressure • Air flow meter • Cold start injector • ECU

DIAGNOSTIC CODES (Cont'd)

Fig. 65a Diagnostic malfunction codes—1989-90 Cressida continued

Code No.	Number of Check engine blinks	System	Diagnosis	Trouble area
*27	(blink pattern)	Sub-Oxygen Sensor Signal	Open or short circuit in sub-oxygen sensor signal (OX2).	• Sub-oxygen sensor circuit • Sub-oxygen sensor • ECU
	(blink pattern)		Open or short circuit in sub-oxygen sensor heater signal (HT).	• Sub-oxygen sensor heater circuit • Sub-oxygen sensor heater • ECU
31	(blink pattern)	Air Flow Meter Signal	Open circuit in VC signal or short circuit between VS and E2 when idle contacts are closed.	• Air flow meter circuit • Air flow meter • ECU
32	(blink pattern)	Air Flow Meter Signal	Open circuit in E2 or short circuit between VC and VS.	• Air flow meter circuit • Air flow meter • ECU
41	(blink pattern)	Throttle Position Sensor Signal	Open or short circuit in throttle position sensor signal (VTA).	• Throttle position sensor circuit • Throttle position sensor • ECU
42	(blink pattern)	Vehicle Speed Sensor Singnal	No "SP1" signal to ECU for 8 seconds when engine speed is above 2,500 rpm and neutral start switch is off.	• No. 1 vehicle speed sensor (Meter side) circuit • No. 1 vehicle speed sensor (Meter side) • ECU
43	(blink pattern)	Starter Signal	No "STA" signal to ECU until engine speed reaches 400 rpm with vehicle not moving.	• Ignition switch circuit • Ignition switch • ECU
52	(blink pattern)	Knock Sensor Singal	Open or short circuit in knock sensor singal (KNK).	• Knock sensor circuit • Knock sensor • ECU
53	(blink pattern)	Knock Control Singal	Knock control program faulty.	• ECU
*71	(blink pattern)	EGR System Malfunction	• EGR gas temp. below predetermined level during EGR operation. • Open circuit in EGR gas temp. sensor signal (THG).	• EGR valve • EGR hose • EGR gas temp. sensor circuit • EGR gas temp. sensor • VSV for EGR • VSV circuit for EGR • ECU
51	(blink pattern)	Switch Condition Signal	No "IDL" signal, "NSW" signal or "A/C" signal to ECU, during diagnosis check for test mode.	• A/C switch circuit • A/C switch • A/C amplifier • Throttle position sensor circuit • Throttle position sensor • Neutral start switch circuit • Neutral start switch • Accelerator pedal and cable • ECU

* California specification vehicles only

DIAGNOSTIC CODES (Cont'd)

Code No.	Number of Check engine Blinks	System	Diagnosis	Trouble area
27		Sub-oxygen Sensor Signal	Open or short circuit in sub-oxygen sensor signal.	• Sub-oxygen sensor circuit • Sub-oxygen sensor • ECU
31		Air Flow Meter Signal	(1) Short circuit between VC and VB, VC and E2, or VS and VC. (2) Open circuit between VC and E2.	• Air flow meter circuit • Air flow meter • ECU
41		Throttle Position Sensor Signal	(1) Open or short circuit in throttle position sensor signal. (2) IDL ON and PSW ON condition continues for several seconds.	• Throttle position sensor circuit • Throttle position sensor • ECU
42		Vehicle Speed Sensor Signal	No "SPD" signal for 8 seconds when engine speed is between 1,500 rpm and 5,000 rpm and coolant temp. is below 80°C (176°F) except when racing the engine	• Vehicle speed sensor circuit • Vehicle speed sensor • ECU
43		Starter Signal	No "STA" signal to ECU unitl engine speed reaches 800 rpm with vehicle not moving	• Ignition switch circuit • Ignition switch • ECU
*71		EGR System Malfunction	EGR gas below predetermined level during EGR operation.	• EGR system (EGR valve, EGR hose etc.,) • EGR gas temp. sensor circuit • EGR gas temp. sensor • ECU
51		Switch Signal	No "IDL" signal, "NSW" signal or "A/C" signal to ECU, with the check terminals E1 and T shorted.	• A/C switch circuit • A/C switch • A/C Amplifire • Throttle position sensor circuit • Throttle position sensor • Neutral start switch circuit • Neutral start switch • Accelerator pedal and cable • ECU

* California vehicles only

Fig. 67 Diagnostic malfunction codes—Van

VACUUM DIAGRAMS

Following are vacuum diagrams for most of the engine and emissions package combinations covered by this manual. Because vacuum circuits will vary based on various engine and vehicle options, always refer first to the vehicle emission control information label, if present. Should the label be missing, or should vehicle be equipped with a different engine from the vehicle's original equipment, refer to the diagrams below for the same or similar configuration.

If you wish to obtain a replacement emissions label, most manufacturers make the labels available for purchase. The labels can usually be ordered from a local dealer.

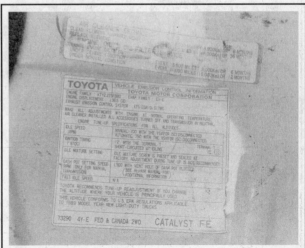

There is a vacuum hose routing sticker located in the engine compartment—Van shown

The emission control label is also located in the engine compartment—Van shown

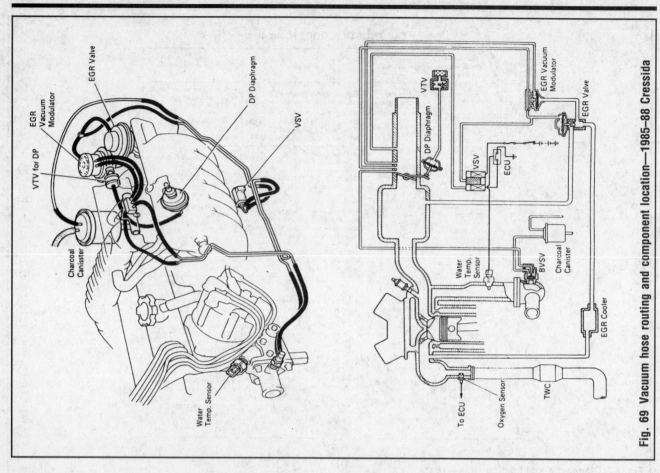

Fig. 69 Vacuum hose routing and component location—1985–88 Cressida

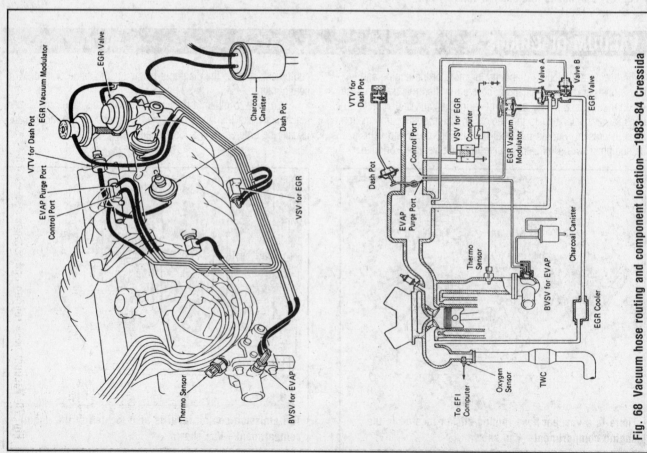

Fig. 68 Vacuum hose routing and component location—1983–84 Cressida

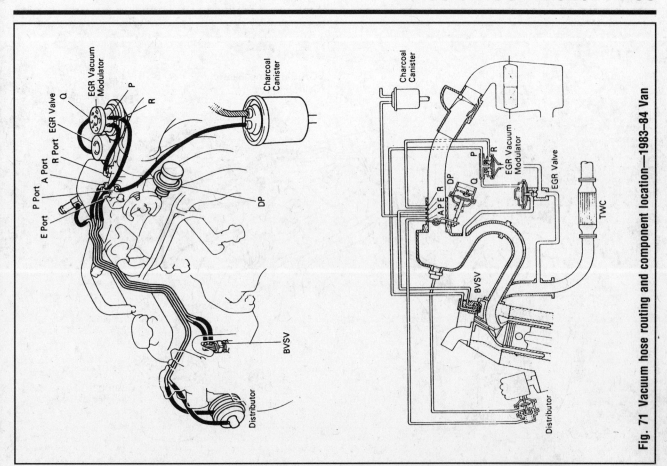

Fig. 71 Vacuum hose routing and component location—1983–84 Van

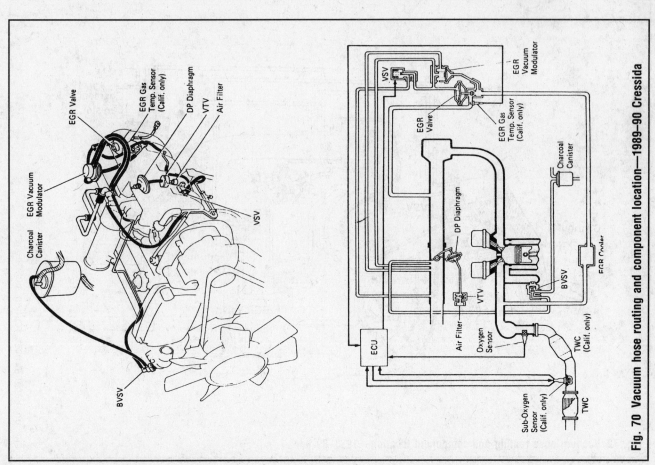

Fig. 70 Vacuum hose routing and component location—1989–90 Cressida

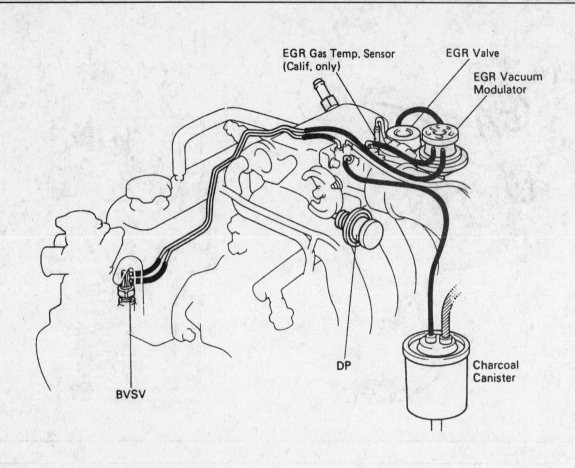

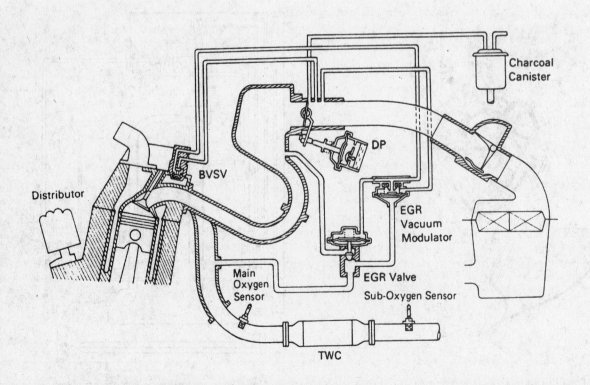

Fig. 72 Vacuum hose routing and component location—1985–89 Van

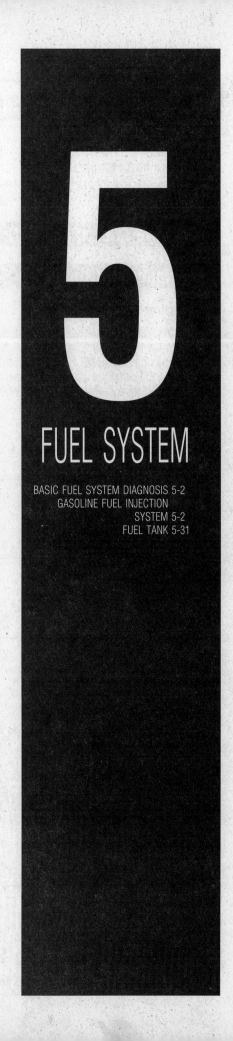

5

FUEL SYSTEM

BASIC FUEL SYSTEM DIAGNOSIS

When there is a problem starting or driving a vehicle, two of the most important checks involve the ignition and the fuel systems. The questions most mechanics attempt to answer first, "is there spark?" and "is there fuel?" will often lead to solving most basic problems. For ignition system diagnosis and testing, please refer to the information on engine electrical components and ignition systems found earlier in this manual. If the ignition system checks out (there is spark), then you must determine if the fuel system is operating properly (is there fuel?).

GASOLINE FUEL INJECTION SYSTEM

Description and Operation

▶ **See Figures 1, 2, 3, 4 and 5**

An electric fuel pump supplies sufficient fuel, under a constant pressure, to the EFI injectors. These injectors inject a metered quantity of fuel into the intake manifold in accordance with signals from the EFI computer. Each injector injects at the same time, one half of the fuel required for ideal combustion with each engine revolution. The air induction system provides sufficient air for the engine operation.

The engines are equipped with a Toyota Computer Control System (TCCS) which centrally controls the electronic fuel injection, electronic spark advance and the exhaust gas recirculation valve. The systems can be diagnosed by means of an Electronic Control Unit (ECU) which employs a microcomputer. The ECU and the TCCS control the following functions:

COMPONENT OPERATION

Electronic Fuel Injection (EFI)

The ECU receives signals from the various sensors indicating changing engine operations conditions such as:

- Intake air volume
- Intake air temperature
- Coolant temperature sensor
- Engine rpm
- Acceleration/deceleration
- Exhaust oxygen content

These signals are utilized by the ECU to determine the injection duration necessary for an optimum air-fuel ratio.

Electronic Spark Advance (ESA)

The ECU is programmed with data for optimum ignition timing during any and all operating conditions. Using the data provided by sensors which monitor various engine functions (rpm, intake air volume, coolant temperature, etc.), the microcomputer (ECU) triggers the spark at precisely the right moment.

Idle Speed Control (ISC)

The ECU is programmed with specific engine speed values to respond to different engine conditions (coolant temperature, air conditioner on/off, etc.). Sensors transmit signals to the ECU which controls the flow of air through the by-pass of the throttle valve and adjusts the idle speed to the specified value.

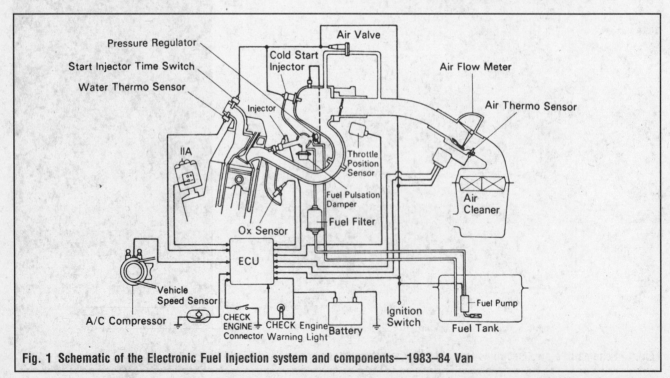

Fig. 1 Schematic of the Electronic Fuel Injection system and components—1983–84 Van

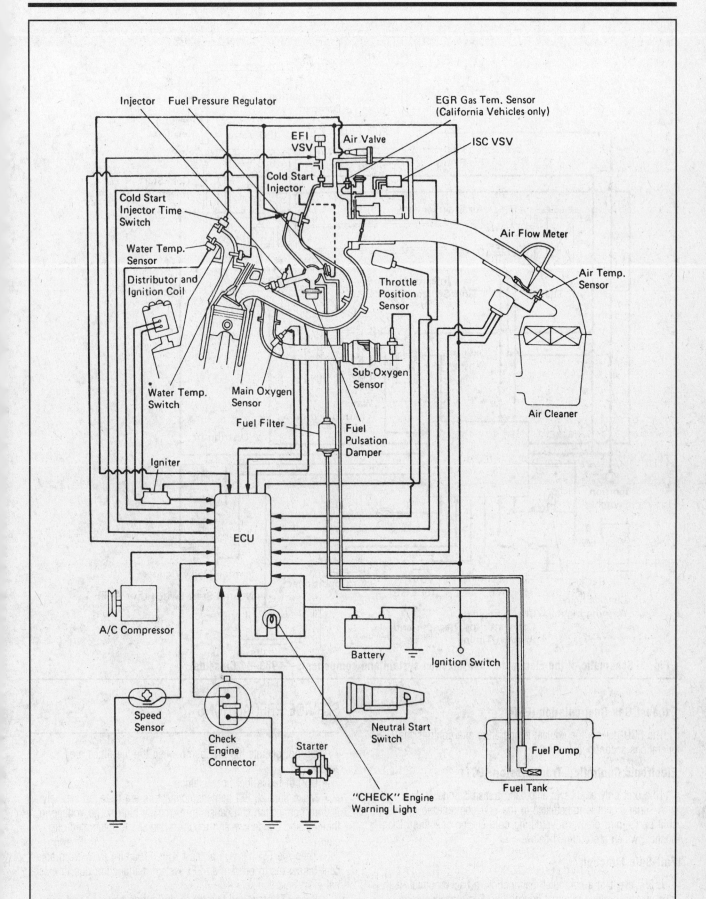

Fig. 2 Schematic of the Electronic Fuel Injection system and components—1985–89 Van

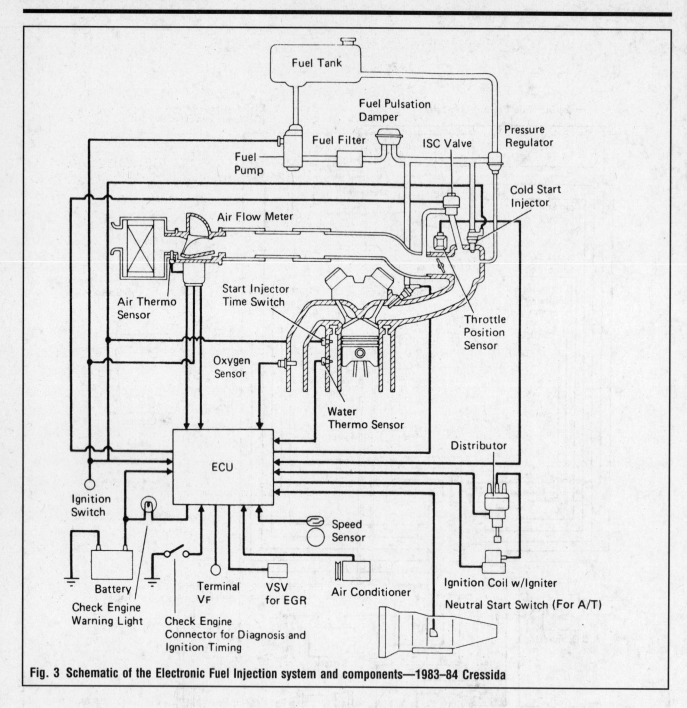

Fig. 3 Schematic of the Electronic Fuel Injection system and components—1983–84 Cressida

Exhaust Gas Recirculation (EGR)

The ECU detects the coolant temperature and controls the EGR operations accordingly.

Electronic Controlled Transmission (ECT)

This unit only applies to automatic transmissions.

A serial signal is transmitted to the ECT computer to prevent shift up to third or overdrive during cold engine operation. Diagnostics, which are outlined below.

Fail-Safe Function

In the event of a computer malfunction, a backup circuit will take over to provide minimal driveability. Simultaneously, the CHECK ENGINE warning light is activated.

SERVICE PRECAUTIONS

- Do not operate the fuel pump when the fuel lines are empty
- Do not reuse fuel hose clamps
- Make sure all EFI harness connectors are fastened securely. A poor connection can cause an extremely high surge voltage in the coil and condenser and result in damage to integrated circuits
- Keep the EFI harness at least 4 in. (100mm) away from adjacent harnesses to prevent an EFI system malfunction due to external electronic "noise"
- Keep EFI parts and harnesses dry during service
- Before attempting to remove any parts, turn **OFF** the ignition

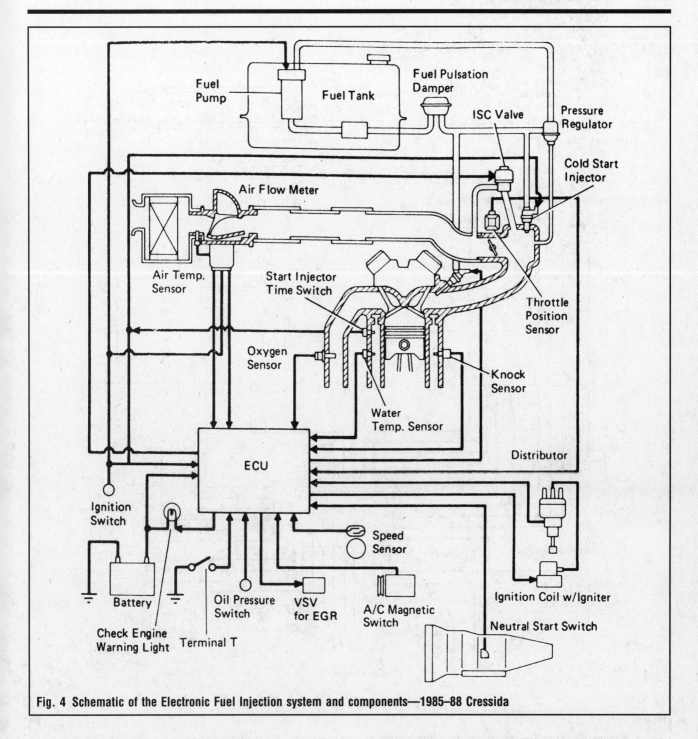

Fig. 4 Schematic of the Electronic Fuel Injection system and components—1985–88 Cressida

switch and disconnect the battery ground cable
- Always use a 12 volt battery as a power source
- Do not attempt to disconnect the battery cables with the engine running
- Do not depress the accelerator pedal when starting
- Do not rev up the engine immediately after starting or just prior to shutdown
- Do not attempt to disassemble the EFI control unit under any circumstances

- If installing a two-way or CB radio, keep the antenna as far as possible away from the electronic control unit. Keep the antenna feeder line at least 8 in. (200mm) away from the EFI harness and do not let the two run parallel for a long distance. Be sure to ground the radio to the vehicle body
- Do not apply battery power directly to injectors
- Handle air flow meter carefully to avoid damage
- Do not disassemble air flow meter or clean meter with any type of detergent

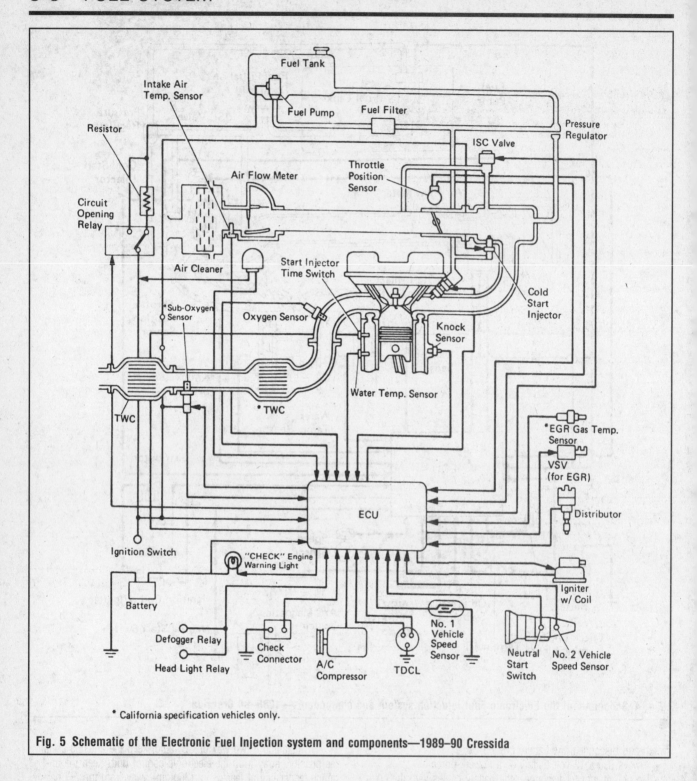

Fig. 5 Schematic of the Electronic Fuel Injection system and components—1989–90 Cressida

* California specification vehicles only.

TESTING PRECAUTIONS

• Before connecting or disconnecting the control unit ECU harness connectors, make sure the ignition switch is **OFF** and the negative battery cable is disconnected to avoid the possibility of damage to the control unit

• When performing ECU input/output signal diagnosis, remove the pin terminal retainer from the connectors to make it easier to insert tester probes into the connector

• When attaching or disconnecting pin connectors from the ECU, take care not to bend or break any pin terminals. Check that there are no bends or breaks on ECU pin terminals before attempting any connections

• Before replacing any ECU, perform the ECU input/output signal diagnosis to make sure the ECU is functioning properly

• After checking through EFI troubleshooting, perform the EFI self-diagnosis and driving test

• When measuring supply voltage of ECU controlled components with a circuit tester, separate one tester probe from another.

If the two tester probes accidentally make contact with each other during measurement, a short circuit will result and damage the power transistor in the ECU

Relieving Fuel System Pressure

1. Remove the fuel pump fuse from the fuse block, or remove the fuel pump relay or disconnect the wiring harness at the fuel tank while the engine is running.
2. The engine should run and then stall when the fuel in the fuel lines is exhausted. When the engine stops, crank the starter for about 3 seconds to be sure that all the fuel pressure in the lines was released.
3. Install the fuel pump fuse, relay and or wiring harness connector after the repairs have been made.

➡**The fuel pressure should be relieved whenever the fuel system is to be opened up for repairs.**

Fuel Pump

TESTING

Fuel Pump Operation

▶ **See Figures 6, 7 and 8**

1. Turn **ON** the ignition switch, but do not start the engine.
2. Short both terminals of the fuel pump connector. Check that there is pressure in the hose to the cold start injector.

➡**At this point, you will hear fuel return noise from the pressure regulator.**

3. Remove the service wire and install the rubber cap on the fuel pump check connector. Turn **OFF** the ignition switch.

4. If there is no pressure check the following components:
• Fusible link
• EFI and Ignition fuses
• Circuit opening relay
• Fuel pump
• Wiring connector

Fuel Pressure Check

1. Disconnect the negative battery cable. Disconnect the wiring from the cold start injector.
2. Place a suitable container or shop towel under the rear end of the delivery pipe.
3. Slowly loosen the union bolt of the cold start injector (on some models it may be necessary to remove the cold start valve in order to connect the pressure gauge) hose and remove the bolt and two gaskets from the delivery pipe.
4. Drain the fuel from the delivery pipe. Install a gasket, pressure gauge (tool SST-09268-45011 or equivalent), another gasket and the union bolt to the delivery pipe.
5. Wipe up any excess gasoline, reconnect the negative battery cable and start the engine.

➡**On the later models short the terminals on the fuel pump check connector (Fp and +B) and turn the ignition switch to the on position, then take a fuel pressure reading.**

6. Disconnect the vacuum sensing hose from the pressure regulator and pinch it off. Measure the fuel pressure at idle. The fuel pressure should be as follows:
• 1983–88 Cressida—33–38 psi.
• 1989–90 Cressida—38–44 psi.
• 1984–89 Van—33–38 psi.

7. If the fuel pressure is too high, replace the pressure regulator.
8. If the fuel pressure is low, check the following components:

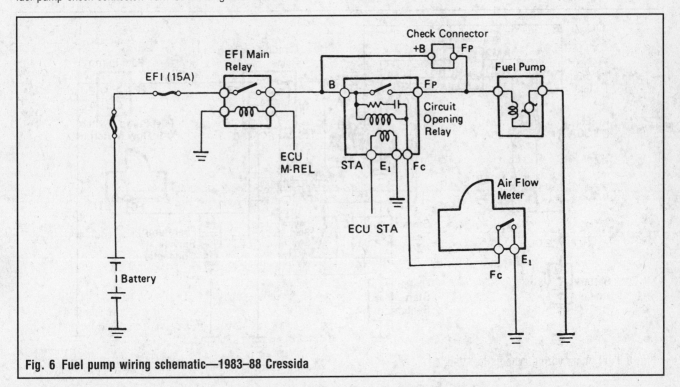

Fig. 6 Fuel pump wiring schematic—1983–88 Cressida

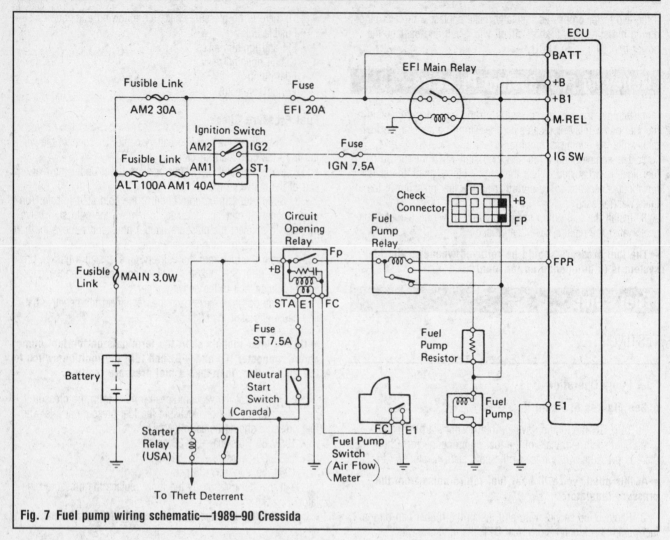

Fig. 7 Fuel pump wiring schematic—1989-90 Cressida

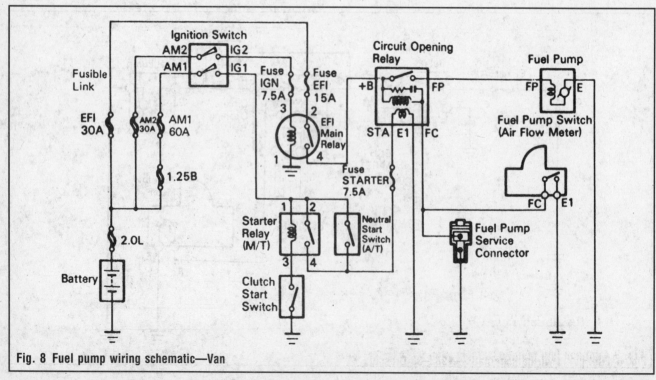

Fig. 8 Fuel pump wiring schematic—Van

- Fuel hoses and fuel connections
- Fuel pump
- Fuel filter
- Pressure regulator

9. Remove the service wire from the check connector (if still installed). Start the engine.

10. Disconnect the vacuum sensing hose from the pressure regulator and pinch it off. Measure the fuel pressure at idle. The fuel pressure should be as follows:
- 1983–88 Cressida—33–38 psi.
- 1989–90 Cressida—38–44 psi.
- 1984–89 Van—33–38 psi.

11. Reconnect the vacuum sensing hose to the pressure regulator. Measure the fuel pressure at idling:
- 1983–88 Cressida—27–31 psi.
- 1989–90 Cressida—33–37 psi.
- 1984–89 Van—28 psi.

12. If there is no fuel pressure, check the vacuum sensing hose and pressure regulator. Stop the engine. Check that the fuel pressure remains above 21 psi. for five minutes after the engine has been shut off.

13. If not within specifications, check the fuel pump, pressure regulator and or the injectors.

14. After checking the fuel pressure, disconnect the battery ground cable and carefully remove the pressure gauge to prevent gasoline from splashing.

15. Using new gaskets, reconnect the cold start injector hose to the delivery pipe (install the cold start injector valve if it was removed). Connect the wiring to the cold start injector. Check for fuel leakage.

REMOVAL & INSTALLATION

▶ **See Figures 9, 10, 11 and 12**

On all models the electric fuel pump is located in the fuel tank usually attached to the fuel sending unit. On some earlier fuel in-jected models, the fuel pump is mounted at the rear of the vehicle (usually located on the frame rail) outside of the gas tank.

1. Disconnect the negative battery cable.

2. Drain the fuel from the fuel tank into a suitable container. Remove the fuel tank assembly from the vehicle.

3. Remove the retaining screws which secure the pump access plate to the fuel tank. Withdraw the plate, gasket and pump assembly.

4. Pull off the lower side of the fuel pump from the fuel pump bracket.

5. Remove the 2 nuts and disconnect the wires from the fuel pump. Disconnect the fuel hose from the fuel pump.

6. Remove the rubber cushion. Using a small prybar, remove the retaining clip and pull out the pump filter.

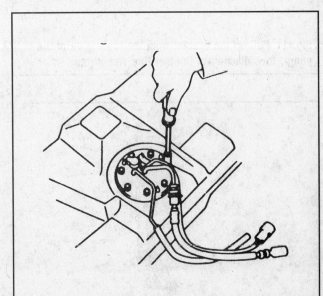

Fig. 10 Remove the fuel pump mounting screws and lift the unit pump bracket and bracket from the gas tank

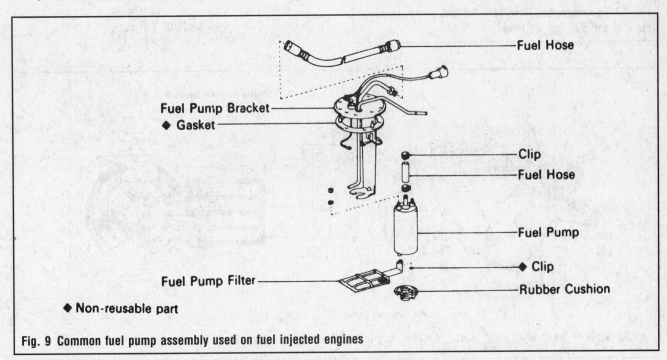

Fuel Hose

Fuel Pump Bracket
◆ Gasket

Clip
Fuel Hose

Fuel Pump

◆ Clip
Rubber Cushion

Fuel Pump Filter

◆ **Non-reusable part**

Fig. 9 Common fuel pump assembly used on fuel injected engines

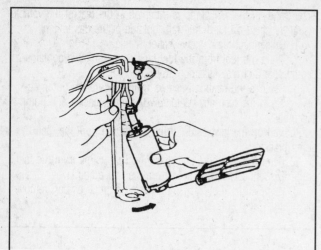

Fig. 11 Pull off the bracket from the lower side of the pump, then disconnect the fuel line and wiring

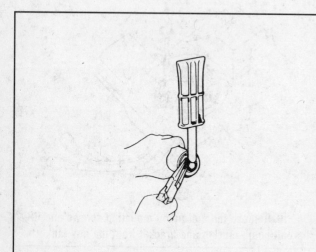

Fig. 12 To remove the filter from the fuel pump, remove the clip and pull out the filter

To install:

7. Install the fuel pump filter with a new clip. Install the rubber cushion.

8. Connect the fuel hose to the outlet port of the fuel pump. Connect the wires to the fuel pump with the 2 retaining buts. Push the lower side of the side of the fuel pump onto the fuel pump bracket and install the fuel pump.

9. Install a new gasket along with the pump bracket retaining plate and screws. Install the bolt of the bracket.

10. Install the fuel pump and refill the tank with fresh gas. Connect the negative battery cable. Start the engine and check for leaks.

Throttle Body

REMOVAL & INSTALLATION

Cressida

▶ **See Figures 13, 14, 15 and 16**

1. Disconnect the negative battery cable. Remove the air intake connector.

2. Drain the coolant system. Disconnect the accelerator connecting rod from the throttle linkage.

✳✳ CAUTION

When draining engine coolant, keep in mind that cats and dogs are attracted to ethylene glycol antifreeze and could drink any that is left in an uncovered container or in puddles on the ground. This will prove fatal in sufficient quantity. Always drain coolant into a sealable container. Coolant should be reused unless it is contaminated or is several years old.

3. Disconnect and label the following hoses:
- The No.1 and No.2 water by-pass hoses
- The PCV hose from the throttle body
- All the necessary emission hoses

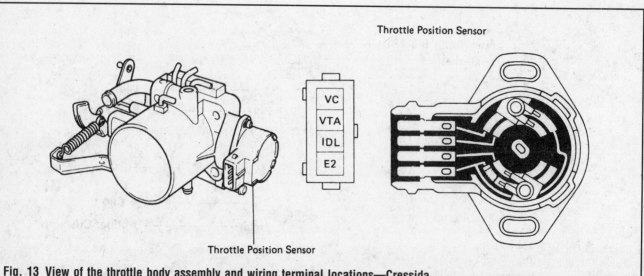

Fig. 13 View of the throttle body assembly and wiring terminal locations—Cressida

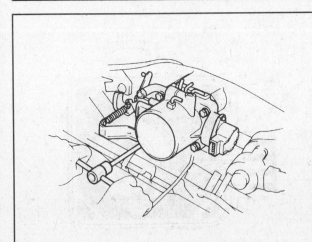

Fig. 14 Remove the throttle body retaining bolts to separate the unit from the engine—Cressida

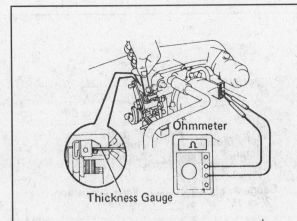

Fig. 15 To test the throttle position sensor, attach a ohmmeter to the sensor terminals. Insert a feeler gage between the stop screw and lever—Cressida

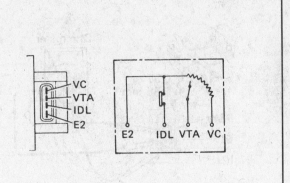

Fig. 16 Throttle position sensor terminal identification—Cressida

4. Disconnect the throttle sensor wiring.

5. Remove the accelerator bracket. Then remove the 4 throttle body retaining bolts and remove the throttle body and gasket. On the 1989–90 Cressida models it will also be necessary to disconnect the No.3 water by-pass hose along with the vacuum transducer valve.

6. Wash and clean the cast parts of the throttle body with a soft brush in carburetor cleaner.

7. Using compressed air, blow all the passages and apertures in the throttle body.

➡**To prevent deterioration, do not clean the throttle position sensor. Check that there is no clearance between the throttle stop screw and throttle lever when the throttle valve is fully closed.**

8. Adjust the throttle position sensor as follows:
   a. Loosen the 2 sensor screws.
   b. Connect the ohmmeter to the throttle position sensor terminals IDL and E2.
   c. Insert a feeler gauge 0.0197 in. (0.50mm) between the throttle stop screw and lever.
   d. Gradually turn the sensor clockwise until the ohmmeter deflects and secure the sensor with the 2 screws.
   e. Insert the feeler gauge in between the throttle stop screw and lever and recheck the continuity between terminals IDL and E2.
   f. With the clearance between the lever and the stop screw at 0.0197 in. (0.50mm) there should be continuity between terminals IDL and E2.
   g. With the clearance between the lever and the stop screw at 0.0354 in. (0.90mm) there should be no continuity between terminals IDL and E2.

9. Replace the throttle position sensor as follows:
   a. Remove the 2 screws retaining the sensor to the throttle body and remove the sensor.
   b. When installing the throttle position sensor, check that the throttle valve is fully closed.
   c. Place the sensor on the throttle body and turn the sensor clockwise and temporarily install the retaining screws. Adjust the throttle sensor and tighten the retaining screws.

To install:

10. Install a new gasket and install the throttle body along with the four bolts. Tighten the bolts to 9 ft. lbs. (13 Nm). On the 1989–90 Cressida models it will also be necessary to reconnect the No.3 water by-pass hose along with the vacuum transducer valve. Connect the throttle sensor wiring.

11. Connect the following hoses:
• The No.1 and No.2 water by-pass hoses
• The PCV hose from the throttle body
• All the necessary emission hoses

12. Install the air intake connector and reconnect the accelerator connecting rod to the throttle linkage. Refill the coolant system.

Van

▶ **See Figures 17 thru 22**

1. Disconnect the negative battery cable.
2. Drain the coolant system. Disconnect the accelerator cable from the throttle body.

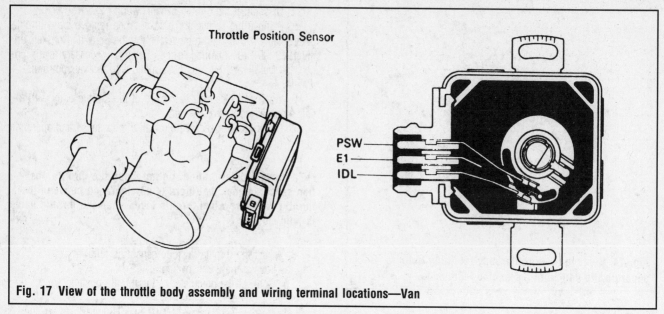

Fig. 17 View of the throttle body assembly and wiring terminal locations—Van

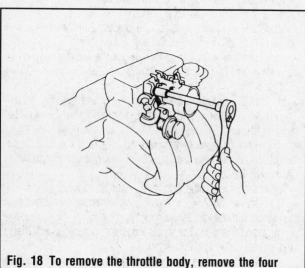

Fig. 18 To remove the throttle body, remove the four mounting bolts—Van

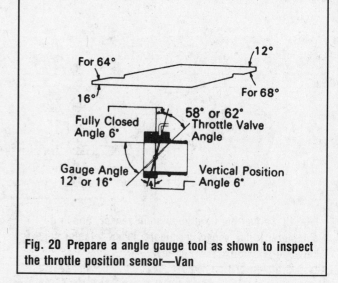

Fig. 20 Prepare a angle gauge tool as shown to inspect the throttle position sensor—Van

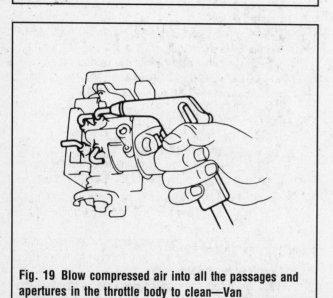

Fig. 19 Blow compressed air into all the passages and apertures in the throttle body to clean—Van

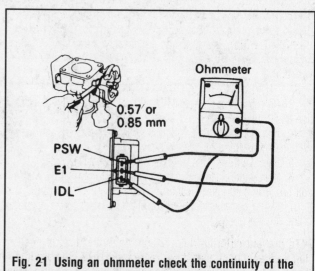

Fig. 21 Using an ohmmeter check the continuity of the throttle position sensor terminals—Van

TPS TERMINAL TESTING

Throttle valve opening angle	Continuity		
	IDL — E1	PSW — E1	IDL – PSW
64° from vertical	No continuity	No continuity	No continuity
68° from vertical	No continuity	Continuity	No continuity

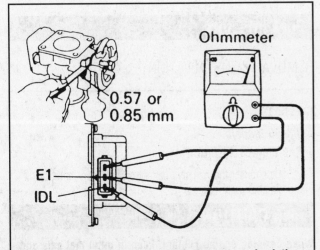

Ohmmeter

0.57 or
0.85 mm

E1

IDL

Fig. 22 Using a feeler gauge and ohmmeter, check the continuity of terminals IDL and E1—Van

TPS FEELER GAUGE TEST

Clearance between lever and stop screw	Continuity (IDL — E1)
0.57 mm (0.0224 in.)	Continuity
0.85 mm (0.0335 in.)	No continuity

✳✳ CAUTION

When draining engine coolant, keep in mind that cats and dogs are attracted to ethylene glycol antifreeze and could drink any that is left in an uncovered container or in puddles on the ground. This will prove fatal in sufficient quantity. Always drain coolant into a sealable container. Coolant should be reused unless it is contaminated or is several years old.

3. Remove the air cleaner hose. Disconnect the throttle position sensor wiring.

4. Remove the 2 water by-pass hoses. Disconnect and tag the vacuum hoses from the throttle body.

5. Remove the 4 nuts, throttle body and gaskets.

6. Wash and clean the cast parts of the throttle body with a soft brush in carburetor cleaner.

7. Using compressed air, blow all the passages and apertures in the throttle body.

➡To prevent deterioration, do not clean the throttle position sensor. Check that there is no clearance between the throttle stop screw and throttle lever when the throttle valve is fully closed.

8. Inspect the throttle position sensor as follows:

a. Prepare an angle gauge as shown in the illustration.

b. Set the throttle valve opening to 64° or 68° from the vertical position (include the throttle valve fully closed angle of 6°. Using an ohmmeter check the continuity between each terminal as follows:

a. With the throttle valve opening angle at 64° from vertical there should be no continuity between terminals IDL-E1, PSW-E1 and IDL-PSW.

b. With the throttle valve opening angle at 68° from vertical there should be no continuity between terminals IDL-E1 and continuity PSW-E1 and no continuity IDL-PSW.

9. Using a feeler gauge, check the continuity between terminals IDL and E1:

c. With the clearance between the lever and the stop screw at 0.0224 in. (0.57mm) there should be continuity between terminals IDL and E1.

d. With the clearance between the lever and the stop screw at 0.0355 in. (0.85mm) there should be no continuity between terminals IDL and E1.

10. If the throttle sensor fails any portion of this these tests, replace the throttle sensor along with the throttle body as a complete unit.

To install:

11. Install a new gasket and the throttle body along with the 4 nuts. Tighten the nuts to 9 ft. lbs. (12 Nm).

12. Connect the vacuum hoses to the throttle body. Install the 2 water by-pass hoses.

13. Connect the throttle position sensor wiring. Install the air cleaner hose.

14. Connect the throttle position sensor wiring. Connect the accelerator cable to the throttle body.

15. Refill the coolant system. Reconnect the negative battery cable and start the vehicle to check the operation and for any fluid leaks.

Throttle Position Sensor

TESTING

Cressida
♦ See Figure 23

1. Disconnect the sensor wiring.

2. Insert a feeler gauge between the throttle stop screw and stop lever.

3. Using an ohmmeter, measure the resistance between each terminal.

4. The resistance readings should be as follows:

a. With the clearance between the lever and the stop screw at 0, the resistance between terminals VTA and E2 should be 0.3–6.3kΩ.

b. With the clearance between the lever and the stop screw a 0. 0197 in. (0.50mm) the resistance between terminals IDL and E2 should be 2.3kΩ or less.

c. With the clearance between the lever and the stop screw a 0. 0354 in. (0.90mm) the resistance between terminals IDL and E2 should be infinity (∞).

d. With the throttle valve fully opened the resistance between terminals VTA and E2 should be 3.5–10.3kΩ.

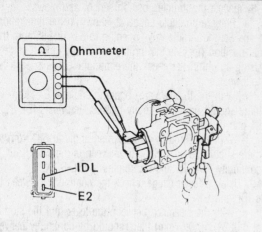

Fig. 23 Inspecting the throttle position sensor on the vehicle—Cressida

e. With the throttle valve fully opened the resistance between terminals VC and E2 should be 4.3–8.3kΩ.

5. If the sensor fails to pass any one of the resistance tests, replace the sensor. If everything proves to be satisfactory, reconnect the sensor connector.

Van

1. Unplug the sensor connector.
2. Insert a feeler gauge between the throttle stop screw and stop lever.
3. Using an ohmmeter, measure the resistance between each terminal.
4. The resistance readings should be as follows:
   a. With the clearance between the lever and the stop screw at 0.0224 in. (57mm) there should be continuity between terminal IDL and E1 and no continuity between terminals PSW-E1 and IDL-PSW.
   b. With the clearance between the lever and the stop screw at 0.0335 in. (85mm) there should be no continuity between ter-

minal IDL and E1 and no continuity between terminals PSW-E1 and IDL-PSW.
   c. With the throttle valve in the fully opened position there should be no continuity between terminal IDL and E1 and continuity between terminals PSW-E1 and no continuity between terminals IDL-PSW.

5. If the sensor fails to pass any one of the resistance tests, replace the sensor. If everything proves to be satisfactory, reconnect the sensor connector.

Fuel Injectors

REMOVAL & INSTALLATION

Cressida

1983–88 Models
▶ **See Figures 24 thru 31**

1. Disconnect the negative battery cable. Drain the coolant into a suitable drain pan.

✳✳ CAUTION

When draining engine coolant, keep in mind that cats and dogs are attracted to ethylene glycol antifreeze and could drink any that is left in an uncovered container or in puddles on the ground. This will prove fatal in sufficient quantity. Always drain coolant into a sealable container. Coolant should be reused unless it is contaminated or is several years old.

2. Remove the air intake chamber as follows:
   a. Disconnect the No.1 water by-pass hose from the ISC valve body.
   b. Disconnect the No.2 water by-pass hose from the throttle body.
   c. Disconnect the air valve hose from the ISC body.
   d. Disconnect the PCV hose from the throttle body.

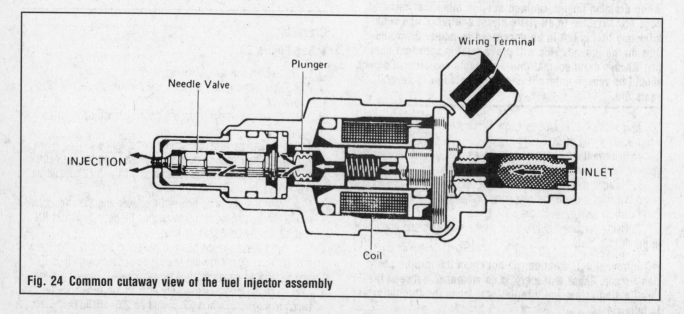

Fig. 24 Common cutaway view of the fuel injector assembly

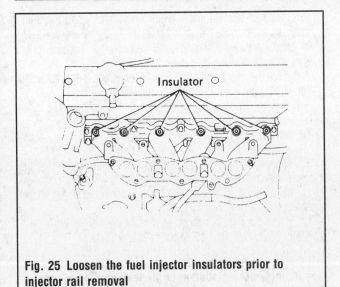

Fig. 25 Loosen the fuel injector insulators prior to injector rail removal

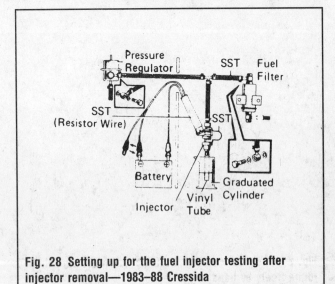

Fig. 28 Setting up for the fuel injector testing after injector removal—1983–88 Cressida

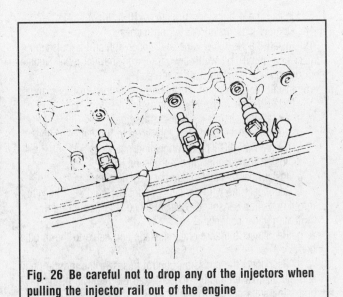

Fig. 26 Be careful not to drop any of the injectors when pulling the injector rail out of the engine

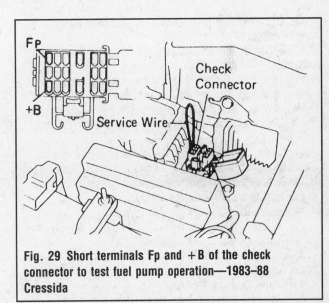

Fig. 29 Short terminals Fp and +B of the check connector to test fuel pump operation—1983–88 Cressida

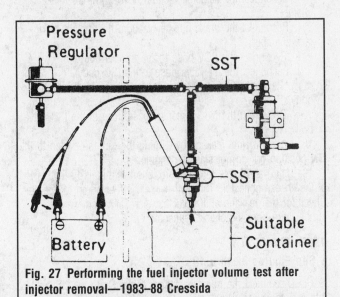

Fig. 27 Performing the fuel injector volume test after injector removal—1983–88 Cressida

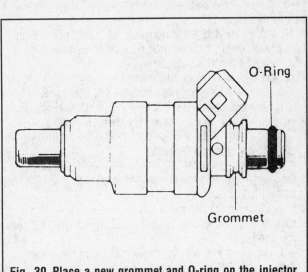

Fig. 30 Place a new grommet and O-Ring on the injector prior to injector installation

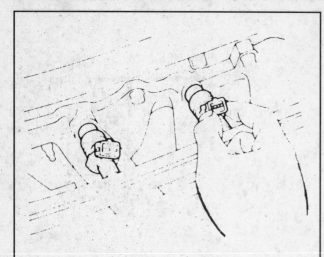

Fig. 31 Once the injectors are installed, make sure they rotate freely by hand

e. Disconnect the brake booster vacuum hose from the air intake chamber.

f. Disconnect the actuator vacuum hose from the air intake chamber.

g. Label and disconnect the emission control hoses from the throttle body and the air intake chamber that will allow the removal of the vacuum pipe subassembly.

h. Disconnect the accelerator linkage and cable from the throttle body.

i. Unplug the wire connections for the cold start injector, throttle position sensor, ISC valve and vacuum switching valve.

j. Remove the air intake chamber stay bracket.

k. Remove the vacuum pipe subassembly.

l. Loosen the EGR pipe connecting nut.

m. Disconnect the cold start fuel hose from the delivery pipe.

n. Remove the air intake chamber.

3. Remove the distributor assembly as previously outlined in Chapter 3.

4. Remove the No.1 fuel pipe.

5. Disconnect and remove the wiring harness from the injectors.

6. Remove the 4 bolts and then remove the delivery pipe with the injectors.

7. When removing the delivery pipe, be careful not to drop the injectors. Do not remove the injector cover. Remove the 6 insulators from the intake manifold.

8. Inspect the injectors as follows:

a. Disconnect the fuel hose from the fuel filter outlet.

b. Connect a suitable union hose (SST#09268-41045) to the fuel filter. Be sure to use the vehicle's fuel filter.

c. Connect a suitable union hose (SST#09268-41045) to the removed fuel pressure regulator.

d. Connect a suitable union hose (SST#09268-41045) to the injector and hold the injector and union with a suitable holding fixture.

e. Place the injector into a suitable measuring cup. Install a suitable vinyl tubing onto the injector to prevent gasoline from splashing out.

f. Reconnect the negative battery cable. Turn the ignition switch to the **ON** position but do not start the engine.

g. Using a suitable jumper wire, short terminals Fp and +B of the check connector. This will cause the fuel pump to operate.

h. Connect some suitable wires to the battery and to the injector so as to make the injector spray. Apply battery voltage for approximately 15 seconds and measure the injection volume with the measuring cup.

i. Test the injector at least 2 or 3 times and if the volume is not within specifications, clean or replace the injector.

j. The volume should be 40–50cc in 15 seconds. The difference between each injector should be less than 6cc.

To install:

9. Install the grommet and a new O-ring to the injector.

10. Apply a thin coat of gasoline to the O-rings and install the injectors into the delivery pipe.

11. Install the 6 insulators into the injector holes of the intake manifold.

12. Install the injectors together with the delivery pipe to the manifold. Make sure that the injectors rotate freely.

➡**If the injectors do not rotate freely, the probable cause may be incorrect installation of the O-rings. Replace the O-rings.**

13. Install the 4 bolts and tighten to 10 ft. lbs. (14 Nm).

14. Connect and install the wiring harness.

15. Install the No.1 fuel pipe and finger-tighten the pulsation damper and union bolt with new gaskets on the fuel pipe. Tighten them being careful not to bend the pipe.

16. Install the distributor as previously outlined in this manual.

17. Install the air intake chamber as follows:

a. Install the air intake chamber assembly.

b. Reconnect the cold start fuel hose to the delivery pipe.

c. Tighten the EGR pipe connecting nut.

d. Install the vacuum pipe subassembly.

e. Install the air intake chamber stay bracket.

f. Reconnect the wire connections for the cold start injector, throttle position sensor, ISC valve connectors and vacuum switching valve connector.

g. Reconnect the accelerator linkage and cable to the throttle body.

h. Reconnect the emission control hoses to the throttle body and the air intake chamber that allowed the removal of the vacuum pipe subassembly.

i. Reconnect the actuator vacuum hose to the air intake chamber.

j. Reconnect the brake booster vacuum hose to the air intake chamber.

k. Reconnect the PCV hose to the throttle body.

l. Reconnect the air valve hose to the ISC body.

m. Reconnect the No.2 water by-pass hose to the throttle body.

n. Reconnect the No.1 water by-pass hose to the ISC valve body.

18. Check for fuel leakage by turning the ignition switch to the **ON** position but do not start the engine.

19. Using a suitable jumper wire, short terminals Fp and +B of the check connector. This will cause the fuel pump to operate. Check for fuel leakage and repair as necessary. Remove the jumper wire from the check connector.

1989–90 MODELS

◆ See Figures 32 thru 40

1. Disconnect the negative battery cable. Drain the coolant into a suitable drain pan.

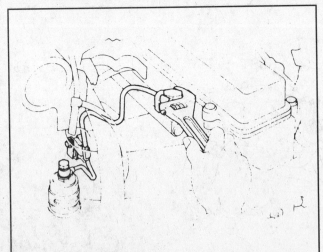

Fig. 32 During fuel injector removal, unbolt the clamp for the No. 1 fuel pipe

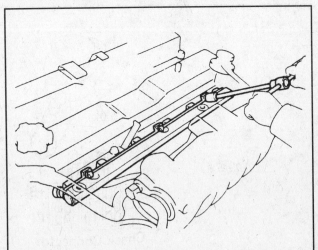

Fig. 35 Remove the 3 bolts retaining the delivery pipe which hold the fuel injectors

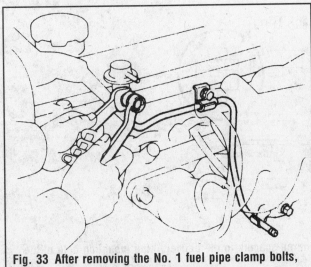

Fig. 33 After removing the No. 1 fuel pipe clamp bolts, remove them on the No. 2 fuel pipe

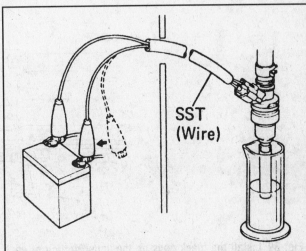

Fig. 36 Performing the fuel injector volume test after injector removal—1989–90 Cressida

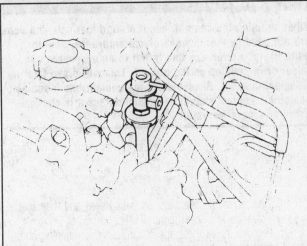

Fig. 34 Loosen the locknut retaining the fuel pressure regulator, then remove the regulator

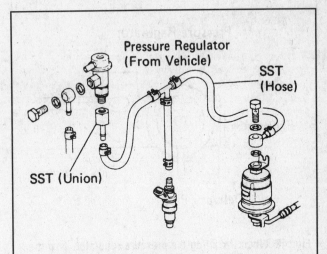

Fig. 37 Setting up for the fuel injector testing after injector removal—1989–90 Cressida

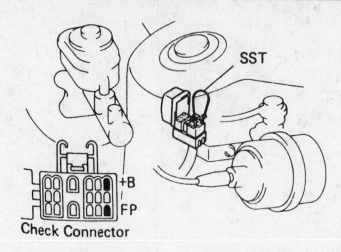

Fig. 38 Short terminals Fp and +B of the check connector to test fuel pump operation—1989–90 Cressida

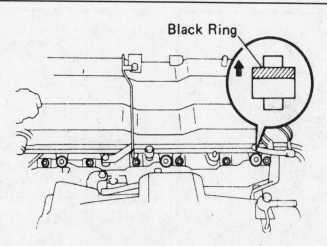

Fig. 39 Install the black rings on the upper portion of each of the three spacers in the delivery pipe mounting hole of the cylinder head

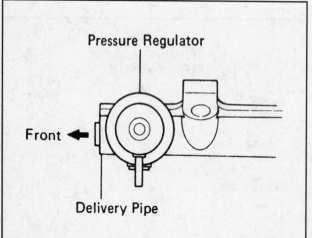

Fig. 40 When installing the pressure regulator, turn the unit clockwise until the vacuum pipe faces in this direction

✳✳ CAUTION

When draining the coolant, keep in mind that cats and dogs are attracted by the ethylene glycol antifreeze, and are quite likely to drink any that is left in an uncovered container or in puddles on the ground. This will prove fatal in sufficient quantity. Always drain the coolant into a sealable container. Coolant should be reused unless it is contaminated or several years old.

2. Remove the throttle body assembly as previously outlined in this section.

3. Remove the ISC valve as follows:

    a. Unplug the two idle speed valve connectors.

    b. Disconnect the two water by pass hoses and the vacuum hoses from the idle speed control valve body.

    c. Remove the two idle speed control valve retaining bolts and remove the valve from the vehicle.

4. Disconnect the cold start injector tube from the fuel delivery pipe as follows:

a. Place a suitable shop towel under the cold start injector.

b. Remove the union bolt and 2 gaskets and disconnect the injector tube.

c. Slowly loosen the union bolt, remove the union bolt, 2 gaskets and fuel tube.

5. Unplug the EGR vacuum switching valve connector. Remove the union bolt and the 2 gaskets from the delivery pipe.

6. Remove the union bolt and 2 gaskets from the fuel filter. Remove the clamp bolt and the No.1 fuel pipe with the vacuum switching valve.

7. Disconnect the vacuum sensing hose. Disconnect the fuel hose from the No.2 fuel pipe.

8. Remove the union bolt and 2 gaskets the fuel pressure regulator.

9. Remove the clamp bolts and the No.2 fuel pipe.

10. Loosen the locknut of the fuel pressure regulator and remove the regulator.

11. Remove the 3 bolts and delivery pipe together with the fuel injectors. Be careful not to drop the injectors, when removing the delivery (fuel rail) pipe.

12. Remove the six insulators and three spacers from the cylinder head. Pull the injectors from the delivery pipe.

13. Inspect the injectors as follows:

a. Disconnect the fuel hose from the fuel filter outlet.

b. Connect a suitable union hose (SST#09268-41045) to the fuel filter. Be sure to use the vehicle's fuel filter.

c. Connect a suitable union hose (SST#09268-41045) to the removed fuel pressure regulator.

d. Connect a suitable union hose (SST#09268-01045) to the injector and hold the injector and union with a suitable holding fixture.

e. Place the injector into a suitable measuring cup. Install a suitable vinyl tubing onto the injector to prevent gasoline from splashing out.

f. Reconnect the negative battery cable. Turn the ignition switch to the **ON** position but do not start the engine.

g. Using a suitable jumper wire, short terminals Fp and +B of the check connector. This will cause the fuel pump to operate.

h. Connect some suitable wires to the battery and to the injector so as to make the injector spray. Apply battery voltage for approximately 15 seconds and measure the injection volume with the measuring cup.

i. Test the injector at least 2 or 3 times and if the volume is not within specifications, clean or replace the injector.

j. The volume should be 69–85cc in 15 seconds. The difference between each injector should be less than 9cc.

To install:

14. Install the grommet and a new O-ring to the injector.

15. Apply a thin coat of gasoline to the O-rings and install the injectors into the delivery pipe. Be sure to turn the injector left and right while installing them into the delivery pipe.

16. Install the 6 insulators into the injector holes of the cylinder head. Install the black rings on the upper portion of each of the 3 spacers. Then install the spacers on the delivery pipe mounting hole of the cylinder head.

17. Install the injectors together with the delivery pipe to the cylinder head. Make sure that the injectors rotate freely.

→**If the injectors do not rotate freely, the probable cause may be incorrect installation of the O-rings. Replace the O-rings.**

18. Position the injector connector upward. Install the 3 bolts and tighten them to 13 ft. lbs. (18 Nm).

19. Install the fuel pressure regulator as follows:

a. Fully loosen the locknut of the pressure regulator.

b. Apply a light coat of gasoline to a new O-ring and install it to the pressure regulator.

c. Thrust the pressure regulator completely into the delivery pipe by hand.

d. Turn the fuel pressure regulator counterclockwise until the vacuum pipe faces in the direction indicated in the figure.

e. Tighten the locknut to 18 ft. lbs (25 Nm).

20. Install the No.2 fuel pipe with the 2 clamp bolts. Connect the pipe with the union and new gaskets. Tighten the union bolt to 18 ft. lbs. (25 Nm). Connect the fuel return line.

21. Connect the No.3 PCV hose. Connect the vacuum sensing hose.

22. Install the No.1 fuel pipe with the vacuum switching valve with the clamp bolt. Connect the pipe to the fuel filter with the union bolt and new gaskets. Tighten the union bolt to 22 ft. lbs. (29 Nm).

23. Connect the fuel pipe to delivery pipe with the union bolt and new gaskets. Tighten the union bolt to 29 ft. lbs. (39 Nm).

24. Install the cold start injector tube to the fuel delivery pipe.

25. Attach the injector connectors.

26. Install the idle speed control valve assembly.

27. Install the throttle body assembly.

28. Refill the cooling system. Reconnect the negative battery cable.

29. Check for fuel leakage by turning the ignition switch to the **ON** position but do not start the engine.

30. Using a suitable jumper wire, short terminals Fp and +B of the check connector. This will cause the fuel pump to operate. Check for fuel leakage and repair as necessary. Remove the jumper wire from the check connector.

Van

▶ **See Figures 41, 42, 43 and 44**

1. Disconnect the negative battery cable.

2. Drain the coolant system. Disconnect the accelerator cable from the throttle linkage.

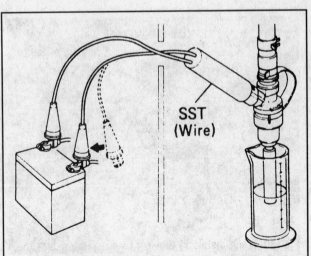

Fig. 41 Performing the fuel injector volume test after injector removal—Van

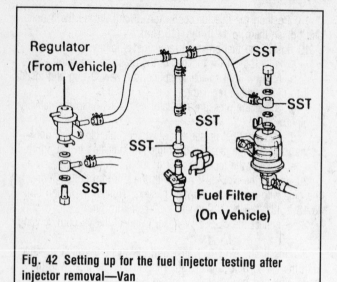

Fig. 42 Setting up for the fuel injector testing after injector removal—Van

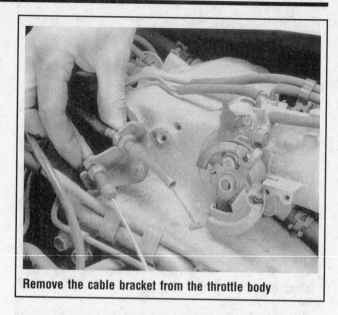

Remove the cable bracket from the throttle body

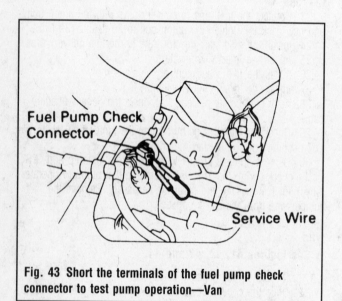

Fig. 43 Short the terminals of the fuel pump check connector to test pump operation—Van

When removing the fuel injectors begin by, disconnecting the throttle cable

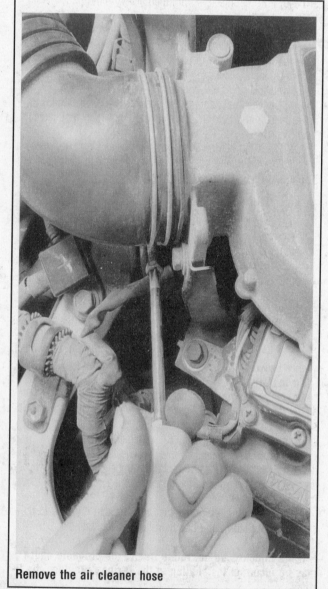

Remove the air cleaner hose

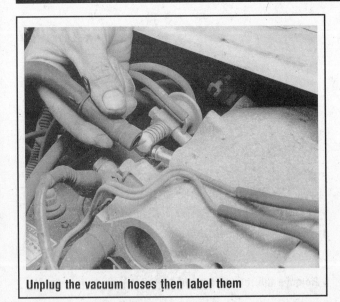

Unplug the vacuum hoses then label them

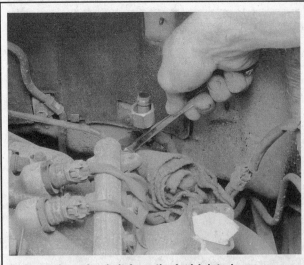

Remove the union bolt from the fuel inlet pipe

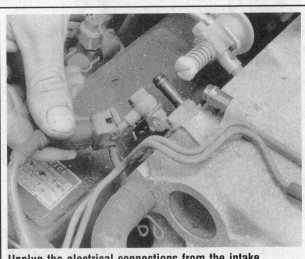

Unplug the electrical connections from the intake chamber

Loosen the pulsation damper . . .

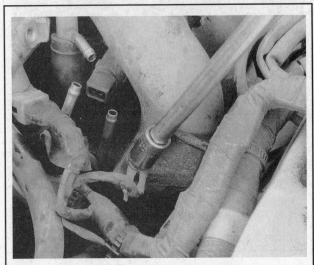

Remove the intake chamber mounting nuts

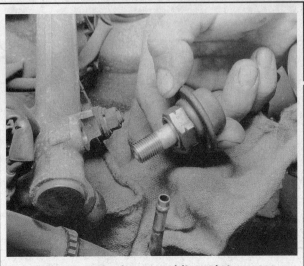

. . . and remove the damper and its gaskets

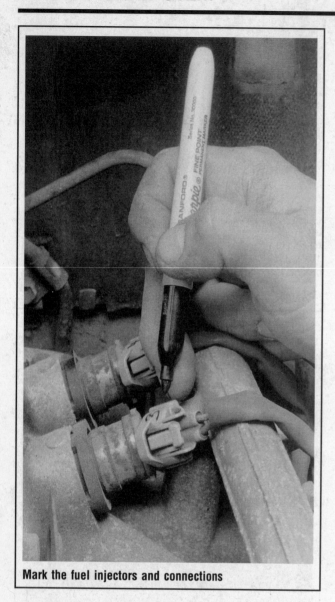

Mark the fuel injectors and connections

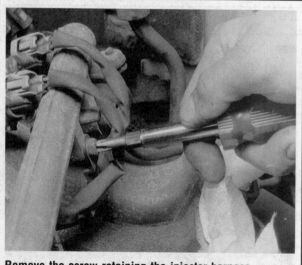

Remove the screw retaining the injector harness

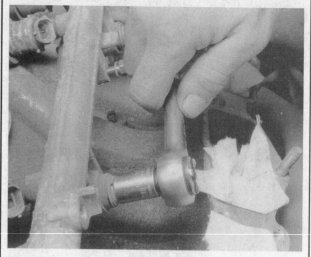

Remove the retainers securing the delivery pipe

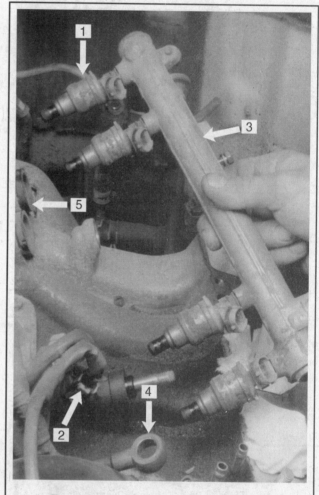

1. Fuel injector
2. Injector harness
3. Fuel delivery pipe
4. Union
5. Insulator

Remove the delivery pipe along with the fuel injectors

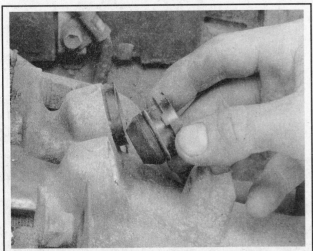

Pull out the insulators, inspect and replace if they are damaged

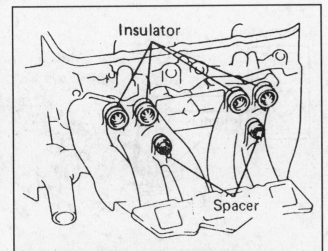

Fig. 44 Before installing the fuel injectors, place the spacers and insulators into the intake manifold—Van

✳✳ CAUTION

When draining the coolant, keep in mind that cats and dogs are attracted by the ethylene glycol antifreeze, and are quite likely to drink any that is left in an uncovered container or in puddles on the ground. This will prove fatal in sufficient quantity. Always drain the coolant into a sealable container. Coolant should be reused unless it is contaminated or several years old.

3. Disconnect the throttle cable from the throttle linkage on models equipped with an automatic transmission.

4. Remove the air cleaner hose. Label and disconnect the following:
- Cold start injector connector
- Air valve connector
- PCV hoses
- Brake booster vacuum hose
- Charcoal canister
- Emission control hoses

5. Remove the 2 nuts from the air intake chamber. Remove the union nut from the exhaust manifold and EGR valve.

6. Disconnect the cold start injector fuel pipe, the water by-pass hoses and the pressure regulator hose.

7. Remove the air intake chamber brackets. Use a 12mm socket wrench to remove the rear air intake chamber bracket.

8. Remove the air intake chamber with the air valve. Use 10mm and 12mm socket wrenches to remove the air intake chamber with the air vent.

9. Disconnect the fuel inlet pipe and remove the pulsation damper and 2 gaskets.

10. Remove the fuel outlet pipe and remove the union bolt and 2 gaskets.

11. Disconnect the fuel inlet and outlet pipes from the delivery pipe. Remove the bolt, nut and delivery pipe together with the fuel injectors. Be careful not to drop the injectors, when removing the delivery (fuel rail) pipe.

12. Remove the 4 insulators and 2 spacers from the intake manifold. Pull the injectors from the delivery pipe.

13. Inspect the injectors as follows:

   a. Disconnect the fuel hose from the fuel filter outlet.

   b. Connect a suitable union hose (SST#09268-41045 or equivalent) to the fuel filter. Be sure to use the vehicle's fuel filter.

   c. Connect a suitable union hose (SST#09268-41045 or equivalent) to the removed fuel pressure regulator.

   d. Connect a suitable union hose (SST#09268-41045 or equivalent) to the injector and hold the injector and union with a suitable holding fixture.

   e. Place the injector into a suitable measuring cup. Install a suitable vinyl tubing onto the injector to prevent gasoline from splashing out.

   f. Reconnect the negative battery cable. Turn the ignition switch to the **ON** position but do not start the engine.

   g. Using a suitable jumper wire, short terminals of the fuel pump check connector. This will cause the fuel pump to operate.

   h. Connect some suitable wires to the battery and to the injector so as to make the injector spray. Apply battery voltage for approximately 15 seconds and measure the injection volume with the measuring cup.

   i. Test the injector at least 2 or 3 times and if the volume is not within specifications, clean or replace the injector.

   j. The volume should be 45–55cc in 15 seconds. The difference between each injector should be less than 5cc.

To install:

14. Install the grommet and a new O-ring to the injector.

15. Apply a thin coat of gasoline to the O-rings and install the injectors into the delivery pipe. Be sure to turn the injector left and right while installing them into the delivery pipe.

16. Install the 4 insulators ad 2 spacers into the injector holes of the intake manifold.

17. Install the injectors together with the delivery pipe to the intake manifold. Make sure that the injectors rotate freely.

➡**If the injectors do not rotate freely, the probable cause may be incorrect installation of the O-rings. Replace the O-rings.**

18. Install the fuel delivery pipe with the bolt and nut.

19. Connect the inlet pipe with the pulsation damper and 2 gaskets. Tighten the pulsation damper to 22 ft. lbs. (29 Nm).

20. Connect the outlet pipe with the union bolt and 2 new gaskets. Tighten the union bolt to 14 ft. lbs. (20 Nm).

21. Install the air intake chamber with the air valve. Use 10mm and 12mm socket wrenches to install the air intake chamber with the air vent.

22. Install the air intake chamber brackets. Use a 12mm socket wrench to install the rear air intake chamber bracket.

23. Reconnect the cold start injector fuel pipe, the water bypass hoses and the pressure regulator hose.

24. Install the 2 nuts to the air intake chamber. Install the union nut to the exhaust manifold and EGR valve.

25. Install the air cleaner hose. Reconnect the following hoses and connectors:
- Cold start injector connector
- Air valve connector
- PCV hoses
- Brake booster vacuum hose
- Charcoal canister
- Emission control hoses

26. Connect the accelerator cable and adjust it.

27. On models equipped with automatic transmissions, connect the throttle cable and adjust it.

28. Connect the negative battery cable. Refill the coolant system.

29. Check for fuel leakage by turning the ignition switch to the **ON** position but do not start the engine.

30. Using a suitable jumper wire, short the terminals of the fuel pump check connector. This will cause the fuel pump to operate. Check for fuel leakage and repair as necessary. Remove the jumper wire from the check connector.

TESTING

▶ **See Figures 45, 46 and 47**

1. With the engine running or cranking, use a sound scope or a large metal rod to check that there is normal operating noise in proportion to the engine rpm.

2. If you do not own a sound scope, you can check the injector transmission with you finger. Be sure that the engine is not hot.

3. If no sound or an unusual sound is heard, check the wiring connector, injector or injection signal from the ECU.

4. Unplug the wiring connector on the fuel injector.

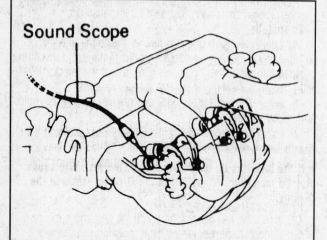

Fig. 45 To test the injector on the vehicle, use a sound scope to inspect for any irregular operating noise

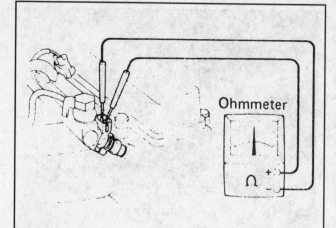

Fig. 46 If no sound is heard on the scope test, check the continuity with an ohmmeter of the fuel injector—Cressida

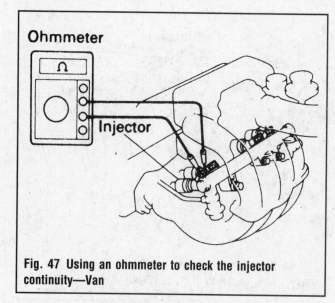

Fig. 47 Using an ohmmeter to check the injector continuity—Van

5. Using an ohmmeter, check the continuity of both terminals.

6. The ohmmeter reading should be as follows:
- 1983–88 Cressida—1.5–3.0Ω
- 1989–90 Cressida—14.0Ω
- 1984–87 Van—1.5–3.0Ω
- 1988–89 Van—1.1–2.2Ω

7. If the resistance is not as specified, replace the injector.

Cold Start Injector

REMOVAL & INSTALLATION

Cressida

▶ **See Figures 48, 49, 50 and 51**

1. Disconnect the negative battery cable.

2. Place a suitable container along with a shop towel under the cold start injector.

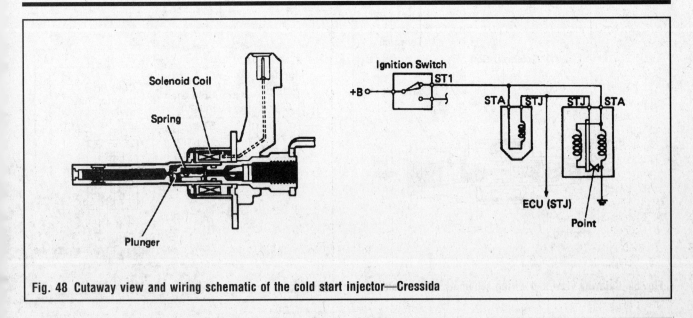

Fig. 48 Cutaway view and wiring schematic of the cold start injector—Cressida

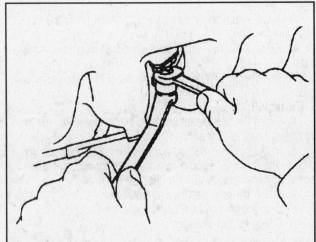

Fig. 49 Remove the union bolt and gaskets, and remove the injector tube for the cold start injector—Cressida

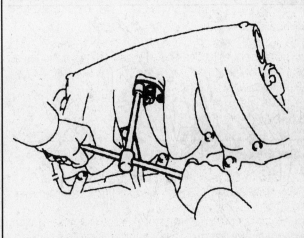

Fig. 51 Remove the two cold start injector mounting bolts—Cressida

3. Remove the union bolt and two gaskets, then disconnect the injector tube.

4. Slowly loosen the union bolt.

5. Remove the bolts retaining the cold start injector and gasket, then disconnect the cold start injector wiring.

To install:

6. Attach the cold start injector wiring.

7. Install new gaskets and injector. Tighten the mounting bolts to 48 inch lbs. (5 Nm).

8. Install the injector tube to the delivery pipe and cold start injector with new gaskets and union bolts. Tighten the delivery bolt side to 22 ft. lbs. (29 Nm) and the cold start injector side to 13 ft. lbs. (18 Nm).

9. Connect the negative battery cable.

10. Check for fuel leaks.

Van

▶ **See Figures 52, 53 and 54**

1. Disconnect the negative battery cable.
2. Unplug the cold start injector connector.

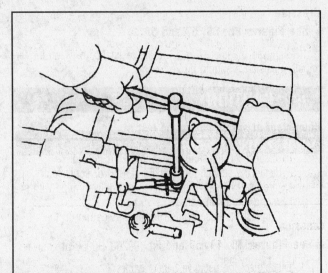

Fig. 50 Remove the union bolt, gaskets, and the fuel tube for the cold start injector—Cressida

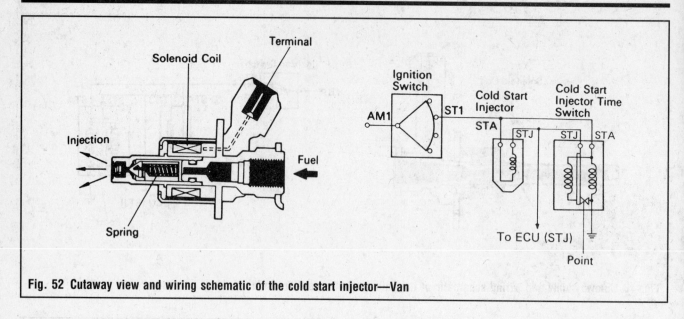

Fig. 52 Cutaway view and wiring schematic of the cold start injector—Van

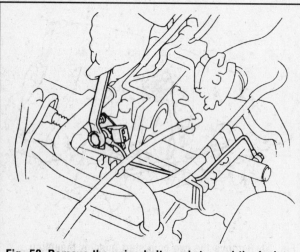

Fig. 53 Remove the union bolt, gaskets, and the fuel pipe for the cold start injector—Van

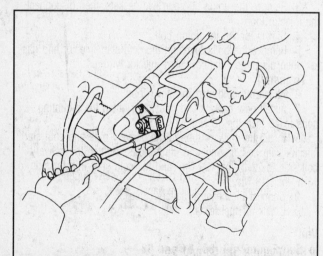

Fig. 54 Disconnect the cold start injector wiring, then remove the two injector mounting bolts—Van

3. Place a suitable container or shop towel under the cold start injector pipe.

4. Remove the two union bolts, cold start injector and gaskets.

5. Remove the two bolts retaining the cold start injector and gasket.

To install:

6. Install the new gasket and cold start injector, tighten the mounting bolts to 52 inch lbs. (6 Nm).

7. Install new gaskets and reconnect the cold start injector pipe to the delivery pipe and cold start injector with the union bolts. Tighten the bolts to 14 ft. lbs. (20 Nm).

8. Attach the cold start injector connector.

9. Connect the negative battery cable.

10. Check for fuel leakage.

TESTING

Cressida

▶ **See Figures 55, 56, 57 and 58**

1. Using an ohmmeter, measure the resistance between the terminals. Resistance should be 2–4 ohms.

✳✳ CAUTION

Keep clear of sparks during the test.

2. To inspect the injection of the cold start injector.

a. Install the service tool (09268–41045 or equivalent) which are two unions to the injector and delivery pipe with new gaskets and the union bolts.

b. Connect the hose portion of the service tool to the unions.

c. Connect the service tool wire (09268–30050 or equivalent) to the injector.

d. Place a suitable container under the injector to catch any spilt fuel.

e. Reconnect the negative battery cable.

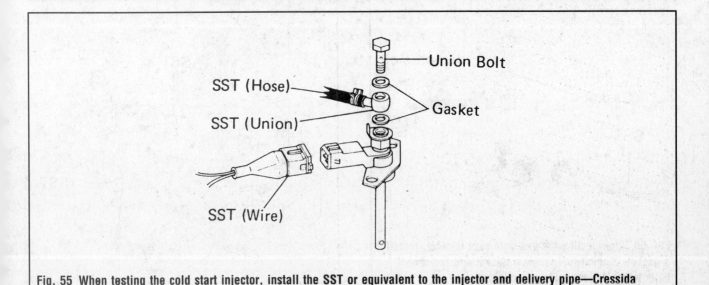

Fig. 55 When testing the cold start injector, install the SST or equivalent to the injector and delivery pipe—Cressida

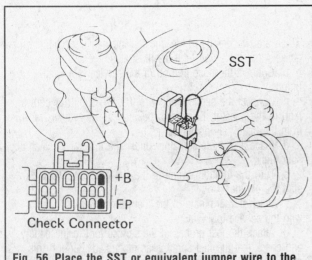

Fig. 56 Place the SST or equivalent jumper wire to the check connector terminals +B and FP—Cressida

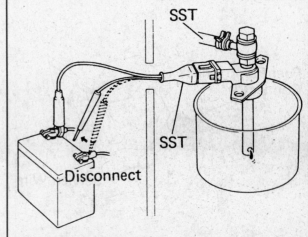

Fig. 58 Inspecting the injector leakage, less than one drop per minute should flow

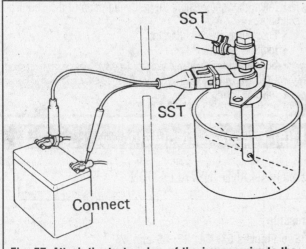

Fig. 57 Attach the test probes of the jumper wire to the battery, and check for proper fuel spray—Cressida

f. Turn the ignition switch to the **ON** position. **DO NOT** start the engine.

g. Using tool 09843–18020 or equivalent, connect terminals B+ and FP of the check connector.

h. Connect the test probes of the tool to the battery, and check the fuel spray. This should be done in the shortest time possible.

3. Inspect the injector leakage:

a. In the condition above, disconnect the test probes of the service tool wire from the battery and check fuel leakage from the injector.

b. The fuel drop should be one drop per minute.

c. Disconnect the negative battery cable.

d. Remove the service tools and wire.

Van

♦ **See Figures 59, 60, 61 and 62**

1. To inspect the injection of the cold start injector:

a. Install the service tool (09268–41045 or equivalent)

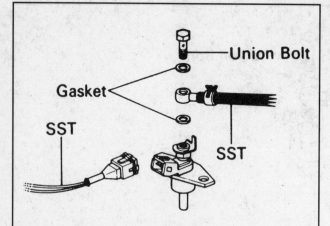

Fig. 59 When testing the Van cold start injector, install a gasket, a union tool, another gasket and two union bolts to the delivery pipe and injector

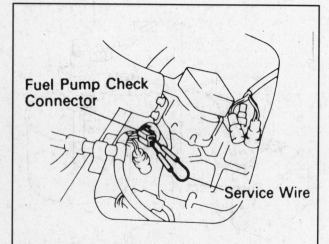

Fig. 60 Connect the terminals of the fuel pump check connector with a service wire—Van

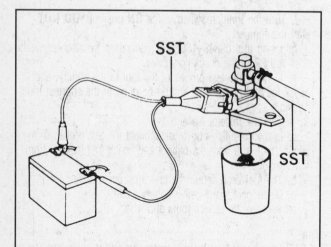

Fig. 61 Attach the test probes of the jumper wire to the battery, and check for proper fuel spray—Van

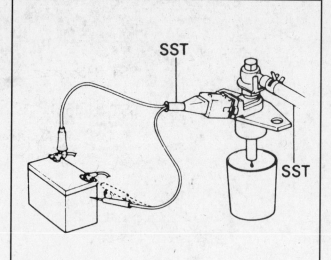

Fig. 62 Inspecting the injector knozzle leakage, one drop or less should flow per minute—Van

which are two unions to the injector and delivery pipe with new gaskets and the union bolts as illustrated.

b. Connect the hose portion of the service tool to the unions.

c. Connect the service tool wire (09268–30050 or equivalent) to the injector. Be sure to position the injector as far away from the battery as possible.

d. Place a suitable container under the injector to catch any spilt fuel.

e. Turn the ignition switch to the **ON** position. **DO NOT** start the engine.

f. Attach the terminals of the fuel pump check connector with the service tool wire.

g. Attach the test probes of the service tool to the battery and check that the fuel spray is as illustrated. Perform this check within the shortest possible time.

h. Disconnect the test probes from the battery and check the fuel drops one drop or less per minute from the injector nozzle.

i. After checking, restore the following parts to their original condition:
• Fuel pump check connector
• Ignition switch
• Service tools
• Cold start injector
• Injector wiring

Fuel Pressure Regulator

REMOVAL AND INSTALLATION

Cressida
▶ **See Figures 63, 64, 65, 66 and 67**

1. Disconnect the No. 3 PCV hose.
2. Disconnect the vacuum sensing hose.

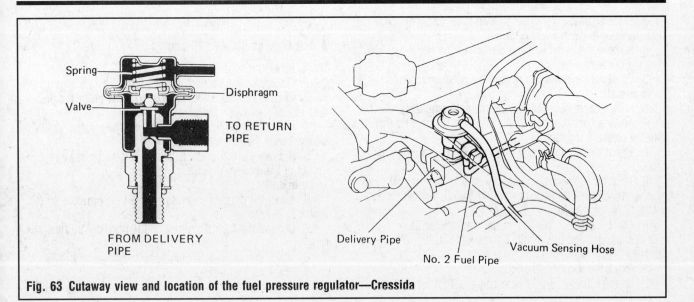

Fig. 63 Cutaway view and location of the fuel pressure regulator—Cressida

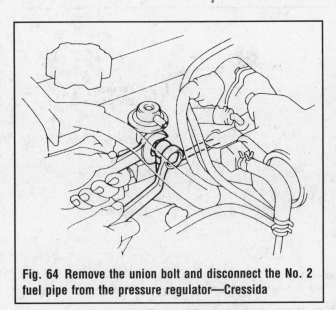

Fig. 64 Remove the union bolt and disconnect the No. 2 fuel pipe from the pressure regulator—Cressida

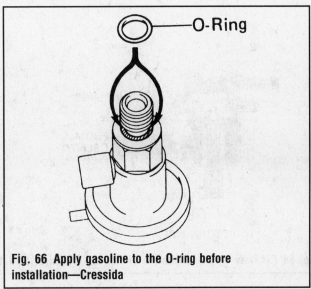

Fig. 66 Apply gasoline to the O-ring before installation—Cressida

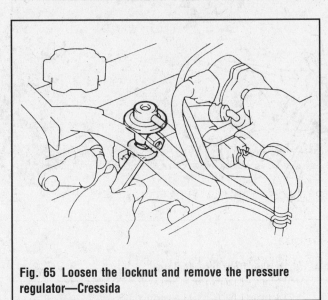

Fig. 65 Loosen the locknut and remove the pressure regulator—Cressida

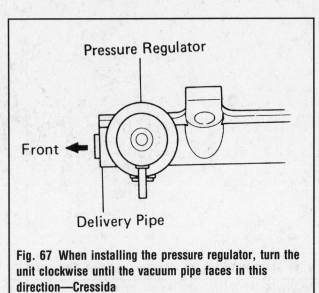

Fig. 67 When installing the pressure regulator, turn the unit clockwise until the vacuum pipe faces in this direction—Cressida

3. Place a suitable container or shop towel under the pressure regulator to catch any spilt fuel.

4. Remove the union bolt and disconnect the No. 2 fuel pipe from the pressure regulator.

5. Loosen the locknut and remove the pressure regulator.

To install:

6. Fully loosen the locknut of the pressure regulator.

7. Apply a light coat of gasoline to a new O-ring, and install it to the pressure regulator.

8. Thrust the regulator completely into the delivery pipe by hand.

9. Turn the regulator counterclockwise until the vacuum pipe faces in the direction indicated in the illustration. Tighten the locknut to 18 ft. lbs. (25 Nm).

10. Attach the No. 2 fuel pipe to the pressure regulator with new gaskets and union bolt. Tighten to 18 ft. lbs. (25 Nm).

11. Attach the vacuum sensing hose.

12. Connect the No. 3 PCV hose and check for fuel leakage.

Van

▶ See Figures 68, 69, 70 and 71

1. Raise and support the vehicle.

2. Disconnect the vacuum sensing hose.

3. Place a suitable container or shop towel under the pressure regulator to catch any spilt fuel.

4. Disconnect the fuel return pipe from the pressure regulator, slowly loosen the fuel return pipe.

5. Remove the two union bolts and pull the pressure regulator out of the delivery pipe.

To install:

6. Install the pressure regulator, tighten the two bolts to 52 inch lbs. (6 Nm).

7. Connect the fuel return pipe and tighten to 14 ft. lbs. (20 Nm).

8. Attach the vacuum sensing hose.

9. Check for fuel leakage.

10. Lower the vehicle.

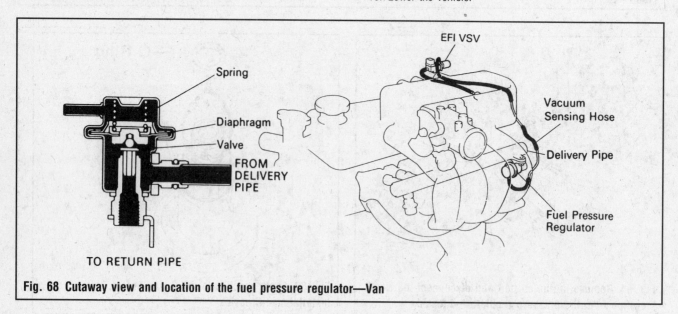

Fig. 68 Cutaway view and location of the fuel pressure regulator—Van

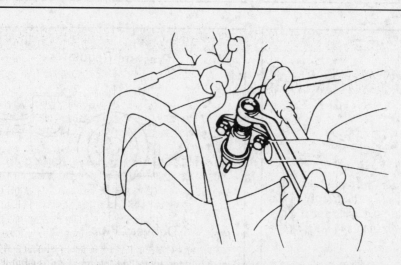

Fig. 69 When removing the pressure regulator, disconnect the fuel return pipe from the regulator

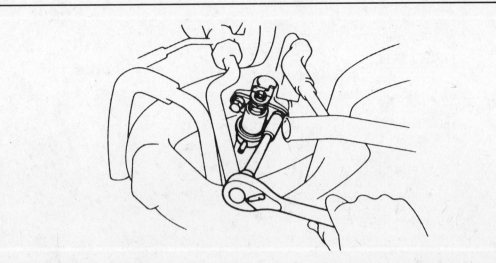

Fig. 70 Remove the two mounting bolts and remove the fuel pressure regulator from the delivery pipe—Van

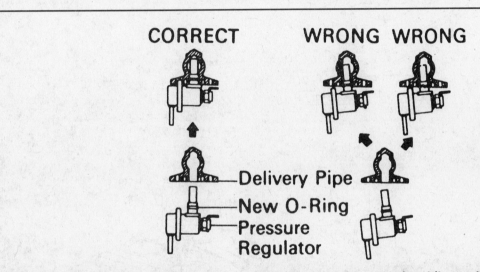

Fig. 71 When installing the pressure regulator on the delivery pipe, be sure to insert it correctly—Van

FUEL TANK

Tank Assembly

REMOVAL & INSTALLATION

▶ **See Figures 72, 73 and 74**

➡**The fuel tank is usually mounted at the rear of the vehicle. If it is necessary to work on the fuel tank or its components and fittings, either in or out of the vehicle, the ignition must be switched to the OFF position and the negative battery cable disconnected.**

1. Raise and safely support the vehicle. Remove all fuel tank safety covers and or tank protectors.

2. Before removing the fuel tank, the fuel should be drained out of the tank into a suitable gasoline safe container. It should

be noted that some models are equipped with a drain plug on the fuel tank.

3. In effort to make the fuel tank filler neck more accessible during the removal procedure, remove the tire and wheel assembly from the side of the vehicle that the fuel tank filler neck is located on.

4. Place a suitable jack under the center of the fuel tank, be sure to use a flat piece of wood between the jack cradle and the fuel tank so as to prevent damaging the fuel tank. Spray the fuel tank retaining strap bolts and nuts with a suitable penetrating fluid.

5. Loosen the fuel tank restraining strap retaining bolts and nuts, but do not remove at this time. Slowly lower the jack so as to take up the slack in the fuel tank restraining straps.

6. If so equipped, remove the trim panel in the trunk then reach through the hole and disconnect the fuel evaporative emission control hose and the fuel gauge/fuel pump sending unit wiring.

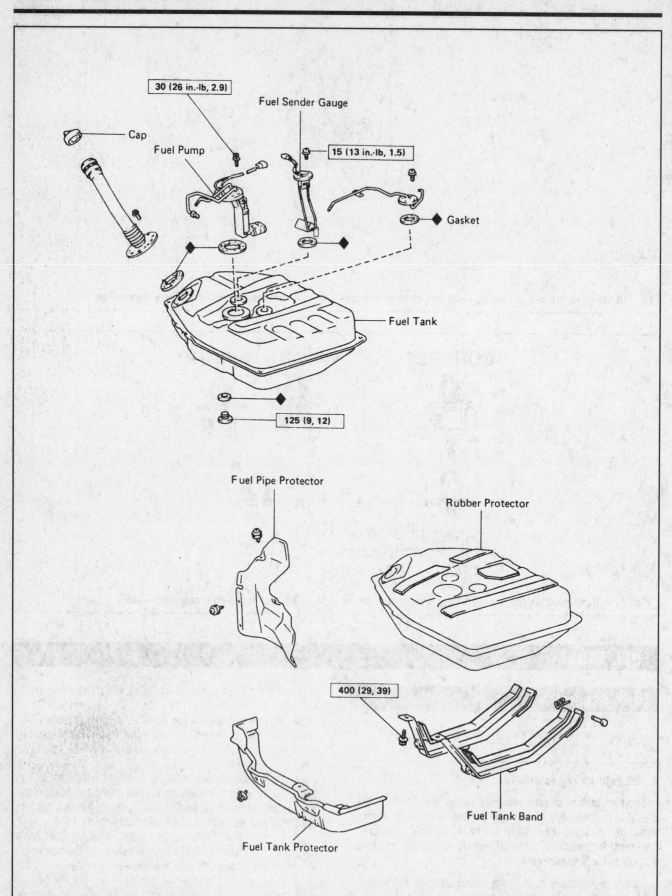

Fig. 72 View of the fuel tank and related components—1983–88 Cressida

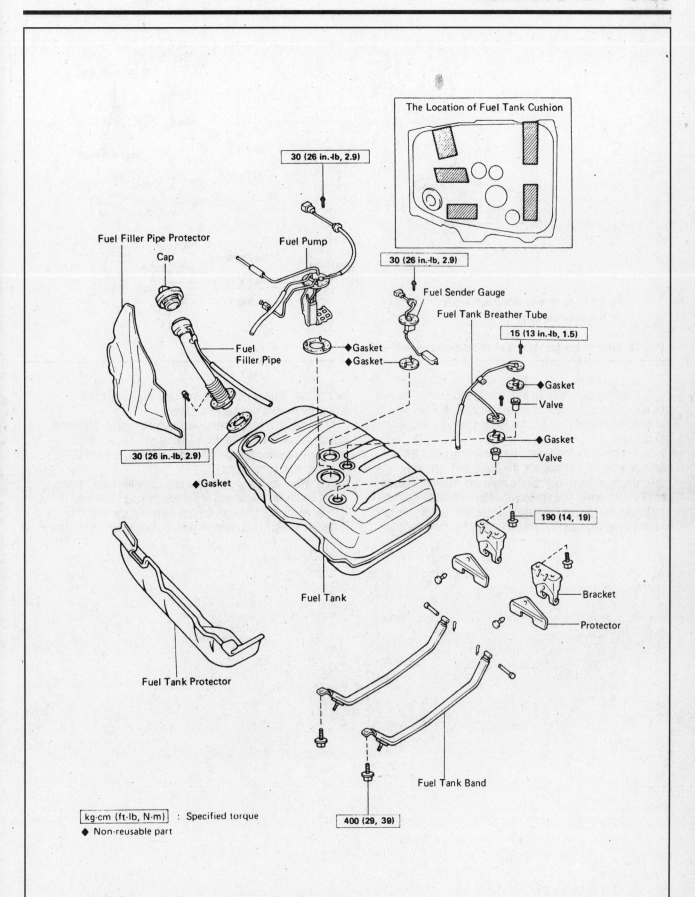

The Location of Fuel Tank Cushion

30 (26 in.-lb, 2.9)

Fuel Pump

30 (26 in.-lb, 2.9)

Fuel Filler Pipe Protector

Cap

Fuel Sender Gauge

Fuel Tank Breather Tube

15 (13 in.-lb, 1.5)

Fuel Filler Pipe

Gasket

Gasket

Gasket

Valve

Gasket

Valve

30 (26 in.-lb, 2.9)

Gasket

190 (14, 19)

Fuel Tank

Bracket

Protector

Fuel Tank Protector

Fuel Tank Band

kg·cm (ft-lb, N·m) : Specified torque

◆ Non-reusable part

400 (29, 39)

Fig. 73 View of the fuel tank and related components—1988–90 Cressida

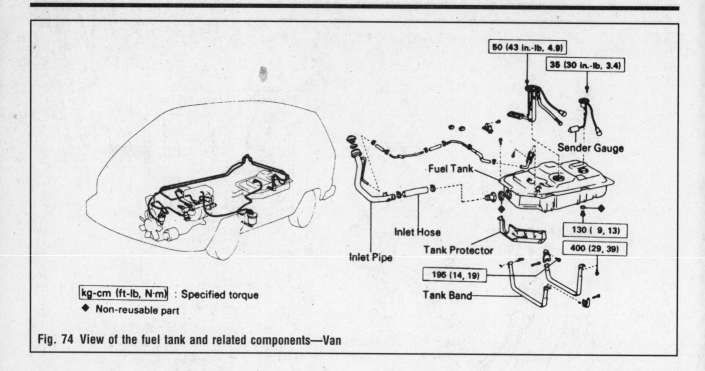

Fig. 74 View of the fuel tank and related components—Van

7. If not equipped with an easy access panel, lower the fuel tank enough to gain access so as to disconnect the fuel evaporative emission control hose and the fuel gauge/fuel pump sending unit wiring.

8. Working from inside the wheel well, disconnect the fuel filler pipe from the fuel tank and the inlet pipe in the body.

9. Disconnect and separate the main and return fuel hoses from their respective tank connecting lines underneath the car.

10. With the tank still supported by the jack, remove the tank strap retaining bolts and or nuts and slowly but carefully lower the fuel tank. Remove and lines that may still be attached or hindering the removal process in any way.

11. Installation is the reverse order of the removal procedure. Be sure to pay attention to the following:

a. Always use new gaskets when replacing the fuel tank or an fuel tank components.

b. When reinstalling; be sure to include the rubber protectors on the upper surfaces of the fuel tank and tank band.

c. Be sure to check all the fuel lines and connection for cracks, leakage or connection deformation. Repair as necessary.

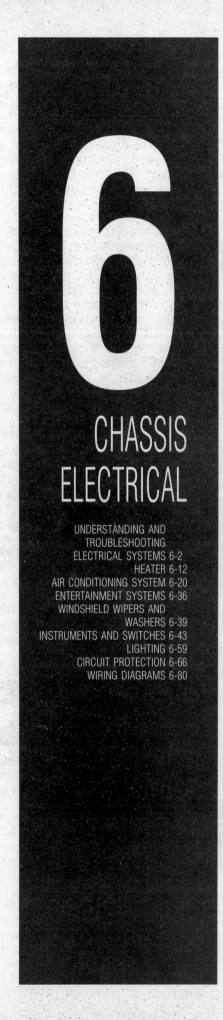

6

CHASSIS
ELECTRICAL

UNDERSTANDING AND TROUBLESHOOTING ELECTRICAL SYSTEMS

Over the years import and domestic manufacturers have incorporated electronic control systems into their production lines. In fact, electronic control systems are so prevalent that all new cars and trucks built today are equipped with at least one on-board computer. These electronic components (with no moving parts) should theoretically last the life of the vehicle, provided that nothing external happens to damage the circuits or memory chips.

While it is true that electronic components should never wear out, in the real world malfunctions do occur. It is also true that any computer-based system is extremely sensitive to electrical voltages and cannot tolerate careless or haphazard testing/service procedures. An inexperienced individual can literally cause major damage looking for a minor problem by using the wrong kind of test equipment or connecting test leads/connectors with the ignition switch **ON**. When selecting test equipment, make sure the manufacturer's instructions state that the tester is compatible with whatever type of system is being serviced. Read all instructions carefully and double check all test points before installing probes or making any test connections.

The following section outlines basic diagnosis techniques for dealing with automotive electrical systems. Along with a general explanation of the various types of test equipment available to aid in servicing modern automotive systems, basic repair techniques for wiring harnesses and connectors are also given. Read the basic information before attempting any repairs or testing. This will provide the background of information necessary to avoid the most common and obvious mistakes that can cost both time and money. Although the replacement and testing procedures are simple in themselves, the systems are not, and unless one has a thorough understanding of all components and their function within a particular system, the logical test sequence these systems demand cannot be followed. Minor malfunctions can make a big difference, so it is important to know how each component affects the operation of the overall system in order to find the ultimate cause of a problem without replacing good components unnecessarily. It is not enough to use the correct test equipment; the test equipment must be used correctly.

Safety Precautions

✳✳ CAUTION

Whenever working on or around any electrical or electronic systems, always observe these general precautions to prevent the possibility of personal injury or damage to electronic components.

• Never install or remove battery cables with the key **ON** or the engine running. Jumper cables should be connected with the key **OFF** to avoid power surges that can damage electronic control units. Engines equipped with computer controlled systems should avoid both giving and getting jump starts due to the possibility of serious damage to components from arcing in the engine compartment if connections are made with the ignition **ON**.

• Always remove the battery cables before charging the battery. Never use a high output charger on an installed battery or attempt to use any type of "hot shot" (24 volt) starting aid.

• Exercise care when inserting test probes into connectors to insure good contact without damaging the connector or spreading the pins. Always probe connectors from the rear (wire) side, NOT the pin side, to avoid accidental shorting of terminals during test procedures.

• Never remove or attach wiring harness connectors with the ignition switch **ON**, especially to an electronic control unit.

• Do not drop any components during service procedures and never apply 12 volts directly to any component (like a solenoid or relay) unless instructed specifically to do so. Some component electrical windings are designed to safely handle only 4 or 5 volts and can be destroyed in seconds if 12 volts are applied directly to the connector.

• Remove the electronic control unit if the vehicle is to be placed in an environment where temperatures exceed approximately 176°F (80°C), such as a paint spray booth or when arc/gas welding near the control unit location.

Understanding Basic Electricity

Understanding the basic theory of electricity makes electrical troubleshooting much easier. Several gauges are used in electrical troubleshooting to see inside the circuit being tested. Without a basic understanding, it will be difficult to understand testing procedures.

THE WATER ANALOGY

Electricity is the flow of electrons—hypothetical particles thought to constitute the basic stuff of electricity. Many people have been taught electrical theory using an analogy with water. In a comparison with water flowing in a pipe, the electrons would be the water. As the flow of water can be measured, the flow of electricity can be measured. The unit of measurement is amperes, frequently abbreviated amps. An ammeter will measure the actual amount of current flowing in the circuit.

Just as the water pressure is measured in units such as pounds per square inch, electrical pressure is measured in volts. When a voltmeter's two probes are placed on two live portions of an electrical circuit with different electrical pressures, current will flow through the voltmeter and produce a reading which indicates the difference in electrical pressure between the two parts of the circuit.

While increasing the voltage in a circuit will increase the flow of current, the actual flow depends not only on voltage, but on the resistance of the circuit. The standard unit for measuring circuit resistance is an ohm, measured by an ohmmeter. The ohmmeter is somewhat similar to an ammeter, but incorporates its own source of power so that a standard voltage is always present.

CIRCUITS

An actual electric circuit consists of four basic parts. These are: the power source, such as a generator or battery; a hot wire, which conducts the electricity under a relatively high voltage to the component supplied by the circuit; the load, such as a lamp, motor, resistor or relay coil; and the ground wire, which carries the current back to the source under very low voltage. In such a circuit the bulk of the resistance exists between the point where the hot wire is connected to the load, and the point where the load is grounded. In an automobile, the vehicle's frame or body, which is made of steel, is used as a part of the ground circuit for many of the electrical devices.

Remember that, in electrical testing, the voltmeter is connected in parallel with the circuit being tested (without disconnecting any wires) and measures the difference in voltage between the locations of the two probes; that the ammeter is connected in series with the load (the circuit is separated at one point and the ammeter inserted so it becomes a part of the circuit); and the ohmmeter is self-powered, so that all the power in the circuit should be off and the portion of the circuit to be measured contacted at either end by one of the probes of the meter.

For any electrical system to operate, it must make a complete circuit. This simply means that the power flow from the battery must make a complete circle. When an electrical component is operating, power flows from the battery to the component, passes through the component causing it to perform it to function (such as lighting a light bulb) and then returns to the battery through the ground of the circuit. This ground is usually (but not always) the metal part of the vehicle on which the electrical component is mounted.

Perhaps the easiest way to visualize this is to think of connecting a light bulb with two wires attached to it to your vehicle's battery. The battery in your vehicle has two posts (negative and positive). If one of the two wires attached to the light bulb was attached to the negative post of the battery and the other wire was attached to the positive post of the battery, you would have a complete circuit. Current from the battery would flow out one post, through the wire attached to it and then to the light bulb, where it would pass through causing it to light. It would then leave the light bulb, travel through the other wire, and return to the other post of the battery.

AUTOMOTIVE CIRCUITS

The normal automotive circuit differs from this simple example in two ways. First, instead of having a return wire from the bulb to the battery, the light bulb return the current to the battery through the chassis of the vehicle. Since the negative battery cable is attached to the chassis and the chassis is made of electrically conductive metal, the chassis of the vehicle can serve as a ground wire to complete the circuit. Secondly, most automotive circuits contain switches to turn components on and off.

Some electrical components which require a large amount of current to operate also have a relay in their circuit. Since these circuits carry a large amount of current, the thickness of the wire in the circuit (gauge size) is also greater. If this large wire were connected from the component to the control switch on the instrument panel, and then back to the component, a voltage drop would occur in the circuit. To prevent this potential drop in voltage, an electromagnetic switch (relay) is used. The large wires in the circuit are connected from the vehicle battery to one side of the relay, and from the opposite side of the relay to the component. The relay is normally open, preventing current from passing through the circuit. An additional, smaller wire is connected from the relay to the control switch for the circuit. When the control switch is turned on, it grounds the smaller wire from the relay and completes the circuit.

SHORT CIRCUITS

If you were to disconnect the light bulb (from the previous example of a light-bulb being connected to the battery by two wires) from the wires and touch the two wires together (please take our word for this; don't try it), the result will be a shower of sparks. A similar thing happens (on a smaller scale) when the power supply wire to a component or the electrical component itself becomes grounded before the normal ground connection for the circuit. To prevent damage to the system, the fuse for the circuit blows to interrupt the circuit—protecting the components from damage. Because grounding a wire from a power source makes a complete circuit—less the required component to use the power—the phenomenon is called a short circuit. The most common causes of short circuits are: the rubber insulation on a wire breaking or rubbing through to expose the current carrying core of the wire to a metal part of the car, or a shorted switch.

Some electrical systems on the vehicle are protected by a circuit breaker which is, basically, a self-repairing fuse. When either of the described events takes place in a system which is protected by a circuit breaker, the circuit breaker opens the circuit the same way a fuse does. However, when either the short is removed from the circuit or the surge subsides, the circuit breaker resets itself and does not have to be replaced as a fuse does.

Troubleshooting

When diagnosing a specific problem, organized troubleshooting is a must. The complexity of a modern automobile demands that you approach any problem in a logical, organized manner. There are certain troubleshooting techniques that are standard:

1. Establish when the problem occurs. Does the problem appear only under certain conditions? Were there any noises, odors, or other unusual symptoms?

2. Isolate the problem area. To do this, make some simple tests and observations; then eliminate the systems that are working properly. Check for obvious problems such as broken wires, dirty connections or split/disconnected vacuum hoses. Always check the obvious before assuming something complicated is the cause.

3. Test for problems systematically to determine the cause once the problem area is isolated. Are all the components functioning properly? Is there power going to electrical switches and motors? Is there vacuum at vacuum switches and/or actuators? Is there a mechanical problem such as bent linkage or loose mounting screws? Performing careful, systematic checks will often turn up most causes on the first inspection without wasting time checking components that have little or no relationship to the problem.

4. Test all repairs after the work is done to make sure that the problem is fixed. Some causes can be traced to more than one component, so a careful verification of repair work is important in order to pick up additional malfunctions that may cause a problem to reappear or a different problem to arise. A blown fuse, for example, is a simple problem that may require more than another fuse to repair. If you don't look for a problem that caused a fuse to blow, a shorted wire (for example) may go undetected.

Experience has shown that most problems tend to be the result of a fairly simple and obvious cause, such as loose or corroded connectors or air leaks in the intake system. This makes careful inspection of components during testing essential to quick and accurate troubleshooting.

BASIC TROUBLESHOOTING THEORY

Electrical problems generally fall into one of three areas:
• The component that is not functioning is not receiving current.
• The component itself is not functioning.
• The component is not properly grounded.

Problems that fall into the first category are by far the most complicated. It is the current supply system to the component which contains all the switches, relay, fuses, etc.

The electrical system can be checked with a test light and a jumper wire. A test light is a device that looks like a pointed screwdriver with a wire attached to it. It has a light bulb in its handle. A jumper wire is a piece of insulated wire with an alligator clip attached to each end.

If a light bulb is not working, you must follow a systematic plan to determine which of the three causes is the villain.

1. Turn on the switch that controls the inoperable bulb.
2. Disconnect the power supply wire from the bulb.
3. Attach the ground wire to the test light to a good metal ground.
4. Touch the probe end of the test light to the end of the power supply wire that was disconnected from the bulb. If the bulb is receiving current, the test light will go on.

➡**If the bulb is one which works only when the ignition key is turned on (turn signal), make sure the key is turned on.**

If the test light does not go on, then the problem is in the circuit between the battery and the bulb. As mentioned before, this includes all the switches, fuses, and relays in the system. Turn to a wiring diagram and find the bulb on the diagram. Follow the wire that runs back to the battery. The problem is an open circuit between the battery and the bulb. If the fuse is blown and, when replaced, immediately blows again, there is a short circuit in the system which must be located and repaired. If there is a switch in the system, bypass it with a jumper wire. This is done by connecting one end of the jumper wire to the power supply wire into the switch and the other end of the jumper wire to the wire coming out of the switch. If the test light illuminates with the jumper wire installed, the switch or whatever was bypassed is defective.

➡**Never substitute the jumper wire for the bulb, as the bulb is the component required to use the power from the power source.**

5. If the bulb in the test light goes on, then the current is getting to the bulb that is not working in the car. This eliminates the first of the three possible causes. Connect the power supply wire and connect a jumper wire from the bulb to a good metal ground. Do this with the switch which controls the bulb works with jumper wire installed, then it has a bad ground. This is usually caused by the metal area on which the bulb mounts to the vehicle being coated with some type of foreign matter.
6. If neither test located the source of the trouble, then the light bulb itself is defective.

The above test procedure can be applied to any of the components of the chassis electrical system by substituting the component that is not working for the light bulb. Remember that for any electrical system to work, all connections must be clean and tight.

TEST EQUIPMENT

➡**Pinpointing the exact cause of trouble in an electrical system can sometimes only be accomplished by the use of special test equipment. The following describes different types of commonly used test equipment and explains how to use them in diagnosis. In addition to the information covered below, the tool manufacturer's instructions booklet (provided with the tester) should be read and clearly understood before attempting any test procedures.**

Jumper Wires

Jumper wires are simple, yet extremely valuable, pieces of test equipment. They are basically test wires which are used to bypass sections of a circuit. The simplest type of jumper wire is a length of multi-strand wire with an alligator clip at each end. Jumper wires are usually fabricated from lengths of standard automotive wire and whatever type of connector (alligator clip, spade connector or pin connector) that is required for the particular vehicle being tested. The well equipped tool box will have several different styles of jumper wires in several different lengths. Some jumper wires are made with three or more terminals coming from a common splice for special purpose testing. In cramped, hard-to-reach areas it is advisable to have insulated boots over the jumper wire terminals in order to prevent accidental grounding, sparks, and possible fire, especially when testing fuel system components.

Jumper wires are used primarily to locate open electrical circuits, on either the ground (−) side of the circuit or on the hot (+) side. If an electrical component fails to operate, connect the jumper wire between the component and a good ground. If the component operates only with the jumper installed, the ground circuit is open. If the ground circuit is good, but the component does not operate, the circuit between the power feed and component may be open. By moving the jumper wire successively back from the lamp toward the power source, you can isolate the area of the circuit where the open is located. When the component stops functioning, or the power is cut off, the open is in the segment of wire between the jumper and the point previously tested.

You can sometimes connect the jumper wire directly from the

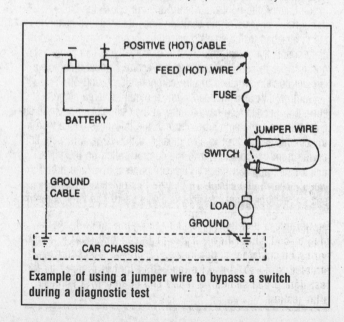

Example of using a jumper wire to bypass a switch during a diagnostic test

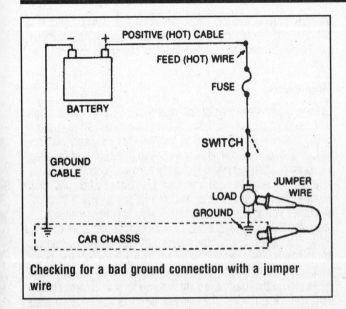

Checking for a bad ground connection with a jumper wire

battery to the hot terminal of the component, but first make sure the component uses 12 volts in operation. Some electrical components, such as fuel injectors, are designed to operate on about 4 volts and running 12 volts directly to the injector terminals can cause damage.

By inserting an in-line fuse holder between a set of test leads, a fused jumper wire can be used for bypassing open circuits. Use a 5 amp fuse to provide protection against voltage spikes. When in doubt, use a voltmeter to check the voltage input to the component and measure how much voltage is normally being applied.

✳✳ CAUTION

Never use jumpers made from wire that is of lighter gauge than that which is used in the circuit under test. If the jumper wire is of too small a gauge, it may overheat and possibly melt. Never use jumpers to bypass high resistance loads in a circuit. Bypassing resistances, in effect, creates a short circuit. This may, in turn, cause damage and fire. Jumper wires should only be used to bypass lengths of wire.

Unpowered Test Lights

The 12 volt test light is used to check circuits and components while electrical current is flowing through them. It is used for voltage and ground tests. Twelve volt test lights come in different styles but all have three main parts; a ground clip, a probe, and a light. The most commonly used 12 volt test lights have pick-type probes. To use a 12 volt test light, connect the ground clip to a good ground and probe wherever necessary with the pick. The pick should be sharp so that it can be probed into tight spaces.

✳✳ CAUTION

Do not use a test light to probe electronic ignition spark plug or coil wires. Never use a pick-type test light to probe wiring on computer controlled systems unless specifically instructed to do so. Any wire insulation that is pierced by the test light probe should be taped and sealed with silicone after testing.

Like the jumper wire, the 12 volt test light is used to isolate opens in circuits. But, whereas the jumper wire is used to bypass the open to operate the load, the 12 volt test light is used to locate the presence of voltage in a circuit. If the test light glows, you know that there is power up to that point; if the 12 volt test light does not glow when its probe is inserted into the wire or connector, you know that there is an open circuit (no power). Move the test light in successive steps back toward the power source until the light in the handle does glow. When it glows, the open is between the probe and point which was probed previously.

➡**The test light does not detect that 12 volts (or any particular amount of voltage) is present; it only detects that some voltage is present. It is advisable before using the test light to touch its terminals across the battery posts to make sure the light is operating properly.**

Self-Powered Test Lights

The self-powered test light usually contains a 1.5 volt penlight battery. One type of self-powered test light is similar in design to the 12 volt unit. This type has both the battery and the light in the handle, along with a pick-type probe tip. The second type has the light toward the open tip, so that the light illuminates the contact point. The self-powered test light is a dual purpose piece of test equipment. It can be used to test for either open or short circuits when power is isolated from the circuit (continuity test). A powered test light should not be used on any computer controlled system or component unless specifically instructed to do so. Many engine sensors can be destroyed by even this small amount of voltage applied directly to the terminals.

Voltmeters

A voltmeter is used to measure voltage at any point in a circuit, or to measure the voltage drop across any part of a circuit. It can also be used to check continuity in a wire or circuit by indicating current flow from one end to the other. Analog voltmeters usually have various scales on the meter dial and a selector switch to allow the selection of different voltages. The voltmeter has a positive and a negative lead. To avoid damage to the meter, always connect the negative lead to the negative (−) side of the circuit (to ground or nearest the ground side of the circuit) and connect the positive lead to the positive (+) side of the circuit (to the power source or the nearest power source). Note that the negative voltmeter lead will always be black and that the positive voltmeter will always be some color other than black (usually red).

Depending on how the voltmeter is connected into the circuit, it has several uses. A voltmeter can be connected either in parallel or in series with a circuit and it has a very high resistance to current flow. When connected in parallel, only a small amount of current will flow through the voltmeter current path; the rest will flow through the normal circuit current path and the circuit will work normally. When the voltmeter is connected in series with a circuit, only a small amount of current can flow through the circuit. The circuit will not work properly, but the voltmeter reading will show if the circuit is complete or not.

Ohmmeters

The ohmmeter is designed to read resistance (which is measured in ohms or Ω) in a circuit or component. Although there are several different styles of ohmmeters, all analog meters will usually have a selector switch which permits the measurement of different ranges of resistance (usually the selector switch allows the multiplication of the meter reading by 10, 100, 1000, and 10,000). A calibration knob allows the meter to be set at zero for accurate measurement. Since all ohmmeters are powered by an internal battery, the ohmmeter can be used as a self-powered test light. When the ohmmeter is connected, current from the ohmmeter flows through the circuit or component being tested. Since the ohmmeter's internal resistance and voltage are known values, the amount of current flow through the meter depends on the resistance of the circuit or component being tested.

The ohmmeter can be used to perform a continuity test for opens or shorts (either by observation of the meter needle or as a self-powered test light), and to read actual resistance in a circuit. It should be noted that the ohmmeter is used to check the resistance of a component or wire while there is no voltage applied to the circuit. Current flow from an outside voltage source (such as the vehicle battery) can damage the ohmmeter, so the circuit or component should be isolated from the vehicle electrical system before any testing is done. Since the ohmmeter uses its own voltage source, either lead can be connected to any test point.

➡**When checking diodes or other solid state components, the ohmmeter leads can only be connected one way in order to measure current flow in a single direction. Make sure the positive (+) and negative (−) terminal connections are as described in the test procedures to verify the one-way diode operation.**

In using the meter for making continuity checks, do not be concerned with the actual resistance readings. Zero resistance, or any ohm reading, indicates continuity in the circuit. Infinite resistance indicates an open in the circuit. A high resistance reading where there should be none indicates a problem in the circuit. Checks for short circuits are made in the same manner as checks for open circuits except that the circuit must be isolated from both power and normal ground. Infinite resistance indicates no continuity to ground, while zero resistance indicates a dead short to ground.

Ammeters

An ammeter measures the amount of current flowing through a circuit in units called amperes or amps. Amperes are units of electron flow which indicate how fast the electrons are flowing through the circuit. Since Ohms Law dictates that current flow in a circuit is equal to the circuit voltage divided by the total circuit resistance, increasing voltage also increases the current level (amps). Likewise, any decrease in resistance will increase the amount of amps in a circuit. At normal operating voltage, most circuits have a characteristic amount of amperes, called "current draw" which can be measured using an ammeter. By referring to a specified current draw rating, measuring the amperes, and comparing the two values, one can determine what is happening within the circuit to aid in diagnosis. An open circuit, for example, will not allow any current to flow so the ammeter reading will be zero. More current flows through a heavily loaded circuit or when the charging system is operating.

An ammeter is always connected in series with the circuit being tested. All of the current that normally flows through the circuit must also flow through the ammeter; if there is any other path for the current to follow, the ammeter reading will not be accurate. The ammeter itself has very little resistance to current flow and therefore will not affect the circuit, but it will measure current draw only when the circuit is closed and electricity is flowing. Excessive current draw can blow fuses and drain the battery, while a reduced current draw can cause motors to run slowly, lights to dim and other components to not operate properly. The ammeter can help diagnose these conditions by locating the cause of the high or low reading.

Multimeters

Different combinations of test meters can be built into a single unit designed for specific tests. Some of the more common combination test devices are known as Volt/Amp testers, Tach/Dwell meters, or Digital Multimeters. The Volt/Amp tester is used for charging system, starting system or battery tests and consists of a voltmeter, an ammeter and a variable resistance carbon pile. The voltmeter will usually have at least two ranges for use with 6, 12 and/or 24 volt systems. The ammeter also has more than one range for testing various levels of battery loads and starter current draw. The carbon pile can be adjusted to offer different amounts of resistance. The Volt/Amp tester has heavy leads to carry large amounts of current and many later models have an inductive ammeter pickup that clamps around the wire to simplify test connections. On some models, the ammeter also has a zero-center scale to allow testing of charging and starting systems without switching leads or polarity. A digital multimeter is a voltmeter, ammeter and ohmmeter combined in an instrument which gives a digital readout. These are often used when testing solid state circuits because of their high input impedance (usually 10 megohms or more).

The tach/dwell meter that combines a tachometer and a dwell (cam angle) meter is a specialized kind of voltmeter. The tachometer scale is marked to show engine speed in rpm and the dwell scale is marked to show degrees of distributor shaft rotation. In most electronic ignition systems, dwell is determined by the control unit, but the dwell meter can also be used to check the duty cycle (operation) of some electronic engine control systems. Some tach/dwell meters are powered by an internal battery, while others take their power from the vehicle battery in use. The battery powered testers usually require calibration (much like an ohmmeter) before testing.

TESTING

Open Circuits

To use the self-powered test light or a multimeter to check for open circuits, first isolate the circuit from the vehicle's 12 volt power source by disconnecting the battery or wiring harness connector. Connect the test light or ohmmeter ground clip to a good ground and probe sections of the circuit sequentially with the test light. (start from either end of the circuit). If the light is out/or there is infinite resistance, the open is between the probe and the circuit ground. If the light is on/or the meter shows continuity, the open is between the probe and end of the circuit toward the power source.

Short Circuits

By isolating the circuit both from power and from ground, and using a self-powered test light or multimeter, you can check for shorts to ground in the circuit. Isolate the circuit from power and ground. Connect the test light or ohmmeter ground clip to a good ground and probe any easy-to-reach test point in the circuit. If the light comes on or there is continuity, there is a short somewhere in the circuit. To isolate the short, probe a test point at either end of the isolated circuit (the light should be on/there should be continuity). Leave the test light probe engaged and open connectors, switches, remove parts, etc., sequentially, until the light goes out/continuity is broken. When the light goes out, the short is between the last circuit component opened and the previous circuit opened.

➡**The battery in the test light and does not provide much current. A weak battery may not provide enough power to illuminate the test light even when a complete circuit is made (especially if there are high resistances in the circuit). Always make sure that the test battery is strong. To check the battery, briefly touch the ground clip to the probe; if the light glows brightly the battery is strong enough for testing. Never use a self-powered test light to perform checks for opens or shorts when power is applied to the electrical system under test. The 12 volt vehicle power will quickly burn out the light bulb in the test light.**

Available Voltage Measurement

Set the voltmeter selector switch to the 20V position and connect the meter negative lead to the negative post of the battery. Connect the positive meter lead to the positive post of the battery and turn the ignition switch **ON** to provide a load. Read the voltage on the meter or digital display. A well charged battery should register over 12 volts. If the meter reads below 11.5 volts, the battery power may be insufficient to operate the electrical system properly. This test determines voltage available from the battery and should be the first step in any electrical trouble diagnosis procedure. Many electrical problems, especially on computer controlled systems, can be caused by a low state of charge in the battery. Excessive corrosion at the battery cable terminals can cause a poor contact that will prevent proper charging and full battery current flow.

Normal battery voltage is 12 volts when fully charged. When the battery is supplying current to one or more circuits it is said to be "under load." When everything is off the electrical system is under a "no-load" condition. A fully charged battery may show about 12.5 volts at no load; will drop to 12 volts under medium load; and will drop even lower under heavy load. If the battery is partially discharged the voltage decrease under heavy load may be excessive, even though the battery shows 12 volts or more at no load. When allowed to discharge further, the battery's available voltage under load will decrease more severely. For this reason, it is important that the battery be fully charged during all testing procedures to avoid errors in diagnosis and incorrect test results.

Voltage Drop

When current flows through a resistance, the voltage beyond the resistance is reduced (the larger the current, the greater the reduction in voltage). When no current is flowing, there is no voltage drop because there is no current flow. All points in the circuit which are connected to the power source are at the same voltage as the power source. The total voltage drop always equals the total source voltage. In a long circuit with many connectors, a series of small, unwanted voltage drops due to corrosion at the connectors can add up to a total loss of voltage which impairs the operation of the normal loads in the circuit. The maximum allowable voltage drop under load is critical, especially if there is more than one high resistance problem in a circuit because all voltage drops are cumulative. A small drop is normal due to the resistance of the conductors.

INDIRECT COMPUTATION OF VOLTAGE DROPS

1. Set the voltmeter selector switch to the 20 volt position.
2. Connect the meter negative lead to a good ground.
3. While operating the circuit, probe all loads in the circuit with the positive meter lead and observe the voltage readings. A drop should be noticed after the first load. But, there should be little or no voltage drop before the first load.

DIRECT MEASUREMENT OF VOLTAGE DROPS

1. Set the voltmeter switch to the 20 volt position.
2. Connect the voltmeter negative lead to the ground side of the load to be measured.
3. Connect the positive lead to the positive side of the resistance or load to be measured.
4. Read the voltage drop directly on the 20 volt scale.
Too high a voltage indicates too high a resistance. If, for example, a blower motor runs too slowly, you can determine if perhaps there is too high a resistance in the resistor pack. By taking voltage drop readings in all parts of the circuit, you can isolate the problem. Too low a voltage drop indicates too low a resistance. Take the blower motor for example again. If a blower motor runs too fast in the MED and/or LOW position, the problem might be isolated in the resistor pack by taking voltage drop readings in all parts of the circuit to locate a possibly shorted resistor.

HIGH RESISTANCE TESTING

1. Set the voltmeter selector switch to the 4 volt position.
2. Connect the voltmeter positive lead to the positive post of the battery.
3. Turn on the headlights and heater blower to provide a load.
4. Probe various points in the circuit with the negative voltmeter lead.
5. Read the voltage drop on the 4 volt scale. Some average maximum allowable voltage drops are:
- FUSE PANEL: 0.7 volts
- IGNITION SWITCH: 0.5 volts
- HEADLIGHT SWITCH: 0.7 volts
- IGNITION COIL (+): 0.5 volts
- ANY OTHER LOAD: 1.3 volts

➡**Voltage drops are all measured while a load is operating; without current flow, there will be no voltage drop.**

Resistance Measurement

The batteries in an ohmmeter will weaken with age and temperature, so the ohmmeter must be calibrated or "zeroed" before taking measurements. To zero the meter, place the selector switch in its lowest range and touch the two ohmmeter leads together. Turn the calibration knob until the meter needle is exactly on zero.

➡**All analog (needle) type ohmmeters must be zeroed before use, but some digital ohmmeter models are automatically calibrated when the switch is turned on. Self-calibrating digital ohmmeters do not have an adjusting knob, but its a good idea to check for a zero readout before use by touching the leads together. All computer controlled systems require the use of a digital ohmmeter with at least 10 megohms impedance for testing. Before any test procedures are attempted, make sure the ohmmeter used is compatible with the electrical system or damage to the on-board computer could result.**

To measure resistance, first isolate the circuit from the vehicle power source by disconnecting the battery cables or the harness connector. Make sure the key is **OFF** when disconnecting any components or the battery. Where necessary, also isolate at least one side of the circuit to be checked in order to avoid reading parallel resistances. Parallel circuit resistances will always give a lower reading than the actual resistance of either of the branches. When measuring the resistance of parallel circuits, the total resistance will always be lower than the smallest resistance in the circuit. Connect the meter leads to both sides of the circuit (wire or component) and read the actual measured ohms on the meter scale. Make sure the selector switch is set to the proper ohm scale for the circuit being tested to avoid misreading the ohmmeter test value.

✳✳ WARNING

Never use an ohmmeter with power applied to the circuit. Like the self-powered test light, the ohmmeter is designed to operate on its own power supply. The normal 12 volt automotive electrical system current could damage the meter!

Wiring Harnesses

The average automobile contains about ½ mile of wiring, with hundreds of individual connections. To protect the many wires from damage and to keep them from becoming a confusing tangle, they are organized into bundles, enclosed in plastic or taped together and called wiring harnesses. Different harnesses serve different parts of the vehicle. Individual wires are color coded to help trace them through a harness where sections are hidden from view.

Automotive wiring or circuit conductors can be in any one of three forms:
1. Single strand wire
2. Multi-strand wire
3. Printed circuitry

Single strand wire has a solid metal core and is usually used inside such components as alternators, motors, relays and other devices. Multi-strand wire has a core made of many small strands of wire twisted together into a single conductor. Most of the wiring in an automotive electrical system is made up of multi-strand wire, either as a single conductor or grouped together in a harness. All wiring is color coded on the insulator, either as a solid color or as a colored wire with an identification stripe. A printed circuit is a thin film of copper or other conductor that is printed on an insulator backing. Occasionally, a printed circuit is sandwiched between two sheets of plastic for more protection and flexibility. A complete printed circuit, consisting of conductors, insulating material and connectors for lamps or other components is called a printed circuit board. Printed circuitry is used in place of individual wires or harnesses in places where space is limited, such as behind instrument panels.

Since automotive electrical systems are very sensitive to changes in resistance, the selection of properly sized wires is critical when systems are repaired. A loose or corroded connection or a replacement wire that is too small for the circuit will add extra resistance and an additional voltage drop to the circuit. A ten percent voltage drop can result in slow or erratic motor operation, for example, even though the circuit is complete. The wire gauge number is an expression of the cross-section area of the conduc-

tor. The most common system for expressing wire size is the American Wire Gauge (AWG) system.

Gauge numbers are assigned to conductors of various cross-section areas. As gauge number increases, area decreases and the conductor becomes smaller. A 5 gauge conductor is smaller than a 1 gauge conductor and a 10 gauge is smaller than a 5 gauge. As the cross-section area of a conductor decreases, resistance increases and so does the gauge number. A conductor with a higher gauge number will carry less current than a conductor with a lower gauge number.

➡ **Gauge wire size refers to the size of the conductor, not the size of the complete wire. It is possible to have two wires of the same gauge with different diameters because one may have thicker insulation than the other.**

12 volt automotive electrical systems generally use 10, 12, 14, 16 and 18 gauge wire. Main power distribution circuits and larger accessories usually use 10 and 12 gauge wire. Battery cables are usually 4 or 6 gauge, although 1 and 2 gauge wires are occasionally used. Wire length must also be considered when making repairs to a circuit. As conductor length increases, so does resistance. An 18 gauge wire, for example, can carry a 10 amp load for 10 feet without excessive voltage drop; however if a 15 foot wire is required for the same 10 amp load, it must be a 16 gauge wire.

An electrical schematic shows the electrical current paths when a circuit is operating properly. It is essential to understand how a circuit works before trying to figure out why it doesn't. Schematics break the entire electrical system down into individual circuits and show only one particular circuit. In a schematic, no attempt is made to represent wiring and components as they physically appear on the vehicle; switches and other components are shown as simply as possible. Face views of harness connectors show the cavity or terminal locations in all multi-pin connectors to help locate test points.

If you need to backprobe a connector while it is on the component, the order of the terminals must be mentally reversed. The wire color code can help in this situation, as well as a keyway, lock tab or other reference mark.

WIRING REPAIR

Soldering is a quick, efficient method of joining metals permanently. Everyone who has the occasion to make wiring repairs should know how to solder. Electrical connections that are soldered are far less likely to come apart and will conduct electricity much better than connections that are only "pig-tailed" together. The most popular (and preferred) method of soldering is with an electrical soldering gun. Soldering irons are available in many sizes and wattage ratings. Irons with higher wattage ratings deliver higher temperatures and recover lost heat faster. A small soldering iron rated for no more than 50 watts is recommended, especially on electrical systems where excess heat can damage the components being soldered.

There are three ingredients necessary for successful soldering; proper flux, good solder and sufficient heat. A soldering flux is necessary to clean the metal of tarnish, prepare it for soldering and to enable the solder to spread into tiny crevices. When soldering, always use a rosin core solder which is non-corrosive and will not attract moisture once the job is finished. Other types of flux (acid core) will leave a residue that will attract moisture and cause the wires to corrode. Tin is a unique metal with a low melting point. In a molten state, it dissolves and alloys easily with many metals. Solder is made by mixing tin with lead. The most common proportions are 40/60, 50/50 and 60/40, with the percentage of tin listed first. Low priced solders usually contain less tin, making them very difficult for a beginner to use because more heat is required to melt the solder. A common solder is 40/60 which is well suited for all-around general use, but 60/40 melts easier and is preferred for electrical work.

Soldering Techniques

Successful soldering requires that the metals to be joined be heated to a temperature that will melt the solder, usually 360–460°F (182–238°C). Contrary to popular belief, the purpose of the soldering iron is not to melt the solder itself, but to heat the parts being soldered to a temperature high enough to melt the solder when it is touched to the work. Melting flux-cored solder on the soldering iron will usually destroy the effectiveness of the flux.

➡**Soldering tips are made of copper for good heat conductivity, but must be "tinned" regularly for quick transference of heat to the project and to prevent the solder from sticking to the iron. To "tin" the iron, simply heat it and touch the flux-cored solder to the tip; the solder will flow over the hot tip. Wipe the excess off with a clean rag, but be careful as the iron will be hot.**

After some use, the tip may become pitted. If so, simply dress the tip smooth with a smooth file and "tin" the tip again. Flux-cored solder will remove oxides but rust, bits of insulation and oil or grease must be removed with a wire brush or emery cloth. For maximum strength in soldered parts, the joint must start off clean and tight. Weak joints will result in gaps too wide for the solder to bridge.

If a separate soldering flux is used, it should be brushed or swabbed on only those areas that are to be soldered. Most solders contain a core of flux and separate fluxing is unnecessary. Hold the work to be soldered firmly. It is best to solder on a wooden board, because a metal vise will only rob the piece to be soldered of heat and make it difficult to melt the solder. Hold the soldering tip with the broadest face against the work to be soldered. Apply solder under the tip close to the work, using enough solder to give a heavy film between the iron and the piece being soldered, while moving slowly and making sure the solder melts properly. Keep the work level or the solder will run to the lowest part and favor the thicker parts, because these require more heat to melt the solder. If the soldering tip overheats (the solder coating on the face of the tip burns up), it should be retinned. Once the soldering is completed, let the soldered joint stand until cool. Tape and seal all soldered wire splices after the repair has cooled.

Wire Harness Connectors

Most connectors in the engine compartment or that are otherwise exposed to the elements are protected against moisture and dirt which could create oxidation and deposits on the terminals.

These special connectors are weather-proof. All repairs require the use of a special terminal and the tool required to service it. This tool is used to remove the pin and sleeve terminals. If removal is attempted with an ordinary pick, there is a good chance that the terminal will be bent or deformed. Unlike standard blade type terminals, these weather-proof terminals cannot be straight-ened once they are bent. Make certain that the connectors are properly seated and all of the sealing rings are in place when connecting leads. On some models, a hinge-type flap provides a backup or secondary locking feature for the terminals. Most secondary locks are used to improve connector reliability by retaining the terminals if the small terminal lock tangs are not positioned properly.

Molded-on connectors require complete replacement of the connection. This means splicing a new connector assembly into the harness. All splices should be soldered to insure proper contact. Use care when probing the connections or replacing terminals in them as it is possible to short between opposite terminals. If this happens to the wrong terminal pair, it is possible to damage certain components. Always use jumper wires between connectors for circuit checking and never probe through weatherproof seals.

Open circuits are often difficult to locate by sight because corrosion or terminal misalignment are hidden by the connectors. Merely wiggling a connector on a sensor or in the wiring harness may correct the open circuit condition. This should always be considered when an open circuit or a failed sensor is indicated. Intermittent problems may also be caused by oxidized or loose connections. When using a circuit tester for diagnosis, always probe connections from the wire side. Be careful not to damage sealed connectors with test probes.

All wiring harnesses should be replaced with identical parts, using the same gauge wire and connectors. When signal wires are spliced into a harness, use wire with high temperature insulation only. It is seldom necessary to replace a complete harness. If replacement is necessary, pay close attention to insure proper harness routing. Secure the harness with suitable plastic wire clamps to prevent vibrations from causing the harness to wear in spots or contact any hot components.

➡**Weatherproof connectors cannot be replaced with standard connectors. Instructions are provided with replacement connector and terminal packages. Some wire harnesses have mounting indicators (usually pieces of colored tape) to mark where the harness is to be secured.**

In making wiring repairs, its important that you always replace damaged wires with wiring of the same gauge as the wire being replaced. The heavier the wire, the smaller the gauge number. Wires are color-coded to aid in identification and whenever possible the same color coded wire should be used for replacement. A wire stripping and crimping tool is necessary to install solderless terminal connectors. Test all crimps by pulling on the wires; it should not be possible to pull the wires out of a good crimp.

Wires which are open, exposed or otherwise damaged are repaired by simple splicing. Where possible, if the wiring harness is accessible and the damaged place in the wire can be located, it is best to open the harness and check for all possible damage. In an inaccessible harness, the wire must be bypassed with a new insert, usually taped to the outside of the old harness.

When replacing fusible links, be sure to use fusible link wire, NOT ordinary automotive wire. Make sure the fusible segment is of the same gauge and construction as the one being replaced and double the stripped end when crimping the terminal connector for a good contact. The melted (open) fusible link segment of the wiring harness should be cut off as close to the harness as possible, then a new segment spliced in as described. In the case of a damaged fusible link that feeds two harness wires, the harness connections should be replaced with two fusible link wires so that each circuit will have its own separate protection.

➡️Most of the problems caused in the wiring harness are due to bad ground connections. Always check all vehicle ground connections for corrosion or looseness before performing any power feed checks to eliminate the chance of a bad ground affecting the circuit.

Hard-Shell Connectors

Unlike molded connectors, the terminal contacts in hard-shell connectors can be replaced. Weatherproof hard-shell connectors with the leads molded into the shell have non-replaceable terminal ends. Replacement usually involves the use of a special terminal removal tool that depresses the locking tangs (barbs) on the connector terminal and allows the connector to be removed from the rear of the shell. The connector shell should be replaced if it shows any evidence of burning, melting, cracks, or breaks. Replace individual terminals that are burnt, corroded, distorted or loose.

➡️The insulation crimp must be tight to prevent the insulation from sliding back on the wire when the wire is pulled. The insulation must be visibly compressed under the crimp tabs, and the ends of the crimp should be turned in for a firm grip on the insulation.

The wire crimp must be made with all wire strands inside the crimp. The terminal must be fully compressed on the wire strands with the ends of the crimp tabs turned in to make a firm grip on the wire. Check all connections with an ohmmeter to insure a good contact. There should be no measurable resistance between the wire and the terminal when connected.

Fusible Links

The fuse link is a short length of special, Hypalon (high temperature) insulated wire, integral with the engine compartment wiring harness and should not be confused with standard wire. It is several wire gauges smaller than the circuit which it protects. Under no circumstances should a fuse link replacement repair be made using a length of standard wire cut from bulk stock or from another wiring harness.

To repair any blown fuse link use the following procedure:

1. Determine which circuit is damaged, its location and the cause of the open fuse link. If the damaged fuse link is one of three fed by a common No. 10 or 12 gauge feed wire, determine the specific affected circuit.
2. Disconnect the negative battery cable.
3. Cut the damaged fuse link from the wiring harness and discard it. If the fuse link is one of three circuits fed by a single feed wire, cut it out of the harness at each splice end and discard it.
4. Identify and procure the proper fuse link with butt connectors for attaching the fuse link to the harness.

➡️Heat shrink tubing must be slipped over the wire before crimping and soldering the connection.

5. To repair any fuse link in a 3-link group with one feed:
  a. After cutting the open link out of the harness, cut each of the remaining undamaged fuse links close to the feed wire weld.
  b. Strip approximately ½ in. (13mm) of insulation from the detached ends of the two good fuse links. Insert two wire ends into one end of a butt connector, then carefully push one stripped end of the replacement fuse link into the same end of the butt connector and crimp all three firmly together.

➡️Care must be taken when fitting the three fuse links into the butt connector as the internal diameter is a snug fit for three wires. Make sure to use a proper crimping tool. Pliers, side cutters, etc. will not apply the proper crimp to retain the wires and withstand a pull test.

  c. After crimping the butt connector to the three fuse links, cut the weld portion from the feed wire and strip approximately ½ in. (13mm) of insulation from the cut end. Insert the stripped end into the open end of the butt connector and crimp very firmly.
  d. To attach the remaining end of the replacement fuse link, strip approximately ½ in. (13mm) of insulation from the wire end of the circuit from which the blown fuse link was removed, and firmly crimp a butt connector or equivalent to the stripped wire. Then, insert the end of the replacement link into the other end of the butt connector and crimp firmly.
  e. Using rosin core solder with a consistency of 60 percent tin and 40 percent lead, solder the connectors and the wires at the repairs then insulate with electrical tape or heat shrink tubing.
6. To replace any fuse link on a single circuit in a harness, cut out the damaged portion, strip approximately ½ in. (13mm) of insulation from the two wire ends and attach the appropriate replacement fuse link to the stripped wire ends with two proper size butt connectors. Solder the connectors and wires, then insulate.
7. To repair any fuse link which has an eyelet terminal on one end such as the charging circuit, cut off the open fuse link behind the weld, strip approximately ½ in. (13mm) of insulation from the cut end and attach the appropriate new eyelet fuse link to the cut stripped wire with an appropriate size butt connector. Solder the connectors and wires at the repair, then insulate.
8. Connect the negative battery cable to the battery and test the system for proper operation.

➡️Do not mistake a resistor wire for a fuse link. The resistor wire is generally longer and has print stating, "Resistor-don't cut or splice."

When attaching a single No. 16, 17, 18 or 20 gauge fuse link to a heavy gauge wire, always double the stripped wire end of the fuse link before inserting and crimping it into the butt connector for positive wire retention.

Add-On Electrical Equipment

The electrical system in your vehicle is designed to perform under reasonable operating conditions without interference between components. Before any additional electrical equipment is installed, it is recommended that you consult your dealer or a reputable repair facility that is familiar with the vehicle and its systems.

If the vehicle is equipped with mobile radio equipment and/or mobile telephone, it may have an effect upon the operation of any on-board computer control modules. Radio Frequency Interference (RFI) from the communications system can be picked up by the vehicle's wiring harnesses and conducted into the control module, giving it the wrong messages at the wrong time. Although well shielded against RFI, the computer should be further protected by taking the following measures:

• Install the antenna as far as possible from the control module. For instance, if the module is located behind the center console area, then the antenna should be mounted at the rear of the vehicle.

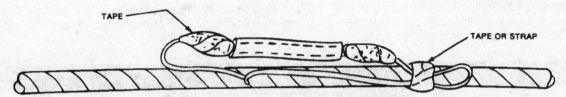

REMOVE EXISTING VINYL TUBE SHIELDING
REINSTALL OVER FUSE LINK BEFORE CRIMPING
FUSE LINK TO WIRE ENDS

TYPICAL REPAIR USING THE SPECIAL #17 GA. (9.00" LONG-YELLOW) FUSE LINK REQUIRED FOR THE AIR/COND.
CIRCUITS (2) #687E and #261A LOCATED IN THE ENGINE COMPARTMENT

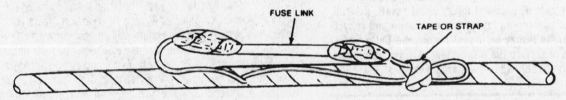

TYPICAL REPAIR FOR ANY IN-LINE FUSE LINK USING THE SPECIFIED GAUGE FUSE LINK FOR THE SPECIFIC CIRCUIT

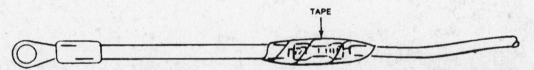

TYPICAL REPAIR USING THE EYELET TERMINAL FUSE LINK OF THE SPECIFIED GAUGE FOR ATTACHMENT TO A CIRCUIT WIRE END

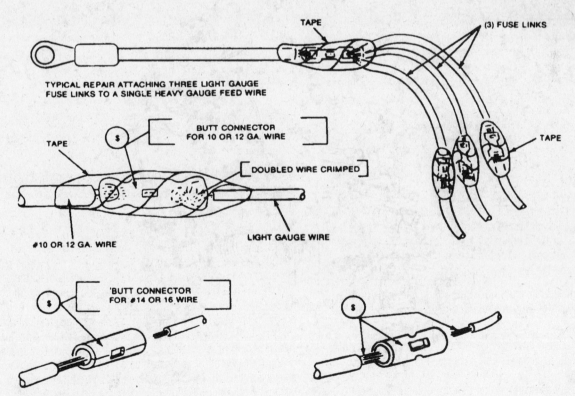

FUSIBLE LINK REPAIR PROCEDURE

General fusible link repair—never replace a fusible link with regular wire or a fusible link rated at a higher amperage than the one being replaced

• Keep the antenna wiring a minimum of eight inches away from any wiring running to control modules and from the module itself. NEVER wind the antenna wire around any other wiring.

• Mount the equipment as far from the control module as possible. Be very careful during installation not to drill through any wires or short a wire harness with a mounting screw.

• Insure that the electrical feed wire(s) to the equipment are properly and tightly connected. Loose connectors can cause interference.

• Make certain that the equipment is properly grounded to the vehicle. Poor grounding can damage expensive equipment.

HEATER

✵✵ CAUTION

Please refer to Section 1 before discharging the compressor or disconnecting air conditioning lines. Damage to the air conditioning system or personal injury could result. Consult your local laws concerning refrigerant discharge and recycling. In many areas it may be illegal for anyone but a certified technician to service the A/C system. Always use an approved recovery station when discharging the air conditioning.

General Information

▶ See Figure 1

The blend-air type heater system is used on all models. The blend-air method on vehicles without air condition uses a controlled flow system with the engine coolant flow controlled through the heater core, with the use of a heater coolant shut-off valve. The temperature of the heated air entering the passenger compartment is controlled by regulating, with the temperature control lever and blend door, the quantity of air which flows through

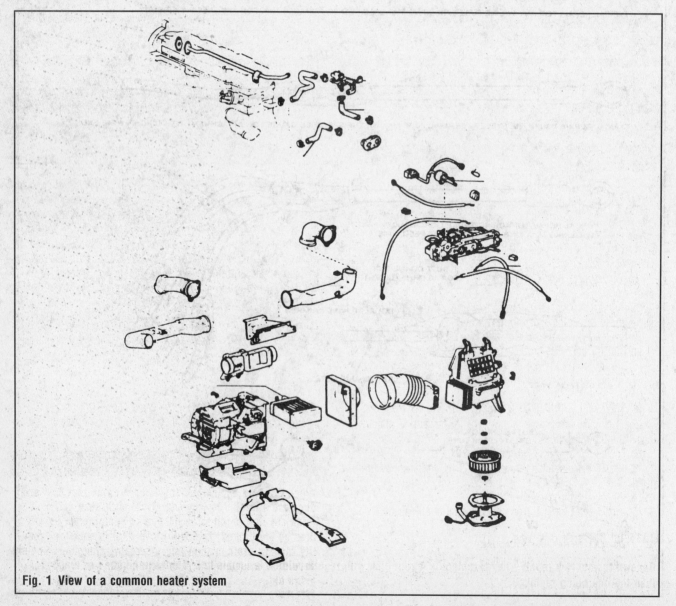

Fig. 1 View of a common heater system

the heater core air passages or fins, then blending the heated air with a controlled amount of cool fresh air which bypasses the heater core. The air flow for the heating system is through the cowl air intake and into the heating system. Defroster operation is controlled by the air control lever and cable, or vacuum servo motor, moving the defroster damper to direct heated air to the defroster outlets.

Blower Motor

➡**On the later Toyota models, with factory installed air conditioning, the air conditioner assembly and heater assembly utilize the same blower. The blower motor is integral with the heater assembly and therefore in most cases the blower motor must be removed from the A/C heater case assembly when the assembly has been removed from the vehicle. However there may be an exception to this rule on some models. In those cases the procedure below may be used as a general guide. Some mounting and wiring may differ from model to model from the procedures detailed below. Many Toyota vehicles have dealer installed air conditioning. This type system may use a separate blower motor just for the air conditioning. The procedures that follow are for factory air conditioning.**

Due to the lack of information available at the time of this publication, a general blower motor removal and installation procedure is outlined. The removal steps can be altered as required.

REMOVAL & INSTALLATION

1983–84 Cressida

1. Disconnect the negative battery cable.
2. Remove the instrument panel undercover and cowl side trim panel.
3. Remove the air duct and the glove box.
4. Disconnect the heater control cable from the blower motor and remove the blower duct.
5. Separate the heater relay from the heater relay electrical connector.
6. Remove the retaining screws from the blower motor assembly. Remove the assembly from the vehicle.
7. Remove the blower motor from the blower motor assembly.
   To install:
8. Install the blower motor to the blower motor assembly.
9. Install the blower motor assembly and install the retaining screws.
10. Attach the heater relay connector to the heater relay.
11. Reconnect the heater control cable to the blower motor and install the blower duct.
12. Install the air duct and the glove box.
13. Install the instrument panel undercover and cowl side trim panel.
14. Reconnect the negative battery cable.
15. Check the blower for proper operation at all speeds.

1985–90 Cressida and Van

1. Disconnect the negative battery cable.
2. Remove the screws that secure the blower motor retainer to the blower motor.

3. Remove the glove box.
4. Remove the heating duct that is between the blower motor assembly and the heater assembly.
5. Unplug the blower motor electrical connection from the blower motor.
6. Disconnect the heater selector control cable at the blower motor assembly.
7. Remove the nuts and bolts that attach the blower motor assembly to the blower motor case and remove the blower motor from the vehicle.
   To install:
8. Install the blower motor into the blower motor case assembly.
9. Install the blower motor assembly and install the retaining screws.
10. Attach the heater selector control cable at the blower motor assembly.
11. Attach the blower motor electrical connection to the blower motor.
12. Install the heating duct that is between the blower motor assembly and the heater assembly.
13. Install the glove box.
14. Install and tighten the blower motor retainer and screws that secure the retainer to the motor.
15. Reconnect the negative battery cable.
16. Check the blower for proper operation at all speeds.

Heater Core

REMOVAL & INSTALLATION

➡**On some of the Toyota models, the air conditioner assembly is integral with the heater assembly (including the heater core) and, therefore, the heater core removal may differ from the procedures detailed below. In some cases, it may be necessary to remove the A/C-heater housing and assembly to remove the heater core. Vehicles with factory installed air conditioning vary from those with dealer installed air conditioning. The following procedures are for factory installed air conditioning.**

Due to the lack of information available at the time of this publication, a general blower motor removal and installation procedure is outlined. The removal steps can be altered as required.

Cressida

1. Disconnect the negative battery cable. Drain the coolant system into a suitable drain pan. Remove the hood release and the fuel lid release levers.

✳✳ CAUTION

When draining engine coolant, keep in mind that cats and dogs are attracted to ethylene glycol antifreeze and could drink any that is left in an uncovered container or in puddles on the ground. This will prove fatal in sufficient quantity. Always drain coolant into a sealable container. Coolant should be reused unless it is contaminated or is several years old.

2. Remove the left-hand instrument panel undercover and lower center pad. Remove the finish plate, then remove the radio assembly.

3. Remove the heater control knobs, heater control panel and ashtray.

4. Remove the right side instrument panel undercover, glove box door and glove box. On 1989–90 models, remove the A/C amplifier or wiring harness, if necessary.

5. Remove the front pillar garnish, cluster finish panel and instrument cluster gauge assembly.

6. Remove the safety pad and side defroster hose. Remove the heater assembly air ducts.

7. Remove the lower pad reinforcement and remove the front seats. Remove the center console assembly and the cowl side trim panel.

8. Remove the scuff plate, then position the floor carpeting aside. Remove the rear heater duct, if equipped and heater control assembly.

9. Disconnect the heater hoses from the heater core assembly, remove the heater core grommet.

10. Remove the blower motor duct, center duct and instrument panel brace. Remove the heater core assembly from the vehicle.

11. Remove the nuts securing the heater core to the heater core assembly and remove the core.

To install:

12. Install the heater core into the heater case assembly. Install the nuts securing the heater core to the heater core assembly.

13. Install the heater core assembly into the vehicle. Install the blower motor duct, center duct and instrument panel brace.

14. Reconnect the heater hoses to the heater core assembly, install the heater core grommet.

15. Install the heater control assembly (if so equipped) and install the rear heater duct. Install the floor carpeting along with the scuff plate.

16. Install the center console assembly and the cowl rip panel. Install the lower pad reinforcement and install the front seats.

17. Install the heater assembly air ducts. Install the safety pad and side defroster hose.

18. Install the front pillar garnish, cluster finish panel and instrument cluster gauge assembly.

19. Install the right side instrument panel undercover, glove box door and glove box. On 1989–90 models, install the A/C amplifier or wiring harness, if necessary.

20. Install the heater control knobs, heater control panel and ashtray.

21. Install the radio assembly and finish plate. Install the left-hand instrument panel undercover and lower center pad.

22. Install the hood release and the fuel lid release levers. Reconnect the negative battery cable. Refill the coolant system, start the vehicle and check for coolant leaks.

Van

The heater core is incorporated into the cooling assembly housing and therefore cannot be removed with out removing the cool-

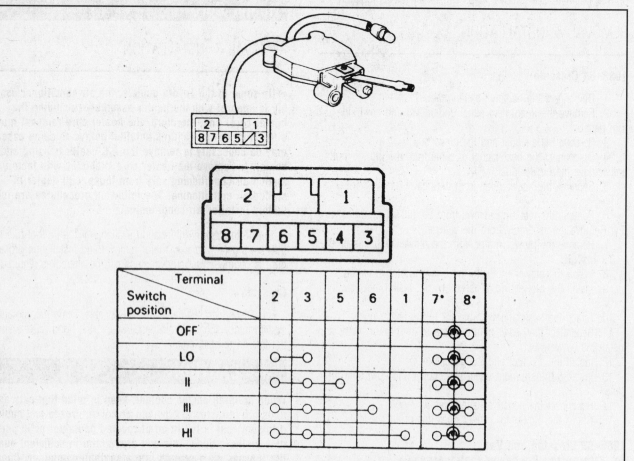

* For illumination light

Fig. 2 Inspecting the heater control assembly for resistance—Van

ing unit assembly and splitting the case into two halves. Refer to evaporator removal and installation for heater core removal procedures on vehicles equipped with air conditioning.

Control Assembly

REMOVAL & INSTALLATION

➡ **Due to differences in optional equipment, the removal steps can be altered as required.**

1. Disconnect the negative battery cable.
2. Remove the air conditioning switch trim cluster from the instrument panel.
3. Remove the air conditioning switch retaining screws as required.
4. Tag and disconnect the electrical wiring from the rear of the switch assembly.
5. Remove the switch from the vehicle.
6. Using a volt and ohmmeter, check the continuity between the terminals for each switch position and proper voltage (as shown in the charts). If specifications are incorrect, replace the air conditioning control switch.
7. Installation is the reverse of the removal procedure. Check system for proper operation.

Vent Control Switch

REMOVAL & INSTALLATION

▶ **See Figures 2, 3 and 4**

1. Disconnect the negative battery cable.
2. Remove the necessary instrument cluster in order to gain access to the vent control switch.
3. Remove the heater control cables. Remove the vent mode switch connector.
4. Check the continuity between the terminal at the vent mode

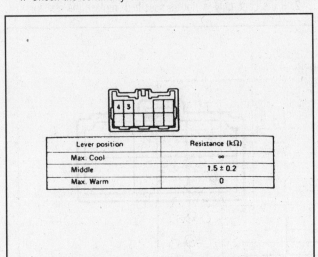

Fig. 3 Inspecting the heater control assembly for resistance—Cressida

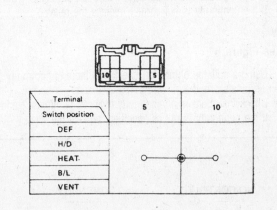

Fig. 4 Pin connectors for resistance inspection of the air vent mode switch—Cressida

position using an ohmmeter. If there is no continuity, replace the switch.
5. Installation is the reverse of the removal procedure.

Component Testing and Inspection

➡ **Due to optional equipment, the number or types of relays or other components will vary by model.**

HEATER MAIN RELAY

Continuity

CRESSIDA

▶ **See Figure 5**

1. Using a suitable ohmmeter, check that there is continuity between terminals 1 and 3.
2. Check that there is continuity between terminals 2 and 4.

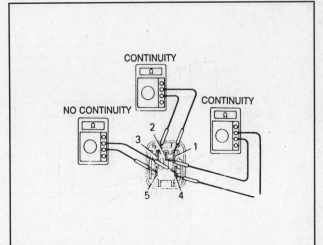

Fig. 5 Using an ohmmeter, test the heater relay continuity—Cressida

3. Check that there is no continuity between terminals 4 and 5.
4. If the continuity is not correct, replace the relay.

VAN
▶ See Figure 6

1. Using a suitable ohmmeter, check that there is continuity between terminals 1 and 3.
2. Check that there is no continuity between terminals 2 and 4.
3. If the continuity is not as specified, replace the relay.

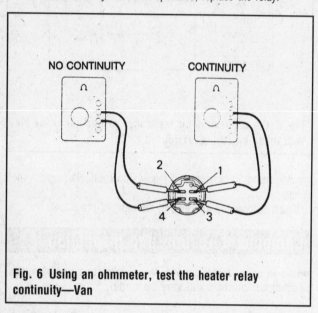

Fig. 6 Using an ohmmeter, test the heater relay continuity—Van

Operation

CRESSIDA
▶ See Figure 7

1. Apply battery voltage across terminals 1 and 3 of the relay connector.
2. Using a suitable ohmmeter, check that there is continuity between terminals 4 and 5.
3. Check that there is no continuity between terminals 5 and 6.

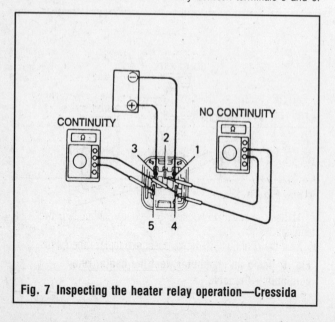

Fig. 7 Inspecting the heater relay operation—Cressida

4. If the operation of the relay is not as just described, replace the relay.

VAN
▶ See Figure 8

1. Apply battery voltage across terminals 1 and 3 of the relay connector.
2. Using a suitable ohmmeter, check that there is continuity between terminals 2 and 4.
3. If the operation of the relay is not as just described, replace the relay.

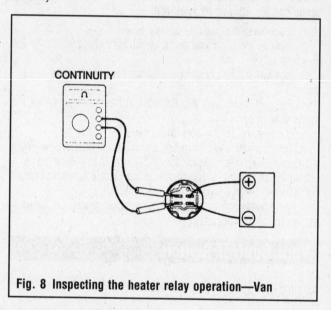

Fig. 8 Inspecting the heater relay operation—Van

BLOWER RESISTOR

CRESSIDA
▶ See Figure 9

1. Using a suitable ohmmeter, check that there is continuity between terminals 5 and 6.
2. If the continuity is not as specified, replace the resistor.

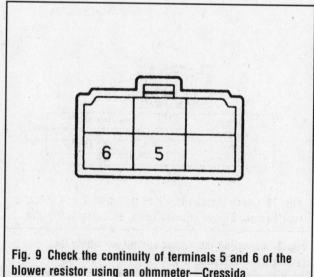

Fig. 9 Check the continuity of terminals 5 and 6 of the blower resistor using an ohmmeter—Cressida

VAN

▶ **See Figure 10 and 11**

1. Using a suitable ohmmeter, check that there is continuity between terminals 2 and 4 (terminals 2 and 3 on the rear heater blower resistor, if so equipped).
2. If the continuity is not as specified, replace the resistor.

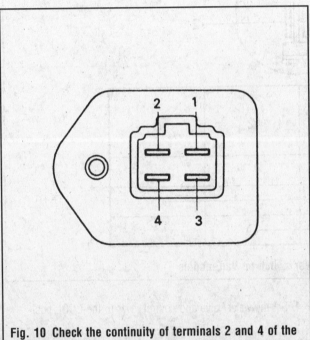

Fig. 10 Check the continuity of terminals 2 and 4 of the front heaters blower resistor using an ohmmeter—Van

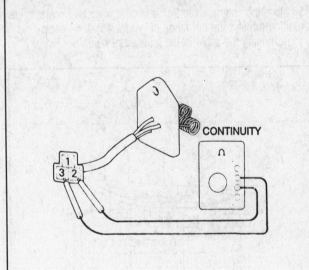

Fig. 11 Check the continuity of terminals 2 and 3 of the rear heaters blower resistor using an ohmmeter—Van

NO. 1 AND NO. 2 REAR HEATER SWITCHES

▶ **See Figure 12**

1. Using a suitable ohmmeter, check for continuity between the terminals.
2. If the continuity is not as specified, replace the switch.

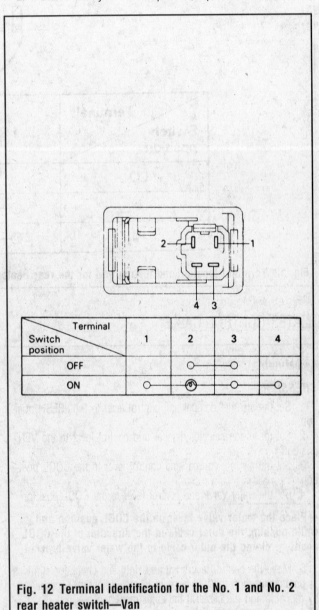

Switch position \ Terminal	1	2	3	4
OFF		o	o	
ON	o	o	o	o

Fig. 12 Terminal identification for the No. 1 and No. 2 rear heater switch—Van

REAR HEATER BLOWER SWITCH

▶ **See Figure 13**

1. Using a suitable ohmmeter, check for continuity between the terminals.
2. If the continuity is not as specified, replace the switch.

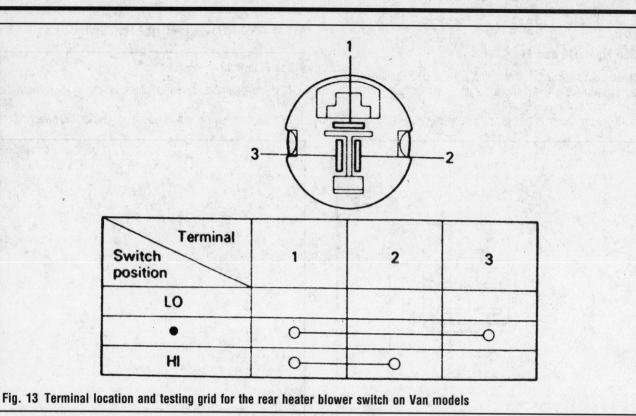

Switch position	Terminal	1	2	3
LO				
●		○——————————————○		
HI		○——————○		

Fig. 13 Terminal location and testing grid for the rear heater blower switch on Van models

HEATER CONTROL CABLE

Adjustment

CRESSIDA

1. Set the air inlet damper and control lever to the FRESH position.
2. Set the mode selector damper and control lever to the VENT position.
3. Set the air mix damper and control lever to the COOL position.
4. Set the water valve and control lever to the COOL position.

➡**Place the water valve lever on the COOL position and while pushing the outer cable in the direction of the COOL position, clamp the outer cable to the water valve bracket.**

5. Move the control levers left and right and check for stiffness or binding through the full range of levers. Adjust as necessary, by repositioning the cable in the adjustment clip.

VAN—FRONT HEATER

▶ **See Figures 14 and 15**

1. Set the air inlet damper and control lever to the FRESH position.
2. Set the mode selector damper and control lever to the FACE position.
3. Set the air mix damper and control lever to the COOL position.

4. Set the water valve and control lever to the COOL position.

➡**Place the water valve lever on the COOL position and while pushing the outer cable in the direction of the COOL position, clamp the outer cable to the water valve bracket.**

5. Move the control levers left and right and check for stiffness or binding through the full range of levers. Adjust as necessary, by repositioning the cable in the adjustment clip.

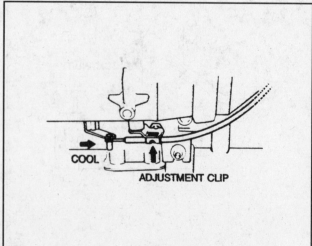

Fig. 14 Adjustment clip location for the front heater cable which regulates the air mix damper—Van

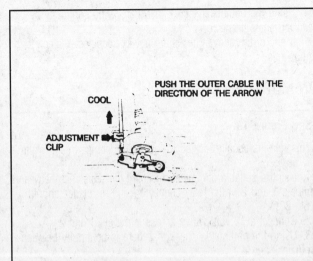

Fig. 15 Adjusting the front heater cable after positioning the water valve—Van

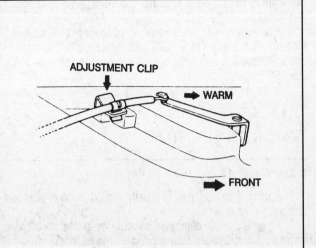

Fig. 17 Adjusting the rear heater cable which regulates the air mix damper—Van

VAN—REAR HEATER

▶ **See Figures 16 and 17**

1. Set the mode selector damper and control lever to the FACE position.

2. Set the air mix damper and control lever to the WARM position.

3. Move the control levers left and right and check for stiffness or binding through the full range of levers. Adjust as necessary, by repositioning the cable in the adjustment clip.

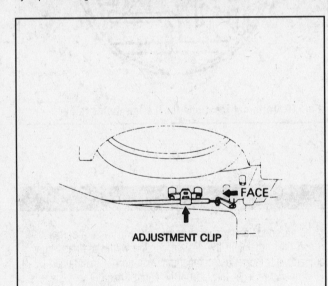

Fig. 16 Adjusting the rear heater cable which regulates the mode selector damper—Van

ELECTRIC COOLING FAN

➡The following procedures are to be used on vehicles equipped with a single cooling fan assembly only. If the vehicle is equipped with a dual fan system (one for the radiator and one for the A/C condenser), refer to the A/C condenser fan tests located in Section 3.

Operation

TEMPERATURE BELOW 181°F (82°C)

1. Turn the ignition switch to the **ON** position. If the fan runs, then check the fan relay and temperature switch. Check for a separated connector or a severed wire between the relay and temperature switch.

2. Disconnect the temperature switch wire and check to see if the fan rotates.

3. If the fan does not move, check the fan relay, fan motor, ignition relay and fuse. Check for a short circuit between the fan relay and temperature switch.

TEMPERATURE ABOVE 194°F (90°C)

1. Start the engine and raise the engine rpm so as to raise the engine coolant temperature above 194°F (90°C).

2. Confirm that the fan rotates, if the fan does not rotate, replace the temperature switch.

TEMPERATURE SWITCH

1. Remove the temperature switch, which is usually located in the lower tank of the radiator.

2. Place the switch into a suitable container of coolant which is at or above 194°F (90°C). Using a suitable ohmmeter, check

that there is no continuity when the coolant temperature is above 194°F (90°C).

3. Place the switch into a container of coolant of which the temperature is below 181°F (83°C). Using a suitable ohmmeter, check that there is continuity when the coolant temperature is below 181°F (83°C).

4. If the temperature switch fails any part of this inspection, replace it with a new one.

IGNITION (OR CUTOUT) RELAY

▶ See Figure 18

This relay, if so equipped, is usually located in the engine compartment in the relay box.

1. Using a suitable ohmmeter, measure the resistance between terminals 1 and 2 of the relay connector. The resistance should be 50–80Ω.

2. Connect a 12 volt battery across terminals 1 and 2.

3. Using the ohmmeter, check that there is continuity between terminals 3 and 4.

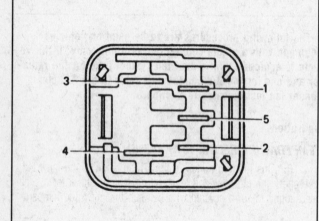

Fig. 18 Terminal locations for the ignition or cutout relay

4. Using the ohmmeter, check that there is no continuity between terminals 4 and 5.

5. If any of the above checks are not as specified, replace the ignition relay.

FAN MOTOR RELAY

▶ See Figure 19

This relay is usually located in the engine compartment in the relay box.

1. Using a suitable ohmmeter, measure the resistance between terminals 1 and 2 of the relay connector. The resistance should be 50–80Ω.

2. Connect a 12 volt battery across terminals 1 and 2.

3. Using the ohmmeter, check that there is continuity between terminals 3 and 4.

4. If any of the above checks are not as specified, replace the fan motor relay.

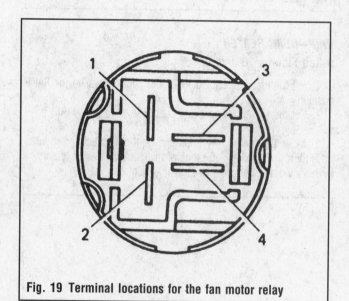

Fig. 19 Terminal locations for the fan motor relay

AIR CONDITIONING SYSTEM

General Information

✳✳ CAUTION

Please refer to Section 1 before discharging the compressor or disconnecting air conditioning lines. Damage to the air conditioning system or personal injury could result. Consult your local laws concerning refrigerant discharge and recycling. In many areas it may be illegal for anyone but a certified technician to service the A/C system. Always use an approved recovery station when discharging the air conditioning.

The air conditioning system is designed to cycle a compressor on and off to maintain the desired cooling within the passenger compartment. Passenger compartment comfort is maintained by the temperature lever located on the control head. The system is also designed to prevent the evaporator from freezing.

When an air conditioning mode is selected, electrical current is sent to the compressor clutch coil. The clutch plate and the hub assembly is then drawn rearward which engages the pulley. The clutch plate and the pulley are then locked together and act as a single unit. This in turn drives the compressor shaft which compresses low pressure refrigerant vapor from the evaporator into high pressure. The compressor also circulates refrigerant oil and refrigerant through the air conditioner system. On most models, the compressor is equipped with a cut-off solenoid which will shut the compressor off momentarily under certain conditions. These include wide-open throttle and low idle speeds.

The switches on the control head are used to control the operation of the air conditioning system.

Moving the control lever to the **A/C MAX** or **A/C NORM** position energizes the compressor clutch circuit, closes the heater water valve (if equipped) and partially open the recirculating air door.

When the temperature control lever is moved to **COOL** position, a vacuum switch mounted on the control panel directs vacuum to the vacuum-operated water valve in the heater input line, stopping the flow of coolant. The control also moves the blend-air door, stopping or regulating the flow of air through the heater core. Operating the system in **MAX A/C** position provides 100% recirculated air with no heated air, on most vehicles.

System Components

OPERATION

♦ **See Figures 20 thru 25**

Heater Water Valve

Most models are equipped with a bypass heater water valve. When the air conditioning is turned **ON,** or heater is turned **OFF,** the vacuum operated heater valve closes off the hot water flow to the heater core.

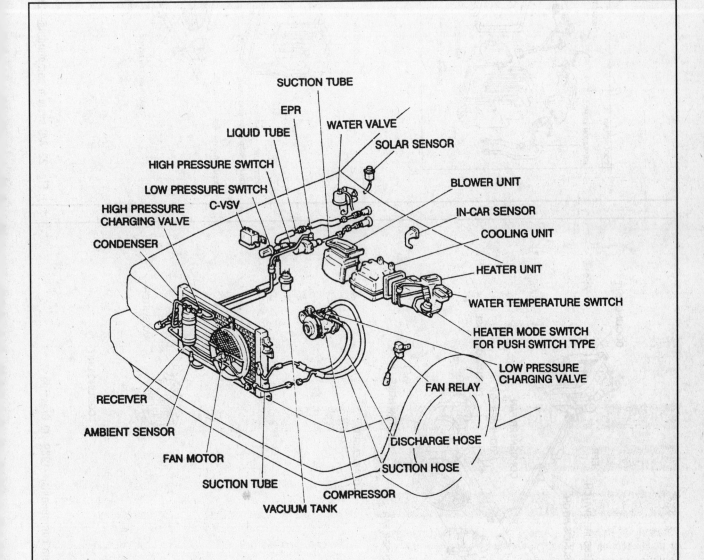

Fig. 20 A/C and heater system components—1983–88 Cressida

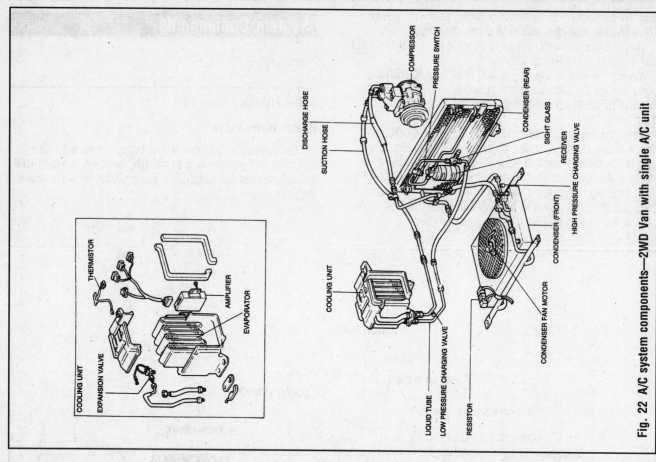

Fig. 22 A/C system components—2WD Van with single A/C unit

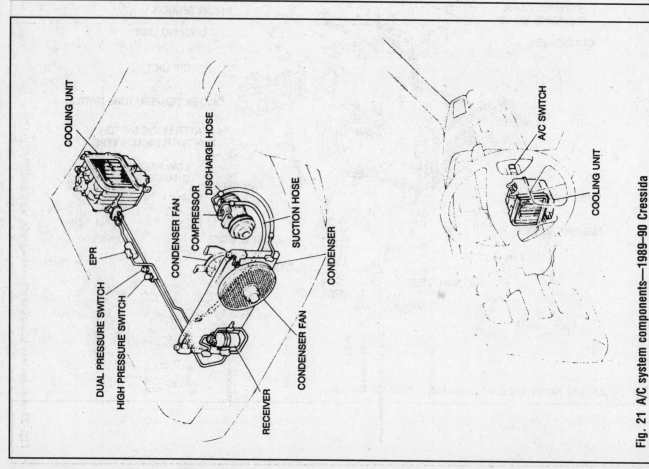

Fig. 21 A/C system components—1989–90 Cressida

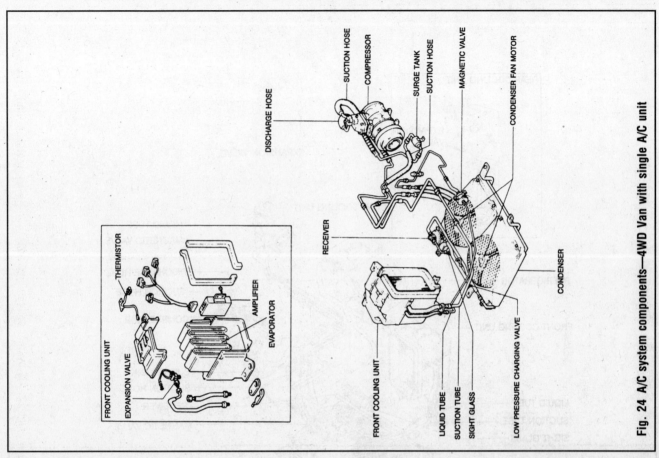

Fig. 24 A/C system components—4WD Van with single A/C unit

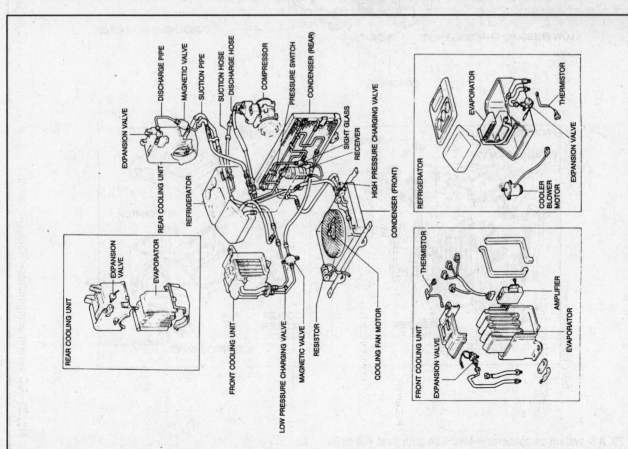

Fig. 23 A/C system components—2WD Van with dual A/C units

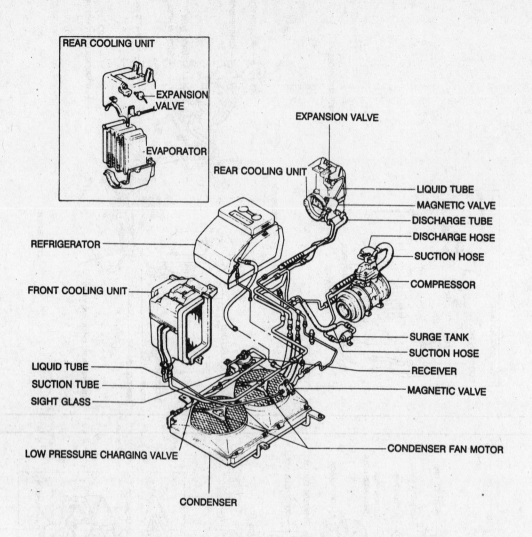

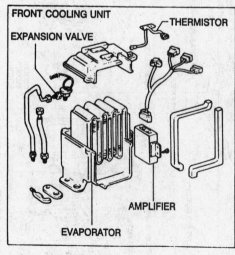

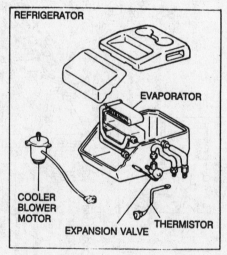

Fig. 25 A/C system components—4WD Van with dual A/C units

Low Pressure Switch

The low pressure switch is designed to shut off the compressor should the pressure in the system be too low to maintain proper lubrication.

➡**The compressor used with this system is a high speed unit and requires lubrication at all times. Do not override or bypass the low pressure switch when the system is not capable of maintaining sufficient pressure to circulate the lubricant.**

Dual and High Pressure Switch

The dual and high pressure switches are designed to protect the system and compressor from excessively high and low pressures. Should the pressure in the system be too low to maintain proper lubrication or be excessively high, the compressor is shut off.

Receiver/Drier

▶ **See Figure 26**

The receiver/drier is a reservoir used to store refrigerant required by the system. The receiver/drier should provide an adequate and steady flow of liquid refrigerant to the expansion valve. The receiver/drier contains a dessicant to remove moisture from the system and the assembly should be replaced anytime the system has been opened to the atmosphere, due to the immediate entrance of moisture and foreign material.

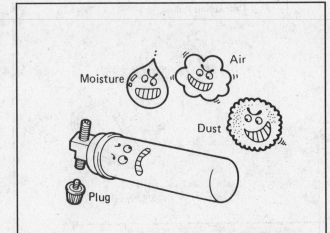

Fig. 26 Do not remove the plugs located on the side of the receiver/drier unit until you are ready to install it

Condenser

The condenser is mounted in front of the radiator core to allow air to flow over the cooling fins and remove the heat from the refrigerant, allowing the refrigerant to condense (liquefy).

Evaporator

The evaporator is encased in a housing and is mounted under the dash panel. The evaporator is used as an air cooler and dehumidifier. The heat in the air passing over the evaporator fins, transfers or gives up its heat to the boiling refrigerant within the evaporator coil. As the air is cooled, the moisture in the air condenses on the evaporator core and is drained off as water.

Expansion Valve

▶ **See Figures 27, 28 and 29**

The thermostatic expansion valve is located at the inlet of the evaporator and meters the refrigerant into the evaporator coil, so as to maintain the proper flow for the various evaporator heat load requirements encountered during the vehicle operation. The metering action of the expansion valve is controlled by the temperature sensing bulb, mounted on the outlet (suction) side of the evaporator.

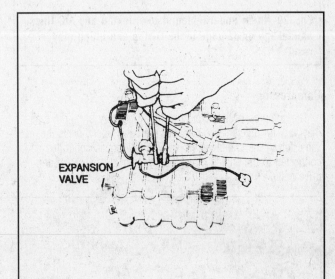

Fig. 27 Use one wrench to hold the expansion valve and one to remove the A/C line

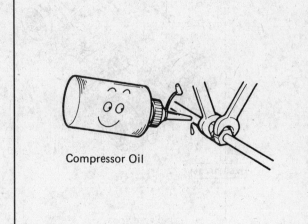

Fig. 28 Apply a few drops of compressor oil to the O-ring fitting to prevent leaking

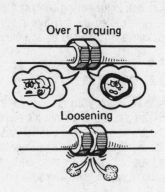

Fig. 29 Never undertighten or overtighten any A/C lines, as leakage or damage to the O-ring and fitting may result

Compressor

The compressor is a typical belt driven rotary unit. The type may vary on different vehicles, but the basic operation is the same for all the compressors. The compressor is controlled and connected to the engine through a electromagnetic clutch and drive belt.

Service Valves

There are 2 service access gauge port valves on the system. The high pressure discharge port is located in the discharge line near the condenser. This port requires the use of a high pressure gauge adapter. The other service port (low pressure side) is located on the low pressure side of the system and is used to measure evaporator pressure.

Compressor

REMOVAL & INSTALLATION

▶ **See Figures 30 and 31**

1. Run the engine at idle speed with the A/C on for 10 minutes.
2. Stop the engine.
3. Disconnect the negative battery cable.
4. Unplug the clutch lead wire from the harness.
5. Have an authorized service station discharge the refrigerant from the cooling system.
6. Disconnect the two hoses from the compressor service valves. Cap the opening fitting immediately to keep moisture out of the system.

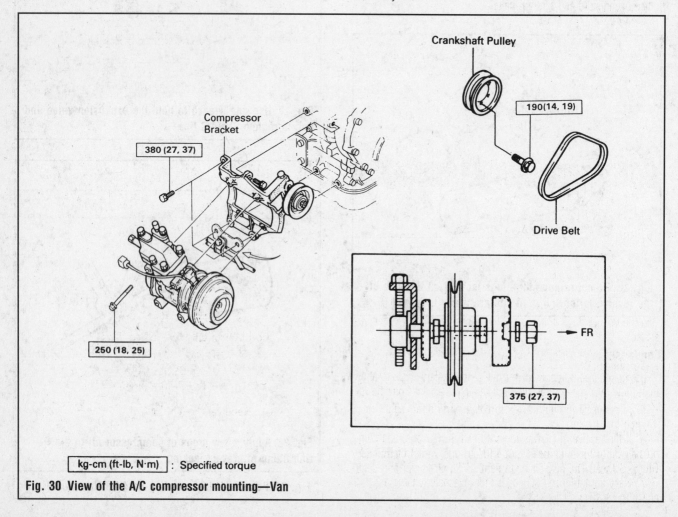

kg-cm (ft-lb, N·m) : Specified torque

Fig. 30 View of the A/C compressor mounting—Van

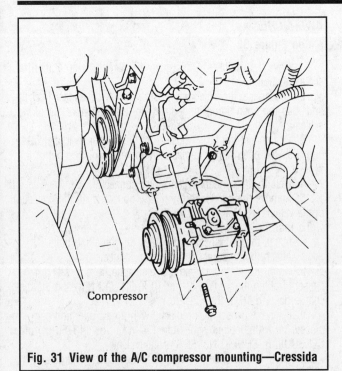

Fig. 31 View of the A/C compressor mounting—Cressida

7. Loosen the drive belt and remove the compressor mounting bolts and compressor.

To install:

8. Install the compressor with the mounting bolts.
9. Install the drive belt.
10. Attach the two hoses to the compressor service valves. Tighten both discharge and suction lines to 16–18 ft. lbs. (22–25 Nm).
11. Connect the clutch lead wire to the wiring harness.
12. Connect the negative battery cable.
13. Have the A/C system evacuated, charged and check for leaks by an authorized service station.

Receiver/Drier

REMOVAL & INSTALLATION

▶ **See Figures 32, 33 and 34**

1. Have the vehicle's A/C system discharged by an authorized service station.
2. Disconnect the two liquid tubes from the receiver/drier unit. Cap the open fittings immediately to keep moisture out of the system.
3. Remove the receiver/drier from the bracket.

To install:

4. Position the receiver/drier into the bracket. Do not remove the plugs until you are ready for connection.
5. Attach the two liquid tubes to the receiver/drier, tighten to 47 inch lbs. (5 Nm).
6. If the receiver/drier was replaced with a new one, add compressor oil to the compressor. Add 0.7 fl. oz. (20 cc) of DENSO-OIL 6, SUNISO No. 5GS or equivalent.
7. Have an authorized service station evacuate, charge and check the system for leaks.

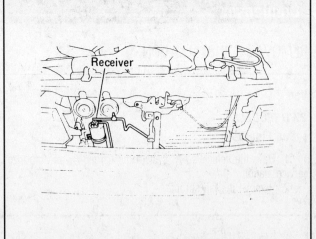

Fig. 32 The receiver/drier is located at the front right side of the vehicle, near the horns on Cressida models

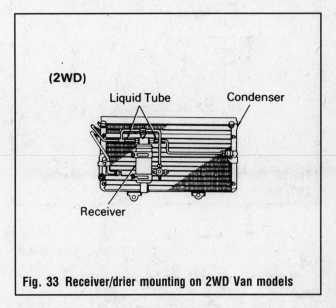

Fig. 33 Receiver/drier mounting on 2WD Van models

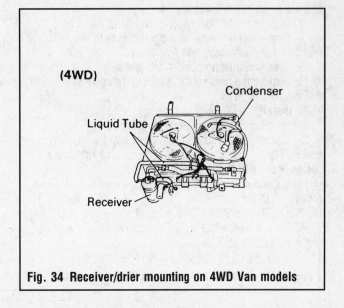

Fig. 34 Receiver/drier mounting on 4WD Van models

Condenser

REMOVAL & INSTALLATION

Van

2WD MODELS

▶ See Figure 35

1. Have the vehicle's A/C system discharged by an authorized service station.
2. Remove the fan shroud.

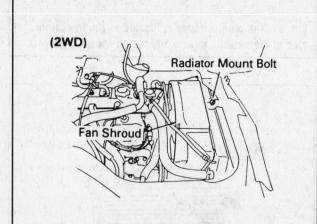

Fig. 35 The radiator mount bolts retain the condenser—2WD Van

3. Remove the radiator mount bolts.
4. Disconnect the discharge hose from the condenser inlet fitting.
5. Disconnect the liquid hose from the condenser outlet fitting.
6. Remove the condenser mounting bolts and nuts, lift the unit out of the engine compartment.
7. Disconnect the liquid hose from the sight glass.
8. Disconnect the three discharge hoses from the condenser inlet fitting and discharge tube.
9. Disconnect the pressure switch lead wire.
10. Remove the bolts retaining the rear housing, then remove the rear housing.
   To install:
11. Install in the reverse sequence of removal.
12. Connect the liquid hose and discharge hose to the condenser. Tighten the liquid hose to 10 ft. lbs. (13 Nm) and the discharge hose to 16 ft. lbs. (22 Nm).
13. If the condenser was replaced with a new one, add compressor oil to the compressor. Add 1.4–1.7 fl. oz. (40–50 cc) of DENSOOIL 6, SUNISO No. 5GS or equivalent.
14. Have an authorized service station evacuate, charge and check the system for leaks.

4WD MODELS

▶ See Figure 36

1. Have the vehicle's A/C system discharged by an authorized service station.
2. Disconnect the discharge hose from the condenser inlet fitting. Cap the open fitting immediately to keep moisture out of the system.
3. Disconnect the liquid hose from the condenser outlet fitting. Cap the open fitting immediately to keep moisture out of the system.
4. Unplug the condenser fan motor connector.
5. Remove the condenser mounting bolts and lift the unit out of the vehicle.
   To install:
6. Install the condenser and tighten the mounting bolts.
7. Attach the compressor fan motor connector.
8. Connect the liquid hose and discharge hose to the condenser. Tighten the liquid hose to 10 ft. lbs. (13 Nm) and the discharge hose to 16 ft. lbs. (22 Nm).
9. If the condenser was replaced with a new one, add compressor oil to the compressor. Add 1.4–1.7 fl. oz. (40–50 cc) of DENSOOIL 6, SUNISO No. 5GS or equivalent.
10. Have an authorized service station evacuate, charge and check the system for leaks.

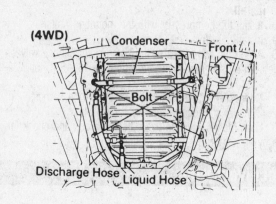

Fig. 36 There are four bolts retaining the condenser in 4WD Van models

Cressida

▶ See Figures 37 and 38

1. Have the vehicle's A/C system discharged by an authorized service station.
2. Remove the following parts:
- Front grille
- Hood lock and center brace
- Horn
- Receiver/drier
- Bumper

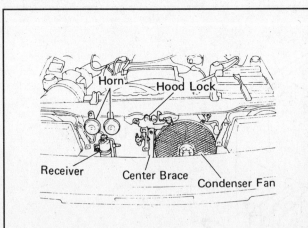

Fig. 37 Remove the indicated parts to access the condenser in Cressida models

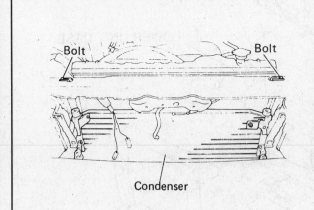

Fig. 38 There are four mounting bolts retaining the condenser in Cressida models

- Condenser fan
- Oil cooler (the oil cooler hoses do not remove)

3. Disconnect the liquid line tube and discharge hose from the condenser' outlet fitting. Cap the open fitting immediately to keep moisture out of the system.

4. Remove the ambient sensor. Unbolt and remove the condenser.

To install:

5. Install the condenser and tighten the mounting bolts.

6. Install the ambient sensor.

7. Attach the liquid and discharge hose to the condenser. Tighten the liquid tube to 17 ft. lbs. (21 Nm) and the discharge hose to 18 ft. lbs. (25 Nm).

8. Install the following parts:
- Front grille
- Hood lock and center brace
- Horn
- Receiver/drier
- Bumper
- Condenser fan
- Oil cooler

9. If the condenser was replaced with a new one, add compressor oil to the compressor. Add 1.4–1.7 fl. oz. (40–50 cc) of DENSOOIL 6, SUNISO No. 5GS or equivalent.

10. Have an authorized service station evacuate, charge and check the system for leaks.

Evaporator Core

✳✳ CAUTION

Please refer to Section 1 before discharging the compressor or disconnecting air conditioning lines. Damage to the air conditioning system or personal injury could result. Consult your local laws concerning refrigerant discharge and recycling. In many areas it may be illegal for anyone but a certified technician to service the A/C system. Always use an approved recovery station when discharging the air conditioning.

REMOVAL & INSTALLATION

➡The following procedures are for factory installed air conditioned vehicles, as opposed to dealer or aftermarket installed air conditioning systems.

Cressida

♦ See Figures 39 and 40

1. Disconnect the negative battery cable. Discharge the refrigerant system.

2. Disconnect the suction flexible hose from the cooling unit outlet fitting.

3. Disconnect the liquid line from the cooling unit inlet fitting. Cap the open fittings immediately to keep the moisture out of the system.

4. Remove the grommets from the inlet and outlet fittings.

5. Remove the glove box with the under cover. Unplug all necessary connectors, such as the pressure switch connector and the A/C harness.

6. Remove the cooling unit attaching nuts and bolts. Remove the cooling unit from the vehicle.

7. Place the cooling unit on a suitable work bench and unscrew the thermistor, if so equipped.

8. Using suitable tools, remove the lower cooling unit case clamps and retaining screws.

9. Unplug the connectors and wire harness. Remove the upper cooling unit case retainer screws and clips. Remove the upper case from the evaporator.

10. Remove the heat insulator and the clamp from the outlet tube. Disconnect the liquid line from the inlet fitting of the expansion valve.

11. Disconnect the expansion valve from the inlet fitting of the evaporator. Remove the pressure switch (if so equipped) if required and remove the evaporator from the cooling unit.

➡Before installing the evaporator, check the evaporator fins for blockage. If the fins are clogged, clean them with compressed air. Never use water to clean the evaporator. Check the fittings for cracks and or scratches and repair as necessary.

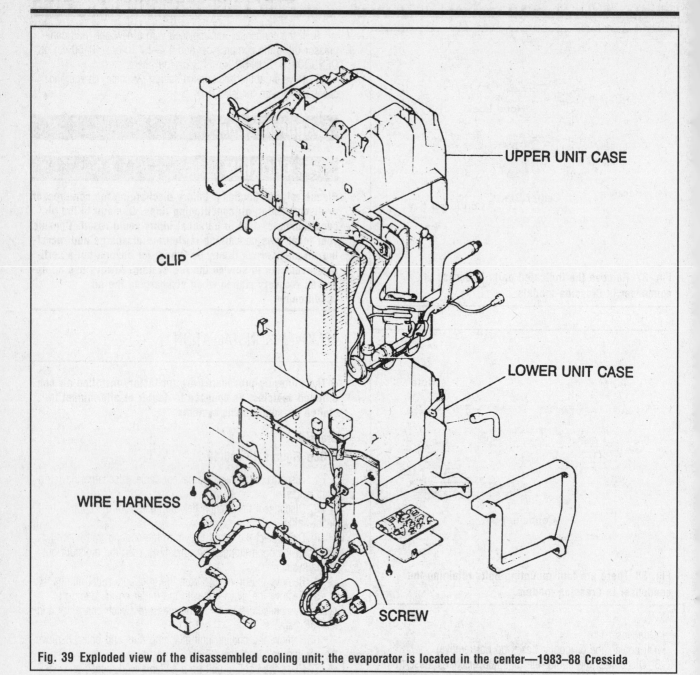

Fig. 39 Exploded view of the disassembled cooling unit; the evaporator is located in the center—1983–88 Cressida

To install:

10. Connect the expansion valve to the inlet fitting of the evaporator and tighten to 17 ft. lbs. Be sure that the O-ring is positioned on the tube fitting.

11. Connect the liquid line tube to the inlet fitting on the expansion valve. Tighten the nut to 10 ft. lbs.

12. Install the pressure switch, if removed. Tighten to 10 ft. lbs. Install the clamp and heat insulator to the outlet tube.

13. Install the upper and lower cases on the evaporator. Install the thermistor.

14. Install the A/C wiring harness to the cooling unit and all other necessary components.

15. Install the cooling unit assembly and its retaining nuts and bolts. Be careful not to pinch the wiring harness while installing the cooling unit.

16. Install the glove box and the grommets on the inlet and outlet fittings.

17. Connect the liquid line to the cooling unit inlet fittings and tighten to 10 ft. lbs.

18. If the evaporator was replaced, add 1.4–1.7 oz. of compressor oil to the compressor. Connect the negative battery cable.

19. Evacuate the A/C system. Have an authorized service station recharge the system, operate it and check for leaks.

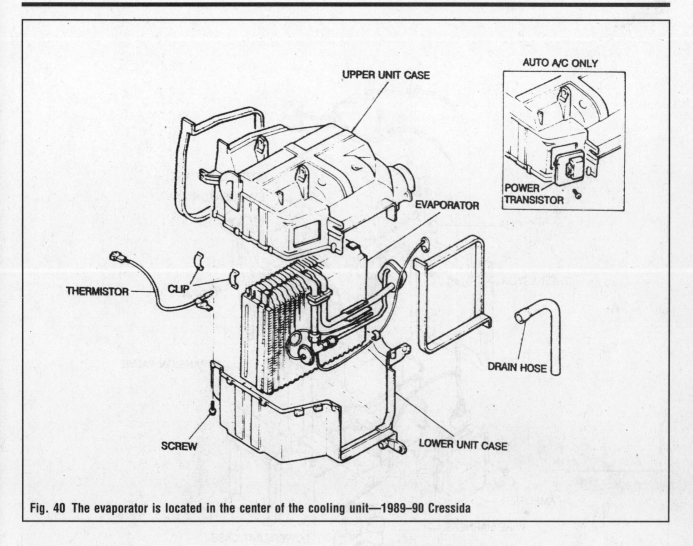

Fig. 40 The evaporator is located in the center of the cooling unit—1989–90 Cressida

Van

FRONT COOLING UNIT

▶ **See Figures 41, 42 and 43**

1. Disconnect the negative battery cable. Discharge the refrigerant system.

2. Disconnect the suction flexible hose from the cooling unit outlet fitting.

3. Disconnect the liquid line from the cooling unit inlet fitting. Cap the open fittings immediately to keep the moisture out of the system.

4. Remove the grommets from the inlet and outlet fittings.

5. Remove the glove box with the under cover. Unplug all necessary connectors, such as the pressure switch connector and the A/C harness.

6. Remove the cooling unit attaching nuts and bolts. Remove the cooling unit from the vehicle.

7. Place the cooling unit on a suitable work bench and disassemble it as follows:

   a. Unplug the connectors at the cooling unit case.
   b. Remove the amplifier.
   c. Remove the wire harness.
   d. Remove the 7 case retaining clips.
   e. Remove the case retaining screws.
   f. Remove the upper case unit.
   g. Remove the thermistor along with the thermistor holder.
   h. Remove the lower case unit.
   i. Disconnect the liquid tube from the inlet fitting of the expansion valve.
   j. Remove the packing and the heat sensing tube from the suction tube of the evaporator.
   k. Remove the expansion valve.

➡**Before installing the evaporator, check the evaporator fins for blockage. If the fins are clogged, clean them with compressed air. Never use water to clean the evaporator. Check the fittings for cracks and or scratches and repair as necessary.**

To install:

8. Connect the expansion valve to the inlet fitting of the evaporator and tighten to 17 ft. lbs. Be sure that the O-ring is positioned on the tube fitting.

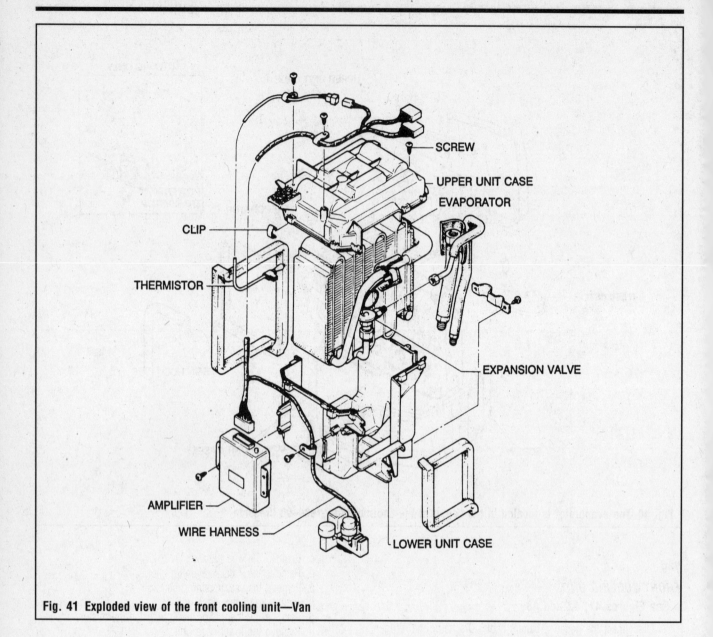

Fig. 41 Exploded view of the front cooling unit—Van

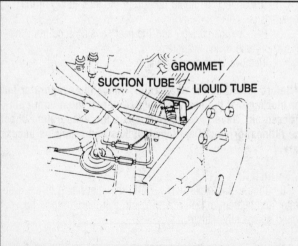

Fig. 42 Disconnect the suction and liquid lines from the front cooling unit—Van

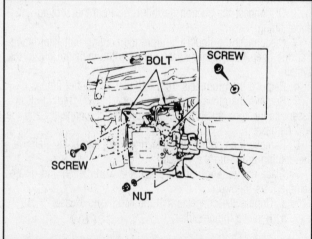

Fig. 43 Unfasten the cooling unit nuts and bolts, then remove the unit from the vehicle—Van

9. Install the holder to the suction tube with the heat sensitizing tube. Connect the liquid line tube to the inlet fitting on the expansion valve. Tighten the nut to 10 ft. lbs.

10. Reassemble the cooling unit assembly as follows:
   a. Install the lower case unit.
   b. Install the thermistor along with the thermistor holder.
   c. Install the upper case unit.
   d. Install the case retaining screws.
   e. Install the 7 case retaining clips.
   f. Install the wire harness.
   g. Install the amplifier.
   h. Attach the connectors at the cooling unit case.

11. Install the cooling unit assembly and its retaining nuts and bolts. Be careful not to pinch the wiring harness while installing the cooling unit. Attach all the necessary connectors.

12. Install the glove box along with the under cover. Install the grommets on the inlet and outlet fittings.

13. Connect the liquid line to the cooling unit inlet fittings and tighten to 10 ft. lbs. Connect the suction tube to the cooling unit outlet fitting, tighten to 24 ft. lbs.

14. If the evaporator was replaced, add 1.4–1.7 oz. of compressor oil to the compressor. Connect the negative battery cable.

15. Evacuate the A/C system. Have an authorized service station recharge the system, operate it and check for leaks.

REAR COOLING UNIT
▶ See Figures 44, 45, 46 and 47

1. Disconnect the negative battery cable. Discharge the refrigerant system.

2. Disconnect the suction flexible hose from the cooling unit outlet fitting.

3. Disconnect the liquid line from the cooling unit inlet fitting. Cap the open fittings immediately to keep the moisture out of the system.

4. Remove the grommets from the inlet and outlet fittings.

5. Remove the magnetic valve.

6. Remove the rear blower unit.

7. Disconnect the suction tube. Remove the 4 rear cooling unit retaining bolts and remove the rear cooling unit assembly.

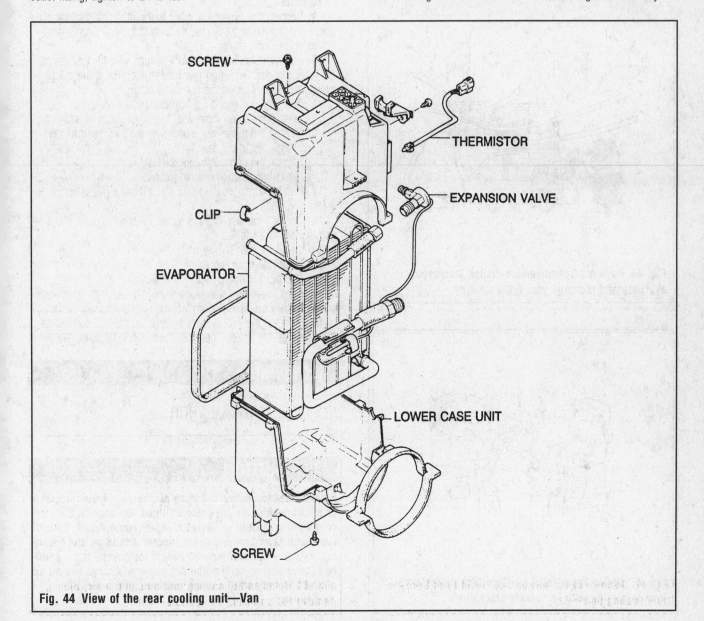

Fig. 44 View of the rear cooling unit—Van

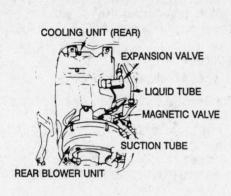

Fig. 45 Remove the necessary components to gain access to the rear cooling unit—Van

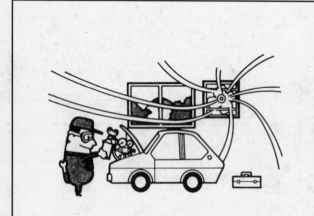

Fig. 46 Have a certified service station discharge, evacuate and recharge your A/C system

Fig. 47 Unlike these fools, certified technicians are knowledgeable with refrigerant precautions

8. Place the cooling unit on a suitable work bench and disassemble it as follows:

   a. Unplug the connectors at the cooling unit case.

   b. Disconnect the liquid tube from the inlet fitting of the expansion valve.

   c. Remove the packing and the heat sensing tube from the suction tube of the evaporator.

   d. Remove the expansion valve.

   e. Remove the 5 case retaining clips.

   f. Remove the case retaining screws.

   g. Remove the upper case unit.

   h. Remove the thermistor along with the thermistor holder.

   i. Remove the lower case unit.

➡**Before installing the evaporator, check the evaporator fins for blockage. If the fins are clogged, clean them with compressed air. Never use water to clean the evaporator. Check the fittings for cracks and or scratches and repair as necessary.**

To install:

9. Connect the expansion valve to the inlet fitting of the evaporator and tighten to 17 ft. lbs. Be sure that the O-ring is positioned on the tube fitting.

10. Install the holder to the suction tube with the heat sensitizing tube. Connect the liquid line tube to the inlet fitting on the expansion valve. Tighten the nut to 10 ft. lbs.

11. Reassemble the cooling unit assembly as follows:

   a. Install the lower case unit.

   b. Install the thermistor along with the thermistor holder.

   c. Install the upper case unit.

   d. Install the case retaining screws.

   e. Install the 5 case retaining clips.

12. Install the rear cooling unit into the vehicle and install the 4 retaining bolts.

13. Connect the suction tube to the rear cooling unit outlet fitting, tighten to 24 ft. lbs.

14. Install the rear blower unit.

15. Install the magnetic valve.

16. Connect the liquid tubes 10 ft. lbs.

17. If the evaporator was replaced, add 1.4–1.7 oz. of compressor oil to the compressor. Connect the negative battery cable.

18. Evacuate the A/C system. Have an authorized service station recharge the system, operate it and check for leaks.

Refrigerator

REMOVAL & INSTALLATION

✳✳ CAUTION

Please refer to Section 1 before discharging the compressor or disconnecting air conditioning lines. Damage to the air conditioning system or personal injury could result. Consult your local laws concerning refrigerant discharge and recycling. In many areas it may be illegal for anyone but a certified technician to service the A/C system. Always use an approved recovery station when discharging the air conditioning.

◗ **See Figures 48, 49, 50 and 51**

1. Disconnect the negative battery cable. Discharge the refrigerant system.

2. Remove the 3 screws from the refrigerator side cover and remove the side cover.

3. Remove the 2 and 6-pin connectors from the refrigerator control unit.

4. Remove the suction and liquid lines from the refrigerator.

5. Remove the refrigerator mounting bolts and remove the refrigerator.

6. Inspect the refrigerant lines and hoses going to the refrigerator for cracks and other damage. Replace as necessary.

7. Connect the negative battery cable.

8. Evacuate the A/C system. Have an authorized service station recharge the system, operate it and check for leaks.

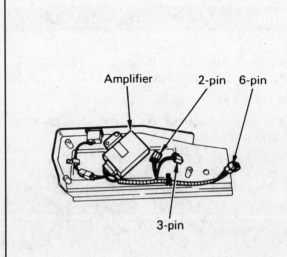

Fig. 50 Disengage the 2-pin, 3-pin and 6-pin connectors from the refrigerator harness

Fig. 48 The refrigerator is located between the seats in the front of the vehicle

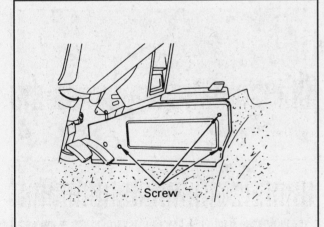

Fig. 49 Remove the refrigerator side cover screws, then remove the cover

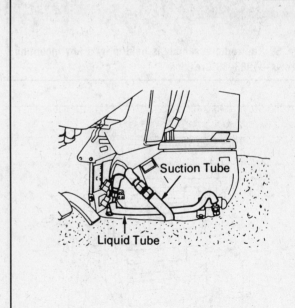

Fig. 51 Disconnect the suction and liquid lines for the refrigerator

ENTERTAINMENT SYSTEMS

Radio

REMOVAL & INSTALLATION

◆ See Figures 52, 53 and 54

➡Due to optional equipment, the removal steps can be altered as required.

1. Disconnect the negative battery cable.
2. Remove the ashtray and cigarette lighter, if required.
3. Remove the center cluster finish panel and clips.

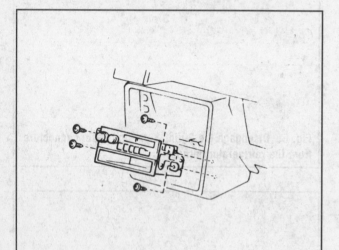

Fig. 52 The radio assembly is held in by a few mounting screws—1983-88 Cressida

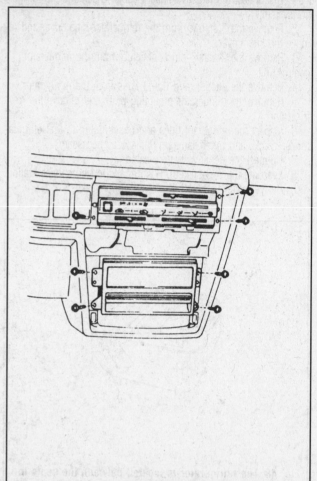

Fig. 54 Radio mounting on the Van models

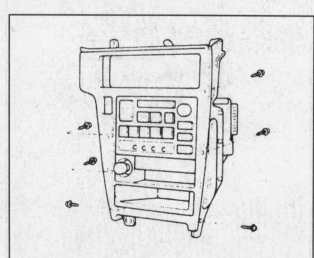

Fig. 53 A large finish panel surrounds the radio unit on 1989-90 Cressida models

To remove the radio from the dash, pull out the ashtray

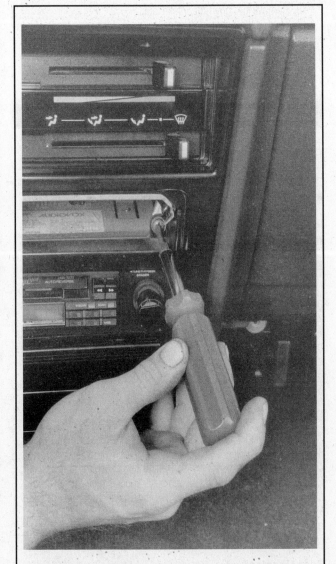

Unscrew and separate the trim panel with the lighter assembly from the dash

Unplug the radio wiring from the back of the unit

Disconnect the lighter wiring from the rear of the unit

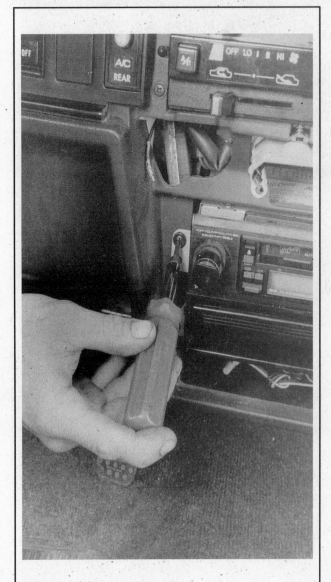

Unscrew the radio from the dash . . .

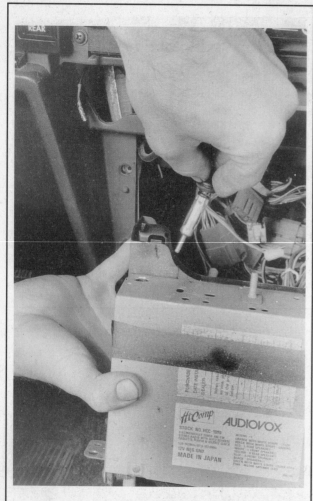

. . . then disconnect the antenna lead from the back of the radio

4. Remove the radio finish panel. Unplug any connectors at this time that can be reached including the cigarette lighter wire (if so equipped). On the models equipped with an ashtray in this area, remove the ashtray retainer screws along with the retainer.

5. Detach the antenna lead from the jack on the radio case.

6. Remove the cowl air intake duct.

7. Detach the power and speaker leads. Label the leads for assembly reference.

8. Remove the radio support nuts and bolts.

9. Remove the radio from beneath the dashboard.

10. Installation is the reverse of the removal procedure.

Speakers

REMOVAL & INSTALLATION

▶ **See Figure 54a**

➡ **Always disconnect the negative battery cable before attempting to remove the speakers.**

Dash Mounted

Dash mounted speakers can be accessed after removing the appropriate trim panel. These panels are usually retained by screws and clips. Be sure you have removed all of the attaching screws before prying the panel from the dash. Do not use excessive force on the panel as this will only lead to damage. Once the panel has been removed, loosen the speaker attaching bolts/screws, then pull the speaker from the dash and unplug the electrical connection.

Door Mounted

Door mounted speakers can be accessed after removing the door panel. These panels are usually retained by screws and clips. Be sure you have removed all of the attaching screws before prying the panel from the door. A special tool can be purchased for this purpose. Do not use excessive force on the panel as this will only lead to damage. Once the panel has been removed, loosen the speaker attaching bolts/screws, then pull the speaker from its mount and unplug the electrical connection.

Rear Mounted

Removing the rear speakers involves basically the same procedure as the front speakers. Remove the appropriate trim panel, then remove the speaker. The rear speakers on some models can be accessed from inside the rear hatch.

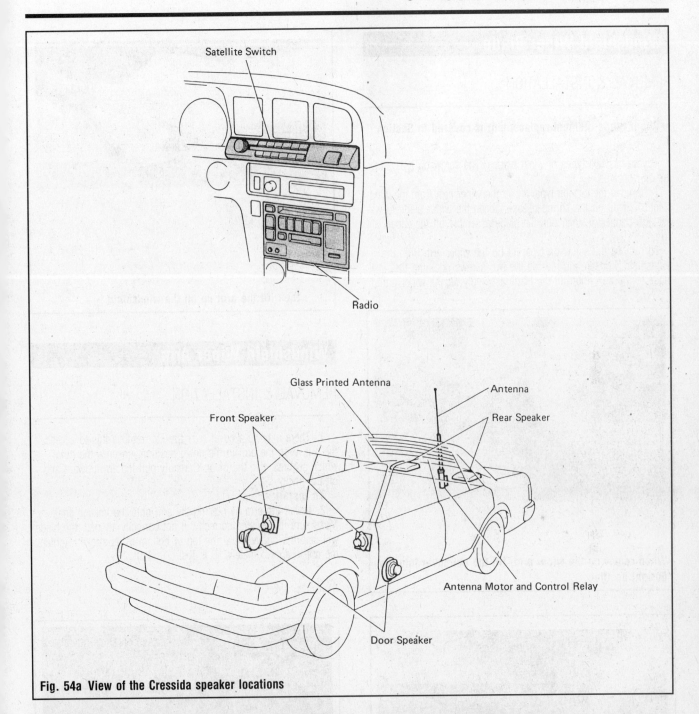

Fig. 54a **View of the Cressida speaker locations**

WINDSHIELD WIPERS AND WASHERS

General Information

➡️**Due to the lack of information available at the time of this publication, a general windshield wiper assembly removal and installation procedure is outlined. The removal steps can be altered as required.**

For maximum effectiveness and longest element life, the windshield and wiper blades should be kept clean. Dirt, tree sap, road tar and so on will cause streaking, smearing and blade deterioration if left on the glass. It is advisable to wash the windshield

carefully with a commercial glass cleaner at least once a month. Wipe off the rubber blades with the wet rag afterwards. Do not attempt to move the wipers by hand; damage to the motor and drive mechanism will result.

If the blades are found to be cracked, broken or torn, they should be replaced immediately. Replacement intervals will vary with usage, although ozone deterioration usually limits blade life to about one year. If the wiper pattern is smeared or streaked, or if the blade chatters across the glass, the elements should be replaced. It is easiest and most sensible to replace the elements in pairs.

Windshield Wiper Blade

REMOVAL & INSTALLATION

→Wiper blade element replacement is covered in Section 1.

Toyota has two types of wiper blades. The screw-on type and the clip-on type.

To remove the clip-on type, lift up the wiper arm from the windshield. Lift up on the spring release tab on the wiper blade-to-wiper arm connector, then pull the blade assembly off the wiper arm.

To remove the screw-on type, lift up the wiper arm from the windshield. Loosen and remove the two screws retaining the blade to the arm, then lift the blade assembly off the wiper arm.

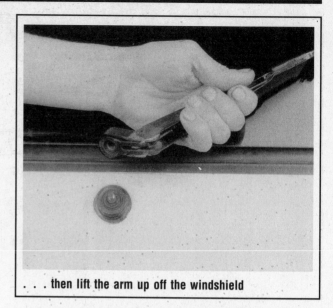

. . . then lift the arm up off the windshield

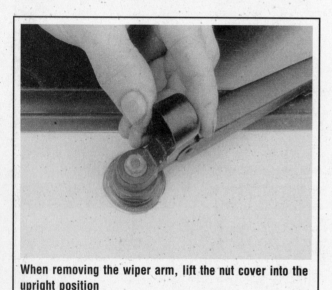

When removing the wiper arm, lift the nut cover into the upright position

Windshield Wiper Arm

REMOVAL & INSTALLATION

1. There may be a cover over the nut, remove this to access the nut. With the arm in the down position, unscrew the nut which secures it to the pivot. Carefully pull the arm upward and off the pivot.

To install:

2. Install the arm by placing the arm onto the linkage shaft. Make sure it is seated correctly; if not correctly aligned, the blade will slap the bodywork at the top or bottom of its stroke. Tighten the nut to approximately 15 ft. lbs. (20 Nm).

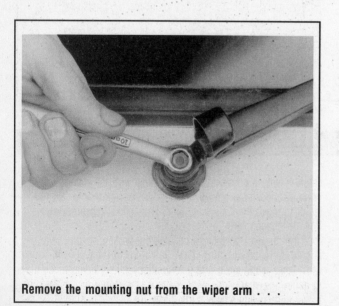

Remove the mounting nut from the wiper arm . . .

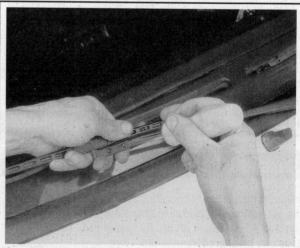

To remove the wiper blade from the wiper arm, remove the mounting screws

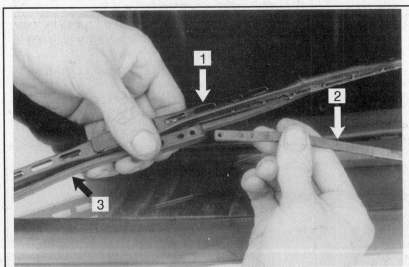

1. Wiper blade
2. Wiper arm
3. Wiper insert

Lift the blade off the arm and replace as necessary

➡If one wiper arm does not move when turned on or only moves a little bit, check the retaining nut at the bottom of the arm. The extra effort of moving snow or wet leaves off the glass can cause the nut to come loose—the pivot will move without moving the arm.

Windshield Wiper Motor

REMOVAL & INSTALLATION

Cressida

1. Remove the access hole cover.
2. Separate the wiper and motor by prying gently with a small prybar.
3. Remove the wiper arms and the linkage mounting nuts. Push the linkage pivot ports into the ventilators.
4. Remove the wiper arms and the linkage mounting nuts. Push the linkage pivot ports into the ventilators.
5. Loosen the wiper link connectors at their ends and with the linkage from the cowl ventilator.
6. Start the wiper motor and turn the ignition key to the **OFF** position when the crank is a position best suited for removal of the motor.

➡The wiper motor is difficult to remove when it is in the parked position. If the motor is turned off at the wiper switch, it will automatically return to this position.

7. Unplug the wiper motor connector.
8. Loosen the motor mounting bolts and withdraw the motor.
9. Installation is the reverse of the removal procedure. Be sure to install the wiper motor with it in the park position by connecting the multi-connector and operating the wiper control switch. Assemble the crank.

Van

1. Disconnect the negative battery cable.
2. Unplug the wiring connector from the wiper motor.

3. Remove the wiper motor retaining bolts that secure the motor to the firewall in the engine compartment.
4. Pull the motor away from the firewall so as to allow enough room to be able to remove the wiper crank arm retaining nut.
5. Once the crank arm nut has been removed, use a suitable tool and pry the wiper arm linkage from the crank arm.
6. Remove the motor from the vehicle.
7. To install reverse the removal procedure. Connect the negative battery cable and check the operation of the wiper motor.

Wiper Linkage

REMOVAL & INSTALLATION

1. Disconnect the negative battery cable.
2. Remove the wiper motor assembly.
3. Remove the wiper arms by removing their retaining nuts and working them off their shafts.
4. Remove the wiper shaft nuts and spacers. Push the shafts down into the body cavity. Pull the linkage out of the cavity through the wiper motor hole.
5. To install reverse the removal procedure. Install the wiper motor assembly. Connect the negative battery cable and check the operation of the wiper motor.

Rear Window Wiper Motor

REMOVAL & INSTALLATION

Cressida

1. Disconnect the negative battery cable.
2. Remove the wiper arm and rear door trim cover.
3. Unplug the wiper motor wire connector.
4. Remove the wiper motor bracket attaching bolts and the wiper motor along with the bracket.
5. To install reverse the removal procedure. Connect the negative battery cable and check the operation of the wiper motor.

Van

1. Disconnect the negative battery cable.
2. At the rear of the vehicle, remove the wiper motor cover panel.
3. Remove the wiper arm from the wiper motor.
4. Unplug the electrical connector from the wiper motor.
5. Remove the wiper motor-to-door bolts and the motor from the vehicle.
6. To install reverse the removal procedure. Connect the negative battery cable and check the operation of the wiper motor.

INSPECTION

▸ **See Figures 55 and 56**

1. Unplug the connector from the wiper motor.
2. To inspect the motor operation in low speed, connect the positive lead from the battery to terminal 2. Connect the negative lead to the motor body.
3. If the motor operates at low speed, the motor is working properly.
4. To inspect the motor operation in high speed, connect the positive lead from the battery to terminal 1. Connect the negative lead to the motor body.
5. If the motor operates at high speed, the motor is working properly.
6. To inspect the motor operates, stopping at the stop position, use the following procedure:
   a. Operate the motor at low speed.

b. Stop the motor operation anywhere except the stop position by disconnecting terminal 2.
c. Connect terminals 2 and 3. Connect the positive lead from battery to terminal 4.
d. Check that the motor stops running at the stop position after the motor operates again.

7. If the motor fails any of these operational test, replace it with a new one.

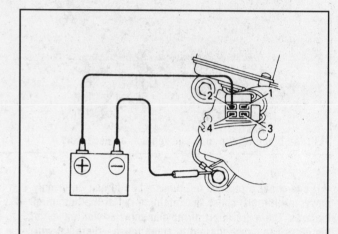

Fig. 55 Attach the positive lead of the battery to terminal 2 and the negative lead to the motor body to test the wiper motor operation

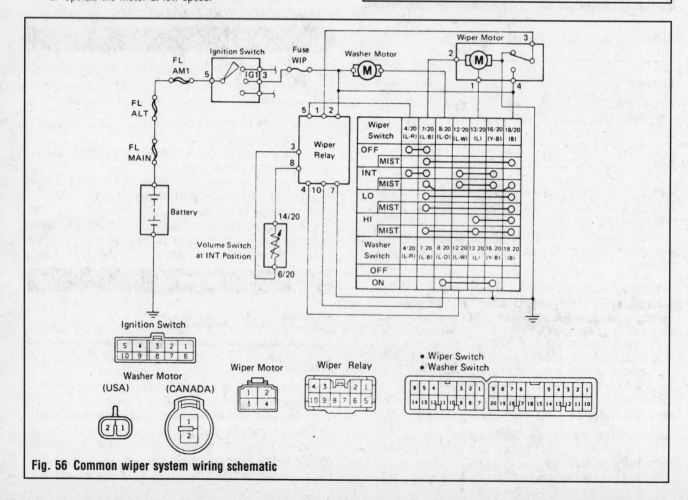

Fig. 56 Common wiper system wiring schematic

INSTRUMENTS AND SWITCHES

➡On the Toyota models covered in this manual, all of the instrument panel, cluster, console and other components associated with the instrument panel are covered in the removal and installation procedure of what Toyota refers to as the Instrument Safety Pad. Therefore, most of the information pertaining to the instrument panel and its components is covered under the Instrument Safety Pad removal and installation procedures.

Instrument Safety Pad

REMOVAL & INSTALLATION

Cressida

1983–88 MODELS

◆ **See Figures 57 thru 64**

1. Disconnect the negative battery cable.
2. Remove the steering wheel as outlined in Section 8.
3. Remove the glove box as follows:
   a. Remove the glove box check arm retaining screw and check arm assembly.
   b. Remove the compartment door retaining screws and compartment door.
   c. Remove the door lock striker.
   d. Remove the compartment retaining screws and the compartment. Disconnect the compartment light connector.
4. Remove the 4 screws from the glove box bracket and remove the bracket.
5. To remove the lower finish panel on the passenger's side remove the bolt from the CD amplifier, if so equipped.
6. Remove the passenger's side lower finish panel retaining bolts, nuts and screws. Pull off the lower finish panel along with the under cover.
7. Remove the hood release lever retaining screws and remove the hood release lever.
8. Remove the lower steering column cover retaining screws and remove the cover.
9. To remove the lower finish panel on the driver's side (USA models), pry off the cruise control switch. Unplug the switch connector and remove it. Pry off the speaker panel and remove the retaining bolts hidden behind the speaker panel. Remove the lower finish panel retaining bolts, nuts and screws. Pull off the lower finish panel and unplug any connectors.
10. To remove the lower finish panel on the driver's side (Canadian models), push out the headlight cleaner switch from the reverse side of the dash panel. Push out the cruise control main switch and defogger switch. Unplug the switch connectors and remove them. Remove the lower finish panel retaining bolts, nuts and screws. Pull off the lower finish panel and disconnect the light control rheostat switch.
11. Remove the air duct assembly.
12. Remove the left and right front speaker retaining screws, disconnect the wiring and remove the speakers.
13. Pry and pull off the defroster button. Then pry out the heater control panel.

14. Remove the center cluster finish panel retaining screws and remove the finish panel. Unplug the wiring.
15. Remove the radio retaining screws and remove the radio. Disconnect the radio wiring and pull out the antenna cord.
16. Remove the screws from the satellite switches (if so equipped) unplug the connectors and remove the switches.
17. Remove the instrument cluster finish panel retaining screws, pull out the panel, disconnect the harness wiring and remove the cluster finish panel.
18. Remove the combination meter retaining screws, disconnect the connectors and remove the meter assembly.
19. Remove the heater controller retaining screws and controller.
20. Disconnect the wiring and heater vacuum tube connectors.
21. Unplug the light sensor connector, solar sensor for A/C, In-car sensor for A/C and glove box courtesy switch connectors.
22. Disconnect the hose from the aspirator for the A/C.
23. Remove the nut and screws from the instrument panel stay bracket.
24. Remove the nut and screws from the instrument panel No. 1, instrument panel mounting bracket and remove the bracket.
25. Remove the instrument safety pad retaining bolts, nuts and screws.

➡The safety pad has a boss on the reverse side for clamping onto the clip on the body side. Therefore, when removing it, pull upward at an angle.

26. Disconnect the defroster ducts from the safety pad.
To install:
27. Reconnect the defroster ducts to the safety pad.

➡The safety pad has a boss on the reverse side for clamping onto the clip on the body side. Therefore, when installing it, push downward at an angle.

28. Install the instrument safety pad retaining bolts, nuts and screws.
29. Install the No. 1 instrument panel mounting bracket and install the retaining nuts and screws.
30. Install the instrument panel stay bracket and the retaining nut and screws.
31. Reconnect the hose to the aspirator for the A/C.
32. Reattach the light sensor, solar sensor for A/C, In-car sensor for A/C and glove box courtesy switch connectors.
33. Reconnect the wiring connectors and heater vacuum tube connectors.
34. Install the heater controller and the retaining screws.
35. Plug-in the combination meter connectors, install the meter and the retaining screws.
36. Reconnect the instrument cluster finish panel wiring, then install the cluster finish panel and retaining screws.
37. Reattach the connectors to the satellite switches (if so equipped) install the switches and retaining screws.
38. Reconnect the radio wiring and the antenna cord. Install the radio and the retaining screws.
39. Reattach the center cluster finish panel connectors, install the finish panel and the retaining screws.
40. Push in the heater control panel. Push back into place the defroster button.

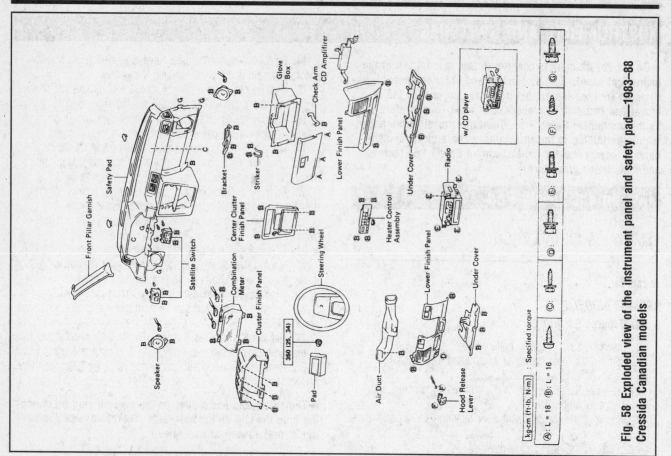

Fig. 58 Exploded view of the instrument panel and safety pad—1983–88 Cressida Canadian models

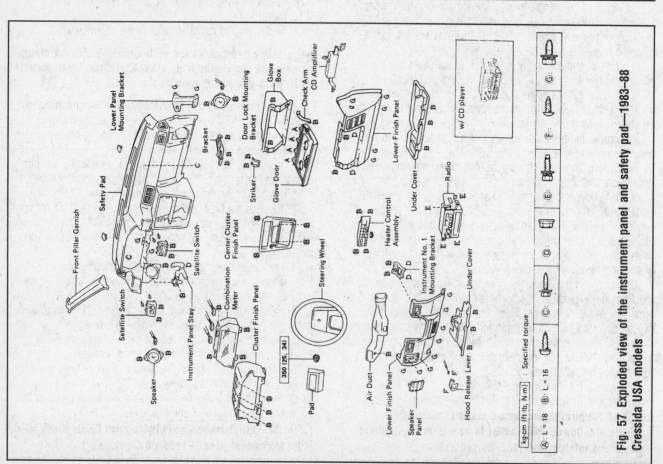

Fig. 57 Exploded view of the instrument panel and safety pad—1983–88 Cressida USA models

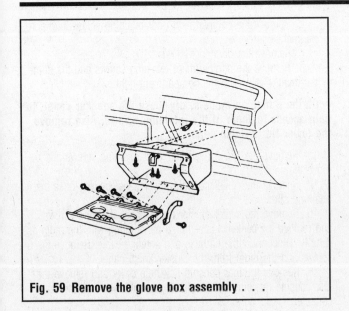

Fig. 59 Remove the glove box assembly . . .

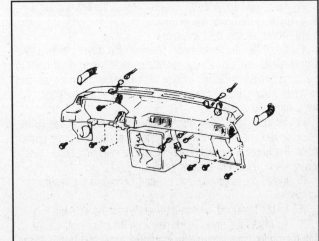

Fig. 62 Instrument panel and safety pad retaining screw locations—1983–88 Cressida

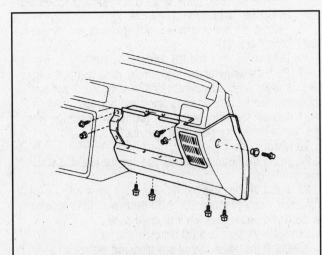

Fig. 60 . . . then remove the lower finish panel on the passengers side—1983–88 Cressida

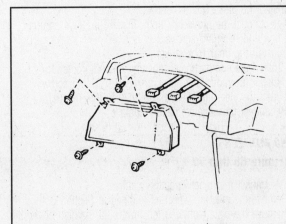

Fig. 63 Remove the mounting screws and unfasten the wiring harnesses leading to the combination meter—1983–88 Cressida

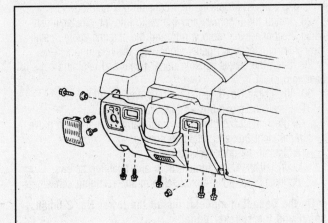

Fig. 61 Remove the mounting screws retaining the drivers side lower finish panel to access the instrument panel and safety pad—1983–88 Cressida

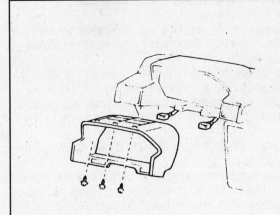

Fig. 64 Three screws retain the cluster finish panel to the instrument panel—1983–88 Cressida

41. Reconnect the speaker harness, install the left and right front speakers and retaining screws.

42. Install the air duct assembly.

43. To install the lower finish panel on the driver's side (Canadian models), reattach all the switch connectors and push back in place the headlight cleaner switch, cruise control main switch and defogger switch. Install the lower finish panel along with the bolts, nuts and screws.

44. To install the lower finish panel on the driver's side (USA models), reconnect all wiring and install the cruise control switch. Install the lower finish panel and install the retaining bolts, nuts and screws. Install the speaker panels.

45. Install the lower steering column cover and the retaining screws.

46. Install the hood release lever and retaining screws.

47. To install the lower finish panel on the passenger's side, install the under cover along with the finish panel and install the retaining bolts, nuts and screws. Install the bolt to the CD amplifier, if so equipped.

48. Install the glove box bracket and the 4 screws to the glove box bracket.

49. Install the glove box as follows:

a. Reconnect the glove box light. Install the glove compartment box and retaining screws.

b. Install the door lock striker.

c. Install the compartment door and retaining screws.

d. Install the glove box check arm and retaining screw.

50. Install the steering wheel as outlined in this manual.

51. Reconnect the negative battery cable.

1989–90 MODELS

♦ **See Figure 65 thru 73**

1. Disconnect the negative battery cable.

2. Remove the steering wheel as outlined in Section 8.

3. Remove the right front and left front pillar garnish covers, by prying them out by hand.

4. Remove the steering column cover retaining screws and remove the steering column cover.

5. Using a suitable prytool, pry loose the 4 cluster finish lower panel clips and remove the cluster finish lower panel. Disconnect any related wiring.

6. Remove the No. 1 under cover retaining screws and remove the under cover panel.

7. Remove the engine hood release lever retaining screws and remove the release lever. Disconnect the release cable from the lever, if so equipped.

8. To remove the lower finish panel on the driver's side, pry off the speaker panel and remove the retaining bolts hidden behind speaker panel. Remove the lower finish panel retaining bolts, nuts and screws. Pull off the lower finish panel and unplug any connectors.

9. Remove the No. 2 heater air duct retaining screws and remove the air duct.

10. Remove the remote control mirror switch and disconnect the wiring. Remove the instrument cluster finish panel retaining screws and cluster finish panel. Disconnect all the wiring.

11. Remove the combination meter retaining screws and remove the combination meter. Disconnect the related wiring.

12. Remove the glove box as follows:

a. Remove the glove box check arm retaining screw and check arm assembly.

b. Remove the compartment door retaining screws and compartment door.

c. Remove the door lock striker.

d. Remove the compartment retaining screws and the compartment. Disconnect the compartment light.

➡**On the Canadian models, pry loose the speaker panel, to gain access to some of the retaining screws. Also remove the lower No. 2 finish panel.**

13. Remove the No. 3 heater air duct retaining screws and remove the air duct.

14. Remove the center console upper panel by pry loose the 4 retaining clips.

15. Remove the center cluster finish panel retaining screws and remove the center cluster finish panel along with the radio assembly. Disconnect the harness and antenna cable. Remove the 6 screws and the radio from the cluster finish panel.

16. Remove the rear console box hole cover and remove the rear console retaining nuts, bolts and screws. Remove the rear console.

17. Remove the finish lower center panel retaining screws and remove the panel. Unplug the connectors.

18. Remove the heater control retaining screws and remove the heater control assembly.

19. Remove the right and left defroster nozzles.

20. Push the pawls of the speedometer cable and pull it from the instrument panel. Remove the bolt from the No. 3 and the screw from the No. 2 instrument safety pad retainers.

21. Remove the instrument safety pad retaining screws, nuts and bolts. Remove the safety pad from the vehicle.

To install:

22. Install the instrument safety pad and the retaining screws, nuts and bolts.

23. Install the bolt into the No. 3 and the screw into the No. 2 instrument safety pad retainers. Push the pawls of the speedometer cable and push it into the instrument panel.

24. Install the right and left defroster nozzles.

25. Install the heater control assembly and the retaining screws.

26. Reconnect the wiring and install the finish lower center panel along with the retaining screws.

27. Install the rear console box along with the retaining nuts, bolts and screws. Install the rear console box hole cover.

28. Install the 6 screws and the radio into the cluster finish panel. Reconnect the radio wiring and the antenna cable. Install the center cluster finish panel along with the retaining screws.

29. Snap the center console upper panel and retaining clips back into place.

30. Install the No. 3 heater air duct and retaining screws.

31. Install the glove box as follows:

a. Reconnect the glove box light harness. Install the glove compartment box and retaining screws.

b. Install the door lock striker.

c. Install the compartment door and retaining screws.

d. Install the glove box check arm and retaining screw.

➡**On the Canadian models, install the lower No. 2 finish panel and the speaker panel.**

32. Attach the wiring and install the combination meter and retaining screws.

33. Reattach all the connectors. Install the instrument cluster finish panel and retaining. Install the remote control mirror switch.

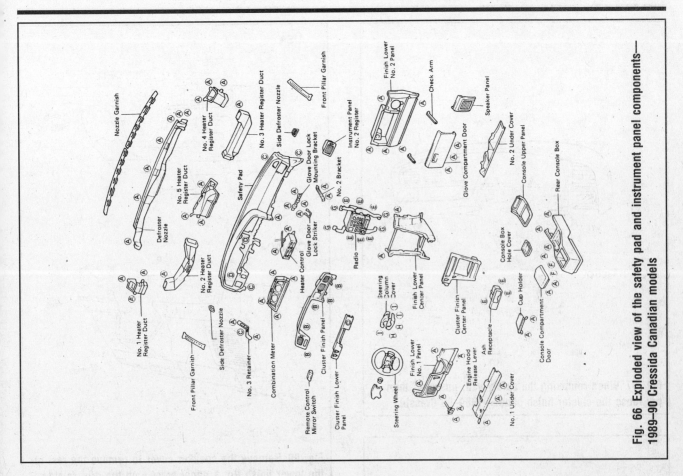

Fig. 66 Exploded view of the safety pad and instrument panel components— 1989–90 Cressida Canadian models

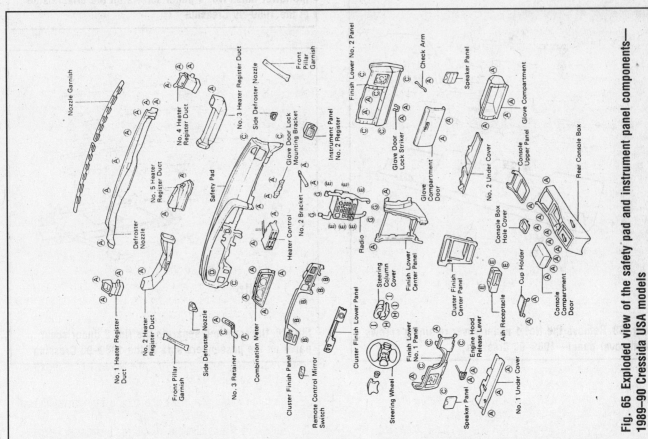

Fig. 65 Exploded view of the safety pad and instrument panel components— 1989–90 Cressida USA models

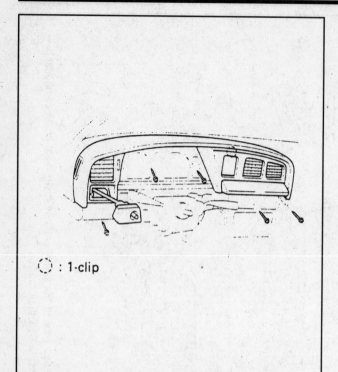

◌ : 1-clip

Fig. 67 When removing the safety pad, unscrew, then pry loose the cluster finish panel—1989–90 Cressida

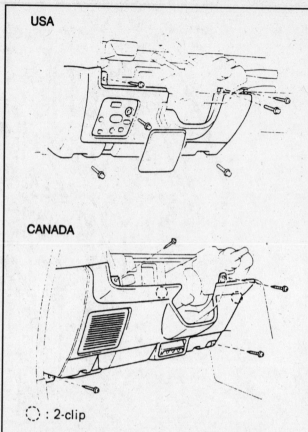

USA

CANADA

◌ : 2-clip

Fig. 69 Remove the speaker cover to remove the rest of the lower finish No. 1 panel screws on the drivers side of the 1989–90 Cressida

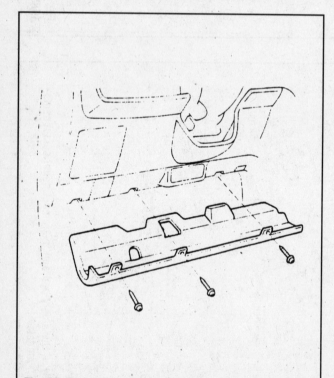

Fig. 68 Remove the No. 1 under cover retaining screws and cover panel—1989–90 Cressida

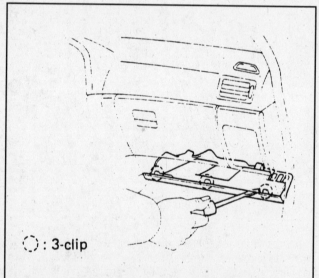

◌ : 3-clip

Fig. 70 Unscrew and separate the No. 2 under cover panel on the passengers side of the 1989–90 Cressida

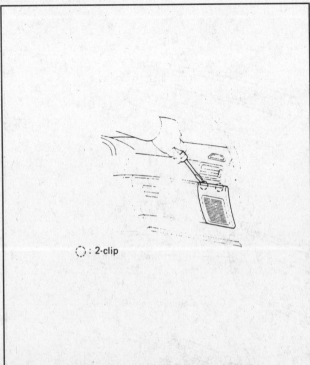

Fig. 71 Pry the lower finish (No. 2) panel off the passengers side near the glove box—1989–90 Cressida Canadian models

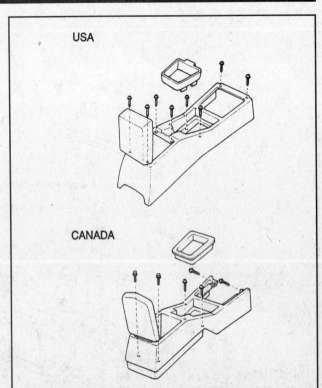

Fig. 72 Remove the center console retaining screws and lift the unit out of the vehicle—1989–90 Cressida

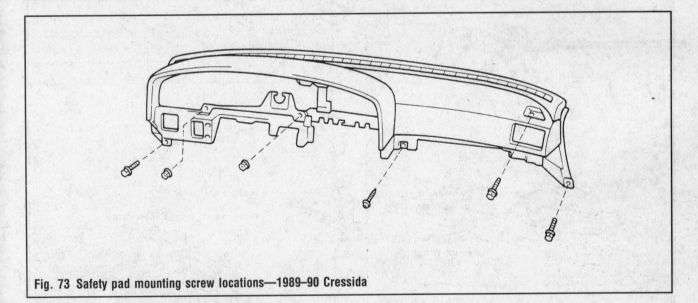

Fig. 73 Safety pad mounting screw locations—1989–90 Cressida

34. Install the No. 2 heater air duct and retaining screws.
35. To install the lower finish panel on the driver's side, reconnect all wiring. Install the lower finish panel and install the retaining bolts, nuts and screws. Install the speaker panels.
36. Reconnect the engine hood release cable to the release lever, if so equipped. Install the engine hood release lever and retaining screws.
37. Install the No. 1 under cover panel and retaining screws.
38. Snap the 4 cluster finish lower panel clips and panel back into place.
39. Install the steering column cover and retaining screws.

40. Install the right front and left front pillar garnish covers, by snapping them into place.
41. Install the steering wheel as outlined in this manual.
42. Reconnect the negative battery cable.

Van

▶ **See Figures 74 thru 79**

1. Disconnect the negative battery cable.
2. Remove the steering wheel as outlined in Section 8.
3. Remove the lower finish panel retaining screws and remove the finish panel.

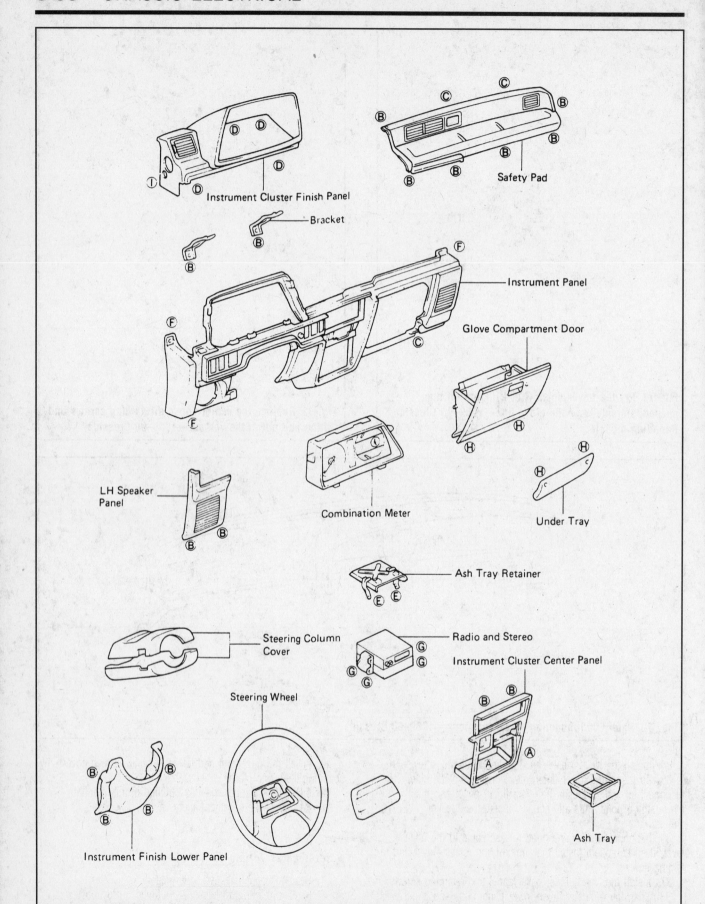

Fig. 74 Exploded view of the safety pad and instrument panel—Van

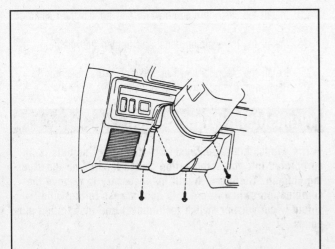

Fig. 75 Remove the steering column lower finish panel on the Van models

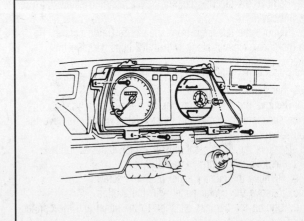

Fig. 77 Unscrew the combination meter attached to the instrument panel—Van

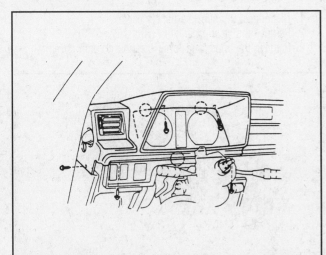

Fig. 76 Remove the instrument panel cluster finish panel—Van

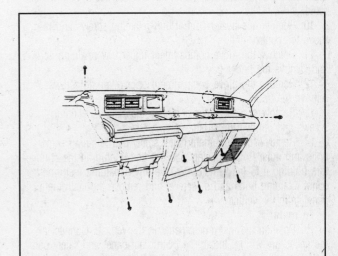

Fig. 78 The safety pad can be unscrewed and removed—Van

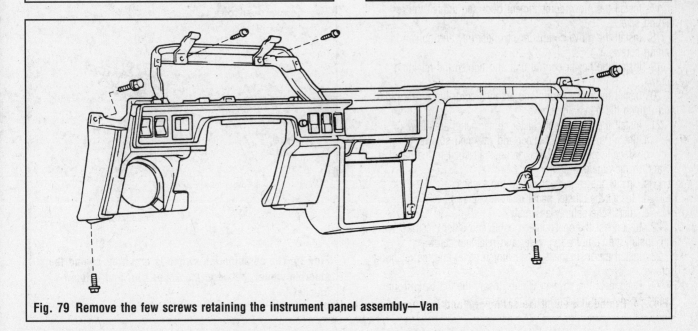

Fig. 79 Remove the few screws retaining the instrument panel assembly—Van

4. Remove the steering column cover retaining screws and remove the cover.

5. Remove the left-hand front speaker retaining screws. Remove the speaker panel along with the 2 clips. Unplug the speaker connectors.

6. Remove the instrument cluster finish panel retaining screws then remove the panel.

7. Remove the combination meter retaining screws. Disconnect the speedometer cable and other related wiring. Remove the combination meter.

8. Remove the instrument cluster center panel as follows:
   a. Remove the ashtray assembly.
   b. Remove the cluster panel retaining screws.
   c. Remove the center panel with the 2 clips.
   d. Unplug the harness attached to the panel and the connector to the cigarette lighter.
   e. Remove the ashtray retainer screws and remove the retainer.

9. Remove the radio retaining screws, pull the radio out and disconnect the harness along with the antenna cable. Remove the radio.

10. Remove the heater control unit retaining screws and remove the control unit.

11. Remove the glove compartment under tray retaining screws and remove the under tray.

12. Remove the glove compartment door retaining screws, then remove the door.

13. Remove the glove compartment latch striker retaining screws and remove the striker.

14. Remove the instrument panel safety pad retaining screw bolts and nuts. Pull the safety pad out and unplug all the connectors holding it to the vehicle. Remove any remaining instrument panel retaining bolts and or screws and remove the instrument panel from the vehicle.

To install:

15. Position the instrument panel in the vehicle. Connect all the necessary wiring. Install the instrument panel and safety pad retaining bolts, nuts and screws.

16. Install the glove compartment latch striker and tighten the retaining screws.

17. Install the glove compartment door and tighten the retaining screws.

18. Install the glove compartment under tray and tighten the retaining screws.

19. Install the heater control unit and tighten the retaining screws.

20. Install the radio wiring and antenna cord. Install the radio and tighten the retaining screws.

21. Install the instrument cluster center panel as follows:
   a. Install the ashtray retainer and retaining screws.
   b. Reconnect the electrical harness attached to the panel and to the cigarette lighter.
   c. Install the center panel with the 2 clips.
   d. Install the cluster panel retaining screws.
   e. Install the ashtray assembly.

22. Reconnect the speedometer cable and other electrical wiring. Install the combination meter and retaining screws.

23. Install the instrument cluster finish panel and the retaining screws.

24. Reconnect the speaker wiring. Install the left-hand front speaker panel and tighten the retaining screws.

25. Install the steering column cover and tighten the retaining screws.

26. Install the lower finish panel and tighten the retaining screws.

27. Install the steering wheel as outlined in this Section 8.

28. Reconnect the negative battery cable.

Windshield Wiper Switch

➡**The windshield wiper/washer switch on all models is incorporated into the combination switch located on the steering column. Therefore, it will be necessary to remove the combination switch in order to gain access to the windshield wiper/washer switch for removal and installation purposes.**

REMOVAL & INSTALLATION

◆ **See Figures 80 and 81**

1. Disconnect the negative battery cable.
2. Remove the steering column garnish.
3. Remove the upper and lower steering column covers.

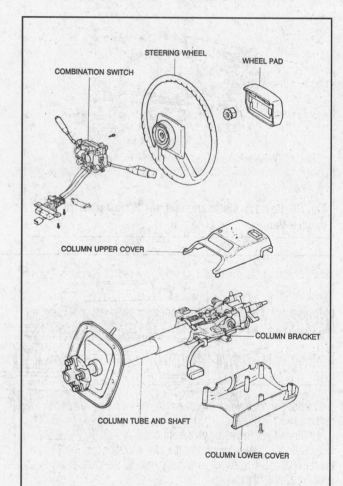

Fig. 80 The combination switch is mounted behind the steering wheel, between the upper trim and column bracket

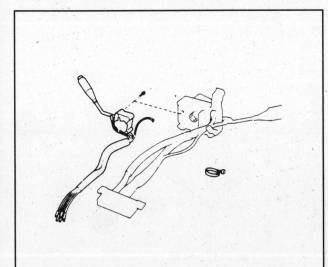

Fig. 81 The windshield wiper and washer switch is usually screwed into the side of the combination switch

4. Remove the steering wheel as outlined in Section 8.

5. Trace the switch wiring harness to the multi-connector. Push in the lock levers and pull apart the connectors.

6. On vehicles equipped with Toyota Electronic Modulated Suspension (TEMS), remove the steering sensor.

7. Unscrew the mounting screws and slide the combination switch from the steering column. For additional details on Combination Switch removal and installation, refer to Section 8.

8. Remove the windshield wiper/washer switch as follows:

a. Remove the terminals from the connectors.

b. Remove the terminals from the horn contact.

c. Remove the windshield wiper/washer switch retaining bolts and remove the switch.

To install:

9. Install the windshield wiper/washer switch and retaining bolts.

10. Install the terminals to the horn contact.

11. Install the terminals to the connectors.

12. Installation of the combination switch is the reverse of the removal procedure. Check all switch functions for proper operation.

Rear Wiper Switch

REMOVAL & INSTALLATION

If equipped with a rear wiper switch, it is usually located in the center of the dash area.

1. Disconnect the negative battery cable.

2. Using a small prytool, pry the rear wiper switch loose from the dash panel. The switch is usually held to the dash panel by 2 small retaining clips.

3. Disconnect the electrical wiring from the rear of the switch and remove the switch.

4. Installation of the rear wiper switch is the reverse of the removal procedure. Check the switch functions for proper operation.

Headlight Switch

→The headlight switch on all models is incorporated into the combination switch located on the steering column. Therefore, it will be necessary to remove the combination switch in order to gain access to the headlight switch for removal and installation purposes.

REMOVAL & INSTALLATION

◆ **See Figures 82 and 83**

1. Disconnect the negative battery cable.

2. Remove the steering column garnish.

3. Remove the upper and lower steering column covers.

4. Remove the steering wheel as outlined in Section 8.

5. Trace the switch wiring harness to the multi-connector. Push in the lock levers and pull apart the connectors.

6. On vehicles equipped with Toyota Electronic Modulated Suspension (TEMS), remove the steering sensor.

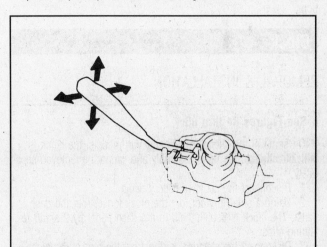

Fig. 82 The combination switch can be moved up and down for the turn signals, as well as to and for the headlights high and low beams

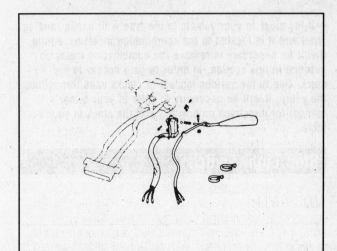

Fig. 83 The common headlight switch has a ball type end which fits into the bracket on the combination switch

7. Unscrew the mounting screws and slide the combination switch from the steering column. For additional details on Combination Switch removal and installation, refer to Section 8.

8. Remove the headlight switch as follows:

   a. Remove the terminals from the headlight switch connector.

   b. Remove the light control switch retaining screws and the light control switch.

   c. Remove the headlight control switch retaining screws and the headlight control switch.

To install:

9. Install the headlight dimmer control switch and retaining screws.

10. Insert the spring into the lever and install the lever with the retaining screw and nut.

11. Place the ball on the spring, position the lever at HI and install the plate.

12. Insure the switch operates smoothly.

13. Attach the terminals to the headlight switch connector.

14. Installation of the combination switch is the reverse of the removal procedure. Check all switch functions for proper operation.

Clock

REMOVAL & INSTALLATION

◆ **See Figures 84 thru 85**

On some of the later Cressida and Van models, the clock is built directly into the radio assembly and cannot be removed separately.

1. Disconnect the negative battery cable.

2. Using a small prytool, pry the clock loose from the dash panel. The clock is usually held to the dash panel by 2 small retaining clips.

3. Disconnect the electrical wiring from the rear of the clock and remove the clock.

4. Installation of the clock is the reverse of the removal procedure. Check the clock functions for proper operation. Reset the clock.

➡**If the clock in your vehicle is the type with hands (analog type) and it is located in the combination meter assembly, it will be necessary to remove the combination meter as outlined in this section, in order to gain access to the clock. Due to the various models of clocks used throughout the years, it will be necessary to refer to your owner's manual for directions on how to reset the clock in your vehicle.**

Stop Light Switch

ADJUSTMENT

1. Remove the instrument lower finish panel and the air duct if required to gain access to the stop light switch.

2. Disconnect the stop light switch.

3. Loosen the switch locknut.

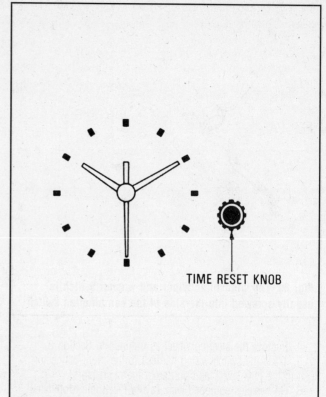

Fig. 84 To set the clock hands on a conventional type clock, pull the knob and turn it clockwise

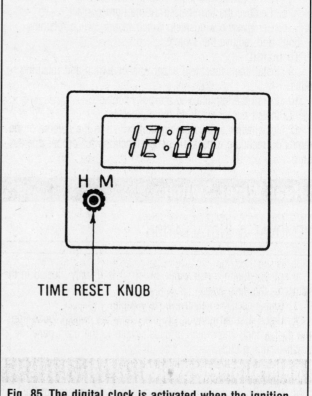

Fig. 85 The digital clock is activated when the ignition key is in the ON or ACC position

4. Turn the stop light switch until the end of the switch lightly contacts the pedal stopper.

5. Hold the switch and tighten the locknut.

6. Connect the switch.

7. Depress the brake pedal and verify that the brake lights illuminate.

8. Install the air duct and the lower finish panel, if removed.

REMOVAL & INSTALLATION

1. Disconnect the negative battery cable.

2. Remove the instrument lower finish panel and the air duct if required to gain access to the stop light switch.

3. Disconnect the stop light switch.

4. Remove the switch mounting nut, then slide the switch from the mounting bracket on the pedal.

To install:

5. Install the switch into the mounting bracket and adjust as described above.

6. Connect the switch.

7. Depress the brake pedal and verify that the brake lights illuminate.

8. Install the air duct and the lower finish panel, if removed.

Clutch Switch

ADJUSTMENT

1. Attempt to start the engine when the clutch pedal is released. The engine should not start.

2. Depress the clutch pedal fully and attempt to start the engine. The engine should start.

3. If the engine does not start, depress the clutch pedal fully. With the clutch pedal depressed, loosen the switch locknut.

4. Use the adjusting nut to turn the switch until the tip of the switch contacts the clutch pedal stop.

5. Tighten the locknut and attempt to start the engine. Re-adjust as necessary.

6. If the switch cannot be adjusted, check the switch continuity with a suitable ohmmeter. There should be continuity between the switch terminals when the switch is on (tip pushed in) and no continuity when the switch is off (tip released). If the continuity is not as specified, replace the switch.

REMOVAL & INSTALLATION

1. Disconnect the negative battery cable.

2. Unplug the switch connector.

3. Remove the switch adjusting nut.

4. Withdraw the switch from the mounting bracket.

5. Installation is the reverse of the removal procedure. Adjust the switch.

Neutral Safety Switch

The shift lever is adjusted properly if the engine will not start in any position other than **N** or **P**.

ADJUSTMENT

▶ **See Figure 86 thru 90**

1. Loosen the neutral start switch bolt. Position the selector in the **N** position.

2. Align the switch shaft groove with the neutral base line which is located on the switch.

3. Tighten the bolt to 48 inch lbs. (5 Nm).

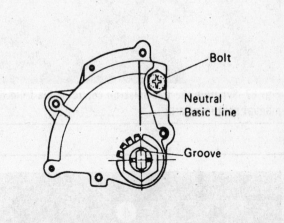

Fig. 86 Align the shaft groove with the base line of the neutral safety switch to align

REMOVAL & INSTALLATION

1. Disconnect the negative battery cable.

2. Unplug the switch wiring connectors.

3. Disconnect the transmission control cable from the manual shift lever.

4. Remove the manual shift lever.

5. Pry the C-washer from the manual shaft nut. Discard the washer and replace with new.

Fig. 86a Remove the bolt retaining the shift lever and the transmission control cable for the neutral switch

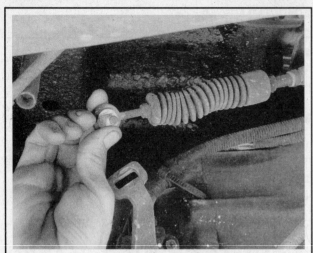

Fig. 87 Separate the transmission control cable from the manual shift lever arm

Fig. 87a Unbolt the manual shift lever . . .

1. Neutral safety switch
2. Manual shaft nut
3. Manual shift lever
4. Transmission control cable

Fig. 88 . . . and separate it from the neutral safety switch

Fig. 88a Remove the manual shaft nut . . .

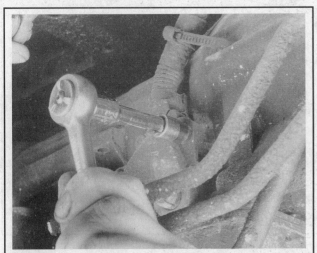

Fig. 89 . . . then remove the retaining bolts from the neutral safety switch

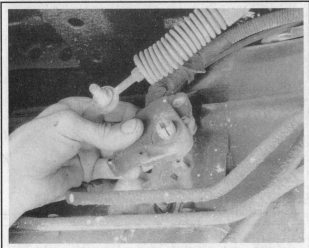

Fig. 90 Pull the neutral safety switch off the automatic transmission and replace as necessary

6. Remove the manual shaft nut and washer.

7. Remove the manual shaft lever packing, if so equipped.

8. Remove the retaining bolts and withdraw the switch from the transaxle case.

9. Installation is the reverse of the removal procedure. Adjust the switch.

Speedometer Cable

REMOVAL & INSTALLATION

▶ **See Figures 91 and 92**

The speedometer cable connects a rotating gear within the transmission to the dashboard speedometer/odometer assembly. The dashboard unit interprets the number of turns made by the cable and displays the information as miles per hour and total mileage.

Assuming that the transmission contains the correct gear for the vehicle, the accuracy of the speedometer depends primarily on tire condition and tire diameter. Badly worn tires (too small in diameter) or over-inflation (too large in diameter) can affect the speedometer reading. Replacement tires of the incorrect overall diameter (such as oversize snow tires) can also affect the readings.

Generally, manufacturers state that speedometer/odometer error of plus or minus 10% is considered normal due to wear and other variables. Stated another way, if you drove the vehicle over a measured 1 mile course and the odometer showed anything between 0.9 and 1.1 miles, the error is considered normal. If you plan to do any checking, always use a measured course such as mileposts on an Interstate highway or turnpike. Never use another vehicle for comparison; the other vehicle's inherent error may further cloud your readings.

The speedometer cable can become dry or develop a kink within its case. As it turns, the ticking or light knocking noise it makes can easily lead an owner to chase engine related problems in error. If such a noise is heard, carefully watch the speedometer needle during the speed range in which the noise is heard. Generally, the needle will jump or deflect each time the cable binds. The needle motion may be very small and hard to notice; a helper in the back seat should look over the driver's shoulder at the speedometer while the driver concentrates on driving.

➡**The slightest bind in the speedometer cable can cause unpredictable behavior in the cruise control system. If the cruise control exhibits intermittent surging or loss of set speed symptoms, check the speedometer cable first.**

Some cables do not attach directly to the speedometer assembly but rather to an electrical pulse generator. These pulses may be used for the meter and mileage signal. Additionally, the electric signals representing the speed of the vehicles can be used by the fuel injection control unit, the cruise control unit and other components.

1. Remove the instrument cluster and disconnect the cable at the speedometer. On some models it may be possible to disconnect the cable by reaching under the dash. Some connectors screw onto the back of the speedometer; others are held by plastic clips.

2. Disconnect the other end of the speedometer cable at the transmission extension housing and pull the cable from its jacket

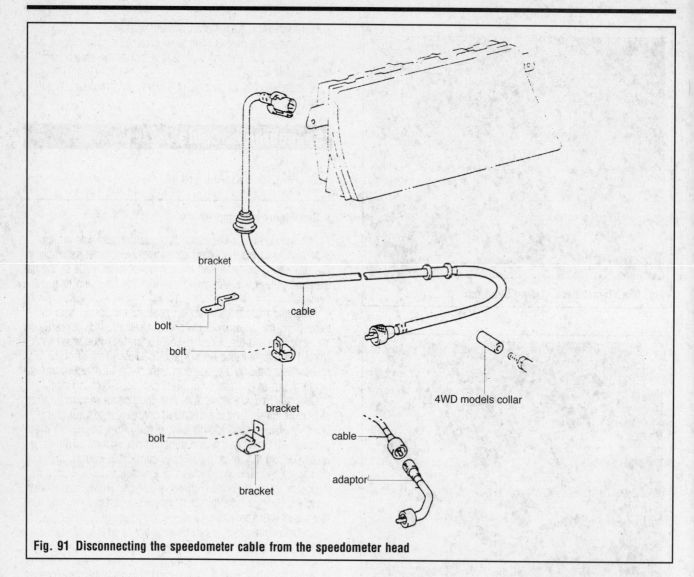

bracket

bolt

cable

bolt

bracket

bolt

bracket

4WD models collar

cable

adaptor

Fig. 91 Disconnecting the speedometer cable from the speedometer head

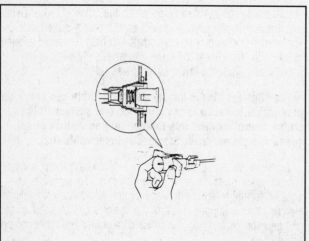

Fig. 92 The plastic retainer must be pushed down to release the speedometer cable on some models

Unscrew the speedometer cable end attached to the transmission

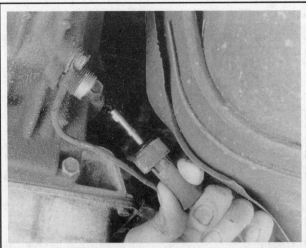

Pull the speedometer cable end out of the transmission extension housing

at the transmission end. If you are replacing the cable because it is broken, don't forget to remove both pieces of broken cable.

To install:

3. Lubricate the new cable with graphite speedometer cable lubricant, and feed it into the cable jacket from the lower end.

4. Connect the cable to the transmission, then to the speedometer. Note that both ends of the cable are square; the ends must fit properly in the fittings.

5. Plug the electrical connector into the instrument cluster, and replace the cluster if it was removed.

LIGHTING

Headlights

REMOVAL & INSTALLATION

♦ See Figure 93

Van

1. Disconnect the negative battery cable.
2. Loosen the retaining screws and remove the front cornering light unit.

3. Remove the headlight door together with the front fog light unit, unplugging the connector.

➡**Before replacement, make sure both the headlight and the fog light switches are off.**

4. If the connector is tight wiggle it. Loosen the retainer screws and remove the sealed beam unit together with the retaining ring. Unplug the connector.

➡**Never attempt to remove the headlight aim adjusting screws.**

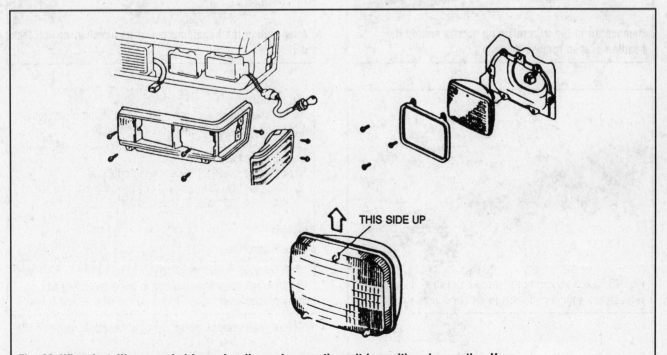

THIS SIDE UP

Fig. 93 When installing a sealed beam headlamp, be sure the unit is positioned correctly—Van

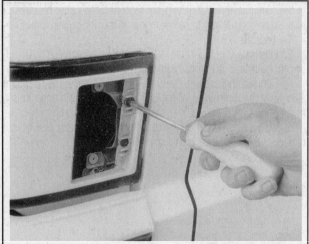

To remove a headlamp on the Van, remove the cornering lamp, then unscrew the headlamp trim

This will enable you to pull the retaining ring off the headlamp

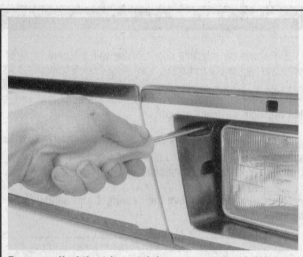

Remove all of the trim retaining screws around the headlamp, then remove the trim

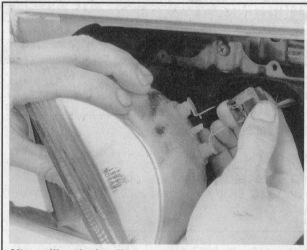

After pulling the headlamp out of its housing, unplug the wiring

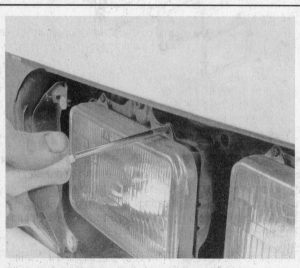

Remove the headlamp retaining ring screws

To install:

5. Install a new sealed beam unit with a single protrusion on the glass face upward, plugging in the connector.
6. Put the retaining ring on the sealed beam unit and tighten the retaining screws.
7. Install the headlight door and fog light unit.
8. Install the front cornering light unit and the retaining screws.
9. Reconnect the negative battery cable.

Cressida

▶ See Figure 94

1. Disconnect the negative battery cable.
2. Working behind the headlight in the engine compartment, unplug the connector while depressing the lock release.

➡Before replacement, make sure the headlight switch is off.

3. If the connector is tight, wiggle it. Turn the bulb retaining ring counterclockwise and remove the bulb.

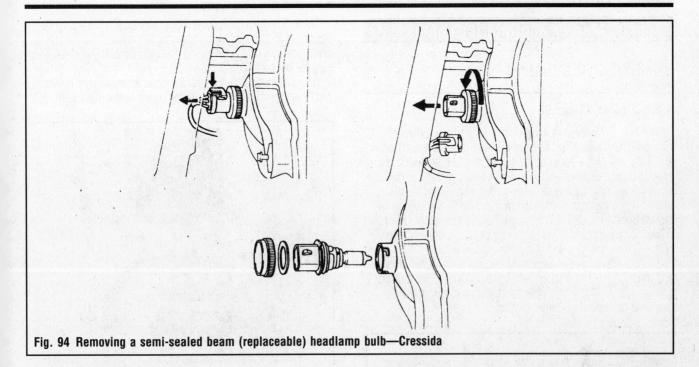

Fig. 94 Removing a semi-sealed beam (replaceable) headlamp bulb—Cressida

The single end bulbs are removed by pressing in and turning counterclockwise. The double end bulbs (or wedge base bulbs) can be pulled straight out of the holder clip.

To install:

4. Align the cutouts of the bulb socket with the protrusions of the headlight body.

➡**Try not to touch the glass portion of these bulbs with your bare hand; if so, clean the glass with alcohol and a clean rag. When replacing a bulb, make sure to use the same bulb numbers and wattage ratings given on the base of the bulb.**

5. Insert the bulb and fasten its retaining ring. Attach the electrical connector.

AIMING

The head lamps should be aimed using a special alignment tool, however this procedure may be used for temporary adjustment. Local regulations may vary regarding head lamp aiming, consult with your local authorities.

1. Verify the tires are at their proper inflation pressure. Clean the head lamp lenses and make sure there are no heavy loads in the trunk. The gas tank should be filled.

2. Position the vehicle on a level surface facing a flat wall 25 ft. (7.7m) away.

3. Measure and record the distance from the floor to the center of the head lamp. Place a strip of tape across the wall at this same height.

4. Place strips of tape on the wall, perpendicular to the first measurement, indicating the vehicle centerline and the centerline of both head lamps.

5. Rock the vehicle side-to-side a few times to allow the suspension to stabilize.

6. Turn the lights on, adjust the head lamps to achieve a high intensity pattern.

Fog Light Bulbs

REMOVAL & INSTALLATION

1. Disconnect the negative battery cable.

2. Loosen the retaining screws and remove the front cornering light unit.

3. Remove the headlight door together with the front fog light unit, unplugging the connector.

➡**Before replacement, make sure both the headlight and the fog light switches are off.**

4. If the connector is tight wiggle it. Remove the rubber cover over the fog light bulb.

5. Release the bulb retaining spring and remove the bulb.

To install:

6. Install a new bulb and the bulb retaining spring. To install the bulb, align the cutouts of the bulb base with the protrusions of the reflector.

7. Install the rubber cover with the tab upward and snuggle on the boss. Insert the connector.

8. Install the headlight door and fog light unit.

9. Install the front cornering light unit and the retaining screws.

10. Reconnect the negative battery cable.

➡**Try not to touch the glass portion of these bulbs with your bare hand, if so clean the glass with alcohol and a clean rag. When replacing a bulb, make sure to use the same bulb numbers and wattage ratings given on the base of bulb. A fog light bulb with the wattage rating of 35 should be used.**

The single end bulbs are removed by pressing in and turning counterclockwise. The double end bulbs or the wedge base bulbs can be pulled straight out of the holder clip.

Signal, Marker and Interior Lamps

REMOVAL & INSTALLATION

▶ **See Figures 95 thru 98**

The lens is removed to allow access to the bulb. External lenses usually have a rubber gasket around them to keep dust and water out of the housing; the gasket must be present and in good condition at reinstallation. Exterior lenses and the larger interior ones are held by one or more screws which must be removed. Once the lens is removed from the body, the bulb is removed from the socket and replaced. For the rear lamps, front marker lamps and some front turn signals, the socket and bulb is removed from the lens with a counter-clockwise turn.

Smaller interior lenses usually fit in place with plastic clips and must be pried or popped out of place. A small, flat, plastic tool is ideal for this job; if other tools are used, care must be taken not to break the lens or the clip.

The bulbs used on Toyotas are all US standard and may be purchased at any auto store or dealer. Because of the variety of lamps used on any vehicle, take the old one with you when shopping for the replacement.

On some models the lens can be replaced separately. On others, you have to replace the lens with the plastic backing attached.

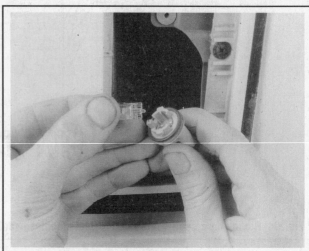

Fig. 95b **Pull the bulb straight out of its socket. Inspect the bulb, and replace if necessary**

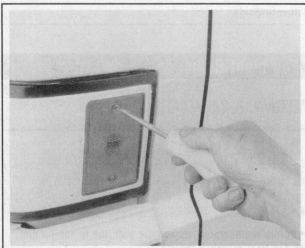

Fig. 95 **Cornering lamps are screwed into the headlamp trim bezel on the side of the vehicle**

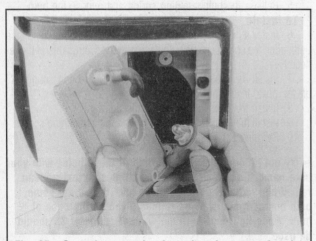

Fig. 95a **Once the cornering lamp lens is removed, twist the socket assembly 1/4 turn counterclockwise, then separate it from the lens**

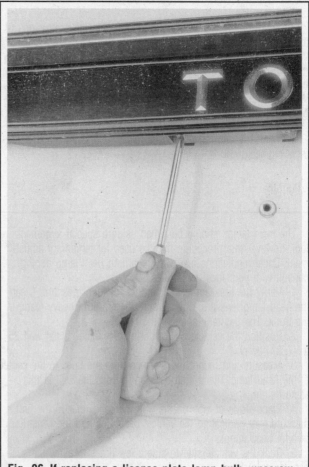

Fig. 96 **If replacing a license plate lamp bulb, unscrew the lens . . .**

Fig. 96a . . . then pull the assembly out

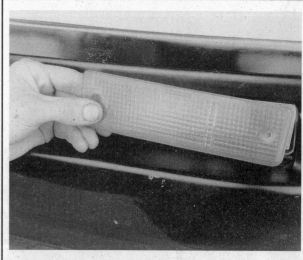

Fig. 97a Remove the turn signal lens, then . . .

Fig. 96b If the license plate lamp bulb needs replacement, gently depress and turn slightly, then pull it out of the socket

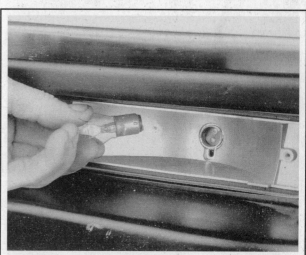

Fig. 97b . . . gently depress and turn the bulb slightly counterclockwise, then pull it out

Fig. 97 Turn signal bulbs can be replaced by removing the lens mounting screws

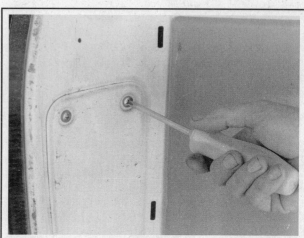

Fig 98 Tail lamps on the Van models are replaced by removing the inner metal panel on the interior of the vehicle

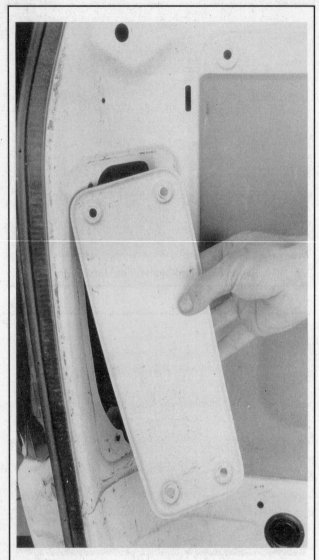

Fig 98a The metal panel covers all of the tail lamp wiring and houses the lamp assembly—Van

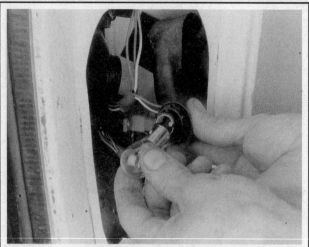

Fig 98c . . . then gently depress the bulb and twist 1/8 turn counterclockwise before pulling it out

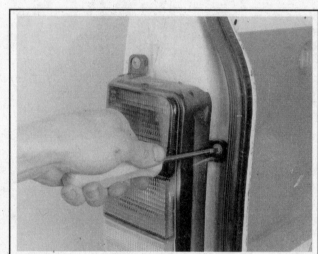

Fig 98d From the exterior with the liftgate open, remove the tail lamp retaining screws

1. Bulb socket
2. Bulb
3. Tail lamp housing

Fig 98b To replace a tail lamp bulb, twist the socket assembly counterclockwise, and remove it from the housing . . .

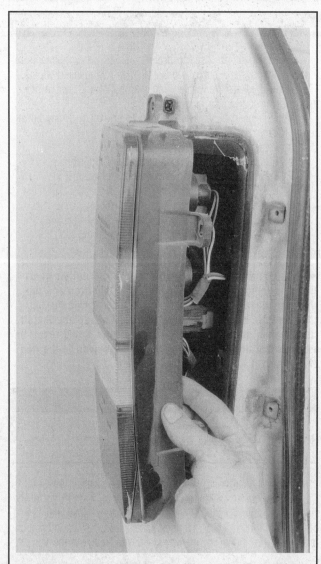

Fig 98e Pull the tail lamp assembly off the rear body panel . . .

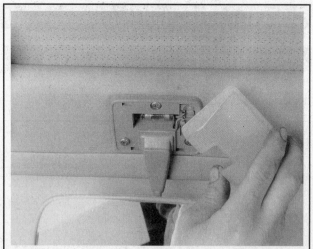

When replacing the interior map light bulb on some models, unsnap the lens from the rear view mirror

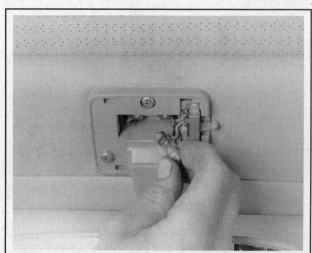

With your fingers, gently spread the sockets clips and pull the bulb out

Fig 98f . . . and unplug the harness attached to the lamp—Van

CIRCUIT PROTECTION

Circuit Breakers

RESETTING & REPLACEMENT

▶ **See Figures 99 and 100**

Circuit breakers operate when a circuit overload exceeds its rated amperage. Once operated, they automatically reset after a certain period of time.

There are two kinds of circuit breaker, as previously mentioned, one type will reset itself. The second will not reset itself until the problem in the circuit has been repaired.

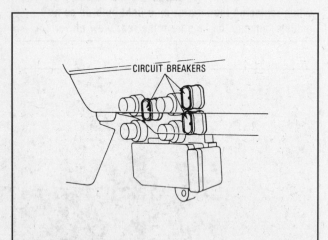

Fig. 99 Circuit breakers are usually located in the fuse block, either in the engine compartment or inside the vehicle

Circuit breakers are used to protect the various components of the electrical system, such as headlights and windshield wipers. The circuit breakers are located either in the control switch or mounted on or near the fuse panel.

If a circuit breaker has been tripped (overloaded) it may be reset as follows:

   a. Remove the circuit breaker in question.
   b. Unlock the stopper and pull out the circuit breaker.
   c. Insert a needle into the reset hole and push it in.
   d. Using a suitable ohmmeter, check to be sure that there is continuity on both sides of the circuit breaker.
   e. If there is no continuity, replace the circuit breaker.
   f. Assemble the circuit breaker in its case and install the circuit breaker.

➡**If the circuit breaker continues to trip (cut out), a short circuit is indicated. The system must be checked and the short circuit repaired. Do not ever try to override the short circuit with a higher amp circuit breaker or replace the circuit breaker with a solid metal object. This would result in an electrical fire in the wiring harness involved in the line of that circuit breaker.**

Turn Signal and Hazard Flasher

REPLACEMENT

The turn signal/hazard warning flasher relay on the 1983–88 Cressida is located under the instrument panel, to the right of the steering column. On the 1989–90 Cressida this same relay is located behind the driver's side kick panel on top of the integration relay. The turn signal/hazard warning flasher relay on the Van

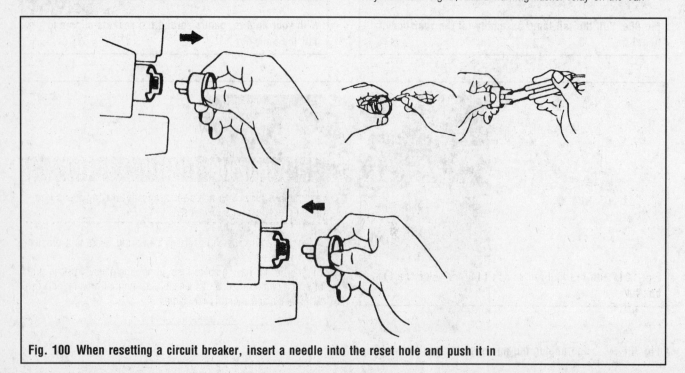

Fig. 100 When resetting a circuit breaker, insert a needle into the reset hole and push it in

models is located under the right-hand side of the instrument panel above the left side of the fuse/relay block.

To replace a relay or flasher, simply pull the relay or flasher out of the fuse block by hand and place the new one in the same position.

Fuses

REPLACEMENT

▶ **See Figures 101, 102 and 103**

The fuse panels on the Cressida are located behind the passenger's side kick panel, the driver's side kick panel and in the engine compartment near the driver's side strut tower. The fuse panel on the Van models is located under the right-hand side of the instrument panel.

Fuses are a one-time circuit protection. If a circuit is overloaded or shorts, the fuse will blow thus protecting the circuit. A fuse will continue to blow until the circuit is repaired.

1. Turn the ignition switch off and open the fuse box lid.

   a. If any light or electrical component does not work, your vehicle may have a blown fuse.

   b. Determine which fuse may be causing the problem. The lid of the fuse box shows the name of the circuit for each fuse.

2. Be sure the inoperative component is off. Pull a suspected fuse straight out with the pull-out tool and inspect it. If the fuse has blown, push a new one into the clips.

   a. Look carefully at the fuse. If the thin wire is broken, the

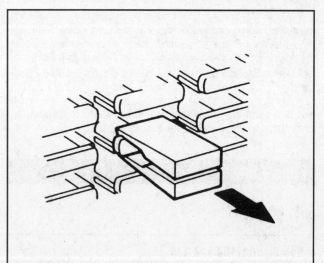

Fig. 102 Remove the suspected fuse with the pull-out tool and inspect it

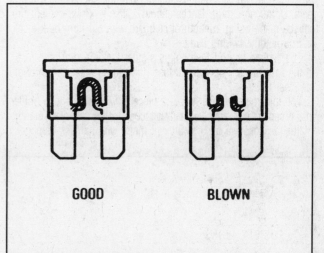

GOOD   BLOWN

Fig. 103 A fuse can be checked by looking at the element and inspecting it for a break

fuse has blown. If you are not sure or if it is too dark to see, try replacing the suspected fuse with one you know is good.

   b. Install only a fuse with an amperage rating designated on the fuse box lid.

❊❊ WARNING

Never use a fuse with a higher amperage rating nor some other object in place of a fuse.

   c. If the new fuse immediately blows out, there is a problem with the electrical system.

If you do not have a spare fuse, in an emergency you can pull out a fuse, which may be dispensable for normal driving, and use it if its amperage rating is the same.

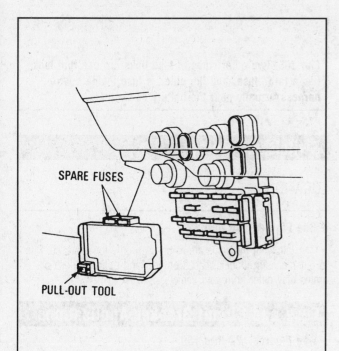

SPARE FUSES

PULL-OUT TOOL

Fig. 101 Turn the ignition switch OFF and open the fuse box lid

If you cannot use one of the same amperage, use one with a lower than, but as close as possible to, the same rating. If the amperage is lower than that specified, the fuse might blow out again but this does not indicate anything wrong. Be sure to get a correct fuse as soon as possible and return the substitute to its original clips.

➡**It is a good idea to purchase a set of spare fuses and keep them in your vehicle for emergencies.**

Fuse Link

REPLACEMENT

◗ See Figures 104 and 105

One type of fuse link is a short length of special, Hypalon (high temperature) insulated wire, integral with the engine compartment wiring harness and should not be confused with standard wire. It is several wire gauges smaller than the circuit which it protects. Under no circumstances should a fuse link replacement repair be made using a length of standard wire cut from bulk stock or from another wiring harness.

The second type of fuse link is similar looking to a large fuse in the fuse block. This type of fuse link can be inspected through the clear top.

The third type of fuse link is a piece of wire with a fuse holder in the center of it, which usually attaches to the battery or starter.

Fusible links are used to prevent major wire harness damage

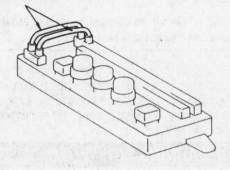

Fig. 104 One type of fuse link is a piece of special wire made to withstand the electrical current going through the circuit

in the event of a short circuit or an overload condition in the wiring circuits that are normally not fused, due to carrying high amperage loads or because of their locations within the wiring harness. Each fusible link is of a fixed value for a specific electrical load and should a fusible link fail, the cause of the failure must be determined and repaired prior to installing a new fusible link of the same value.

The fusible link can be located near the battery and or starter motor and also may be incorporated into the fuse block.

➡**For a more extensive look at the computers, relays and switch locations, refer to the illustration provided in this section.**

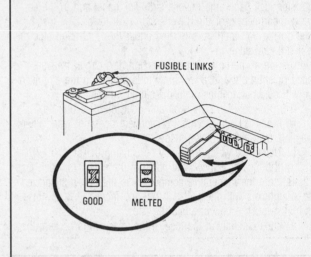

Fig. 105 Two other types of fuse links are one that looks like a large fuse, and the other, a fuse inside a wire harness, usually near the battery or starter

Switch and Relay

LOCATIONS

◗ See Figures 106 thru 121

The following diagrams are to be used only for reference. Due to differences in models, based on year and options, these diagrams may differ from your vehicle.

Fuse and Circuit Breaker Applications

◗ See Figures 122 thru 130

The following diagrams are to be used as a reference for locations. To obtain the exact fuse type, look in your owner's manual or on the label under the lid of each fuse box.

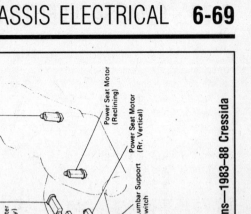

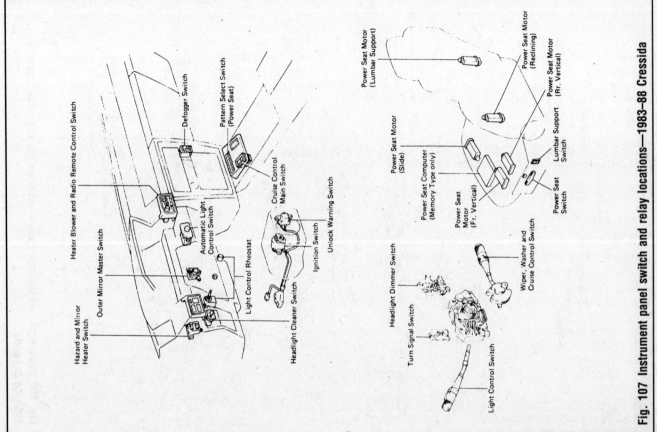

Fig. 107 Instrument panel switch and relay locations—1983–88 Cressida

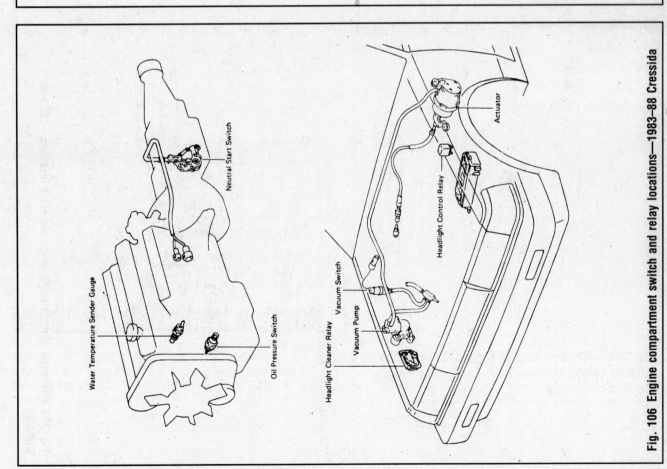

Fig. 106 Engine compartment switch and relay locations—1983–88 Cressida

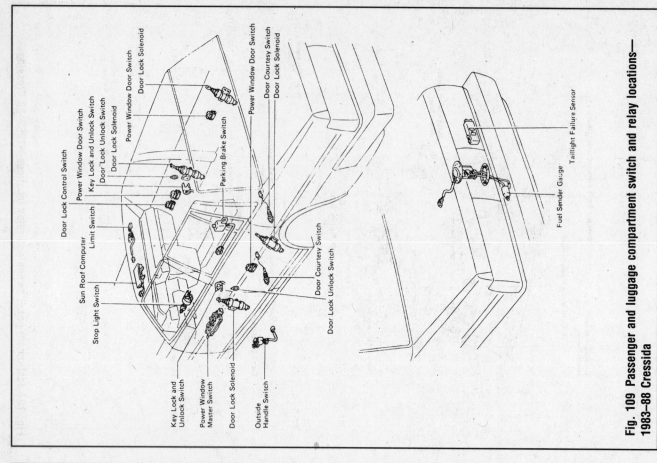

Fig. 109 Passenger and luggage compartment switch and relay locations—1983–88 Cressida

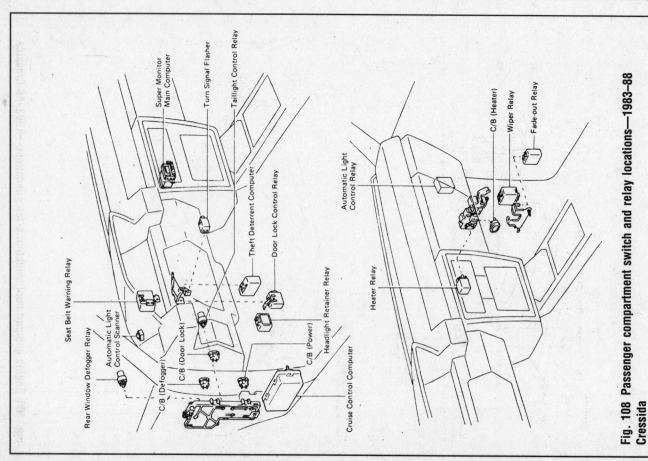

Fig. 108 Passenger compartment switch and relay locations—1983–88 Cressida

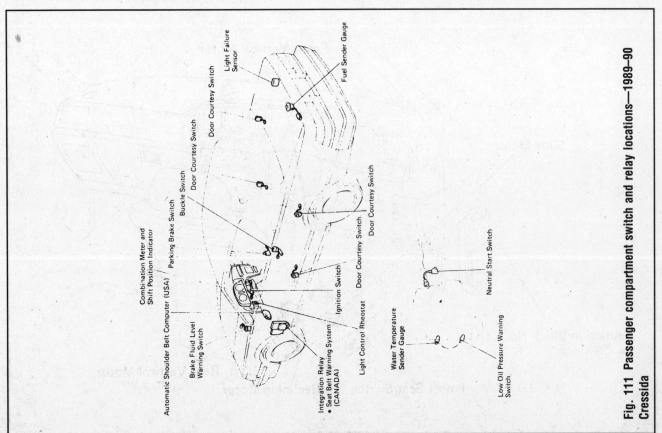

Fig. 111 Passenger compartment switch and relay locations—1989–90 Cressida

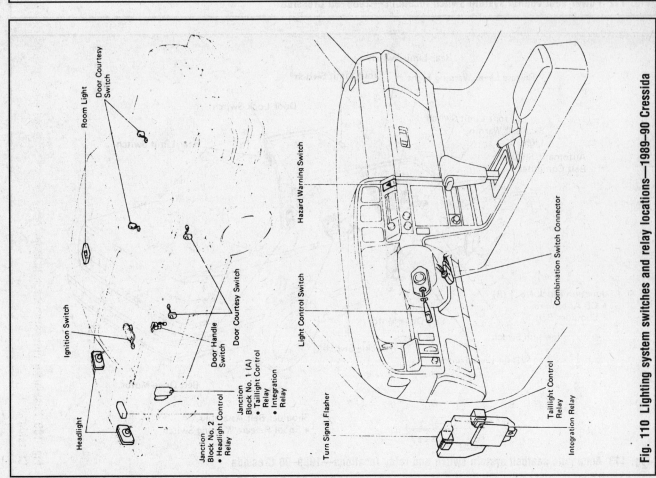

Fig. 110 Lighting system switches and relay locations—1989–90 Cressida

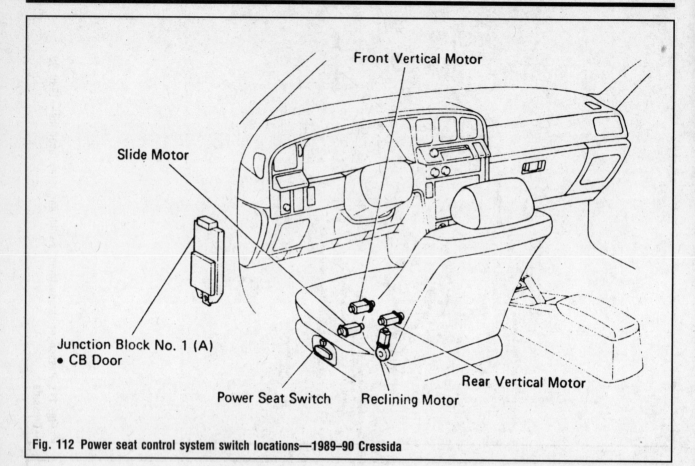

Fig. 112 Power seat control system switch locations—1989–90 Cressida

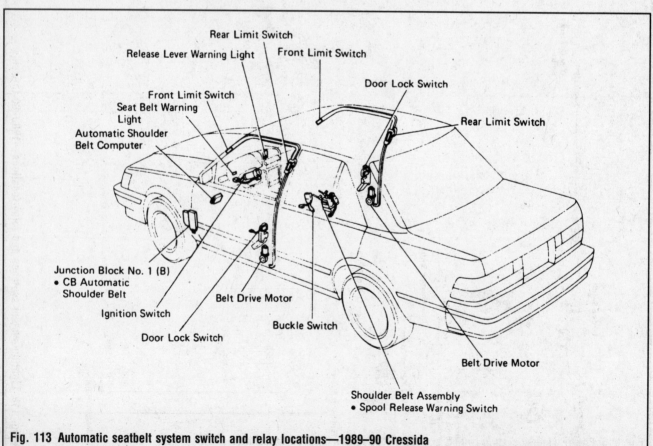

Fig. 113 Automatic seatbelt system switch and relay locations—1989–90 Cressida

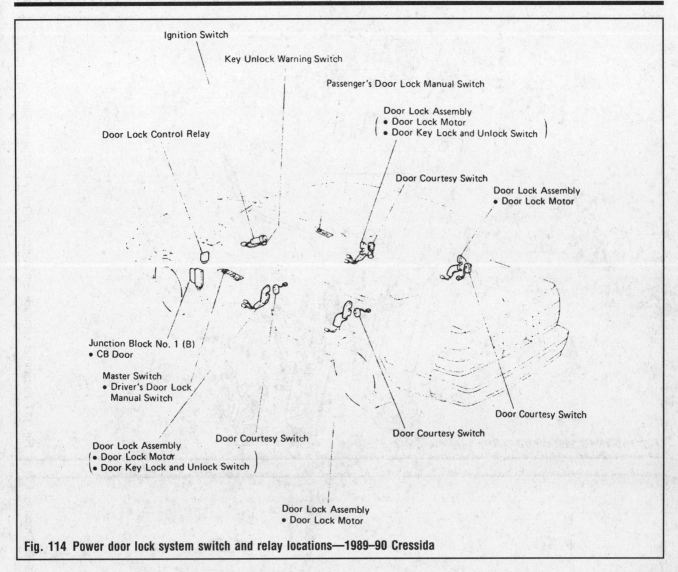

Ignition Switch

Key Unlock Warning Switch

Passenger's Door Lock Manual Switch

Door Lock Assembly
• Door Lock Motor
• Door Key Lock and Unlock Switch)

Door Lock Control Relay

Door Courtesy Switch

Door Lock Assembly
• Door Lock Motor

Junction Block No. 1 (B)
• CB Door

Master Switch
• Driver's Door Lock
  Manual Switch

Door Courtesy Switch

Door Lock Assembly
(• Door Lock Motor
(• Door Key Lock and Unlock Switch)

Door Courtesy Switch

Door Courtesy Switch

Door Lock Assembly
• Door Lock Motor

Fig. 114 Power door lock system switch and relay locations—1989–90 Cressida

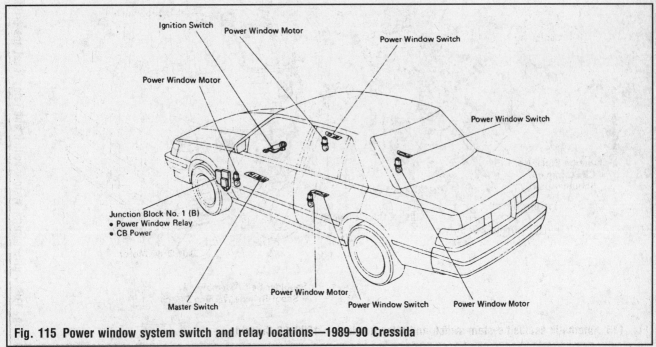

Ignition Switch   Power Window Motor

Power Window Switch

Power Window Motor

Power Window Switch

Junction Block No. 1 (B)
• Power Window Relay
• CB Power

Master Switch

Power Window Motor

Power Window Switch   Power Window Motor

Fig. 115 Power window system switch and relay locations—1989–90 Cressida

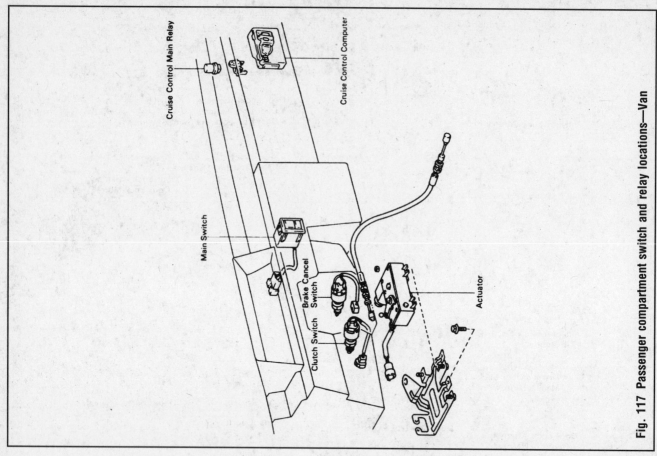

Fig. 117 Passenger compartment switch and relay locations—Van

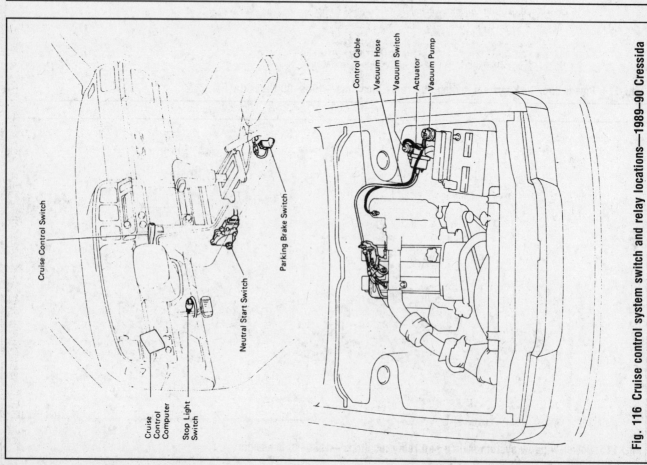

Fig. 116 Cruise control system switch and relay locations—1989—90 Cressida

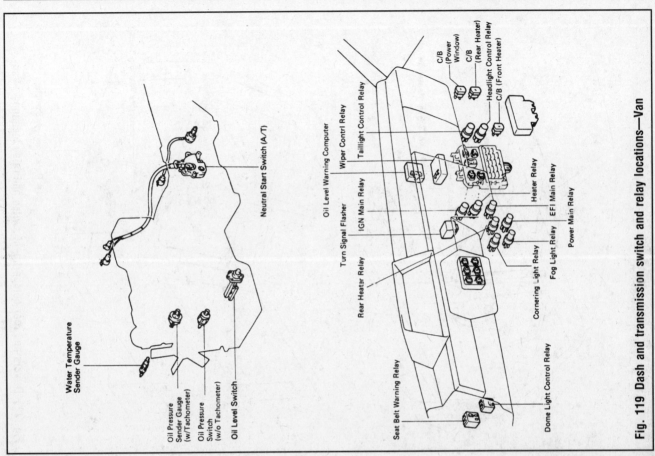

Fig. 119 Dash and transmission switch and relay locations—Van

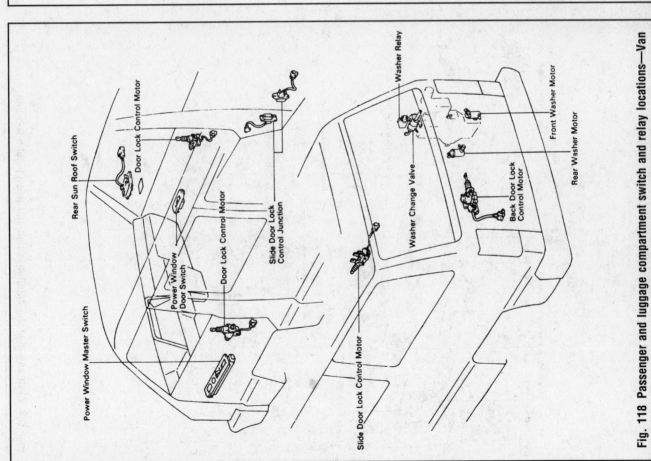

Fig. 118 Passenger and luggage compartment switch and relay locations—Van

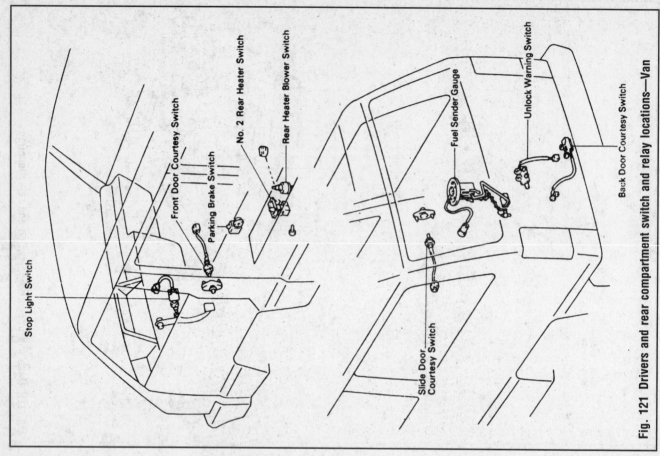

Fig. 121 Drivers and rear compartment switch and relay locations—Van

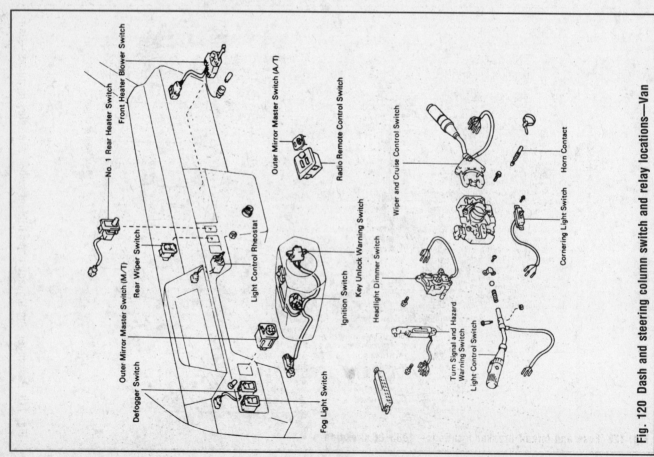

Fig. 120 Dash and steering column switch and relay locations—Van

Fuses

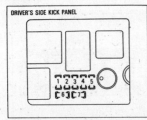

DRIVER'S SIDE KICK PANEL

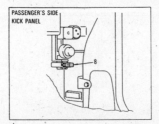

PASSENGER'S SIDE KICK PANEL

ENGINE COMPARTMENT

1.TURN 7.5 A: Turn signal lights and turn signal indicator lights

2.CRUISE CONT.L 15 A: Automatic transmission overdrive solenoid, cruise control system, power antenna, and rear window wiper and washer

3.GAUGES 7.5 A: Air conditioner main relay, automatic shoulder belt control system, back-up lights, brake system warning light, engine temperature gauge, fuel gauge, low engine coolant level warning light, low fuel level warning light, low oil pressure warning light, low windshield washer fluid level warning light, oil pressure gauge, power window relay, rear light failure warning light, seat belt reminder light and buzzer (Canada), seat belt warning light and buzzer (U.S.A.), tachometer, voltmeter, engine electrical system warning light and automatic transmission control system

4. DOME 5 A: Clock, interior light, luggage compartment light, open door warning light, personal lights, power antenna, trunk room light and vanity light

5. IGN 7.5 A: Discharge warning light and electronic fuel injection control system

6. RADIO 7.5 A: Clock, radio and stereo cassette tape player

7. CIG 15 A: Cigarette lighter and power antenna

8. 10 A: Air conditioner

9. CHARGE 7.5 A: Alternator (L terminal)

10. ENGINE 15 A: Alternator (IG terminal)

11. HAZ.HORN 15 A: Emergency flashers, emergency flasher indicator lights, horns and radio

12. TAIL 15 A: Automatic transmission selector light, glovebox light, instrument panel lights, license plate lights, parking lights, rear light failure warning light, rear side marker lights and tail lights

13. HEAD (RH) 15 A: Right-hand headlights and high beam indicator light

14. HEAD (LH) 15 A: Left-hand headlights and high beam indicator light

15. EFI.ECD 15 A: Electronic fuel injection control system

16. WIPER 20 A: Windshield wipers and washer

17. STOP 15 A: Stop lights

Fig. 122 Fuse and circuit breaker locations—1983–84 Cressida

Fuses and circuit breakers

DRIVER'S SIDE KICK PANEL

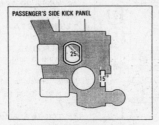

PASSENGER'S SIDE KICK PANEL

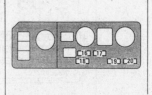

ENGINE COMPARTMENT

Fuses

1. RADIO 7.5 A: Radio, cassette tape player, Compact Disc player, power antenna, power rear view mirrors

2. IGN 7.5 A: Discharge warning light, emission control system, electronic fuel injection system

3. ECU + B 15 A: Power rear view mirrors, automatic light control system

4. STOP 15 A: Stop lights, cruise control system cancel device, anti-lock brake system

5. TAIL 15 A: Tail lights, parking lights, side marker lights, license plate lights, instrument panel lights, glovebox light

6. CIG 15 A: Cigarette lighter, clock, shift lock system

7. ST 7.5 A: Electronic fuel injection system, cruise control system, shift lock system

8. ECU-IG 15 A: Charging system, cruise control system, environmental control system, power steering control system, shift lock system, automatic light control system

9. FOG 15 A: No circuit

10. ENG 15 A: Charging system, discharge warning light

11. WIPER 20 A: Windshield wipers and washer, headlight cleaner

12. TURN 7.5 A: Turn signal lights

13. GAUGE 7.5 A: Gauges and meters, warning lights and buzzers (except discharge and open door warning lights), back-up lights, electronically controlled automatic transmission system, automatic transmission overdrive system, rear window defogger, power door lock system, power windows, automatic shoulder belts

14. HTR-MIR 10 A: Rear view mirror heater

15. 10 A: Environmental cooling system

16. HEAD (RH) 15 A: Right-hand headlight

17. HEAD (LH) 15 A: Left-hand headlight

18. HAZ-HORN 15 A: Emergency flashers, horns

19. DOME 20 A: Interior light, personal lights, door courtesy lights, ignition switch light, digital clock display, open door warning light, trunk room light, power rear view mirrors, electric sun roof, automatic light control system, radio, cassette tape player, Compact Disc player, power antenna

20. EFI 20 A: Electronic fuel injection system, emission control system

Circuit breakers

21. 30 A: Power windows, electric sun roof

22. 30 A: Rear window defogger

23. 30 A: Automatic shoulder belts

24. 20 A: Power door lock system

25. 40 A: Environmental control system

Fig. 123 Fuse and circuit breaker locations—1985–88 Cressida

Fuses and circuit breakers

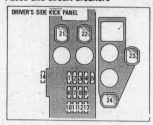
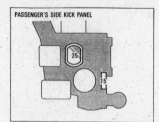

Fuses

1. RADIO 7.5 A: Radio, cassette tape player, Compact Disc player, power antenna, power rear view mirrors

2. IGN 7.5 A: Discharge warning light, emission control system, electronic fuel injection system

3. ECU + B 15 A: Power rear view mirrors, automatic light control system

4. STOP 15 A: Stop lights, cruise control system cancel device, anti-lock brake system

5. TAIL 15 A: Tail lights, parking lights, side marker lights, license plate lights, instrument panel lights, glovebox light

6. CIG 15 A: Cigarette lighter, clock, shift lock system

7. ST 7.5 A: Electronic fuel injection system, cruise control system, shift lock system

8. ECU-IG 15 A: Charging system, cruise control system, environmental control system, power steering control system, shift lock system, automatic light control system

9. FOG 15 A: No circuit

10. ENG 15 A: Charging system, discharge warning light

11. WIPER 20 A: Windshield wipers and washer, headlight cleaner

12. TURN 7.5 A: Turn signal lights

13. GAUGE 7.5 A: Gauges and meters, warning lights and buzzers (except discharge and open door warning lights), back-up lights, electronically controlled automatic transmission system, automatic transmission overdrive system, rear window defogger, power door lock system, power windows, automatic shoulder belts

14. HTR-MIR 10 A: Rear view mirror heater

15. 10 A: Environmental cooling system

16. HEAD (RH) 15 A: Right-hand headlight

17. HEAD (LH) 15 A: Left-hand headlight

18. HAZ-HORN 15 A: Emergency flashers, horns

19. DOME 20 A: Interior light, personal lights, door courtesy lights, ignition switch light, digital clock display, open door warning light, trunk room light, power rear view mirrors, electric sun roof, automatic light control system, radio, cassette tape player, Compact Disc player, power antenna

20. EFI 20 A: Electronic fuel injection system, emission control system

Circuit breakers

21. 30 A: Power windows, electric sun roof

22. 30 A: Rear window defogger

23. 30 A: Automatic shoulder belts

24. 20 A: Power door lock system

25. 40 A: Environmental control system

Fig. 124 Fuse and circuit breaker locations—1989–90 Cressida

Fuses and circuit breakers

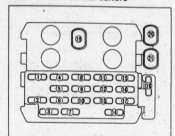

Fuses

1. IGN 7.5 A: Discharge warning light, EFI main relay, ignition main relay

2. ENGINE 7.5 A: Alternator voltage regulator (IG terminal)

3. RADIO 7.5 A: Clock (digital type), radio, stereo cassette tape player

4. STOP 15 A: Cruise control system, stop lights

5. DOME 7.5 A: Clock, interior lights, key reminder buzzer, open door warning light, personal lights, door courtesy lights, tailgate light, step light

6. A.C 15 A: Air conditioner, cooler, front heater main relay, rear heater main relay

7. CIG 15 A: Cigarette lighters

8. GAUGE 7.5 A: Back-up lights, brake system warning light, engine temperature gauge, fuel gauge, low engine coolant level warning light, low engine oil level warning light, low fuel level warning light, oil pressure gauge, overdrive main relay, power window and electric sun roof relay, seat belt reminder light and buzzer, tachometer, unlocked tailgate reminder light

9. ECU-IG 10 A: Cruise control system

10. WIPER 20 A: Rear window wiper and washer, windshield wipers and washer

11. CHARGE 7.5 A: Electronic fuel injection control system

12. DEFOG 15 A: Rear window defogger, rear window defogger indicator light

13. TURN 7.5 A: Turn signal indicator lights, turn signal lights

14. HAZ-HORN 15 A: Emergency flashers, horns

15. TAIL 15 A: Automatic transmission shift position indicator light, instrument panel lights, license plate lights, parking lights, side marker lights, tail lights

16. HEAD (LH) 15 A: High beam indicator light, left-hand headlights

17. HEAD (RH) 15 A: High beam indicator light, right-hand headlights

18. EFI 15 A: Electronic fuel injection control system

Circuit breakers

19. 30 A: Front heater blower motor

20. 20 A: Electric sun roof, power windows, power door lock

21. 20 A: Rear heater blower motor

Fig. 125 Fuse and circuit breaker locations—1983–86 Van

Fuses and circuit breakers

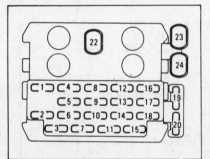

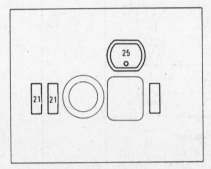

Fuses

1. IGN 7.5 A: Charging system, discharge warning light, emission control system, electronic fuel injection system

2. ENGINE 7.5 A: Charging system, emission control system

3. RADIO 7.5 A: Radio, cassette tape player, graphic equalizer

4. STOP 15 A: Stop lights, cruise control system cancel device

5. DOME 7.5 A: Interior lights, personal lights, door courtesy lights, tailgate light, step light, clock, open door warning light

6. A.C 15 A: Environmental cooling system

7. CIG 15 A: Cigarette lighter

8. GAUGE 7.5 A: Gauges and meters, warning lights and buzzer (except discharge and open door warning lights), back-up lights, automatic transmission overdrive system, electric sun roof, power windows

9. ECU. IG 10 A: Cruise control system

10. WIPER 20 A: Windshield wipers and washer, rear window wiper and washer

11. FOG 15 A: Front fog lights

12. CHARGE 7.5 A: Charging system, discharge warning light, electronic fuel injection system

13. DEFOG 15 A: Rear window defogger

14. TURN 7.5 A: Turn signal lights

15. HAZ-HORN 15 A: Emergency flashers, horns

16. TAIL 15 A: Tail lights, parking lights, license plate lights, front cornering lights, instrument panel lights

17. HEAD (LH) 15 A: Left-hand headlights

18. HEAD (RH) 15 A: Right-hand headlights

19. EFI 15 A: Electronic fuel injection system

20. ST 15 A: Starter system

21. 15 A: Environmental cooling system

Circuit breakers

22. 30 A: Environmental control system (front)

23. 20 A: Electric sun roof, power windows, power door lock system

24. 20 A: Environmental control system (rear)

25. 30 A: Environmental cooling system (four-wheel drive models only)

Fig. 126 Fuse and circuit breaker locations—1987–89 Van

WIRING DIAGRAMS

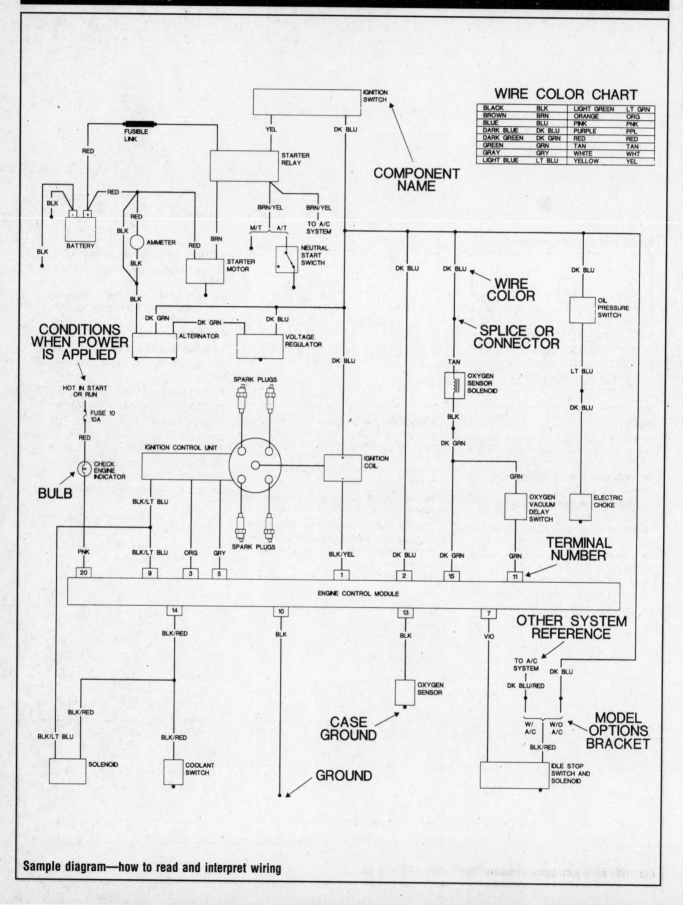

Sample diagram—how to read and interpret wiring

WIRING DIAGRAM SYMBOLS

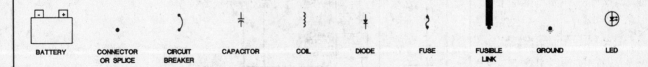

BATTERY   CONNECTOR OR SPLICE   CIRCUIT BREAKER   CAPACITOR   COIL   DIODE   FUSE   FUSIBLE LINK   GROUND   LED

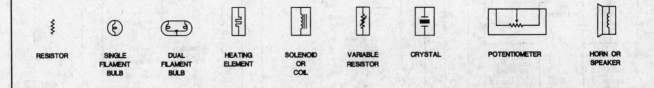

RESISTOR   SINGLE FILAMENT BULB   DUAL FILAMENT BULB   HEATING ELEMENT   SOLENOID OR COIL   VARIABLE RESISTOR   CRYSTAL   POTENTIOMETER   HORN OR SPEAKER

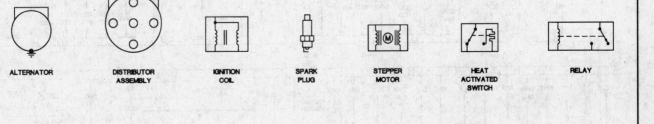

ALTERNATOR   DISTRIBUTOR ASSEMBLY   IGNITION COIL   SPARK PLUG   STEPPER MOTOR   HEAT ACTIVATED SWITCH   RELAY

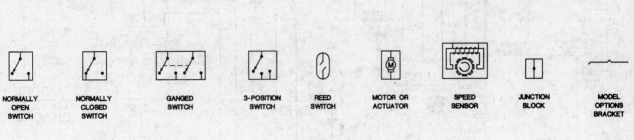

NORMALLY OPEN SWITCH   NORMALLY CLOSED SWITCH   GANGED SWITCH   3-POSITION SWITCH   REED SWITCH   MOTOR OR ACTUATOR   SPEED SENSOR   JUNCTION BLOCK   MODEL OPTIONS BRACKET

Common wiring diagram symbols

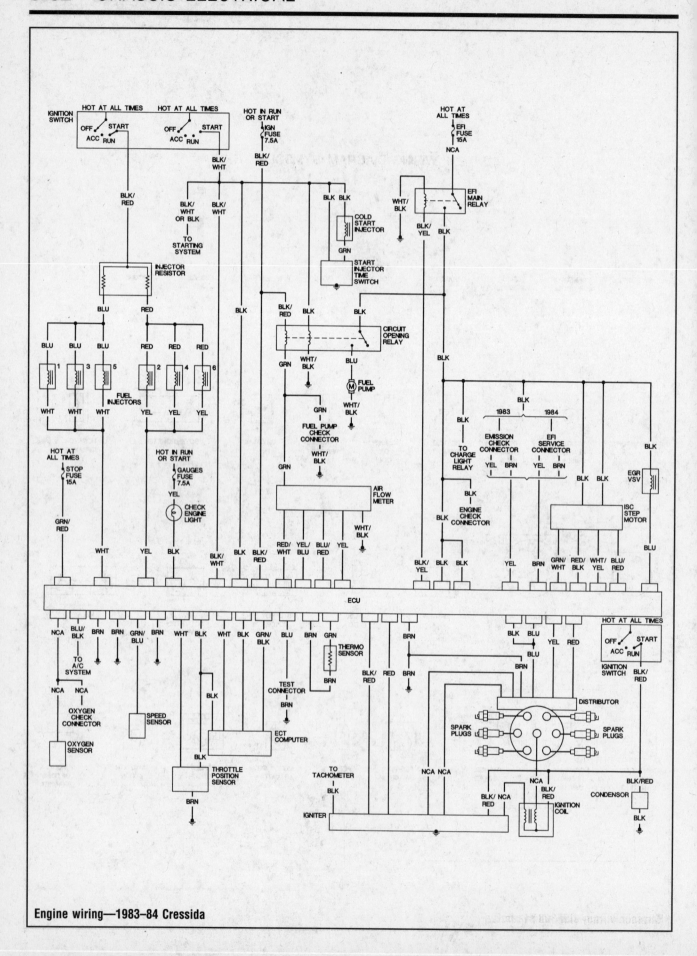

Engine wiring—1983–84 Cressida

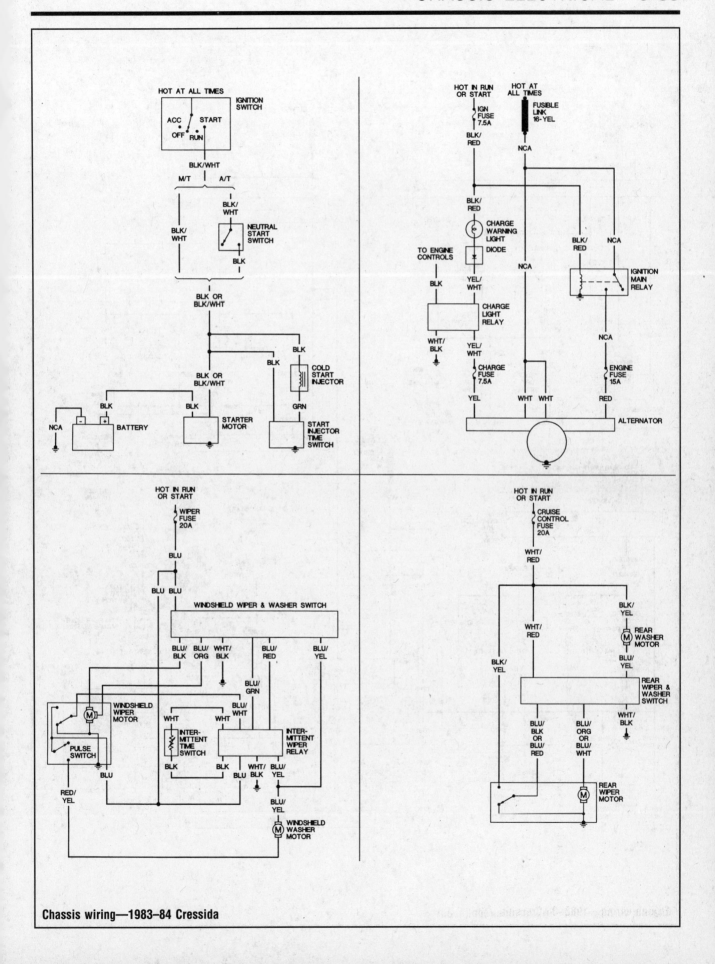

Chassis wiring—1983–84 Cressida

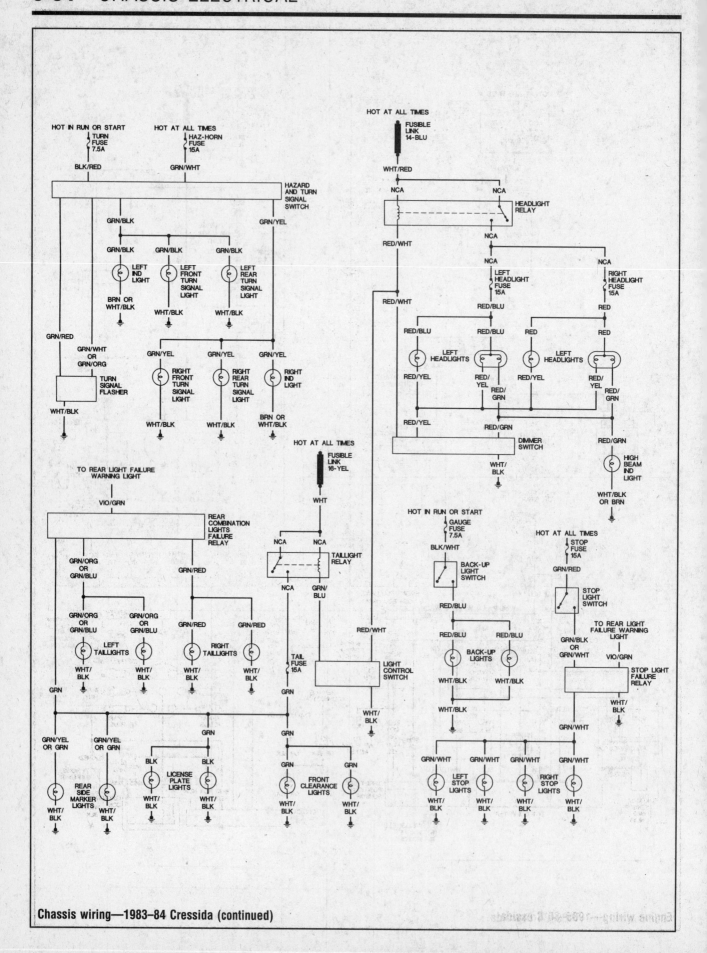

Chassis wiring—1983-84 Cressida (continued)

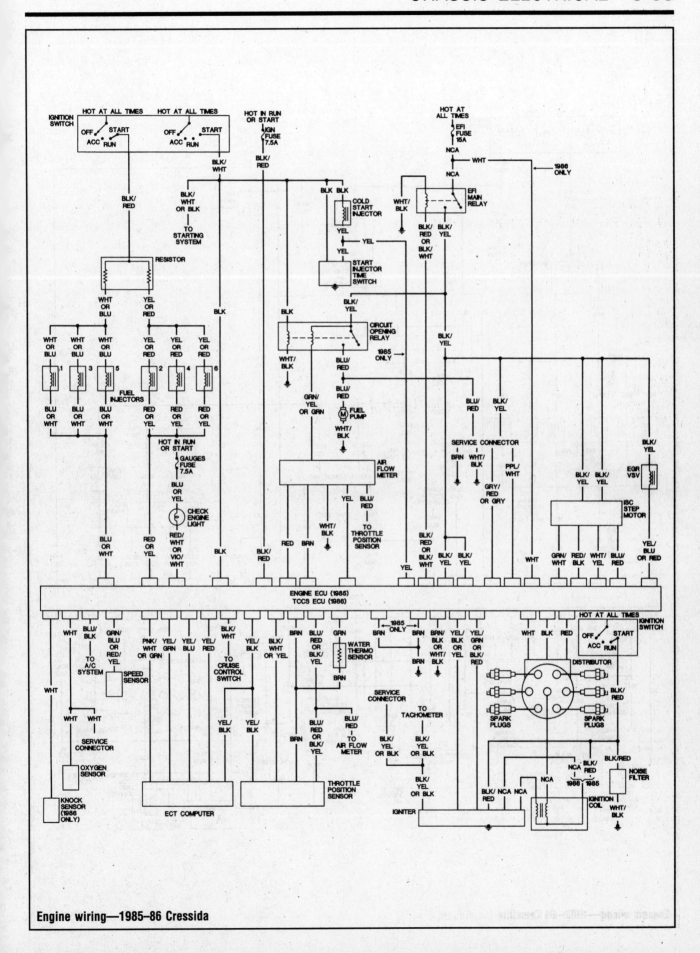

Engine wiring—1985–86 Cressida

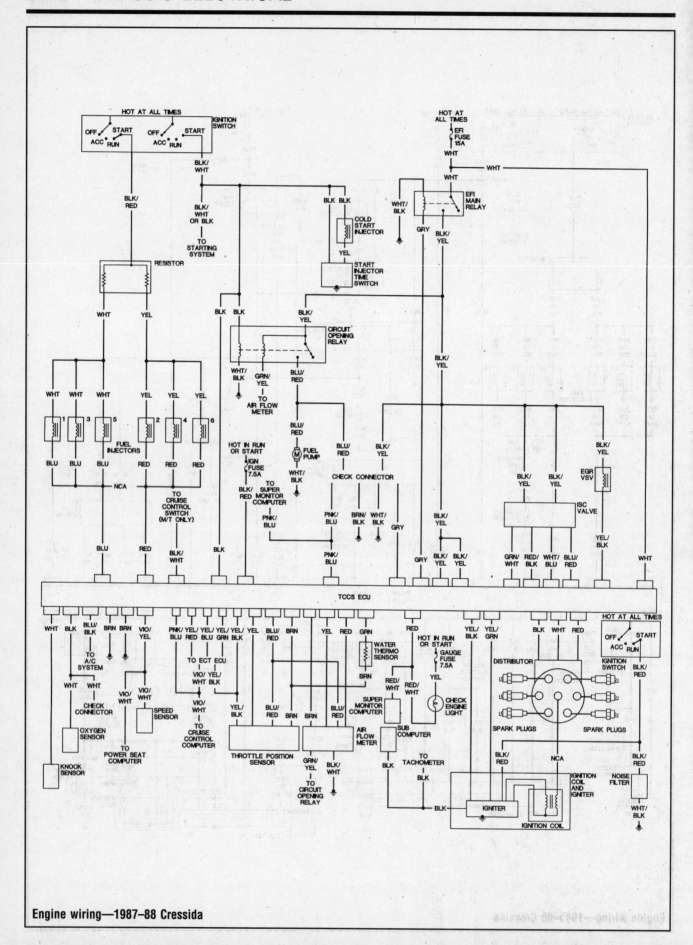

Engine wiring—1987–88 Cressida

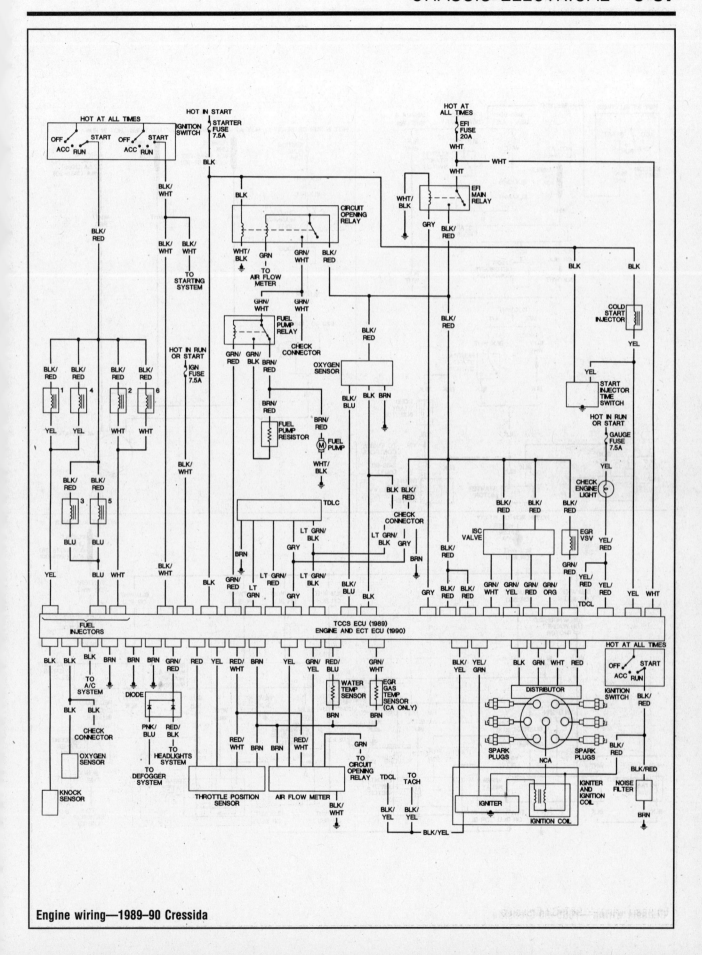

Engine wiring—1989–90 Cressida

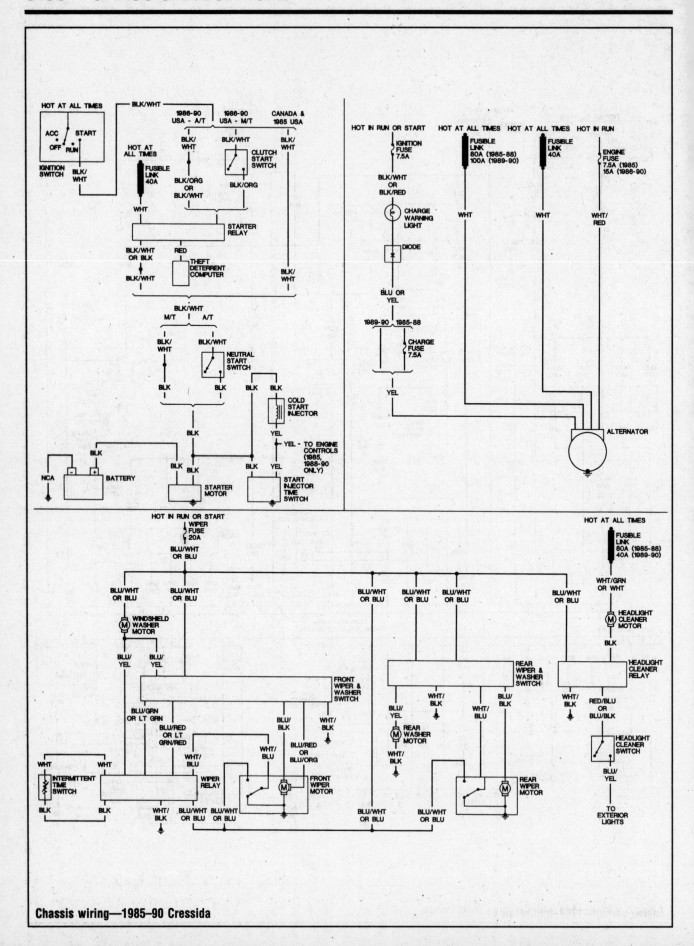

Chassis wiring—1985–90 Cressida

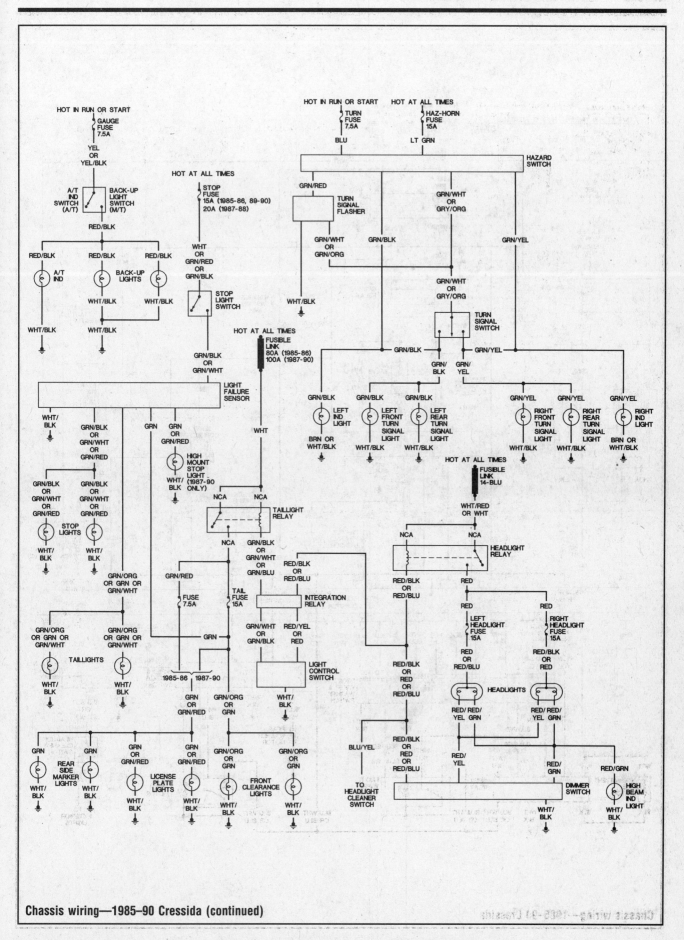

Chassis wiring—1985–90 Cressida (continued)

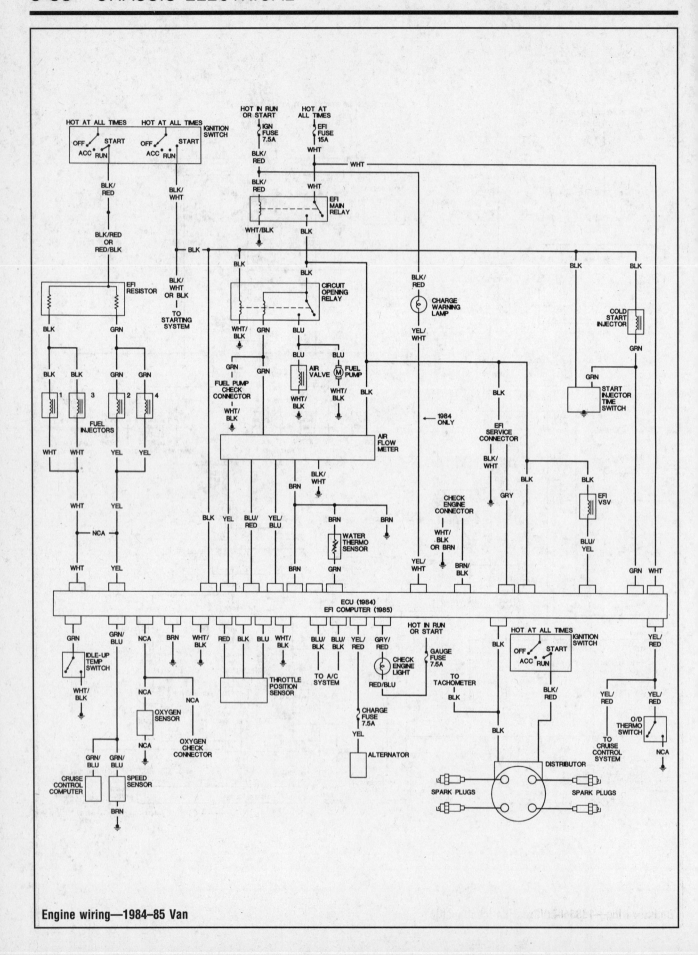

Engine wiring—1984-85 Van

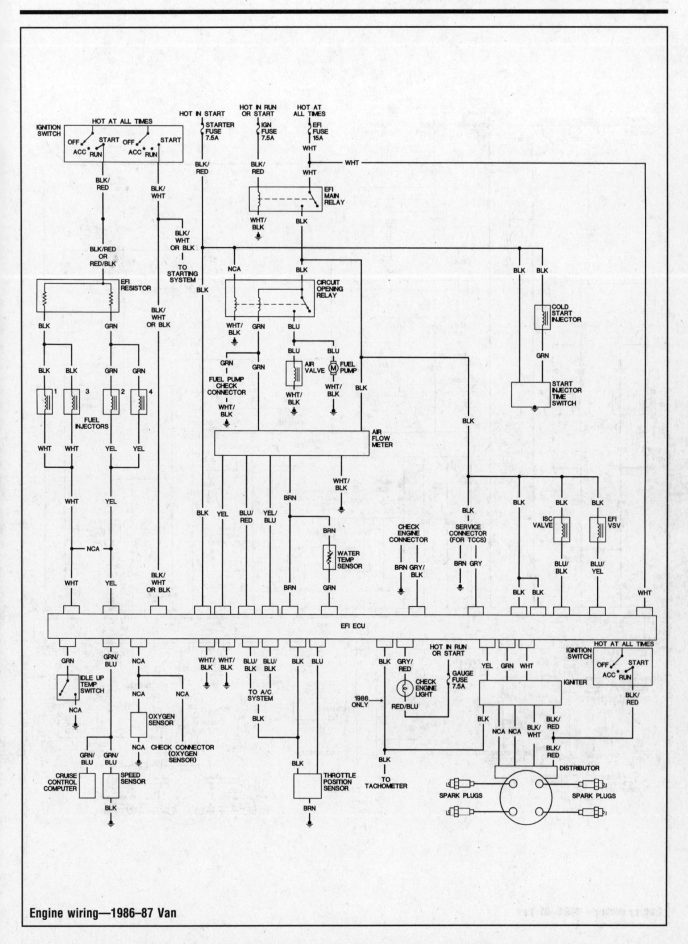

Engine wiring—1986-87 Van

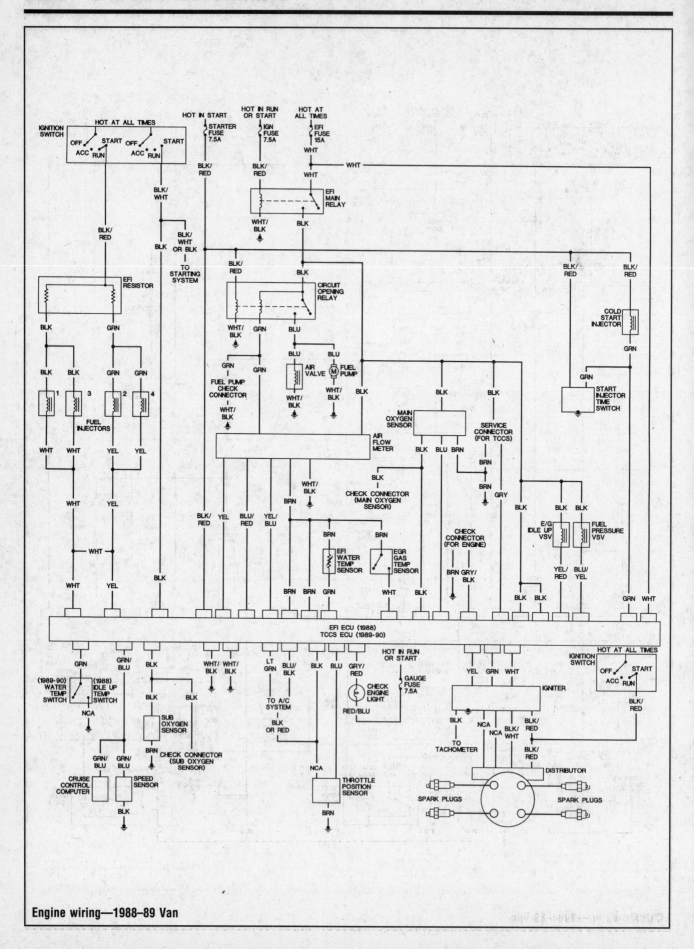

Engine wiring—1988–89 Van

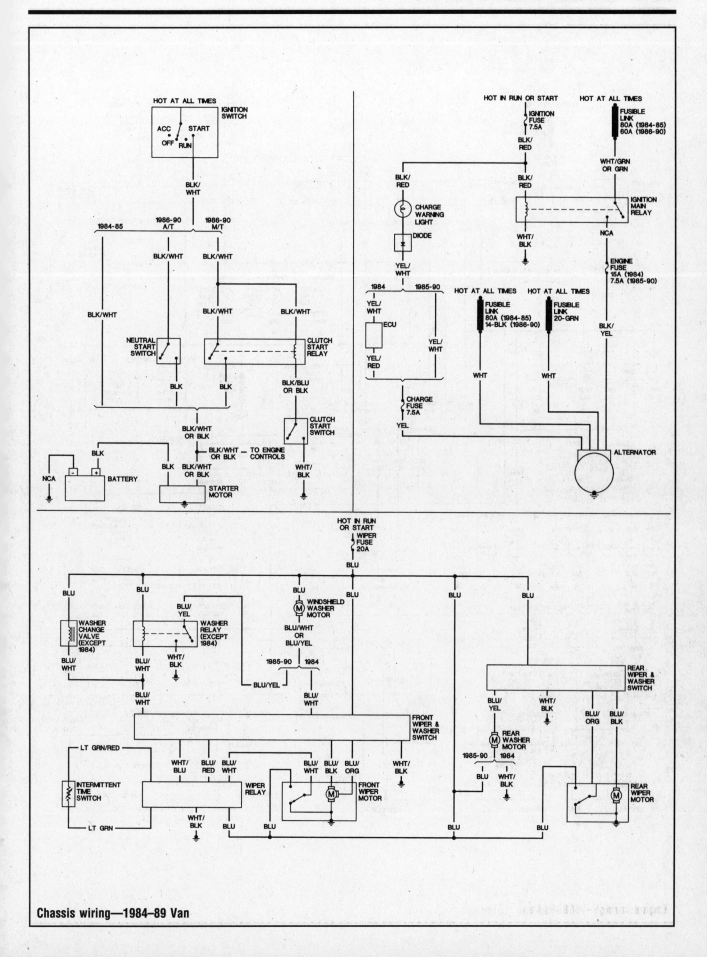

Chassis wiring—1984–89 Van

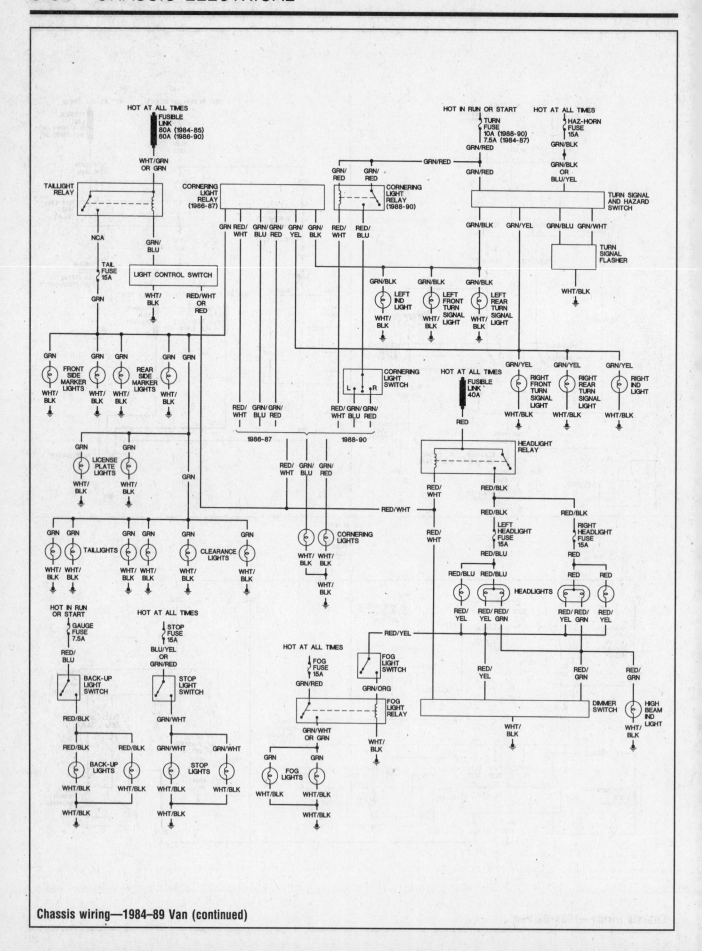

Chassis wiring—1984–89 Van (continued)

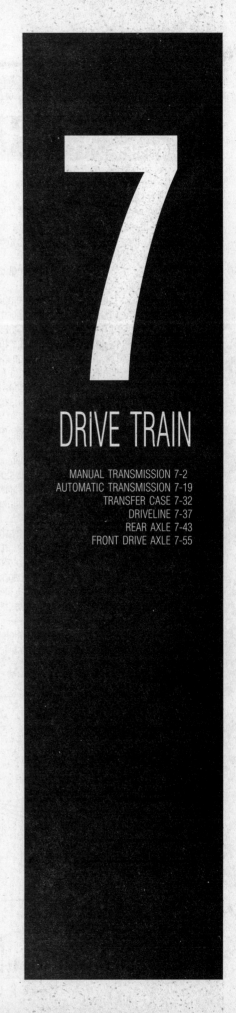

7
DRIVE TRAIN

MANUAL TRANSMISSION

Understanding the Manual Transmission

Because of the way an internal combustion engine breathes, it can produce torque (or twisting force) only within a narrow speed range. Most overhead valve pushrod engines must turn at about 2500 rpm to produce their peak torque. Often by 4500 rpm, they are producing so little torque that continued increases in engine speed produce no power increases.

The torque peak on overhead camshaft engines is, generally, much higher, but much narrower.

The manual transmission and clutch are employed to vary the relationship between engine RPM and the speed of the wheels so that adequate power can be produced under all circumstances. The clutch allows engine torque to be applied to the transmission input shaft gradually, due to mechanical slippage. The vehicle can, consequently, be started smoothly from a full stop.

The transmission changes the ratio between the rotating speeds of the engine and the wheels by the use of gears. 4-speed or 5-speed transmissions are most common. The lower gears allow full engine power to be applied to the rear wheels during acceleration at low speeds.

The clutch driveplate is a thin disc, the center of which is splined to the transmission input shaft. Both sides of the disc are covered with a layer of material which is similar to brake lining and which is capable of allowing slippage without roughness or excessive noise.

The clutch cover is bolted to the engine flywheel and incorporates a diaphragm spring which provides the pressure to engage the clutch. The cover also houses the pressure plate. When the clutch pedal is released, the driven disc is sandwiched between the pressure plate and the smooth surface of the flywheel, thus forcing the disc to turn at the same speed as the engine crankshaft.

The transmission contains a mainshaft which passes all the way through the transmission, from the clutch to the driveshaft.

This shaft is separated at one point, so that front and rear portions can turn at different speeds.

Power is transmitted by a countershaft in the lower gears and reverse. The gears of the countershaft mesh with gears on the mainshaft, allowing power to be carried from one to the other. Countershaft gears are often integral with that shaft, while several of the mainshaft gears can either rotate independently of the shaft or be locked to it. Shifting from one gear to the next causes one of the gears to be freed from rotating with the shaft and locks another to it. Gears are locked and unlocked by internal dog clutches which slide between the center of the gear and the shaft. The forward gears usually employ synchronizers; friction members which smoothly bring gear and shaft to the same speed before the toothed dog clutches are engaged.

Identification

The 1983–87 Cressida uses the W-58 manual transmission and the Van uses the G-53 manual transmission. These transmissions are 5 speed manual transmissions. These units are equipped with constant mesh synchronizers for the forward gears and sliding mesh reverse gear. The G-53 transmission is available in 2WD and 4WD versions.

An identification tag is on the side of the transmission case. Included on the tag is the model number and serial number of the unit.

General Information

Metric tools will be required to service this transmission. Due to the large number of alloy parts used in this transmission, torque specifications should be strictly observed. Before installing capscrews into aluminum parts, dip the bolts into clean transmission fluid as this will prevent the screws from galling the aluminum threads, thus causing damage.

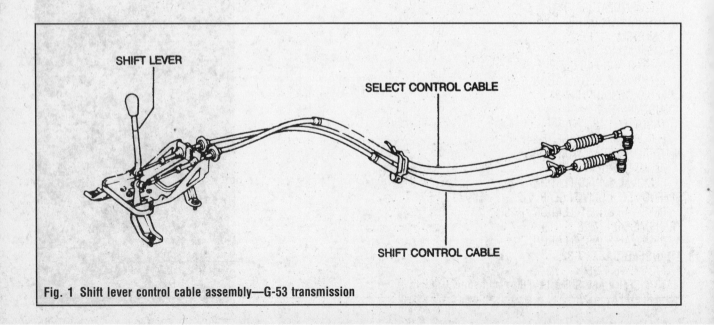

Fig. 1 Shift lever control cable assembly—G-53 transmission

Metric fastener dimensions are very close to the dimensions of the familiar inch system fasteners. For this reason replacement fasteners must have the same measurement and strength as the original fastener.

Do not attempt to interchange metric fasteners for inch system fasteners. Mismatched or incorrect fasteners can cause damage to the automatic transmission unit and possible personal injury. Care should be taken to reuse fasteners in their original locations.

Adjustments

SHIFT LEVER

G-53 Transmission

◗ See Figures 1, 2 and 3

1. Disconnect the negative battery cable. Remove the console assembly.
2. Place the shift lever in **N**.
3. Using a 0.24 in. (6mm) diameter guide pin, check that the guide pin inserts smoothly into the shift lever retainer hole and shift lever inspection hole.

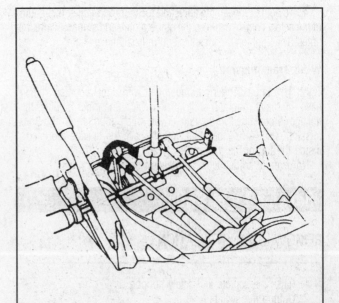

Fig. 2 Loosen the locknuts and adjust the length of the shift lever cable so the guide pin inserts into the holes—G-53 transmission

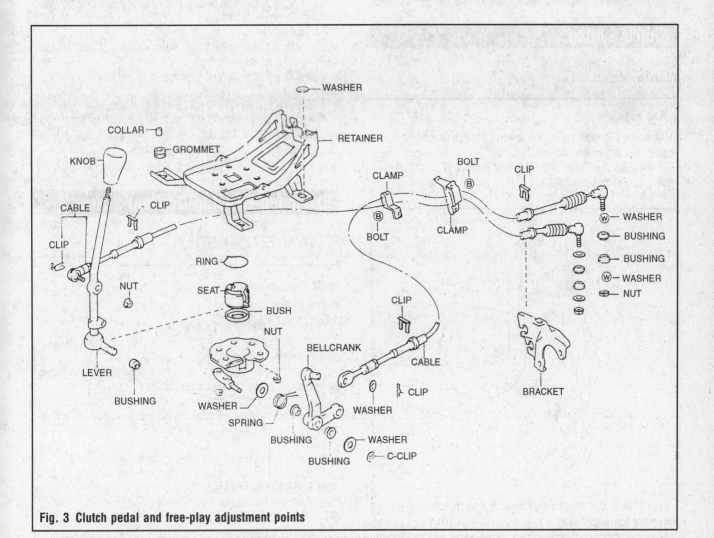

Fig. 3 Clutch pedal and free-play adjustment points

4. To adjust, loosen the adjusting locknuts and adjust the length of the select control cable so the guide pin inserts smoothly into the holes. Then tighten the locknuts and reinstall the console.

W-58 Transmission

All Toyota passenger cars equipped with floor mounted shifters have internally mounted shift linkage. On some older models, the linkage is contained in the side cover which is bolted on the transmission case. All of the other models have the linkage mounted inside the top of the transmission case, itself.

No external adjustments are needed or possible.

Back-up Light Switch

REMOVAL & INSTALLATION

1. Raise the vehicle and safely support.
2. Unplug the switch.
3. Remove the switch. If the plunger is stuck, the switch is defective and should be replaced.
To install:
4. Replace the sealing washer when installing the switch.
5. Lower the vehicle and check the operation of the reverse lights.

Clutch Switch

ADJUSTMENT

▶ **See Figure 4**

1. Attempt to start the engine when the clutch pedal is released. The engine should not start.
2. Depress the clutch pedal fully and attempt to start the engine. The engine should start.

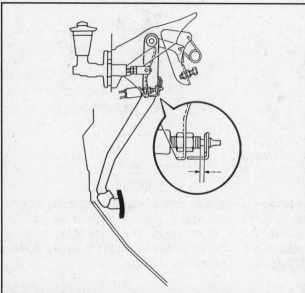

Fig. 4 With the pedal depressed, the switch should contact the pedal stop

3. If the engine does not start, depress the clutch pedal fully. With the clutch pedal depressed, loosen the switch locknut.
4. Use the adjusting nut to turn the switch until the tip of the switch contacts the clutch pedal stop.
5. Tighten the locknut and attempt to start the engine. Re-adjust as necessary.
6. If the switch cannot be adjusted, check the switch continuity with a suitable ohmmeter. There should be continuity between the switch terminals when the switch is on (tip pushed in) and no continuity when the switch is off (tip released). If the continuity is not as specified, replace the switch.

Speedometer Driven Gear

REMOVAL & INSTALLATION

▶ **See Figure 5**

1. Raise the vehicle and safely support.
2. Disconnect the speedometer cable.
3. Remove the speedometer driven gear housing lock plate, then remove the gear from the housing by removing the clip.
4. Using a suitable tool, remove the oil seal from inside the housing sleeve, if necessary.
To install:
5. Install the new seal into the sleeve using seal installer tool 09201-60011, or equivalent.
6. Install the speedometer driven gear to the housing and install the clip.
7. Replace the housing O-ring and coat it with oil.
8. Install the assembly to the transmission and tighten the lock plate bolt to 8 ft. lbs. (11 Nm).
9. Check for proper speedometer operation.

Extension Housing Oil Seal

REMOVAL & INSTALLATION

W-58 Transmission
▶ **See Figure 6**

1. Raise the vehicle and safely support.
2. Matchmark the driveshaft flange to the companion flange on the differential. Remove the nuts and bolts.
3. Position a suitable drain pan under the transmission where the driveshaft enters the extension housing.
4. Pull the driveshaft yoke from the transmission.
5. Remove the dust deflector. Using a suitable prying tool, remove the seal.
To install:
6. Install the new seal and the dust deflector.
7. Install the driveshaft yoke to the extension housing.
8. Install the rear flange to the differential companion flange aligning the matchmarks. Torque the nuts to 54 ft. lbs. (74 Nm).
9. Refill the transmission with the proper lubricant.

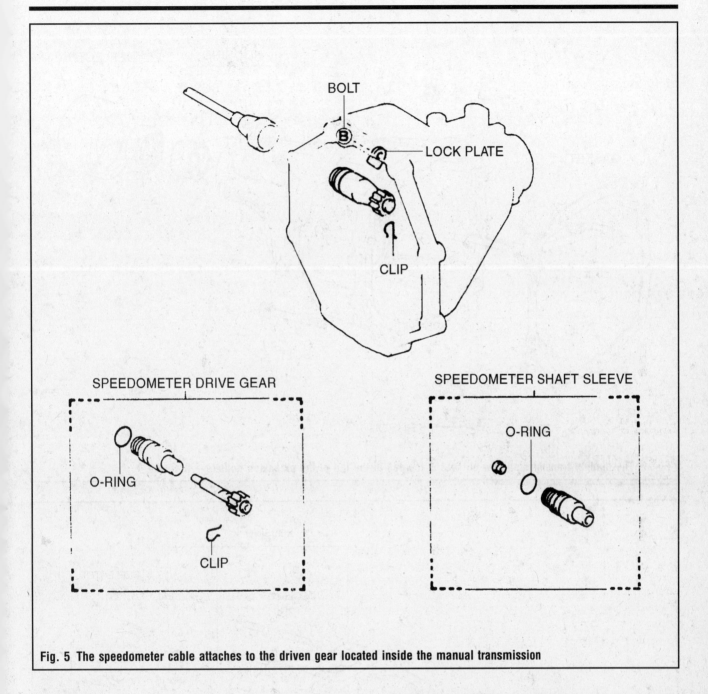

BOLT

LOCK PLATE

CLIP

SPEEDOMETER DRIVE GEAR

O-RING

CLIP

SPEEDOMETER SHAFT SLEEVE

O-RING

Fig. 5 The speedometer cable attaches to the driven gear located inside the manual transmission

G-53 Transmission

2WD MODELS

▶ **See Figure 7**

1. Raise and safely support the vehicle.
2. Matchmark the driveshaft flange-to-differential flange. Remove the nuts and bolts.
3. Remove the center bearing support-to-chassis bolts.
4. Position a drain pan under the extension housing and pull the driveshaft from the extension housing.
5. Remove the dust deflector. Using a prybar, pry the seal from the end of the extension housing.

To install:

6. Using a seal driver tool, drive a new seal into the extension housing. Install the dust deflector.

7. Install the driveshaft yoke-to-extension housing.
8. Align the center bearing support-to-chassis and loosely install the bolts.
9. Align the driveshaft flange-to-differential flange matchmarks and tighten the nuts/bolts to 54 ft. lbs. (74 Nm).

➡**Before torquing the center support bearing bolts, adjust the bearing bracket so it is at a right angle to the driveshaft. Also, make sure the center line of the center bearing is adjusted to the center line of the bracket when the vehicle is in a no-load condition.**

10. Tighten the center support bearing bolts to 27 ft. lbs. (36 Nm).
11. Refill the transmission with the proper lubricant.

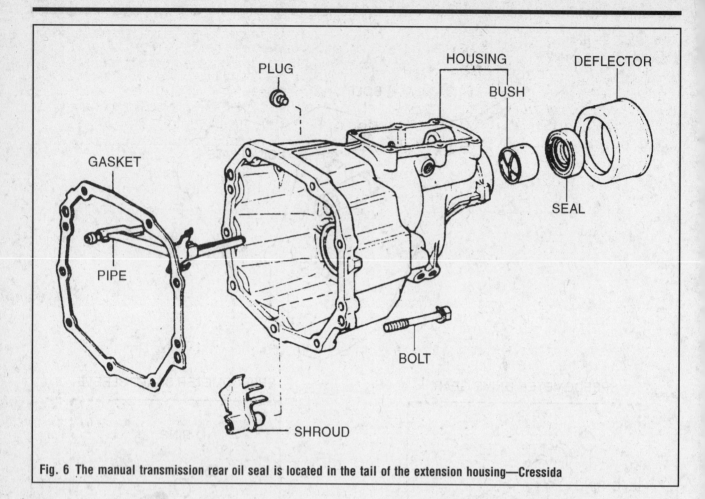

Fig. 6 The manual transmission rear oil seal is located in the tail of the extension housing—Cressida

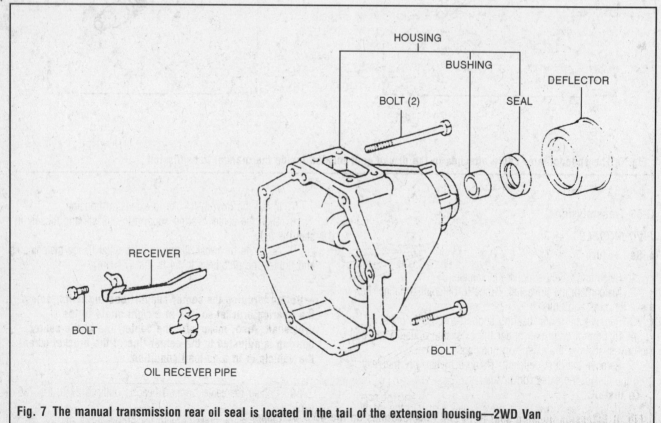

Fig. 7 The manual transmission rear oil seal is located in the tail of the extension housing—2WD Van

4WD MODELS—REAR

▶ **See Figure 8**

1. Raise and safely support the vehicle.
2. Matchmark the rear driveshaft flange-to-rear differential flange and the rear driveshaft flange-to-transfer case flange. Remove the nuts/bolts.

3. Remove the center bearing support-to-chassis bolts and the driveshaft from the vehicle.
4. Position a drain pan under the transfer case.
5. Remove the rear companion flange by performing the following procedures:

   a. Using a hammer and a chisel, loosen the staked part of the companion flange nut.

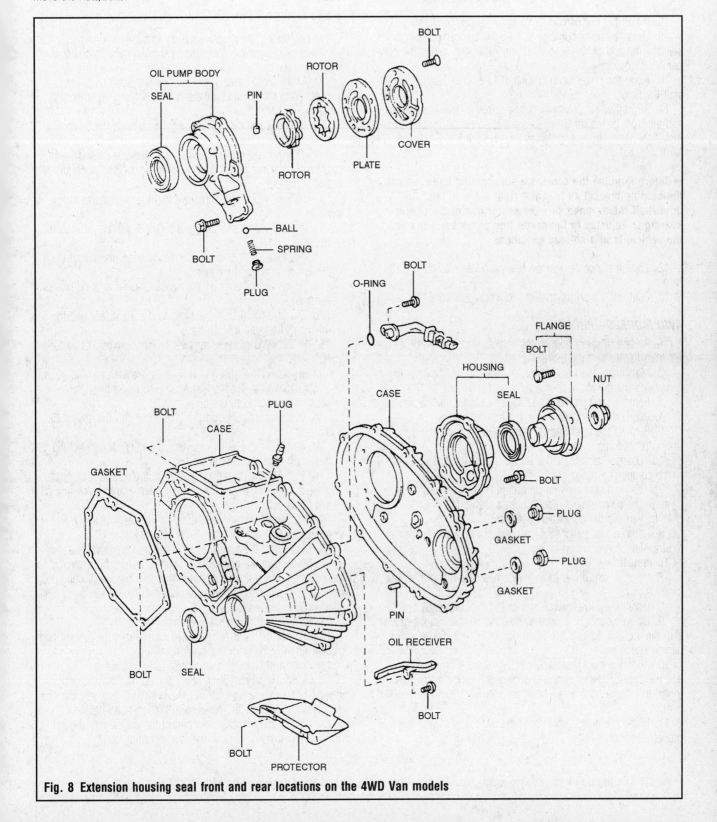

Fig. 8 Extension housing seal front and rear locations on the 4WD Van models

b. Using a spanner wrench to hold the companion flange, remove the companion flange-to-output shaft nut.

c. Remove the companion flange.

6. Using a seal puller tool, pull the oil seal from the rear of the transfer case.

To install:

7. Using a seal driver tool, drive a new seal into the transfer case.

8. Install the companion flange onto the output shaft.

9. Using a spanner wrench to hold the companion flange, install the nut and tighten it to 90 ft. lbs. (123 Nm). Stake the companion flange nut.

10. Align the center bearing support-to-chassis and loosely install the bolts.

11. Align the rear driveshaft flange-to-rear differential flange and the front driveshaft flange-to-companion flange matchmarks. Install the flange bolts and tighten the nuts/bolts to 54 ft. lbs. (74 Nm).

➡**Before torquing the center support bearing bolts, adjust the bearing bracket so it is at a right angle to the driveshaft. Also, make sure the center line of the center bearing is adjusted to the center line of the bracket when the vehicle is in a no-load condition.**

12. Tighten the center support bearing bolts to 27 ft. lbs. (36 Nm).

13. Refill the transmission with the proper lubricant.

4WD MODELS—FRONT

1. Raise and safely support the vehicle. Remove the dust covers from the front of the transfer case.

2. Matchmark the front driveshaft flange-to-front differential flange and the driveshaft-to-transfer case flange.

3. Remove the nuts/bolts and the driveshaft from the vehicle.

4. Position a drain pan under the transfer case.

5. Remove the front transfer case flange by performing the following procedures:

a. Using a hammer and a chisel, loosen the staked part of the companion flange nut.

b. Using a spanner wrench to hold the companion flange, remove the companion flange-to-output shaft nut.

c. Remove the companion flange.

6. Using a seal puller tool, pull the oil seal from the rear of the transfer case.

To install:

7. Using a seal driver tool, drive a new seal into the transfer case.

8. Install the companion flange onto the output shaft.

9. Using a spanner wrench to hold the companion flange, install the nut and tighten it to 90 ft. lbs. (123 Nm). Stake the companion flange nut.

10. Align the front driveshaft flange-to-front differential flange and the front driveshaft flange-to-companion flange matchmarks. Install the flange bolts and tighten the nuts/bolts to 54 ft. lbs. (74 Nm).

11. Install the dust covers. Refill the transmission with the proper lubricant.

Transmission Assembly

REMOVAL & INSTALLATION

Van

◆ **See Figures 9 thru 14**

1. Disconnect the negative battery terminal.

2. Raise the vehicle and support safely. Drain the transmission oil.

3. On the 2WD models, remove the driveshaft as follows:

a. Place matchmarks on the differential and the driveshaft flange.

b. Remove the 4 bolts and nuts, disconnect the driveshaft from the differential.

c. Pull out the driveshaft yoke from the transmission and place a container under the extension housing to catch any oil that spills out.

4. On the 4WD models, remove the rear driveshafts as follows:

a. Place matchmarks on the differential and the driveshaft flange.

b. Remove the 4 bolts, washers and nuts, disconnect the driveshaft from the differential.

c. Place matchmarks on the transfer case and the driveshaft flanges.

d. Remove the 4 bolts, washers and nuts, disconnect the driveshaft from the transfer case.

5. On the 4WD models, remove the front driveshafts as follows:

a. Remove the 2 differential support bracket retaining bolts.

b. Remove the 4 bolts and nuts, disconnect the differential support member from the body.

c. Place matchmarks on the differential and the driveshaft flanges.

d. Remove the 4 bolts, washers and nuts, disconnect the driveshaft from the differential.

e. Pull out the driveshaft yoke from the transfer case and place a container under the extension housing to catch any oil that spills out.

6. Disconnect the reverse light and transfer indicator switches, if equipped.

7. Disconnect the speedometer cable and ground cable.

8. Disconnect the transmission control cables by removing the nuts and removing the retainers from the bracket. If equipped with 4WD, disconnect the transfer control cable by removing the retaining clip and washer.

9. Remove the clutch slave cylinder.

10. Remove the front exhaust pipe clamp from the bracket and disconnect the pipe from the exhaust manifold.

11. Remove the starter and control cable bracket.

12. Using the proper equipment, jack up the transmission enough to take the weight off of the mount and remove either the rear mount (2WD) or the rear mount through bolt (4WD).

13. On the 2WD models, disconnect the engine rear mounting. On the 4WD models, remove the rear mounting bolt.

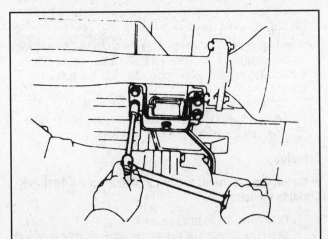

Fig. 9 When removing the manual transmission on the 2WD Van, the rear engine mount must be unbolted from the vehicle

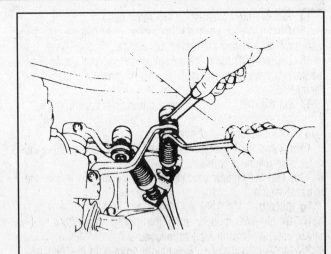

Fig. 12 On the 2WD Van models, disconnect and remove the transmission case control cables

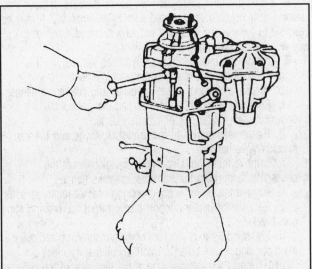

Fig. 10 On the 4WD Van, matchmark the transfer case and separate it from the manual transmission

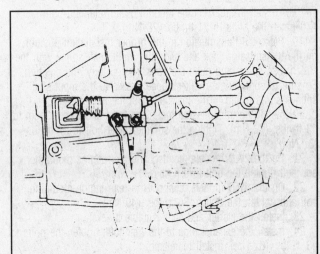

Fig. 13 On all Van models, remove the clutch slave cylinder from the manual transmission assembly

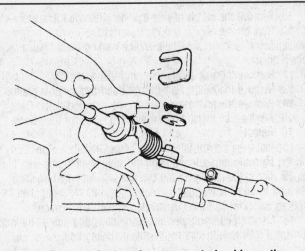

Fig. 11 Remove the transfer case control cable on the 4WD Van models during manual transmission removal

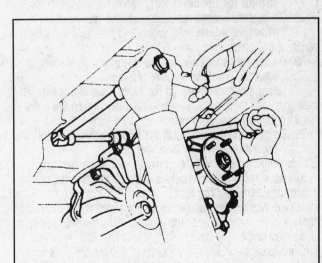

Fig. 14 Prior to transmission removal, remove the rear engine mount on the 4WD Van

14. Remove the transmission mounting bolts.

15. On the 2WD lower the transmission jack, pull the transmission down and toward the rear of the vehicle.

16. On the 4WD lower the transmission jack, pull the transmission and transfer case assembly down and toward the rear of the vehicle.

17. On the 4WD models, remove the transfer case from the transmission as follows:

    a. Remove the rear engine mounting.

    b. Stand the transmission straight up and remove the transfer case retaining bolts.

    c. Pull the transfer case straight up and remove it from the transmission.

To install:

18. On the 4WD models, install the transfer case with a new gasket onto the transmission as follows:

    a. Install the transfer case straight down onto the transmission.

    b. Install the transfer case retaining bolts and tighten them to 27 ft. lbs. (37 Nm). Be sure to apply a suitable thread sealer to the 2 front bolts.

    c. Install the rear engine mounting and retaining bolts. Tighten the bolts to 21 ft. lbs. (28 Nm).

19. Place the transmission in the proper installation position on the transmission jack and align the input shaft spline with the clutch disc spline and push the transmission fully into position. Be sure to apply some multi-purpose grease to the input shaft splines so as to aid in the installation of the transmission.

20. Install the transmission mounting bolts and torque them to 53 ft. lbs. (72 Nm). Tighten the stiffener plate bolt to 27 ft. lbs. (37 Nm).

21. On the 2WD models, connect the rear engine mounting bolt and tighten the bolt to 9 ft. lbs. (12 Nm).

22. On the 4WD models, connect the rear engine mounting bolt and tighten the bolt to 36 ft. lbs. (49 Nm).

23. Install the starter and control cable bracket.

24. Install the exhaust pipe to the manifold, tighten the bolts to 46 ft. lbs. (62 Nm). Install the clamp.

25. Install the clutch slave cylinder.

26. Connect the transfer control cable, if equipped and install a new clip.

27. Install the transmission control cables.

28. Connect the speedometer cable and the ground strap.

29. Connect the reverse light switch and transfer indicator switch, if equipped.

30. On the 2WD models install the driveshafts as follows:

    a. Insert the yoke into the transmission.

    b. Align the matchmarks on the flanges and attach the flanges with the 4 bolts, washers and nuts. Tighten the bolts and nuts 54 ft. lbs. (74 Nm).

31. On the 4WD models install the front driveshafts as follows:

    a. Insert the yoke into the transfer case.

    b. Align the matchmarks on the flanges and attach the flanges with the 4 bolts, washers and nuts. Tighten the bolts and nuts 31 ft. lbs. (42 Nm).

    c. Connect the differential support member to the body with the 4 bolts, washers and nuts. Tighten the bolts and nuts 70 ft. lbs. (95 Nm).

    d. Install the 2 bolts to the bracket. Tighten the bolts until they are snug.

32. On the 4WD models, install the rear driveshafts as follows:

    a. Align the matchmarks on the flanges and attach the flanges with the 4 bolts, washers and nuts. Tighten the bolts and nuts 54 ft. lbs. (74 Nm).

    b. Connect the rear driveshaft to the differential by aligning the matchmarks on the flanges and attach the flanges with the 4 bolts, washers and nuts. Tighten the bolts and nuts 54 ft. lbs. (74 Nm).

33. Refill the transmission with the proper lubricant.

34. Lower the vehicle and connect the negative battery cable.

35. Road test the vehicle and check for leaks.

Cressida

➡**Manual transmissions are not available on the 1988–90 Cressida models.**

1. Disconnect the negative battery cable.

2. Drain the radiator and remove the upper radiator hose.

3. Remove the console box assembly.

4. Remove the shift lever assembly.

5. Raise and support the vehicle safely. Drain the transmission fluid.

6. If the vehicle is equipped with power steering, remove the steering gear housing (as outlined later in this manual). It may be possible to remove the gear and properly suspend it out of the way without disconnecting the fluid lines.

7. Remove the intermediate driveshaft as follows:

    a. Remove the driveshaft flange reinforcement.

    b. Place matchmarks on the driveshaft and differential flanges.

    c. Remove the 4 bolts and nuts and disconnect the driveshaft flange from the differential flange.

    d. Place matchmarks on the driveshaft flange and the transmission yoke flange.

    e. Remove the 4 bolts and nuts and disconnect the driveshaft flange from the transmission yoke flange.

    f. Remove the center support bearing bracket retaining bolts.

    g. Remove the center support bearing from the bearing support bracket.

    h. Pull the driveshaft yoke out of the transmission and place a drain pan underneath so as to catch any oil that may leak out.

8. Disconnect the exhaust pipe at the rear side of the converter. Remove the 2 rubber hangers. Remove the pipe clamp from the transmission case.

9. Disconnect the speedometer cable. Disconnect the back-up light switch electrical wiring.

10. Remove the clutch release cylinder. Remove the starter.

11. Support the engine and the transmission using a proper transmission jack and a suitable engine holding fixture (such as a chain hoist).

12. Remove the rear engine crossmember assembly.

13. Remove the exhaust pipe bracket and two stiffener plates.

14. Remove the transmission-to-engine retaining bolts. Carefully lower the transmission down and to the rear of the vehicle.

To install:

15. Place the transmission in the proper installation position on the transmission jack and align the input shaft spline with the clutch disc spline and push the transmission fully into position. Be sure to apply some multi-purpose grease to the input shaft splines so as to aid in the installation of the transmission.

16. Install the transmission mounting bolts and tighten them to 47 ft. lbs. (64 Nm). Install the 2 stiffener bolts and exhaust pipe bracket.

17. Install the rear engine crossmember and bolts. Tighten the bolts to 19 ft. lbs. (25 Nm).

18. Install the starter assembly and the clutch release cylinder.
19. Reconnect the speedometer cable. Attach the back-up light switch electrical connector.
20. Install the pipe clamp to the transmission case. Install the 2 rubber hangers and reconnect the exhaust pipe at the rear side of the converter.
21. Install the intermediate driveshaft as follows:
    a. Install the driveshaft yoke into the transmission assembly.
    b. Install the center support bearing into the bearing support bracket.
    c. Install the center support bearing bracket and retaining bolts. Check that the center line of the center bearing is set to the center line of the bracket when the vehicle is in a no-load condition, adjust as necessary. Tighten the bolts to 30 ft. lbs. (40 Nm).
    d. Reconnect the driveshaft flange to the transmission yoke flange. Install the retaining nuts and bolts and torque them to 31 ft. lbs.
    e. Reconnect the driveshaft flange to the differential flange. Install the retaining nuts and bolts and tighten them to 31 ft. lbs.
    f. Install the driveshaft flange reinforcement.
22. Install the steering gear housing assembly (as outlined later in this manual).
23. Refill the transmission with the proper lubricant.
24. Lower the vehicle. Install the shift lever assembly.
25. Install the console box assembly.
26. Install the upper radiator hose. Close the radiator drain petcock and refill the coolant system.
27. Reconnect the negative battery cable.
28. Road test the vehicle and check for leaks.

✳✳ CAUTION

The clutch driven disc may contain asbestos, which has been determined to be a cancer causing agent. Never clean the clutch surfaces with compressed air. Avoids inhaling any dust from the clutch surface. When cleaning the clutch surfaces, use a commercially available disc brake cleaning fluid.

Understanding the Clutch

The purpose of the clutch is to disconnect and connect engine power at the transmission. A vehicle at rest requires a lot of engine torque to get all that weight moving. An internal combustion engine does not develop a high starting torque (unlike steam engines) so it must be allowed to operate without any load until it builds up enough torque to move the vehicle. To a point, torque increases with engine rpm. The clutch allows the engine to build up torque by physically disconnecting the engine from the transmission, relieving the engine of any load or resistance.

The transfer of engine power to the transmission (the load) must be smooth and gradual; if it weren't, drive line components would wear out or break quickly. This gradual power transfer is made possible by gradually releasing the clutch pedal. The clutch disc and pressure plate are the connecting link between the engine and transmission. When the clutch pedal is released, the disc and plate contact each other (the clutch is engaged) physically joining the engine and transmission. When the pedal is

pushed in, the disc and plate separate (the clutch is disengaged) disconnecting the engine from the transmission.

Most clutch assemblies consists of the flywheel, the clutch disc, the clutch pressure plate, the throw out bearing and fork, the actuating linkage and the pedal. The flywheel and clutch pressure plate (driving members) are connected to the engine crankshaft and rotate with it. The clutch disc is located between the flywheel and pressure plate, and is splined to the transmission shaft. A driving member is one that is attached to the engine and transfers engine power to a driven member (clutch disc) on the transmission shaft. A driving member (pressure plate) rotates (drives) a driven member (clutch disc) on contact and, in so doing, turns the transmission shaft.

There is a circular diaphragm spring within the pressure plate cover (transmission side). In a relaxed state (when the clutch pedal is fully released) this spring is convex; that is, it is dished outward toward the transmission. Pushing in the clutch pedal actuates the attached linkage. Connected to the other end of this is the throw out fork, which hold the throw out bearing. When the clutch pedal is depressed, the clutch linkage pushes the fork and bearing forward to contact the diaphragm spring of the pressure plate. The outer edges of the spring are secured to the pressure plate and are pivoted on rings so that when the center of the spring is compressed by the throw out bearing, the outer edges bow outward and, by so doing, pull the pressure plate in the same direction away from the clutch disc. This action separates the disc from the plate, disengaging the clutch and allowing the transmission to be shifted into another gear. A coil type clutch return spring attached to the clutch pedal arm permits full release of the pedal. Releasing the pedal pulls the throw out bearing away from the diaphragm spring resulting in a reversal of spring position. As bearing pressure is gradually released from the spring center, the outer edges of the spring bow outward, pushing the pressure plate into closer contact with the clutch disc. As the disc and plate move closer together, friction between the two increases and slippage is reduced until, when full spring pressure is applied (by fully releasing the pedal) the speed of the disc and plate are the same. This stops all slipping, creating a direct connection between the plate and disc which results in the transfer of power from the engine to the transmission. The clutch disc is now rotating with the pressure plate at engine speed and, because it is splined to the transmission shaft, the shaft now turns at the same engine speed.

The clutch is operating properly if:
1. It will stall the engine when released with the vehicle held stationary.
2. The shift lever can be moved freely between 1st and reverse gears when the vehicle is stationary and the clutch disengaged.

Adjustments

PEDAL HEIGHT AND CLUTCH FREE-PLAY

▶ **See Figure 15**

The correct pedal height from the floor boards to the clutch pedal should be 6.10–6.54 in. (155–166mm) on the Cressida and 6.73–7.13 in. (171–181mm) on the Van models.

1. Loosen the locknut and turn the stopper bolt until the correct clutch pedal height is obtained.
2. Tighten the locknut.

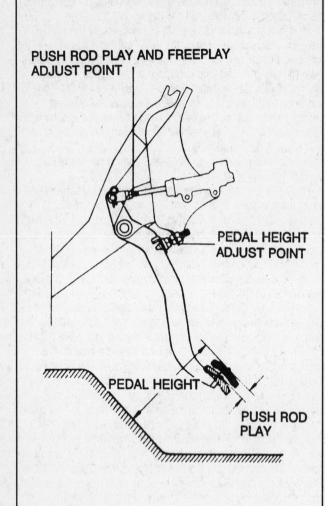

PUSH ROD PLAY AND FREEPLAY
ADJUST POINT

PEDAL HEIGHT
ADJUST POINT

PEDAL HEIGHT

PUSH ROD
PLAY

Fig. 15 Clutch pedal and free-play adjustment points

3. After adjusting the clutch pedal height, check the clutch pedal free-play.

4. Push in on the clutch pedal until the beginning of the clutch resistance is felt. The clutch pedal free-play should be as follows:

  a. The clutch pedal free-play should be 0.20–0.59 in. (5–15mm).

  b. The pushrod play at the pedal should be 0.04–0.20 in. (1–5mm).

5. If it is necessary to adjust the clutch free-play, use the following procedure:

  a. Loosen the locknut and turn the pushrod until the free-play is in the specified range.

  b. Tighten the locknut. After adjusting the free-play, check the pedal height.

6. Check the pedal operation by gently depressing and releasing the clutch pedal, check that engagement and disengagement are smooth.

Clutch Switch

ADJUSTMENT

1. Attempt to start the engine when the clutch pedal is released. The engine should not start.

2. Depress the clutch pedal fully and attempt to start the engine. The engine should start.

3. If the engine does not start, depress the clutch pedal fully. With the clutch pedal depressed, loosen the switch locknut.

4. Use the adjusting nut to turn the switch until the tip of the switch contacts the clutch pedal stop.

5. Tighten the locknut and attempt to start the engine. Re-adjust as necessary.

6. If the switch cannot be adjusted, check the switch continuity with a suitable ohmmeter. There should be continuity between the switch terminals when the switch is on (tip pushed in) and no continuity when the switch is off (tip released). If the continuity is not as specified, replace the switch.

REMOVAL & INSTALLATION

1. Disconnect the negative battery cable.
2. Disconnect the switch connector.
3. Remove the switch adjusting nut.
4. Withdraw the switch from the mounting bracket.
5. Installation is the reverse of the removal procedure. Adjust the switch.

Driven Disc and Pressure Plate

REMOVAL & INSTALLATION

▶ See Figures 16 and 17

✳✳ WARNING

Do not allow grease or oil to get on any of the disc, pressure plate, or flywheel surfaces.

1. Remove the transmission from the car as previously outlined.
2. Place some matchmarks on the clutch cover and flywheel.
3. Loosen the clutch plate retaining bolts one turn at a time until the spring tension is released.

➡**If the screws are released too fast, the clutch assembly will fly apart, causing possible injury or loss of parts.**

4. Remove the retaining bolts and remove the clutch cover and disc from the bellhousing.

5. Unfasten the release fork bearing clips. Withdraw the release bearing hub, complete with the release bearing.

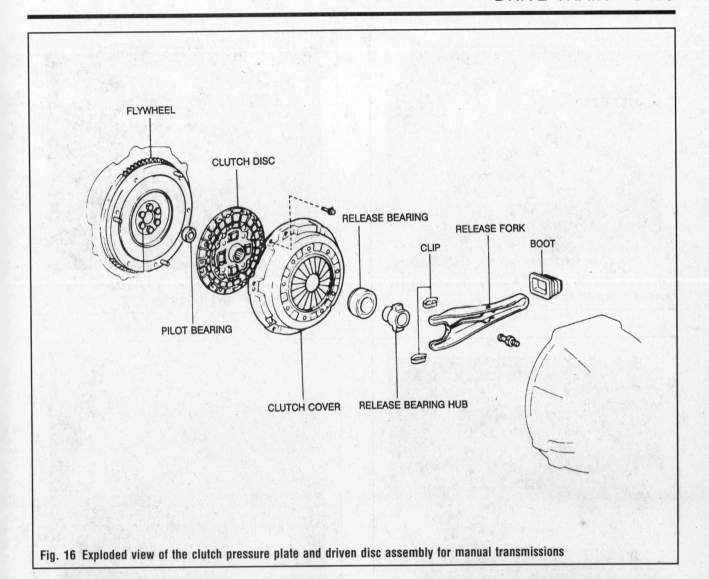

FLYWHEEL

CLUTCH DISC

RELEASE BEARING

RELEASE FORK

CLIP

BOOT

PILOT BEARING

CLUTCH COVER

RELEASE BEARING HUB

Fig. 16 Exploded view of the clutch pressure plate and driven disc assembly for manual transmissions

Typical clutch alignment tool, note how the splines match the transmission's input shaft

Loosen and remove the clutch and pressure plate bolts evenly, a little at a time . . .

. . . then carefully remove the clutch and pressure plate assembly from the flywheel

. . . then remove the flywheel from the crankshaft in order replace it or have it machined

Check across the flywheel surface, it should be flat

Upon installation, it is usually a good idea to apply a thread-locking compound to the flywheel bolts

If necessary, lock the flywheel in place and remove the retaining bolts . . .

Check the pressure plate for excessive wear

Be sure that the flywheel surface is clean, before installing the clutch

You may want to use a thread locking compound on the clutch assembly bolts

Install a clutch alignment arbor, to align the clutch assembly during installation

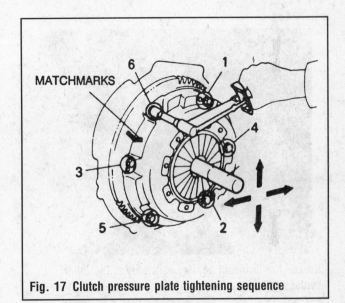

Fig. 17 Clutch pressure plate tightening sequence

Clutch plate installed with the arbor in place

Be sure to use a torque wrench to tighten all bolts

Grease the throwout bearing assembly at the outer contact points

Grease the throwout bearing assembly at the inner contact points

6. Remove the tension spring from the clutch linkage.
7. Remove the release fork and support.
8. Inspect the parts for wear or deterioration. Replace parts as required.

➡ **It should be noted that the pilot bearing (pressed into the flywheel) may have to be replaced if it is showing any signs of heat disfiguring or any other sort of damage. If the pilot bearing is to be removed, it is recommended that a special pilot bearing removal tool be used. This tool can be purchased or rented at any reputable parts house. The pilot bearing may also be removed by removing the flywheel and driving the pilot bearing out of the flywheel from the back side of the flywheel.**

9. Installation is performed in the reverse order of removal. Several points should be noted, however:
   a. Be sure to align the matchmarks on the clutch cover and pressure plate which were made during disassembly.
   b. Apply a thin coating of multipurpose grease to the release bearing hub and release fork contact points. Also, pack the groove inside the clutch hub with multipurpose grease.
   c. Center the clutch disc by using a clutch pilot tool or an old input shaft . Insert the pilot into the end of the input shaft front bearing and bolt the clutch to the flywheel.

➡ **Bolt the clutch assembly to the flywheel in two or three stages, evenly and to the torque specified in the chart below.**

   d. Adjust the clutch as outlined earlier in this section.

Master Cylinder

REMOVAL & INSTALLATION

Cressida
▶ **See Figure 18**

1. Disconnect the negative battery cable.
2. Draw the brake fluid out of the clutch master cylinder with a syringe.

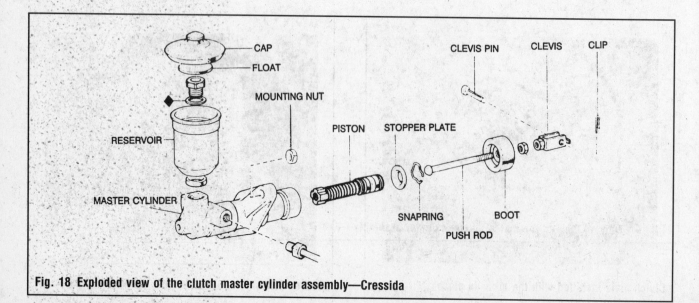

Fig. 18 Exploded view of the clutch master cylinder assembly—Cressida

3. Remove the instrument panel lower finish panel and air duct.
4. Remove the clevis pin and clip.
5. Detach the hydraulic line from the tube.

✳✳ WARNING

Do not spill brake fluid on the painted surfaces of the vehicle.

6. Remove the bolts which secure the master cylinder to the firewall. Pull out the master cylinder assembly from the firewall.

7. Installation is the reverse of removal. Bleed the system as outlined in this section. Adjust the clutch pedal height and freeplay as previously outlined in this section.

Van

▶ **See Figure 19**

1. Disconnect the negative battery cable.
2. Draw the brake fluid out of the clutch master cylinder with a syringe.
3. Remove the clutch master cylinder reservoir cap.
4. Remove the instrument cluster finish panel retaining screws and pull the panel toward you.
5. Remove the combination meter retaining screws.
6. Disconnect the speedometer cable and wiring, then remove the combination meter.

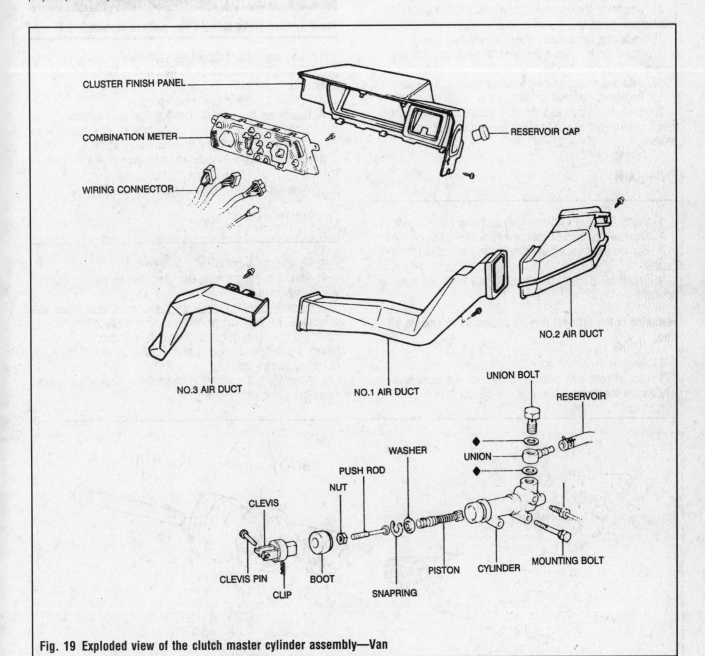

Fig. 19 Exploded view of the clutch master cylinder assembly—Van

7. Remove the 3 air duct assemblies.

8. Remove the clevis pin and clip.

9. Detach the hydraulic lines from the master cylinder and the one going back to the slave cylinder. Do not spill brake fluid on the painted surfaces of the vehicle.

10. Remove the master cylinder retaining bolts. Pull the master cylinder out of the vehicle.

To install:

11. Install the master cylinder assembly and retaining bolts.

12. Attach the hydraulic lines to the master cylinder and slave cylinder.

13. Install the clevis pin and clip.

14. Install the 3 air duct assemblies.

15. Attach the speedometer cable and wiring to the back of the combination meter.

16. Install the combination meter and retaining screws.

17. Install the instrument cluster finish panel and retaining screws.

18. Refill the master cylinder reservoir and install the cap.

19. Reconnect the negative battery cable.

20. Bleed the system as outlined in this section. Adjust the clutch pedal height and free-play as previously outlined in this section.

OVERHAUL

1. Clamp the master cylinder body in a vise with soft jaws.

2. Separate the reservoir assembly from the master cylinder.

3. Remove the snapring and remove the pushrod/piston assembly.

4. Inspect all of the parts and replace any which are worn or defective.

➡**Honing of the cylinder may be necessary to smooth pitting.**

Assembly is performed in the following order:

1. Coat all parts with clean brake fluid, prior to assembly.

2. Install the piston assembly in the cylinder bore.

3. Fit the pushrod over the washer and secure them with the snapring.

4. Install the reservoir.

Slave Cylinder

REMOVAL & INSTALLATION

▶ **See Figure 20**

✳✳ WARNING

Avoid spilling brake fluid on any painted surface.

1. Raise and support the vehicle safely.

2. Remove the gravel shield to gain access to the slave cylinder.

3. Remove the clutch fork return spring.

4. Disconnect the hydraulic line from the slave cylinder.

5. Screw the threaded end of the pushrod in, if necessary in order to allow enough clearance to remove the cylinder.

6. Remove the cylinder attaching nuts and pull out the cylinder.

7. Installation is the reverse of removal.

OVERHAUL

1. Remove the pushrod and rubber boot.

2. Remove the piston, with cup. Don't remove the cup unless you are replacing it.

3. Wash all parts in clean brake fluid. Inspect all parts for wear or damage. The bore can be honed to remove minor imperfections. If it is severely pitted or scored, the cylinder must be replaced. If piston-to-bore clearance is greater than 0.006 in. (0.15mm), replace the unit.

4. Assembly is the reverse of disassembly. Coat all parts with clean brake fluid prior to assembly.

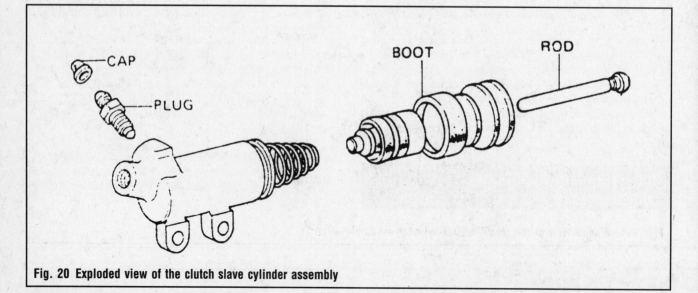

Fig. 20 Exploded view of the clutch slave cylinder assembly

Bleeding Hydraulic System

PROCEDURE

▶ See Figure 21

➡It is more than likely that you will need an assistant in order to be able to bleed the clutch hydraulic system properly.

1. Fill the master cylinder reservoir with brake fluid.

❊❊ WARNING

Do not spill brake fluid on the painted surfaces of the vehicle.

2. Remove the cap and loosen the bleeder plug. Block the outlet hole with your finger.
3. Pump the clutch pedal several times, then take your finger from the hole while depressing the clutch pedal. Allow the air to flow out. Place your finger back over the hole and release the pedal.
4. After fluid pressure can be felt (with your finger), tighten the bleeder plug.
5. Fit a bleeder tube over the plug and place the other end into a clean jar half filled with brake fluid.
6. Depress the clutch pedal, loosen the bleeder plug with a wrench, and allow the fluid to flow into the jar.
7. Tighten the plug and then release the clutch pedal.
8. Repeat Steps 6–7 until no air bubbles are visible in the bleeder tube.
9. When there are no more air bubbles, tighten the plug while keeping the clutch pedal fully depressed. Replace the cap.
10. Fill the master cylinder to the specified level. (See Chapter 1).
11. Check the system for leaks.

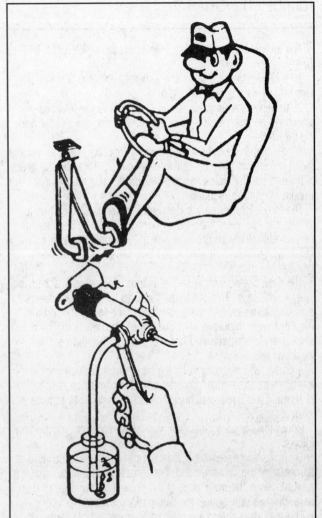

Fig. 21 Have an assistant handy to help bleed the clutch system on manual transmissions

AUTOMATIC TRANSMISSION

➡The automatic transmission, especially the electronically controlled automatic transmission is a very complex piece of equipment and requires a very thorough knowledge and general understanding of hydraulics in order to even considering rebuilding one. Any major repairs that may have to be made to the automatic transmission in your vehicle, should be left in the hands of a qualified factory service technician.

Understanding Automatic Transmissions

The automatic transmission allows engine torque and power to be transmitted to the rear wheels within a narrow range of engine operating speeds. It will allow the engine to turn fast enough to produce plenty of power and torque at very low speeds, while keeping it at a sensible rpm at high vehicle speeds (and it does this job without driver assistance). The transmission uses a light fluid as the medium for the transmission of power. This fluid also works in the operation of various hydraulic control circuits and as a lubricant. Because the transmission fluid performs all of these functions, trouble within the unit can easily travel from one part to another. For this reason, and because of the complexity and unusual operating principles of the transmission, a very sound understanding of the basic principles of operation will simplify troubleshooting.

TORQUE CONVERTER

The torque converter replaces the conventional clutch. It has three functions:

1. It allows the engine to idle with the vehicle at a standstill, even with the transmission in gear.

2. It allows the transmission to shift from range-to-range smoothly, without requiring that the driver close the throttle during the shift.

3. It multiplies engine torque to an increasing extent as vehicle speed drops and throttle opening is increased. This has the effect of making the transmission more responsive and reduces the amount of shifting required.

The torque converter is a metal case which is shaped like a sphere that has been flattened on opposite sides. It is bolted to the rear end of the engine's crankshaft. Generally, the entire metal case rotates at engine speed and serves as the engine's flywheel.

The case contains three sets of blades. One set is attached directly to the case. This set forms the torus or pump. Another set is directly connected to the output shaft, and forms the turbine. The third set is mounted on a hub which, in turn, is mounted on a stationary shaft through a one-way clutch. This third set is known as the stator.

A pump, which is driven by the converter hub at engine speed, keeps the torque converter full of transmission fluid at all times. Fluid flows continuously through the unit to provide cooling.

Under low speed acceleration, the torque converter functions as follows:

The torus is turning faster than the turbine. It picks up fluid at the center of the converter and, through centrifugal force, slings it outward. Since the outer edge of the converter moves faster than the portions at the center, the fluid picks up speed.

The fluid then enters the outer edge of the turbine blades. It then travels back toward the center of the converter case along the turbine blades. In impinging upon the turbine blades, the fluid loses the energy picked up in the torus.

If the fluid was now returned directly into the torus, both halves of the converter would have to turn at approximately the same speed at all times, and torque input and output would both be the same.

In flowing through the torus and turbine, the fluid picks up two types of flow, or flow in two separate directions. It flows through the turbine blades, and it spins with the engine. The stator, whose blades are stationary when the vehicle is being accelerated at low speeds, converts one type of flow into another. Instead of allowing the fluid to flow straight back into the torus, the stator's curved blades turn the fluid almost 90° toward the direction of rotation of the engine. Thus the fluid does not flow as fast toward the torus, but is already spinning when the torus picks it up. This has the effect of allowing the torus to turn much faster than the turbine. This difference in speed may be compared to the difference in speed between the smaller and larger gears in any gear train. The result is that engine power output is higher, and engine torque is multiplied.

As the speed of the turbine increases, the fluid spins faster and faster in the direction of engine rotation. As a result, the ability of the stator to redirect the fluid flow is reduced. Under cruising conditions, the stator is eventually forced to rotate on its one-way clutch in the direction of engine rotation. Under these conditions, the torque converter begins to behave almost like a solid shaft, with the torus and turbine speeds being almost equal.

PLANETARY GEARBOX

The ability of the torque converter to multiply engine torque is limited. Also, the unit tends to be more efficient when the turbine is rotating at relatively high speeds. Therefore, a planetary gearbox is used to carry the power output of the turbine to the driveshaft.

Planetary gears function very similarly to conventional transmission gears. However, their construction is different in that three elements make up one gear system, and, in that all three elements are different from one another. The three elements are: an outer gear that is shaped like a hoop, with teeth cut into the inner surface; a sun gear, mounted on a shaft and located at the very center of the outer gear; and a set of three planet gears, held by pins in a ring-like planet carrier, meshing with both the sun gear and the outer gear. Either the outer gear or the sun gear may be held stationary, providing more than one possible torque multiplication factor for each set of gears. Also, if all three gears are forced to rotate at the same speed, the gearset forms, in effect, a solid shaft.

Most automatics use the planetary gears to provide various reductions ratios. Bands and clutches are used to hold various portions of the gearsets to the transmission case or to the shaft on which they are mounted. Shifting is accomplished, then, by changing the portion of each planetary gearset which is held to the transmission case or to the shaft.

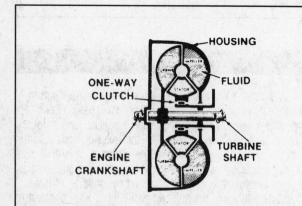

The torque converter housing is rotated by the engine's crankshaft, and turns the impeller—The impeller then spins the turbine, which gives motion to the turbine shaft, driving the gears

SERVOS AND ACCUMULATORS

The servos are hydraulic pistons and cylinders. They resemble the hydraulic actuators used on many other machines, such as bulldozers. Hydraulic fluid enters the cylinder, under pressure, and forces the piston to move to engage the band or clutches.

The accumulators are used to cushion the engagement of the servos. The transmission fluid must pass through the accumulator on the way to the servo. The accumulator housing contains a thin piston which is sprung away from the discharge passage of the accumulator. When fluid passes through the accumulator on the way to the servo, it must move the piston against spring pressure, and this action smooths out the action of the servo.

HYDRAULIC CONTROL SYSTEM

The hydraulic pressure used to operate the servos comes from the main transmission oil pump. This fluid is channeled to the various servos through the shift valves. There is generally a manual shift valve which is operated by the transmission selector lever and an automatic shift valve for each automatic upshift the transmission provides.

➡**Many new transmissions are electronically controlled. On these models, electrical solenoids are used to better control the hydraulic fluid. Usually, the solenoids are regulated by an electronic control module.**

There are two pressures which affect the operation of these valves. One is the governor pressure which is effected by vehicle speed. The other is the modulator pressure which is effected by intake manifold vacuum or throttle position. Governor pressure rises with an increase in vehicle speed, and modulator pressure rises as the throttle is opened wider. By responding to these two pressures, the shift valves cause the upshift points to be delayed with increased throttle opening to make the best use of the engine's power output.

Most transmissions also make use of an auxiliary circuit for

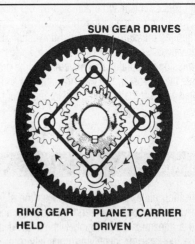
Planetary gears in the maxium reduction (low) range. The ring gear is held and a lower gear ratio is obtained

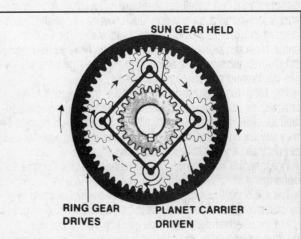
Planetary gears in the minimum reduction (drive) range. The ring gear is allowed to revolve, providing a higher gear ratio

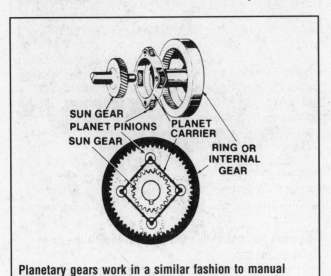
Planetary gears work in a similar fashion to manual transmission gears, but are composed of three parts

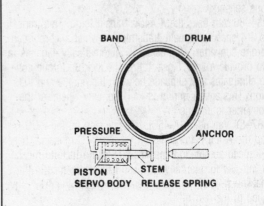
Servos, operated by pressure, are used to apply or release the bands, to either hold the ring gear or allow it to rotate

downshifting. This circuit may be actuated by the throttle linkage the vacuum line which actuates the modulator, by a cable or by a solenoid. It applies pressure to a special downshift surface on the shift valve or valves.

The transmission modulator also governs the line pressure, used to actuate the servos. In this way, the clutches and bands will be actuated with a force matching the torque output of the engine.

Identification

An identification plate is usually located on the side of the transmission with the model and serial number stamped on the plate. Should a transmission be found without an identification plate, examine the case for identifying code letters or digits. Also, obtain the vehicle model and serial number before obtaining replacement parts.

The 1983–85 Cressida uses the A-43DL transmission. This transmission is a 4 speed automatic transmission which incorporated a lock-up torque converter. This converter automatically engages in 3rd gear to provide a 1 to 1 gear ratio. The lock-up torque converter also eliminates any slippage between the engine and the transmission. This action improves fuel economy whenever the lock-up converter is engaged.

The 1986–87 Cressida uses the A-43DE transmission. This transmission is a 4 speed automatic transmission which incorporated a solenoid that is electronically controlled which permits a more precise control of the shift points and torque converter lock-up operation. It will also allow improved response to road changes, engine conditions, driver demands and will improve fuel economy.

The 1988–90 Cressida uses the A-340E transmission. This transmission is a 4 speed automatic transmission which is controlled by selecting the appropriate position from a console mounted selector lever mounted on the passenger compartment floor with a push button overdrive control switch. A power/economy switch is included to further increase the driveability of the vehicle. The on board computer determines the shift and lock-up points of the transmission as well as the speed change range of the transfer system based upon the input data signals received from various sensors.

The 1984–86 Van uses the A-44DL transmission. This transmission is a 4 speed automatic transmission which incorporated a lock-up torque converter. This converter automatically engages in 3rd gear to provide a 1 to 1 gear ratio. The lock-up torque converter also eliminates any slippage between the engine and the transmission. This action improves fuel economy whenever the lock-up converter is engaged.

The 1987–89 Van use a A-45DL transmission on the 2WD models and the A-45DF transmission on the 4WD models. These units are 4 speed automatic transmissions with a lock-up mechanism built into the torque converter. The basic difference in the 2 units is that the A-45DF unit as a transfer case for the 4WD drive train attached to the rear of it.

On all electronically controlled transmissions, the computer system measures the vehicle speed and angle of the fuel injection throttle valve. These measurements are then fed to the electroni-

cally controlled transmission computer where they are analyzed. The computer then selects the best gear and shift speed to match the driving conditions. The computer also monitors engine temperature, brake pedal position, shift lever position and the shift pattern select switches which are located either on the shift lever or the dash panel. This monitoring allows for slight modifications in the shifting program.

The on board computer which controls the operation of the electronically controlled automatic transmission on the basis of the accelerator pedal opening angle and vehicle speed, will automatically shift the transmission in the gear best suited for any given driving condition.

Fluid Pan and Filter

REMOVAL & INSTALLATION

1. Raise the car and safely support it on jackstands.
2. Place a suitable drain pan underneath the transmission oil pan. Remove the drain plug or if not equipped with a drain plug, loosen the oil pan mounting bolts and allow the fluid to drain until it reaches the level of the pan flange. Remove the attaching bolts, leaving one end attached so that the pan will tip and the rest of the fluid will drain.
3. Remove the oil pan. Thoroughly clean the pan. Remove the old gasket. Make sure that the gasket mounting surfaces are clean.
4. Remove the transmission filter screen retaining bolt. Remove the screen.

To install:

5. Install a new filter screen and O-ring. Place a new gasket on the pan and install the pan to the transmission.
6. Fill the transmission to the correct level. Remove the jackstands and lower the car to the ground. The drain and refill level is 2.5 quarts of Dexron® II transmission fluid.

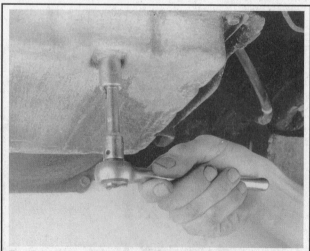

To drain the automatic transmission, loosen the drain plug on the pan

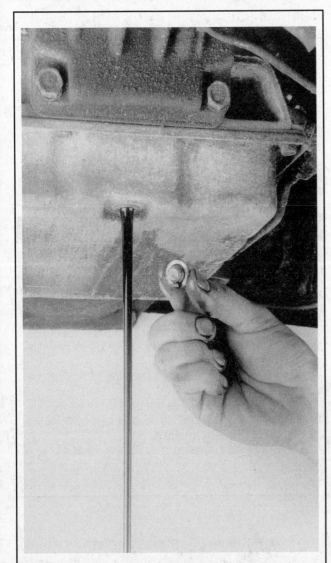

Remove the plug from the pan and allow the fluid to drain

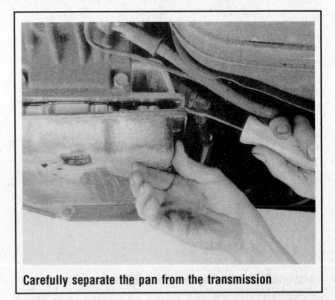

Carefully separate the pan from the transmission

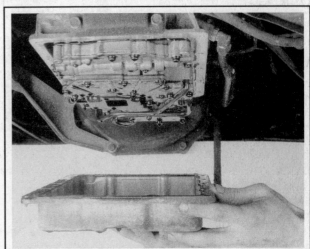

Lower the automatic transmission pan and check for any metal shavings

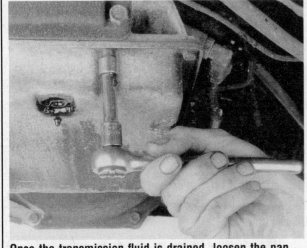

Once the transmission fluid is drained, loosen the pan mounting bolts

Remove and clean the magnets and the pan

The filter is secured by several small bolts

Remove the filter retaining bolts . . .

. . . then lower the filter to clean or replace it

FLUID CONDITION

Pull the transmission dipstick out. Observe the color and odor of the transmission fluid. The color should be red not brown or black. An odor can sometimes indicate an overheating condition, clutch disc or band failure.

Wipe the dipstick with a clean white rag. Examine the stain on the rag for specks of solids (metal or dirt) and for signs of contaminates (antifreeze, gum or varnish condition).

If examination shows evidence of metal specks or antifreeze contamination transmission removal and inspection may be necessary.

Adjustments

THROTTLE CABLE

▶ **See Figure 22**

1. Push on the accelerator connecting rod and check that the throttle valve opens fully. If the throttle valve does not open fully, adjust the accelerator link.
2. Fully depress the accelerator. Loosen the cable adjustment locknuts.
3. Adjust the cable housing so that the distance between the end of the boot and the stopper on the cable is correct. The distance should be 0–0.04 in. (0–1mm).
4. Tighten the cable adjusting nuts. Recheck the adjustments.

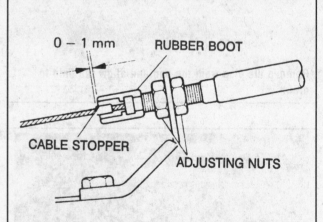

Fig. 22 Adjust the throttle cable housing so that the distance between the end of the boot and stopper on the cable are correct

FLOOR SHIFT LINKAGE

▶ **See Figure 23**

1. Raise and safely support the vehicle.
2. Working from underneath the vehicle, loosen the nuts on the shift linkage connecting rod.

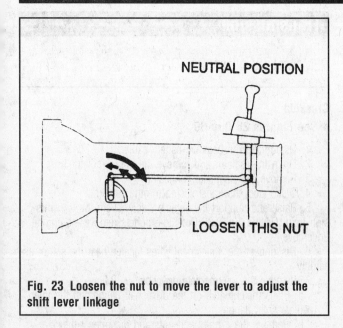

Fig. 23 Loosen the nut to move the lever to adjust the shift lever linkage

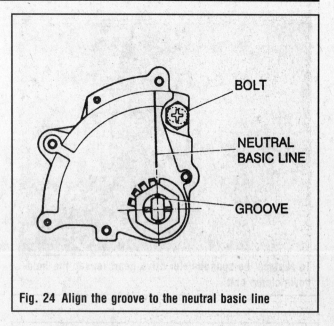

Fig. 24 Align the groove to the neutral basic line

3. Push the manual lever fully toward the front of the vehicle.

4. Return the lever 3 notches to the NEUTRAL position.

5. Set the shift selector at the N position.

6. While holding the selectors lightly toward the R position, tighten the connecting rod nut.

7. When shifting the shift lever from the N position to the other positions, check that the lever can be shifted smoothly and accurately to each position and that the position indicator correctly indicates the position.

Neutral Safety Switch

ADJUSTMENT

▸ **See Figure 24**

The shift lever is adjusted properly if the engine will not start in any position other than **N** or **P**.

1. Loosen the neutral start switch bolt. Position the selector in the **N** position.

2. Align the switch shaft groove with the neutral base line which is located on the switch.

3. Tighten the bolt to 48 inch lbs. (5.4 Nm).

REMOVAL & INSTALLATION

1. Disconnect the negative battery cable. Remove the center console box (shift lever) assembly, if necessary.

2. Unplug the switch wiring connectors.

3. Disconnect the transmission control cable from the manual shift lever.

4. Remove the manual shift lever.

5. Pry the C-washer from the manual shaft nut. Discard the washer and replace with new.

6. Remove the manual shaft nut and washer.

7. Remove the manual shaft lever packing, if so equipped.

8. Remove the retaining bolts and withdraw the switch from the transmission case.

9. Installation is the reverse of the removal procedure. Adjust the switch.

Speedometer Driven Gear

REMOVAL & INSTALLATION

1. Raise the vehicle and safely support.

2. Disconnect the speedometer cable.

3. Remove the speedometer driven gear housing lock plate, then remove the gear from the housing by removing the clip.

4. Using a suitable tool, remove the oil seal from inside the housing sleeve, if necessary.

To install:

5. Install the new seal into the sleeve using seal installer tool 09201-60011, or equivalent.

6. Install the speedometer driven gear to the housing and install the clip.

7. Replace the housing O-ring and coat it with oil.

8. Install the assembly to the transmission and tighten the lock plate bolt to 8 ft. lbs. (11 Nm).

9. Check for proper speedometer operation.

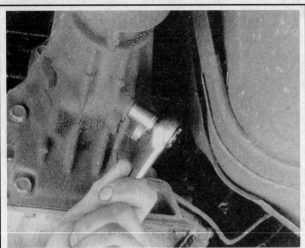

To replace the speedometer drive gear, loosen the hold-down clamp bolt

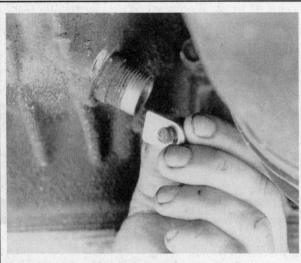

Set the ground wire aside and remove the clamp

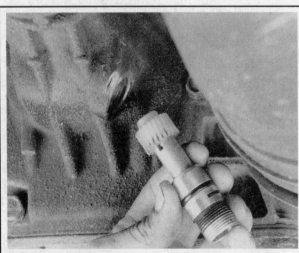

Pull the speedometer driven gear straight out of the extension housing. Inspect the gear teeth for wear

Transmission

REMOVAL & INSTALLATION

Cressida

◗ See Figures 25 thru 30

1. Disconnect the negative battery cable.
2. Drain the radiator and remove the upper radiator hose.
3. Remove the air intake connector.
4. Disconnect the transmission throttle cable(s).
5. Raise and support the vehicle safely. Drain the transmission fluid. On the 1989–90 Cressida models remove the engine undercover.
6. Disconnect the 3 electrical wires located near the starter assembly.
7. Remove the intermediate driveshaft as follows:
   a. Place matchmarks on the driveshaft flange and the intermediate shaft flange.
   b. Remove the 4 bolts and nuts and disconnect the driveshaft flange from the intermediate shaft flange.
   c. Remove the center support bearing bracket retaining bolts.
   d. Remove the intermediate shaft.
8. Disconnect the exhaust pipe at the rear side of the converter. Remove the 2 rubber hangers. Remove the pipe clamp from the transmission case. Remove the front exhaust pipe from the exhaust manifold.
9. Disconnect the oil cooler lines. Remove the oil filler tube.
10. Disconnect the shift linkage at the rear on the transmission.
11. Disconnect the speedometer cable.
12. Remove both stiffener plates and converter cover from the transmission housing and cylinder block.
13. Support the engine and the transmission using a proper transmission jack and a suitable engine holding fixture (such as a chain hoist).
14. Raise the engine enough to remove the weight from the rear support crossmember. Remove the rear support crossmember assembly along with the ground strap.
15. Using a suitable flywheel turning tool, turn the flywheel enough to gain access to the torque converter mounting bolts and remove the 6 bolts.
16. Place a suitable shop rag between the steering gear housing and the engine oil pan to prevent damage.
17. Remove the starter assembly.
18. Remove the transmission-to-engine retaining bolts. Carefully lower the transmission down and to the rear of the vehicle. Be careful not to snap the throttle cable or neutral start switch wiring.
19. Place a drain pan under the transmission and pull the torque converter straight out and off, allow the fluid to run into the pan.

To install:

20. Apply grease to the center hub of the torque converter and the pilot hole in the crankshaft. Install the torque converter onto the transmission.

➡**Using calipers and a straight edge, measure from the installed surface of the torque converter to the front surface of the transmission housing. The correct distance should be 1.043 in. (26.5mm). If the distance is less than specified, check for an improper converter installation.**

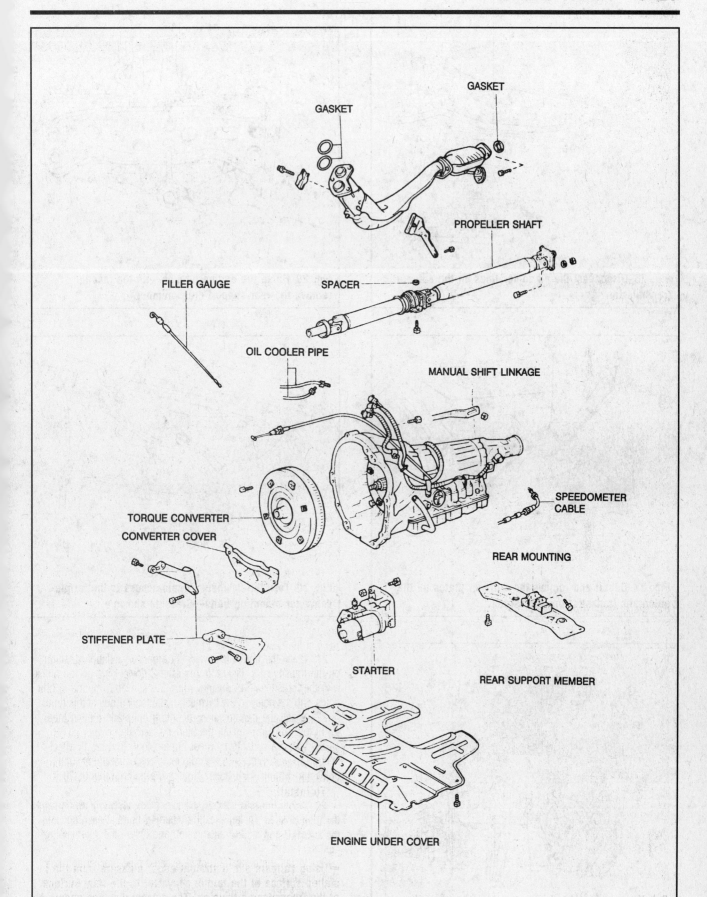

Fig. 25 Exploded view of the automatic transmission mounting—A-340E Cressida

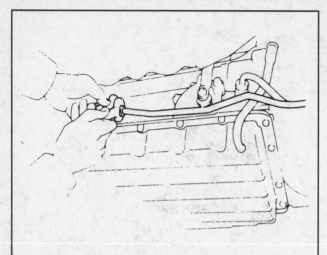

Fig. 26 Disconnect the oil cooler lines on the automatic transmission

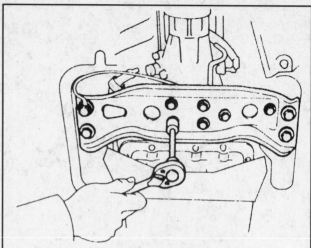

Fig. 29 Raise the engine enough with the jack to remove the rear support crossmember

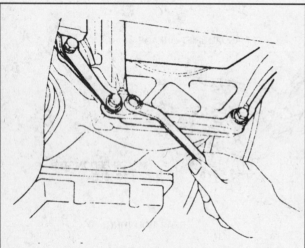

Fig. 27 Unbolt and remove the stiffener plates on the automatic transmission—Cressida

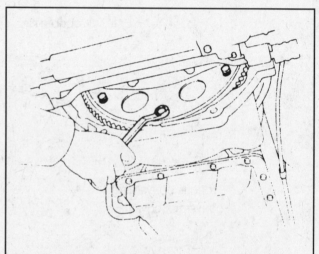

Fig. 30 Turn the flywheel to gain access to the torque converter mounting bolts—Cressida shown

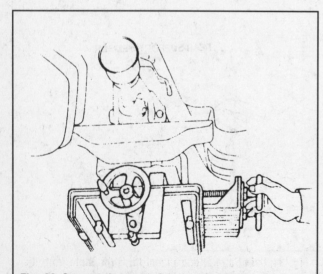

Fig. 28 Support the transmission with a jack

21. Place the transmission in the proper installation position on the transmission jack and align the 2 dowel pins on the block with the transmission housing. Align the converter mounting bolt holes with the holes in the flywheel. Install only 1 bolt at this time.

22. Install the transmission mounting bolts and tighten them to 47 ft. lbs. (64 Nm). Install the starter assembly.

23. Using a suitable flywheel turning tool, turn the flywheel enough to gain access to the torque converter mounting bolt holes and install the 6 bolts. Tighten the bolts evenly to 20 ft. lbs. (27 Nm).

24. Install the rear support crossmember assembly along with the ground strap. Install 2 of the retaining bolts at each end of the support. Lower the transmission and install the 4 remaining mounting bolts.

25. Install the converter cover, exhaust pipe bracket and both stiffener plates.

26. Attach the speedometer cable.

27. Reconnect the shift linkage at the rear connection on the transmission.

28. Reconnect the oil filler tube. Reconnect the oil cooler lines. Tighten the lines to 25 ft. lbs. (34 Nm).

29. Install the front exhaust pipe to the exhaust manifold. Install the pipe clamp to the transmission case along with the 2 rubber hangers. Reconnect the exhaust pipe at the rear side of the converter.

30. Install the intermediate driveshaft as follows:

    a. Install the intermediate shaft.

    b. Install the center support bearing bracket and retaining bolts. Tighten the bolts to 30 ft. lbs. (40 Nm).

    c. Install the driveshaft flange onto the intermediate shaft flange. Tighten the bolts to 31 ft. lbs. (42 Nm).

31. Reconnect the 3 electrical wires located near the starter assembly.

32. Install the engine under cover, if so equipped. Lower the vehicle safely. Refill the transmission fluid.

33. Reconnect the transmission throttle cable(s).

34. Install the air intake connector.

35. Install the upper radiator hose. Refill the radiator and cooling system.

36. Reconnect the negative battery cable.

37. Start the engine check the transmission fluid level and add as necessary. Road test the vehicle and check for leaks.

2WD Van

▶ **See Figures 31 thru 42**

1. Disconnect the battery ground.
2. Disconnect the throttle cable.
3. Disconnect all wires attached to the transmission.
4. Raise and support the vehicle on jackstands.
5. Drain the fluid.
6. Matchmark and remove the driveshaft.
7. Disconnect the exhaust pipe clamp from the transmission case. Remove the exhaust pipe clamp.
8. Disconnect the shift cable from the transmission.
9. Disconnect the speedometer cable.
10. Disconnect the oil cooler lines.
11. Remove the starter.
12. Support the transmission with a floor jack.

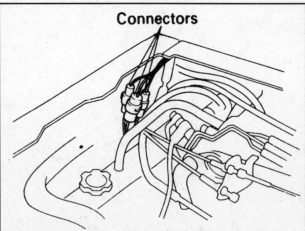

Fig. 32 Unplug the neutral safety switch, back-up light and overdrive solenoid connectors on the 2WD automatic transmission

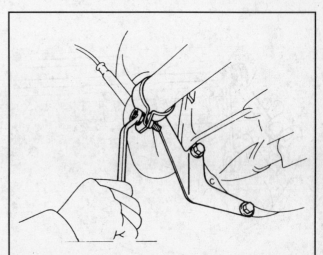

Fig. 33 Remove the exhaust pipe clamp on the 2WD Van models

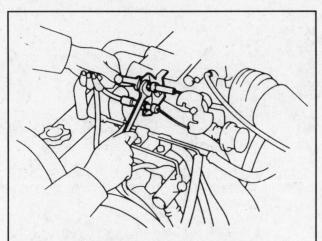

Fig. 31 On the 2WD Van automatic transmission, disconnect the throttle cable by loosening the adjusting nuts

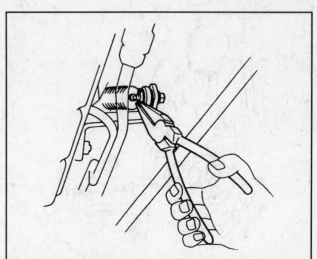

Fig. 34 Using pliers, disconnect the shift cable from the automatic transmission

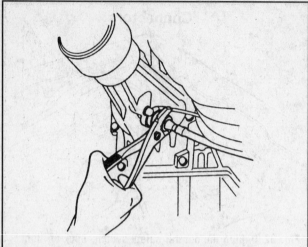

Fig. 35 Next on the 2WD automatic Van models, disconnect the speedometer cable

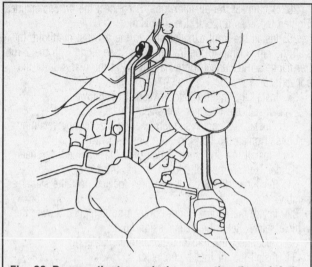

Fig. 38 Remove the transmission mounting through-bolt

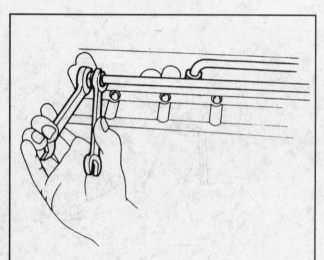

Fig. 36 Using two wrenches, loosen the nuts retaining the two oil cooler lines

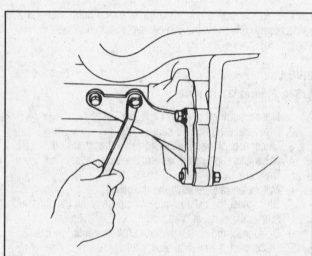

Fig. 39 Unbolt the stiffener plates from the automatic transmission housing

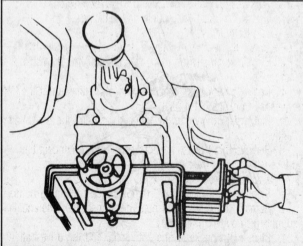

Fig. 37 Support the 2WD automatic transmission with a suitable jack

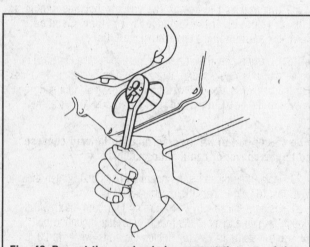

Fig. 40 Pry out the service hole cover at the rear of the engine; turn the crankshaft to gain access to the converter bolts

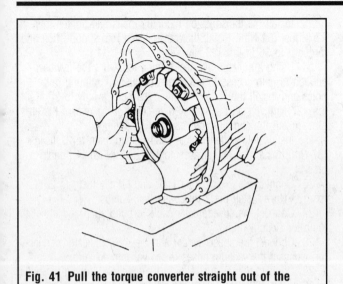

Fig. 41 Pull the torque converter straight out of the housing

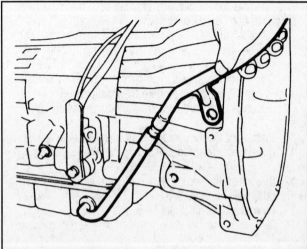

Fig. 42 Unbolt and remove the filler tube on the automatic transmission

13. Support the fuel tank on jackstands, remove the fuel tank mounting bolts, and, remove the rear transmission support bolt.

14. Remove the two stiffener plates from the transmission.

15. Pry out the service hole cover at the torque converter housing. Using a suitable flywheel turning tool, turn the flywheel enough to gain access to the torque converter mounting bolt holes and remove the 6 bolts.

16. Remove the transmission-to-engine bolts then slowly and carefully guide the transmission away from the engine. Be careful not to snap the throttle cable or neutral start switch wiring.

17. Place a drain pan under the transmission and pull the torque converter straight out and off, allow the fluid to run into the pan.

To install:

18. Apply grease to the center hub of the torque converter and the pilot hole in the crankshaft. Install the torque converter onto the transmission.

➡**Using calipers and a straight edge, measure from the installed surface of the torque converter to the front surface of the transmission housing. The correct distance should be 1.02 in. (26 mm). If the distance is less than specified, check for an improper converter installation.**

19. Place the transmission in the proper installation position on the transmission jack and align the 2 dowel pins on the block with the transmission housing. Align the converter mounting bolt holes with the holes in the flywheel. Install only 1 bolt at this time.

➡**Be careful not to tilt the transmission forward because the torque converter could slide out.**

20. Install the transmission mounting bolts and tighten them to 47 ft. lbs. (64 Nm). Install the starter assembly.

21. Using a suitable flywheel turning tool, turn the flywheel enough to gain access to the torque converter mounting bolt holes and install the 6 bolts. Tighten the bolts evenly to 20 ft. lbs. (27 Nm). Install the service hole cover at the rear of the engine. Install the engine under cover, if so equipped.

22. Install both stiffener plates and tighten them to 27 ft. lbs. (37 Nm).

23. Install the transmission rear support bolt and tighten it to 36 ft. lbs. (49 Nm).

24. Connect the 2 oil cooler lines and tighten them to 25 ft. lbs. (34 Nm). Install the 2 oil cooler line clamps.

25. Connect the speedometer cable. Connect the shift cable to the transmission.

26. Install the exhaust pipe clamp.

27. Install the driveshaft.

28. Lower the vehicle and unplug all wiring connectors.

29. Connect and adjust the transmission throttle cable. Refill the transmission fluid.

30. Reconnect the negative battery cable.

31. Start the engine, check the transmission fluid level and add as necessary. Road test the vehicle and check for leaks.

4WD Van

1. Disconnect the battery ground.
2. Disconnect the throttle cable.
3. Disconnect all wires attached to the transmission.
4. Raise and support the vehicle on jackstands.
5. Drain the fluid.
6. Remove the rear driveshafts as follows:
  a. Place matchmarks on the differential and the driveshaft flange.
  b. Remove the 4 bolts, washers and nuts, disconnect the driveshaft from the differential.
  c. Place matchmarks on the transfer case and the driveshaft flanges.
  d. Remove the 4 bolts, washers and nuts, disconnect the driveshaft from the transfer case.
7. Remove the front driveshafts as follows:
  a. Remove the 2 differential support bracket retaining bolts.
  b. Remove the 4 bolts and nuts, disconnect the differential support member from the body.
  c. Place matchmarks on the differential and the driveshaft flanges.

d. Remove the 4 bolts, washers and nuts, disconnect the driveshaft from the differential.

e. Pull out the driveshaft yoke from the transfer case and place a container under the extension housing to catch any oil that spills out.

8. Disconnect the exhaust pipe clamp from the transmission case. Remove the exhaust pipe from the manifold.

9. Disconnect the shift cable from the transmission outer lever.

10. Disconnect the vacuum hoses from the vacuum actuator.

11. Disconnect the speed sensor and the 4WD indicator wiring.

12. Disconnect the speedometer cable, ground strap and transfer indicator switch.

13. Disconnect the oil cooler lines.

14. Remove the control cable bracket from the transmission housing.

15. Remove the starter assembly.

16. Support the transmission with a floor jack.

17. Remove the rear transmission support bolt. Remove the two stiffener plates from the transmission.

18. Pry out the service hole cover at the torque converter housing. Using a suitable flywheel turning tool, turn the flywheel enough to gain access to the torque converter mounting bolt holes and remove the 6 bolts.

19. Remove the transmission-to-engine bolts and slowly and carefully guide the transmission away from the engine. Be careful not to snap the throttle cable or neutral start switch wiring.

20. Place a drain pan under the transmission and pull the torque converter straight out and off, allow the fluid to run into the pan.

To install:

21. Apply grease to the center hub of the torque converter and the pilot hole in the crankshaft. Install the torque converter onto the transmission.

➡**Using calipers and a straight edge, measure from the installed surface of the torque converter to the front surface of the transmission housing. The correct distance should be 1.07 in. (27 mm). If the distance is less than specified, check for an improper converter installation.**

22. Place the transmission in the proper installation position on the transmission jack and align the 2 dowel pins on the block with the transmission housing. Align the converter mounting bolt holes with the holes in the flywheel. Install only 1 bolt at this time.

➡**Be careful not to tilt the transmission forward because the torque converter could slide out.**

23. Install the transmission mounting bolts and tighten them to 47 ft. lbs. (64 Nm). Install the transmission rear support bolt and torque it to 36 ft. lbs. (49 Nm).

24. Using a suitable flywheel turning tool, turn the flywheel enough to gain access to the torque converter mounting bolt holes and install the 6 bolts. Tighten the bolts evenly to 20 ft. lbs. (27 Nm). Install the service hole cover at the rear of the engine. Install the engine under cover, if so equipped.

25. Install both stiffener plates and tighten them to 27 ft. lbs. (37 Nm). Install the starter assembly. Install the control cable bracket.

26. Connect the 2 oil cooler lines and tighten them to 25 ft. lbs. (34 Nm). Install the 2 oil cooler line clamps.

27. Connect the speedometer cable, ground strap and transfer indicator switch wiring.

28. Connect the speed sensor and the 4WD indicator connector. Connect the vacuum hoses to the vacuum actuator.

29. Connect the exhaust pipe to the manifold, tighten the bolts to 46 ft. lbs. (62 Nm). Install the exhaust pipe clamp.

30. Connect the transmission shift cable. Connect the ATF thermo sensor wiring.

31. Install the front driveshafts as follows:

a. Insert the yoke into the transfer case.

b. Align the matchmarks on the flanges and connect the flanges with the 4 bolts, washers and nuts. Tighten the bolts and nuts 31 ft. lbs. (42 Nm).

c. Connect the differential support member to the body with the 4 bolts, washers and nuts. Tighten the bolts and nuts 70 ft. lbs. (95 Nm).

d. Install the 2 bolts to the bracket. Tighten the bolts until they are snug.

32. Install the rear driveshafts as follows:

a. Align the matchmarks on the flanges and connect the flanges with the 4 bolts, washers and nuts. Tighten the bolts and nuts 54 ft. lbs. (74 Nm).

b. Connect the rear driveshaft to the differential by aligning the matchmarks on the flanges and attach the flanges with the 4 bolts, washers and nuts. Tighten the bolts and nuts 54 ft. lbs. (74 Nm).

33. Refill the transmission with the proper lubricant.

34. Lower the vehicle and attach all the disconnected wiring.

35. Connect and adjust the transmission throttle cable.

36. Reconnect the negative battery cable.

37. Start the engine check the transmission fluid level and add as necessary. Road test the vehicle and check for leaks.

TRANSFER CASE

♦ **See Figures 43 and 44**

The 1986–89 Van has an optional 4WD system that incorporates this transfer case unit. There is also an optional electronically controlled transfer case unit that can be order when purchasing the Van.

The transfer case, especially the electronically controlled transfer case is a very complex piece of equipment and requires a very thorough knowledge and general understanding of hydraulics in order to even considering rebuilding one. Any major repairs that may have to be made to the transfer case in your vehicle, should be left in the hands of a qualified factory service technician.

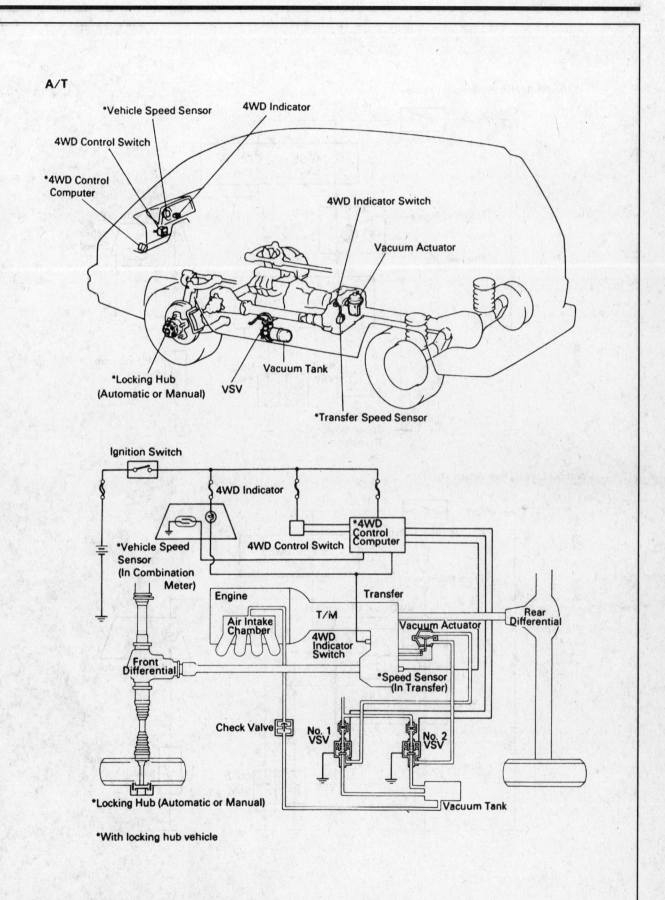

Fig. 43 View of the electrical shift type system—Van

With Locking Hub (Automatic) Vehicle

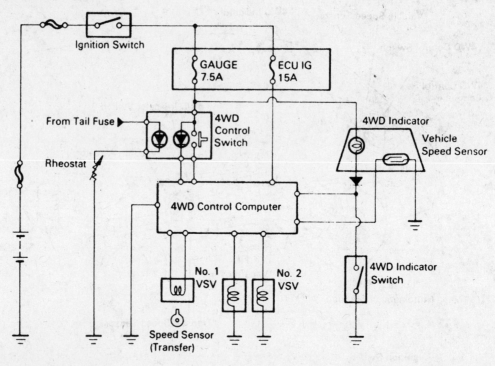

Without Locking Hub Vehicle (A/T)

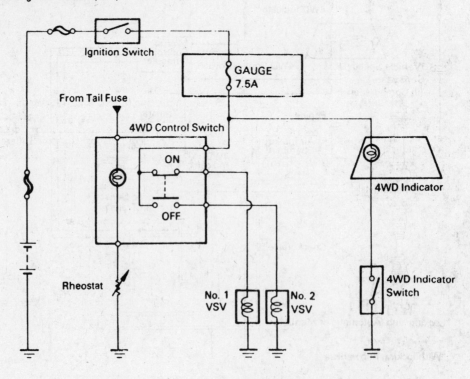

Fig. 44 Wiring schematic of the electrical shift transfer case assembly—Van

Adjustment

TRANSFER CASE SHIFT LEVER FREE-PLAY

1. Shift the transfer lever into the H4 position.
2. Loosen the 3 detent plate installation bolts.
3. Pull the top of the shift lever with a force of 4.4–8.8 lb.
4. Adjust the clearance between the detent plate H4 stopper surface and the shift lever so that it is 0.04 in. (1 mm) or less. Then tighten the detent plate installation bolts.

Transfer Case

REMOVAL & INSTALLATION

▶ **See Figures 45 thru 53**

1. Disconnect the battery ground.
2. Raise and support the vehicle on jackstands.
3. Remove the transfer case protector. Drain the fluid.
4. Remove the rear driveshafts as follows:
   a. Place matchmarks on the differential and the driveshaft flange.
   b. Remove the 4 bolts, washers and nuts, disconnect the driveshaft from the differential.
   c. Place matchmarks on the transfer case and the driveshaft flanges.
   d. Remove the 4 bolts, washers and nuts, disconnect the driveshaft from the transfer case.
5. Remove the front driveshafts as follows:
   a. Remove the 2 differential support bracket retaining bolts.
   b. Remove the 4 bolts and nuts, disconnect the differential support member from the body.
   c. Place matchmarks on the differential and the driveshaft flanges.
   d. Remove the 4 bolts, washers and nuts, disconnect the driveshaft from the differential.

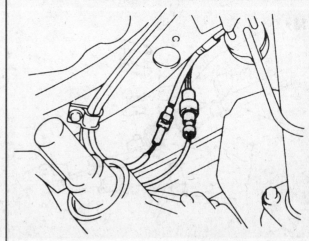

Fig. 46 Disconnect the transfer case indicator switch and speed sensor if equipped

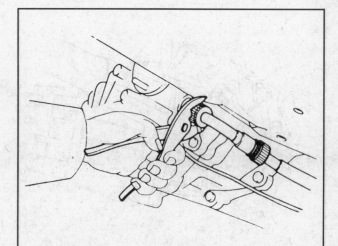

Fig. 47 Using pliers, disconnect then place aside the speedometer cable and ground strap

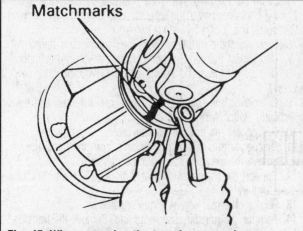

Fig. 45 When removing the transfer case, place matchmarks on the differential and driveshaft flange, then remove the retaining bolts

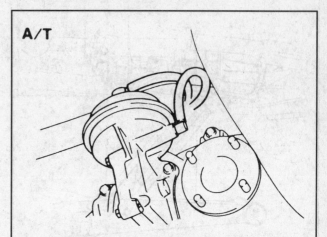

Fig. 48 When removing the transfer case on automatic models, disconnect the vacuum hoses leading to the acuator

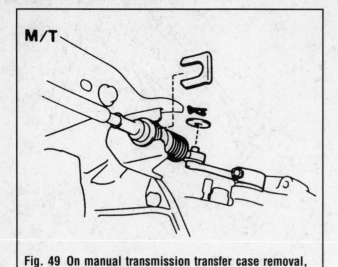

Fig. 49 On manual transmission transfer case removal, disconnect the transfer control cable

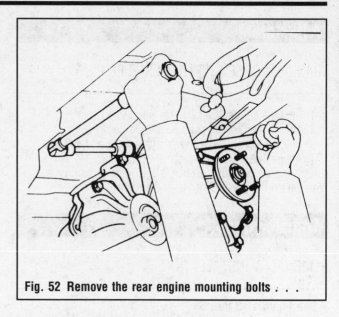

Fig. 52 Remove the rear engine mounting bolts . . .

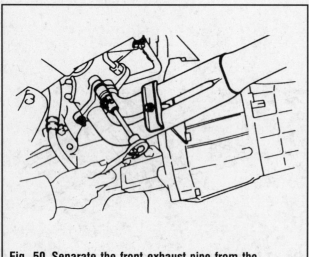

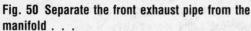

Fig. 50 Separate the front exhaust pipe from the manifold . . .

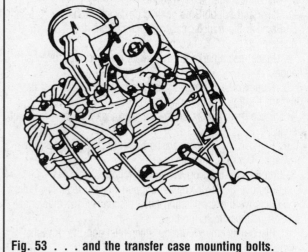

Fig. 53 . . . and the transfer case mounting bolts. Remove the transfer case assembly from the vehicle

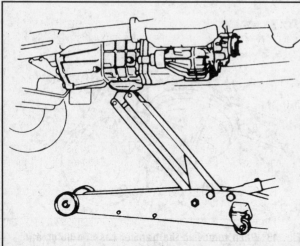

Fig. 51 . . . then raise the transmission up enough to remove the weight from the rear mounting

e. Pull out the driveshaft yoke from the transfer case and place a container under the extension housing to catch any oil that spills out.

6. Disconnect the shift cable from the transmission outer lever.

7. Disconnect the vacuum hoses from the vacuum actuator.

8. Disconnect the speed sensor and the 4WD indicator connectors.

9. Disconnect the speedometer cable, ground strap and transfer indicator switch wiring.

10. Disconnect the transfer control cable.

11. Disconnect the exhaust pipe clamp from the transmission case. Remove the exhaust pipe from the manifold.

12. Support the transmission with a floor jack. Raise the transmission slightly.

13. Remove the rear engine mounting bolt.

14. Remove the transfer case mounting. Remove the transfer case by pulling the transfer case toward the rear of the vehicle.

To install:

15. Install a new transfer case gasket to the transfer case adaptor.

16. Align the input shaft spline with the transmission output

shaft and push the transfer case fully into position. Apply a suitable thread sealer to the first 2 front bolts. Install the bolts and torque them to 27 ft. lbs. (37 Nm).

17. Install the rear engine mounting bolt and torque it to 36 ft. lbs. (49 Nm).

18. Connect the exhaust front pipe to the exhaust manifold. Tighten the bolts to 46 ft. lbs. (62 Nm). Install the front exhaust pipe clamp to the bracket.

19. Connect the transfer control cable.

20. Connect the vacuum hoses to the vacuum actuator.

21. Connect the speedometer cable and ground strap.

22. Attach the transfer indicator switch and speed sensor connector.

23. Install the front driveshafts as follows:

   a. Insert the yoke into the transfer case.

   b. Align the matchmarks on the flanges and connect the flanges with the 4 bolts, washers and nuts. Tighten the bolts and nuts 31 ft. lbs. (42 Nm).

   c. Connect the differential support member to the body with the 4 bolts, washers and nuts. Tighten the bolts and nuts 70 ft. lbs. (95 Nm).

   d. Install the 2 bolts to the bracket. Tighten the bolts until they are snug.

24. Install the rear driveshafts as follows:

   a. Align the matchmarks on the flanges and connect the flanges with the 4 bolts, washers and nuts. Tighten the bolts and nuts 54 ft. lbs. (74 Nm).

   b. Connect the rear driveshaft to the differential by aligning the matchmarks on the flanges and connect the flanges with the 4 bolts, washers and nuts. Tighten the bolts and nuts 54 ft. lbs. (74 Nm).

25. Refill the transfer case with the proper lubricant.

26. Lower the vehicle and connect all the disconnected wiring.

27. Reconnect the negative battery cable.

28. Start the engine check the transmission fluid level and add as necessary. Road test the vehicle and check for leaks.

DRIVELINE

Driveshaft and U-Joints

REMOVAL & INSTALLATION

Cressida

FRONT AND INTERMEDIATE
▶ See Figure 54

1. Disconnect the negative battery cable and raise and support the vehicle safely. Remove the driveshaft flange reinforcement.

2. Place matchmarks on the driveshaft and differential flanges.

3. Remove the 4 bolts and nuts and disconnect the driveshaft flange from the differential flange.

4. Place matchmarks on the driveshaft flange and the transmission yoke flange.

5. Remove the 4 bolts and nuts and disconnect the driveshaft flange from the transmission yoke flange.

6. Remove the center support bearing bracket retaining bolts.

7. Remove the center support bearing from the bearing support bracket.

8. Pull the driveshaft yoke out of the transmission and place a drain pan underneath so as to catch any oil that may leak out.

To install:

9. Install the driveshaft yoke into the transmission assembly.

10. Install the center support bearing into the bearing support bracket.

11. Install the center support bearing bracket and retaining bolts. Check that the center line of the center bearing is set to the center line of the bracket when the vehicle is in a no-load condition, adjust as necessary. Tighten the bolts to 30 ft. lbs. (40 Nm).

12. Reconnect the driveshaft flange to the transmission yoke flange. Install the retaining nuts and bolts and tighten them to 31 ft. lbs. (42 Nm).

13. Reconnect the driveshaft flange to the differential flange. Install the retaining nuts and bolts and tighten them to 31 ft. lbs. (42 Nm).

14. Install the driveshaft flange reinforcement.

15. Refill the transmission with the proper lubricant.

16. Lower the vehicle and connect the negative battery cable.

17. Road test the vehicle and check for leaks.

REAR

1. Disconnect the negative battery cable and raise and support the vehicle safely. Remove the driveshaft flange reinforcement.

2. Place matchmarks on the driveshaft and differential flanges.

3. Remove the 4 bolts and disconnect the driveshaft flange from the differential flange.

4. Place matchmarks on the driveshaft and center flanges.

5. Remove the 4 bolts and disconnect the driveshaft flange from the center flange.

To install:

6. Align the matchmarks and install the driveshaft flange to the center flange. Install the 4 retaining bolts and tighten them to 51–54 ft. lbs. (69–74 Nm).

7. Align the matchmarks and install the driveshaft flange to the differential. Install the 4 retaining bolts and tighten them to 51–54 ft. lbs. (69–74 Nm).

8. Install the driveshaft flange reinforcement. Lower the vehicle and install the negative battery cable.

2WD Van
▶ See Figure 55

1. Disconnect the negative battery cable and raise and support the vehicle safely. Place matchmarks on the differential and the driveshaft flange.

2. Remove the 4 bolts and nuts, disconnect the driveshaft from the differential.

3. Pull out the driveshaft yoke from the transmission and place a container under the extension housing to catch any oil that spills out.

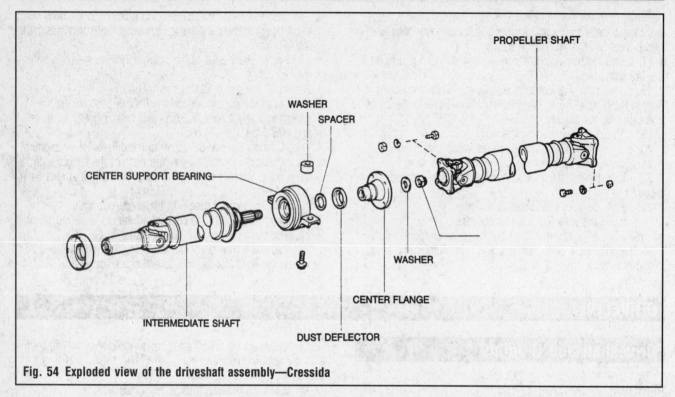

Fig. 54 Exploded view of the driveshaft assembly—Cressida

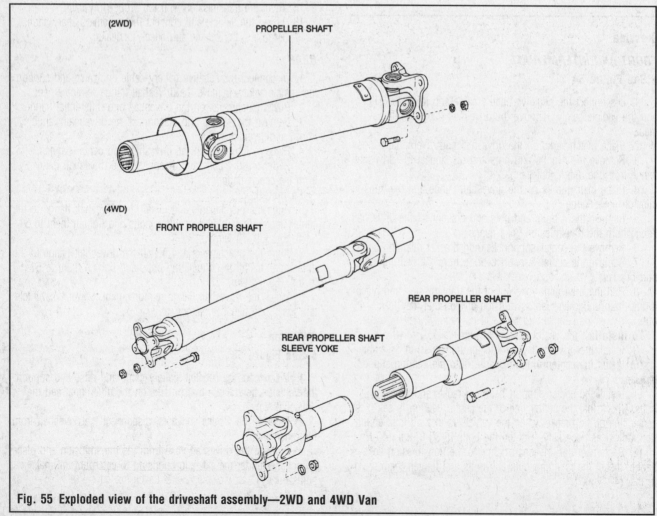

Fig. 55 Exploded view of the driveshaft assembly—2WD and 4WD Van

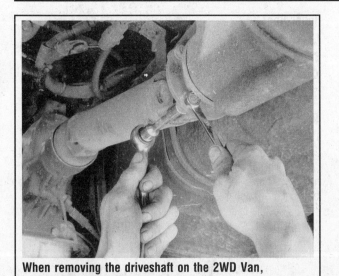

When removing the driveshaft on the 2WD Van, matchmark and unbolt the flange

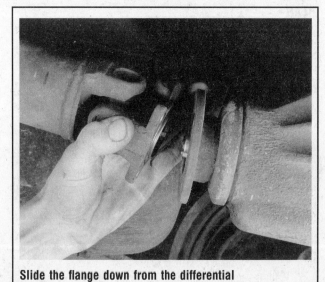

Slide the flange down from the differential

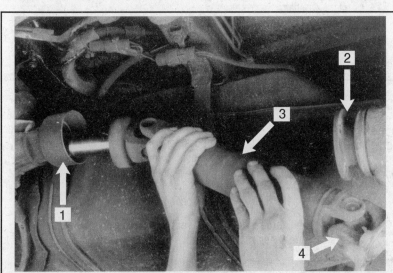

1. Transmission extension housing
2. Differential flange
3. Drive shaft
4. U-joint

Once the one end of the driveshaft is separated, slide the yoke from the other end of the driveshaft out of the transmission

To install:
4. Insert the yoke into the transmission.

5. Align the matchmarks on the flanges and connect the flanges with the 4 bolts, washers and nuts. Tighten the bolts and nuts 54 ft. lbs. (74 Nm).

6. Refill the transmission with the proper lubricant.

7. Lower the vehicle and connect the negative battery cable.

8. Road test the vehicle and check for leaks.

4WD Van

FRONT

1. Disconnect the negative battery cable and raise and support the vehicle safely. Remove the 2 differential support bracket retaining bolts.

2. Remove the 4 bolts and nuts, disconnect the differential support member from the body.

3. Place matchmarks on the differential and the driveshaft flanges.

4. Remove the 4 bolts, washers and nuts, disconnect the driveshaft from the differential.

5. Pull out the driveshaft yoke from the transfer case and place a container under the extension housing to catch any oil that spills out.

To install:
6. Insert the yoke into the transfer case.

7. Align the matchmarks on the flanges and connect the flanges with the 4 bolts, washers and nuts. Tighten the bolts and nuts 31 ft. lbs. (42 Nm).

8. Connect the differential support member to the body with the 4 bolts, washers and nuts. Tighten the bolts and nuts 70 ft. lbs. (95 Nm).

9. Install the 2 bolts to the bracket. Tighten the bolts until they are snug.

10. Refill the transmission with the proper lubricant.

11. Lower the vehicle and connect the negative battery cable.

12. Road test the vehicle and check for leaks.

REAR

1. Disconnect the negative battery cable and raise and support the vehicle safely. Place matchmarks on the differential and the driveshaft flange.
2. Remove the 4 bolts, washers and nuts, disconnect the driveshaft from the differential.
3. Place matchmarks on the transfer case and the driveshaft flanges.
4. Remove the 4 bolts, washers and nuts, disconnect the driveshaft from the transfer case.

To install:

5. Align the matchmarks on the flanges and connect the flanges with the 4 bolts, washers and nuts. Tighten the bolts and nuts 54 ft. lbs. (74 Nm).
6. Connect the rear driveshaft to the differential by aligning the matchmarks on the flanges and connect the flanges with the 4 bolts, washers and nuts. Tighten the bolts and nuts 54 ft. lbs. (74 Nm).
7. Refill the transmission with the proper lubricant.
8. Lower the vehicle and connect the negative battery cable.
9. Road test the vehicle and check for leaks.

U-JOINT OVERHAUL

1. Matchmark the yoke and the driveshaft.
2. Remove the lock rings from the bearings.
3. Position the yoke on vise jaws. Using a bearing remover and a hammer, gently tap the remover until the bearing is driven out of the yoke about 12mm.
4. Place the tool in the vise and drive the yoke away from the tool until the bearing is removed.
5. Repeat Steps 3 and 4 for the other bearings.
6. Check for worn or damaged parts. Inspect the bearing journal surfaces for wear.

To install:

7. Install the bearing cups, seals, and O-rings in the spider.
8. Grease the spider and the bearings.
9. Position the spider in the yoke.
10. Start the bearings in the yoke and then press them into place, using a vise.
11. Repeat Step 4 for the other bearings.
12. If the axial play of the spider is greater than 0.05mm, select lock rings which will provide the correct play. Be sure that the lock rings are the same size on both sides or driveshaft noise and vibration will result
13. Check the U-joint assembly for smooth operation.

CV-Joint And Boot

OVERHAUL

➡When replacing a CV-boot, be aware of the transmission type, transmission axle ratio, engine size, CV-joint type, right-hand or left side and inboard or outboard end. The following section should be used as a guide or an aid in rebuilding the CV-joints on the either end of the driveshaft.

Inner Boot

➡There are two different types of inboard CV-joints (Double Offset Joint and Tripod-Type) requiring different removal procedures.

DOUBLE OFFSET TYPE

▶ See Figure 56

1. Disconnect the negative battery cable.
2. Remove driveshaft assembly from vehicle. Place driveshaft in vise. Do not allow vice jaws to contact the boot or its clamp. The vise should be equipped with jaw caps to prevent damage to any machined surfaces.
3. Cut the large boot clamp using side cutters and peel away from the boot. After removing the clamp, roll boot back over shaft.
4. Remove wire ring ball retainer.
5. Remove outer race.
6. Pull inner race assembly out until it rests on the circlip. Using snapring pliers, spread stop ring and move it back on shaft.
7. Slide inner race assembly down the shaft to allow access to the circlip. Remove circlip.
8. Remove inner race assembly. Remove boot.

➡Circlips must not be reused. Replace with new circlips before assembly.

9. When replacing damaged CV-boots, the grease should be checked for contamination. If the CV-joints were operating satisfactorily and the grease does not appear to be contaminated, add grease and replace the boot. If the lubricant appears contaminated, proceed with a complete CV-joint disassembly and inspection.
10. Remove balls by prying from cage.

➡Exercise care to prevent scratching or other damage to the inner race or cage.

11. Rotate inner race to align lands with cage windows. Lift inner race out through the wider end of the cage.

To install:

12. Clean all parts (except boots) in a suitable solvent.
13. Inspect all CV-joint parts for excessive wear, looseness, pitting, rust and cracks.

➡CV-joint components are matched during assembly. If inspection reveals damage or wear the entire joint must be replaced as an assembly. Do not replace a joint merely because the parts appear polished. Shiny areas in ball races and on the cage spheres are normal.

14. Install a new circlip, supplies with the service kit, in groove nearest end of shaft. Do not over-expand or twist circlip during installation.
15. Install inner race in the cage. The race is installed through the large end of the cage with the circlip counterbore facing the large end of the cage.
16. With the cage and inner race properly aligned, install the balls by pressing through the cage windows with the heel of the hand.
17. Assemble inner race and cage assembly in outer race.
18. Push the inner race and cage assembly by hand, into the outer race. Install with inner race chamber facing out.

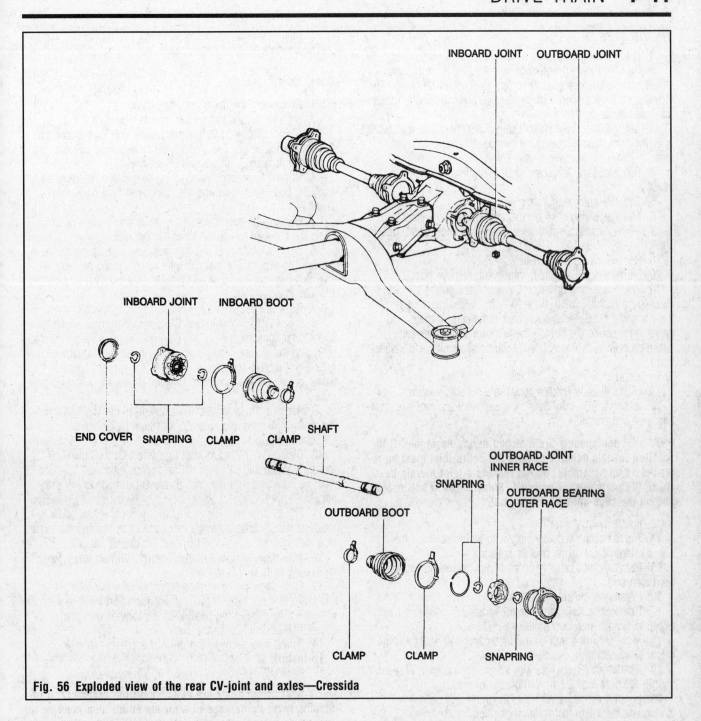

Fig. 56 Exploded view of the rear CV-joint and axles—Cressida

19. Install ball retainer into groove inside of outer race.
20. Install new CV-boot.
21. Tighten clamp securely but not to the point where the clamp bridge is cut or the boot is damaged.
22. Position stop ring and new circlip into grooves on shaft.
23. Fill CV-joint outer race with 3.2 oz. (90 grams) of grease, the spread 1.4 oz. (40 grams) of grease evenly inside boot for a total combined fill of 4.6 oz. (130 grams).
24. With boot peeled back, install CV-joint using soft tipped hammer. Ensure splins are aligned prior to installing CV-joint onto shaft.
25. Remove all excess grease from the CV-joint external surfaces.

26. Position boot over CV-joint. Before installing boot clamp, move CV-joint in or out, as necessary, to adjust to the proper length.

→Insert a suitable tool between the boot and outer bearing race and allow the trapped air to escape from the boot. The air should be released from the boot only after adjusting to the proper dimensions.

27. Ensure boot is seated in its groove and clamp in position.
28. Tighten clamp securely but not to the point where the clamp bridge is cut or the boot is damaged.
29. Install driveshaft assembly in vehicle.
30. Connect negative battery cable.

TRIPOD TYPE

1. Disconnect the negative battery cable.
2. Remove halfshaft assembly from vehicle. Place halfshaft in vice. Do not allow vise jaws to contact the boot or its clamp. The vise should be equipped with jaw caps to prevent damage to any machined surfaces.
3. Cut the large boot clamp using side cutters and peel away from the boot. After removing the clamp, roll boot back over shaft.
4. Bend retaining tabs back slightly to allow for tripod removal.
5. Separate outer race from tripod.
6. Move stop ring back on shaft using snapring pliers.
7. Move tripod assembly back on shaft to allow access to circlip.
8. Remove circlip from shaft.
9. Remove tripod assembly from shaft. Remove boot.
10. When replacing damaged CV-boots, the grease should be checked for contamination. If the CV-joints were operating satisfactorily and the grease does not appear to be contaminated, add grease and replace the boot. If the lubricant appears contaminated, proceed with a complete CV-joint disassembly and inspection.

To install:
11. Clean all parts (except boots) in a suitable solvent.
12. Inspect all CV-joint parts for excessive wear, looseness, pitting, rust and cracks.

➡**CV-joint components are matched during assembly. If inspection reveals damage or wear the entire joint must be replaced as an assembly. Do not replace a joint merely because the parts appear polished. Shiny areas in ball races and on the cage spheres are normal.**

13. Install new CV-boot.
14. Tighten clamp securely but not to the point where the clamp bridge is cut or the boot is damaged.
15. Install tripod assembly on shaft with chamfered side toward stop ring.
16. Install new circlip.
17. Compress circlip and slide tripod assembly forward over circlip to expose stop ring groove.
18. Move stop ring into groove using snapring pliers. Ensure it is fully seated in groove.
19. Fill CV-joint outer race with 3.5 oz. (100 grams) of grease and fill CV boot with 2.1 oz. (60 grams) of grease.
20. Install outer race over tripod assembly and bend 6 retaining tabs back into their original position.
21. Remove all excess grease from CV-joint external surfaces. Position boot over CV-joint. Move CV-joint in and out as necessary, to adjust to proper length.

➡**Insert a suitable tool between the boot and outer bearing race and allow the trapped air to escape from the boot. The air should be released from the boot only after adjusting to the proper dimensions.**

22. Ensure boot is seated in its groove and clamp in position.
23. Tighten clamp securely but not to the point where the clamp bridge is cut or the boot is damaged.
24. Install a new circlip, supplied with service kit, in groove nearest end of shaft by starting one end in the groove and working clip over stub shaft end and into groove.
25. Install halfshaft assembly in vehicle.
26. Connect negative battery cable.

Outer Boot

1. Disconnect the negative battery cable.
2. Remove halfshaft assembly from vehicle.
3. Place halfshaft in vice. Do not allow vise jaws to contact the boot or its clamp. The vise should be equipped with jaw caps to prevent damage to any machined surfaces.
4. Cut the large boot clamp using side cutters and peel away from the boot. After removing the clamp, roll boot back over shaft.
5. Support the interconnecting shaft in a soft jaw vise and angle the CV-joint to expose inner bearing race.
6. Using a brass drift and hammer, give a sharp tap to the inner bearing race to dislodge the internal circlip and separate he CV-joint from the interconnecting shaft. Take care not to drop the CV-joint at separation.
7. Remove the boot.
8. When replacing damaged CV-boots, the grease should be checked for contamination. If the CV-joints were operating satisfactorily and the grease does not appear to be contaminated, add grease and replace the boot. If the lubricant appears contaminated, proceed with a complete CV-joint disassembly and inspection.
9. Remove circlip located near the end of the shaft. Discard the circlip. Use new clip supplied with boot replacement kit and CV-joint overhaul kit.
10. Clamp CV-joint stub shaft in a vise with the outer face facing up. Care should be taken not to damage dust seal. The vise must be equipped with jaw caps to prevent damage to the shaft splines.
11. Press down on inner race until it tilts enough to allow removal of ball. A tight assembly can be tilted by tapping the inner race with wooden dowel and hammer. Do not hit the cage.
12. With cage sufficiently tilted, remove ball from cage. Remove all 6 balls in this manner.
13. Pivot cage and inner race assembly until it is straight up and down in outer race. Align cage windows with outer race lands while pivoting the bearing cage. With the cage pivoted and aligned, lift assembly from the outer race.
14. Rotate inner race up and out of the cage.

To install:
15. Clean all parts (except boots) in a suitable solvent.
16. Inspect all CV-joint parts for excessive wear, looseness, pitting, rust and cracks.

➡**CV-joint components are matched during assembly. If inspection reveals damage or wear the entire joint must be replaced as an assembly. Do not replace a joint merely because the parts appear polished. Shiny areas in ball races and on the cage spheres are normal.**

17. Apply a light coating of grease on inner and outer ball races. Install the inner race in cage.
18. Install inner race and cage assembly in the outer race.
19. Install the assembly vertically and pivot 90° into position.
20. Align cage and inner race with outer race. Tilt inner race and cage and install one of the 6 balls. Repeat this process until the remaining balls are installed.
21. Install new CV-joint boot.

22. Tighten clamp securely but not to the point where the clamp bridge is cut or the boot is damaged.

23. Install the stop ring, if removed.

24. Install a new circlip, supplied with the service kit, in groove nearest the end of the shaft.

25. Pack CV-joint with grease. Any grease remaining in tube should be spread evenly inside boot.

26. With the boot "peeled" back, position CV-joint on shaft and tap into position using a plastic tipped hammer.

27. Remove all excess grease from the CV-joint external surfaces.

28. Position boot over CV-joint.

29. Ensure boot is seated in its groove and clamp into position.

30. Tighten clamp securely but not to the point where the clamp bridge is cut or the boot is damaged.

31. Install halfshaft assembly in vehicle.

32. Connect negative battery cable.

DUST DEFLECTOR REPLACEMENT

➡**The dust deflector should be replaced only if inspection determines it to be cracked, broken or deteriorated.**

Remove the old deflector. Soak the new dust deflector in a container of hot water and let it soak for five to ten minutes. Position the dust deflector over the sleeve with the ribbed side facing the CV joint.

REAR AXLE

Understanding Rear Axles

The rear axle is a special type of transmission that reduces the speed of the drive from the engine and transmission and divides the power to the rear wheels. Power enters the rear axle from the driveshaft via the companion flange. The flange is mounted on the drive pinion shaft. The drive pinion shaft and gear which carry the power into the differential turn at engine speed. The gear on the end of the pinion shaft drives a large ring gear the axis of rotation of which is 90° away from the pinion. The pinion and gear reduce the gear ratio of the axle, and change the direction of rotation to turn the axle shafts which drive both wheels. The rear axle gear ratio is found by dividing the number of pinion gear teeth into the number of ring gear teeth.

The ring gear drives the differential case. The case provides the two mounting points for the ends of a pinion shaft on which are mounted two pinion gears. The pinion gears drive the two side gears, one of which is located on the inner end of each axle shaft.

By driving the axle shafts through the arrangement, the differential allows the outer drive wheel to turn faster than the inner drive wheel in a turn.

The main drive pinion and the side bearings, which bear the weight of the differential case, are shimmed to provide proper bearing preload, and to position the pinion and ring gears properly.

➡**The proper adjustment of the relationship of the ring and pinion gears is critical. It should be attempted only by those with extensive equipment and/or experience.**

Limited slip differentials include clutches which tend to link each axle shaft to the differential case. Clutches may be engaged either by spring action or by pressure produced by the torque on the axles during a turn. During turning on a dry pavement, the effects of the clutches are overcome, and each wheel turns at the required speed. When slippage occurs at either wheel, however, the clutches will transmit some of the power to the wheel which has the greater amount of traction. Because of the presence of clutches, limited slip units require a special lubricant.

Determining Axle Ratio

The drive axle of a car is said to have a certain axle ratio. This number (usually a whole number and a decimal fraction) is actually a comparison of the number of gear teeth on the ring gear and the pinion gear. For example, a 4.11 rear means that theoretically, there are 4.11 teeth on the ring gear and one tooth on the pinion gear or, put another way, the driveshaft must turn 4.11 times to turn the wheels once. Actually, on a 4.11 rear, there might be 37 teeth on the ring gear and 9 teeth on the pinion gear. By dividing the number of teeth on the pinion gear into the number of teeth on the ring gear, the numerical axle ratio (4.11) is obtained. This also provides a good method of ascertaining exactly what axle ratio one is dealing with.

Another method of determining gear ratio is to jack up and support the car so that both rear wheels are off the ground. Make a chalk mark on the rear wheel and the driveshaft. Put the transmission in neutral. Turn the rear wheel one complete turn and count the number of turns that the driveshaft makes. The number of turns that the driveshaft makes in one complete revolution of the rear wheel is an approximation of the rear axle ratio.

Axle Shaft, Bearing and Seal

REMOVAL & INSTALLATION

1983–87 Cressida

4 LINK TYPE AXLE SHAFT

◆ **See Figure 57**

1. Raise the rear of the car and support it securely by using jackstands.

✳✳ CAUTION

Be sure that the vehicle is securely supported. Remember, you will be working underneath it.

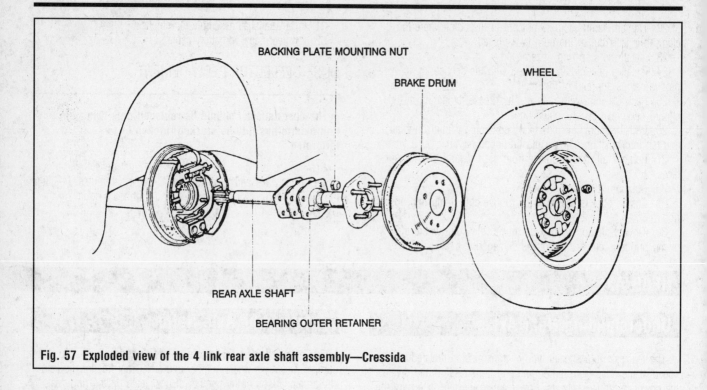

Fig. 57 Exploded view of the 4 link rear axle shaft assembly—Cressida

2. Drain the oil from the axle housing.

3. Remove the wheel cover, unfasten the lug nuts, and remove the wheel.

4. Punch matchmarks on the brake drum and the axle shaft to maintain rotational balance.

5. Remove the brake drum and related components, as outlined in this manual.

6. Remove the rear bearing retaining nut, if so equipped.

7. Remove the brake backing plate attachment nuts through the access holes in the rear axle shaft flange.

8. Use a slide hammer with a suitable adapter to withdraw the axle shaft from its housing.

✳✳ WARNING

Use care not to damage the oil seal when removing the axle shaft.

9. Repeat the procedure for the axle shaft on the opposite side. Be careful not to mix the components of the two sides.

10. Remove the rear axle bearing and inner retainer as follows:

a. Using a suitable grinder, grind down the inner retainer. Using a hammer and chisel, cut off the retainer and remove it from the shaft.

b. Using a suitable hydraulic press, press the rear axle bearing off of the shaft.

c. Using the same press, press on the bearing outer retainer and new bearing.

d. Heat the bearing inner retainer in a container of heated oil 302°F [150°C].

e. With the inner retainer still hot, press the retainer onto the rear axle shaft. Be sure that there is no oil or grease on the rear axle shaft or retainer. Face the non-beveled side of the inner retainer toward the bearing.

11. Using a suitable seal puller, remove the rear axle oil seal.

Apply some suitable multipurpose grease to the new seal and using a suitable seal driver, install the new oil seal.

12. Installation is performed in the reverse order of removal.

a. Place the bearing retainer and gasket on the axle shaft. Install the retainer and gasket with the notches pointing downward.

b. Install the rear axle coat the lips of the rear housing oil seal with multipurpose grease prior to installation of the rear axle shaft.

c. Install the rear axle into the axle housing along with 4 new self locking nuts. Tighten the nuts to 48 ft. lbs. (66 Nm). Be careful not to damage the oil seal. Also when installing the rear axle shaft, be careful not to hit or deform the oil deflector inside the axle housing.

1983–88 Cressida

IRS TYPE REAR AXLE SHAFT

▶ **See Figure 58**

1. Raise and safely support the vehicle.

2. Remove the rear wheel and tire assembly. Remove the disc brake caliper from the rear axle carrier and suspend it with wire. Remove the rotor disc.

3. Remove the rear driveshaft (disconnect the rear axle shaft side only).

4. Disconnect the axle driveshaft from the axle flange and lower the axle driveshaft out of the way.

5. Apply the parking brake completely (pulled up as far as possible).

6. Remove the axle flange nut.

➡**The axle flange nut is staked in place. It will be necessary to loosen the staked part of the nut with a hammer and chisel, prior to loosening the nut. Be sure to remove the washer from the axle shaft or it will not be possible to use the axle flange removal tool in the next Step.**

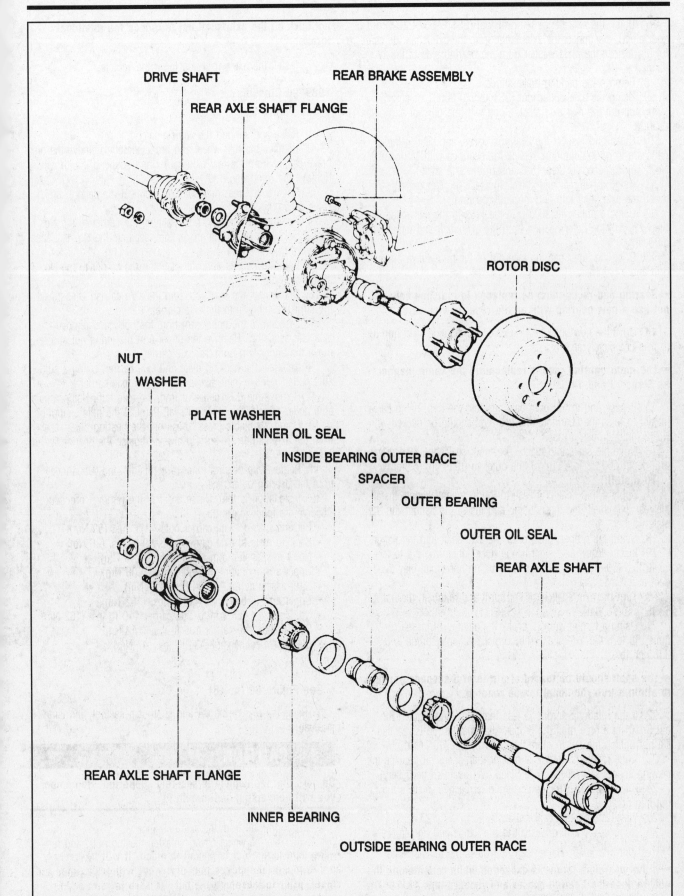

Fig. 58 Exploded view of the Independent Rear Suspension (IRS) rear axle shaft assembly—1983–88 Cressida

7. Using the axle flange removal tool (SST 09557-22022 or equivalent), disconnect the axle flange from the axle shaft. Be careful not to lose the plate washer from the bearing side of the flange.

8. Remove the parking brake shoes.

9. Using the axle puller tool (SST 09520-00031 or equivalent), pull out the rear axle shaft, along with the oil seal and outer bearing.

10. Clean and inspect the bearings, races, and seal. If these parts are in good condition, repack the bearings with MP grease No. 2 and proceed to Step 16 to install the axle shaft.

11. Using a hammer and chisel, increase the clearance between the axle shaft hub and the outer bearing.

12. Using a puller installed with the jaws in the gap made in Step 11, pull the outer bearing from the axle shaft and remove the oil seal.

13. Drive the outer bearing race out of the hub with a brass drift and a hammer.

➡**Bearing and races must be replaced in matched sets. Do not use a new bearing with an old race, or vice-versa.**

14. Drive the new outer bearing race into the axle shaft hub until it is completely seated.

➡**The inner bearing race is replaced in the same manner as Steps 13 and 14.**

15. Repack and install both bearings into the hub, being careful not to miss the bearings. The bearings should be packed with No. 2 multipurpose grease.

16. Drive the seals into place. The inner seal should be driven to a depth of 1.22 in. (31mm); the outer to 0.217 in. (5.5mm).

To install:

17. Apply a thin coat of grease to the axle shaft flange. Install the rear axle shaft into the housing and install the flange with the plate washer.

18. Using the proper tools, draw the axle shaft into the flange.

19. Install a new axle shaft flange nut. Tighten the nut to 22–36 ft. lbs. (30–49 Nm). There should be no horizontal play evident at the axle shaft.

20. Turn the axle shaft back and forth and retighten the nut to 58 ft. lbs. (78 Nm).

21. Using a torque wrench, check the amount of torque required to turn the axle shaft. The correct rotational torque is 0.9–3.5 inch lbs.

➡**The shaft should be turned at a rate of 6 seconds per turn to attain a true rotational torque reading.**

22. If the rotational torque is less than specified, tighten the nut 5–10° at a time until the proper rotational torque is reached. Do not tighten the nut to more than 145 ft. lbs. (196 Nm).

23. If the rotational torque is greater than specified, replace the bearing spacer and repeat those Steps over again (if necessary).

24. After the proper rotational torque is reached, restake the nut into position.

25. Install the parking brake shoes.

26. Connect the axle driveshaft to the flange and tighten the nuts to 51 ft. lbs. (69 Nm).

➡**If the maximum torque is exceeded while retightening the nut, replace the bearing spacer and repeat Steps 18–20. Do not back off the axle shaft nut to reduce the rotational torque.**

27. Install the rear wheel and lower the vehicle.

1989–90 Cressida

➡ **See Figure 59**

1. Raise and support the vehicle safely.

2. Remove the rear wheel and tire assembly. Remove the disc brake caliper from the rear axle carrier and suspend it with wire. Remove the rotor disc.

3. Remove the rear driveshaft. Disconnect the parking brake cable assembly.

4. Remove the bolt and nut attaching the carrier to the No. 1 suspension arm. Using the proper tool, separate the No. 1 suspension arm from the axle carrier.

5. Remove the bolt and nut attaching the carrier to the No. 2 suspension arm.

6. Disconnect the strut rod from the axle carrier. Disconnect the strut assembly from the axle carrier.

7. Disconnect the upper arm from the body and remove the axle hub assembly. Remove the upper arm mounting nut and remove the upper arm from the axle carrier.

8. Separate the backing plate and axle carrier. Using a suitable puller, remove the upper arm from the axle carrier.

9. Remove the dust deflector from the axle hub. Using a suitable puller remove the inner oil seal. Remove the hole snapring.

10. Using a suitable press, press out the bearing outer race from the axle carrier. Be sure to always replace the bearing as an assembly.

11. Remove the bearing inner race (inside) and 2 bearings from the bearing outer race.

12. Installation is the reverse order of the removal procedure. Observe the following torques:

- Backing plate-to-axle carrier nuts-43 ft. lbs. (58 Nm)
- Backing plate-to-axle carrier bolts-19 ft. lbs. (26 Nm)
- No. 1 suspension arm nut 36 ft. lbs. (49 Nm)
- Upper arm mounting nut-80 ft. lbs. (108 Nm)
- Strut assembly nut-101 ft. lbs. (137 Nm)
- Upper arm-to-body bolt-119 ft. lbs. (162 Nm)
- No. 2 suspension arm to axle carrier 119 ft. lbs. (162 Nm)
- Strut rod-to-axle carrier-105 ft. lbs. (142 Nm)
- Disc brake caliper bolts-34 ft. lbs. (47 Nm)

Van

➡ **See Figure 60 (p. 48)**

1. Raise the rear of the car and support it securely by using jackstands.

✳✳ CAUTION

Be sure that the vehicle is securely supported. Remember, you will be working underneath it.

2. Drain the oil from the axle housing.

3. Remove the wheel cover, unfasten the lug nuts, and remove the wheel.

4. Punch matchmarks on the brake drum and the axle shaft to maintain rotational balance.

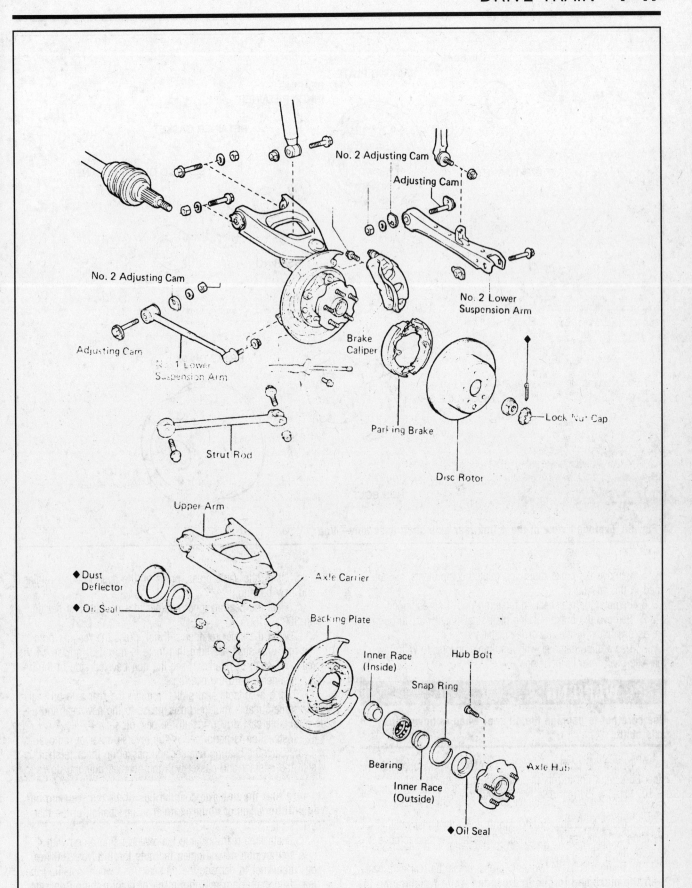

Fig. 59 Exploded view of the Independent Rear Suspension (IRS) rear axle shaft assembly—1989–90 Cressida

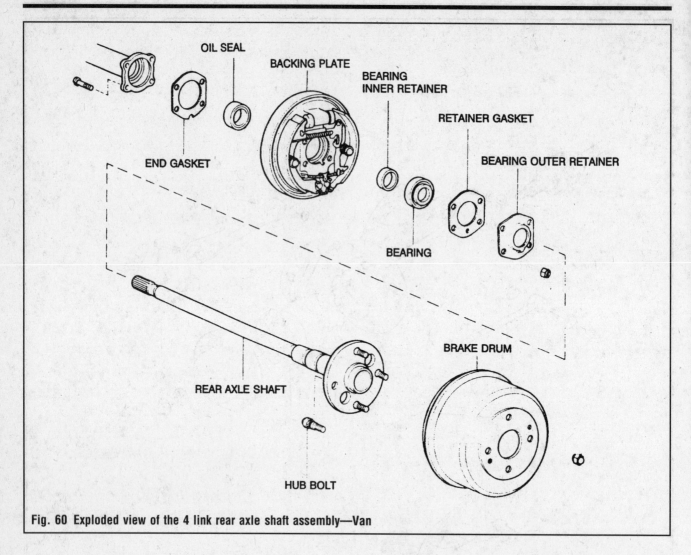

OIL SEAL

BACKING PLATE

BEARING INNER RETAINER

RETAINER GASKET

BEARING OUTER RETAINER

END GASKET

BEARING

BRAKE DRUM

REAR AXLE SHAFT

HUB BOLT

Fig. 60 Exploded view of the 4 link rear axle shaft assembly—Van

5. Remove the brake drum and related components, as outlined in this manual.

6. Remove the rear bearing retaining nut, if so equipped.

7. Remove the brake backing plate attachment nuts through the access holes in the rear axle shaft flange.

8. Use a slide hammer with a suitable adapter to withdraw the axle shaft from its housing.

✳✳ WARNING

Use care not to damage the oil seal when removing the axle shaft.

9. Repeat the procedure for the axle shaft on the opposite side. Be careful not to mix the components of the two sides.

10. Remove the rear axle bearing and inner retainer as follows:

    a. Using a suitable grinder, grind down the inner retainer. Using a hammer and chisel, cut off the retainer and remove it from the shaft.

    b. Using a suitable hydraulic press, press the rear axle bearing off of the shaft.

    c. Using the same press, press on the bearing outer retainer and new bearing.

    d. Heat the bearing inner retainer in a container of heated oil 302°F [150°C].

    e. With the inner retainer still hot, press the retainer onto the rear axle shaft. Be sure that there is no oil or grease on the rear axle shaft or retainer. Face the non-beveled side of the inner retainer toward the bearing.

11. Using a suitable seal puller, remove the rear axle oil seal. Apply some suitable multipurpose grease to the new seal and using a suitable seal driver, install the new oil seal.

12. Installation is performed in the reverse order of removal.

    a. Place the bearing retainer and gasket on the axle shaft. Install the retainer and gasket with the notches pointing downward.

    b. Install the rear axle coat the lips of the rear housing oil seal with multipurpose grease prior to installation of the rear axle shaft.

    c. Install the rear axle into the axle housing along with 4 new self locking nuts. Tighten the nuts to 48 ft. lbs. (66 Nm). Be careful not to damage the oil seal. Also when installing the rear axle shaft, be careful not to hit or deform the oil deflector inside the axle housing.

Differential Carrier

REMOVAL & INSTALLATION

1983–88 Cressida

CONVENTIONAL

▶ **See Figure 61**

1. Raise and support the vehicle safely.
2. Remove the drain plug and drain the differential oil.
3. Remove the rear axle shaft assembly as outlined earlier in this section.
4. Disconnect the driveshaft from the differential as outlined earlier in this section.
5. Remove the differential carrier assembly retaining bolts and remove the carrier assembly from the vehicle.
6. Installation is the reverse order of the removal procedure. Be sure to use a new gasket during the installation procedure and refill the differential with the proper amount of the gear oil.

IRS TYPE DIFFERENTIAL

▶ **See Figures 62 and 63**

1. Raise and support the vehicle safely.
2. Remove the drain plug and drain the differential oil.
3. Disconnect rear driveshafts.
4. Disconnect the driveshaft flange from the companion flange.
5. Remove the cushion mounting bolt from the differential support member.
6. Jack up the differential with a transmission jack and remove the carrier bolts.
7. Lower the differential carrier on the jack. When lowering the carrier, be careful that the differential does not separate.
8. Installation is the reverse order of the removal procedure. Be sure to use a new gasket during the installation procedure. Tighten the carrier retaining bolts to 61 ft. lbs. (83 Nm). Tighten the cushion mounting bolts to the differential support member to 51 ft. lbs. (69 Nm). Refill the differential with the proper amount of the gear oil.

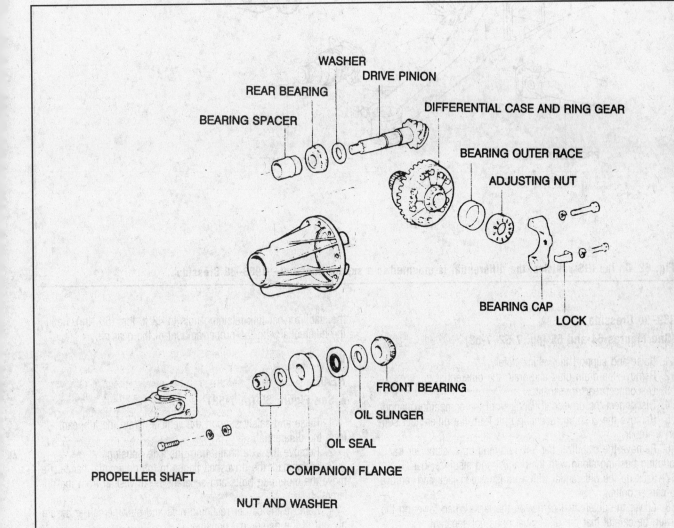

Fig. 61 Exploded view of the conventional differential carrier assembly—Cressida

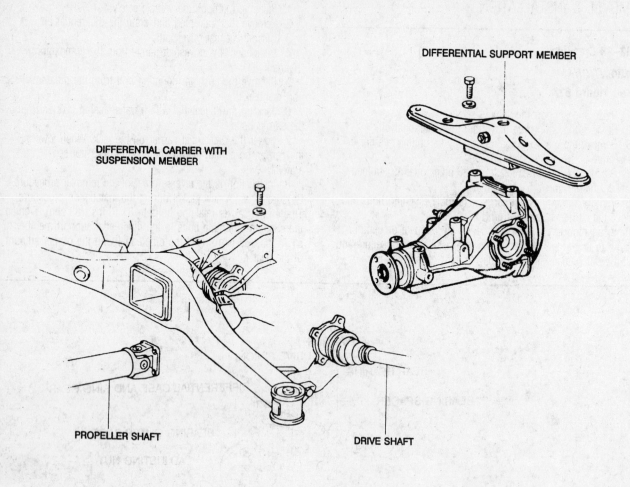

DIFFERENTIAL SUPPORT MEMBER

DIFFERENTIAL CARRIER WITH
SUSPENSION MEMBER

PROPELLER SHAFT

DRIVE SHAFT

Fig. 62 On the IRS vehicles, the differential is mounted to a support member—1983–88 Cressida

1989–90 Cressida

▶ **See Figures 64 and 65 (pp. 7-52–7-53)**

1. Raise and support the vehicle safely.
2. Remove the drain plug and drain the differential oil.
3. Disconnect rear driveshafts.
4. Disconnect the driveshaft flange from the companion flange.
5. Remove the cushion mounting bolt from the differential support member.
6. Remove the stabilizer bar link retaining nuts, stabilizer bar mounting bushing along with the bracket and stabilizer bar.
7. Jack up the differential with a transmission jack and remove the carrier bolts.
8. Lower the differential carrier on the jack. When lowering the carrier, be careful that the differential does not separate.
9. Installation is the reverse order of the removal procedure. Be sure to use a new gasket during the installation procedure. Tighten the carrier retaining bolts to 71 ft. lbs. (96 Nm). Tighten

the stabilizer bar link retaining nuts to 43 ft. lbs. (58 Nm). Refill the differential with the proper amount of the gear oil.

Van

REAR

▶ **See Figure 66 (p. 7-53)**

1. Raise and safely support the vehicle. Drain the lubricant from the differential.
2. Remove the axle shafts from the axle housing.
3. Matchmark the driveshaft flange to the differential flange. Remove the mounting bolts and separate the driveshaft from the differential.
4. Remove the carrier retaining nuts and pull the carrier assembly out of the differential housing.
5. When installing, use new gaskets and reverse the removal procedures. Tighten the differential-to-axle nuts to 23 ft. lbs. and the driveshaft flange-to-differential flange nuts/bolts to 31 ft. lbs.

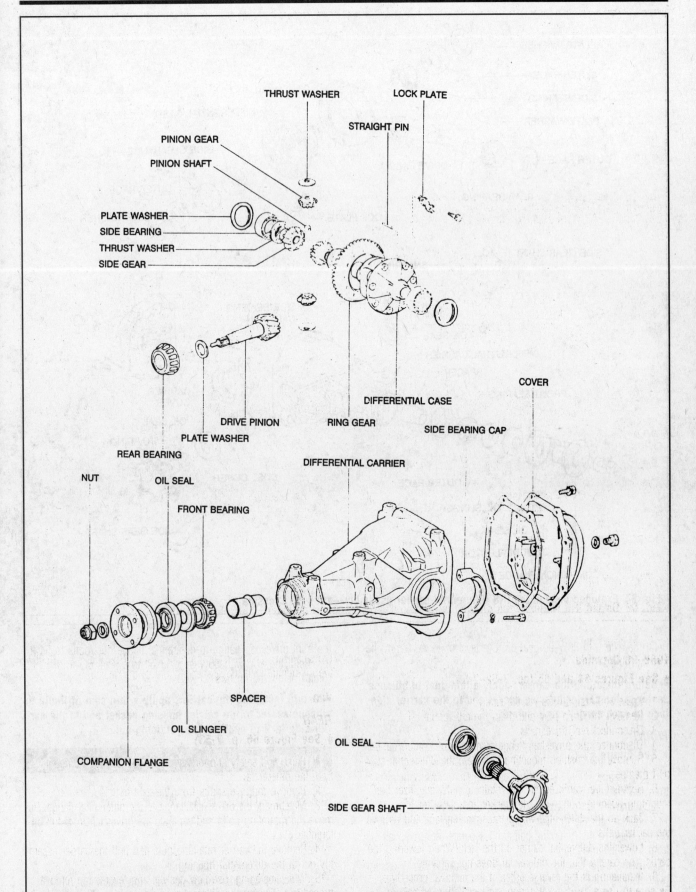

Fig. 63 Exploded view of the IRS differential carrier assembly—1983–88 Cressida

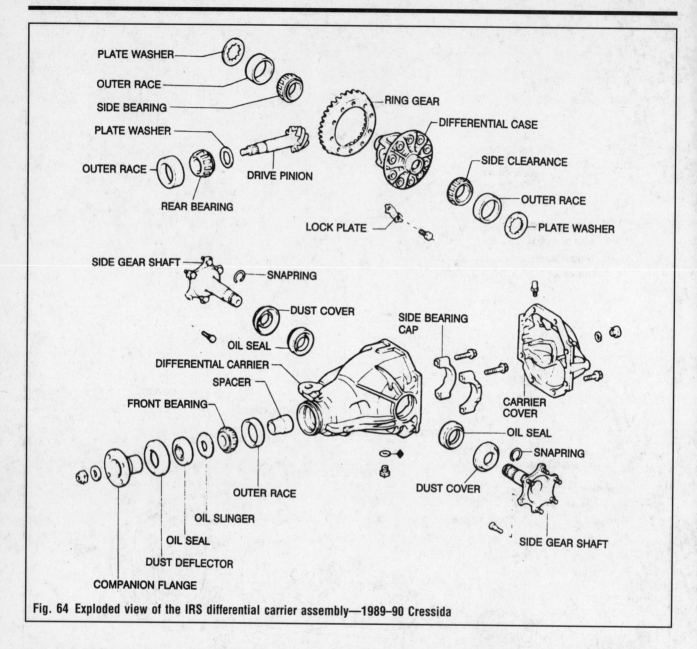

PLATE WASHER
OUTER RACE
SIDE BEARING
PLATE WASHER
OUTER RACE
REAR BEARING
DRIVE PINION
RING GEAR
DIFFERENTIAL CASE
SIDE CLEARANCE
OUTER RACE
PLATE WASHER
LOCK PLATE
SIDE GEAR SHAFT
SNAPRING
DUST COVER
OIL SEAL
DIFFERENTIAL CARRIER
SPACER
FRONT BEARING
OUTER RACE
OIL SLINGER
OIL SEAL
DUST DEFLECTOR
COMPANION FLANGE
SIDE BEARING CAP
CARRIER COVER
OIL SEAL
SNAPRING
DUST COVER
SIDE GEAR SHAFT

Fig. 64 Exploded view of the IRS differential carrier assembly—1989–90 Cressida

Refill the axle with 80W-90 gear oil to a level of ¼ in. (6mm) below the fill hole.

➡ **Before installing the carrier, apply a thin coat of silicone sealer to the carrier housing gasket and to the carrier side face of each carrier retaining nut.**

FRONT

◆ **See Figure 67 (p. 54)**

1. Raise and safely support the vehicle. Drain the lubricant from the differential.
2. Remove the front axle shafts from the axle housing.
3. Matchmark the front driveshaft flange to the differential flange. Remove the mounting bolts and separate the driveshaft from the differential.
4. Remove the carrier retaining nuts and pull the carrier assembly out of the differential housing.
5. When installing, use new gaskets and reverse the removal procedures. Tighten the differential-to-axle nuts to 19 ft. lbs. and

the front driveshaft flange-to-differential flange nuts/bolts to 54 ft. lbs. Refill the axle with 80W-90 gear oil to a level of ¼ in. (6mm) below the fill hole.

➡ **Before installing the carrier, apply a thin coat of liquid or silicone sealer to the carrier housing gasket and to the carrier side face of each carrier retaining nut.**

Pinion Seal

REMOVAL & INSTALLATION

Cressida

1. Raise and support the vehicle safely.
2. Remove the drain plug and drain the differential oil.
3. Disconnect the driveshaft flange from the differential companion flange.

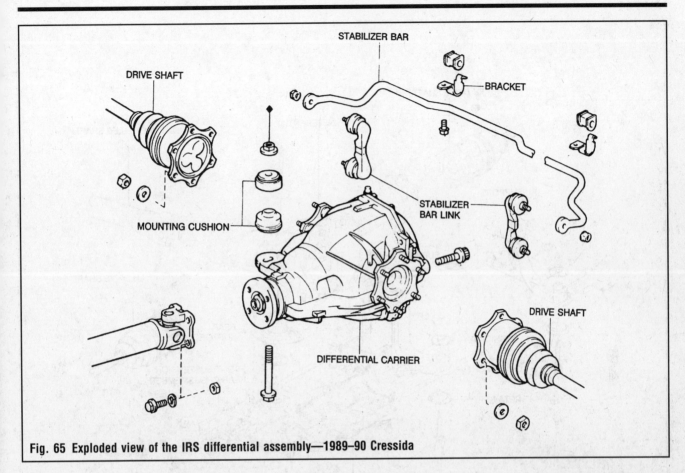

Fig. 65 Exploded view of the IRS differential assembly—1989–90 Cressida

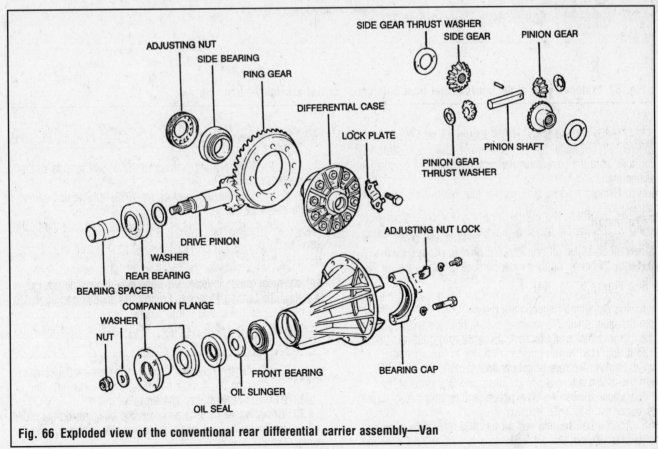

Fig. 66 Exploded view of the conventional rear differential carrier assembly—Van

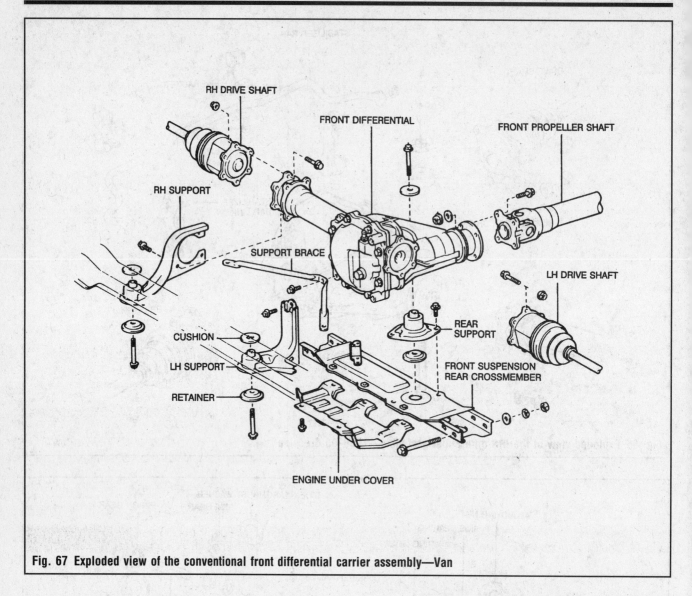

Fig. 67 Exploded view of the conventional front differential carrier assembly—Van

4. Using a hammer and chisel, loosen the staked part of the differential companion flange retaining nut. Using a suitable holding tool, hold the companion flange and remove the companion flange nut.

5. Using a suitable seal removal tool, remove the oil seal and oil slinger.

To install:

6. Install the oil slinger. Using a suitable seal driver, drive in a new oil seal. The oil seal installed drive in depth should be 0.039 in. (1.0mm). Apply a multi-purpose grease to the oil seal lip.

7. Install the companion flange. Coat the threads of the flange retaining nut with a multipurpose grease.

8. Using a suitable retaining tool to hold the flange, tighten the flange retaining nut to 80 ft. lbs. (108 Nm) 1989–90 Cressida 134 ft. lbs. (181 Nm).

9. Adjust the front bearing preload as follows:

a. Using a torque wrench, measure the preload of the backlash between the drive pinion and the ring gear.

b. The new bearing preload for 1983–88 Cressida should be 14–19 inch lbs.

c. The new bearing preload for 1989–90 Cressida should be 4–7 inch lbs.

d. The used bearing preload for 1983–88 Cressida should be 7–10 inch lbs.

e. The used bearing preload for 1989–90 Cressida should be 3–5 inch lbs.

f. If the preload is greater than specified, replace the bearing spacer.

g. If the preload is less than specified, retighten the nut to 9 ft. lbs. at a time until the specified reload is reached. If the maximum torque is exceeded while retightening the nut, replace the bearing spacer and repeat the preload procedure. Do not back off the pinion nut to reduce the preload. The maximum torque is 174 ft. lbs. (235 Nm), 1989–90 Cressida 250 ft. lbs. (338 Nm).

10. Stake the companion flange retaining nut.

11. Reconnect the driveshaft flange to the differential companion flange. Tighten the 4 bolts and nuts to 31 ft. lbs. (42 Nm), 1989–90 Cressida 54 ft. lbs. (74 Nm).

12. Complete the installation procedure by reversing the order of the removal procedure. Refill the differential with the proper amount of the gear oil.

Van

1. Raise and safely support the vehicle.
2. Matchmark and remove the driveshaft.
3. Remove the companion flange from the differential.
4. Using puller 09308-10010 or equivalent, remove the oil seal from the housing.
5. Remove the oil slinger.
6. Remove the bearing and spacer.

To Install:

7. Install the bearing spacer and bearing.

➡**Lubricate the seal lips with multipurpose grease before installing it.**

8. Install the oil slinger and using seal installer 09554-30011 or equivalent, install the oil seal.
9. Drive the seal into place, to a depth of 0.59 in. (15mm) below the housing lip for 7.5 in. (190.5mm) axles and 0.39 in. (10mm) below the lip for 8 in. (203.2mm) axles.
10. Install the companion flange and install the driveshaft.
11. Lower the vehicle.

Axle Housing

REMOVAL & INSTALLATION

Van

FRONT 4WD VEHICLES

1. Raise and safely support the vehicle.
2. Matchmark and remove the front driveshaft.

FRONT DRIVE AXLE

Halfshaft

REMOVAL & INSTALLATION

4WD Van

♦ **See Figure 68**

1. Remove the 4WD hub (with the flange) from the axle hub.
2. Raise and safely support the vehicle. Remove the wheel and tire assembly.
3. Disconnect and plug the brake line from the caliper. Remove the caliper from the axle hub.
4. Using a drift punch and a hammer, drive the lock washer tabs away from the locknut.
5. Remove the locknut from the halfshaft. Remove the lock washer, the adjusting nut, the thrust washer, the outer bearing and the axle hub/disc assembly from the vehicle.
6. Remove the knuckle spindle bolts, the dust seal and the dust cover. Using a brass bar and a hammer, tap the steering spindle from the steering knuckle.
7. Turn the halfshaft until a flat spot on the outer shaft is in the upper position, then pull the halfshaft from the steering knuckle.

3. Disconnect the axle shafts from the axle assembly.
4. Disconnect vacuum hoses, if equipped with automatic locking hubs.
5. Disconnect the 4WD indicator. Remove the front differential mounting bolt.
6. Support the axle housing with a suitable jack and remove the rear mounting bolts.

To install:

7. Install the differential in position under the vehicle.
8. Install the rear mounting bolts and tighten to 123 ft. lbs. (167 Nm).
9. Install the front mounting bolt and tighten to 108 ft. lbs. (147 Nm).
10. Connect vacuum hoses and the 4WD indicator.
11. Install the axle shafts and the driveshaft, aligning matchmarks made during removal.
12. Refill the axle with the correct oil and lower the vehicle.

REAR—4WD VEHICLE

1. Raise and safely support the vehicle.
2. Remove the tire and wheel assemblies.
3. Support the axle housing with a suitable jack.
4. Disconnect the shock absorber lower bolts.
5. Disconnect the stabilizer bar and lateral rod. Also, disconnect the upper and lower control arms.
6. Remove the brake lines from the axle housing.
7. Slowly lower the axle housing from the vehicle.
8. Installation is the reverse of the removal procedure. Observe the following torques:
   a. Shock absorber bottom bolts-27 ft. lbs. (37 Nm) 2WD, 94 ft. lbs. (127 Nm) 4WD vehicles.
   b. Upper control arm bolts-105 ft. lbs. (142 Nm).
   c. Lower control arm bolts-105 ft. lbs. (142 Nm).
   d. Stabilizer bar bolts-19 ft. lbs. (25 Nm).

8. Using a slide hammer, pull the oil seal from the axle housing.
9. Using a clean shop towel, wipe the grease from inside the steering knuckle housing and the halfshaft.

To install:

10. Using an oil seal installation tool, drive a new oil seal into the axle housing until it seats.
11. Install the halfshaft into the axle housing.
12. Using multi-purpose grease, fill the steering knuckle cavity to about ¾ full.
13. To complete the installation, use new seals/gaskets and reverse the removal procedures.
14. Tighten the steering spindle-to-steering knuckle bolts to 38 ft. lbs., the axle hub adjusting nut to 18 ft. lbs., the axle hub locknut to 33 ft. lbs., the free wheel/locking hub nuts to 23 ft. lbs. and the brake caliper to 65 ft. lbs.

➡**To install the wheel bearings with the axle hub, tighten the adjusting nut to 43 ft. lbs., turn the axle hub (back and forth, several times), loosen the nut and retighten the adjusting nut to 18 ft. lbs.**

15. Install the wheel and tire assembly. Lower the vehicle.

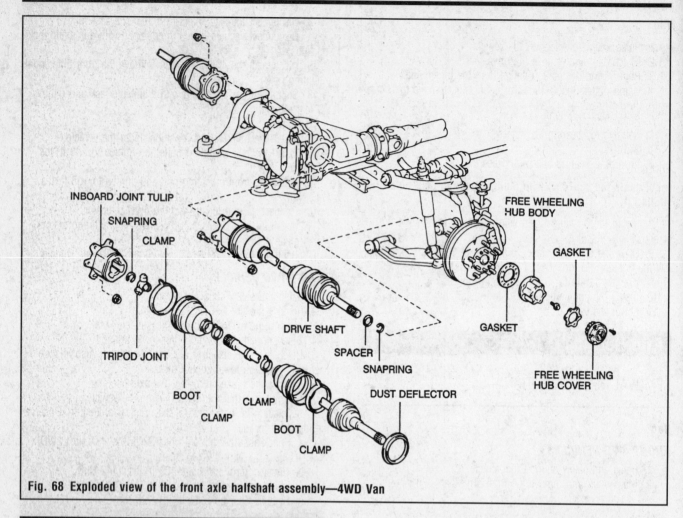

INBOARD JOINT TULIP

SNAPRING

CLAMP

TRIPOD JOINT

BOOT

CLAMP

CLAMP

BOOT

CLAMP

DRIVE SHAFT

SPACER

SNAPRING

DUST DEFLECTOR

FREE WHEELING HUB BODY

GASKET

GASKET

FREE WHEELING HUB COVER

Fig. 68 Exploded view of the front axle halfshaft assembly—4WD Van

Axle Bearing

REMOVAL & INSTALLATION

4WD Van

1. Raise and safely support the vehicle. Remove the 4WD hubs.
2. Using a small prybar, pry the grease seal from the rear of the disc/hub assembly, then remove the inner bearing from the assembly.
3. Using a shop cloth, wipe the grease from inside the disc/hub assembly.
4. Using a brass drift, drive the outer bearing races from each side of the disc/hub assembly.
5. Using solvent, clean all of the parts and blow dry with compressed air.
To install:
6. Using a bearing installation tool, drive the outer races into the disc/hub assembly until they seat against the shoulder.

7. Using multi-purpose grease, coat the area between the races and pack the bearings.
8. Place the inner bearing into the rear of the disc/hub assembly. Using a bearing installation tool, drive a new grease seal into the rear of the disc/hub assembly until it is flush with the housing.
9. Install the disc/hub assembly onto the axle shaft, the outer bearing, the thrust washer and the adjusting nut.
10. To adjust the bearing preload, perform the following:
   a. Tighten the adjusting nut to 43 ft. lbs.
   b. Turn the disc/hub assembly 2–3 times, from the left to the right.
   c. Loosen the adjusting nut until it can be turned by hand.
   d. Retighten the adjusting nut to 18 ft. lbs.
   e. Install the lock washer and the locknut. Tighten the locknut to 33 ft. lbs.
   f. Check that the bearing has no play.
   g. Using a spring gauge, connect it to a wheel stud, the gauge should be held horizontal, then measure the rotating force, it should be 6–12 lbs.

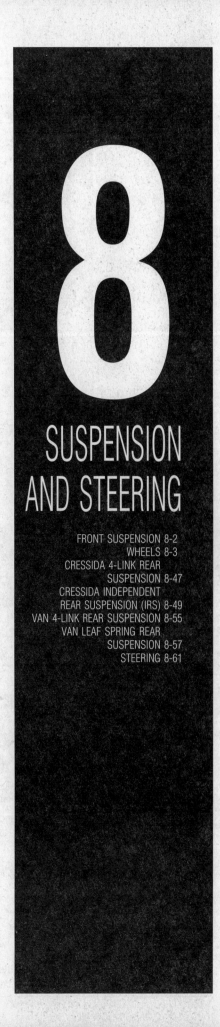

8

SUSPENSION
AND STEERING

FRONT SUSPENSION

FRONT SUSPENSION COMPONENTS - 2WD VAN

1. Ball joint
2. Tie rod
3. Lower control arm
4. Stabilizer bar
5. Stabilizer bar link
6. Stabilizer bar bracket
7. Strut bar

When removing the steering wheel, unscrew the horn pad . . .

WHEELS

Wheel Assembly

REMOVAL & INSTALLATION

▶ **See Figures 1 thru 12**

1. Apply the parking brake and block the opposite wheel.
2. If equipped with an automatic transmission, place the selector lever in **P.** For manual transmission models, place the shifter in Reverse.
3. If equipped, remove the wheel cover or hub cap.
4. Break loose the lug nuts. If a nut is stuck, never use heat to loosen it or damage to the wheel and bearings may occur. If the nuts are seized, one or two heavy hammer blows directly on the end of the bolt head usually loosens the rust. Be careful as continued pounding will likely damage the brake drum or rotor.

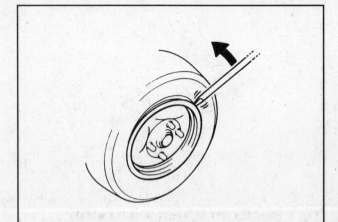

Fig. 3 Remove the trim ring on the outer side of the wheel (if equipped)

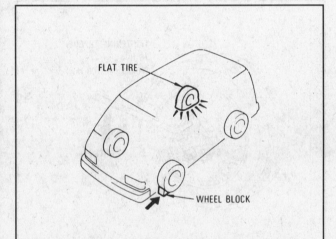

Fig. 1 Always block the wheel diagonally opposite the flat tire to keep the vehicle from rolling when raised

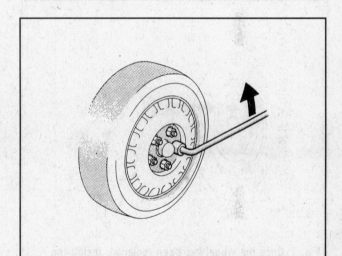

Fig. 4 Loosen all of the lug nuts in this direction

Fig. 2 Remove the hub cap by prying with the beveled end of the wheel nut wrench tool

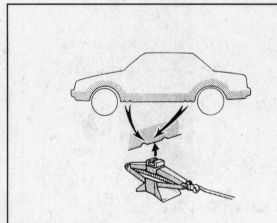

Fig. 5 Position a jack in the proper location after the lug nuts have been loosened

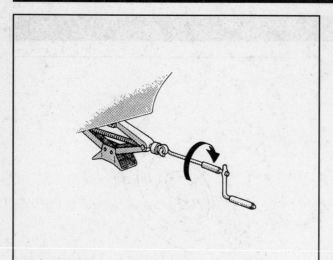

Fig. 6 Raise the jack high enough so the wheel clearance is just up off the ground

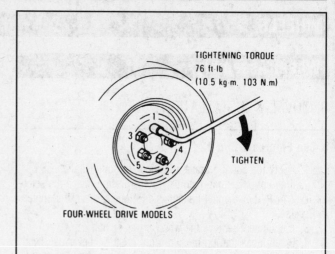

TIGHTENING TORQUE
76 ft-lb
(10.5 kg·m, 103 N.m)

TIGHTEN

FOUR-WHEEL DRIVE MODELS

Fig. 9 Tighten the lug nuts on the 4WD Van models in this order

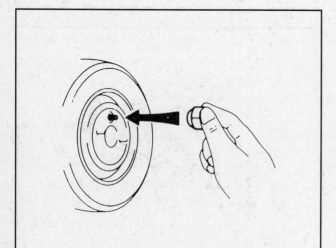

Fig. 7 Once the wheel has been replaced, install the wheel on the vehicle and finger-tighten the lug nuts

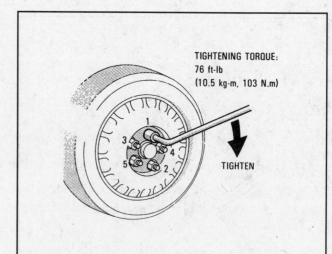

TIGHTENING TORQUE:
76 ft-lb
(10.5 kg-m, 103 N.m)

TIGHTEN

Fig. 10 On Cressida models, tighten the lug nuts as shown

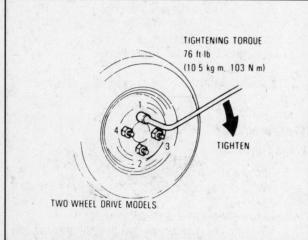

TIGHTENING TORQUE
76 ft-lb
(10.5 kg·m, 103 N·m)

TIGHTEN

TWO WHEEL DRIVE MODELS

Fig. 8 Lower the vehicle and tighten the lug nuts in correct order—2WD Van

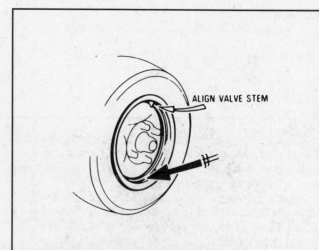

ALIGN VALVE STEM

Fig. 11 Place the trim ring on the wheel with the valve stem aligned properly

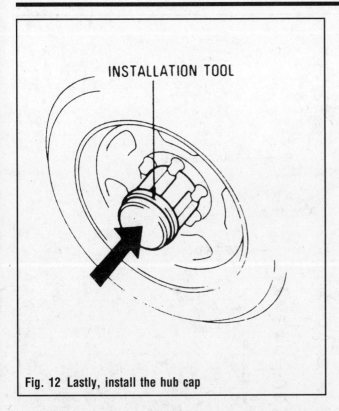

INSTALLATION TOOL

Fig. 12 Lastly, install the hub cap

5. Raise the vehicle until the tire is clear of the ground. Support the vehicle safely using jackstands.

6. Remove the lug nuts and the tire and wheel assembly.

To install:

7. Make sure the wheel and hub mating surfaces as well as the wheel lug studs are clean and free of all foreign material. Always remove rust from the wheel mounting surfaces and the brake rotors/drums. Failure to to so may cause the lug nuts to loosen in service.

8. Position the wheel on the hub or drum and hand-tighten the lug nuts. Tighten all the lug nuts, in a crisscross pattern, until they are snug.

9. Remove the supports, if any, and lower the vehicle. Tighten the lug nuts, in a crisscross pattern. Always use a torque wrench to achieve the proper lug nut torque and to prevent stretching the wheel studs.

10. Repeat the torque pattern to assure proper wheel tightening.

11. If equipped, install the hub cap or wheel cover.

INSPECTION

Check the wheels for any damage. They must be replaced if they are bent, dented, heavily rusted, have elongated bolt holes, or have excessive lateral or radial run-out. Wheels with excessive run-out may cause a high-speed vehicle vibration.

Replacement wheels must be of the same load capacity, diameter, width, offset and mounting configuration as the original wheels. Using the wrong wheels may affect wheel bearing life, ground and tire clearance, or speedometer and odometer calibrations.

Strut and Stabilizer Bars

REMOVAL & INSTALLATION

Cressida

1983–88 MODELS

▶ **See Figures 13 thru 19**

1. Disconnect the negative battery cable.
2. Raise and support the vehicle safely.
3. Remove the engine under cover assembly.
4. Disconnect the stabilizer bar from the lower control arms.
5. Remove both stabilizer bar brackets from the strut bar brackets.
6. Remove the strut bar retaining nuts and disconnect the strut bar from the lower arm.
7. Remove the strut bar bracket bolts.
8. On the 1983–84 models, pull out the stabilizer bar through the strut bar bracket hole.
9. On the 1985–88 models, raise the tip of the stabilizer bar and pull out the strut bar. Remove the rear retainer and shim from the strut bar if so equipped.
10. On the 1985–88 models, remove the strut bar bracket retaining bolts and remove the strut bar bracket along with the stabilizer bar.

To install:

11. On the 1985–88 models, install the strut bar bracket with the stabilizer bar. Install the retaining bolts and tighten them to 32 ft. lbs. (43 Nm).
12. On the 1985–88 models, install rear retainer and shim to the strut bar if so equipped. Install the strut bar to the bracket.
13. On the 1983–84 models, install the stabilizer bar through the strut bar bracket hole.
14. Install the strut bar bracket bolts and tighten the bolts to 9 ft. lbs. (13 Nm).
15. Install the strut bar to the lower control arm. Install the retaining nuts and torque them to 43 ft. lbs. (58 Nm).
16. Install both stabilizer bar brackets to the strut bar brackets.
17. Install the stabilizer bar to the lower control arms. Tighten them to 13 ft. lbs. (18 Nm).
18. Install the front retainer and nut to the strut bar. Tighten the nut to 76 ft. lbs. (103 Nm) 1983–84 models and 87 ft. lbs. (118 Nm) on the 1985–88 models.
19. Install the engine under cover assembly.
20. Lower the vehicle safely.
21. Reconnect the negative battery cable. Check the wheel alignment.

1989–90 MODELS

▶ **See Figure 19a**

1. Disconnect the negative battery cable.
2. Raise and support the vehicle safely. Remove the front wheel assembly.
3. Remove the engine under cover assembly.
4. Disconnect the stabilizer bar links from the stabilizer bar.
5. Remove the right and left stabilizer bushings.

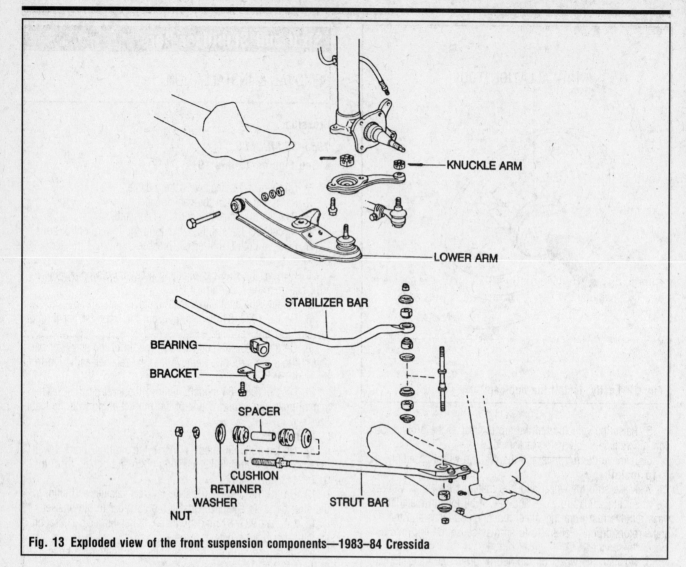

Fig. 13 Exploded view of the front suspension components—1983–84 Cressida

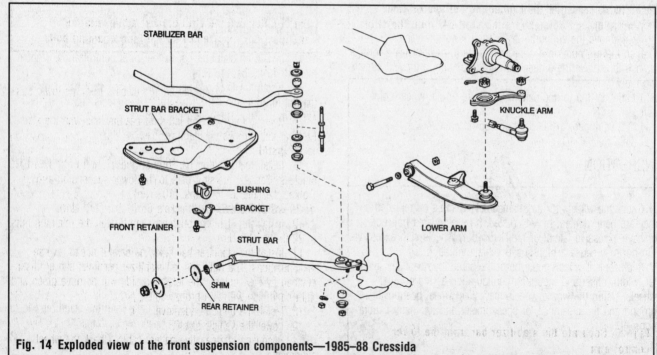

Fig. 14 Exploded view of the front suspension components—1985–88 Cressida

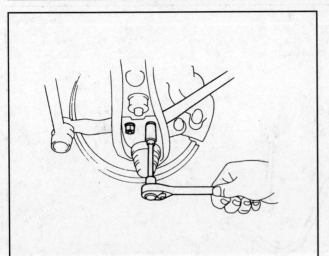

Fig. 15 Disconnect the strut bar from the lower control arm by removing the two nuts from the lower arm

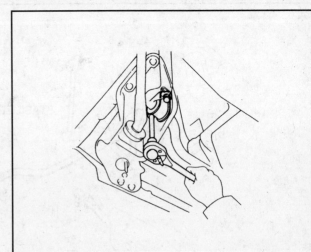

Fig. 18 Remove the stabilizer bracket from the strut bar bracket

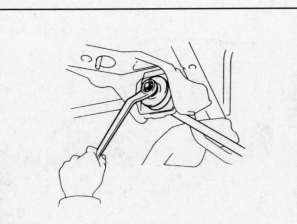

Fig. 16 Remove the front mounting nut and retainer from the bracket to separate the strut bar from the strut bracket

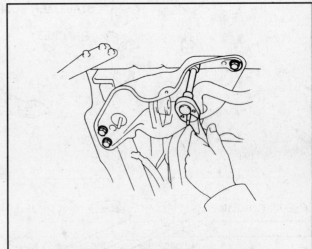

Fig. 19 Remove the strut bracket along with the stabilizer bar after removing the four mounting bolts

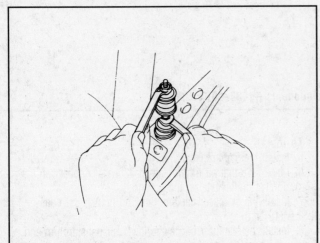

Fig. 17 Separate the stabilizer bar from the lower control arm

6. Disconnect the right and left strut bars from the lower suspension arms.

7. Remove the right and left strut bar brackets with the stabilizer bar and remove the stabilizer bar.

To install:

8. Install the stabilizer bar through the left and right strut bar brackets. Connect the strut bars to the lower suspension arms. Tighten the nuts to 76 ft. lbs. (103 Nm).

9. Install the strut bar brackets 86 ft. lbs. (117 Nm).

10. Install the stabilizer bushings and tighten the retaining nuts to 22 ft. lbs. (29 Nm).

11. Install the stabilizer bar links, be careful not to reverse their positions. The right and left stabilizer bar links can be distinguished by their colors. The left-hand side will be olive green and right-hand side will be a bronze color.

12. Install the engine undercover.

13. Lower the vehicle safely.

14. Reconnect the negative battery cable. Check the wheel alignment.

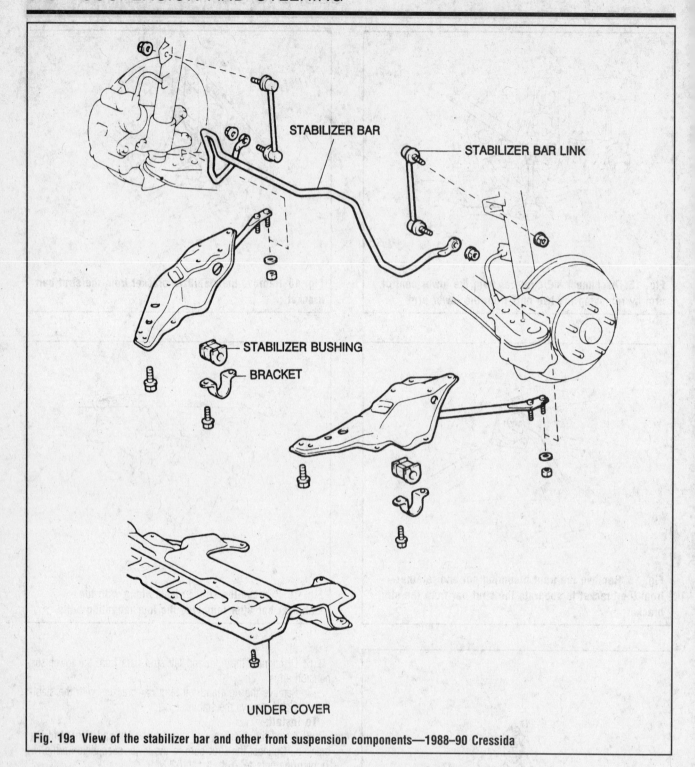

STABILIZER BAR

STABILIZER BAR LINK

STABILIZER BUSHING

BRACKET

UNDER COVER

Fig. 19a View of the stabilizer bar and other front suspension components—1988–90 Cressida

Van

STABILIZER BAR

▶ **See Figures 20, 21, 22, 23 and 24**

1. Raise and safely support the vehicle.
2. Remove the stabilizer bar from the lower suspension arms.
3. Remove the stabilizer bar brackets.
4. Remove the stabilizer bar.

To install:

5. Install the stabilizer bar.
6. Make sure that all torque specifications are done with the full weight of the vehicle on the ground.
7. Install the stabilizer bar brackets and tighten the bolts to 14 ft. lbs. (19 Nm).
8. Install the stabilizer bar to the lower suspension arm and tighten the nuts leaving a distance of 0.51–0.63 in. (13–16 mm).
9. Test drive the vehicle and check the front end alignment.

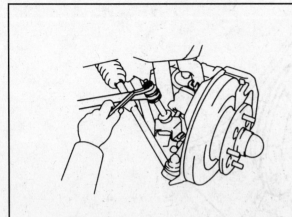

Fig. 20 When removing the 2WD Van stabilizer bar, remove the nuts and cushions holding both sides of the bar to the lower arms

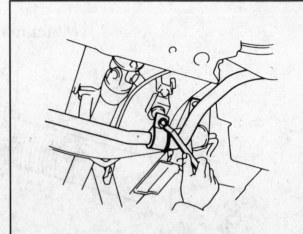

Fig. 23 The 4WD model is similar to the 2WD Vans when removing the brackets holding the stabilizer bar

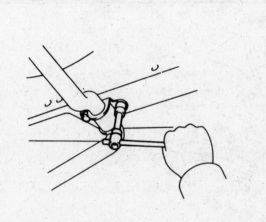

Fig. 21 On 2WD Vans remove both bar cushions and brackets, then remove the bar

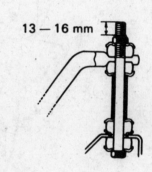

Fig. 24 When installing the stabilizer bar, tighten the nuts and make sure the distance between the nut and top stud is between 13–16mm

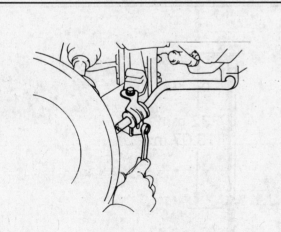

Fig. 22 On the 4WD Vans, remove the bolts retaining the stabilizer bar to the lower control arm

STRUT BAR

▶ See Figures 25, 26, 27, 28 and 29

1. Remove the stabilizer bar as noted earlier in this section.
2. Remove the stabilizer bar bracket from the lower control arm.
3. Place matchmarks on the strut bar.
4. Remove the rear nut from the strut bar.
5. Remove the nuts retaining the strut bar from the lower control arm, then remove the strut bar.

To install:

6. If reusing the old arm, install the front nut and align the matchmarks on the strut bar.
7. If using a new strut bar, install the front nut the standard distance 13.07 in. (332mm).
8. Install the strut bar to the bracket by installing the washer and bushing to the bar. Attach the strut bar to the bracket. Install the collar, bushing and washer to the strut bar. Finger-tighten the rear nut.

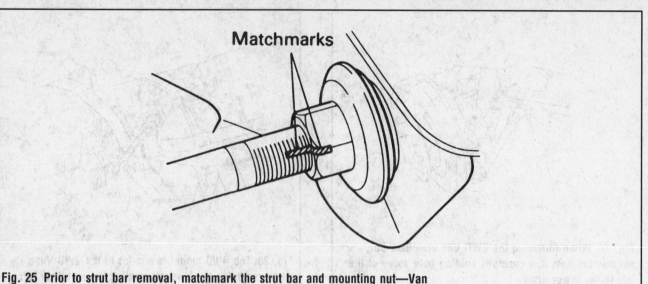

Fig. 25 Prior to strut bar removal, matchmark the strut bar and mounting nut—Van

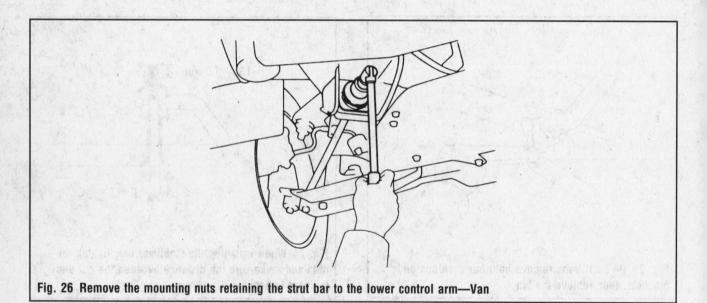

Fig. 26 Remove the mounting nuts retaining the strut bar to the lower control arm—Van

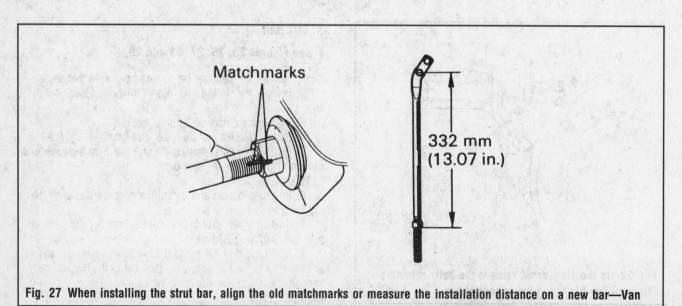

Fig. 27 When installing the strut bar, align the old matchmarks or measure the installation distance on a new bar—Van

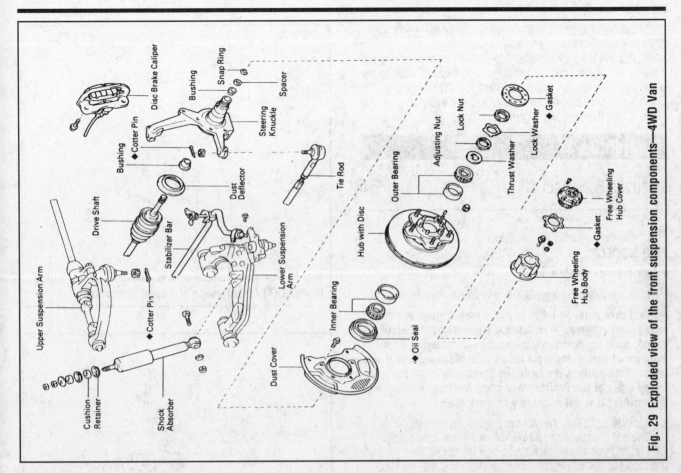

Fig. 29 Exploded view of the front suspension components—4WD Van

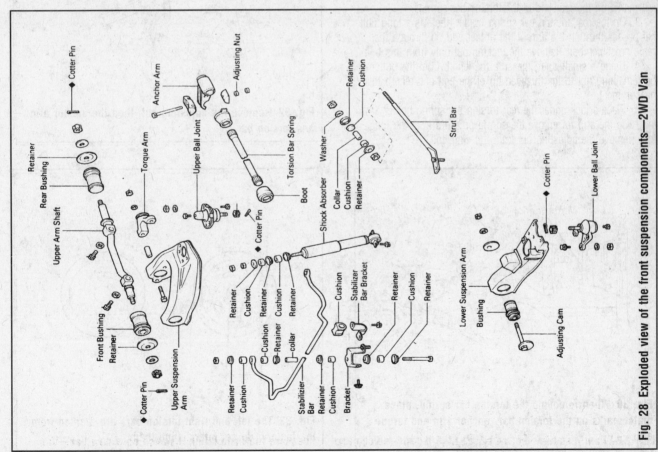

Fig. 28 Exploded view of the front suspension components—2WD Van

9. Connect the strut bar to the lower control arm and tighten to 49 ft. lbs. (67 Nm).

10. Remove the stands placed into position when removing the stabilizer bar and bounce the vehicle up and down to stabilize the suspension. Tighten the rear nut to 89 ft. lbs. (121 Nm).

11. Install the stabilizer bar bracket and stabilizer bar.

12. Check the front end alignment.

Torsion Bars

REMOVAL & INSTALLATION

Van

2WD MODELS

◆ See Figures 30 thru 36

These vehicles are equipped with torsion bar front springs.

➡Great care must be taken to make sure springs are not mixed after removal. It is strongly suggested that before removal, each spring be marked with paint, showing front and rear of spring and from which side of the vehicle it was taken. If the springs are installed backwards or on the wrong sides of the vehicle, they could fracture. If replacing the springs, it is not necessary to mark them.

1. Raise and safely support the front of the vehicle.

2. Slide the boot from the rear of torsion bar spring, then paint an alignment mark from the torsion bar spring onto the anchor arm and the torque arm. There are right and left identification marks on the rear end of the torsion bar springs.

3. On the rear torsion bar spring holder, there is a long bolt that passes through the arm of the holder and up through the frame crossmember. Remove the locking nut only from this bolt.

4. Using a small ruler, measure the length from the bottom of the remaining nut to the threaded tip of the bolt and record this measurement.

5. Place a jack under the rear torsion bar spring holder arm and raise the arm to remove the spring pressure from the long bolt. Remove the adjusting nut from the long bolt.

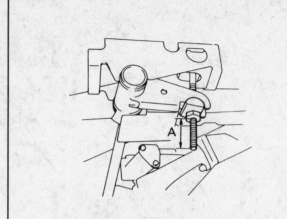
Fig. 31 Remove the locknut and measure the protruding bolt end (A) for reference of ground clearance

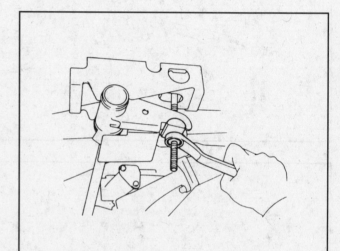
Fig. 32 Remove the adjusting nut, then the anchor arm and torsion bar

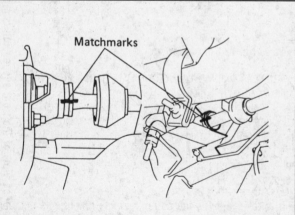
Fig. 30 When removing the torsion bar spring, place matchmarks on the torsion bar, anchor arm and torque arm

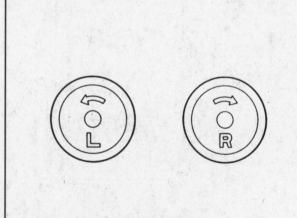
Fig. 33 The left and right torsion bars are marked from the factory, do not interchange them

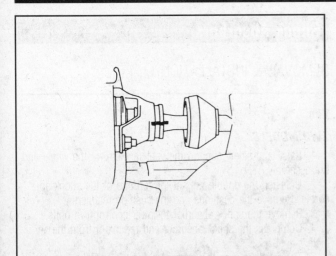

Fig. 34 If installing a new torsion bar, apply light lithium based grease to the spline of the torsion bar

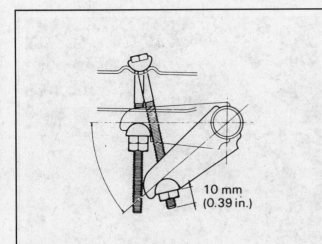

Fig. 35 On new torsion bar installation, the bolt end protrusion should measure about 0.39 in. (10mm)

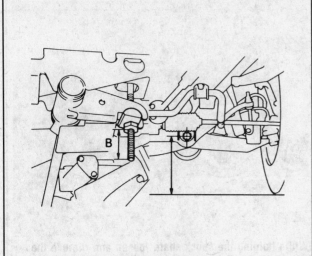

Fig. 36 Adjust the height at bolt (B)

6. Slowly lower the jack.

7. Remove the long bolt, the spacers, the anchor arm and the torsion bar spring. The torsion bar should be easily pulled out of the anchor and the torque arms.

➡**Inspect all parts for wear damage or cracks. Check the boots for rips and wear. Inspect the splined ends of the torsion bar spring and the splined holes in the rear holder and the front torque arm for damage. Replace as necessary.**

To install:

8. Coat the splined ends of the torsion bar with multi-purpose grease.

9. If installing the old torsion bars, perform the following:

a. Slide the front of the torsion bar spring into the torque arm, making sure that the alignment marks are matched.

b. Slide the anchor arm onto the rear of the torsion bar spring, making sure that the alignment marks are matched. Install the long bolt and it's spacers.

c. Tighten the adjusting nut so that it is the same length as it was before removal.

➡**Do not install the locknut.**

10. When installing a new torsion bar spring, perform the following:

a. Raise the front of the vehicle, replace the wheel and tire assembly, place a wooden block, 7½ in. (191mm) high, under the front tire. Lower the jack until the clearance between the spring bumper (on the lower control arm) and the frame is ½ in. (13mm).

b. Slide the front of the torsion bar spring into the torque arm.

c. Install the anchor arm into the rear of the torsion bar spring, then the long bolt and the spacers. the distance from the top of the upper spacer to the tip of the threaded end of bolt is 8–28mm (0.310–1.100 in.).

➡**Make sure the bolt and bottom spacer are snugly in the holder arm while measuring.**

d. Remove the wooden block and lower the vehicle until it rests on the jackstands.

e. Install and tighten the adjusting nut until the distance from the bottom of the nut to the tip of the threaded end of the bolt is 68.5–89mm (2.7–3.5 in.).

➡**Do not install the locknut.**

11. Apply multi-purpose grease to the boot lips, then refit the boots to the torque and the anchor arms.

12. Lower the vehicle to the floor and bounce it several times to settle the suspension. With the wheels on the ground, measure the distance from the ground to the center of the lower control arm-to-frame shaft. Adjust the vehicle height using the adjusting nut on the anchor arm. The height should be approximately 262mm (10.31 in.).

➡**If, after achieving the correct vehicle height, the distance from the bottom of the adjusting nut to the top of the threaded end of the long bolt is not within 68.5–89mm (2.7–3.5 in.), change the position of the anchor arm-to-tension bar spring spline and reassemble.**

13. Install and tighten the locknut on the long bolt to 61 ft. lbs.

➡ Make sure the adjusting nut does not move when tightening locknut.

4WD MODELS

➡ Great care must be taken to make sure springs are not mixed after removal. It is strongly suggested that before removal, each spring be marked with paint, showing front and rear of spring and from which side of the vehicle it was taken. If the springs are installed backwards or on the wrong sides of the vehicle, they could fracture. If replacing the springs, it is not necessary to mark them.

1. Raise and safely support the vehicle.
2. Using a piece of chalk, remove the boots, then, matchmark the torsion bar spring, the anchor arm and the torque arm.
3. Remove the locknut.
4. Measure the protruding length of the adjusting arm bolt (from the nut to the end of the bolt).

➡ The adjusting arm bolt measurement is used as a reference to establish the chassis ground clearance.

5. Remove the adjusting nut, the anchor arm and the torsion bar spring.

➡ When installing the torsion bar springs, be sure to check the left/right indicating marks on the rear end of the springs; be careful not to interchange the springs.

To install:
6. Using molybdenum disulphide lithium base grease, apply a coat to the torsion bar spring splines.
7. If installing a used torsion bar spring, perform the following procedures:
   a. Align the matchmarks and attach the torsion bar spring to the torque arm.
   b. Align the matchmarks and attach the anchor arm to the torsion bar spring.
   c. Tighten the adjusting nut until the bolt protrusion is the same as it was before.
8. If installing a new torsion bar spring, perform the following procedures:
   a. Make sure the upper and lower arms rebound.
   b. Install the boots onto the torsion bar spring.
   c. Install one end of the torsion bar spring to the torque arm.
   d. Install the torsion bar spring onto the opposite end of the anchor arm.
   e. Finger-tighten the adjusting nut until the adjusting bolt protrudes about 39.8mm (1.570 in.).
   f. Tighten the adjusting nut until the adjusting bolt protrudes about 61mm (2.400 in.).
   g. Install the wheel(s) and lower the vehicle. Bounce the front of the vehicle to stabilize the suspension.
9. To adjust the ground clearance, turn the adjusting nut until the center of the cam plate nut (located of the front end of the lower suspension arm) is 252.5mm (9.940 in.) above the ground.
10. After adjusting the ground clearance, tighten the locknut to 58 ft. lbs. then, install the boots.

Shock Absorbers

REMOVAL & INSTALLATION

Van

2WD MODELS

1. Raise and safely support the vehicle. Remove the wheel and tire assembly.
2. Unfasten the double nuts at the top end of the shock absorber. Remove the cushions and the cushion retainers.
3. Remove the shock absorber-to-lower control arm bolts.
4. Compress the shock absorber and remove it from the vehicle.
5. To install, reverse the removal procedures. Tighten the shock absorber-to-lower control arm bolts to 13 ft. lbs. and the shock absorber-to-body nuts to 19 ft. lbs.

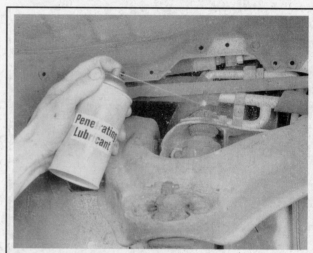

Before removing the shock absorbers, spray a penetrating lubricant on the threads

While holding the shock shaft, loosen and remove the two mounting nuts

Remove the bottom shock absorber-to-lower control arm bolts, then pull the absorber from the vehicle

4WD MODELS

♦ See Figures 37 and 38

1. Raise and safely support the vehicle. Remove the wheel and tire assembly.
2. Unfasten the double nuts at the top end of the shock absorber. Remove the cushions and the cushion retainers.
3. Remove the shock absorber-to-axle housing bolt.
4. Compress the shock absorber and remove it from the vehicle.
5. To install, reverse the removal procedures. Tighten the shock absorber-to-suspension arm nut/bolt 70 ft. lbs. and the shock absorber-to-body nuts to 19 ft. lbs.

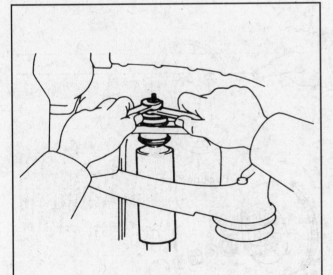

Fig. 37 Remove the locknut and second mounting nut on the upper shock mount—Van

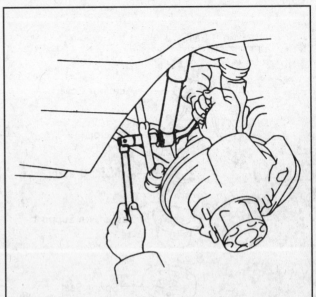

Fig. 38 On the lower shock portion, remove the bolt, spring washer and nut

MacPherson Struts

REMOVAL & INSTALLATION

Cressida

1983–88 MODELS

♦ See Figure 39

1. Remove the hubcap and loosen the lug nuts.
2. Raise and support the vehicle safely.

✳✳ WARNING

Do not support the weight of the vehicle on the suspension arm; the arm will deform under its weight.

3. Unfasten the lug nuts and remove the wheel.
4. Remove the union bolt and 2 washers and disconnect the front brake line from the disc brake caliper. Remove the clip from the brake hose and pull off the brake hose from the brake hose bracket.
5. Remove the caliper and wire it out of the way. Matchmark the strut lower bracket and camber adjust cam if equipped.
6. Disconnect and remove the TEMS (if so equipped) actuator from the top of the strut on late Cressida.
7. Remove the three nuts and lock washers from the top of the strut inside the engine compartment.
8. Remove the bolts and nuts which attach the strut lower end to the steering knuckle lower arm and the lower control arm. Push the arm downward slightly, then remove the strut assembly.
9. Remove the front strut and axle hub assembly and place it in a suitable vise. The strut must be mounted in a vise for further disassembly. It must not be mounted by the shock absorber shell

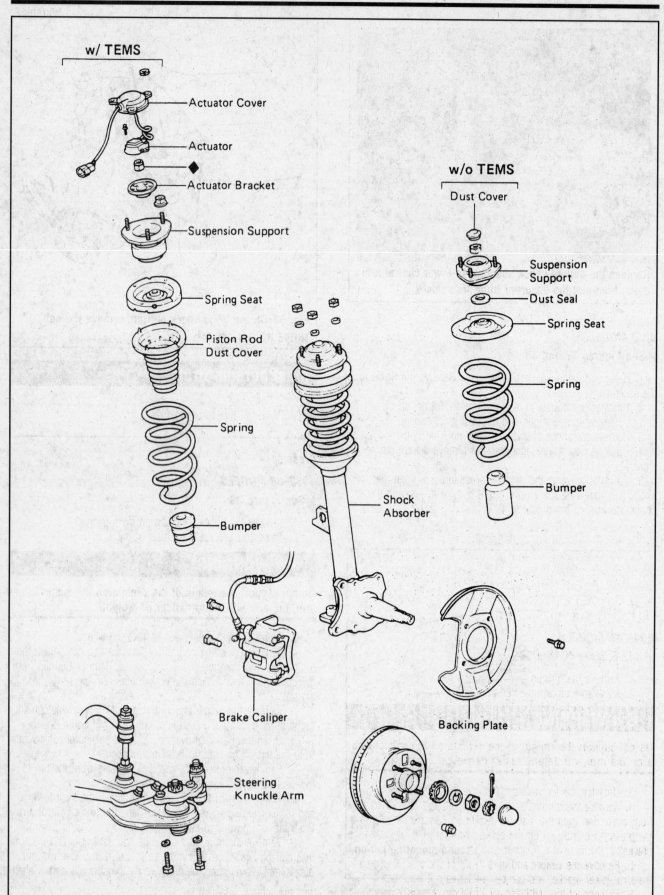

Fig. 39 Exploded view of the front axle strut assembly components—1983–88 Cressida

as this part is machined perfectly round and can easily be distorted. A special tool is available from Toyota for this purpose, or you can obtain this coil spring compression tool from your local parts dealer.

10. Using a spring compression tool designed for this purpose, the spring must be compressed so there is no tension on the upper seat.

✳✳ WARNING

Failure to fully compress the spring and hold it securely before performing the next step is extremely hazardous.

11. Hold the shock absorber seat (at top) with a large spanner wrench, and remove the nut from the top of the shock absorber.

12. Remove upper support, upper seat, dust cover, and spring.

13. Install the compressed spring onto the new strut cartridge being sure to align the hole in the upper suspension support with the shock absorber piston or end, so that they fit properly.

14. Always use a new nut and nylon washer on the shock absorber piston rod end when securing it to the upper suspension support. Tighten the nut to 29–40 ft. lbs. (39–54 Nm).

➡**Do not use an impact wrench to tighten the nut.**

15. Coat the suspension support bearing with multipurpose grease prior to installation. Pack the space in the upper support with multipurpose grease, also, after installation.

To install:

16. Push the arm downward slightly, and then install the strut assembly. Install the bolts and nuts which attach the strut lower end to the steering knuckle lower arm. Torque them to 58 ft. lbs. (86 Nm).

17. Install the three nuts and lock washers to the top of the strut inside the engine compartment. Torque them to 22–32 ft. lbs.

18. Reconnect and install the TEMS (if so equipped) actuator to the top of the strut on late Cressida.

19. Install the brake caliper and brake pad assembly. Tighten the brake caliper slide pin bolts to 62–68 ft. lbs. Reconnect the brake lines and bleed the brake system.

20. Reinstall the wheel assembly. Lower the vehicle and road test the vehicle.

1989–90 MODELS

◆ **See Figures 40 thru 51**

1. Remove the hubcap and loosen the lug nuts.
2. Raise and support the vehicle safely.

✳✳ WARNING

Do not support the weight of the vehicle on the suspension arm; the arm will deform under its weight.

3. Unfasten the lug nuts and remove the wheel.

4. Remove the union bolt and 2 washers and disconnect the front brake line from the disc brake caliper. Remove the clip from the brake hose and pull off the brake hose from the brake hose bracket.

5. Remove the caliper and wire it out of the way. Matchmark the strut lower bracket and camber adjust cam if equipped.

6. Disconnect the stabilizer bar link from the strut assembly.

7. Remove the antilock brake system speed sensor from the strut assembly, if so equipped.

8. Remove the front axle hub assembly.

9. Remove the dust cover retaining bolts and remove the dust cover.

10. Disconnect the lower control arm from the strut assembly.

11. Remove the three nuts and lock washers from the top of the strut inside the engine compartment.

12. Remove the bolts and nuts which attach the strut lower end to the steering knuckle lower arm and the lower control arm. Push the arm downward slightly, and then remove the strut assembly.

13. Remove the front strut and axle hub assembly and place it in a suitable vise. The strut must be mounted in a vise for further disassembly. It must not be mounted by the shock absorber shell as this part is machined perfectly round and can easily be distorted. A special tool is available from Toyota for this purpose, or you can obtain this coil spring compression tool from your local parts dealer.

14. Using a spring compression tool designed for this purpose, the spring must be compressed so there is no tension on the upper seat.

✳✳ WARNING

Failure to fully compress the spring and hold it securely before performing the next step is extremely hazardous.

15. Hold the shock absorber seat (at top) with a large spanner wrench, and remove the nut from the top of the shock absorber.

16. Remove upper support, upper seat, dust cover, and spring.

17. Install the compressed spring onto the new strut cartridge being sure top align the hole in the upper suspension support with the shock absorber piston or end, so that they fit properly.

18. Always use a new nut and nylon washer on the shock absorber piston rod end when securing it to the upper suspension support. Tighten the nut to 34 ft. lbs. (47 Nm).

➡**Do not use an impact wrench to tighten the nut.**

19. Coat the suspension support bearing with multipurpose grease prior to installation. Pack the space in the upper support with multipurpose grease, also, after installation.

To install:

20. Push the arm downward slightly, and then install the strut assembly. Install the bolts and nuts which attach the strut lower end to the steering knuckle lower arm. Tighten them to 80 ft. lbs. (108 Nm).

21. Install the three nuts and lock washers to the top of the strut inside the engine compartment. Tighten them to 32 ft. lbs. (43 Nm).

22. Install the dust cover.

23. Install the front axle hub assembly.

24. Install the ABS speed sensor assembly.

25. Install the brake caliper and brake pad assembly. Tighten the brake caliper slide pin bolts to 67 ft. lbs. (91 Nm). Reconnect the brake lines and bleed the brake system.

26. Connect the stabilizer bar link to the shock absorber. Tighten the bolts and nuts to 70 ft. lbs. (95 Nm).

27. Reinstall the wheel assembly. Lower the vehicle and road test the vehicle.

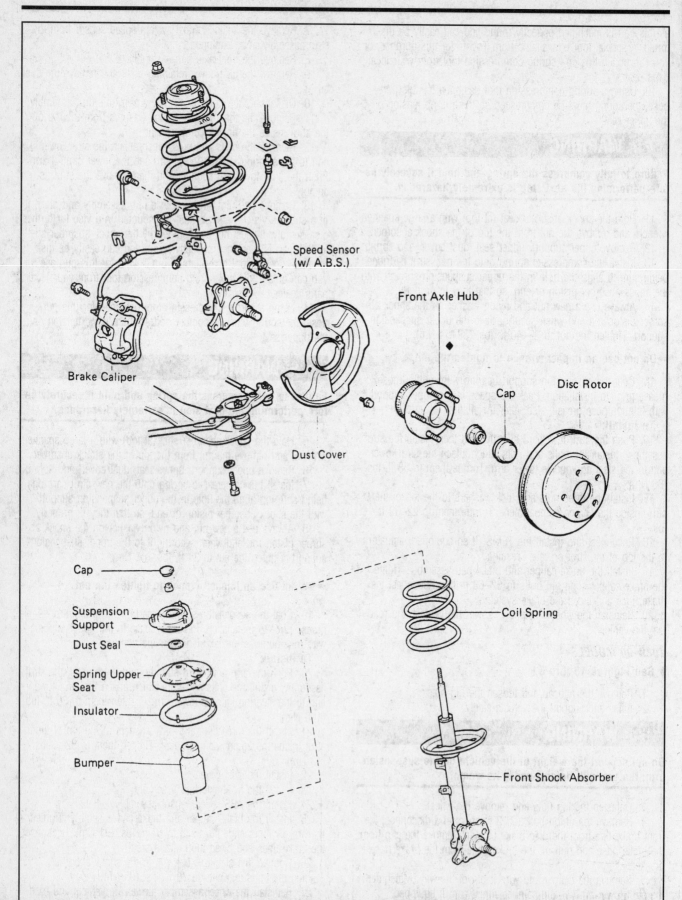

Speed Sensor (w/ A.B.S.)

Front Axle Hub

Disc Rotor

Cap

Brake Caliper

Dust Cover

Cap

Suspension Support

Dust Seal

Spring Upper Seat

Insulator

Bumper

Coil Spring

Front Shock Absorber

Fig. 40 Exploded view of the front axle strut assembly components—1989–90 Cressida

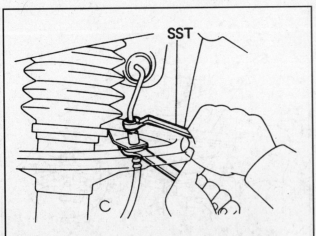

Fig. 41 When removing the strut assembly from the vehicle, disconnect the brake line—1988–90 Cressida shown

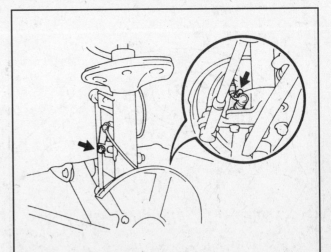

Fig. 44 On ABS models, disconnect the speed sensor from the strut assembly—Cressida

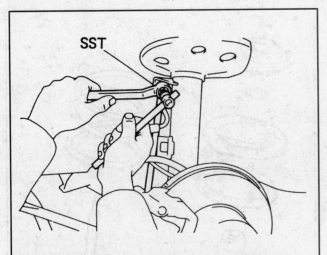

Fig. 42 Disconnect the stabilizer bar linkage from the strut assembly— 1988–90 Cressida

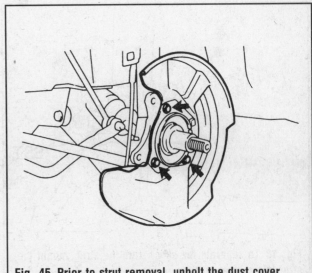

Fig. 45 Prior to strut removal, unbolt the dust cover

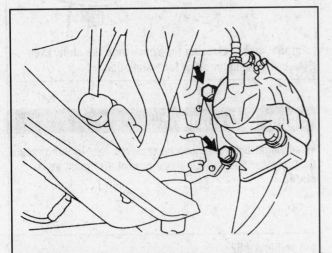

Fig. 43 When removing the strut, the two caliper mounting bolts must be removed—1988–90 Cressida

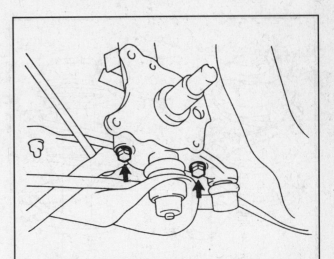

Fig. 46 The lower control arm bolts retaining the strut must be removed

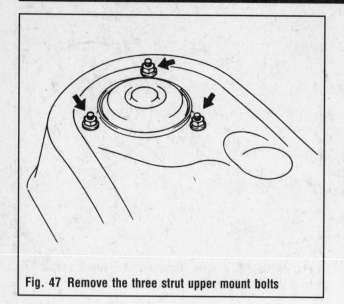

Fig. 47 Remove the three strut upper mount bolts

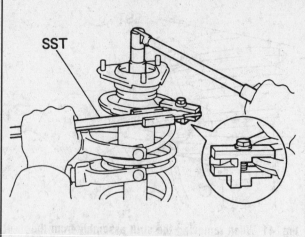

Fig. 50 Hold the spring upper seat and remove the nut to separate the spring from the shock

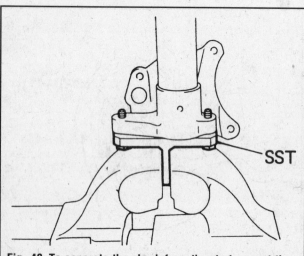

Fig. 48 To separate the shock from the strut, mount the strut into a vise . . .

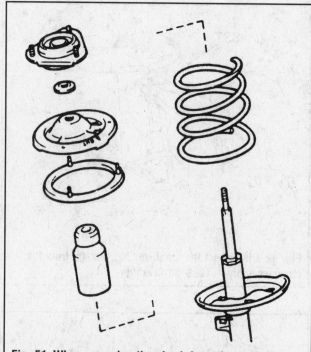

Fig. 51 When removing the shock from the strut, keep the components in order for installation

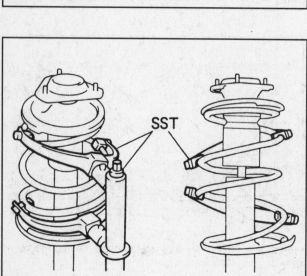

Fig. 49 . . . then compress the coil spring

Upper Ball Joints

➡Individual ball joints can be removed only in Van models. On Cressida models, the entire control arm must be replaced.

INSPECTION

◆ See Figure 52

1. Raise the lower control arm and check for excess play.
2. If the ball joints are within specifications and a looseness

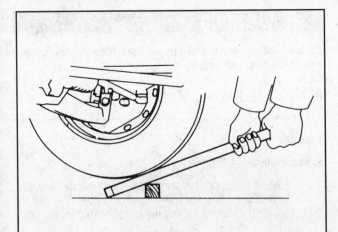

Fig. 52 With the aid of a prybar and block of wood, check the upper ball joint for excessive play—Van

problem still exists, check the other suspension parts (wheel bearings, tie rods and etc.).

3. The bottom of the tire should not move more than 5mm (0.20 in.) when the tire is pushed and pulled inward and outward. The tire should not move more than 2.3mm (0.090 in.) up and down.

4. If the play is greater than these figures, replace the ball joint.

REMOVAL & INSTALLATION

1. Raise and safely support the vehicle. Remove the wheel and tire assembly.

2. Support the lower control arm with a floor jack.

3. Remove the brake caliper and support it out of the way, with a wire.

4. Using a ball joint removal tool, separate the tie rod end from the knuckle arm.

5. Remove the ball joint-to-control arm mounting bolts and separate the joint from the arm.

6. To install, reverse the removal procedures. Tighten the ball joint-to-upper control arm bolts 22 ft. lbs. (2WD Van), the ball joint-to-lower control arm bolts to 49 ft. lbs. (Van), and the lower ball joint-to-steering knuckle nut to 76 ft. lbs. (2WD Van) or 83 ft. lbs. (4WD Van).

➡**Be sure to grease the ball joints before moving the vehicle.**

Lower Ball Joint

➡**Individual ball joints can be replaced only in Van models. On Cressida models, the entire control arm must be replaced.**

INSPECTION

▶ **See Figure 53**

1. Raise the lower control arm and check for excess play.

2. If the ball joints are within specifications and a looseness problem still exists, check the other suspension parts (wheel bearings, tie rods and etc.).

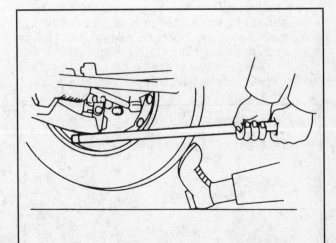

Fig. 53 When inspecting the lower ball joint for play, move the lower control arm up and down—Van

3. The bottom of the tire should not move more than 5mm (0.200 in.) when the tire is pushed and pulled inward and outward. The tire should not move more than 2.3mm (0.090 in.) up and down.

4. The upper ball joint should be replaced if a distinct looseness is felt when turning the ball joint stud with the steering knuckle removed.

REMOVAL & INSTALLATION

1. Raise and safely support the vehicle. Remove the wheel and tire assembly.

2. Support the lower control arm with a floor jack.

3. Remove the brake caliper and support it out of the way, with a wire.

4. Using a ball joint removal tool, separate the tie rod end from the knuckle arm.

5. Using a ball joint removal tool, separate the upper ball joint from the steering knuckle.

6. Remove the ball joint-to-control arm mounting bolts and separate the joint from the arm.

7. To install, reverse the removal procedures. Tighten the ball joint-to-upper control arm bolts 22 ft. lbs. (2WD Van), the upper ball joint to steering knuckle nut to 58 ft. lbs. (2WD Van) or 83 ft. lbs. (4WD Van).

➡**Be sure to grease the ball joints before moving the vehicle.**

Lower Control Arm/Ball Joints

INSPECTION

Cressida

Raise the front end and position a piece of wood under the wheel and lower the vehicle until there is an ½ load on the strut. Check the front wheel play. Replace the lower ball joint if the play at the wheel rim exceeds 2.5mm (0.1 in.) vertical motion or 6mm (0.25 in.) horizontal motion. Be sure the dust covers are not torn and that they are securely glued to the ball joints.

✳✳ WARNING

Do not jack up the control arm on Cressida vehicles; damage to the arm will result.

REMOVAL & INSTALLATION

Cressida

▶ **See Figures 54 thru 62**

1. Raise and support the vehicle safely. Remove the wheels.
2. Remove the 2 knuckle arm-to-strut bolts, pull down on the control arm and disconnect it and the knuckle arm from the strut.

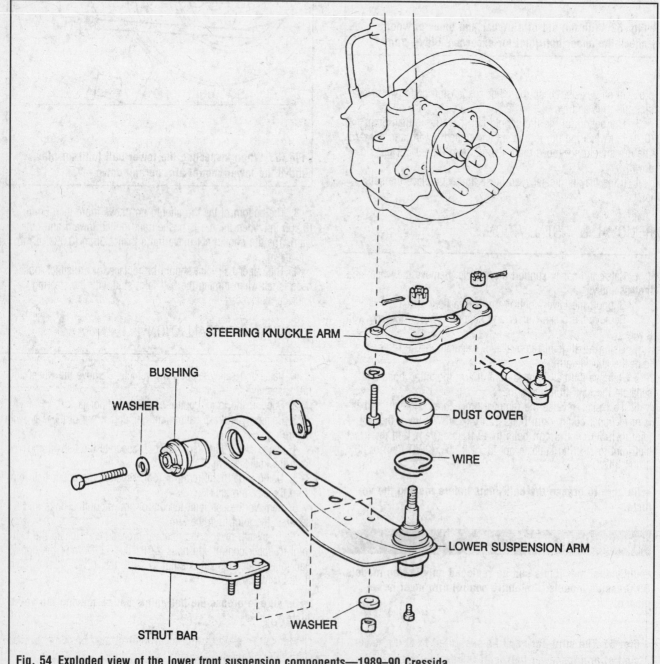

STEERING KNUCKLE ARM

BUSHING

WASHER

DUST COVER

WIRE

LOWER SUSPENSION ARM

STRUT BAR

WASHER

Fig. 54 Exploded view of the lower front suspension components—1989–90 Cressida

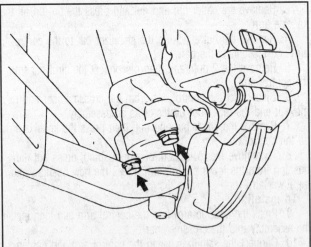

Fig. 55 When removing the lower ball joint, unbolt the shock absorber from the lower control arm—Cressida

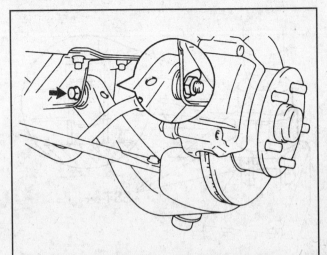

Fig. 58 Next, unbolt the lower control arm and remove the arm along with the steering knuckle—Cressida

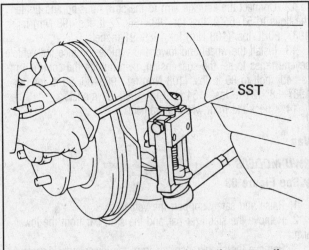

Fig. 56 Remove the cotter pin and nut, then press the tie rod end from the steering knuckle—Cressida

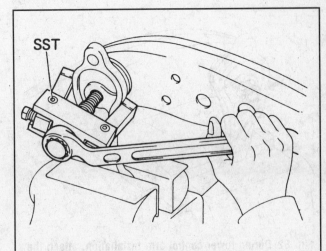

Fig. 59 Press the knuckle arm off the lower control arm—Cressida

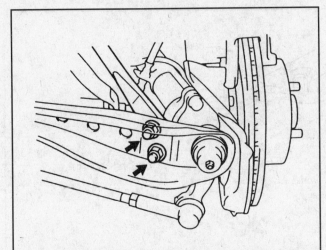

Fig. 57 The strut bar must be separated from the lower control arm for lower ball joint removal—Cressida

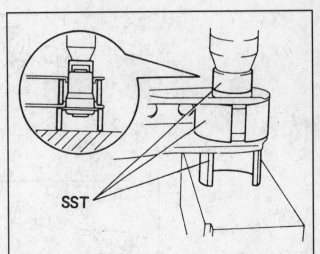

Fig. 60 To replace the lower control arm bushing, press the old one out—Cressida

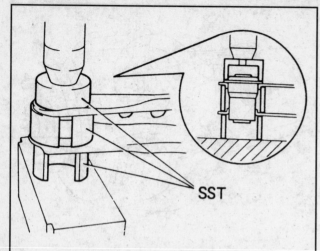

Fig. 61 Using the same press, install a new bushing into the lower control arm—Cressida

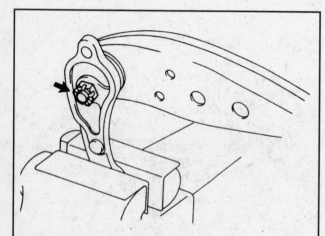

Fig. 62 During lower control arm installation, attach the steering knuckle and tighten the nut to 67 ft. lbs. (91 Nm)

3. Remove the cotter pin and nut and press the tie rod off the knuckle arm.

4. Remove the nut attaching the stabilizer bar to the control arm and disconnect the bar.

5. Remove the 2 nuts and then disconnect the strut bar from the control arm.

6. Disconnect the control arm from the crossmember and remove it and the rack boot protector as an assembly.

7. Remove the cotter pin and nut, then press the knuckle arm off the control arm.

8. To remove the lower control arm bushing, press out the bushing from the lower control arm. Press the new bushing into the lower arm.

To install:

9. Press the knuckle arm into the control arm and then install the assembly into the crossmember.

10. Connect the stabilizer bar to the control arm and tighten the nut to 13 ft. lbs. (18 Nm).

11. Connect the strut bar to the control arm and tighten the nuts to 44–43 ft. lbs. (60 Nm) for 1983–1987; 54 ft. lbs. (73 Nm) for 1988; 76 ft. lbs. (103 Nm) for 1989–91 models.

12. Connect the knuckle arm to the strut housing and tighten the bolts to 51–65 ft. lbs. for 1983–86; 72 ft. lbs. (98 Nm) for 1987; 80 ft. lbs. (108 Nm) for 1988–91 models.

13. Install the wheel and lower the vehicle. Bounce the vehicle several times to set the suspension, then tighten the control arm-to-body bolt to 80 ft. lbs. (108 Nm) for 1983–86; 90 ft. lbs. for 1987–88; 121 ft. lbs. (164 Nm) for 1989–91 models.

14. Check the front wheel alignment.

Van

2WD MODELS

▶ **See Figure 63**

1. Raise and safely support the vehicle.

2. Remove the stabilizer bar and the strut bar from the lower arm.

3. Remove the shock absorber from the lower arm. If necessary, disconnect the tie rod end from the steering knuckle.

4. From the lower ball joint, remove the cotter pin and the nut.

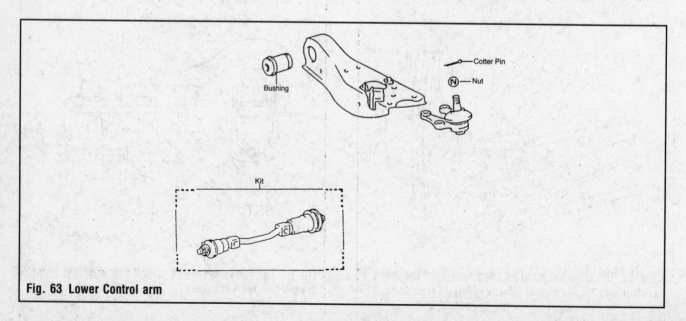

Fig. 63 Lower Control arm

Using a ball joint removal tool, press the ball joint from the lower control arm.

➡️**If the lower ball joint is not to be replaced, simply unbolt it from the lower control arm. It is not necessary to separate the ball joint from the steering knuckle.**

5. Using a piece of chalk, matchmark the adjusting cam of the lower control arm.

6. Remove the adjusting cam, the nut and the lower control arm.

7. To install, reverse the removal procedures. Align the cam matchmarks and finger-tighten the nut. Tighten the ball joint-to-lower control arm nuts/bolts to 49 ft. lbs., the lower ball joint-to-steering knuckle nut to 76 ft. lbs., the strut bar-to-lower control arm bolts to 49 ft. lbs., the stabilizer bar-to-lower control arm bolts to 9 ft. lbs., the tie rod end-to-steering knuckle nut to 43 ft. lbs., the lower shock absorber bolt to 13 ft. lbs., upper shock absorber bolt to 19 ft. lbs. and the adjusting cam nut to 152 ft. lbs. Check and/or adjust the front end alignment.

➡️**Do not tighten the control arm bolts fully until the vehicle is lowered and bounced several times.**

4WD MODELS

▸ **See Figure 64**

1. Raise and safely support the vehicle.

2. Remove the stabilizer bar from the lower control arm.

3. Remove the shock absorber from the lower control arm.

4. From the lower ball joint, remove the cotter pin and the nut. Using a ball joint removal tool, press the ball joint from the lower control arm.

➡️**If the lower ball joint is not to be replaced, simply unbolt it from the lower control arm. It is not necessary to separate the ball joint from the steering knuckle.**

5. Using a piece of chalk, matchmark the adjusting cam of the lower control arm.

6. Remove the adjusting cam, the nut and the lower control arm.

7. To install, reverse the removal procedures. Align the cam matchmarks and finger-tighten the nut. Tighten the ball joint-to-lower control arm nuts/bolts to 83 ft. lbs., the stabilizer bar-to-lower control arm bolts to 14 ft. lbs., the tie rod end-to-steering knuckle nut to 43 ft. lbs., the lower shock absorber bolt to 70 ft. lbs. and the adjusting cam nut to 152 ft. lbs. Check and/or adjust the front end alignment.

➡️**Do not tighten the control arm bolts fully until the vehicle is lowered and bounced several times.**

Upper Control Arm

REMOVAL & INSTALLATION

Van

2WD MODELS

▸ **See Figure 65**

1. Raise and safely support the vehicle. Remove the torsion bar spring.

2. Remove the cool air intake duct.

3. Remove the upper control arm-to-upper ball joint nuts/bolts and separate the upper control arm from the ball joint.

4. Remove the upper control arm-to-chassis bolts and the control arm from the vehicle.

5. To install, reverse the removal procedures. Tighten the upper control arm-to-chassis bolts to 65 ft. lbs. (front) and 112 ft. lbs. (rear), then, the upper control arm-to-ball joint nuts/bolts to 22 ft. lbs. Check and/or adjust the front end alignment.

4WD MODELS

▸ **See Figure 66**

1. Raise and safely support the vehicle. Remove the torsion bar spring. Lower the vehicle.

2. Remove the front-right seat and the console box. Discon-

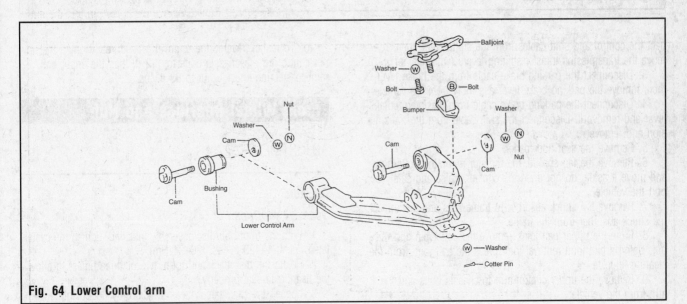

Fig. 64 Lower Control arm

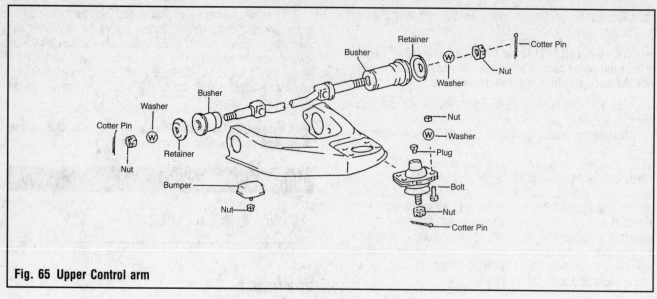

Fig. 65 Upper Control arm

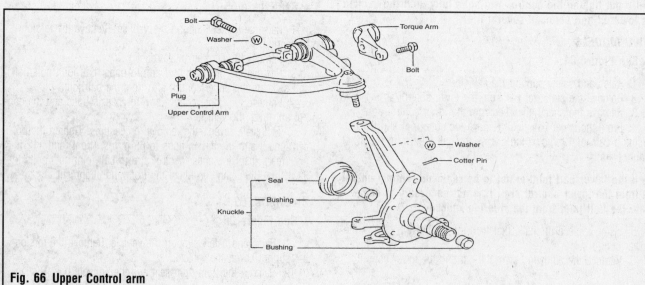

Fig. 66 Upper Control arm

nect the control and shift cables from the shift levers, then, remove the transmission/transfer shifting levers (with retainer).

3. Disconnect the parking brake cable from the brake lever, then, remove the parking brake lever assembly from the vehicle.

4. Disconnect the parking brake cable from the intermediate lever and remove it. Disconnect the shift cable from the transmission and remove it.

5. Remove the seat floor panel.

6. Remove the fan shroud, the radiator mounting bolts/nuts and move it aside; do not drain the coolant. Raise and safely support the vehicle.

7. Remove the shock absorber-to-frame nuts and disconnect the shock absorber from the frame.

8. From the upper ball joint, remove the cotter pin and the nut. Using a ball joint removal tool, press the ball joint from the steering knuckle.

9. Remove the upper control arm-to-chassis bolts and the arm from the vehicle.

10. To install, reverse the removal procedures. Tighten the upper control arm-to-chassis bolts to 112 ft. lbs., the upper ball joint-to-steering knuckle nut to 83 ft. lbs.

Front Wheel Bearings and Hub

ADJUSTMENT

Cressida

1983–88 MODELS

1. With the front hub/disc assembly installed, tighten the castellated nut to 19–23 ft. lbs. (26–31 Nm).

2. Rotate the disc back and forth, two or three times, to allow the bearing to seat properly.

3. Loosen the castellated nut until it is only finger-tight.

4. Tighten the nut firmly, using a box wrench.

5. Measure the bearing preload with a spring scale attached to a wheel mounting stud. Check it against the specifications in the removal and installation procedure.

6. Install the cotter pin.

➡**If the hole does not align with the nut (or cap) holes, tighten the nut slightly until it does.**

7. Finish installing the brake components and the wheel.

REMOVAL & INSTALLATION

Cressida

1983–88 MODELS

♦ **See Figures 67 thru 79**

1. Raise and support the front of the vehicle safely. Remove the front wheel assemblies.

2. Remove the brake caliper retaining bolts, remove the caliper and suspend it from the fender well with a piece of wire. Do not disconnect the brake lines.

3. Remove the hub grease cap, cotter pin, lock cap, nut and axle hub. Remove the hub and brake disc together with the outer bearing and thrust washer. Be careful not to drop the outer bearing.

4. Using a suitable tool, pry out the oil seal and remove the inner bearing from the brake disc. Throw away the old seal.

5. Inspect the spindle with a magnetic flaw detector and check for damage or cracks.

6. Using a brass rod as a drift, tap the outer bearings race out.

7. Drive out the inner bearing race.

8. Inspect the bearings and the hub for signs of wear or damage. Replace components, as necessary.

To install:

9. Install the inner bearing race an then the outer bearing race, by driving them into place.

➡**Use care not to cock the bearing race in the hub.**

10. Pack the bearings, hub inner well and grease cap with multipurpose grease.

11. Install the inner bearing into the hub.

12. Carefully install a new oil seal with a soft drift.

13. Install the hub on the spindle. Be sure to install all of the washers and nuts which were removed.

14. Adjust the bearing preload as follows:

a. Install the hub nut and torque it to 22 ft. lbs. (29 Nm). Turn the hub right and left 2 or 3 times to allow the bearing to settle.

b. Loosen the nut so there is 0.5–1.0mm (0.020–0.039 in.) play in the hub axial direction.

c. Using a spring tension gauge, measure the rotation friction force on the oil seal. Using a socket in your hand, tighten the nut as tight as possible. Check the preload. In addition to rotation friction force of the oil seal 0–2.3 lb.

d. If the preload is less than specification, tighten the nut slightly and check it again.

e. If the preload is excessive, loosen the nut and using a socket in your hand, retighten it as tight as possible. Check the reload again.

f. Measure the hub axial play 0.05mm (0.0020 in.).

15. Install the lock cap, cotter pin and hub grease cap. If the cotter in holes do not line up, correct by tightening the nut by the smallest amount possible.

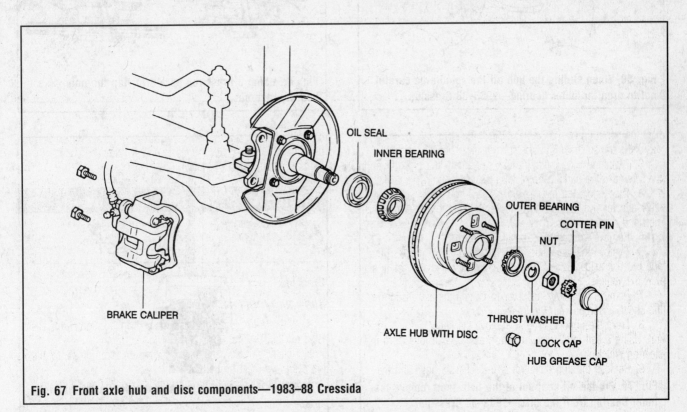

Fig. 67 Front axle hub and disc components—1983–88 Cressida

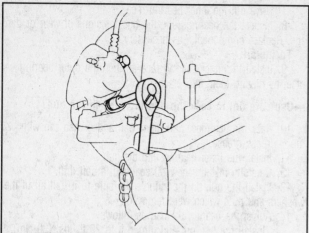

Fig. 68 To remove the front axle hub, the caliper must be unbolted and suspended with a wire. Do not disconnect the brake line

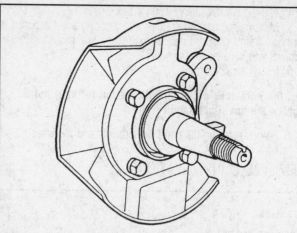

Fig. 71 Once the hub and disc are removed, inspect the spindle for flaws with a magnetic detector—1983–88 Cressida

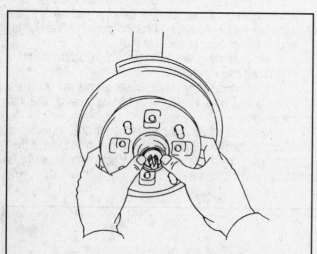

Fig. 69 When sliding the hub off the spindle be careful not to drop the outer bearing—1983–88 Cressida

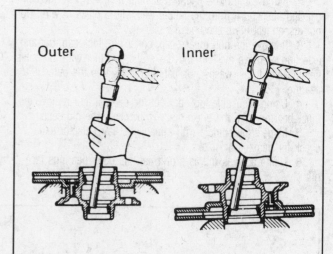

Fig. 72 Using a brass rod as a drift, tap the outer bearing race out . . .

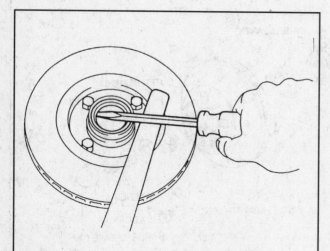

Fig. 70 Pry the oil seal out of the hub, then remove the inner bearing from the disc—1983–88 Cressida

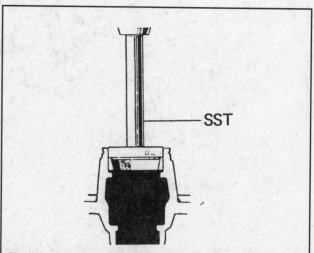

Fig. 73 . . . next drive the new bearing inner race into place

SUSPENSION AND STEERING   8-29

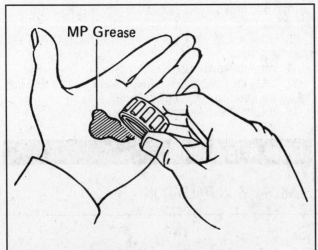

Fig. 74 When installing a new bearing into the hub, pack the bearing with multi-purpose grease

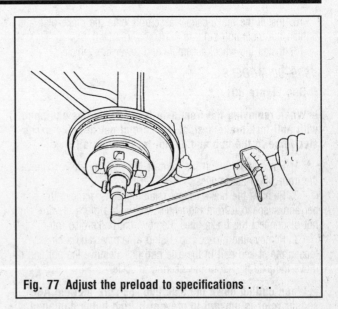

Fig. 77 Adjust the preload to specifications . . .

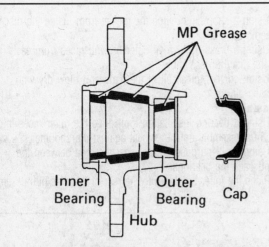

Fig. 75 You must coat other components inside the hub and cap as shown here

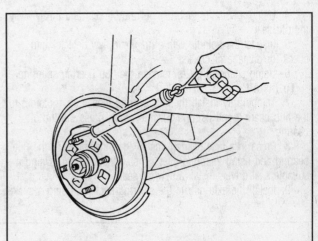

Fig. 78 . . . then using a spring tension gauge, measure the rotation friction force of the oil seal, check preload again

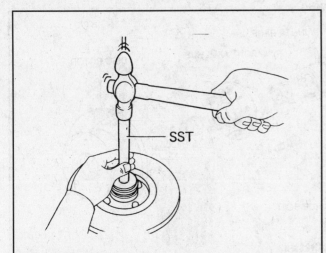

Fig. 76 Drive the inner bearing into the hub, then drive in the new oil seal

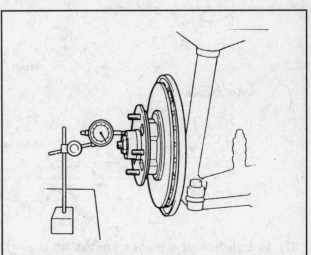

Fig. 79 Using a dial indicator, measure the axial hub play

16. Install the brake caliper assembly onto the brake disc and tighten the mounting bolts to 67 ft. lbs. (91 Nm).

17. Install the wheel assembly and lower the vehicle.

1989–90 MODELS

◆ See Figure 80

➡When removing the front axle hub on vehicles equipped with anti-lock brake system, be careful not to apply excessive force to the hub and do not let the hub fall.

1. Raise and support the front of the vehicle safely. Remove the front wheel assemblies.

2. Remove the brake caliper retaining bolts, remove the caliper and suspend it from the fender well with a piece of wire. Do not disconnect the brake lines. Remove the brake disc rotor.

3. Remove the grease cap. Using a hammer and a chisel, loosen the staked part of the axle hub nut. Remove the nut and remove the axle hub from the steering knuckle.

➡When putting down the axle hub, be sure that the ABS sensor rotor is upward to prevent it from being damaged.

4. Using a suitable tool, pry out the oil seal and throw away the old seal.

5. Inspect the spindle with a magnetic flaw detector and check for damage or cracks.

6. Using snapring pliers, remove the hub bearing snapring.

To install:

7. Temporarily install the hub bearing inner race (outside) to the hub bearing and using a suitable press, press out the old bearing.

8. Press in a new bearing. Install the inner races to the hub bearing and using snapring pliers, install the snapring. Using a suitable seal driver, install a new oil seal.

9. Install the axle hub to the steering knuckle. Using a socket wrench, hold the inner race (outside) to prevent it from getting out of place.

10. Install and tighten a new nut to 108 ft. lbs. (147 Nm) and stake the new nut.

11. Install the grease cap.

12. Install the brake caliper assembly onto the brake disc and tighten the mounting bolts to 67 ft. lbs. (91 Nm).

13. Install the wheel assembly and lower the vehicle.

Front Axle Bearing

REMOVAL & INSTALLATION

Van

1. Raise and safely support the vehicle. Remove the 4WD hubs.

2. Using a small prybar, pry the grease seal from the rear of the disc/hub assembly, then remove the inner bearing from the assembly.

3. Using a shop cloth, wipe the grease from inside the disc/hub assembly.

4. Using a brass drift, drive outer bearing races from each side of the disc/hub assembly.

5. Using solvent, clean all of the parts and blow dry with compressed air.

To install:

6. Using a bearing installation tool, drive the outer races into the disc/hub assembly until they seat against the shoulder.

7. Using multi-purpose grease, coat the area between the races and pack the bearings.

8. Place the inner bearing into the rear of the disc/hub assem-

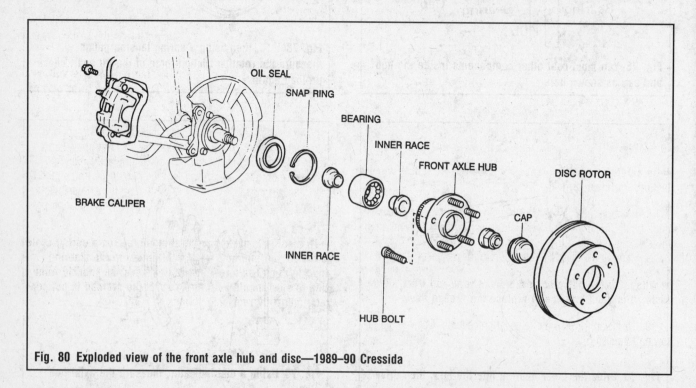

Fig. 80 Exploded view of the front axle hub and disc—1989–90 Cressida

bly. Using a bearing installation tool, drive a new grease seal into the rear of the disc/hub assembly until it is flush with the housing.

9. Install the disc/hub assembly onto the axle shaft, the outer bearing, the thrust washer and the adjusting nut.

10. To adjust the bearing preload, perform the following:

a. Tighten the adjusting nut to 43 ft. lbs.

b. Turn the disc/hub assembly 2–3 times, from the left to the right.

c. Loosen the adjusting nut until it can be turned by hand.

d. Retighten the adjusting nut to 18 ft. lbs.

e. Install the lock washer and the locknut. Tighten the locknut to 33 ft. lbs.

f. Check that the bearing has no play.

g. Using a spring gauge, connect it to a wheel stud, the gauge should be held horizontal, then measure the rotating force, it should be 6–12 lbs.

11. Lower the vehicle.

Front Wheel Hub, Knuckle and Bearing

REMOVAL & INSTALLATION

Van

2WD MODELS

▶ See Figure 81

1. Raise and safely support the vehicle. Remove the wheel and tire assembly.

2. Remove the brake caliper (do not disconnect the brake hose from the caliper) and suspend it on a wire.

3. Remove axle hub dust cap, the cotter pin, the nut lock, the adjusting nut, the thrust washer and the outer bearing, then pull the hub/disc assembly from the axle spindle.

4. Remove the backing plate cotter pins and the mounting nuts or bolts, then the backing plate.

5. Remove steering knuckle arm from the back of the steering knuckle.

6. Remove the nuts, the retainers and the bushings, then the shock absorber from the lower control arm.

7. Support the lower arm with a jack and raise to put pressure on spring.

➡Be careful not to unbalance vehicle support stands when jacking up lower arm.

8. Remove cotter pins, then the upper and lower ball joint nuts. Using a ball joint removal tool, separate the ball joints from the steering knuckle.

9. Remove the steering knuckle from the vehicle.

➡Whenever the hub/disc assembly is removed from the vehicle, it is good practice to replace the grease seal.

10. To install, reverse the removal procedures. Observe the following torques:

- Upper ball joint nut: 58 ft. lbs.
- Lower ball joint nut: 76 ft. lbs.
- Steering knuckle arm-to-steering knuckle bolts: 61 ft. lbs.
- Shock absorber-to-lower control arm nuts: 19 ft. lbs.
- Backing plate-to-steering knuckle bolts: 61 ft. lbs.

11. Adjust the wheel bearing.

4WD MODELS

▶ See Figure 82

1. Remove the front axle shaft assembly from the vehicle.

2. Remove the oil seal retainer and the oil seal set from the rear of the steering knuckle.

3. At the drag link end of the steering knuckle arm, remove the cotter pin. Using the proper tool, remove the plug from the drag link, then disconnect the drag link from the steering knuckle arm.

4. Remove the tie rod-to-steering knuckle, cotter pin and nut. Using the proper ball joint removal tool, separate the tie rod from the steering knuckle arm.

5. Remove the steering knuckle arm-to-steering knuckle (top) nuts and the steering knuckle-to-bearing cap (bottom) nuts. Using a tapered punch, tap the cone washers slits and remove the washers.

➡Do not mix or lose the upper and lower bearing cap shims.

6. Using a bearing removal tool (without a collar), press the steering knuckle arm with the shims from the steering knuckle.

7. Using a bearing removal tool (without a collar), press the bearing cap with the shims from the steering knuckle.

8. Remove the steering knuckle from the vehicle.

To install:

9. To install the steering knuckle, use a suitable tool to support the upper inner bearing. Using a hammer, tap the steering knuckle arm into the bearing inner race.

10. Using the proper tool, support the lower bearing inner race. Using a hammer, tap the bearing cap into the bearing inner race.

➡When installing the drag link-to-steering knuckle arm, tighten the plug all the way, then loosen it 1⅓ turns and secure it with the cotter pin.

11. To install, use gaskets, seals, pack the steering knuckle with multi-purpose grease and reverse the removal procedures. Tighten the steering knuckle arm-to-steering knuckle nuts to 71 ft. lbs., the bearing cap-to-steering knuckle nuts to 71 ft. lbs., the tie rod-to-steering knuckle arm nut to 67 ft. lbs., the axle spindle-to-steering knuckle bolts to 38 ft. lbs. Adjust the wheel bearing preload.

➡To test the knuckle bearing preload, attach a spring scale to the tie rod end hole (at a right angle) in the steering knuckle arm. The force required to move the knuckle from side to side should be 6.6–13 lbs. If the preload is not correct, adjust by replacing shims.

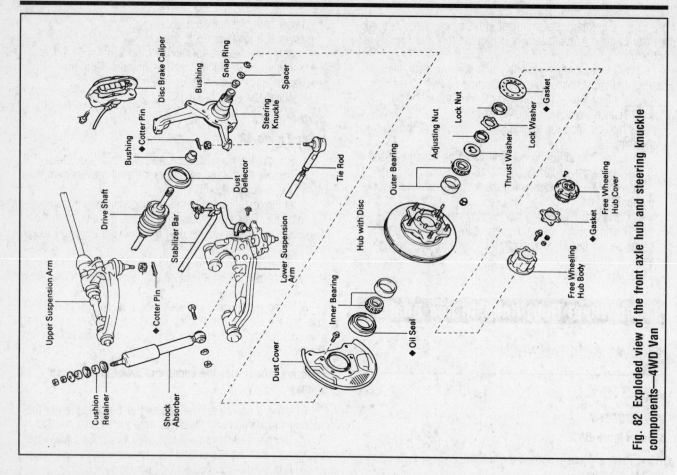

Fig. 82 Exploded view of the front axle hub and steering knuckle components—4WD Van

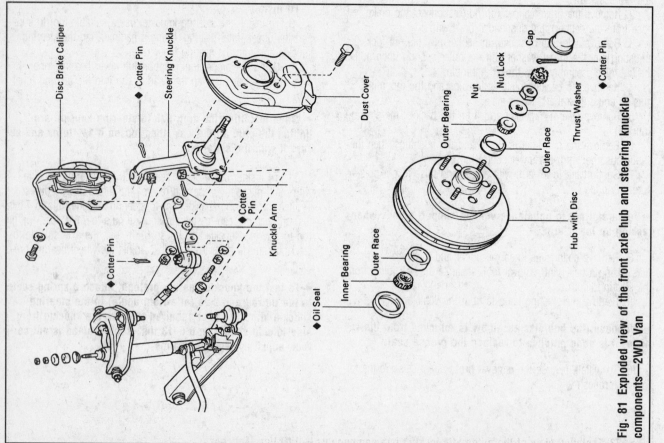

Fig. 81 Exploded view of the front axle hub and steering knuckle components—2WD Van

Locking Hubs

REMOVAL & INSTALLATION

4WD Van

◆ **See Figures 83 thru 110**

1. If equipped with free-wheeling hubs, turn the hub control handle to the **FREE** position.
2. Remove the hub cover bolts and pull off the cover.
3. If equipped with automatic locking hubs, remove the axle bolt with the washer.

4. Using snapring pliers, remove the snapring from the axle shaft.
5. Remove the hub body mounting nuts.
6. Remove the cone washers from the hub body mounting studs by tapping on the washer slits with a tapered punch.
7. Remove the hub body from the axle hub.
8. Apply multi-purpose grease to the inner hub splines.
9. To install, use new gaskets and reverse the removal procedures. Tighten the hub body-to-axle hub nuts to 23 ft. lbs., the plate washer/bolt to 13 ft. lbs. (auto. locking hub) and the hub cover-to-hub body bolts to 7 ft. lbs.

➡**To install the snapring onto the axle shaft, install a bolt into the axle shaft, pull it out and install the snapring.**

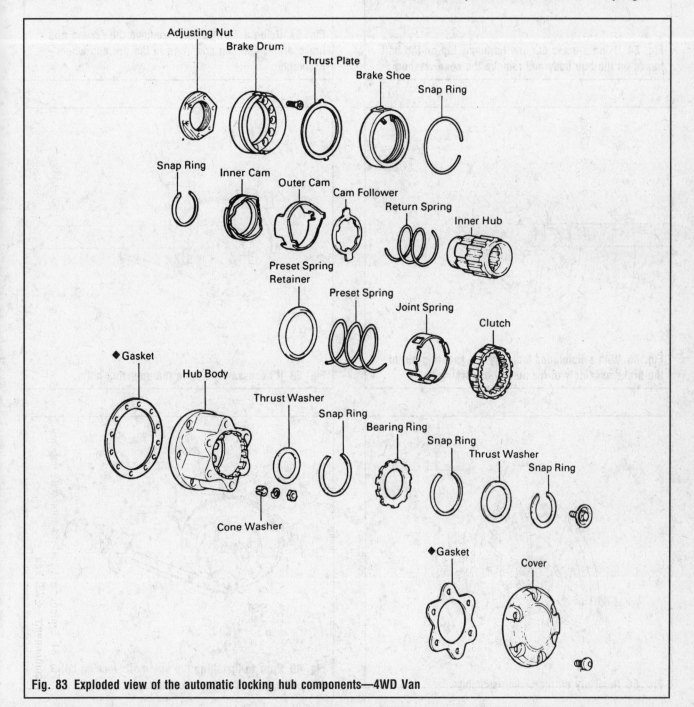

Fig. 83 Exploded view of the automatic locking hub components—4WD Van

Fig. 84 Using a brass bar and hammer, tap on the bolt heads on the hub body and remove the cone washers

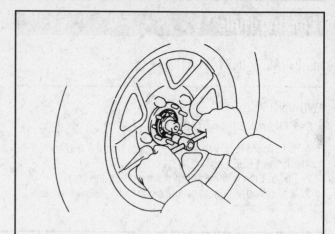

Fig. 87 Using a Torx® socket, remove the screws and brake drum, you can now remove the tire and wheel assembly

Fig. 85 With a flatbladed tool, pry the snapring out of the brake assembly of the automatic locking hub

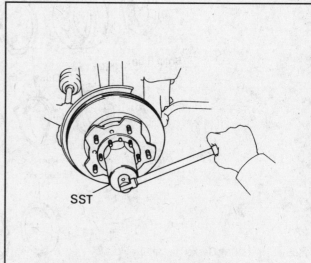

Fig. 88 If necessary, remove the adjusting nut

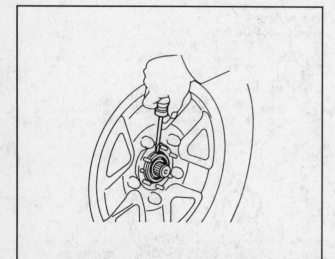

Fig. 86 Next, pry off the brake assembly

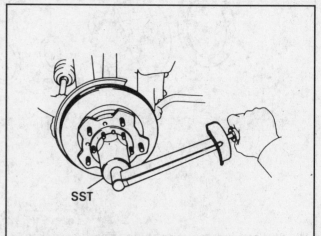

Fig. 89 Prior to installing the automatic locking hub, adjust the preload using a torque wrench . . .

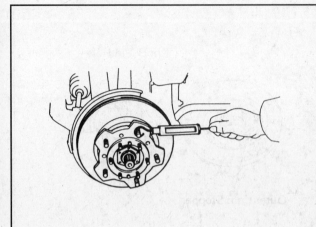

Fig. 90 . . . then, using a spring tension gauge, check the preload

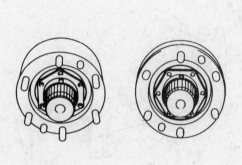

Fig. 91 Install the brake assembly, confirm the holes of the hub and adjusting nut are aligned as shown

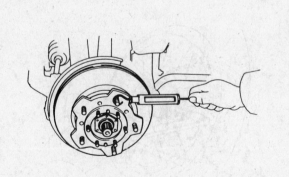

Fig. 92 Use a spring tension gauge again and check the preload. If not within specifications, adjust with the adjusting nut

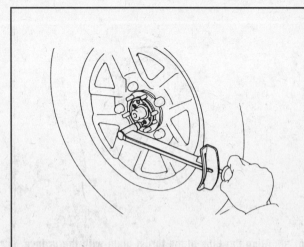

Fig. 93 Next, install the brake drum and tighten the Torx® screws to specifications

Fig. 94 On the automatic locking hub, install the snapring . . .

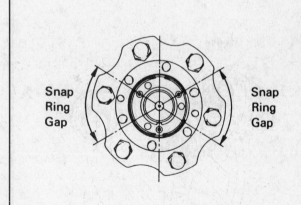

Snap
Ring
Gap

Snap
Ring
Gap

Fig. 95 . . . do not align the snapring gap and the notch of the brake drum

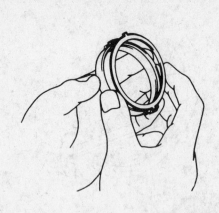

Fig. 96 Align the tabs of the thrust plate with the groove of the thrust plate, then assemble it on the automatic locking hub

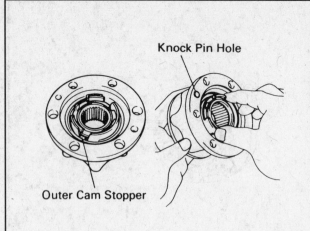

Fig. 99 Check that the outer cam stopper is securely in the inner cam groove

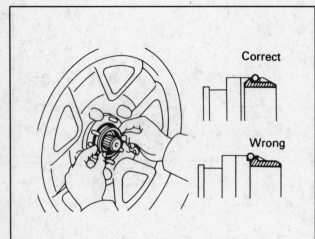

Fig. 97 When installing the brake subassembly to the brake drum, be sure it is aligned correctly

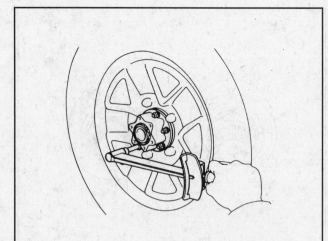

Fig. 100 Install the automatic locking hub body to the axle hub, install the six cone washers and tighten

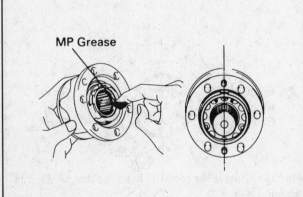

Fig. 98 Install a new gasket to the axle hub, then apply multi-purpose grease to the splines of the automatic locking hub body

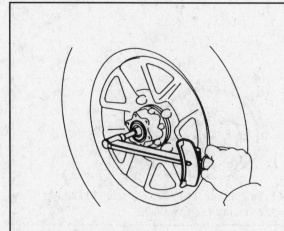

Fig. 101 Install the bolt with washer on the automatic locking hub and tighten

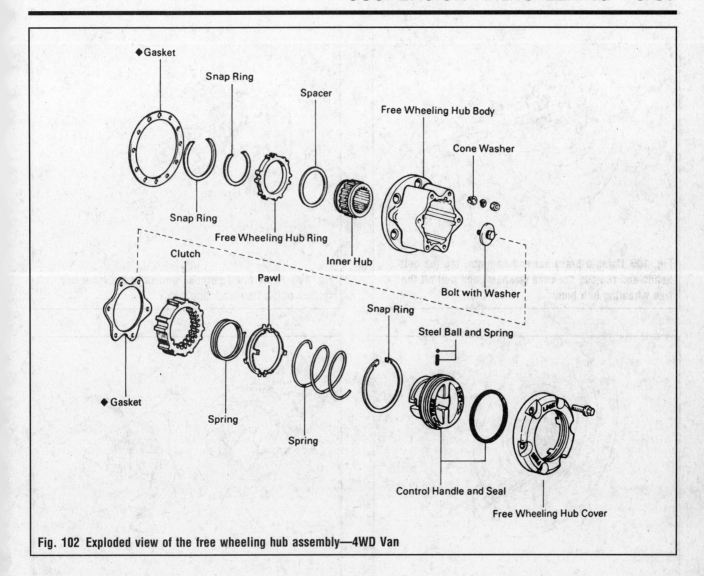

Fig. 102 Exploded view of the free wheeling hub assembly—4WD Van

Fig. 103 Set the free wheeling hub control handle to FREE, then remove the cover bolts

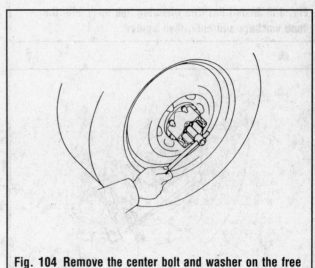

Fig. 104 Remove the center bolt and washer on the free wheeling hub

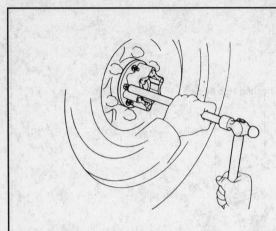

Fig. 105 Using a brass bar and hammer, tap the bolt heads and remove the cone washers, and pull off the free wheeling hub body

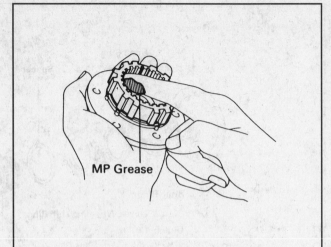

Fig. 108 Apply multi purpose grease to the inner hub splines of the free wheeling hub

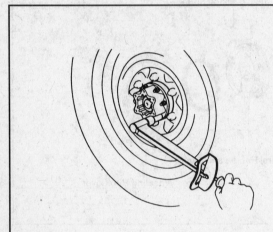

Fig. 106 Install the free wheeling hub body with the cone washers and nuts, then tighten

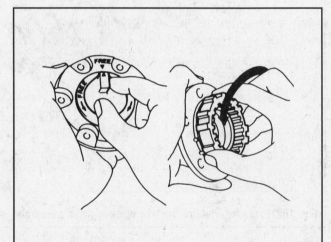

Fig. 109 Set the control handle and clutch to the FREE position of the hub cover. Install a new gasket . . .

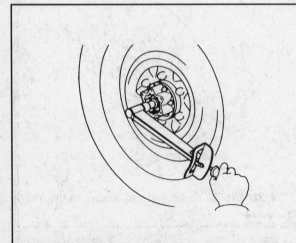

Fig. 107 Install the center bolt with washer and tighten to 13 ft. lbs. (18 Nm) on the free wheeling hub

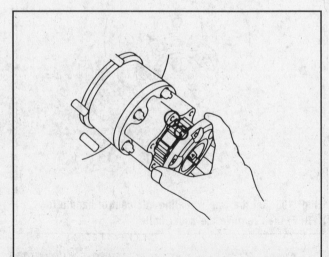

Fig. 110 . . . and place the free wheel hub cover into position and tighten

TROUBLESHOOTING THE AUTOMATIC LOCKING HUB

Problem	Possible cause	Remedy
Will not lock Will not unlock	Brake shoe worn or damaged	Replace brake assembly
	Brake spring weak	Replace brake assembly
	Rubbing between the inner hub and clutch	Replace hub assembly
	Engage/disengagement between the clutch and hub body not smooth	Replace hub assembly
Abnormal noise	Body and clutch loose or damaged	Replace hub assembly
	Loose set bolt on axle shaft and inner hub	Tighten or replace hub assembly
	Loose brake assembly set screw	Replace brake assembly
Brake drag (ALH)	Outer cam worn or damaged	Replace hub assembly
	Front brake dragging	Replace hub assembly

Toyota Electronic Modulated Suspension (TEMS)

DESCRIPTION

♦ **See Figures 111 and 112**

The TEMS system is used to allow the vehicles suspension to be electronically modulated according to the existing driving condi-

tions, allowing for a comfortable and well balanced drive. Damping of the front and rear shock absorbers is controlled automatically to reduce "Squatting" on sudden acceleration and roll when cornering.

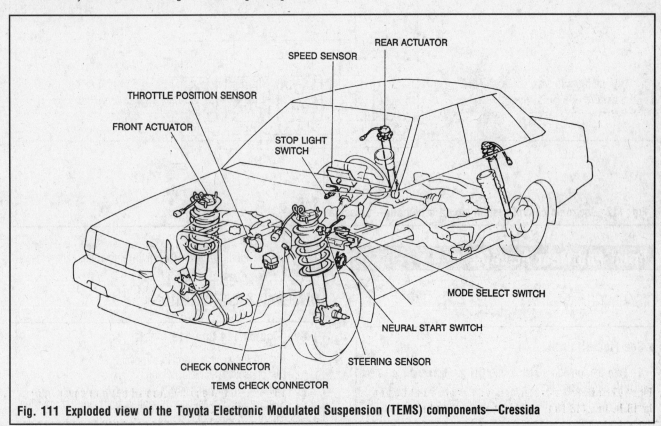

Fig. 111 Exploded view of the Toyota Electronic Modulated Suspension (TEMS) components—Cressida

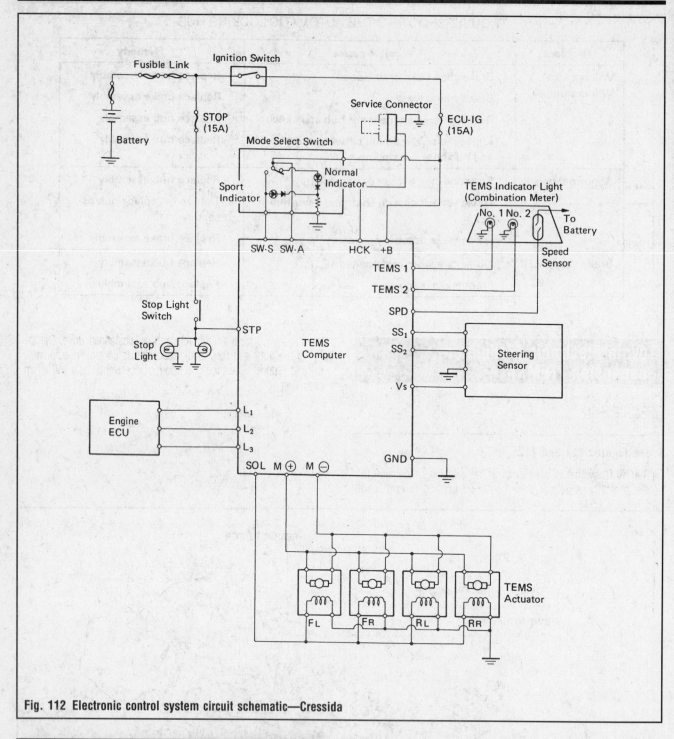

Fig. 112 Electronic control system circuit schematic—Cressida

Front and Rear Actuator

DISARMING

▶ **See Figure 113**

1. Turn the ignition switch to the **ON** position and the select switch to SPORT position.
2. Place a jumper wire in service connector terminals Tem and E2.

3. Turn the ignition switch **OFF** and remove the battery negative terminal.

REMOVAL & INSTALLATION

▶ **See Figures 114 thru 119**

1. Disarm the system prior to removal.
2. Disconnect the actuator wiring.
3. Remove the actuator cover.
4. Remove the two actuator mounting bolts and pull out the actuator from the shock absorber.

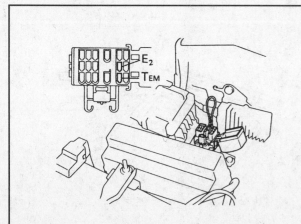

Fig. 113 Use a jumper wire to short circuit the Tem and E2 terminals of the service connector on the TEMS acuator

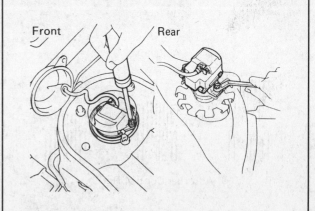

Fig. 115 Remove the actuator mounting bolts and pull the unit out straight to prevent bending the absorber control rod

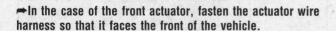

➡Pull the actuator out straight and slowly to prevent bending the absorber control rod.

To install:

5. Position the actuator valve facing toward the hard position.

6. Check that the absorber control rod is facing toward the hard position. If not, use needle-nose pliers to turn it toward that direction.

7. Insert the absorber rod into the groove of the actuator valve, then secure the actuator with two bolts.

➡In the case of the front actuator, fasten the actuator wire harness so that it faces the front of the vehicle.

8. Install the actuator cover and tighten to 10 ft. lbs. (14 Nm).

9. Attach the actuator connector.

10. Remove the service wire from the service connector. Check the TEMS operation.

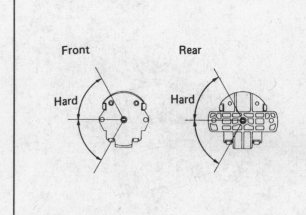

Fig. 116 Position the actuator valve so it is facing toward the hard position

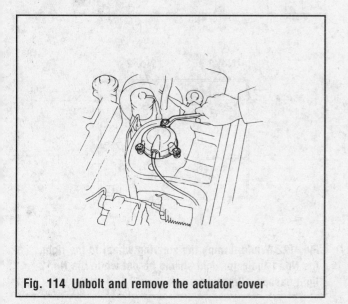

Fig. 114 Unbolt and remove the actuator cover

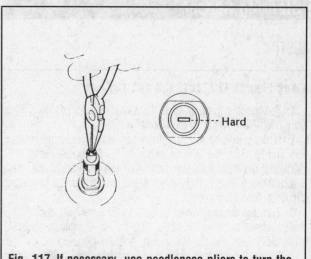

Fig. 117 If necessary, use needlenose pliers to turn the actuator control rod into the correct position

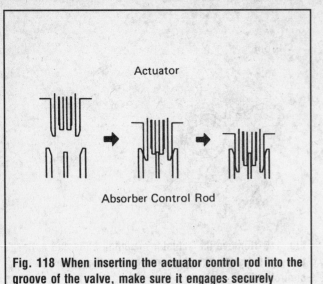

Fig. 118 When inserting the actuator control rod into the groove of the valve, make sure it engages securely

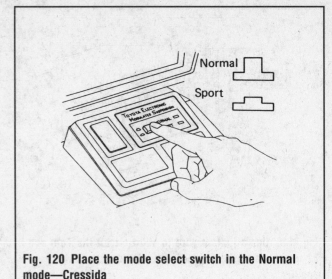

Fig. 120 Place the mode select switch in the Normal mode—Cressida

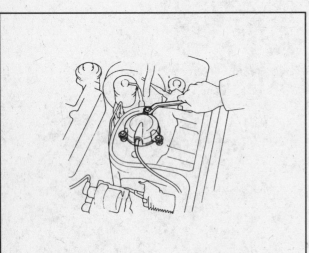

Fig. 119 Install the actuator cover and tighten to specifications

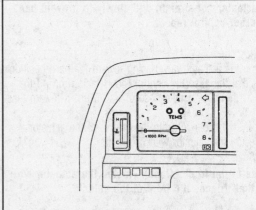

Fig. 121 When testing the TEMS steering sensor indicator light, make sure it flashes after two seconds

Steering Sensor

TESTING

▶ **See Figures 120, 121, 122 and 123**

1. Position the front wheel in the straight-ahead position. Place the mode select switch in the Normal position.

2. Using a jumper wire, short the service connector terminals Tem and E2. Turn the ignition switch to the ON position and check that the indicator lights flash after two seconds. If not, there is a problem with either the mode select switch, service connector circuit or TEMS computer.

3. Turn the steering wheel ¼ turn to the right from the straight-ahead position and check that the No. 2 indicator light (right side) flash and the No. 1 light (left side) goes out.

4. Return the steering wheel to the straight-away position and then ¼ turn to the left, and check that the No. 1 TEMS indicator light (left side) flash and the No. 2 light (right side) goes out.

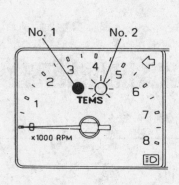

Fig. 122 While turning the steering wheel to the right, the No. 1 indicator light should be out while the No. 2 light flashes—Cressida

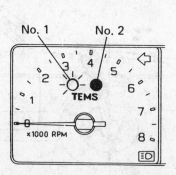

Fig. 123 While turning the steering wheel to the left, the No. 2 indicator light should be out while the No. 1 light flashes—Cressida

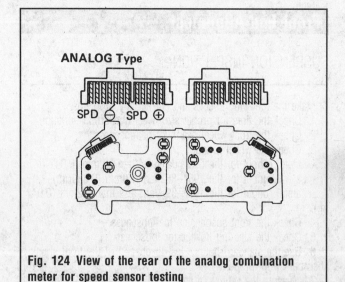

Fig. 124 View of the rear of the analog combination meter for speed sensor testing

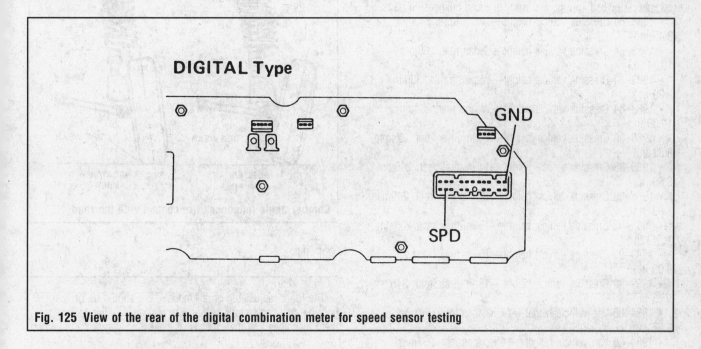

Fig. 125 View of the rear of the digital combination meter for speed sensor testing

5. If the operation is not as specified in the last two steps, inspect for the cause.

Speed Sensor

TESTING

Analog Type
▶ See Figure 124

1. Remove the combination meter.
2. Connect an ohmmeter between the terminals SPD + and SPD −.

3. Revolve the meter shaft and check that the meter needle repeatedly deflects from 0 ohms to infinity ohms.

Digital Type
▶ See Figure 125

1. Remove the combination meter with the attached wire harness.
2. Turn the ignition switch ON.
3. Connect a voltmeter between terminal SPD and GND.
4. Revolve the meter shaft and check that the voltmeter needle repeatedly deflects from 0 volts and 2 volts.

Front End Alignment

SUSPENSION INSPECTION

Make the following checks and correct any problems:
1. Check the tires for proper size, wear and proper inflation.
2. Check the front wheel bearings for looseness.
3. Check the wheel runout.
• Lateral runout for the Cressida: less than 1.2mm (0.047 in.).
• Lateral runout for the 1984–86 Van: 1.0mm (0.039 in.).
• Lateral runout for the 1987–89 Van: less than 1.2mm (0.047 in.).
4. Check the front suspension for looseness.
5. Check the steering linkage for looseness.
6. Use the standard bounce test to check that the front shock absorbers work properly.
7. Measure the vehicle, if the height of the vehicle is not as specified, try to level it by shaking it up or down. If still not correct, check for bad springs and worn or loose suspension parts.
• 1983–84 Cressida vehicle height—Sedan front: 240mm (9.45 in.)
• 1983–84 Cressida vehicle height—Sedan rear: 260mm (10.24 in.)
• 1983–84 Cressida vehicle height—Wagon front: 236mm (9.29 in.)
• 1983–84 Cressida vehicle height—Wagon rear: 264mm (10.39 in.)
• 1985–88 Cressida vehicle height—14 in. tires front: 224mm (8.82 in.)
• 1985–88 Cressida vehicle height—14 in. tires rear: 246mm (9.69 in.)
• 1985–88 Cressida vehicle height—15 in. tires front: 219mm (8.62 in.)
• 1985–88 Cressida vehicle height—15 in. tires rear: 265mm (10.43 in.)
• 1989–90 Cressida vehicle height—15 in. tires front: 231mm (9.09 in.)
• 1989–90 Cressida vehicle height—15 in. tires front: 245mm (9.65 in.)
• 1984–86 Van vehicle height—14 in. tires front: 243mm (9.57 in.)
• 1984–86 Van vehicle height—14 in. tires rear: 267mm (10.51 in.)
• 1987–89 Van vehicle height—14 in. tires front: 234mm (9.21 in.)
• 1987–89 Van vehicle height—14 in. tires rear: 264mm (10.39 in) or 254mm (10.00 in) for the leaf spring type rear suspension
8. When measuring the chassis ground clearance, measure from the ground to the center of the lower suspension arm from the mounting bolt.

CAMBER AND CASTER

The camber and caster is adjustable on all models, but should be perform only by qualified factory technicians who are familiar with alignment machines and their means of measuring degrees and inches.

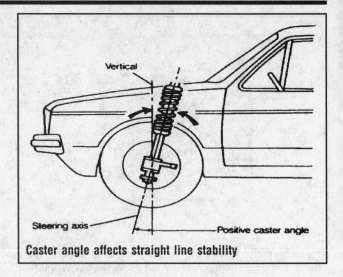

Caster angle affects straight line stability

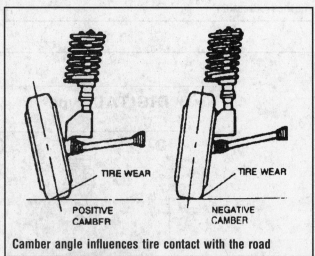

Camber angle influences tire contact with the road

TOE-IN

The toe-in adjustable on all models, but should be perform only by qualified factory technicians who are familiar with alignment machines and their means of measuring degrees and inches.

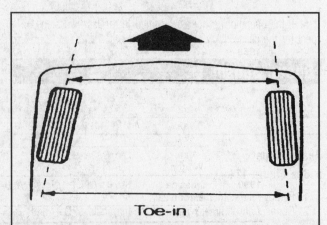

Toe-in means the distance between the wheels is closer at the front than at the rear of the wheels

Wheel Alignment Specifications

Year	Model	Caster Range (deg.)	Caster Pref Setting (deg.)	Camber Range (deg.)	Camber Pref Setting (deg.)	Toe (in.)	Steering Axis Incline (deg.)
1983	Cressida Sedan	2P–3P	$2\frac{1}{2}$P	$\frac{1}{4}$P–$1\frac{1}{4}$P	$\frac{3}{4}$P	$\frac{1}{4}$P	$9\frac{1}{4}$
	Wagon	$1\frac{11}{16}$P–$2\frac{11}{16}$	$2\frac{3}{16}$P	$\frac{5}{16}$P–$1\frac{5}{16}$P	$1\frac{3}{16}$P	$\frac{1}{4}$P	$9\frac{1}{16}$
	Rear	—	—	$\frac{3}{16}$N–$1\frac{3}{16}$P	$\frac{5}{16}$P	$\frac{5}{32}$ (out)	—
1984	Cressida Sedan	2P–3P	$2\frac{1}{2}$P	$\frac{1}{4}$P–$1\frac{1}{4}$P	$\frac{3}{4}$P	$\frac{1}{4}$P	$9\frac{1}{4}$
	Wagon	$1\frac{11}{16}$P–$2\frac{11}{16}$	$2\frac{3}{16}$P	$\frac{5}{16}$P–$1\frac{5}{16}$P	$1\frac{3}{16}$P	$\frac{1}{4}$P	$9\frac{1}{16}$
	Rear	—	—	$\frac{3}{16}$N–$1\frac{3}{16}$P	$\frac{5}{16}$P	$\frac{5}{32}$ (out)	—
	Van	$1\frac{7}{16}$P–$2\frac{9}{16}$P	$2\frac{1}{16}$P	0P–1P	$\frac{1}{2}$P	0	10
1985	Cressida Sedan	$4\frac{5}{16}$P–$5\frac{5}{16}$P	$4\frac{13}{16}$P	$\frac{5}{16}$N–$1\frac{3}{16}$P	$\frac{7}{16}$P	0–0.16	$10\frac{1}{2}$
	Wagon	$3\frac{1}{2}$P–5P	$4\frac{1}{4}$P	$\frac{5}{16}$N–$1\frac{3}{16}$P	$\frac{7}{16}$P	0–0.16	$10\frac{1}{2}$
	Rear	—	—	$\frac{15}{16}$N–$\frac{1}{16}$P	$\frac{7}{16}$P	$\frac{1}{4}$	—
	Van	$1\frac{7}{16}$P–$2\frac{9}{16}$P	$2\frac{1}{16}$P	0P–1P	$\frac{1}{2}$P	0	10
1986	Cressida Sedan	$4\frac{5}{16}$P–$5\frac{5}{16}$P	$4\frac{13}{16}$P	$\frac{5}{16}$N–$1\frac{3}{16}$P	$\frac{7}{16}$P	0–0.16	$10\frac{1}{2}$
	Wagon	$3\frac{1}{2}$P–5P	$4\frac{1}{4}$P	$\frac{5}{16}$N–$1\frac{3}{16}$P	$\frac{7}{16}$P	0–0.16	$10\frac{1}{2}$
	Rear	—	—	$\frac{15}{16}$N–$\frac{1}{16}$P	$\frac{7}{16}$P	$\frac{1}{4}$	—
	Van	2P–3P	$2\frac{1}{2}$P	$\frac{1}{2}$N–$\frac{1}{2}$P	0	0	$10\frac{1}{2}$
1987	Cressida Sedan	$4\frac{5}{16}$P–$5\frac{5}{16}$P	$4\frac{13}{16}$P	$\frac{5}{16}$N–$1\frac{3}{16}$P	$\frac{7}{16}$P	0–0.16	$10\frac{1}{2}$
	Wagon	$3\frac{1}{2}$P–5P	$4\frac{1}{4}$P	$\frac{5}{16}$N–$1\frac{3}{16}$P	$\frac{7}{16}$P	0–0.16	$10\frac{1}{2}$
	Rear	—	—	$\frac{15}{16}$N–$\frac{1}{16}$P	$\frac{7}{16}$P	$\frac{1}{4}$	—
	Van 4x2	2P–3P	$2\frac{1}{2}$P	$\frac{9}{16}$N–$\frac{7}{16}$P	$\frac{1}{16}$N	0	$10\frac{9}{16}$
	Van 4x4	$1\frac{11}{16}$P–$2\frac{9}{16}$P	$2\frac{13}{16}$P	$\frac{5}{16}$N–$1\frac{1}{16}$P	$\frac{3}{16}$P	0	$12\frac{7}{16}$
	Van Wagon	$2\frac{5}{16}$P–$3\frac{5}{16}$P	$2\frac{13}{16}$P	$\frac{9}{16}$N–$\frac{7}{16}$P	$\frac{1}{16}$N	0	$10\frac{9}{16}$
1988	Cressida Sedan	$4\frac{5}{16}$P–$5\frac{5}{16}$P	$4\frac{13}{16}$P	$\frac{5}{16}$N–$1\frac{3}{16}$P	$\frac{7}{16}$P	0–0.16	$10\frac{1}{2}$
	Wagon	$3\frac{1}{2}$P–5P	$4\frac{1}{4}$P	$\frac{5}{16}$N–$1\frac{3}{16}$P	$\frac{7}{16}$P	0–0.16	$10\frac{1}{2}$
	Rear	—	—	$\frac{15}{16}$N–$\frac{1}{16}$P	$\frac{7}{16}$P	$\frac{1}{4}$	—
	Van 4x2	2P–3P	$2\frac{1}{2}$P	$\frac{9}{16}$N–$\frac{7}{16}$P	$\frac{1}{16}$N	0	$10\frac{9}{16}$
	Van 4x4	$1\frac{11}{16}$P–$2\frac{9}{16}$P	$2\frac{13}{16}$P	$\frac{5}{16}$N–$1\frac{1}{16}$P	$\frac{3}{16}$P	0	$12\frac{7}{16}$
	Van Wagon	$2\frac{5}{16}$P–$3\frac{5}{16}$P	$2\frac{13}{16}$P	$\frac{9}{16}$N–$\frac{7}{16}$P	$\frac{1}{16}$N	0	$10\frac{9}{16}$
1989	Cressida Sedan	$6\frac{9}{16}$P–$8\frac{1}{16}$P	$7\frac{5}{16}$P	0P–1P	$\frac{1}{2}$P	$\frac{5}{32}$	$13\frac{3}{16}$
	Rear	—	—	$\frac{1}{2}$N–$\frac{1}{2}$P	0P	$\frac{5}{32}$	—
	Van 4x2	2P–3P	$2\frac{1}{2}$P	$\frac{9}{16}$N–$\frac{7}{16}$P	$\frac{1}{16}$N	0	$10\frac{9}{16}$
	Van 4x4	$1\frac{11}{16}$P–$2\frac{9}{16}$P	$2\frac{13}{16}$P	$\frac{5}{16}$N–$1\frac{1}{16}$P	$\frac{3}{16}$P	0	$12\frac{7}{16}$
	Van Wagon	$2\frac{5}{16}$P–$3\frac{5}{16}$P	$2\frac{13}{16}$P	$\frac{9}{16}$N–$\frac{7}{16}$P	$\frac{1}{16}$N	0	$10\frac{9}{16}$
1990	Cressida Sedan	$6\frac{9}{16}$P–$8\frac{1}{16}$P	$7\frac{5}{16}$P	0P–1P	$\frac{1}{2}$P	$\frac{5}{32}$	$13\frac{3}{16}$
	Rear	—	—	$\frac{1}{2}$N–$\frac{1}{2}$P	0P	$\frac{5}{32}$	—

P Positive
N Negative

FRONT SUSPENSION TROUBLESHOOTING

Problem	Possible cause	Remedy
Wanders/pulls	Tires worn or improperly inflated	Replace tire or inflate tires to proper pressure
	Alignment incorrect	Check front wheel alignment
	Hub bearing worn	Replace hub bearing
	Front or rear suspension parts loose or broken	Tighten or replace suspension parts
	Steering linkage loosen or worn	Tighten or replace steering linkage
	Steering gear out of adjustment or broken	Adjust or repair steering gear
Bottoming	Vehicle overloaded	Check loading
	Shock absorber worn out	Replace shock absorber
	Springs weak	Replace spring
Sways/pitches	Tires improperly inflated	Inflate tires to proper pressure
	Stabilizer bar bent or broken	Inspect stabilizer bar
	Shock absorber worn out	Replace shock absorber
Front wheel shimmy	Tires worn or improperly inflated	Replace tire or inflate tires to proper pressure
	Wheels out of balance	Balance wheels
	Shock absorber worn out	Replace shock absorber
	Alignment incorrect	Check front wheel alignment
	Hub bearings worn	Replace hub bearings
	Ball joints worn	Inspect ball joints
	Steering linkage loosen or worn	Tighten or replace steering linkage
	Steering gear out of adjustment or broken	Adjust or repair steering gear
Abnormal tire wear	Tires improperly inflated	Inflate tires to proper pressure
	Shock absorbers worn out	Replace shock absorber
	Alignment incorrect	Check front wheel alignment
	Suspension parts worn	Replace suspension parts
Oil leak from differential	Oil level too high or wrong grade	Drain and replace oil
	Drive pinion oil seal worn or damaged	Replace oil seal
	Side gear oil seal worn or damaged	Replace oil seal
	Companion flange loose or damaged	Tighten or replace flange
	Side gear shaft damaged	Replace shaft
Noises in axle	Oil level low or wrong grade	Drain and replace oil
	Excessive backlash between pinion and ring or side gear	Check backlash
	Ring gear worn or chipped	Inspect gear
	Pinion or side gears worn or chipped	Inspect gears
	Pinion shaft bearing worn	Replace bearing
	Side bearing worn	Replace bearing
	Differential bearing loose or worn	Tighten or replace bearings

CRESSIDA 4-LINK REAR SUSPENSION

Coil Spring and Shock Absorber

REMOVAL & INSTALLATION

◆ **See Figure 126**

1. Raise and support the rear axle housing and frame safely. Be sure to leave the jack under the rear axle.
2. Remove the bolt holding the shock absorber to the rear axle housing and disconnect the shock absorber.

3. Remove the nut holding the shock absorber to the body and remove the shock absorber. It may be necessary to use a suitable tool to hold the shock absorber so as to be able to remove the retaining nut.
4. Remove the bolts holding the stabilizer bar brackets to the rear axle housing.
5. Remove the nut holding the lateral control rod to the rear axle housing and disconnect the lateral control rod.
6. Start to lower the rear axle. Be careful not to pull the brake line and parking brake cable. While lowering the rear axle housing, remove the coil spring and the upper and lower insulators.

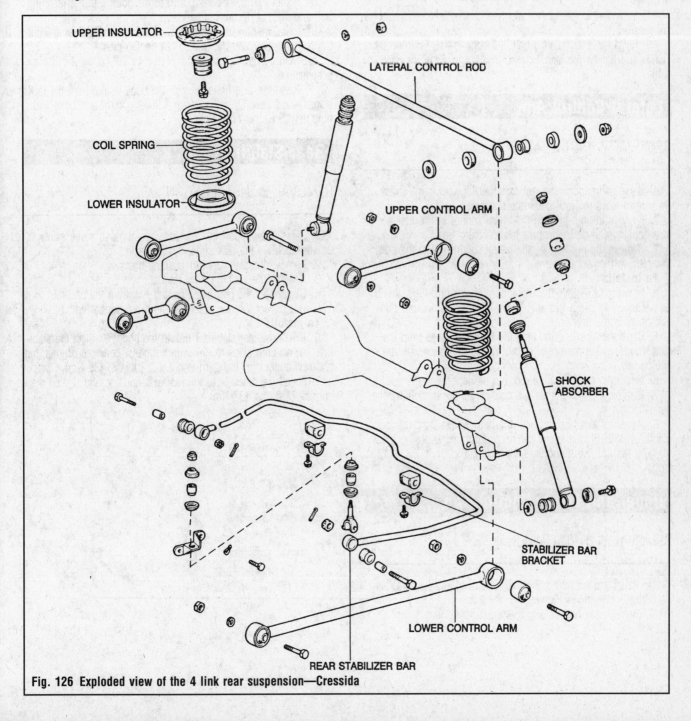

Fig. 126 Exploded view of the 4 link rear suspension—Cressida

To install:

7. Put the lower insulator on the axle housing.

8. Put the upper insulator on the coil spring. Install the coil spring.

9. Check the position of the lower insulator, by jacking up the rear axle housing and checking to see that the lower insulator is installed correctly. If the insulator in not installed correctly, reinstall the coil spring.

10. Install the lateral control rod, but do not tighten the nut.

11. Install the shock absorber to the body and tighten the retaining nut to 18 ft. lbs. (25 Nm).

12. Connect the shock absorber to the rear axle housing with the retaining nut and tighten the nut to 27 ft. lbs. (37 Nm).

13. Install the stabilizer bar bushing brackets to the rear axle housing.

14. Remove the jack stands and bounce the car to stabilize the suspension.

15. Raise the axle housing until the body is free from the jack stands and tighten the lateral control rod nut to 43 ft. lbs. (59 Nm).

Lateral Control Arm

REMOVAL & INSTALLATION

1. Raise and support the rear axle housing and frame safely. Be sure to leave the jack under the rear axle.

2. Remove the nut holding the lateral control rod to the rear axle housing and disconnect the lateral control rod.

3. Remove the nut holding the lateral control rod to the body and remove the lateral control rod.

To install:

4. In order to remove the lateral control arm bushings, it will be necessary to use a hydraulic press to press out the old ones and press in the new ones.

5. Raise the axle housing until the housing is free from the jack stands. Install the lateral control rod to the frame with the retaining nut.

6. Install the lateral control rod, but do not tighten the nut.

7. Remove the jack stands and bounce the car to stabilize the suspension.

8. Raise the axle housing until the body is free from the jack stands and tighten the lateral control rod nut (axle housing side) to 43 ft. lbs. (59 Nm). and the body side nut to 81 ft. lbs. (110 Nm).

Upper and Lower Control Arm

REMOVAL & INSTALLATION

1. Raise and support the rear axle housing and frame safely. Be sure to leave the jack under the rear axle.

2. Remove the bolt holding the upper control arm to the body.

3. Remove the bolt holding the upper control arm to the rear axle housing and remove the control rod.

4. Remove the bolt holding the lower control arm to the body.

5. Remove the bolt holding the lower control arm to the rear axle housing and remove the lower control rod.

To install:

6. In order to remove the lower and upper control arm bushings, it will be necessary to use a hydraulic press to press out the old ones and press in the new ones.

7. Install the upper control arm to the body with the retaining bolt and the nut but do not tighten them.

8. Install the upper control arm to the rear axle housing with the retaining bolt and nut but do not tighten them.

9. Install the lower control arm to the body with the retaining bolt and nut but do not tighten them.

10. Install the lower control arm to the rear axle housing with the retaining bolt and nut but do not tighten them.

11. Remove the jack stands and bounce the car to stabilize the suspension.

12. Raise the axle housing until the body is free from the jack stands and torque all the upper and lower control arm bolts and nuts to 105 ft. lbs. (142 Nm).

Rear Stabilizer Bar

REMOVAL & INSTALLATION

1. Raise and support the rear axle housing and frame safely. Be sure to leave the jack under the rear axle.

2. Remove the stabilizer bar bushing brackets.

3. Remove the bushing from the bar.

4. Disconnect the rear stabilizer bar link from the bracket.

5. Disconnect the rear stabilizer link from the bar end.

To install:

6. Install the rear stabilizer link to the body. Connect the stabilizer bar on both sides to link with the bolts, collars cushions, nut and new cotter pin. Tighten the nut to 22 ft. lbs. (30 Nm).

7. Install the brackets to the rear axle housing and tighten the nuts to 27 ft. lbs. (37 Nm).

CRESSIDA INDEPENDENT REAR SUSPENSION (IRS)

Coil Spring and Shock Absorber

REMOVAL & INSTALLATION

♦ **See Figure 127**

1. Raise and support the rear axle housing and frame safely. Be sure to leave the jack under the rear axle. Remove the rear wheel assembly.
2. Remove the brake hose clip. Disconnect the stabilizer bar end bolt, cushion and retainer from the suspension arm and remove the stabilizer bar end.
3. Remove the drive shaft on the rear axle shaft side only. Leave the jack under the suspension arm.
4. Remove the bolt holding the shock absorber to the rear suspension arm and disconnect the shock absorber.
5. On models without the TEMS system do the following: Remove the shock absorber head cover and locknuts, and remove the shock absorber.
6. On models with the TEMS system do the following:
   a. Remove and inspect the actuator.
   b. Hold the actuator bracket, remove the shock absorber nuts and remove the shock absorber.
7. Start to lower the rear axle. Be careful not to pull the brake line and parking brake cable. While lowering the rear axle housing, remove the coil spring and the upper and lower insulators.
To install:
8. Put the lower insulator on the axle housing. Put the upper insulator on the coil spring. Install the coil spring.
9. Check the position of the lower insulator, by jacking up the rear axle housing and checking to see that the lower insulator is installed correctly. If the insulator in not installed correctly, reinstall the coil spring.
10. On vehicles not equipped with the TEMS system do the following:
    a. Connect the shock absorber to the body with the retaining nuts.
    b. Hold the shaft and tighten the nut to 18 ft. lbs. (25 Nm).
11. On vehicles equipped with the TEMS system do the following:
    a. Install the cushions, retainers and actuator bracket to the shock absorber with the retaining nut.
    b. Hold the bracket and tighten the nut to 20 ft. lbs. (27 Nm). Install the actuator.
12. Connect the shock absorber lower nut and tighten it to 27 ft. lbs. (37 Nm).
13. Connect the stabilizer bar end to the rear suspension. Tighten the bolt to 13 ft. lbs. (18Nm).
14. Install the rear driveshaft assembly.
15. Install the brake hose clips. Install the rear wheel assembly.
16. Remove the jack stands and bounce the car to stabilize the suspension.

Rear Stabilizer Bar

REMOVAL & INSTALLATION

1. Raise and support the rear axle housing and frame safely. Be sure to leave the jack under the rear axle.
2. Remove the stabilizer bar bushing brackets.
3. Remove the stabilizer bar from the arm.
To install:
4. Install the rear stabilizer bar brackets to the body, then tighten the nuts to 27 ft. lbs. (37 Nm).
5. Install the rear stabilizer link to the body. Connect the stabilizer bar on both sides to link with the bolts, collars, cushions and nut. Tighten the bolt to 13 ft. lbs. (18 Nm).

Rear Suspension Arm

REMOVAL & INSTALLATION

1. Raise and support the rear axle housing and frame safely. Be sure to leave the jack under the rear axle.
2. Remove the stabilizer bar from the arm.
3. Disconnect the drive shaft assembly.
4. Remove the rear axle flange and rear axle shaft.
5. Remove the rear brake assembly and rotor disc.
6. Disconnect the parking brake cable.
7. Remove the parking brake with dust cover.
8. Disconnect the brake line.
9. Disconnect the shock absorber from the suspension arm.
10. Remove the coil spring and insulators.
11. Remove the suspension arm retaining bolts. Remove the camber adjusting cam and the suspension arm. Be sure to mark the position when removing the suspension arm.
To install:
12. In order to remove the rear suspension arm bushings, it will be necessary to use a hydraulic press to press out the old ones and press in the new ones.
13. Align the mark at the same position it was before removal. Install the suspension arm and temporarily tighten the bolt.
14. Install the insulators and the coil spring.
15. Install the shock absorber and tighten the nut to 27 ft. lbs. (37 Nm).
16. Install the parking brake with dust cover. Tighten the nut to 105 ft. lbs. (142 Nm) and the bolt to 13 ft. lbs. (18 Nm).
17. Connect the brake line. Connect the parking brake cable.
18. Install the rear axle shaft and rear axle shaft flange.
19. Install the disc rotor and the rear brake assembly. Tighten the bolts to 34 ft. lbs. (47 Nm).
20. Connect the drive shaft.
21. Install the rear stabilizer link to the body. Connect the stabi-

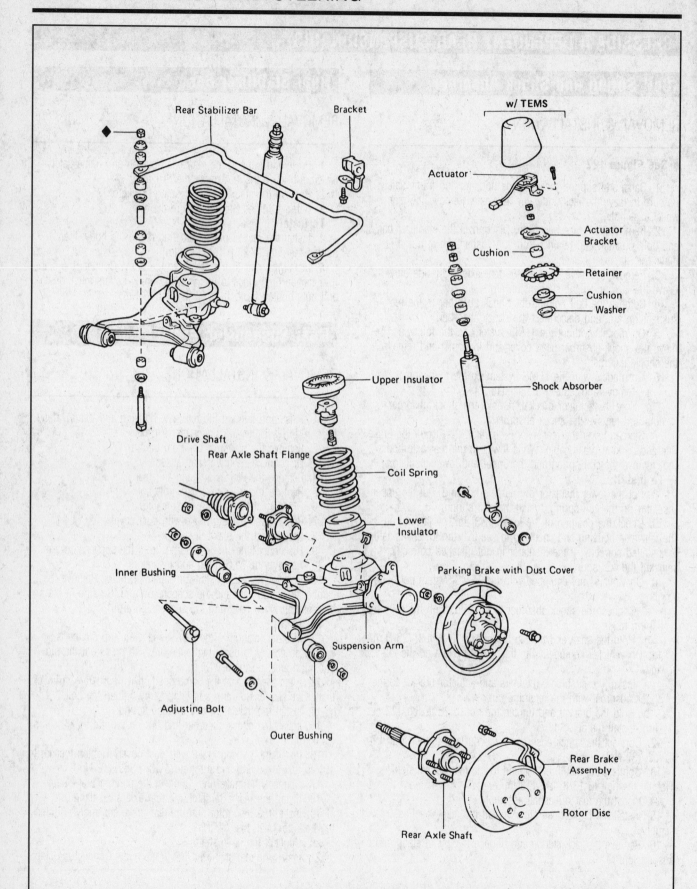

Fig. 127 Exploded view of the Independent Rear Suspension (IRS)—Cressida

lizer bar on both sides to link with the bolts, collars, cushions and nut. Tighten the bolt to 13 ft. lbs. (18 Nm).

22. Install the rear wheel assembly. Remove the jackstands and bounce the car to stabilize the suspension.

23. Tighten the suspension arm bolts to 90 ft. lbs. (123 Nm) on the inside one and 67 ft. lbs. (91 Nm) on the outside one.

24. Bleed the brake system. Be sure to have the rear wheel alignment checked.

MacPherson Strut

REMOVAL & INSTALLATION

▶ **See Figure 128**

1. Raise and support the vehicle safely. Remove the wheels. Remove the strut rod and remove the nut of the shock absorber.

2. Remove the rear seat, speaker grill and interior quarter panel trim (if so equipped) and package tray trim.

3. Disconnect the strut from the axle carrier.

4. Remove the strut cap. Remove the TEMS (Toyota Electronic Modulated Suspension) actuator.

5. Remove the 3 strut mounting nuts from the body and remove the strut assembly.

6. Mount the strut assembly in a suitable vise. Using a suitable spring compressor, compress the coil spring.

7. Remove the strut suspension support nut. Remove the strut suspension support, remove the coil spring and bumper.

To install:

8. Mount the strut in a suitable vise. Using a suitable spring compressor, compress the coil spring.

9. Install the bumper to the strut, align the coil spring end with the lower seat hollow and install the coil spring.

10. Align the strut suspension support hole and piston rod and install it. Align the suspension support with the strut lower bushing.

11. Install the strut suspension support nut and tighten it to 20 ft. lbs. (27 Nm). Connect the strut assembly with the 3 retaining nuts and torque them to 10 ft. lbs. (14 Nm).

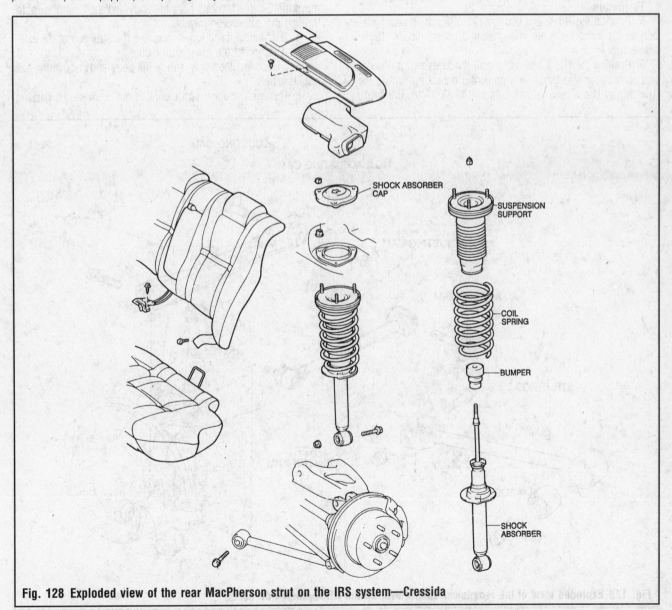

Fig. 128 Exploded view of the rear MacPherson strut on the IRS system—Cressida

12. Connect the strut assembly to the axle carrier and tighten it to 101 ft. lbs. (137 Nm).

13. Install the strut cap. Install the package tray trim, quarter panel trim panel, speaker grille and rear seat.

Lower Control Arm

REMOVAL & INSTALLATION

▶ **See Figure 129**

1. Raise and support the vehicle safely. Remove the wheels.
2. Remove the halfshaft.
3. Remove the nut and disconnect the No. 1 lower arm from the axle carrier. Matchmark the adjusting cam to the body, remove the cam and bolt and then lift out the No. 1 arm.
4. Remove the bolt and nut and disconnect the No. 2 lower arm from the axle carrier. Matchmark the adjusting cam to the body, remove the cam and bolt and then lift out the No. 2 arm.

To install:

5. Position the No. 2 arm and install the adjusting cam and bolt so the matchmarks are in alignment. Connect the arm to the axle carrier.
6. Position the No. 1 arm and install the adjusting cam and bolt so the matchmarks are in alignment. Connect the arm to the axle carrier. Use a new nut and tighten it to 43 ft. lbs. (59 Nm).

7. Install the halfshaft.
8. Install the wheels and lower the vehicle. Bounce it several times to set the suspension and then tighten the body-to-arm bolts and nuts to 134 ft. lbs. (181 Nm). Tighten the No. 2 arm-to-carrier bolt to 119 ft. lbs. (162 Nm). Tighten the No. 1 arm-to-carrier nut to 36 ft. lbs. (49 Nm).
9. Check the rear wheel alignment.

Upper Control Arm

REMOVAL & INSTALLATION

▶ **See Figure 130**

1. Raise and support the rear of the vehicle safely. Remove the wheels.
2. Unbolt the brake caliper and suspend it with wire so it is out of the way. Remove the halfshaft.
3. Disconnect the parking brake cable at the equalizer. Remove the 2 cable brackets from the body and then pull the cable through the suspension member.
4. Disconnect the 2 lower arms and the strut rod at the axle carrier. Disconnect the lower strut mount.
5. Disconnect the upper arm at the body and remove the axle hub assembly.
6. Remove the upper arm mounting nut. Remove the backing

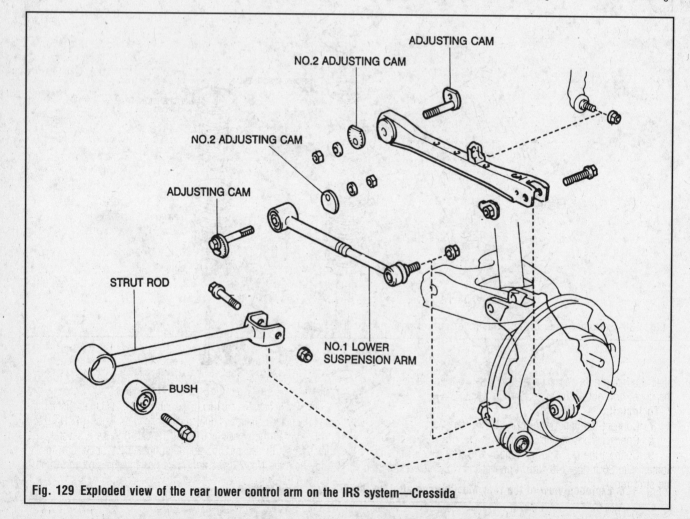

Fig. 129 Exploded view of the rear lower control arm on the IRS system—Cressida

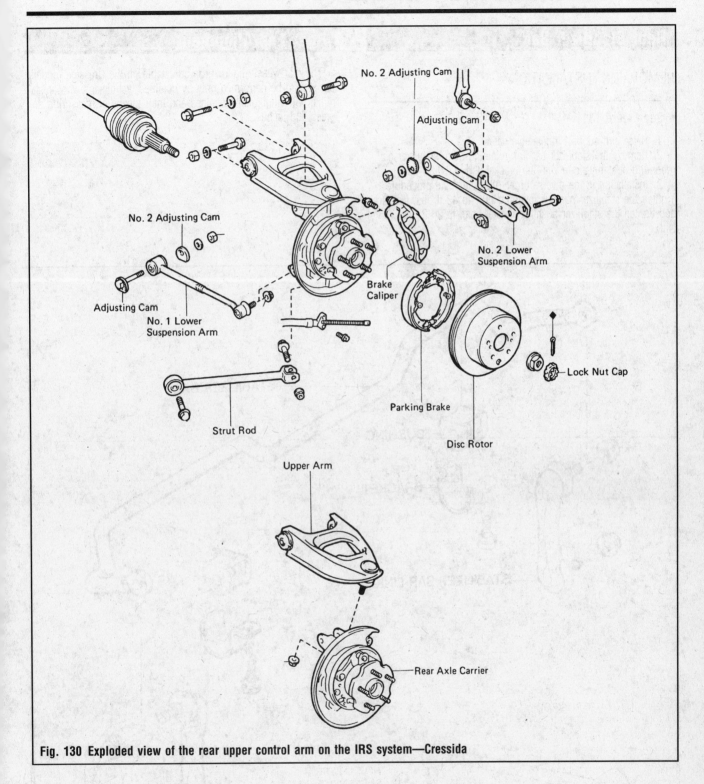

Fig. 130 Exploded view of the rear upper control arm on the IRS system—Cressida

plate mounting nuts and separate the plate from the carrier. Press the upper arm out of the axle carrier.

To install:

7. Connect the upper arm to the body.

8. Connect the axle hub assembly to the arm with a new nut.

9. Connect the No. 1 lower control arm with a new nut and tighten it to 36 ft. lbs. (49 Nm). Connect the No. 2 lower arm and the strut rod.

10. Tighten the upper arm mounting nut to 80 ft. lbs. (108 Nm). Tighten the strut to 101 ft. lbs. (137 Nm).

11. Reconnect the parking brake cable and install the halfshaft. Install the brake caliper and tighten the bolts to 34 ft. lbs. (47 Nm).

12. Install the wheels and lower the car. Bounce it several times to set the suspension and then tighten the upper arm-to-body bolt, the No. 2 lower arm-to-carrier and the strut rod to 119 ft. lbs. (162 Nm).

Rear Stabilizer Bar

REMOVAL & INSTALLATION

▶ See Figure 131

1. Raise and support the vehicle safely.
2. Remove the stabilizer bar link retaining nuts, stabilizer bar mounting bushing along with the bracket and stabilizer bar.
3. Installation is the reverse order of the removal procedure. Tighten the stabilizer bar link retaining nuts to 43 ft. lbs. (58 Nm) and tighten the stabilizer bushing bracket bolts to 26 ft. lbs. (35 Nm).

Rear End Alignment

The rear wheel alignment is adjustable on the Cressida models, but should be performed only by qualified technicians who are familiar with alignment machines and their means of measuring degrees and inches.

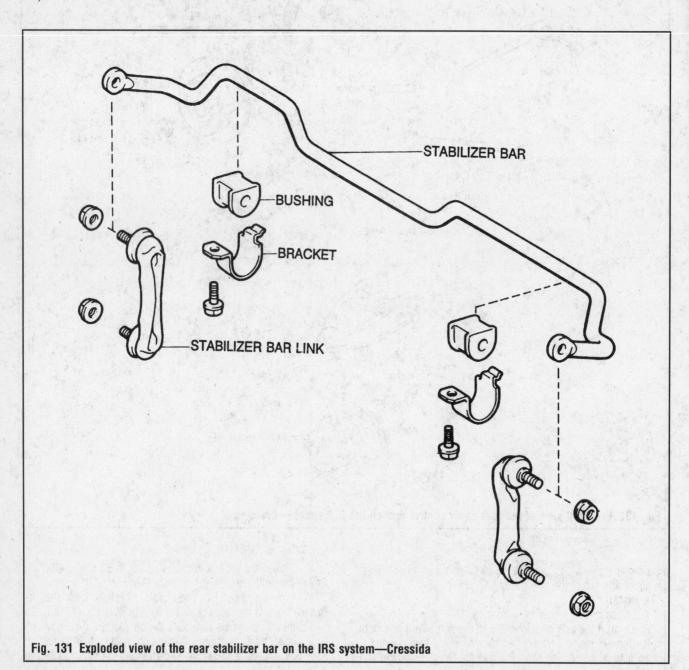

Fig. 131 Exploded view of the rear stabilizer bar on the IRS system—Cressida

VAN 4-LINK REAR SUSPENSION

Shock Absorbers

REMOVAL & INSTALLATION

♦ **See Figure 132**

1. Raise and safely support the vehicle.
2. Remove the shock absorber-to-axle housing bolt.
3. On the upper shock mounting, remove the locknut, the re-

taining nut, the retainers and the rubber bushings from the top of the shock absorber.

➡ **When removing the retaining nut, from the top of the shock absorber, it may be necessary to hold the top of the shock to keep it from turning.**

4. Remove the shock absorber from the vehicle.
5. To install, reverse the removal procedures. Tighten the shock absorber-to-body nut to 16–24 ft. lbs. and the shock absorber-to-axle housing bolt to 27 ft. lbs.

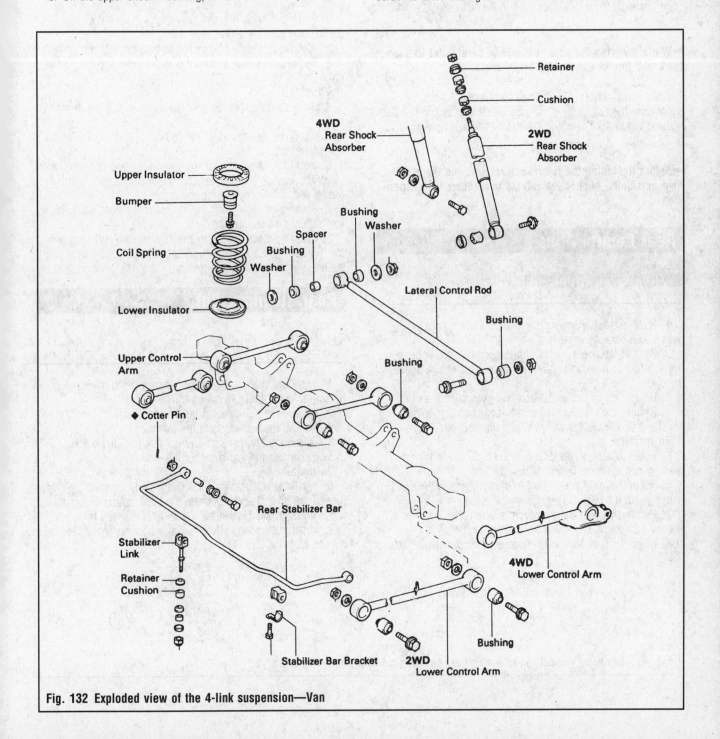

Fig. 132 Exploded view of the 4-link suspension—Van

Coil Spring

REMOVAL & INSTALLATION

1. Raise and safely support the vehicle. Support the axle housing with a floor jack. Remove the wheel and tire assembly.
2. Remove the shock absorber-to-axle housing bolt.
3. Remove the stabilizer-to-axle housing bar bushing bracket bolts.
4. Remove the lateral control arm-to-axle housing nut and disconnect the lateral control arm.
5. Lower the floor jack, then remove the coil spring(s) and the insulators.

➡**While lowering the axle housing, be careful not to snag the brake line of the parking brake cable.**

6. To install, reverse the removal procedures. Tighten the shock absorber bolt to 27 ft. lbs., the lateral control arm-to-axle housing nut to 43 ft. lbs. and the stabilizer-to-axle housing bolts to 27 ft. lbs.

➡**Before tightening the lateral control arm and the stabilizer nuts/bolts, bounce the vehicle to stabilize the suspension.**

Rear Control Arms

REMOVAL & INSTALLATION

1. Raise and safely support the vehicle. Place a floor jack under the axle housing to support it.
2. Remove the upper control arm-to-body bolt, the upper control arm-to-axle housing bolt and the upper control arm from the vehicle.
3. Disconnect the brake line from the lower control arm.
4. Remove the lower control arm-to-body bolt, arm-to-axle housing bolt and the lower control arm from the vehicle.
   To install:
5. Install the upper control arm to the body and to the axle housing with the nuts. Do not tighten the nuts.
6. Install the lower control arm to the body and to the axle housing with the nuts. Do not tighten the nuts.
7. Remove the jack and the supports from under the vehicle. Bounce the vehicle to stabilize the suspension.
8. Using the floor jack under the axle housing, raise the vehi-

cle. Place jackstands under the frame but do not let them touch the frame.
9. To complete the installation, observe the following torques:
- Upper control arm-to-body bolt: 105 ft. lbs.
- Upper control arm-to-axle housing bolt: 105 ft. lbs.
- Lower control arm-to-body bolt: 130 ft. lbs.
- Lower control arm-to-axle housing bolt: 105 ft. lbs.

Lateral Control Rod

REMOVAL & INSTALLATION

1. Raise and safely support the vehicle. Place a floor jack under the axle housing and support it.
2. Remove the lateral control rod-to-axle housing nut.
3. Remove the lateral control rod-to-body nut and the control rod from the vehicle.
   To install:
4. Raise the axle housing until the frame is just free of the jack.
5. Install the lateral control rod-to-body with the nuts. Do not tighten the nut.
6. Install the lateral control rod-to-axle housing in the following order: washer, bushing, spacer, lateral control rod, bushing, washer and nut. Do not tighten the nut.
7. Remove the jack, lower the vehicle to the floor and bounce it to stabilize the suspension.
8. Using the floor jack under the axle housing, raise the vehicle. Tighten the lateral control rod-to-body nut to 81 ft. lbs. and the lateral control rod-to-axle housing nut to 43 ft. lbs.

Rear Stabilizer Bar

REMOVAL & INSTALLATION

1. Raise and support the rear axle housing and frame safely. Be sure to leave the jack under the rear axle.
2. Remove the stabilizer bar bushing brackets.
3. Remove the bushing from the bar.
4. Disconnect the rear stabilizer bar link from the bracket.
5. Disconnect the rear stabilizer link from the bar end.
   To install:
6. Install the rear stabilizer link to the body. Connect the stabilizer bar on both sides to link with the bolts, collars cushions, nut and new cotter pin. Tighten the nut to 19 ft. lbs. (25 Nm).
7. Install the brackets to the rear axle housing and tighten the nuts to 27 ft. lbs. (37 Nm).

VAN LEAF SPRING REAR SUSPENSION

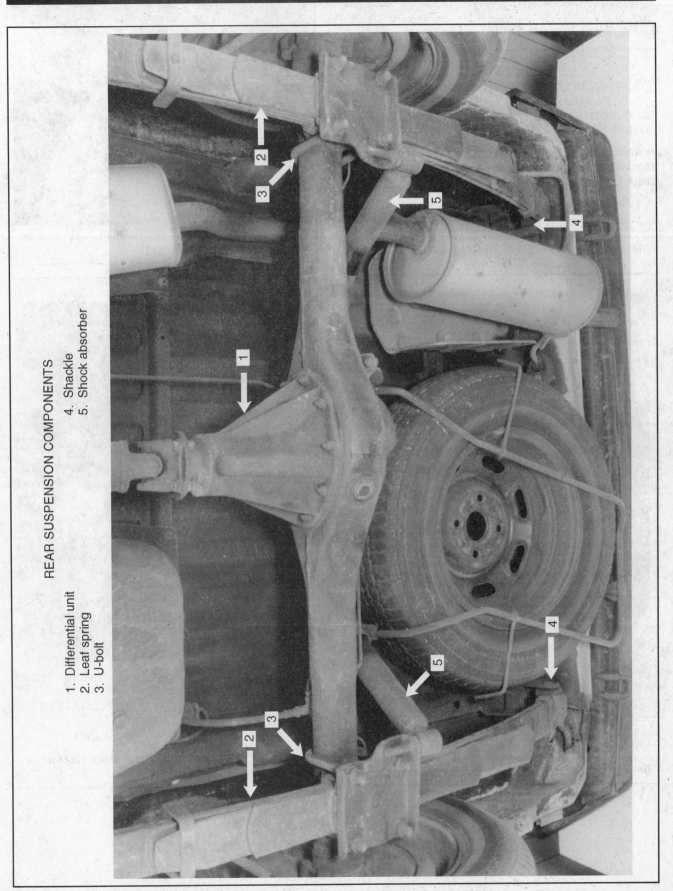

REAR SUSPENSION COMPONENTS

1. Differential unit
2. Leaf spring
3. U-bolt
4. Shackle
5. Shock absorber

Shock Absorber

REMOVAL & INSTALLATION

1. Raise and safely support the vehicle.
2. Remove the shock absorber-to-axle housing bolt.
3. On the upper shock mounting, remove the locknut, the retaining nut, the retainers and the rubber bushings from the top of the shock absorber.

➡**When removing the retaining nut, from the top of the shock absorber, it may be necessary to hold the top of the shock to keep it from turning.**

4. Remove the shock absorber from the vehicle.
5. To install, reverse the removal procedures. Tighten the shock absorber-to-body nut to 16–24 ft. lbs. and the shock absorber-to-axle housing bolt to 27 ft. lbs.

When removing the bottom absorber bolt, make sure the washers comes off with the bolt

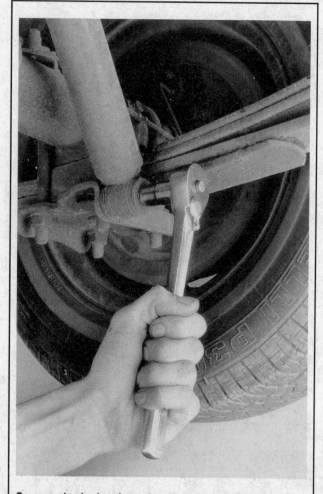

On rear shock absorbers, loosen the lower mounting bolt

1. Spring lower seat
2. Leaf spring
3. Shock absorber
4. Absorber bushing

Remove the lower portion of the rear shock absorber from the spring lower seat

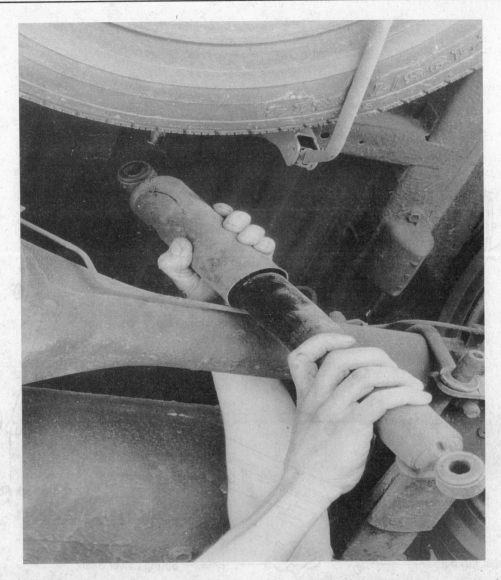

Once the upper and lower retaining bolts are removed, pull the shock absorber from the vehicle

Leaf Springs

REMOVAL & INSTALLATION

▶ **See Figure 133**

1. Raise and safely support the vehicle. Support the axle housing with a floor jack. Remove the wheel and tire assembly.
2. Lower the floor jack to take the tension off of the spring. Remove the shock absorber mounting nuts/bolts and the shock absorber.
3. Remove the cotter pins and the nuts from the lower end of the stabilizer link. Detach the link from the axle housing.
4. Remove the spring-to-axle housing U-bolt nuts, the spring bumper and the U-bolt.

5. At the front of the spring, remove the hanger pin bolt. Disconnect the spring from the bracket.
6. Remove the spring shackle retaining nuts and the spring shackle inner plate, then carefully pry out the spring shackle with a prybar.
7. Remove the spring from the vehicle.
   To install:
8. Install the rubber bushings in the eye of the spring.
9. Align the eye of the spring with the spring hanger bracket and drive the pin through the bracket holes and rubber bushings.

➡**Use soapy water as lubricant (if necessary), to aid in pin installation. Never use oil or grease.**

10. Finger-tighten the spring hanger nuts/bolts.
11. Install the rubber bushings in the spring eye at the opposite end of the spring.

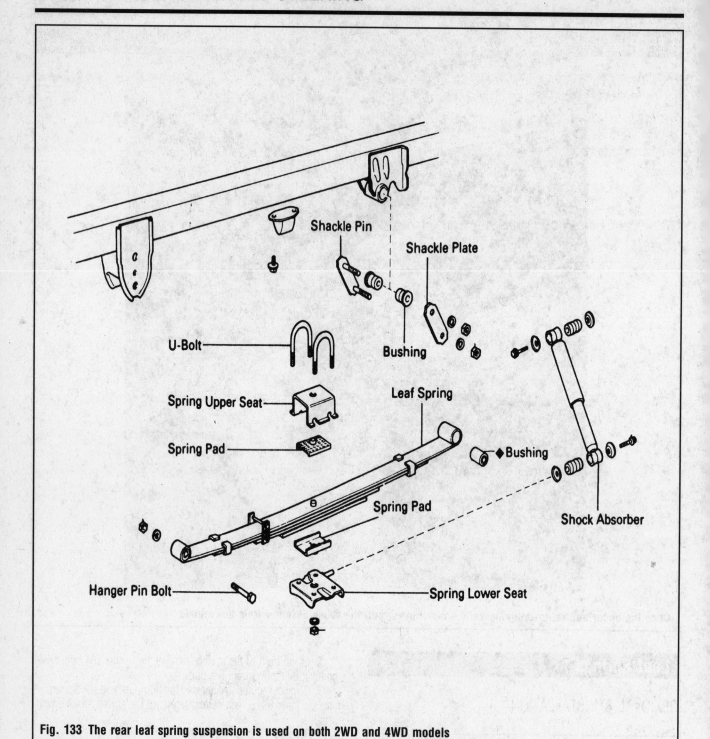

Fig. 133 The rear leaf spring suspension is used on both 2WD and 4WD models

12. Raise the free end of the spring. Install the spring shackle through the bushings and the bracket.

13. Install the shackle inner plate and finger-tighten the retaining nuts.

14. Center the bolt head in the hole which is provided in the spring seat on the axle housing.

15. Fit the U-bolts over the axle housing. Install the lower spring seat (2WD vehicle) or spring bumper (4WD vehicle) and the nuts.

16. To complete the installation, reverse the removal procedures. Tighten the U-bolt nuts to 90 ft. lbs., the hanger pin-to-frame nut to 67 ft. lbs., the shackle pin nuts to 67 ft. lbs., the shock absorber bolts to 47 ft. lbs. (4WD vehicle).

➡When installing the U-bolts, tighten the nuts so that the length of the bolts are equal.

STEERING

Steering Wheel

REMOVAL & INSTALLATION

Cressida

▶ **See Figures 134, 135 and 136**

1. Position the front wheels straight ahead.
2. Unfasten the horn and turn signal multi-connector(s) at the base of the steering column shroud.

3. I equipped with a 3 spoked wheel, loosen the trim pad retaining screws from the back side of the steering wheel. The two spoke steering wheel is removed on the same manner as the three spoke, except that the trim pad should be pried off with a small prybar. Remove the pad by lifting it toward the top of the wheel.
4. Lift the trim pad and horn button assembly from the wheel.
5. Remove the steering wheel hub retaining nut.
6. Scribe matchmarks on the hub and shaft to aid in correct installation.
7. Use a suitable puller to remove the steering wheel.

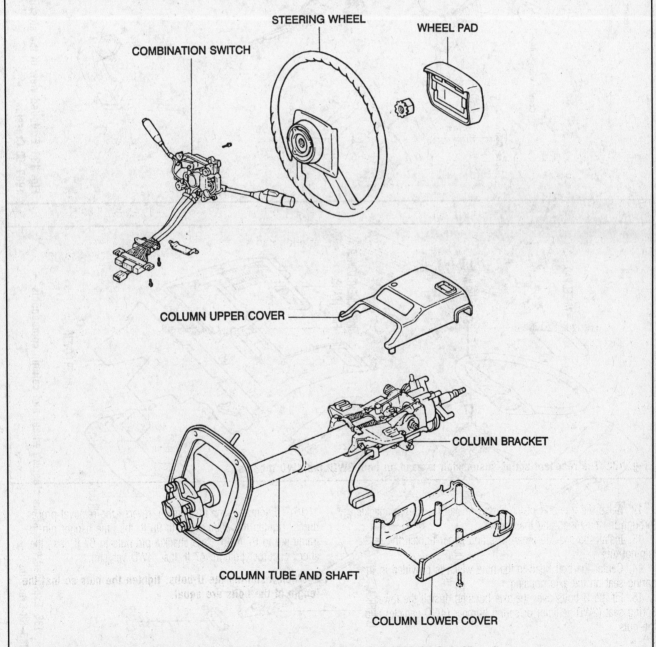

COMBINATION SWITCH

STEERING WHEEL

WHEEL PAD

COLUMN UPPER COVER

COLUMN BRACKET

COLUMN TUBE AND SHAFT

COLUMN LOWER COVER

Fig. 134 Exploded view of the steering wheel and column components—1983–84 Cressida

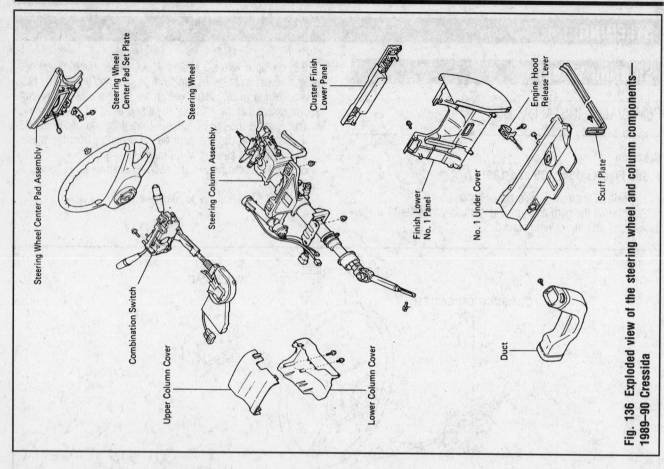

Fig. 136 Exploded view of the steering wheel and column components—1989–90 Cressida

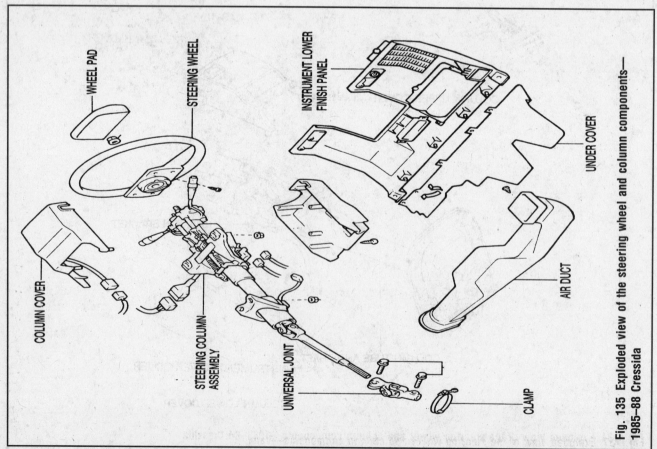

Fig. 135 Exploded view of the steering wheel and column components—1985–88 Cressida

✳✳ WARNING

Do not attempt to remove or install the steering wheel by hammering on it. Damage to the energy-absorbing steering column could result.

8. Installation is the reverse of removal. Tighten the wheel retaining nut to 25 ft. lbs. (34 Nm).

Van

▶ **See Figure 137**

1. Disconnect the negative battery cable.
2. Position the wheels in a straight ahead position.

3. Remove the steering wheel center cover, some vehicles use a screw to retain the cover.
4. Disconnect the horn wire. Matchmark the wheel and the shaft.
5. Remove the steering wheel center nut.
6. Using an appropriate wheel puller tool remove the steering wheel.
7. Installation is the reverse of the removal procedure. Tighten the steering wheel nut to 25 ft. lbs. (34 Nm).

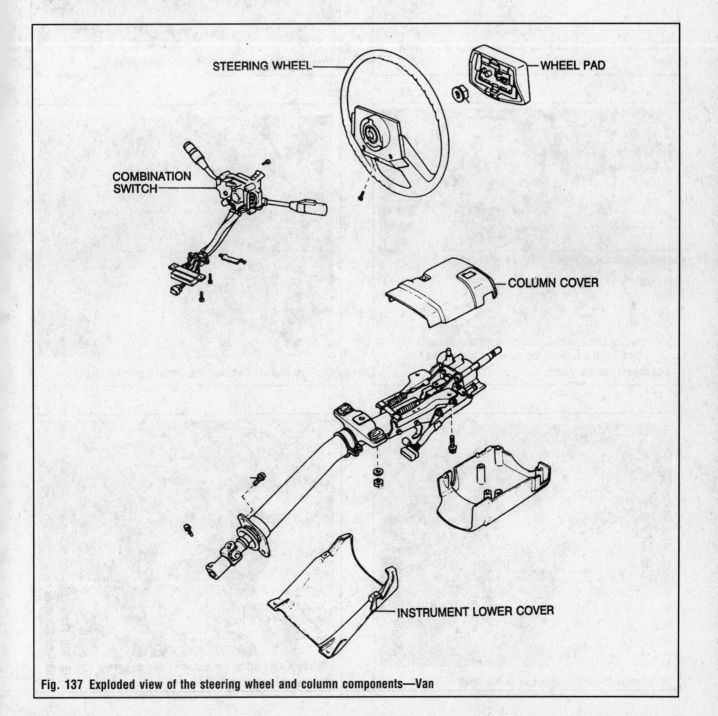

Fig. 137 Exploded view of the steering wheel and column components—Van

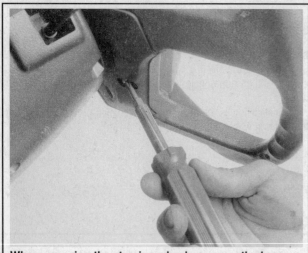

When removing the steering wheel, unscrew the horn pad . . .

Place a socket on the center nut and loosen

. . . then lift the pad off the steering wheel and disconnect the horn wire

Use the puller to extract the wheel from the shaft

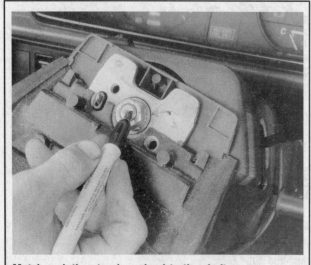

Matchmark the steering wheel to the shaft

Lift the wheel off of the column, and separate any wires that may be attached

Combination Switch

REMOVAL & INSTALLATION

▶ **See Figure 138**

The combination switch is composed of the turn signal, the headlight control, the dimmer, the hazard, the wiper and the washer switches. If the turn signal switch is found to be bad, the combination switch must be replaced as an assembly.

Cressida

1. Disconnect the negative battery cable.
2. Remove the steering column garnish.
3. Remove the upper and lower steering column covers.
4. Remove the steering wheel as outlined in this manual.
5. Trace the switch wiring harness to the multi-connector. Push in the lock levers and pull apart the connectors.
6. On vehicles equipped with Electronic Modulated Suspension (TEMS), remove the steering sensor.
7. Unscrew the mounting screws and slide the combination switch from the steering column.

8. Installation of the combination switch is the reverse of the removal procedure. Check all switch functions for proper operation.

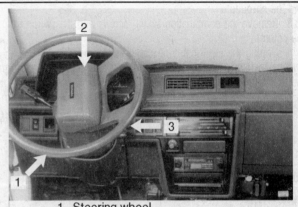

1. Steering wheel
2. Horn pad
3. Ignition lock cylinder (in column)

View of the steering wheel and assorted components—Van

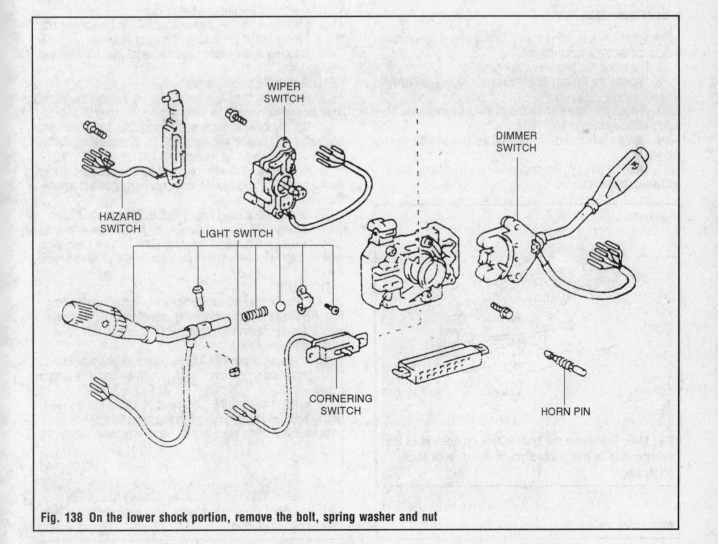

Fig. 138 On the lower shock portion, remove the bolt, spring washer and nut

Van

1. Disconnect the negative battery cable. Remove the steering wheel.

2. Remove the upper and lower steering column shroud screws and the shrouds.

3. Remove the combination switch screws and the switch from the column.

4. Unplug the electrical connector from the combination switch. To remove the wires from the electrical connector, perform the following procedures.

 a. Using a small prybar, insert it into the open end between the locking lugs and the terminal.

 b. Pry the locking lugs upward and pull the terminal out from the rear.

 c. To install the terminals, simply push them into the connector until they lock securely in place.

5. To complete the installation, reverse the removal procedures.

Ignition Lock/Switch

REMOVAL & INSTALLATION

▶ **See Figure 138a**

The ignition lock/switch is usually located behind the combination switch on the steering column.

1. Disconnect the negative battery cable.

2. Unfasten the ignition switch connector underneath the instrument panel.

3. Remove the screws which secure the upper and lower halves of the steering column cover.

4. Turn the lock cylinder to the **ACC** position with the ignition key.

5. Push the lock cylinder stop in with a small, round object (cotter pin, punch, etc.).

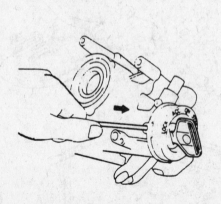

Fig. 138a To remove the ignition lock cylinder, push the cylinder stop in with a small round object, such as a cotter pin

➡**On some vehicles it may be necessary to remove the steering wheel and combination switch first.**

6. Withdraw the lock cylinder from the lock housing while depressing the stop tab.

7. To remove the ignition switch, unfasten its securing screws and withdraw the switch from the lock housing.

 To install:

8. Align the locking cam with the hole in the ignition switch and insert the switch into the lock housing.

9. Secure the switch with its screw(s).

10. Make sure that both the lock cylinder and column lock are in the **ACC** position. Slide the cylinder into the lock housing until the stop tab engages the hole in the lock.

11. Install the steering column covers.

12. Attach the ignition switch connector.

13. Connect the negative battery cable.

Steering Column

REMOVAL & INSTALLATION

▶ **See Figures 139, 140, 141, 142 and 143**

1. Disconnect the negative battery cable.

2. If equipped, remove the universal joint at the steering gear and at the main shaft of the steering column assembly.

3. If equipped, disconnect upper universal joint from the intermediate shaft.

4. Remove the steering wheel.

5. Remove the hood lock control bracket. Remove the instrument lower finish panels, air ducts and column covers.

6. Disconnect all electrical wiring for ignition switch, combination switch, and unlock warning switch key cylinder lamp. Remove the combination switch as necessary.

7. Remove the accelerator rod bracket, if so equipped. Remove the steering column hole cover retaining bolts and remove the cover.

8. Remove the support mounting bolt. Remove the column tube mounting bolts. Pull out steering column. On some vehicles, remove the 2 column bracket mounting nuts. Turn the steering column assembly clockwise and remove it from the vehicle as necessary.

 To install:

9. Place the steering column assembly in the installed position. Tighten all necessary mounting nuts (tighten evenly). Install and tighten all column cover bolts. Tighten column hole cover clamp bolt as necessary.

10. Install combination switch. Reconnect all electrical wiring.

11. Install instrument lower finish panels, air duct and column covers.

12. Install or connect the universal joint. Insure that the retaining bolts are installed through both shaft grooves.

13. Install steering wheel and connect the negative battery cable.

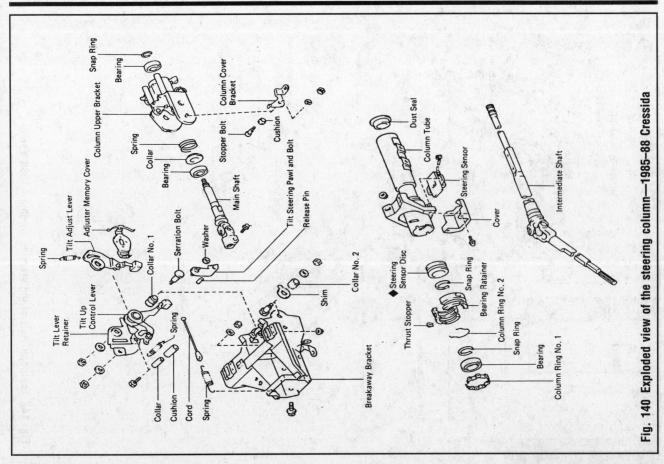

Fig. 140 Exploded view of the steering column—1985–88 Cressida

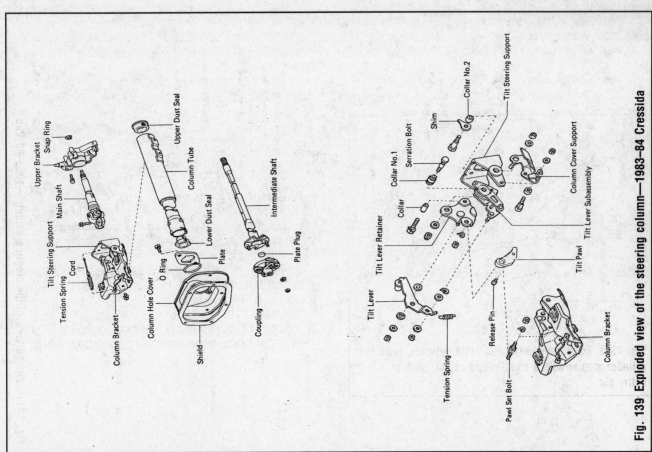

Fig. 139 Exploded view of the steering column—1983–84 Cressida

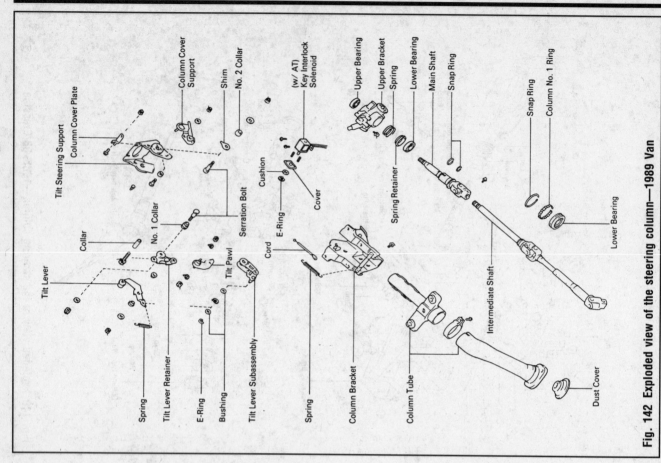

Fig. 142 Exploded view of the steering column—1989 Van

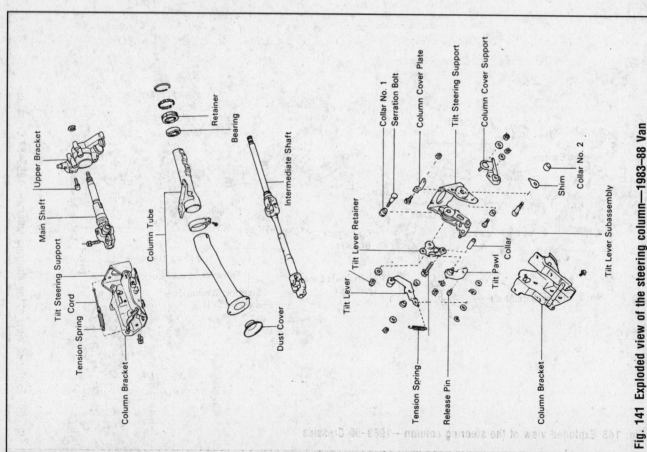

Fig. 141 Exploded view of the steering column—1983-88 Van

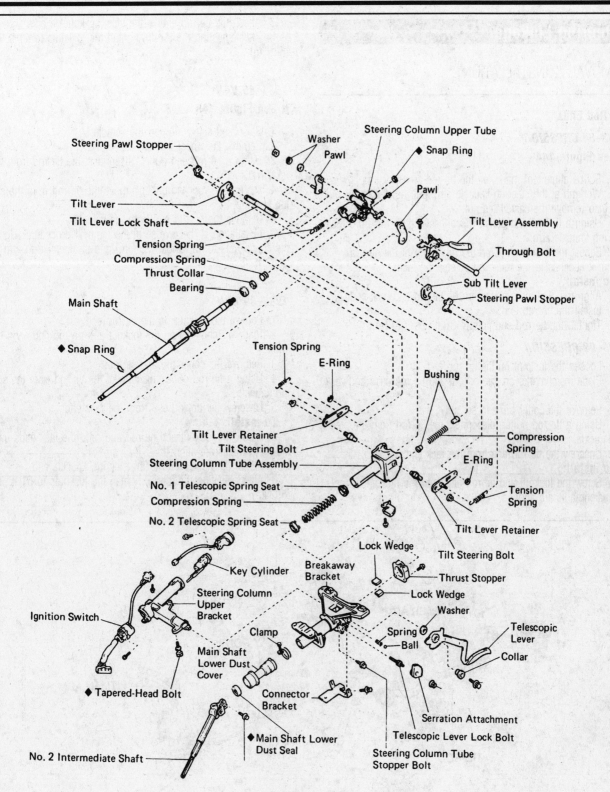

Steering Pawl Stopper

Washer
Pawl

Steering Column Upper Tube

◆ Snap Ring

Pawl

Tilt Lever

Tilt Lever Lock Shaft

Tilt Lever Assembly

Through Bolt

Tension Spring

Compression Spring

Sub Tilt Lever

Thrust Collar

Steering Pawl Stopper

Bearing

Main Shaft

◆ Snap Ring

Tension Spring

E-Ring

Bushing

Compression
Spring

E-Ring

Tilt Lever Retainer

Tilt Steering Bolt

Tension
Spring

Steering Column Tube Assembly

No. 1 Telescopic Spring Seat

Compression Spring

Tilt Lever Retainer

No. 2 Telescopic Spring Seat

Tilt Steering Bolt

Lock Wedge

Thrust Stopper

Key Cylinder

Breakaway
Bracket

Lock Wedge

Washer

Steering Column
Upper
Bracket

Ignition Switch

Telescopic
Lever

Clamp

Spring

Collar

Main Shaft
Lower Dust
Cover

Ball

◆ Tapered-Head Bolt

Connector
Bracket

Serration Attachment

◆ Main Shaft Lower
Dust Seal

Telescopic Lever Lock Bolt

No. 2 Intermediate Shaft

Steering Column Tube
Stopper Bolt

Fig. 143 Exploded view of the steering column—1989–90 Cressida

Steering Linkage

REMOVAL & INSTALLATION

Tie Rod Ends

1983–84 CRESSIDA

▶ **See Figure 144**

1. Scribe alignment marks on the tie rod and rack end.
2. Working at the steering knuckle arm, pull out the cotter pin and then remove the castellated nut.
3. Using a tie rod end puller, disconnect the tie rod from the steering knuckle arm.
4. Repeat the first 2 steps on the other end of the tie rod (where it attaches to the relay rod or steering rack).

To install:

5. Align the alignment marks on the tie rod and rack end.
6. Install the tie rod end.
7. Tighten the tie rod end nuts to 36 ft. lbs. (49 Nm).

1985–90 CRESSIDA

1. Loosen the locknut on the tie rod end.
2. Place matchmarks on the locknut and tie rod ends and rack ends.
3. Remove the cotter pin and set nut.
4. Using a tie rod puller, disconnect the tie rod from the steering knuckle.
5. Unscrew the tie rod end from the rack end.

To install:

6. Screw the locknut and tie rod end onto the rack ends until the matchmarks are aligned.
7. Attach the tie rod end to the steering knuckle end.
8. After adjusting the toe-in, tighten the locknuts to 41 ft. lbs. (56 Nm).

1984–85 VAN

▶ **See Figure 145**

1. Raise and safely support the vehicle.
2. Remove the wheel and tire assembly.
3. Using a tie rod end puller, disconnect the tie rod from the relay rod.
4. Using a tie rod end puller remove the tie rod from the steering knuckle.
5. Remove the tie rod end from the vehicle.
6. Installation is the reverse of the removal procedure. Tighten the clamp nuts to 19 ft. lbs. (25 Nm) and the knuckle-to-arm nuts to 67 ft. lbs.

1986–89 VAN

1. Loosen the locknut on the tie rod end.
2. Place matchmarks on the locknut and tie rod ends and rack ends.
3. Remove the cotter pin and set nut.
4. Using a tie rod puller, disconnect the tie rod from the steering knuckle.
5. Unscrew the tie rod end from the rack end.

To install:

6. Screw the locknut and tie rod end onto the rack ends until the matchmarks are aligned.
7. Attach the tie rod end to the steering knuckle end.
8. After adjusting the toe-in, tighten the locknuts to 51 ft. lbs. (69 Nm).

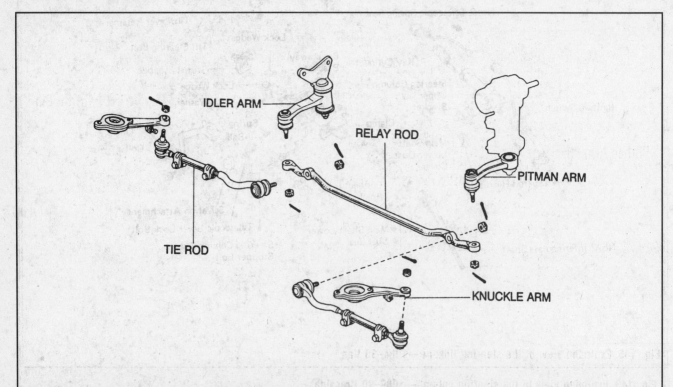

Fig. 144 Exploded view of the steering linkage—1983–84 Cressida

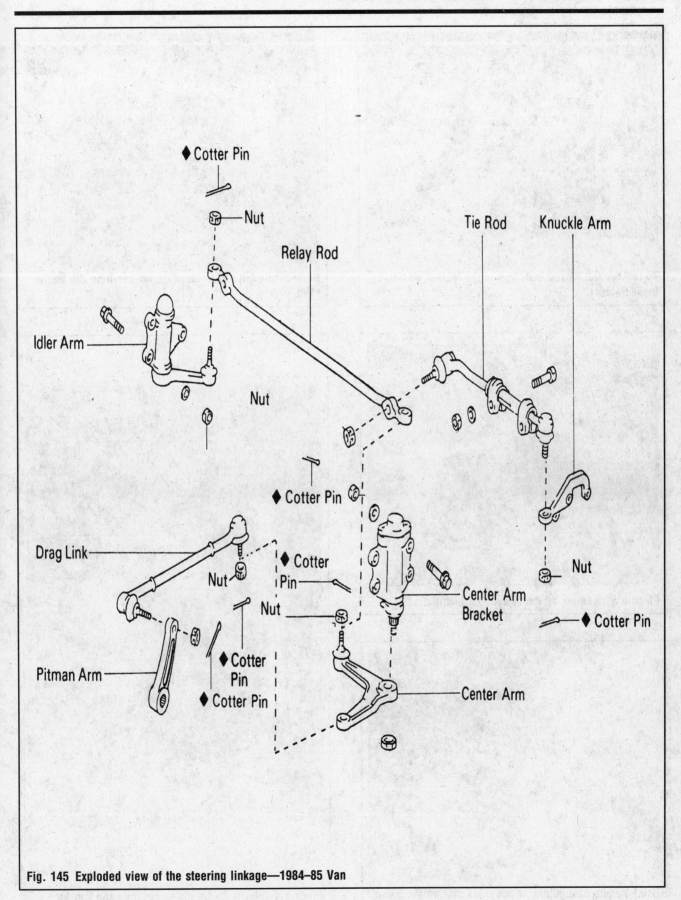

Fig. 145 Exploded view of the steering linkage—1984–85 Van

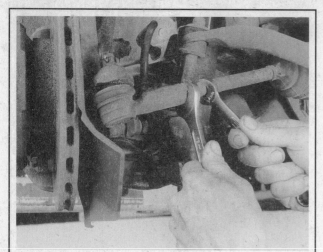

To remove the tie rod end, loosen the locknut on the inner tie rod

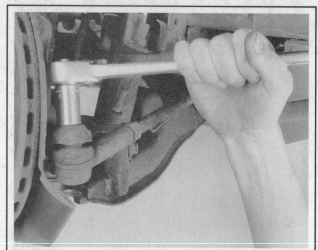

Remove the nut and castellated washer from the end of the tie rod

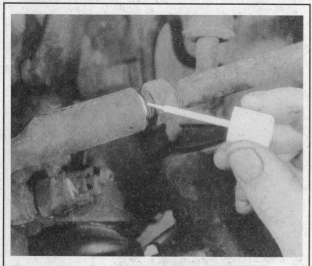

Place a matchmark on the threads for installation

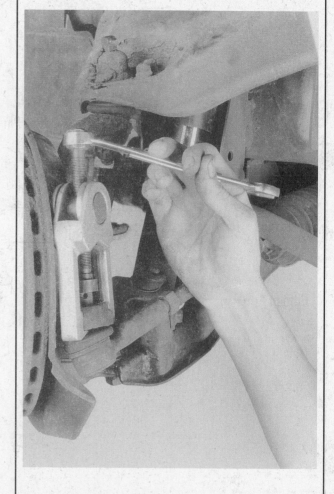

Place a puller on the tie rod to separate the knuckle from the end

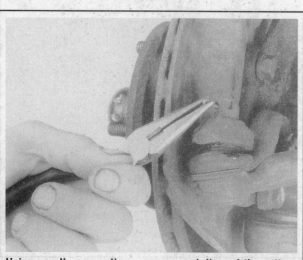

Using needle nose pliers, remove and discard the cotter pin

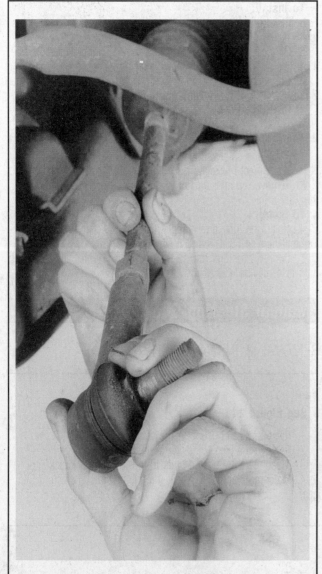

Unscrew the tie rod end from the inner tie rod

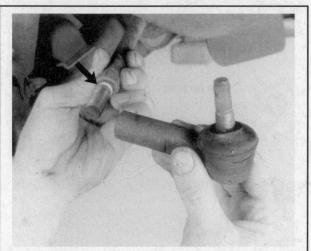

When installing the tie rod end, screw the end in until it meets the matchmark

Pitman Arm

1984–85 VAN

1. Raise and support the vehicle safely.
2. Loosen the pitman arm nut. Disconnect the pitman arm from the sector shaft.
3. Disconnect the drag link from the pitman arm. Inspect the arm for damage and cracks.

To install:

4. Align the marks on the pitman arm and the sector shaft and install the nut. Tighten the drag link nut to 67 ft. lbs. (91 Nm).
5. Tighten the pitman arm nut 90 ft. lbs. (123 Nm).

Relay Rod

1983–84 CRESSIDA

1. Raise and support the vehicle safely. Disconnect the tie rod ends from the knuckle arm.
2. Disconnect the relay rod from the pitman arm and the idler arm.
3. Disconnect tie rods from the relay rod.
4. Inspect the arms for damage and cracks.

To install:

5. Turn the tie rods in the adjusting tube until the measurements are equal. The tie rods should be approximately 320mm (12.60 in.).
6. Turn the tie rods so they cross at approximately 90°.
7. Tighten the adjusting tube clamps to lock the tie rods into position. Torque them to 13 ft. lbs. (17 Nm).
8. Connect the tie rods to the relay rods to the relay rod and tighten the 2 nuts to 43 ft. lbs. (59 Nm).
9. Connect the relay rod to the pitman arm and idler arm. Tighten the 2 nuts to 43 ft. lbs. (59 Nm) and install the cotter pin.
10. Connect the tie rod ends to the knuckle arm and tighten the 2 nuts to 43 ft. lbs. (59 Nm). Install new cotter pins.
11. Check the front wheel alignment.

1984–85 VAN

1. Raise and support the vehicle safely.
2. Disconnect the tie rod ends from the relay rod.
3. Disconnect the relay rod from the center arm and the idler arm.
4. Inspect the arm for damage and cracks.

To install:

5. Connect the relay rod to the center arm. Tighten the mounting nut to 43 ft. lbs. (59 Nm).
6. Connect the relay rod to the idler arm. Tighten the mounting nut to 43 ft. lbs. (59 Nm).
7. Connect the relay rod to the tie rods. Tighten the mounting nut to 43 ft. lbs. (59 Nm).

Knuckle Arm

1984–85 VAN

1. Raise and safely support the vehicle. Remove the front axle hub assembly as previously outlined in this manual.

2. Disconnect the tie rod from the knuckle arm.
3. Remove the knuckle arm.
4. Inspect the knuckle arm for damage and cracks.
To install:
5. Install the knuckle arm to the steering knuckle and torque bolt to 61 ft. lbs. (83 Nm).
6. Connect the tie rod to the knuckle arm. Tighten the mounting nut to 43 ft. lbs. (59 Nm).
7. Install the front axle hub assembly.

Center Arm Bracket

1984–85 VAN

1. Raise and safely support the vehicle.
2. Disconnect the relay rod from the center arm.
3. Disconnect the drag link from the center arm.
4. Remove the nut from the center arm shaft. Using a suitable puller, remove the center arm from the center arm shaft.
5. Remove the center arm bracket retaining bolts and nuts.
To install:
6. Install the center arm bracket nuts and bolts. Tighten them to 58 ft. lbs. (78 Nm).
7. Connect the center arm to the drag link. Tighten the mounting nut to 67 ft. lbs. (91 Nm).
8. Connect the center arm to the relay rod. Tighten the mounting nut to 43 ft. lbs. (59 Nm).

Idler Arm Bracket

1983–84 CRESSIDA

1. Raise and support the vehicle safely.
2. Disconnect the tie rod ends from the knuckle arm.
3. Disconnect the idler arm from the relay rod.
4. Remove the idler arm retaining nuts and remove the idler arm from the body.

To install:
5. Install the idler arm and the retaining nuts. Tighten the nuts to 43 ft. lbs. (59 Nm).
6. Connect the idler arm to the relay rod. Tighten the nuts to 43 ft. lbs. (59 Nm). Install a new cotter pin.
7. Connect the tie rod ends to the knuckle arm and tighten the 2 nuts to 43 ft. lbs. (59 Nm). Install new cotter pins.
8. Check the front wheel alignment.

1984–85 VAN

1. Raise and safely support the vehicle.
2. Disconnect the relay rod from the idler arm.
3. Remove the idler arm bracket nuts and bolts and remove the idler arm.
To install:
4. Install the idler arm along with the bracket nuts and bolts. Tighten them to 58 ft. lbs. (78 Nm).
5. Connect the idler arm to the relay rod. Tighten the mounting nuts to 43 ft. lbs. (59 Nm).

Manual Steering Gear

REMOVAL & INSTALLATION

Van

▶ **See Figure 146**

1. Raise and safely support the vehicle.
2. Remove the wheel and tire assemblies.
3. Disconnect the tie rod ends from the steering knuckle.
4. Matchmark and disconnect the intermediate shaft from the gear.

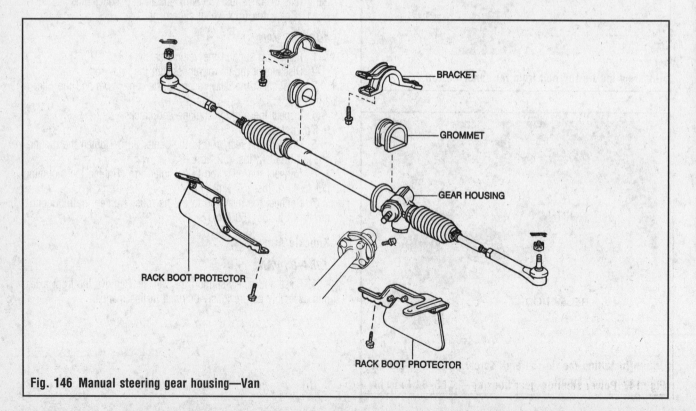

Fig. 146 Manual steering gear housing—Van

5. Remove the retaining bolts from the 2 brackets and slide the rack out from under the vehicle.

6. Installation is the reverse of the removal procedure. Tighten the bracket bolts to 56 ft. lbs. (76 Nm), the coupling bolts to 26 ft. lbs. (35 Nm) and the tie rod bolts to 43 ft. lbs. (59 Nm).

Power Steering Gear

REMOVAL & INSTALLATION

Cressida

1983–84 MODELS

▶ **See Figure 147**

1. Raise and support the vehicle safely and remove the front wheels. Place matchmarks on the coupling and steering column shaft. Remove the coupling bolt.

2. Disconnect the return and pressure lines from the gear housing.

3. Using a suitable puller, remove the relay rod from the pitman arm.

4. Remove the gear housing retaining bolts and remove the gear housing from the vehicle.

To install:

5. Install the gear housing along with the retaining bolts. Tighten the bolts to 43 ft. lbs. (59 Nm).

6. Connect the relay rod to the pitman arm and tighten the nut to 43 ft. lbs. (59 Nm).

7. Tighten the pitman arm nut to 90 ft. lbs. (123 Nm).

8. Tighten the coupling bolt to 18 ft. lbs. (25 Nm).

9. Reconnect the return and pressure lines. Refill the power steering reservoir and bleed the air out of the power steering system.

1985–90 MODELS

▶ **See Figure 148**

1. Raise and support the vehicle safely and remove the front wheels. Place matchmarks on the coupling and steering column shaft. Disconnect the solenoid connectors.

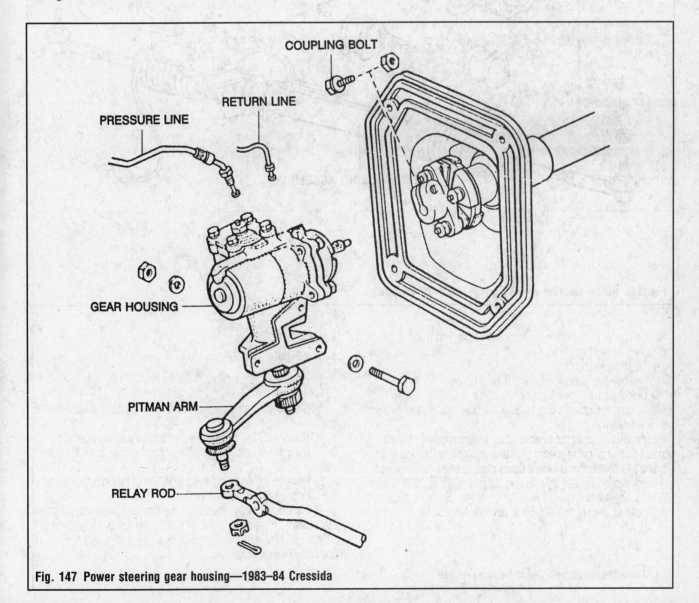

Fig. 147 Power steering gear housing—1983–84 Cressida

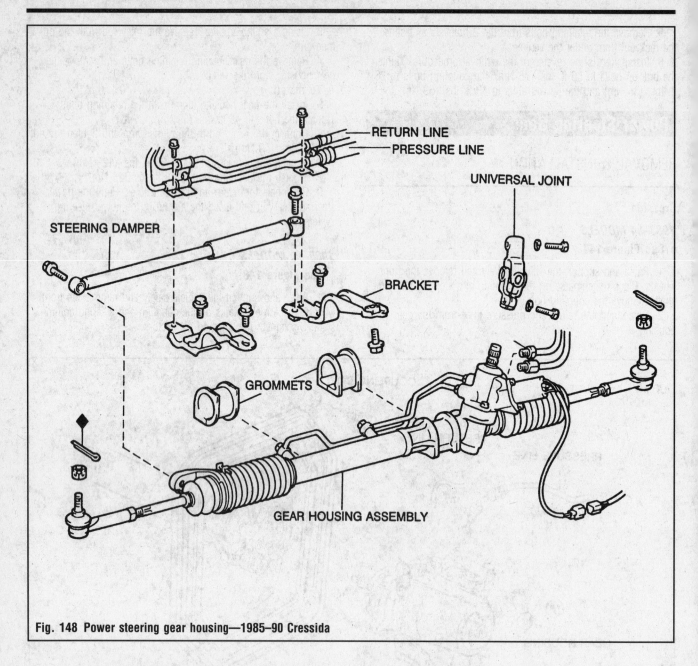

RETURN LINE
PRESSURE LINE
UNIVERSAL JOINT
STEERING DAMPER
BRACKET
GROMMETS
GEAR HOUSING ASSEMBLY

Fig. 148 Power steering gear housing—1985–90 Cressida

2. Disconnect the Pitman arm from the relay rod using a tie rod puller on the Pitman arm set nut. Disconnect the tie rod ends from the steering knuckles.

3. Remove the steering damper, if so equipped.

4. Disconnect the steering gearbox at the coupling. Unbolt the gearbox from the chassis and remove. Remove the grommets from the gear housing.

5. Installation is in the reverse order of removal, with the exception of first aligning the matchmarks and connecting the steering shaft to the coupling before bolting the gearbox into the vehicle permanently. Tighten the steering damper bolts to 20 ft. lbs. (26 Nm). Tighten the tie rod ends to 43 ft. lbs. (59 Nm). Tighten the mounting bracket bolts to 56 ft. lbs. (76 Nm).

Van

♦ **See Figure 149**

1. Raise and safely support the vehicle.

2. Remove the wheel and tire assemblies.

3. Disconnect and plug the power steering fluid lines from the gear.

4. Disconnect the tie rod ends from the steering knuckle.

5. Matchmark and disconnect the intermediate shaft from the gear.

6. Remove the retaining bolts from the 2 brackets and slide the rack out from under the vehicle.

7. Installation is the reverse of the removal procedure. Tighten the bracket bolts to 56 ft. lbs. (76 Nm), the coupling bolts to 26 ft. lbs. (35 Nm) and the tie rod bolts to 43 ft. lbs. (59 Nm).

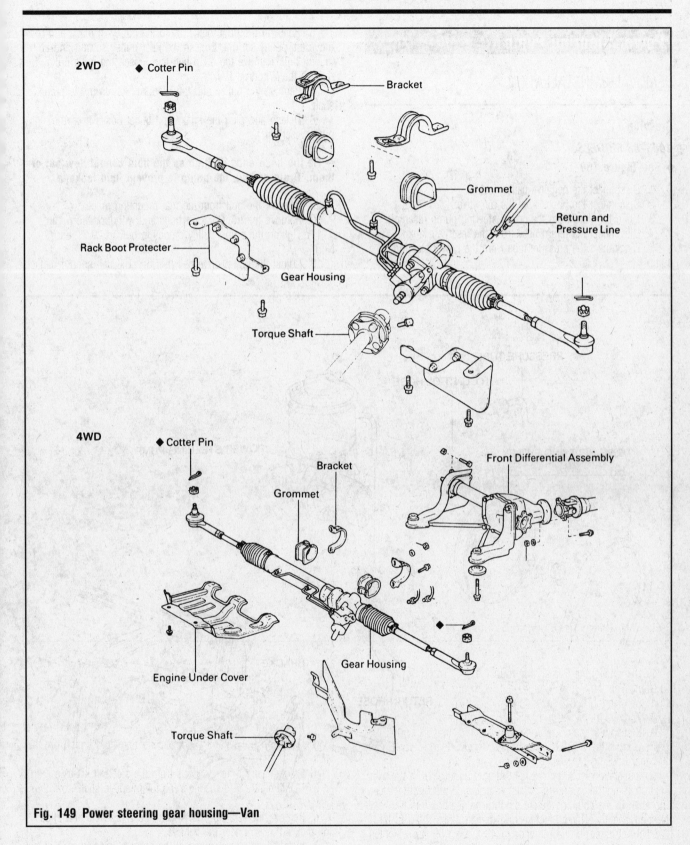

Fig. 149 Power steering gear housing—Van

Power Steering Pump

REMOVAL & INSTALLATION

Cressida

1983–88 MODELS

▶ See Figure 150

1. Disconnect the negative battery cable.
2. Disconnect the hoses from the air valve.
3. Drain the fluid from the power steering pump reservoir.
4. Disconnect the return hose from the reservoir tank.
5. Disconnect the pressure tube from the power steering pump.

6. Push on the drive belt to hold the pulley in place and remove the pulley set nut. Loosen the idler pulley set nut and adjusting bolt. Remove the drive belt and loosen the drive pulley to remove the Woodruff key.
7. Remove the pulley and the Woodruff key from the pump shaft.
8. Detach and plug the intake and outlet hoses from the pump reservoir.

➡Tie the hose ends up high so the fluid cannot flow out of them. Drain or plug the pump to prevent fluid leakage.

9. Remove the bolt from the rear mounting brace.
10. Remove the front bracket bolts and withdraw the pump.
11. Tighten the pump pulley mounting bolt to 29 ft. lbs. (39 Nm).
12. Adjust the pump drive belt tension. The belt should deflect

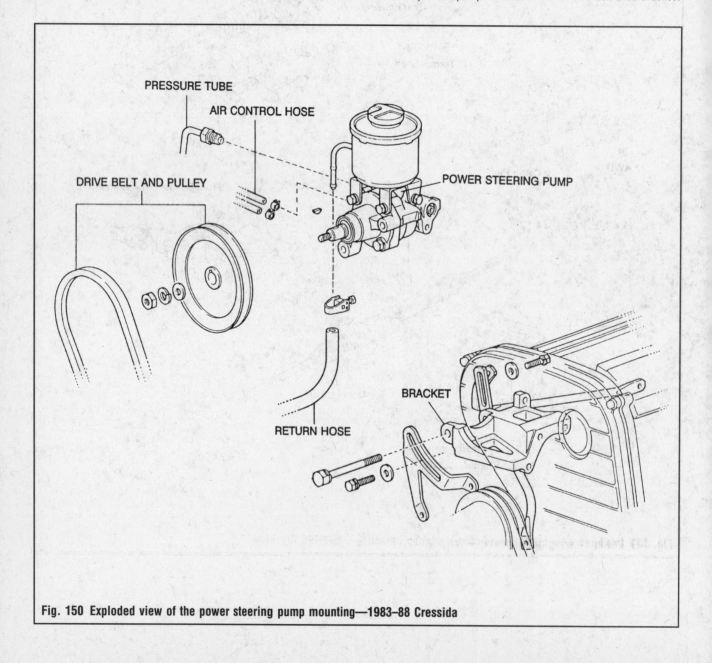

Fig. 150 Exploded view of the power steering pump mounting—1983–88 Cressida

3.3–23mm (0.13–0.93 in.) under thumb pressure applied midway between the air pump and the power steering pump.

13. Fill the reservoir with DEXRON®II automatic transmission fluid. Bleed the air from the system.

1989–90 MODELS

▶ **See Figure 151**

1. Raise and support the vehicle safely. Drain the fluid from the reservoir tank.

2. Disconnect the air hose from the air control tank. Disconnect the return hose from the reservoir tank.

3. Remove the engine under cover. Disconnect and plug the pressure hose from the power steering pump.

4. Holding the power steering pump pulley, remove the pulley set nut. Remove the drive belt adjusting nut.

5. Remove the power steering pump set bolt. Remove the drive belt, pulley and woodruff key.

6. Disconnect the oil cooler hose bracket from the power steering pump. Remove the drive belt adjust bolt and remove the power steering set bolt and power steering pump.

7. Installation is the reverse order of the removal procedure. Be sure to bleed the system upon completion of the installation procedure.

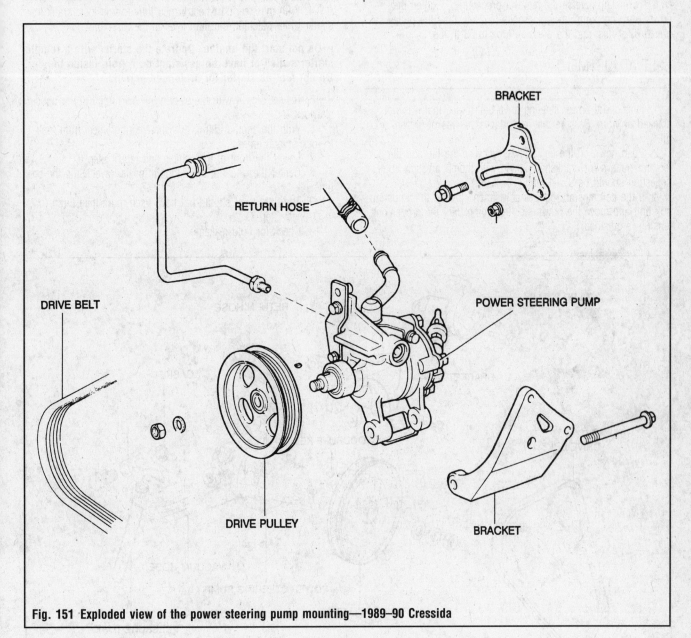

Fig. 151 Exploded view of the power steering pump mounting—1989–90 Cressida

Van

▶ **See Figure 152**

1. Disconnect the negative battery cable. Disconnect the air hoses from the air control valve of the power steering pump.
2. Drain the fluid from the power steering reservoir tank.
3. At the power steering pump, disconnect the return hose and the pressure tube.
4. Loosen the power steering pump adjusting bolt, then, remove the drive belt, the pulley and the woodruff key.
5. Remove the mounting bolts, the power steering pump and the bracket from the vehicle.
6. To install, reverse the removal procedures. Tighten the power steering pump-to-engine bolts to 29 ft. lbs., the pulley set nut to 32 ft. lbs. and the pressure tube to 33 ft. lbs.

BELT ADJUSTMENT

1. Inspect the power steering drive belt to see that it is not cracked or worn. Be sure that its surfaces are free of grease or oil.
2. Push down on the belt halfway between the fan and the alternator pulleys (or crankshaft pulley) with thumb pressure. Belt deflection should be 9.5–13mm (3/8–1/2 in.).
3. If the belt tension requires adjustment, loosen the adjusting link bolt and move the power steering pump until the proper belt tension is obtained.

4. Do not over-tighten the belt, as damage to the power steering pump bearings could result. Tighten the adjusting link bolt.
5. Drive the vehicle and re-check the belt tension. Adjust as necessary.

SYSTEM BLEEDING

1. Raise and support the vehicle safely.
2. Fill the pump reservoir with the proper fluid.
3. Rotate the steering wheel from lock-to-lock several times. Add fluid if necessary.
4. With the steering wheel turned fully to one lock, crank the starter while watching the fluid level in the reservoir.

➡**Do not start the engine. Operate the starter with a remote starter switch or have an assistant do it from inside the car. Do not run the starter for prolonged periods.**

5. Repeat Step 4 with the steering wheel turned to the opposite lock.
6. With the engine idling, turn the steering wheel from lock-to-lock several times.
7. Lower the front of the vehicle and repeat Step 6.
8. Center the wheel at the midpoint of its travel. Stop the engine.
9. The fluid level should not have risen more than 5mm (0.2 in.), repeat Step 7.
10. Check for fluid leakage.

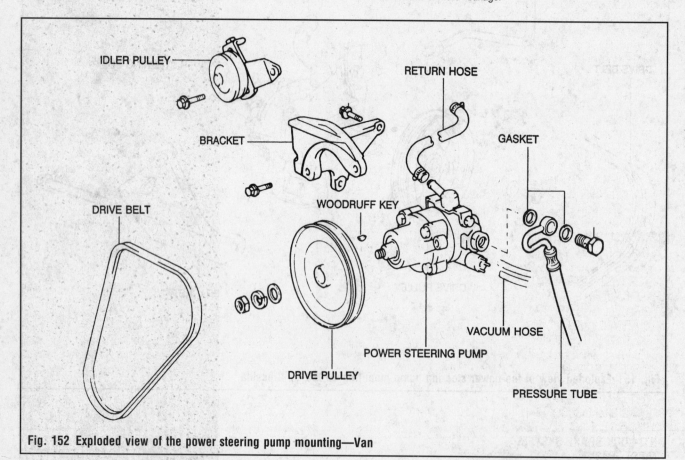

Fig. 152 Exploded view of the power steering pump mounting—Van

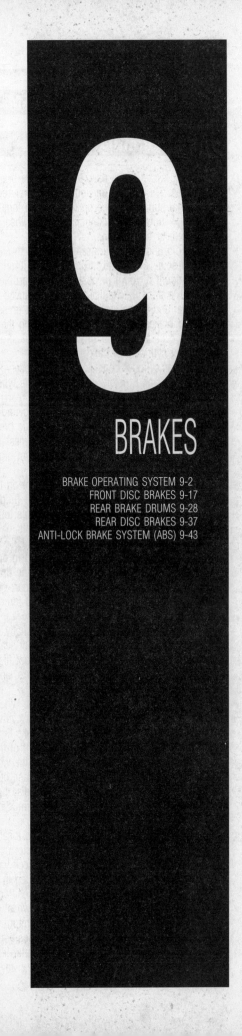

9

BRAKES

BRAKE OPERATING SYSTEM

Basic Operating Principles

Hydraulic systems are used to actuate the brakes of all modern automobiles. The system transports the power required to force the frictional surfaces of the braking system together from the pedal to the individual brake units at each wheel. A hydraulic system is used for two reasons.

First, fluid under pressure can be carried to all parts of an automobile by small pipes and flexible hoses without taking up a significant amount of room or posing routing problems.

Second, a great mechanical advantage can be given to the brake pedal end of the system, and the foot pressure required to actuate the brakes can be reduced by making the surface area of the master cylinder pistons smaller than that of any of the pistons in the wheel cylinders or calipers.

The master cylinder consists of a fluid reservoir along with a double cylinder and piston assembly. Double type master cylinders are designed to separate the front and rear braking systems hydraulically in case of a leak. The master cylinder coverts mechanical motion from the pedal into hydraulic pressure within the lines. This pressure is translated back into mechanical motion at the wheels by either the wheel cylinder (drum brakes) or the caliper (disc brakes).

Steel lines carry the brake fluid to a point on the vehicle's frame near each of the vehicle's wheels. The fluid is then carried to the calipers and wheel cylinders by flexible tubes in order to allow for suspension and steering movements.

In drum brake systems, each wheel cylinder contains two pistons, one at either end, which push outward in opposite directions and force the brake shoe into contact with the drum.

In disc brake systems, the cylinders are part of the calipers. At least one cylinder in each caliper is used to force the brake pads against the disc.

All pistons employ some type of seal, usually made of rubber, to minimize fluid leakage. A rubber dust boot seals the outer end of the cylinder against dust and dirt. The boot fits around the outer end of the piston on disc brake calipers, and around the brake actuating rod on wheel cylinders.

The hydraulic system operates as follows: When at rest, the entire system, from the piston(s) in the master cylinder to those in the wheel cylinders or calipers, is full of brake fluid. Upon application of the brake pedal, fluid trapped in front of the master cylinder piston(s) is forced through the lines to the wheel cylinders. Here, it forces the pistons outward, in the case of drum brakes, and inward toward the disc, in the case of disc brakes. The motion of the pistons is opposed by return springs mounted outside the cylinders in drum brakes, and by spring seals, in disc brakes.

Upon release of the brake pedal, a spring located inside the master cylinder immediately returns the master cylinder pistons to the normal position. The pistons contain check valves and the master cylinder has compensating ports drilled in it. These are uncovered as the pistons reach their normal position. The piston check valves allow fluid to flow toward the wheel cylinders or calipers as the pistons withdraw. Then, as the return springs force the brake pads or shoes into the released position, the excess fluid reservoir through the compensating ports. It is during the time the pedal is in the released position that any fluid that has leaked out of the system will be replaced through the compensating ports.

Dual circuit master cylinders employ two pistons, located one behind the other, in the same cylinder. The primary piston is actuated directly by mechanical linkage from the brake pedal through the power booster. The secondary piston is actuated by fluid trapped between the two pistons. If a leak develops in front of the secondary piston, it moves forward until it bottoms against the front of the master cylinder, and the fluid trapped between the pistons will operate the rear brakes. If the rear brakes develop a leak, the primary piston will move forward until direct contact with the secondary piston takes place, and it will force the secondary piston to actuate the front brakes. In either case, the brake pedal moves farther when the brakes are applied, and less braking power is available.

All dual circuit systems use a switch to warn the driver when only half of the brake system is operational. This switch is usually located in a valve body which is mounted on the firewall or the frame below the master cylinder. A hydraulic piston receives pressure from both circuits, each circuit's pressure being applied to one end of the piston. When the pressures are in balance, the piston remains stationary. When one circuit has a leak, however, the greater pressure in that circuit during application of the brakes will push the piston to one side, closing the switch and activating the brake warning light.

In disc brake systems, this valve body also contains a metering valve and, in some cases, a proportioning valve. The metering valve keeps pressure from traveling to the disc brakes on the front wheels until the brake shoes on the rear wheels have contacted the drums, ensuring that the front brakes will never be used alone. The proportioning valve controls the pressure to the rear brakes to lessen the chance of rear wheel lock-up during very hard braking.

Warning lights may be tested by depressing the brake pedal and holding it while opening one of the wheel cylinder bleeder screws. If this does not cause the light to go on, substitute a new lamp, make continuity checks, and, finally, replace the switch as necessary.

The hydraulic system may be checked for leaks by applying pressure to the pedal gradually and steadily. If the pedal sinks very slowly to the floor, the system has a leak. This is not to be confused with a springy or spongy feel due to the compression of air within the lines. If the system leaks, there will be a gradual change in the position of the pedal with a constant pressure.

Check for leaks along all lines and at wheel cylinders. If no external leaks are apparent, the problem is inside the master cylinder.

DISC BRAKES

Instead of the traditional expanding brakes that press outward against a circular drum, disc brake systems utilize a disc (rotor) with brake pads positioned on either side of it. An easily-seen analogy is the hand brake arrangement on a bicycle. The pads squeeze onto the rim of the bike wheel, slowing its motion. Automobile disc brakes use the identical principle but apply the braking effort to a separate disc instead of the wheel.

The disc (rotor) is a casting, usually equipped with cooling fins between the two braking surfaces. This enables air to circulate between the braking surfaces making them less sensitive to heat buildup and more resistant to fade. Dirt and water do not drastically affect braking action since contaminants are thrown off by the centrifugal action of the rotor or scraped off the by the pads. Also, the equal clamping action of the two brake pads tends to ensure uniform, straight line stops. Disc brakes are inherently self-adjusting. There are three general types of disc brake:

1. A fixed caliper.
2. A floating caliper.
3. A sliding caliper.

The fixed caliper design uses two pistons mounted on either side of the rotor (in each side of the caliper). The caliper is mounted rigidly and does not move.

The sliding and floating designs are quite similar. In fact, these two types are often lumped together. In both designs, the pad on the inside of the rotor is moved into contact with the rotor by hydraulic force. The caliper, which is not held in a fixed position, moves slightly, bringing the outside pad into contact with the rotor. There are various methods of attaching floating calipers. Some pivot at the bottom or top, and some slide on mounting bolts. In any event, the end result is the same.

DRUM BRAKES

Drum brakes employ two brake shoes mounted on a stationary backing plate. These shoes are positioned inside a circular drum which rotates with the wheel assembly. The shoes are held in place by springs. This allows them to slide toward the drums (when they are applied) while keeping the linings and drums in alignment. The shoes are actuated by a wheel cylinder which is mounted at the top of the backing plate. When the brakes are applied, hydraulic pressure forces the wheel cylinder's actuating links outward. Since these links bear directly against the top of the brake shoes, the tops of the shoes are then forced against the inner side of the drum. This action forces the bottoms of the two shoes to contact the brake drum by rotating the entire assembly slightly (known as servo action). When pressure within the wheel cylinder is relaxed, return springs pull the shoes back away from the drum.

Most modern drum brakes are designed to self-adjust themselves during application when the vehicle is moving in reverse. This motion causes both shoes to rotate very slightly with the drum, rocking an adjusting lever, thereby causing rotation of the adjusting screw. Some drum brake systems are designed to self-adjust during application whenever the brakes are applied. This on-board adjustment system reduces the need for maintenance adjustments and keeps both the brake function and pedal feel satisfactory.

POWER BOOSTERS

Virtually all modern vehicles use a vacuum assisted power brake system to multiply the braking force and reduce pedal effort. Since vacuum is always available when the engine is operating, the system is simple and efficient. A vacuum diaphragm is located on the front of the master cylinder and assists the driver in applying the brakes, reducing both the effort and travel he must put into moving the brake pedal.

The vacuum diaphragm housing is normally connected to the intake manifold by a vacuum hose. A check valve is placed at the point where the hose enters the diaphragm housing, so that during periods of low manifold vacuum brakes assist will not be lost.

Depressing the brake pedal closes off the vacuum source and allows atmospheric pressure to enter on one side of the diaphragm. This causes the master cylinder pistons to move and apply the brakes. When the brake pedal is released, vacuum is applied to both sides of the diaphragm and springs return the diaphragm and master cylinder pistons to the released position.

If the vacuum supply fails, the brake pedal rod will contact the end of the master cylinder actuator rod and the system will apply the brakes without any power assistance. The driver will notice that much higher pedal effort is needed to stop the car and that the pedal feels harder than usual.

Vacuum Leak Test

1. Operate the engine at idle without touching the brake pedal for at least one minute.
2. Turn off the engine and wait one minute.
3. Test for the presence of assist vacuum by depressing the brake pedal and releasing it several times. If vacuum is present in the system, light application will produce less and less pedal travel. If there is no vacuum, air is leaking into the system.

System Operation Test

1. With the engine **OFF**, pump the brake pedal until the supply vacuum is entirely gone.
2. Put light, steady pressure on the brake pedal.
3. Start the engine and let it idle. If the system is operating correctly, the brake pedal should fall toward the floor if the constant pressure is maintained.

Power brake systems may be tested for hydraulic leaks just as ordinary systems are tested.

Adjustments

DISC BRAKES

The front and rear disc brakes require no adjustments. Hydraulic pressure maintains the proper pad to disc contact at all times. However, the parking brake shoe on the rear disc brake systems must be adjusted manually.

DRUM BRAKES

◗ **See Figure 1**

The rear drum brakes, on your car, are self adjusting. The only adjustment necessary should be the initial one after new brake shoes have been installed or some type of service work has been done on the rear brake system.

➡**After any brake service, obtain a firm brake pedal before moving the car. Adjusted brakes should not drag. The**

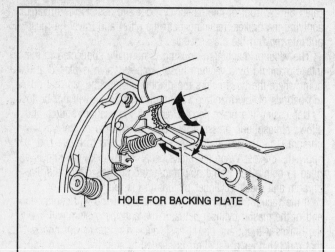

Fig. 1 There is a hole in the backing plate for rear drum brakes to turn the star adjuster

HOLE FOR BACKING PLATE

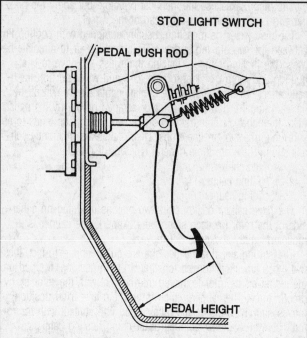

Fig. 2 Pedal height is measured from the floor pad, not the carpet

STOP LIGHT SWITCH
PEDAL PUSH ROD
PEDAL HEIGHT

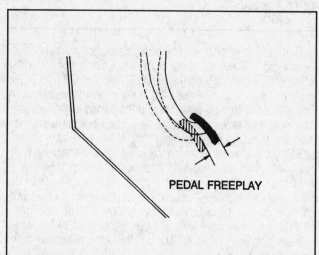

Fig. 3 Pedal free-play is the amount of motion before the brakes are applied

PEDAL FREEPLAY

wheel must turn freely. Be sure the parking brake cables are not to tightly adjusted.

Since no adjustment is necessary, except when service work is done on the rear brakes, we will assume that the car is jacked up and properly supported. If not, then refer to the appropriate sections of this Chapter for the procedures necessary. Adjust the rear brakes as follows:

1. With the vehicle raised and properly supported, remove the inspection plug from the top rear of the brake backing plate.
2. Insert a suitable brake adjusting tool into the inspection hole and turn the star adjuster until the wheel cannot be turn any more.
3. Insert a long narrow rod through the inspection hole and hold the automatic adjusting lever away from the adjusting bolt.
4. Using a suitable brake adjusting tool, insert the tool through the inspection hole and reduce the brake shoe adjustment by turning the star adjuster counterclockwise.
5. Reduce the brake shoe adjustment enough to allow the wheel to spin freely at least one full revolution.
6. Do the same to the other wheel and then lower the vehicle.

PEDAL HEIGHT AND FREE-PLAY

▶ **See Figures 2 and 3**

The correct pedal height from the floor boards to the brake pedal should be 166–176mm (6.54–6.93 in.) for 1983–88 or 157–167mm (6.18–6.57 in.) for 1989–90 on the Cressida, and 148–158mm (5.83–6.22 in.) on the Van models.

1. On the Cressida models, remove the instrument lower finish panel and air duct.
2. Loosen the locknut and turn the stop light switch and the brake cancel switch for the cruise control (if so equipped).
3. Adjust the pedal height by turning the pedal pushrod until the correct brake pedal height is obtained.
4. Return the stop light switch and brake cancel switch until it they lightly contact the pedal stopper.
5. After adjusting the brake pedal height, check the brake pedal free-play.
6. With the engine **OFF,** push in the brake pedal several times

until there is no more vacuum left in the brake booster. Push the pedal in until the beginning of resistance is felt. Measure the distance from the stand still point till the free-play point. The brake pedal free-play should be as follows:

  a. The brake pedal free-play should be 3–6mm (0.12–0.24 in.) on the Cressida models.
  b. The brake pedal free-play should be 1–4mm (0.04–0.138 in.) on the Van models.

7. If it is necessary to adjust the brake pedal free-play, use the following procedure:
  a. Adjust the brake pedal free-play by turning the pedal pushrod.
  b. Start the engine and confirm that the pedal free-play exist.

c. After adjusting the brake pedal free-play, recheck the brake pedal height.

8. Reinstall the air duct and lower instrument finish panel one the Cressida models.

Stoplight Switch

ADJUSTMENT

1. Remove the instrument lower finish panel and the air duct if required to gain access to the stop light switch.
2. Unplug the stoplight switch connector.
3. Loosen the switch locknut.
4. Turn the stoplight switch until the end of the switch lightly contacts the pedal stopper.
5. Hold the switch and tighten the locknut.
6. Attach the switch connector.
7. Depress the brake pedal and verify that the brake lights illuminate.
8. Install the air duct and the lower finish panel, if removed.

REMOVAL & INSTALLATION

1. Disconnect the negative battery cable.
2. Remove the instrument lower finish panel and the air duct if required to gain access to the stop light switch.
3. Unplug the stoplight switch connector.

4. Remove the switch mounting nut, then slide the switch from the mounting bracket on the pedal.

To install:

5. Install the switch into the mounting bracket and adjust as described above.
6. Attach the switch connector.
7. Depress the brake pedal and verify that the brake lights illuminate.
8. Install the air duct and the lower finish panel, if removed.

Master Cylinder

REMOVAL & INSTALLATION

Cressida

▶ **See Figures 4, 5, 6 and 7**

1. Disconnect the negative battery cable. Unplug the level warning switch connector.
2. Draw the brake fluid out of the master cylinder with a syringe.
3. Detach the hydraulic lines from the master cylinder.

✳✳ WARNING

Do not spill brake fluid on the painted surfaces of the vehicle.

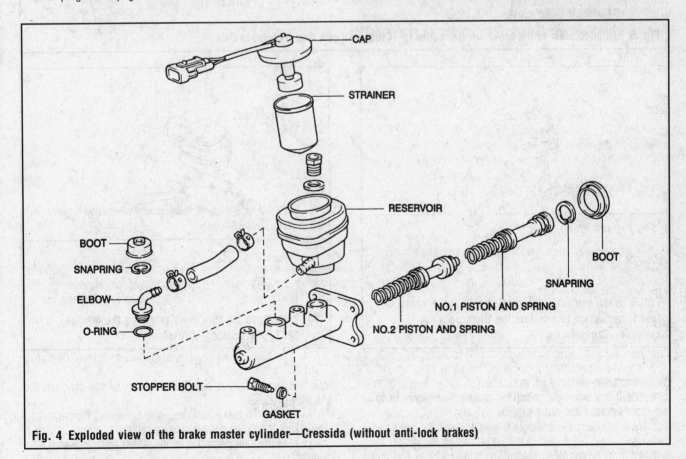

Fig. 4 Exploded view of the brake master cylinder—Cressida (without anti-lock brakes)

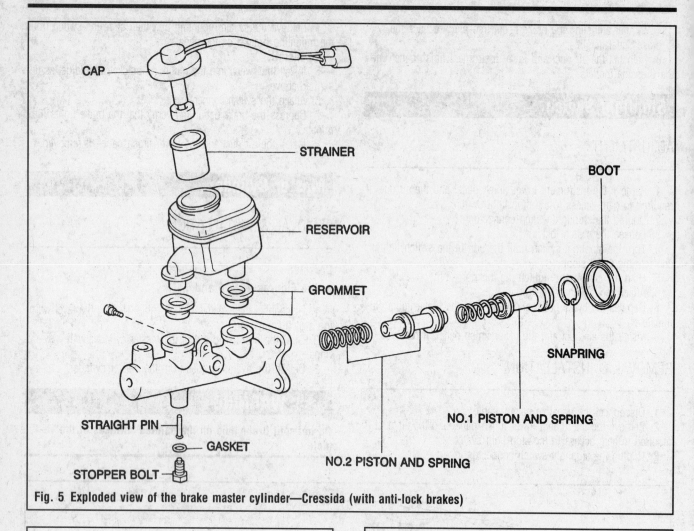

Fig. 5 Exploded view of the brake master cylinder—Cressida (with anti-lock brakes)

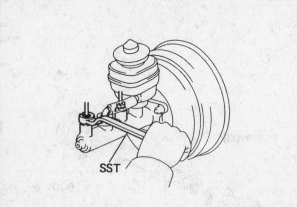

Fig. 6 When removing the master cylinder, a brake line tool is necessary to separate the lines from the cylinder—Cressida

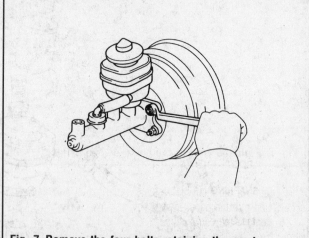

Fig. 7 Remove the four bolts retaining the master cylinder to the booster—Cressida

4. Remove the bolts, nuts and clamp (on the ABS models, remove the 3-way union nut) which secure the master cylinder to the brake booster. Pull out the master cylinder from the brake booster.

5. Installation is the reverse of removal. Bleed the system as outlined in this Chapter.

Van

▶ **See Figure 8**

1. Disconnect the negative battery cable.
2. Draw the brake fluid out of the master cylinder with a syringe.

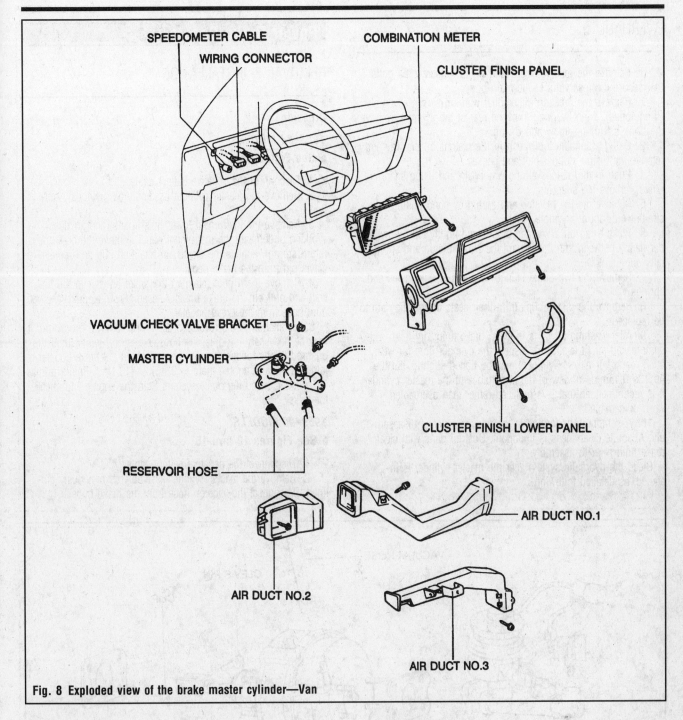

SPEEDOMETER CABLE
WIRING CONNECTOR
COMBINATION METER
CLUSTER FINISH PANEL
VACUUM CHECK VALVE BRACKET
MASTER CYLINDER
CLUSTER FINISH LOWER PANEL
RESERVOIR HOSE
AIR DUCT NO.1
AIR DUCT NO.2
AIR DUCT NO.3

Fig. 8 Exploded view of the brake master cylinder—Van

3. Remove the instrument cluster finish panel retaining screws and pull the panel toward you.

4. Remove the combination meter retaining screws.

5. Disconnect the speedometer cable and wiring, then remove the combination meter.

6. Remove the 3 air duct assemblies.

7. Detach the hydraulic lines from the master cylinder and using pliers, disconnect the 2 reservoir hoses from the master cylinder. Do not spill brake fluid on the painted surfaces of the vehicle.

8. Remove the master cylinder mounting nuts and vacuum check valve bracket. Pull the master cylinder out of the vehicle.

To install:

9. Install the master cylinder assembly, retaining nuts and vacuum check valve bracket.

10. Reconnect the hydraulic lines to the master cylinder and the two reservoir hoses.

11. Install the 3 air duct assemblies.

12. Attach the speedometer cable and wiring connectors to the back of the combination meter.

13. Install the combination meter and retaining screws.

14. Install the instrument cluster finish panel and retaining screws.

15. Refill the master cylinder reservoir and install the cap.

16. Reconnect the negative battery cable.

17. Bleed the brake system.

OVERHAUL

1. Remove the reservoir caps and floats. Unscrew the bolts that secure the reservoirs to the main body.

2. Remove the pressure differential warning switch assembly (if equipped). Then, working from the rear of the cylinder, remove the boot, snapring, elbow and O-ring.

3. Using a suitable tool, push in the pistons all the way and remove the piston stopper bolt and gasket.

4. Push in the pistons all the way again and using snapring pliers, remove the snapring.

5. Remove the No.1 piston and spring by hand pulling it straight out, not at an angle.

6. Place a rag on 2 wooden blocks and lightly tap the cylinder flange between the blocks until the No. 2 piston and spring falls out.

7. Remove the two outlet fittings, washers, check valves and springs.

8. Remove the piston cups from their seats only if they are to be replaced.

9. After washing all parts in clean brake fluid, dry them with compressed air (if available). Inspect the cylinder bore for wear, scuff marks, or nicks. Cylinders may be honed slightly, but the limit is 0.15mm. In view of the importance of the master cylinder, it is recommended that it is replaced rather than overhauled if worn or damaged.

10. Assembly is performed in the reverse order of disassembly. Absolute cleanliness is important. Coat all parts with clean brake fluid prior to assembly.

Bleed the hydraulic system after the master cylinder is installed, as detailed following.

Power Brake Booster

REMOVAL & INSTALLATION

Cressida

1983–88 MODELS
▶ See Figure 9

1. Disconnect the negative battery cable.

2. Remove the master cylinder assembly as previously outlined.

3. Remove the instrument lower finish panel and air duct. Working underneath the instrument panel, remove the brake pedal return spring. Remove the clevis pin retaining clip and remove the clevis pin from the brake pedal.

4. Remove the 4 nuts retaining the brake booster to the firewall and pull out the brake booster assembly. Disconnect the vacuum hose from the brake booster.

5. Installation is the reverse order of the removal procedure. It may be necessary to adjust the booster pushrod length until the pushrod lightly touches the pin head. Tighten the brake booster retaining nuts and tighten them to 9 ft. lbs. (13 Nm). Refill the master cylinder, bleed the brake system. Start the engine and check for leaks.

1989–90 MODELS
▶ See Figures 10 thru 15

1. Disconnect the negative battery cable.

2. Remove the master cylinder assembly as previously outlined. Disconnect the vacuum hose from the brake booster.

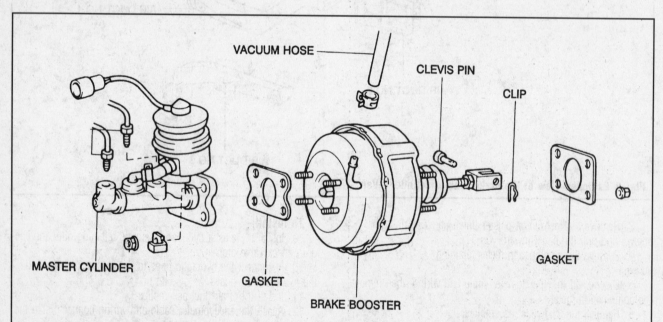

Fig. 9 The brake booster is mounted on the firewall with the master cylinder attached on the front—1983–88 Cressida shown

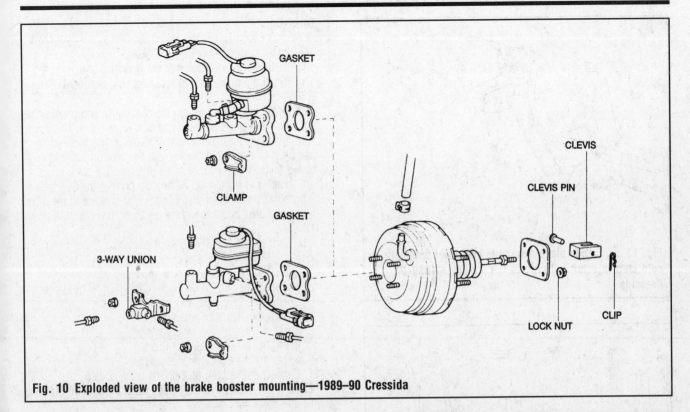

Fig. 10 Exploded view of the brake booster mounting—1989–90 Cressida

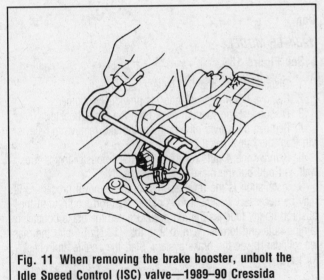

Fig. 11 When removing the brake booster, unbolt the Idle Speed Control (ISC) valve—1989–90 Cressida

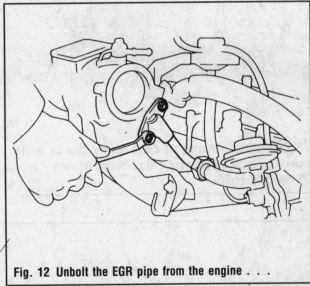

Fig. 12 Unbolt the EGR pipe from the engine . . .

3. Remove the instrument lower finish panel and air duct. Working underneath the instrument panel, remove the brake pedal return spring. Remove the clevis pin retaining clip and remove the clevis pin from the brake pedal.

4. Remove the windshield wiper motor.

5. Remove the brake booster as follows:

  a. Remove the alternator assembly.

  b. Remove the PCV pipe with hose.

  c. Disconnect the No.3 PCV hose from the cylinder head cover.

  d. Remove the 2 bolts retaining the idle speed control valve and remove the valve.

  e. Disconnect the No.3 water by-pass hose from the throttle body.

  f. Remove the EGR pipe retaining bolt and remove the EGR pipe.

  g. Place a suitable container or shop rag under the cold start injector tube. Slowly loosen the 2 union bolts of the cold start injector tube and remove the bolts, 4 gaskets and injector tube.

  h. Remove the 2 bolts and the intake manifold stay bracket.

  i. Remove the air intake chamber and move it forward.

  j. Remove the brake booster retaining bolts, located under the instrument panel.

  k. Remove the clevis yoke off of the operating rod.

  l. Remove the brake booster and gasket.

6. Adjust the booster pushrod length until the pushrod lightly touches the pin head.

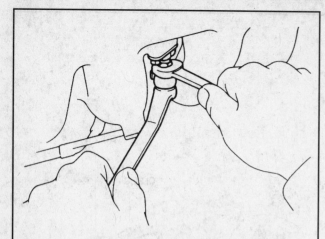

Fig. 13 . . . then place a suitable container under the cold start injector and remove the injector—1989–90 Cressida

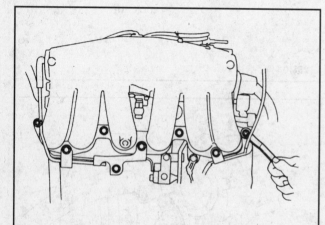

Fig. 14 When removing the brake booster, the air intake chamber must be removed and poitioned forward—1989–90 Cressida

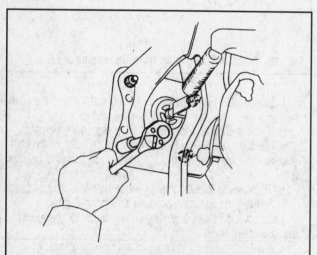

Fig. 15 Remove the booster mounting nuts and clevis, then remove the booster and gasket from the firewall

To install:

7. Install the brake booster as follows:

a. Install the brake booster and gasket.

b. Install the clevis yoke onto the operating arm.

c. Install the brake booster retaining nuts and torque them to 9 ft. lbs. (13 Nm).

d. Install the clevis pin into the clevis yoke and brake pedal and install the clevis pin retaining clip.

e. Install the air intake chamber to the intake manifold. Install the intake manifold bracket and chamber to manifold retaining bolts. Tighten the bolts to 13 ft. lbs. (18 Nm).

f. Install and tighten the installation bolts to the EGR pipe.

g. Install a new cold start injector tube gasket and the tube to the cold start injector. Tighten the union bolts to 13 ft. lbs. (18 Nm).

h. Connect the No. 3 water-to-bypass hose to the throttle body.

i. Install the idle speed control valve and retaining bolts.

j. Connect the No. 3 PCV hose to the cylinder head cover.

k. Install the PCV pipe with hose.

l. Install the alternator assembly.

8. Install the windshield wiper motor.

9. Install the brake pedal return spring.

10. Install the master cylinder assembly.

11. Connect the vacuum hose to the brake booster.

12. Refill the master cylinder, bleed the brake system. Start the engine and check for leaks.

Van

1984–86 MODELS

▶ **See Figure 16**

1. Disconnect the negative battery cable.

2. Remove the master cylinder as previously outlined.

3. Disconnect the vacuum hose from the brake booster.

4. Remove the clevis pin retaining clip and remove the clevis pin from the brake pedal.

5. Remove the 4 nuts retaining the brake booster to the firewall and pull out the brake booster assembly.

6. Installation is the reverse order of the removal procedure. It may be necessary to adjust the booster pushrod length until the pushrod lightly touches the pin head. Tighten the brake booster retaining nuts and torque them to 9 ft. lbs. (13 Nm). Refill the master cylinder, bleed the brake system. Start the engine and check for leaks.

1987–89 MODELS

▶ **See Figure 17**

1. Disconnect the negative battery cable.

2. Remove the master cylinder as previously outlined.

3. Disconnect the vacuum hose from the brake booster.

4. Remove the cluster finish lower panel. Remove the steering column assembly and unplug the 4 connectors.

5. Loosen the clutch pedal installation nut and bolt. Remove the nut and pull out the bolt until the bolt head goes in.

6. Loosen the 2 clutch master cylinder retaining bolts and pull them out until the brake pedal bracket is free from the clutch master cylinder.

7. Pull out the throttle cable from the cable hook.

8. Remove the 3 mounting bolts of the pedal bracket lower side.

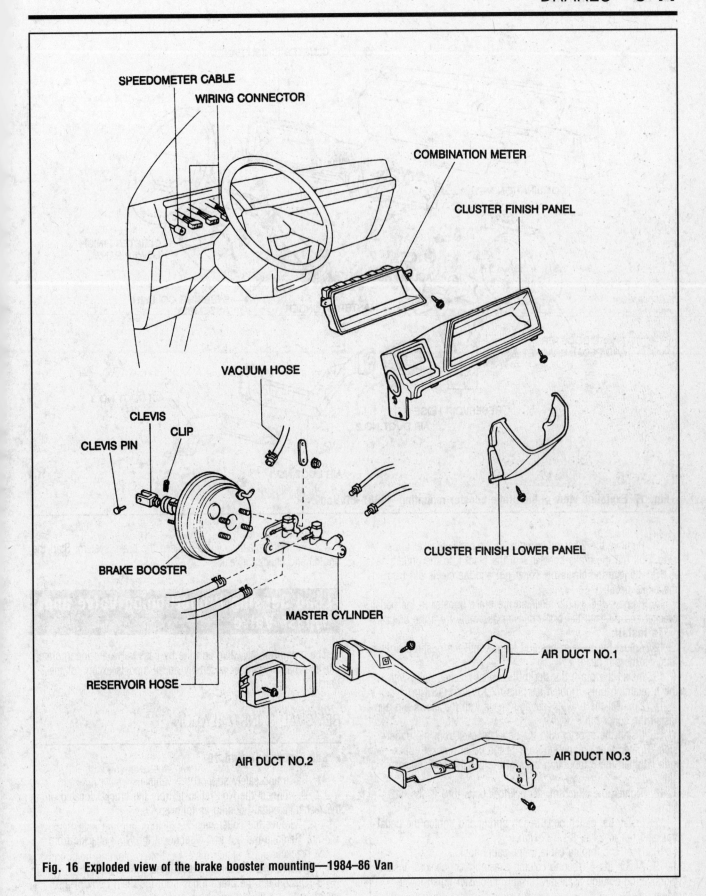

Fig. 16 Exploded view of the brake booster mounting—1984–86 Van

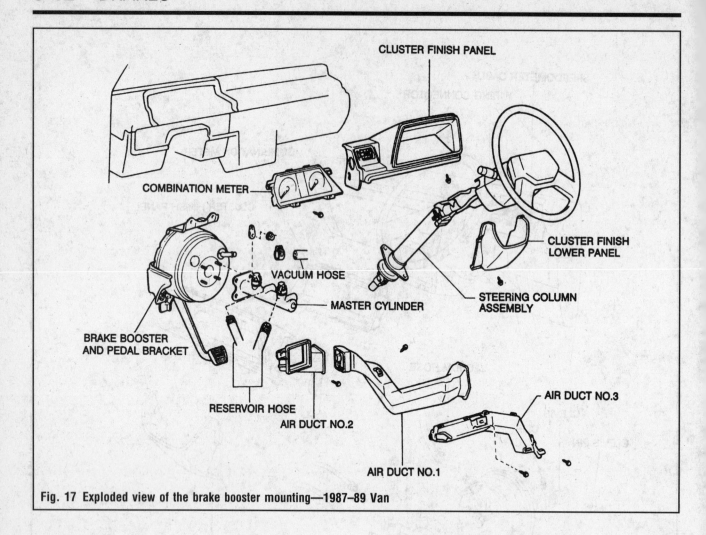

Fig. 17 Exploded view of the brake booster mounting—1987–89 Van

9. Remove the 2 mounting bolts of the pedal bracket upper side. Pull out the brake booster with the bracket to the underside.

10. Remove the clevis pin cotter pin and the clevis pin from the brake pedal.

11. Remove the 4 nuts retaining the brake booster to the pedal bracket and pull out the brake booster assembly from the bracket.

To install:

12. Adjust the booster pushrod length until the pushrod lightly touches the pin head.

13. Install the brake booster to the pedal bracket along with the 4 retaining nuts. Tighten the nuts to 9 ft. lbs. (13 Nm).

14. Connect the brake pedal and clevis with the clevis pin and install the cotter pin.

15. Install the booster with the pedal bracket from the underside. Tighten the 2 mounting bolts of the pedal bracket upper side. Tighten the 3 mounting bolts of the pedal bracket lower side.

16. Tighten the clutch master cylinder bolts to 9 ft. lbs. (13 Nm).

17. Install the clutch pedal return spring and tighten the pedal bolt and nut to 24 ft. lbs. (32 Nm).

18. Hook the throttle cable to the cable hook.

19. Attach the 4 steering column assembly connectors. Install the steering column assembly. Install the cluster finish lower panel.

20. Install the master cylinder assembly.

21. Connect the vacuum hose to brake booster.

22. Refill the master cylinder, bleed the brake system. Start the engine and check for leaks.

Load Sensing Proportioning Valve and Bypass Valve

The proportioning valve and the by-pass valve are incorporated into the master cylinder assembly on all models except for the Van.

REMOVAL & INSTALLATION

▶ **See Figures 18 and 19**

1. Raise and safely support the vehicle.

2. Disconnect the No.2 shackle from the bracket located on the rear differential housing as follows:

  a. Remove the cotter pin.

  b. Remove the nut and disconnect the No.2 shackle from the bracket.

  c. Remove the retainer, 2 bushings and collar.

3. Disconnect the brake tubes from the main body of the valve.

4. Remove the valve bracket mounting bolts and the valve assembly.

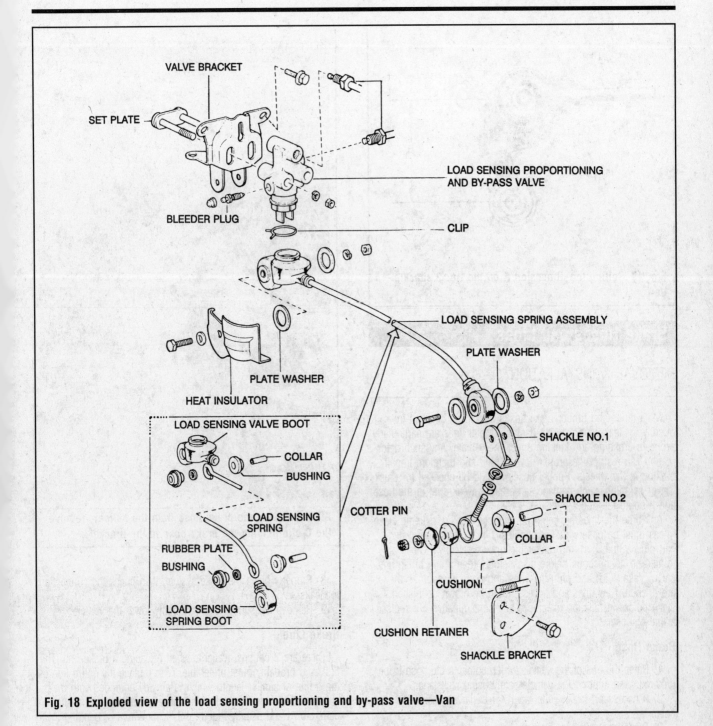

Fig. 18 Exploded view of the load sensing proportioning and by-pass valve—Van

To install:

5. Install the valve assembly to the frame with the 4 retaining nuts. Tighten the nuts to 14 ft. lbs. (19 Nm).

6. Connect the brake tubes.

7. Connect the No.2 shackle to the bracket. Set dimension A (the distance between the No.2 shackle retainer nut and the No.1 shackle retainer bolt) by turning the adjusting nut. The initial setting is 78mm (3.07 in.). Tighten the locknut to 18 ft. lbs. (25 Nm).

8. Install the 2 bushings and a collar to the load sensing spring shackle. Install the load sensing spring to the shackle bracket with a retainer and nut. Tighten the nut to 9 ft. lbs. (13 Nm). Install a new cotter pin.

9. When pulling down the load sensing spring, confirm that the valve piston moves down smoothly. Position the valve body so that the valve piston lightly contacts the load sensing spring. Tighten the valve body mounting nuts to 9 ft. lbs. (13 Nm).

10. Bleed the brake system and check for fluid leakage.

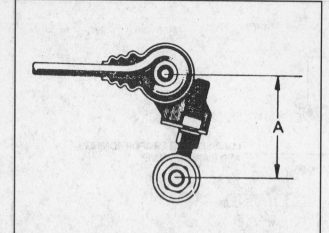

Fig. 19 Setting the dimension A on the No. 2 shackle—Van

Brake Hoses and Lines

REMOVAL & INSTALLATION

Metal lines and rubber brake hoses should be checked frequently for leaks and external damage. Metal lines are particularly prone to crushing and kinking under the vehicle. Any such deformation can restrict the proper flow of fluid and therefore impair braking at the wheels. Rubber hoses should be checked for cracking or scraping; such damage can create a weak spot in the hose and it could fail under pressure.

Any time the lines are removed or disconnected, extreme cleanliness must be observed. The slightest bit of dirt in the system can plug a fluid port and render the brakes defective. Clean all joints and connections before disassembly (use a stiff brush and clean brake fluid) and plug the lines and ports as soon as they are opened. New lines and hoses should be blown or flushed clean before installation to remove any contamination. To replace a line or hose:

Brake Hose

1. Raise the end of the vehicle which contains the hose to be repaired, then support the vehicle safely using jackstands.
2. If necessary, remove the wheel for easier access to the hose.
3. Disconnect the hose from the wheel cylinder or caliper and plug the opening to avoid excessive fluid loss or contamination.
4. Disconnect the hose from the brake line and plug the openings to avoid excessive fluid loss or contamination.
   To install:
5. Install the brake hose to the brake line and tighten to 14 ft. lbs. (19 Nm) for rear brakes or 18 ft. lbs. (24 Nm) for front brakes.
6. If installing a front brake hose, make sure the hose is routed properly.
7. Install the hose to the wheel cylinder or caliper using NEW washers, then tighten the retainer to 36 ft. lbs. (49 Nm).

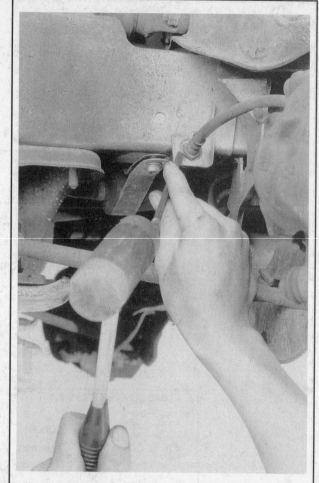

After removing the brake hose from the caliper, remove the C-clip holding the brake hose in the bracket

8. Properly bleed the brake system, then check the connections for leaks.
9. Remove the supports and carefully lower the vehicle.

Brake Line

There are 2 options available when replacing a brake line. The first, and probably most preferable, is to replace the entire line using a line of similar length which is already equipped with machined flared ends. Such lines are usually available from auto parts stores and usually require only a minimum of bending in order to properly fit them to the vehicle. The second option is to bend and flare the entire replacement line (or a repair section of line) using the appropriate tools.

Buying a line with machined flares is usually preferable because of the time and effort saved, not to mention the cost of special tools if they are not readily available. Also, machined flares are usually of a much higher quality than those produced by hand flaring tools or kits.

1. Raise the end of the vehicle which contains the hose to be repaired, then support the vehicle safely using jackstands.
2. Remove the components necessary for access to the brake line which is being replaced.

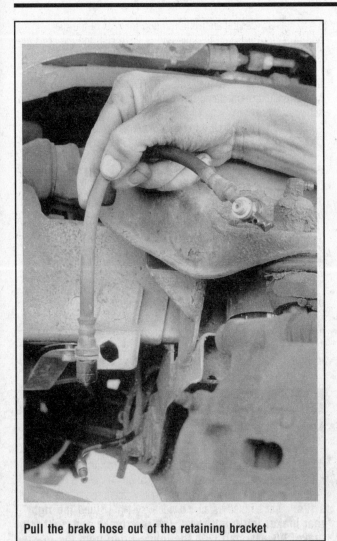

Pull the brake hose out of the retaining bracket

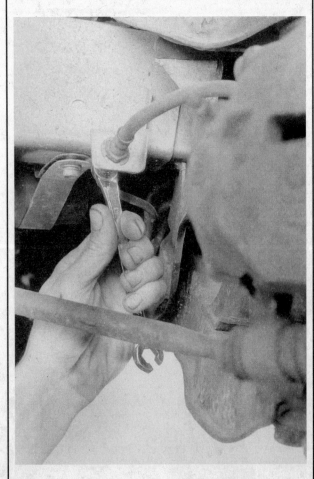

Using a line wrench, separate the brake pipe from the brake hose

3. Disconnect the fittings at each end of the line, then plug the openings to prevent excessive fluid loss or contamination.

4. Trace the line from one end to the other and disconnect the line from any retaining clips, then remove the line from the vehicle.

To install:

5. Try to obtain a replacement line that is the same length as the line that was removed. If the line is longer, you will have to cut it and flare the end. If you have decided to repair a portion of the line, see the procedure on brake line flaring.

6. Use a suitable tubing bender to make the necessary bends in the line. Work slowly and carefully; try to make the bends look as close as possible to those on the line being replaced.

➡**When bending the brake line, be careful not to kink or crack the line. If the brake line becomes kinked or cracked, it must be replaced.**

7. Before installing the brake line, flush it with brake cleaner to remove any dirt or foreign material.

8. Install the line into the vehicle. Be sure to attach the line to the retaining clips, as necessary. Make sure the replacement brake line does not contact any components that could rub the line and cause a leak.

9. Connect the brake line fittings and tighten to 18 ft. lbs. (24 Nm), except for the rear line-to-hose fitting which should be tightened to 14 ft. lbs. (19 Nm).

10. Properly bleed the brake system and check for leaks.

11. Install any removed components, then remove the supports and carefully lower the vehicle.

BRAKE LINE FLARING

Use only brake line tubing approved for automotive use; never use copper tubing. Whenever possible, try to work with brake lines that are already cut to the length needed. These lines are available at most auto parts stores and have machine made flares, the quality of which is hard to duplicate with most of the available inexpensive flaring kits.

When the brakes are applied, there is a great amount of pressure developed in the hyddraulic system. An improperly formed flare can leak with resultant loss of stopping power. If you have never formed a double-flare, take time to familiarize yourself with the flaring kit; practice forming double-flares on scrap tubing until you are satisfied with the results.

The following procedure applies to the SA9193BR flaring kit, but should be similar to commercially available brake-line flaring

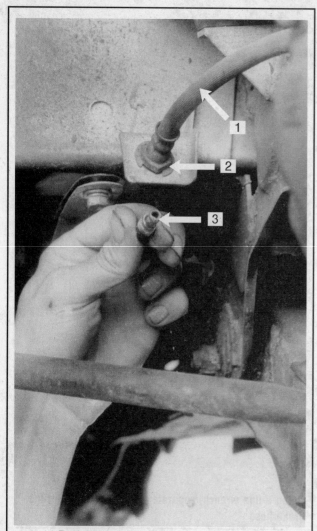

1. Brake hose   2. C-clip   3. Brake pipe

After its loosened, unthread the nut by hand

kits. If these instructions differ in any way from those in your kit, follow the instructions in the kit.

1. Determine the length necessary for the replacement or repair and allow an additional 1/8 in. (3.2mm) for each flare. Select a length of tubing according to the repair/replacement charts in the figure, then cut the brake line to the necessary length using an appropriate saw. Do not use a tubing cutter.

2. Square the end of the tube with a file and chamfer the edges. Remove burrs from the inside and outside diameters of the cut line using a deburring tool.

3. Install the required fittings onto the line.

4. Install SA9193BR, or an equivalent flaring tool, into a vice and install the handle into the operating cam.

5. Loosen the die clamp screw and rotate the locking plate to expose the die carrier opening.

6. Select the required die set (4.75mm DIN) and install in the carrier with the full side of either half facing clamp screw and counter bore of both halves facing punch turret.

7. Insert the prepared line through the rear of the die and push forward until the line end is flush with the die face.

8. Make sure the rear of both halves of the die rest against the hexagon die stops, then rotate the locking place to the fully closed position and clamp the die dirmly by tightening the clamp screw.

9. Rotate the punch turret until the appropriate size (4.75mm DIN) points towards the open end of the line to be flared.

10. Pull the operating handle against the line resistance in order to create the flare, then return the handle to the original position.

11. Release the clamp screw and rotate the locking plate to the open position.

12. Remove the die set and line, then separate by gently tapping both halves on the bench. Inspect the flare for proper size and shape. Measurement should be 0.272–0.286 in. (6.92–7.28mm).

13. If necessary, repeat the steps for the other end of the line or for the end of the line which is being repaired.

14. Bend the replacement line or section using SA91108NE, or an equivalent line bending tool.

15. If repairing the original line, join the old and new sections using a female union and tighten.

Brake System Bleeding

▶ **See Figure 20**

It is necessary to bleed the brake system of air whenever a hydraulic component, of the system, has been rebuilt or replaced, or if the brakes feel spongy during application.

Your car has a diagonally split brake system. Each side of this system must be bled as an individual system. **Bleed the right rear brake, left front brake, left rear brake and right front brake. Always start with the longest line from the master cylinder first.**

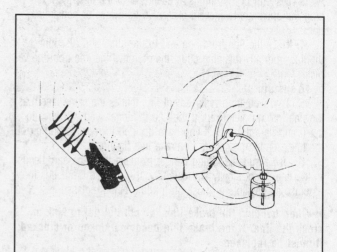

Fig. 20 Have an assistant in the vehicle pump the brake pedal while you bleed the lines

✱✱ WARNING

When bleeding the system(s) never allow the master cylinder to run completely out of brake fluid. Always use DOT 3 heavy duty brake fluid or the equivalent. Never reuse brake fluid that has been drained from the system or that has been allowed to stand in an opened container for an extended period of time. If your car is equipped with power brakes, remove the reserve vacuum stored in the booster by pumping the brake pedal several times before bleeding the brakes.

1. Clean all of the dirt away from the master cylinder filler cap.
2. Raise and support the car on jackstands. Make sure your car is safely supported and it is raised evenly front and back.

➡ **If the master cylinder has been overhauled or if air is present in it, start the bleeding procedure with the master cylinder. Otherwise (and after bleeding the master cylinder), start with the wheel cylinder which is farthest from the master cylinder.**

If the master cylinder has to be bled, it is recommended that the master cylinder be bled while it is off the car if a new one is being installed or it can be bled on the car if the problem is within the brake system. Either way it is recommended that a inexpensive master cylinder bleeding kit be purchased at your local parts dealer. This will make bleeding the master cylinder easier and also help to insure that the master cylinder is bled properly.

To bleed the master cylinder, follow the directions on your bleeding kit or have a friend pump up the brakes while you crack one line at a time on the master cylinder until clear brake fluid runs out of the lines.

3. Starting with the right rear wheel cylinder. Remove the dust cover from the bleeder screw. Place the proper size box wrench over the bleeder fitting and attach a piece of rubber tubing (about three feet long and snug fitting) over the end of the fitting.
4. Submerge the free end of the rubber tube into a container half filled with clean brake fluid.
5. Have a friend pump up the brake pedal and then push down to apply the brakes while you loosen the bleeder screw. When the pedal reaches the bottom of its travel close the bleeder fitting before your friend release the brake pedal.
6. Repeat Step 5 until air bubbles cease to appear in the container in which the tubing is submerged. Tighten the fitting, remove the rubber tubing and replace the dust cover.
7. Repeat Steps 3 through 6 to the left front wheel, then to the left rear and right front.

➡ **Refill the master cylinder after each wheel cylinder or caliper is bled. Be sure the master cylinder top gasket is mounted correctly and the brake fluid level is within the proper limits.**

8. After bleeding the brakes, pump the brake pedal several times, this ensures proper seating of the rear linings and the front caliper pistons.

FRONT DISC BRAKES

✱✱ CAUTION

Some brake pads contain asbestos, which has been determined to be a cancer causing agent. Never clean the brake surfaces with compressed air! Avoid inhaling any dust from any brake surface! When cleaning brake surfaces, use a commercially available brake cleaning fluid.

Disc Brake Pads

INSPECTION

1. Loosen the front wheel lugs slightly, then raise the front of the car and safely support it on jackstands.
2. Remove the front wheel and tire assemblies.
3. The cut out in the top of the front brake caliper allows visual inspection of the disc brake pad. If the lining is worn to within 3mm (⅛ in.) of the metal disc shoe (check local inspection requirements) replace all four pads (both sides). Minimum pad thickness is 1.0mm (0.039 in.).
4. While you are inspecting the brake pads, visually inspect the caliper for hydraulic fluid leaks. If a leak is visible the caliper will have to be rebuilt or replaced.

➡ **If a squealing noise occurs from the front brakes while driving, check the pad wear indicator. If there are traces of the indicator contacting the rotor disc, the pads should be replaced.**

REMOVAL & INSTALLATION

Cressida
◆ **See Figures 21 thru 31**

1. Raise and safely support the front of the vehicle.
2. Remove the front wheel assembly and temporarily fasten the rotor disc with the hub nuts.
3. Remove the sliding main pin from the torque plate. Lift up the brake cylinder and suspend it so the brake hose is not stretched. Do not disconnect the brake hose.

➡ **Be sure to do one side at time, in case of running into a state of confusion you can always look at the untouched side to see where you may have made your mistakes.**

4. Remove the following parts:
   a. The 2 brake pads.
   b. The four anti-squeal shims.
   c. The 2 pad wear indicator plates.
   d. The 4 pad support plates.

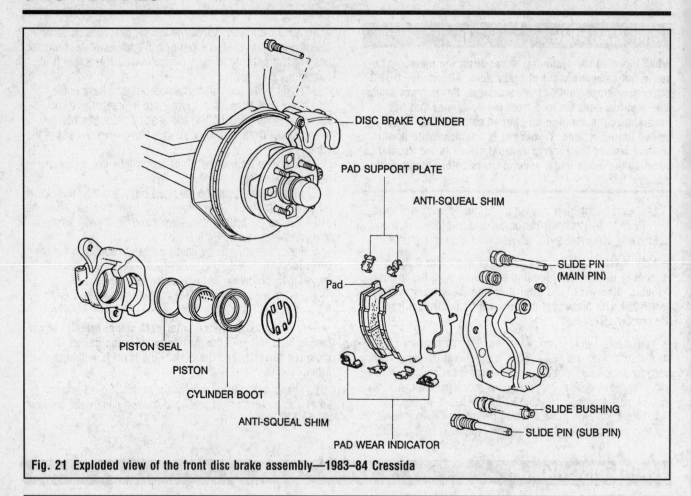

Fig. 21 Exploded view of the front disc brake assembly—1983–84 Cressida

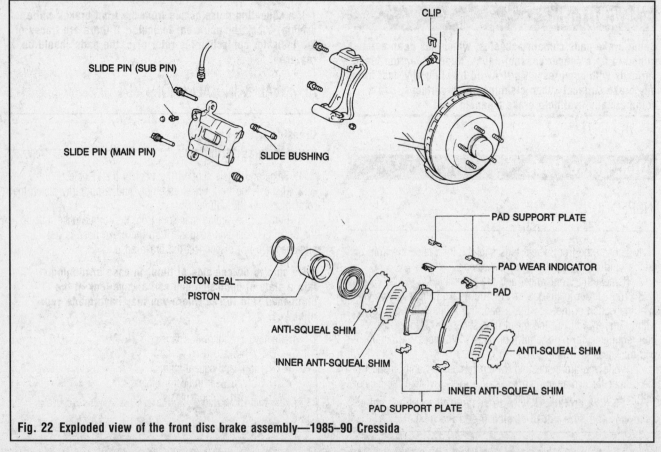

Fig. 22 Exploded view of the front disc brake assembly—1985–90 Cressida

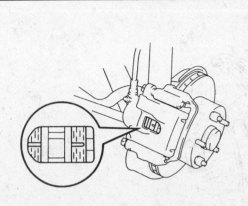

Fig. 23 When replacing front brake pads, inspect the pad thickness through the cylinder inspection hole—Cressida

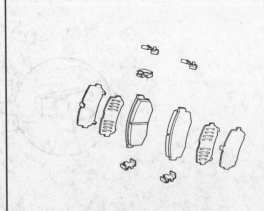

Fig. 26 Remove the pads, antisqueal shims, wear indicator and support plates from the caliper

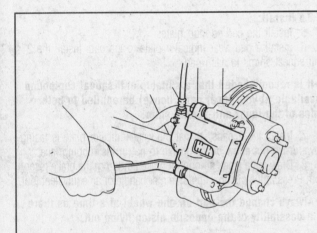

Fig. 24 Remove the sliding main pin from the torque plate and lift the caliper up

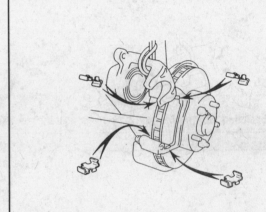

Fig. 27 When installing the new pads, place the support plates on first . . .

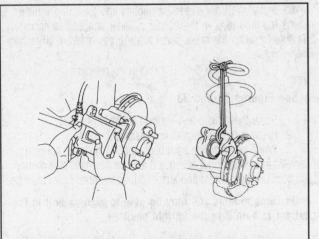

Fig. 25 Use a piece of wire to suspend the caliper out of the way, be sure not to stretch the brake hose

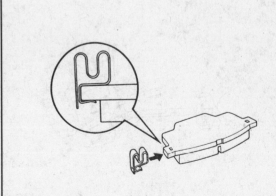

Fig. 28 Install the wear indicators on the inside brake pad

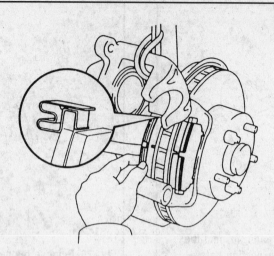

Fig. 29 When installing the pads into the caliper, insert the pads so that the wear indicator is facing upward

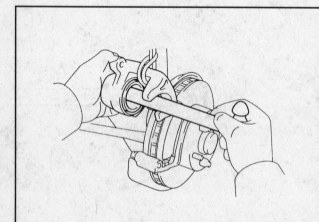

Fig. 30 Press the piston inside the caliper in with a hammer handle, then insert the cylinder on the pad assembly

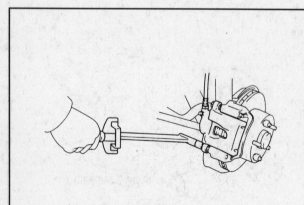

Fig. 31 Install and tighten the sliding main pin, be careful that the plug in the torque plate does not come loose

To install:

5. Install the pad support plates.

6. Install a pad wear indicator plate to the pad. Install the 2 anti-squeal shims to each pad.

➡**It is recommended that a suitable anti-squeal compound (available at your local parts house) be applied to both sides of the inner anti-squeal shim.**

7. Install the 2 pads so that the wear indicator plate is facing upward. Do not allow oil or grease to get in the rubbing face.

8. Draw out a small amount of brake fluid from the brake reservoir. Press in the piston with a hammer handle or an equivalent tool.

➡**Always change the pad on one wheel at a time as there is a possibility of the opposite piston flying out.**

9. Insert the brake cylinder carefully so the boot is not wedged. Install and tighten the sliding main pin. Tighten the pin to 65 ft. lbs. (88 Nm).

➡**When installing the sliding main pin, be careful that the plug installed in the torque plate does not come loose.**

10. Install the front wheel assemblies and lower the vehicle. Check the fluid level in the master cylinder and add as necessary. Be sure to pump the brake pedal a few times before road testing the vehicle.

Van

▶ **See Figures 32 and 33**

1. Raise the vehicle and support it safely.
2. Remove the wheel and tire assembly.
3. When servicing the front pads, loosen the brake caliper upper side mounting bolt. Loosen and remove the lower side mounting bolt. Lift the cylinder and suspend it so the hose is not stretched.

➡**On some models you may be able to place a bolt in the caliper to hold it in the upright position.**

4. When servicing the rear pads, it will be necessary to remove both upper and lower side caliper mounting bolts. Do not disconnect the brake hose. Remove the anti-squeal springs, brake pads, anti-squeal shims and pad support plates.

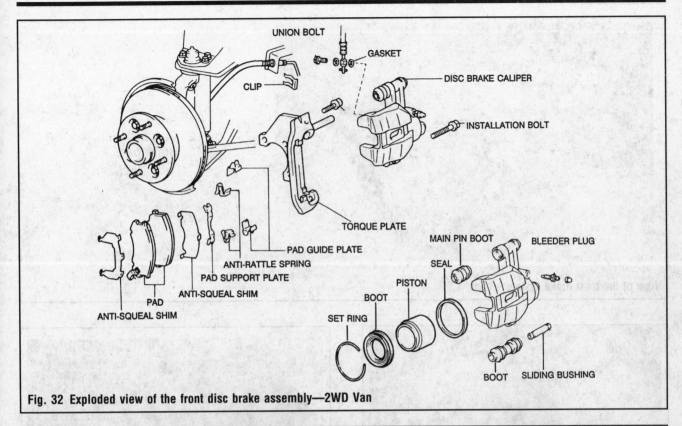

Fig. 32 Exploded view of the front disc brake assembly—2WD Van

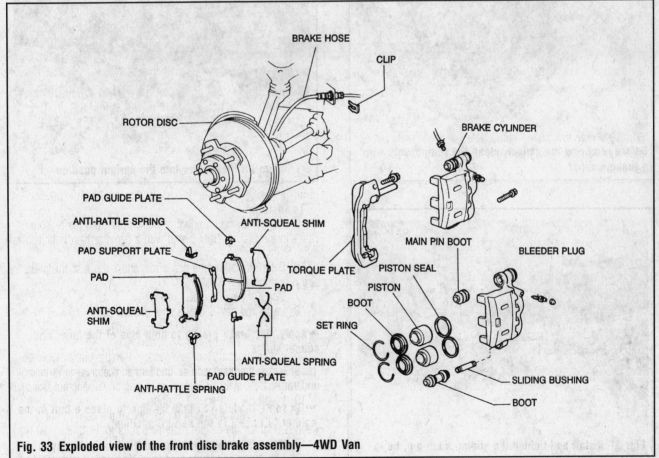

Fig. 33 Exploded view of the front disc brake assembly—4WD Van

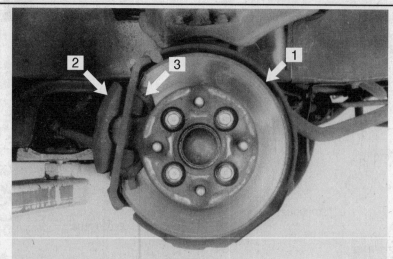

1. Rotor
2. Caliper
3. Brake pad

View of the front brake system—Van

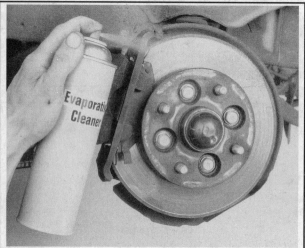

Before removing the caliper, clean the components with a brake cleaner

. . . then lift the caliper into the upright position

Remove the lower caliper mounting bolt . . .

To install:

5. Siphon a small amount of brake fluid from the reservoir. Press in the brake caliper piston with a hammer handle or equivalent.

6. Before installing the new pads, check the disc thickness and disc runout.

7. Install the pad support plates.

8. Install the anti-squeal shims to each pad.

➥Apply disc brake grease to both side of the inner anti-squeal shims.

9. Install the disc pads so the wear indicator plate is facing underneath.

10. Install the anti-squeal springs.

11. Carefully install the brake caliper so the boot is not wedged. Tighten the caliper mounting bolts to 14 ft. lbs. (20 Nm).

12. Install the wheel and tire assembly.

13. Check and adjust the fluid level. Apply the brake pedal several times.

14. Road test the vehicle for proper operation.

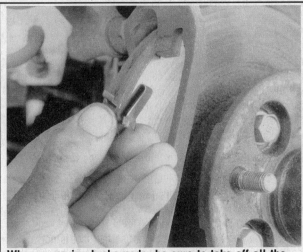

Place a bolt into the caliper as shown, then remove the brake pads

When removing brake pads, be sure to take off all the old clips and inspect them for wear

Brake Caliper

REMOVAL & INSTALLATION

Cressida

1. Raise and support the vehicle safely.
2. Remove the front wheels.
3. Disconnect the brake hose from the caliper. Plug the end of the hose to prevent loss of fluid.
4. Remove the bolts that attach the caliper to the torque plate.
5. Lift up and remove the caliper assembly.

To install:

6. Grease the caliper slides and bolts with lithium grease or equivalent. Install the caliper and secure with the bolts, torque to 18 ft. lbs. (25 Nm).
7. Reconnect the brake hose to the caliper, using new washers if equipped.
8. Fill the brake system to the proper level and bleed the brake system.
9. Install the tire and wheel assembly.
10. Add brake fluid to the reservoir to fill to the correct level. Check for leaks and proper brake operation.

Van

1. Raise the vehicle and support it safely.
2. Remove the wheel and tire assembly.
3. Place a suitable container into position to catch the brake fluid.
4. Disconnect the brake hose.
5. Remove the caliper mounting bolts and remove the caliper.
6. Remove the anti-rattle springs, pads, anti-squeal springs, pad guide plates and support plate.

To install:

7. Install the anti-rattle springs, pads, anti-squeal springs, pad guide plates and support plate.
8. Install the caliper. Tighten the caliper mounting bolts to 14 ft. lbs. (20 Nm) 2 WD and 90 ft. lbs. (123 Nm) on 4WD.
9. Connect the brake hose.
10. Fill the brake reservoir and bleed the brake system.
11. Check for fluid leakage.
12. Install the wheel and tire assembly.
13. Road test the vehicle for proper operation.

OVERHAUL

Sliding Caliper (Single Piston)

1. Place the caliper in a suitable holding fixture. Put a piece of cloth or an equivalent between the piston and cylinder.
2. Apply compressed air through the bleeder hole in the caliper to remove the piston and cylinder boot from the piston.

➡**Do not place your fingers in front of the piston when using the compressed air. It is best to have the piston forced out of the caliper into a hard plastic bucket in order of avoid injury.**

3. Remove the piston seal from the brake caliper.

4. Apply lithium soap based glycol grease to all the moving parts in the caliper.

5. Install the piston seal in the caliper.

6. Install the piston and the cylinder boot in the cylinder.

7. Install the pin boot into the sliding main pin side. Using a plastic bar, install the cylinder sliding bushing into the sliding sub pin side.

8. Install the brake pad assemblies.

9. Install the brake caliper to the rotor. Install and tighten the 2 sliding pins to 65 ft. lbs. (88 Nm).

10. Connect the flexible hose to the cylinder and brake caliper. Install the brake hose clip and make sure the hose is not twisted. Bleed the brake system.

11. Install the wheel assemblies and lower the vehicle. Check the fluid level in the master cylinder and add as necessary. Be sure to pump the brake pedal a few times before road testing the vehicle.

Fixed Caliper (Dual Piston)

1. Remove the caliper as previously described.

✳✳ WARNING

The caliper halves must not be separated. If brake fluid leaks from the bridge seal, replace the caliper assembly.

2. Clean the caliper assembly of all accumulated mud and dust.

3. Remove the retaining rings. Remove the dust covers.

4. Hold one piston with a finger so that it will not come out and gradually apply air pressure to the brake line fitting. This should cause the other piston to come out, but if the piston you are holding begins moving before the other, switch your finger over and remove the more movable one first.

5. Carefully remove the other piston.

6. With a finger, carefully remove both piston seals.

7. Thoroughly clean all parts in brake fluid.

8. Inspect, as follows:

   a. Check cylinder walls for damage or excessive wear. Light rust, etc., should be removed with fine emery paper. If the wall is heavily rusted, replace the caliper assembly.

   b. Inspect the pad, as previously described.

   c. Inspect the piston for uneven wear, damage or any rust. Replace the piston if there is any rust, as it is chrome plated and cannot be cleaned.

   d. Replace piston seals and dust covers.

9. Coat the piston seal with brake fluid and carefully install the piston seal.

10. Install the dust seal onto the piston. Coat the piston with brake fluid. Install the piston and seal assembly and install the retaining ring.

11. Repeat Steps 9 and 10 for the other piston.

12. Install the caliper assembly. Fill the master cylinder and bleed the system.

Brake Disc Rotor

REMOVAL & INSTALLATION

Cressida

▶ **See Figure 34**

1. Remove the front wheel covers and loosen the lug nuts.

2. Raise and safely support the vehicle safely. Remove the front wheels.

3. Remove the brake caliper mounting bolts and caliper from the steering knuckle. Use a suitable piece of wire to support the brake caliper assembly. Do not disconnect the brake hose.

4. Remove the hub grease cap, cotter pin, lock cap, nut and axle hub.

5. Remove the hub and brake disc (rotor) together with the outer bearing and thrust washer. Be careful not to drop the outer bearing.

To install:

6. Place the axle hub and brake disc rotor on the spindle. Install the outer bearing and thrust washer.

7. Install and tighten the locknut to 22 ft. lbs.

8. Turn the hub right and left 2 or 3 times to allow the bearing to settle.

9. Loosen the locknut so that there is 0.5–1.0mm (0.020–0.039 in.) play in the axial direction. Using the socket in your hand, tighten the nut as tight as possible.

10. Install lock cap, cotter pin and hub grease cap. If the cotter pin hole does not lineup correct by tightening the nut by the smallest amount possible.

11. Install the brake caliper on the disc, tighten the mounting bolts to specification.

12. Install the wheel assemblies. Lower the vehicle and apply the brake pedal several times before road testing the vehicle.

Van

2WD MODELS

1. Raise the vehicle and support it safely.

2. Remove the wheel and tire assembly.

3. Remove the brake caliper. Use a piece of wire or string to hang it out of the way. Do not allow the caliper to hang by the hose.

4. Remove the grease cap, cotter pin nut lock and bearing from the spindle.

5. Remove the hub and rotor assembly from the steering knuckle.

6. Remove the bolts securing the rotor to the hub and remove the rotor.

To install:

7. Before installing the rotor, thoroughly clean and repack the wheel bearings, using Multi-purpose (MP) grease. Coat inside the hub and cap with MP grease.

8. Install a new bearing seal. Coat the seal lip with MP grease.

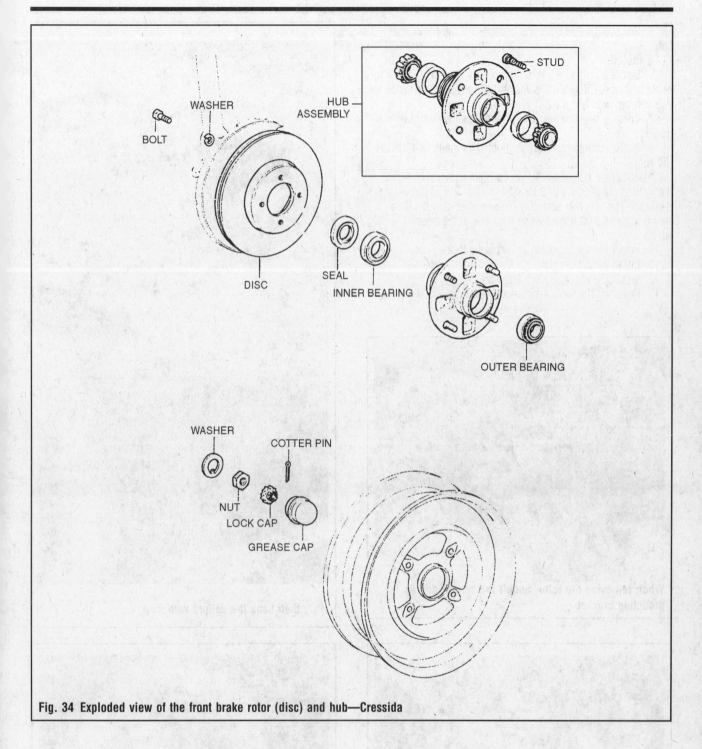

Fig. 34 Exploded view of the front brake rotor (disc) and hub—Cressida

9. Install the rotor on the hub, tighten the bolts to 47 ft. lbs. (64 Nm).

10. Install the hub assembly on the spindle and adjust the bearing preload.

11. Install the nut lock, cotter pin and grease cap.

12. Install the brake caliper.

13. Install the wheel and tire assembly and lower the vehicle to the floor.

4WD MODELS

1. Raise the vehicle and support it safely.

2. Remove the wheel and tire assembly.

3. Remove the brake caliper. Use a piece of wire or string to hang it out of the way. Do not allow the caliper to hang by the hose.

4. Remove automatic or free wheeling hub. Remove the locknut, adjusting nut and thrust washer. Remove the hub with disc together with the outer bearing.

5. Remove the five bolts and separate the rotor from the hub.

To install:

6. Before installing the rotor, thoroughly clean and repack the wheel bearings, using Multi-purpose (MP) grease. Coat inside the hub and cap with MP grease.

7. Install a new bearing seal. Coat the seal lip with MP grease.

8. Install the rotor on the hub, tighten the bolts to 47 ft. lbs. (64 Nm).

9. Install the hub assembly on the steering knuckle. Adjust the bearing preload to 4.6–8 lbs. (21–35 N). This is the weight needed to start the hub assembly moving when pulled with a spring scale at a 90 degree angle from one of the wheel studs.

10. Install the free wheeling or automatic locking hub.

11. Install the brake caliper.

12. Install the wheel and tire assembly.

13. Road test the vehicle for proper operation.

. . . then hang the caliper with wire

When removing the rotor, unbolt the caliper and its mounting bracket

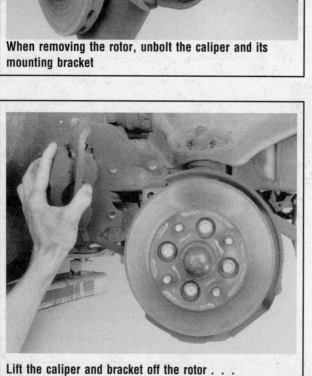

Lift the caliper and bracket off the rotor . . .

Pry off the grease cap . . .

INSPECTION

Examine the disc. If it is worn, warped or scored, it must be replaced. Check the thickness of the disc against the specifications given in the Disc and Pad Specifications chart. If it is below specifications, replace it. Use a micrometer to measure the thickness.

The disc run-out should be measured before the disc is removed and again, after the disc is installed. Use a dial indicator mounted on a stand to determine run-out. If run-out exceeds 0.15mm (all models), replace the disc.

➡**Be sure that the wheel bearing nut is properly tightened. If it is not, an inaccurate run-out reading may be obtained. If different run-out readings are obtained with the same disc, between removal and installation, this is probably the cause.**

Remove the nut lock and washer from the spindle

. . . then remove and discard the cotter pin

Dont forget to remove the wheel bearing from the spindle when removing the rotor

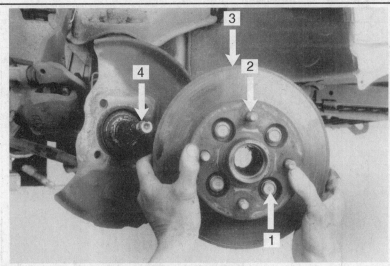

Slide the hub and rotor assembly off the spindle

1. Hub retaining bolts
2. Wheel studs
3. Rotor
4. Spindle

REAR BRAKE DRUMS

✳✳ CAUTION

Some brake shoes contain asbestos, which has been determined to be a cancer causing agent. Never clean the brake surfaces with compressed air! Avoid inhaling any dust from any brake surface! When cleaning brake surfaces, use a commercially available brake cleaning fluid.

Rear Brake Drum

REMOVAL & INSTALLATION

▶ See Figures 35 and 36

1. Remove the hub cap (if used) and loosen the lug nuts. Release the parking brake.
2. Block the front wheels, raise the rear of the car, and support it with jackstands.

✳✳ CAUTION

Support the vehicle securely.

3. Remove the lug nuts and the wheel.
4. Unfasten the brake drum retaining screws if equipped.

5. Tap the drum lightly with a mallet in order to free it. If the drum is difficult to remove use the following procedure. But first be sure that the parking brake is released.
   a. Insert a long narrow rod through the inspection hole and hold the automatic adjusting lever away from the adjusting bolt.
   b. Using a suitable brake adjusting tool, insert the tool through the inspection hole and reduce the brake shoe adjustment by turning the star adjuster counterclockwise.
   c. Reduce the brake shoe adjustment enough to allow the wheel to spin freely and pull off the brake drum.

✳✳ WARNING

Don't depress the brake pedal once the drum has been removed.

6. Inspect the brake drum as detailed following.
7. Brake drum installation is performed in the reverse order of removal.

INSPECTION

▶ See Figures 37 and 38

1. Clean the drum.
2. Inspect the drum for scoring, cracks, grooves and out-of-roundness. Replace or turn the drum, as required.

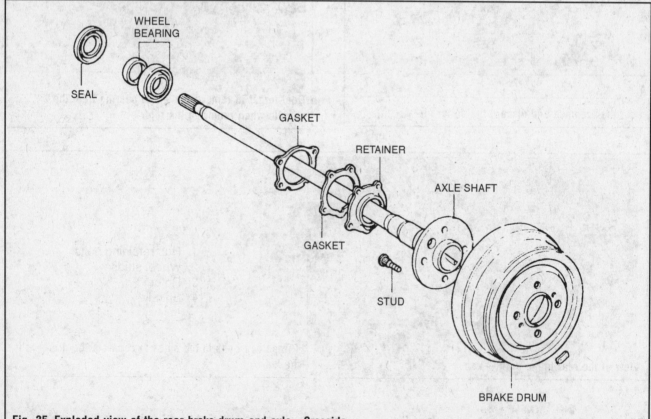

Fig. 35 Exploded view of the rear brake drum and axle—Cressida

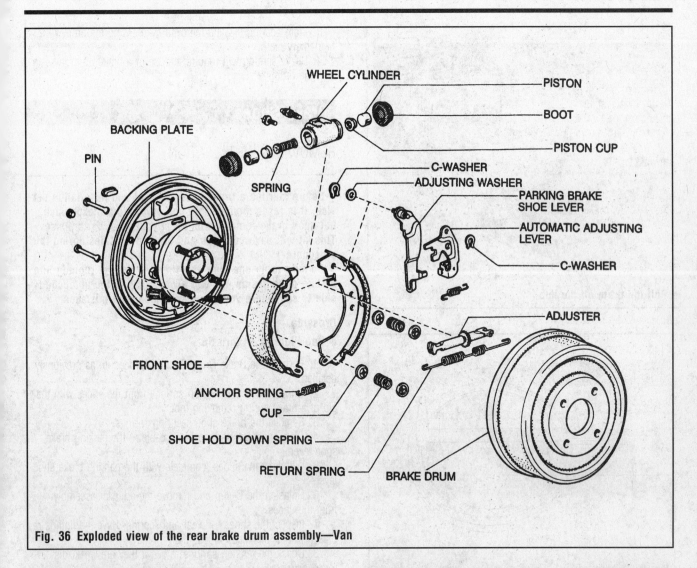

WHEEL CYLINDER
PISTON
BOOT
PISTON CUP
BACKING PLATE
PIN
C-WASHER
ADJUSTING WASHER
PARKING BRAKE SHOE LEVER
AUTOMATIC ADJUSTING LEVER
C-WASHER
SPRING
ADJUSTER
FRONT SHOE
ANCHOR SPRING
CUP
SHOE HOLD DOWN SPRING
RETURN SPRING
BRAKE DRUM

Fig. 36 Exploded view of the rear brake drum assembly—Van

View of the rear brake drum—Van

Thread two bolts in the holes to separate the drum from the hub

Pull the drum off the hub

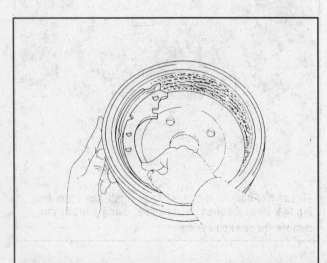

Fig. 37 Use a H-gauge caliper to measure the inside diameter of the brake drum

Fig. 38 Inspect the brake lining and drum contact, then if necessary, lathe the drum

3. Light scoring may be removed by dressing the drum with fine emery cloth.

4. Heavy scoring will require the use of a brake drum lathe to turn the drum.

Brake Shoes

REMOVAL & INSTALLATION

➡ **Before starting a brake shoe removal and installation service, it is recommended that you purchase a inexpensive but good brake removal tool kit at your local parts house. This kit will save you time and bruised knuckles during this procedure.**

Be sure to do one side at a time, in case of running into a state of confusion you can always look at the untouched side to see where you may have made your mistakes.

Cressida

▶ **See Figures 39 thru 55**

1. Perform the Brake Drum Removal procedure as previously detailed.

2. Unhook the shoe tension springs from the shoes with the aid of a brake spring removing tool.

3. Remove the brake shoe securing springs.

4. Disconnect the parking brake cable at the parking brake shoe lever.

5. Withdraw the shoes, complete with the parking brake shoe lever.

6. Unfasten the C-clip and remove the adjuster assembly from the shoes.

7. Inspect the shoes for wear and scoring. Have the linings replaced if their thickness is less than 1mm.

8. Check the tension springs to see if they are weak, distorted or rusted.

9. Inspect the teeth on the automatic adjuster wheel for chipping or other damage.

➡ **Grease the point of the shoe which slides against the backing plate. Do not get grease on the linings.**

10. Installation is performed in the following order:

   a. Attach the parking brake shoe lever and the automatic adjuster lever to the rear side of the shoe.

   b. Fasten the parking brake cable to the lever on the brake shoe. c. Install the automatic adjuster and fit the tension spring on the adjuster lever.

   d. Install the securing spring on the rear shoe and then install the securing spring on the front shoe.

➡ **The tension spring should be installed on the anchor, before performing Step d.**

   e. Hook one end of the tension spring over the rear shoe with the tool used during removal. Hook the other end over the front shoe.

✳✳ WARNING

Be sure that the wheel cylinder boots are not being pinched in the ends of the shoes.

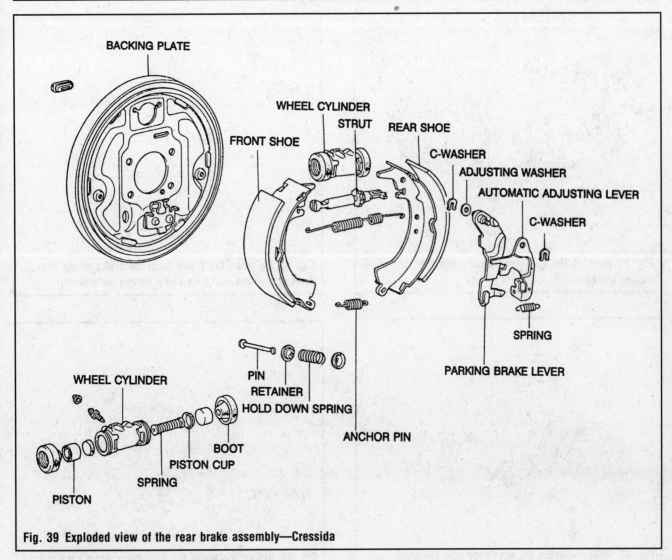

Fig. 39 Exploded view of the rear brake assembly—Cressida

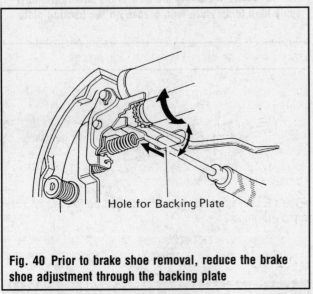

Fig. 40 Prior to brake shoe removal, reduce the brake shoe adjustment through the backing plate

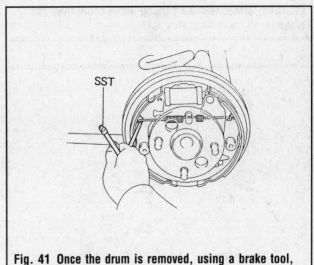

Fig. 41 Once the drum is removed, using a brake tool, remove the tension spring

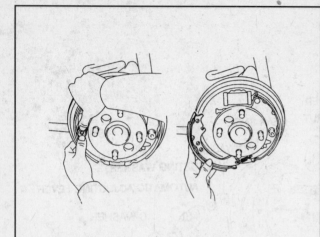

Fig. 42 Remove the hold-down spring and the front shoe anchor spring

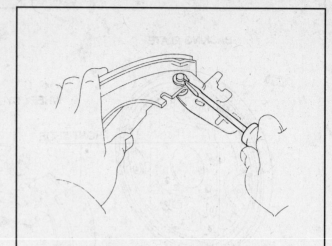

Fig. 45 Unfasten the C-clip from the brake shoes and discard, always use a new clip during installation

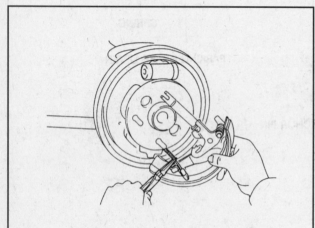

Fig. 43 After removing the rear shoe with the strut attached, disconnect the parking brake cable from the lever

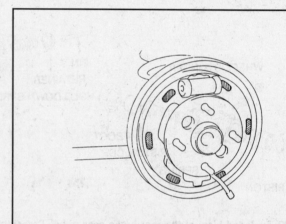

Fig. 46 Before installing the new brake shoe assembly, apply high tempreture type grease on the backing plate . . .

Fig. 44 Remove the strut from the rear brake shoe

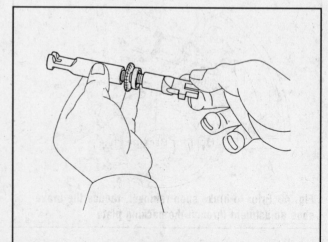

Fig. 47 . . . apply some of the grease to the adjuster also

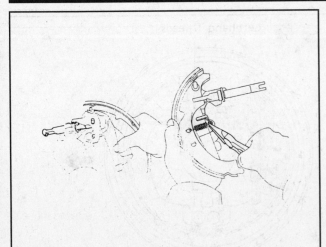

Fig. 48 Install the strut and adjuster lever spring on the rear shoe . . .

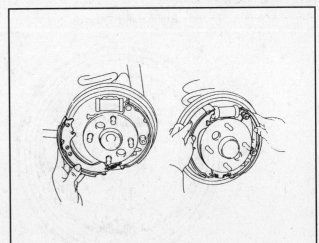

Fig. 51 When installing the shoes, place the anchor spring between the front and rear shoes

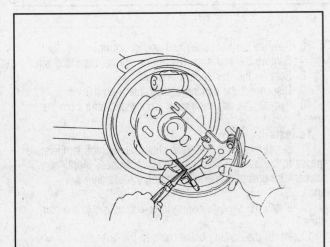

Fig. 49 . . . then connect the parking brake cable to the lever

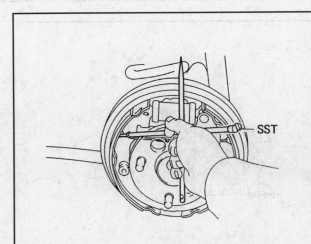

Fig. 52 Install the shoe hold-down spring and pin, then use a brake tool to install the tension spring

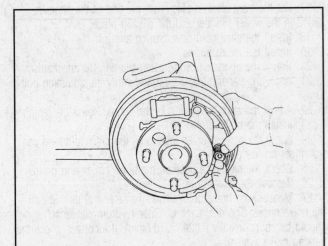

Fig. 50 Install the pin and the shoe hold-down spring on the backing plate

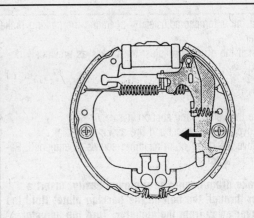

Fig. 53 Check the operation of the automatic adjuster mechanism, be sure the bolt turns while pulling the lever up

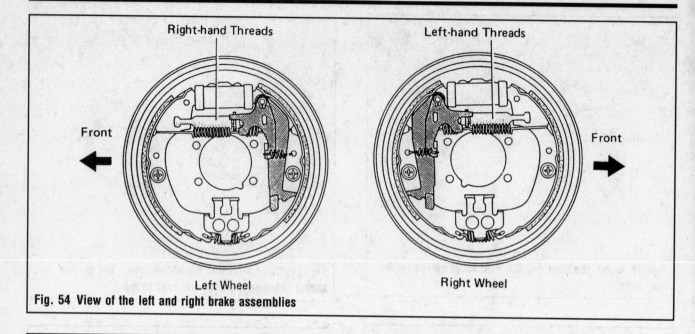

Fig. 54 View of the left and right brake assemblies

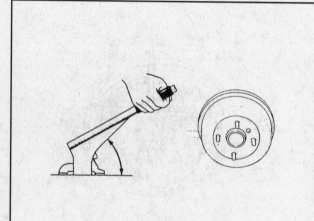

Fig. 55 After brake shoe installation, pull the parking brake lever all the way up several times for adjustment

f. Test the automatic adjuster by operating the parking brake shoe lever.

g. Install the drum and adjust the brakes as previously detailed.

Van

1. Raise the vehicle and support it safely.
2. Remove the rear wheel and tire assembly.
3. Remove the brake drum retaining screws, if equipped. Remove the brake drum.

➡**If the brake drum cannot be removed easily, insert a screwdriver through the hole in the backing plate. Hold the adjuster lever away from the adjuster. Turn the adjuster with another tool to increase the clearance between the drum and shoe.**

4. Remove the front shoe return spring.
5. Remove the hold-down spring, cups and pin.

6. Remove the front shoe and anchor spring.
7. Remove the rear shoe hold-down spring, cups and pin.
8. Remove the rear shoe with strut.
9. Disconnect the parking brake cable from the lever.
10. Remove the adjusting lever, spring and strut from the rear shoe.

To install:

11. Before installing the brake shoes, apply high temperature grease to the backing plate shoe contact surfaces. Apply high temperature grease to the adjuster bolt threads and ends.
12. Install the strut, adjusting lever and spring to the rear shoe.
13. Install the parking brake cable to the lever.
14. Set the rear shoe in place with the end of the shoe inserted in the wheel cylinder and the other end in the anchor plate.
15. Install the pin and shoe hold-down springs.
16. Install the anchor spring between the front rear shoes.
17. Set the front shoe in place with the end of the shoe inserted in the wheel cylinder and the strut in place.
18. Install the shoe hold-down spring and pin.
19. Install the return spring.
20. Check the operation of the automatic adjuster mechanism.
21. Apply the parking brake lever and verify the adjusting bolt turns.
22. Adjust the strut to where it is the shortest possible length.
23. Install the brake drum.
24. Apply the parking brake lever until the clicking sound can no longer be heard.
25. Check the clearance between the brake shoes and drum.
26. Remove the brake drum.
27. Measure the brake drum inside diameter and diameter of the brake shoes. The difference is "Shoe-to-drum clearance" and should be approximately 0.024 in. (0.6mm). If incorrect, check the parking brake system.
28. Install the brake drum.
29. Install the rear wheel and tire assembly.
30. Road test the vehicle for proper operation.

View of the rear brake shoe assembly—Van

Be careful not to drop the spring and washer

To remove the brake shoe assemblies, start by removing the return spring

Pull the pin out from behind the backing plate

Using a brake tool, remove the hold-down spring

Remove the front brake shoe and anchor spring

Using the brake tool again, remove the rear brake shoe hold-down spring

. . . then remove the star adjuster

When removing the rear shoe assembly . . .

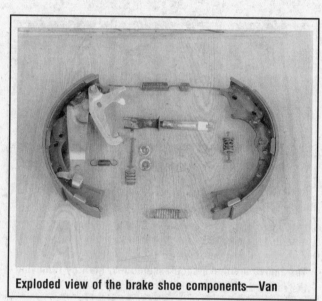

Exploded view of the brake shoe components—Van

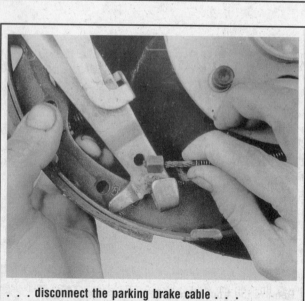

. . . disconnect the parking brake cable . . .

Wheel Cylinder

REMOVAL & INSTALLATION

▶ **See Figure 56**

1. Plug the master cylinder inlet to prevent hydraulic fluid from leaking.
2. Remove the brake drums and shoes as detailed in the appropriate preceding section.
3. Working from behind the backing plate, disconnect the hydraulic line from the wheel cylinder.
4. Unfasten the screws retaining the wheel cylinder and withdraw the cylinder.
5. Installation is performed in the reverse order of removal. Bleed the brake system after installation. However, once the hydraulic line has been disconnected from the wheel cylinder, the union seat must be replaced.

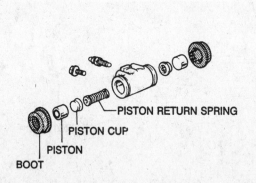

Fig. 56 Exploded view of the wheel cylinder assembly on drum brake models

6. To replace the seat, proceed in the following manner:

a. Use a screw extractor with a diameter of 2.5mm and having reverse threads, to remove the union seat from the wheel cylinder.

b. Drive in the new union seat with an 8mm bar, used as a drift.

c. Remember to bleed the brake system after completing wheel cylinder, brake shoe and drum installation.

REAR DISC BRAKES

✳✳ CAUTION

Some brake pads contain asbestos, which has been determined to be a cancer causing agent. Never clean the brake surfaces with compressed air! Avoid inhaling any dust from any brake surface! When cleaning brake surfaces, use a commercially available brake cleaning fluid.

Disc Brake Pads

INSPECTION

1. Loosen the rear wheel lugs slightly, then raise the rear of the car and safely support it on jackstands.

2. Remove the rear wheel and tire assemblies.

3. The cut out in the top of the rear brake caliper allows visual inspection of the disc brake pad. If the lining is worn to within 3mm (⅛ in.) of the metal disc shoe (check local inspection requirements) replace all four pads (both sides). Minimum pad thickness is 1.0mm (0.039 in.).

4. While you are inspecting the brake pads, visually inspect the caliper for hydraulic fluid leaks. If a leak is visible the caliper will have to be rebuilt or replaced.

➡️**If a squealing noise occurs from the rear brakes while driving, check the pad wear indicator. If there are traces of**

OVERHAUL

It is not necessary to remove the wheel cylinder from the backing plate if it is only to be inspected or rebuilt.

1. Remove the brake drum and shoes. Remove the wheel cylinder only if it is going to be replaced.

2. Remove the rubber boots from either end of the wheel cylinder.

3. Withdraw the piston and cup assemblies.

4. Take the compression spring out of the wheel cylinder body.

5. Remove the bleeder plug (and ball), if necessary.

6. Check all components for wear or damage. Inspect the bore for signs of wear, scoring, and/or scuffing. If in doubt, replace or hone the wheel cylinder (with a special hone). The limit for honing a cylinder is 0.127mm oversize. Wash all the residue from the cylinder bore with clean brake fluid and blow dry.

Assembly is performed in the following order:

1. Soak all components in clean brake fluid, or coat them with the rubber grease supplied in the wheel cylinder rebuilding kit.

2. Install the spring, cups (recesses toward the center), and pistons in the cylinder body, in that order.

3. Insert the boots over the ends of the cylinder.

4. Install the bleeder plug (and ball), if removed.

5. Assemble the brake shoes and install the drum.

6. Bleed the brake system after installation.

the indicator contacting the rotor disc, the pads should be replaced.

REMOVAL & INSTALLATION

Cressida

1983–84 MODELS
▸ **See Figure 57**

1. Raise and safely support the rear of the vehicle.

2. Remove the rear wheel assembly and temporarily fasten the rotor disc with the hub nuts.

➡️**Be sure to do one side at a time, in case of running into a state of confusion you can always look at the untouched side to see where you may have made your mistakes.**

3. Remove the pad protector.

4. Remove the No. 2 anti-rattle spring.

5. Hold the No. 1 anti-rattle spring and remove the hole pin of the lower side.

6. Remove the No. 1 anti-rattle spring and the other hole pin.

7. Remove the brake pads and the anti-squeal shims.

To install:

8. Draw out a small amount of brake fluid from the brake reservoir. Press in the piston with a hammer handle or an equivalent tool.

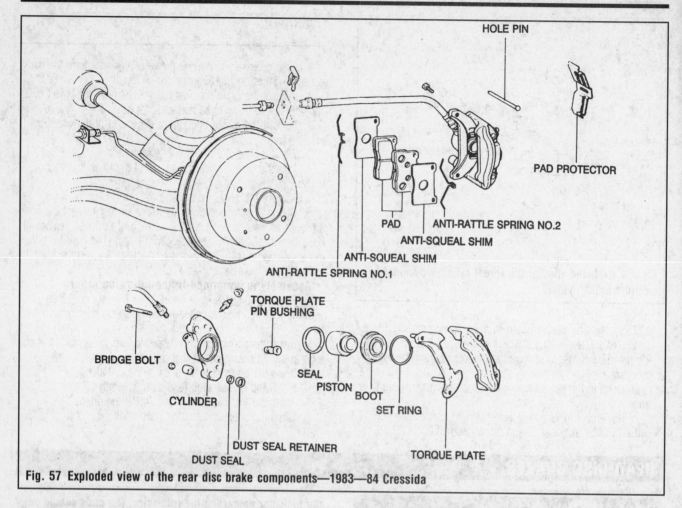

Fig. 57 Exploded view of the rear disc brake components—1983—84 Cressida

➡**Always change the pad on one wheel at a time as there is a possibility of the opposite piston flying out.**

9. Assemble the anti-squeal shims. Install the brake pads with the anti-squeal shims. Do not allow oil or grease to get in the rubbing face.

➡**It recommended that a suitable anti-squeal compound (available at your local parts house) be applied to both sides of the inner anti-squeal shim.**

10. Install the hole pin to the upper side. Install the No. 1 anti-rattle spring and hold its lower end.
11. Install the other hole pin.
12. Install the No. 2 anti-rattle spring.
13. Install the pad protector.
14. Install the rear wheel assemblies and lower the vehicle. Check the fluid level in the master cylinder and add as necessary. Be sure to pump the brake pedal a few times before road testing the vehicle.

1985–90 MODELS
◆ **See Figure 58**

1. Raise and safely support the rear of the vehicle.
2. Remove the rear wheel assembly and temporarily fasten the rotor disc with the hub nuts.
3. Remove the sliding main pin from the torque plate (on some models it may be necessary to remove the sliding sub pin

as well. Lift up the brake cylinder and suspend it so the brake hose is not stretched. Do not disconnect the brake hose.

➡**Be sure to do one side at a time, in case of running into a state of confusion you can always look at the untouched side to see were you may have made your mistakes.**

4. Remove the following parts:
   a. The 2 brake pads.
   b. The four anti-squeal shims.
   c. The 1 pad wear indicator plates.
   d. The 2 pad support plates.

To install:

5. Install the pad support plates.
6. Install a pad wear indicator plate to the pad. Install the 2 anti-squeal shims to each pad.

➡**It recommended that a suitable anti-squeal compound (available at your local parts house) be applied to both sides of the inner anti-squeal shim.**

7. Install the 2 pads so that the wear indicator plate is facing upward. Do not allow oil or grease to get in the rubbing face.
8. Draw out a small amount of brake fluid from the brake reservoir. Press in the piston with a hammer handle or an equivalent tool.

➡**Always change the pad on one wheel at a time as there is a possibility of the opposite piston flying out.**

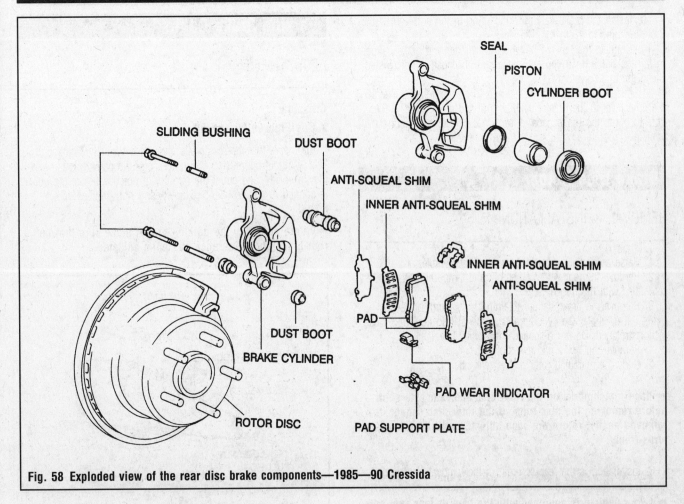

Fig. 58 Exploded view of the rear disc brake components—1985—90 Cressida

9. Insert the brake cylinder carefully so the boot is not wedged. Install and tighten the sliding main pin. Tighten the pin to 18 ft. lbs. (25 Nm).

➡ **When installing the sliding main pin, be careful that the plug installed in the torque plate does not come loose.**

10. Install the rear wheel assemblies and lower the vehicle. Check the fluid level in the master cylinder and add as necessary. Be sure to pump the brake pedal a few times before road testing the vehicle.

Brake Caliper

REMOVAL & INSTALLATION

1. Raise and safely support the rear of the vehicle.
2. Remove the rear wheel assembly and temporarily fasten the rotor disc with the hub nuts.
3. Using a suitable brake line wrench disconnect the flexible hose from the brake tube and the brake caliper. Remove the clip from the flexible hose.
4. Remove the 2 caliper retaining bolts from the torque plate. Lift up and remove the brake caliper. Remove the brake pad assembly.

5. Installation is the reverse order of the removal procedure. Be sure to bleed the brake system after the job is complete.

OVERHAUL

1. Place the caliper in a suitable holding fixture. Put a piece of cloth or an equivalent between the piston and cylinder.
2. Apply compressed air through the bleeder hole in the caliper to remove the piston and cylinder boot from the piston.

➡ **Do not place your fingers in front of the piston when using the compressed air. It is best to have the piston forced out of the caliper into a hard plastic bucket in order to avoid injury.**

3. Remove the piston seal from the brake caliper.
4. Apply lithium soap based glycol grease to all the moving parts in the caliper.
5. Install the piston seal in the caliper.
6. Install the piston and the cylinder boot in the cylinder.
7. Install the pin boot into the sliding main pin side. Using a plastic bar, install the cylinder sliding bushing into the sliding sub pin side.
8. Install the brake pad assemblies.

9. Install the brake caliper to the rotor. Install and tighten the 2 sliding pins to 18 ft. lbs. (25 Nm).

10. Connect the flexible hose to the cylinder and brake caliper. Install the brake hose clip and make sure the hose is not twisted. Bleed the brake system.

11. Install the wheel assembles and lower the vehicle. Check the fluid level in the master cylinder and add as necessary. Be sure to pump the brake pedal a few times before road testing the vehicle.

Brake Disc Rotor

REMOVAL & INSTALLATION

1. Raise and safely support the rear of the vehicle.
2. Remove the rear wheel assembly and temporarily fasten the rotor disc with the hub nuts.
3. Remove the brake caliper retaining bolts from the torque plate. Lift up the brake cylinder and suspend it so the brake hose is not stretched. Do not disconnect the brake hose.
4. Remove the brake pad assembly.
5. Slide the rear disc rotor off the rear axle.

➡**Place matchmarks on the rotor disc and rear axle shaft before removing the disc rotor. If the rotor disc cannot be removed easily, return the shoe adjuster until the wheel turns freely.**

6. Installation is the reverse order of the removal procedure.

➡**If your vehicle is equipped with the type of rear axle set-up that won't allow the disc rotor to come free without re-moving the rear wheel bearing, you will be in need for more extensive coverage of the brake disc rotor removal and installation. Refer to the Rear Drive Axle section in Chapter 7 of this manual.**

INSPECTION

Examine the disc. If it is worn, warped or scored, it must be replaced. Check the thickness of the disc against the specifications given in the Disc and Pad Specifications chart. If it is below specifications, replace it. Use a micrometer to measure the thickness.

The disc run-out should be measured before the disc is removed and again, after the disc is installed. Use a dial indicator mounted on a stand to determine run-out. If run-out exceeds 0.15mm (all models), replace the disc.

➡**Be sure that the wheel bearing nut is properly tightened. If it is not, an inaccurate run-out reading may be obtained. If different run-out readings are obtained with the same disc, between removal and installation, this is probably the cause.**

Parking Brake Cable

ADJUSTMENT

Cressida

◆ **See Figures 59 and 60**

1. Ensure that the rear brake shoes are correctly adjusted.
2. Without depressing the button, pull the parking brake handle up slowly, and count the number of notches before the brake is applied. It should take 5–8 notches. If not, proceed with Step 3.

➡**Before adjusting the parking brake, make sure that the rear brake shoe clearance has been adjusted.**

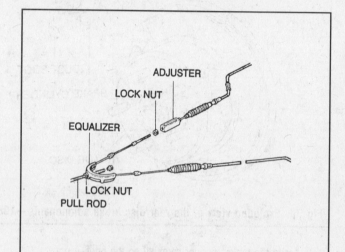

Fig. 59 Exploded view of the parking brake cable on rear drum models—Cressida

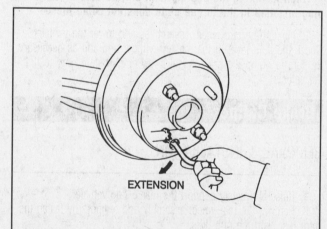

Fig. 60 On rear disc models, remove the adjuster hole cover. Turn the adjuster to expand the brake shoes until the rotor locks—Cressida

3. The following adjustment is for the 1983–84 Cressida with the rear drum brake set-up:

    a. Raise and safely support the vehicle. Working from underneath of the car, loosen the locknut on the parking brake equalizer.

    b. Screw the adjusting nut in, just enough so that the parking brake cables have no slack.

    c. Hold the adjusting nut in this position while tightening the locknut.

    d. Check the rotation of the rear wheels, with the parking brake off, to be sure that the brake shoes aren't dragging.

4. The following adjustment is for the Cressida with the rear disc brake set-up:

    a. Raise and safely support the vehicle. Remove the rear wheel assembly.

    b. Temporarily install the hub nuts.

    c. Remove the parking brake adjustment hole plug.

    d. Using a suitable brake adjusting tool, turn the brake adjuster so as to expand the brake shoes until the disc rotor locks.

    e. Return the adjuster 8 notches. Install the hole plug.

5. Install the rear wheel assembly and lower the vehicle.

Van

♦ **See Figure 61**

1. Raise and safely support the rear of the vehicle.
2. Remove the shift knob and the console box.
3. At the parking brake handle, loosen the cable locknut. Pull the hand brake upward about 7–9 (6–8 on the YR29 series) clicks.
4. Turn the adjust nut until the rear wheels can no longer be turned, then, tighten the locknut.
5. Install the console and the shift knob.

Parking Brake Shoes

REMOVAL & INSTALLATION

♦ **See Figures 62 thru 68**

➡**Parking brake shoes are only used on Cressida models.**

1. Raise and safely support the rear of the vehicle.
2. Remove the rear wheel assembly and temporarily fasten the rotor disc with the hub nuts.
3. Remove the brake caliper retaining bolts from the torque plate. Lift up the brake cylinder and suspend it so the brake hose is not stretched. Do not disconnect the brake hose.
4. Remove the brake pad assembly.
5. Slide the rear disc rotor off the rear axle.

➡**Place a matchmarks on the rotor disc and rear axle shaft before removing the disc rotor. If the rotor disc cannot be removed easily, return the shoe adjuster until the wheel turns freely.**

6. Using the proper brake tool, remove the shoe return springs.
7. Remove the shoe strut with springs.

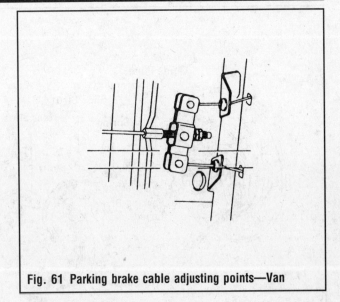

Fig. 61 Parking brake cable adjusting points—Van

8. Slide out the front shoe and remove the shoe adjuster.
9. Disconnect the tension spring and remove the front shoe.
10. Slide out the rear shoe.
11. Disconnect the tension spring and remove the rear shoe.
12. Disconnect the parking brake cable from the parking brake shoe lever.
13. Remove the brake shoe hold-down spring cups, springs and pins.

➡**Using a feeler gauge, measure the clearance between the parking brake shoe and lever. Standard clearance is less than 0.35mm (0.0138 in.). If the clearance is not within specification, replace the shim with one of the correct size 0.3mm or 0.6mm (0.012 in., 0.024 in.). Remove the parking brake lever, and install the correct size shim. Install the parking brake lever with a new C-washer. Re-measure the clearance.**

To install:

14. Apply a high temperature grease to the sliding surfaces of the shoe. Also apply the grease to the threads on the adjuster.
15. Install the shoe hold-down springs, cups and pins. Connect the parking brake cable to the parking brake lever of the rear shoe.
16. Slide in the rear shoe between the shoe hold-down spring cup and backing late. Do not allow oil or grease to get on the rubbing surface.
17. Install the tension spring to the rear shoe.
18. Install the front shoe to the tension spring. Install the adjuster between the front and rear shoes.
19. Slide in the front shoe between the shoe hold-down spring cup and backing plate.
20. Install the strut with the spring forward.
21. Using a suitable brake tool, install the front return spring and then install the rear return spring.
22. Align the matchmarks and install the rotor disc.
23. Adjust the parking brake.
24. Install the rear caliper assembly and tighten the caliper retaining bolts to 34 ft. lbs. (47 Nm).
25. Install the rear wheel assembly and lower the vehicle.

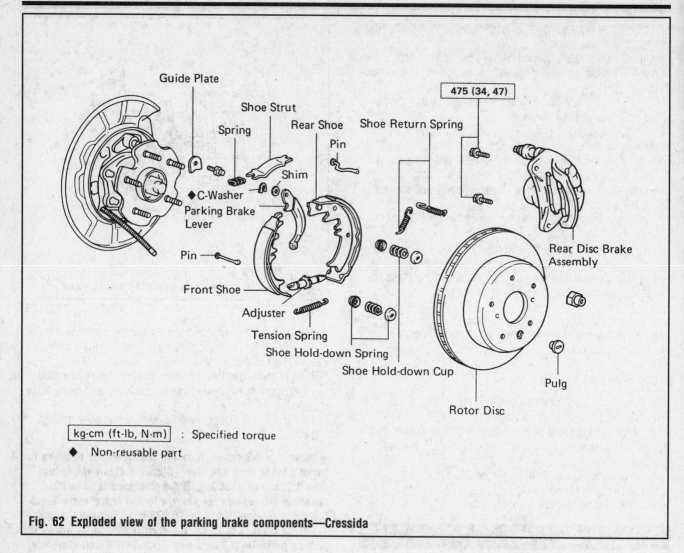

Fig. 62 Exploded view of the parking brake components—Cressida

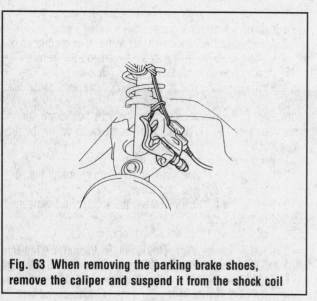

Fig. 63 When removing the parking brake shoes, remove the caliper and suspend it from the shock coil

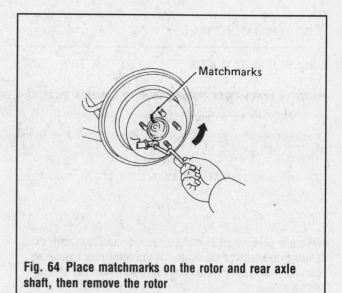

Fig. 64 Place matchmarks on the rotor and rear axle shaft, then remove the rotor

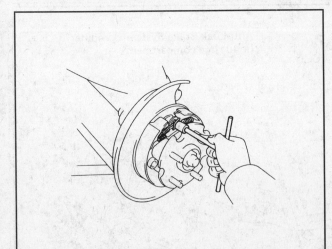

Fig. 65 Using a brake tool, remove the shoe return springs on the parking brake

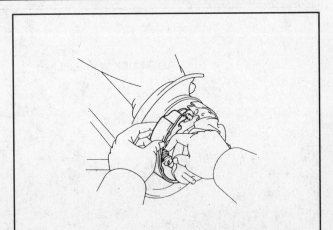

Fig. 67 Slide the front shoe out and remove the adjuster, then disconnect the tension spring and remove the front shoe

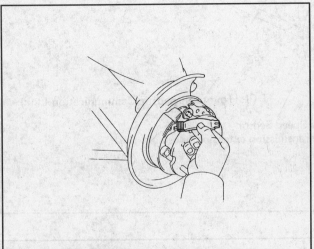

Fig. 66 When removing the parking brake strut, make sure the spring is attached

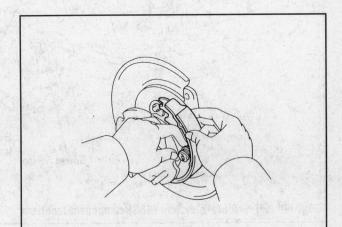

Fig. 68 When removing the rear shoe, separate the tension spring and disconnect the parking brake cable from the lever

ANTI-LOCK BRAKE SYSTEM (ABS)

Description and Operation

▶ See Figures 69, 70 and 71

The ABS system is only offered on the 1989–90 Cressida models.

The ABS is a brake system which controls the wheel cylinder hydraulic pressure of all 4 wheels during sudden braking and braking on slippery road surfaces, preventing the wheels from locking. The ABS system enables steering around an obstacle with a greater degree of certainly even when panic braking. It also enables stopping in a panic brake while keeping the effect upon the stability and steerability to a minimum, even on curves.

The functions of the ABS is to help maintain directional stability and vehicle steerability on most road conditions. However the system cannot prevent the vehicle from skidding if the cornering speed limit is exceeded.

In case a malfunction occurs, a diagnosis function and fail safe system have been adopted for the ABS to increase serviceability.

➡**Due to the severe degree of technology incorporated into this Anti-Lock Brake System On Board Diagnosis System. It is highly recommended that any repairs or problems that occur to the ABS system that your vehicle is equipped with, be handled by a factory trained and authorizes technician.**

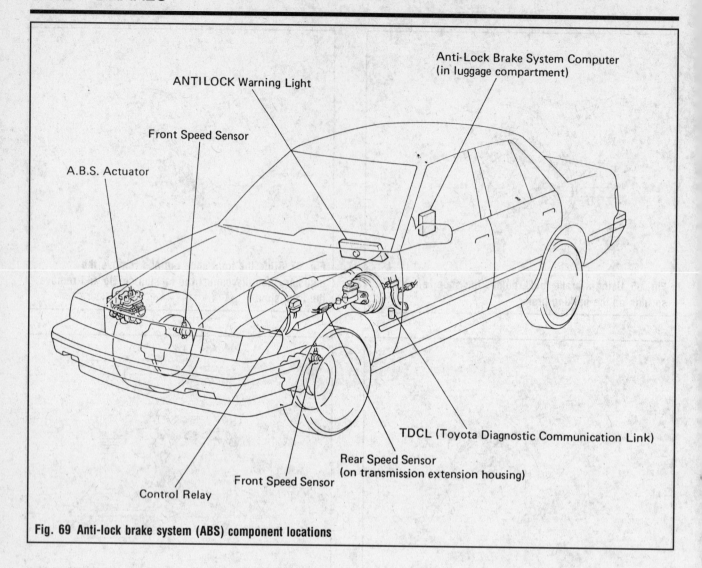

Fig. 69 Anti-lock brake system (ABS) component locations

Component	Function
Front Speed Sensor	Detects the wheel speed of each of the left and right front wheels.
Rear Speed Sensor	Detects the average wheel speed of the left and right rear wheels.
ANTILOCK Warning Light	Lights up to alert the driver when trouble has occured in the Anti-lock Brake System.
A.B.S. Actuator	Controls the brake fluid pressure to each disc brake cylinder through signals from the computer.
Anti-lock Brake System Computer	From the wheel speed signals from each sensor, it calculates acceleration, deceleration and slip values and sends signals to the actuator to control brake fluid pressure.

Fig. 70 Anti-lock brake system (ABS) component functions

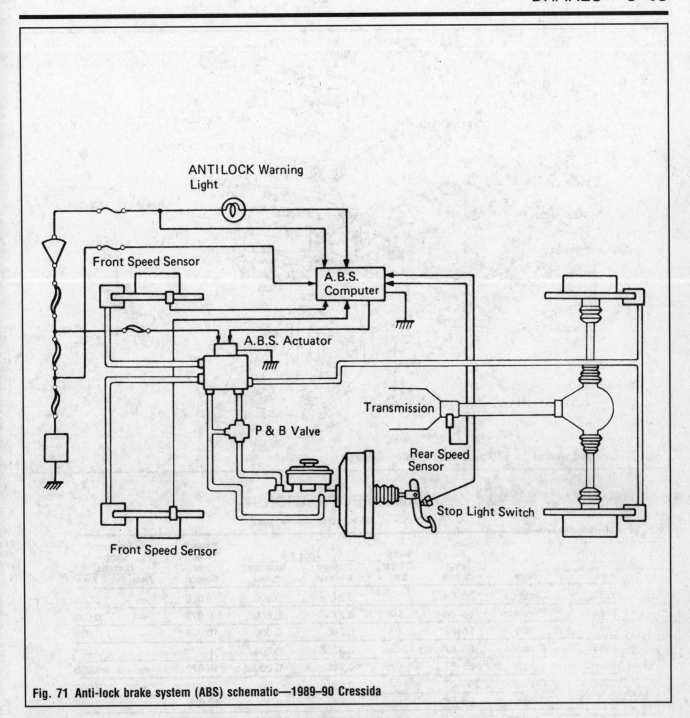

Fig. 71 Anti-lock brake system (ABS) schematic—1989–90 Cressida

Anti-Lock Brake Actuator

REMOVAL & INSTALLATION

▶ See Figure 72

1. Remove the brake fluid from the master cylinder with a syringe.
2. Remove the air cleaner.
3. Remove the plastic cover from the actuator.
4. Unplug the electrical connectors from the actuator.
5. Disconnect the hydraulic lines from the actuator. Plug the lines to prevent loss of fluid.
6. Remove the actuator bracket retaining bolts and remove the actuator along with the bracket.
7. Installation is the reverse of the removal procedure. Fill and bleed the system.
8. Check the system operation.

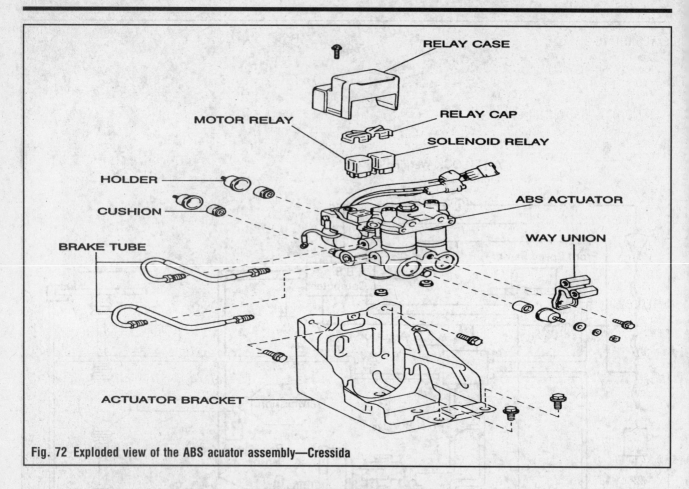

Fig. 72 Exploded view of the ABS acuator assembly—Cressida

BRAKE SPECIFICATIONS

All specifications in inches unless noted.

Years	Model	Lug Nut Torque (ft. lbs.)	Master Cylinder Bore	Brake Disc		Standard Brake Drum Diameter	Minimum Lining Thickness	
				Minimum Thickness	Maximum Runout		Front	Rear
1983	Cressida	66–86	①	0.87 ②	0.006	9.079	—	0.039
1984	Cressida	66–86	①	0.87 ②	0.006	9.079	—	0.039
	Van	65–87	①	0.748	0.006	10.079	—	0.039
1985	Cressida	65–87	①	0.87 ②	0.006	—	—	—
	Van	65–87	①	0.748	0.006	10.079	—	0.039
1986	Cressida	65–87	①	0.83 ③	0.006	9.079	—	0.039
	Van	65–87	①	0.748	0.006	10.079	—	0.039
1987	Cressida	76	①	0.87 ③	0.006	9.079	—	0.039
	Van	65–87	①	0.79 ④	0.006	10.079	—	0.039
1988	Cressida	76	①	0.87 ②	0.006	—	—	—
	Van	65–87	①	0.79 ④	0.006	10.079	—	0.039
1989	Cressida	76	①	0.87 ②	0.006	—	—	—
	Van	65–87	①	0.79 ④	0.006	10.079	—	0.039
1990	Cressida	76	①	0.87 ②	0.006	—	—	—

① Not specified by the manufacturer
② Rear disc—0.71
③ Rear disc—0.67
④ Front disc 4WD—0.98

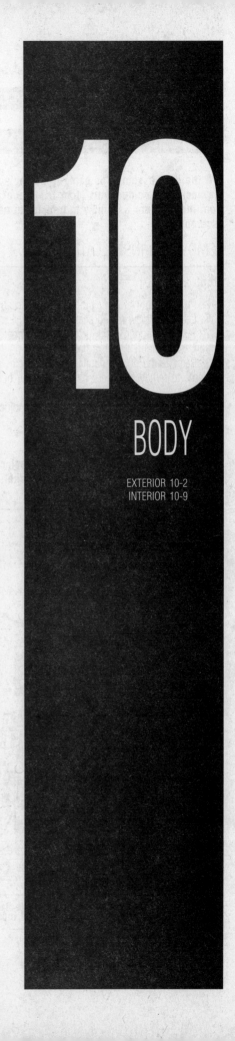

10
BODY

EXTERIOR

Door

➡ If the door assembly is going to be replaced remove all the necessary components (door trim panel, handle, etc.) from the old door assembly to transfer to new door assembly.

REMOVAL & INSTALLATION

Front

1. Pull the door stopper pin upward while pushing in on the claw. Leave the claw raised after removing the pin.
2. Place a wooden block or equivalent under the door for protection and support it with a floor jack.
3. Remove the door mounting bolts (special box wrenches are available to remove the door hinge mounting bolts) and remove the door.
4. Installation is the reverse of removal. Adjust the door as necessary.

Rear

➡ If the door assembly is going to be replaced, remove all the necessary components (door trim panel, handle, etc.)

from the old door assembly to transfer to the new door assembly.

1. Remove the door stopper pin.
2. Remove the door mounting bolts and remove the door.
3. Installation is the reverse of removal. Adjust the door as necessary.

ADJUSTMENT

▶ **See Figures 1 thru 6**

1. To adjust the door in the forward/rearward and vertical directions, loosen the body side hinge bolts and move the door to the desired position.
2. To adjust the door in the left/right (in/out) and vertical directions, loosen the door side hinge bolts and move the door to the desired position.
3. Adjust the door lock striker (check that the door fit and door lock linkages are adjusted correctly) as necessary by slightly loosening the striker mounting screws, and hitting the striker lightly with a hammer or equivalent. Tighten the striker mounting screws.

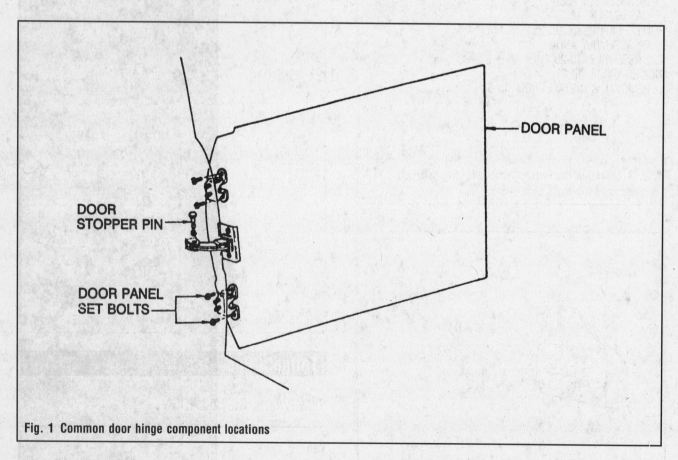

Fig. 1 Common door hinge component locations

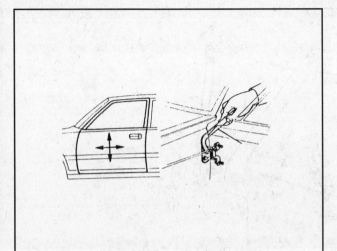

Fig. 2 Adjusting the forward/rearward and vertical directions of the front door—Cressida

Fig. 3 Adjusting the forward/rearward and vertical directions of the front door—Van

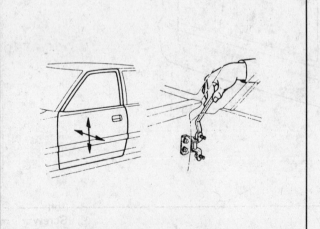

Fig. 4 Adjusting the left/right (in/out) and vertical directions of the front door—Cressida

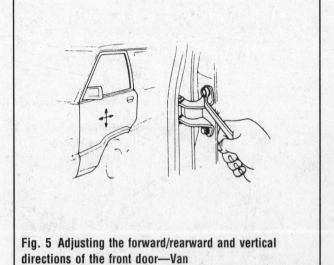

Fig. 5 Adjusting the forward/rearward and vertical directions of the front door—Van

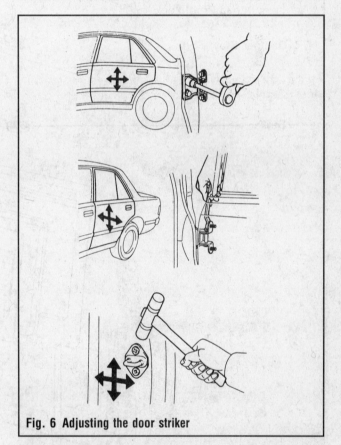

Fig. 6 Adjusting the door striker

Tailgate/Back Door

REMOVAL & INSTALLATION

Van

▶ **See Figure 7**

1. Place a wooden block or equivalent under the door for protection and support it with a floor jack.

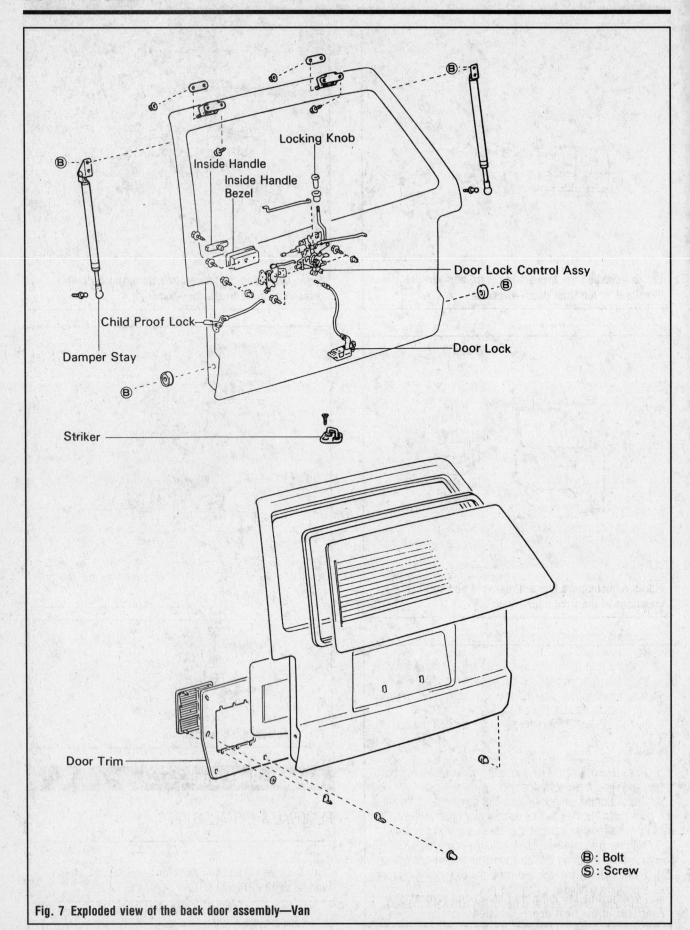

Locking Knob

Inside Handle

Inside Handle
Bezel

Door Lock Control Assy

Child Proof Lock

Door Lock

Damper Stay

Striker

Door Trim

Ⓑ: Bolt
Ⓢ: Screw

Fig. 7 Exploded view of the back door assembly—Van

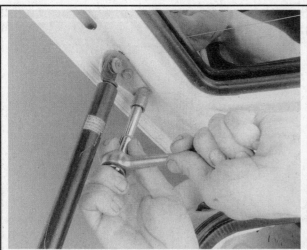

Before removing the tailgate (back door), the damper shocks must be removed

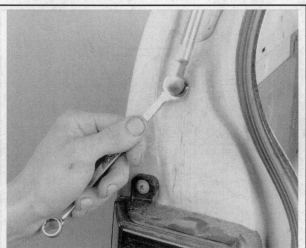

Have an assistant help hold the door when you remove the shocks on each side

2. Disconnect the air (shock absorber) damper stays from the rear door assembly.

3. With the help of an assistant, hold the door steady on the floor jack while removing the top back door hinge retaining nuts.

4. Carefully lower the jack and lower the door down to ground level and carefully remove it from the jack.

5. Installation is the reverse order of the removal procedure.

Cressida

1. Place a wooden block or equivalent under the door for protection and support it with a floor jack.

2. Disconnect the air (shock absorber) damper stays from the rear door assembly. Remove the damper stay upper end from the back door. Remove the damper stay lower end from the body.

3. With the help of an assistant, hold the door steady on the floor jack while removing the top back door hinge retaining nuts.

4. Carefully lower the jack and lower the door down to ground level and carefully remove it from the jack.

5. Installation is the reverse order of the removal procedure.

ADJUSTMENT

Van

▶ **See Figures 8 and 9**

1. To adjust the door in the forward/rearward and left/right directions, loosen the door hinge bolts and move the door to the desired position.

2. Adjust the door lock striker (check that the door fit and door lock linkages are adjusted correctly) as necessary by slightly loosening the striker mounting screws, and hitting the striker lightly with a hammer or equivalent. Tighten the striker mounting screws.

Cressida

1. To make the door forward and rearward and left/right directions:

Adjust the door by loosening the door side hinge bolts or body side hinge nuts.

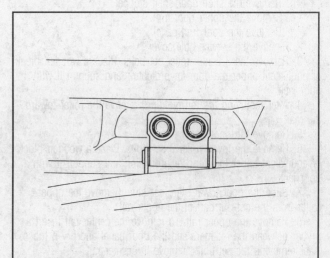

Fig. 8 To adjust the back door forward/rearward and left/right, loosen the hinge bolts—Van

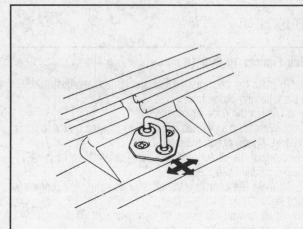

Fig. 9 Loosen the striker setscrews and tap the striker with a hammer to adjust

2. To make the door vertical adjustment use the following procedure:

Adjust the door by increasing or decreasing the number of shims. Be sure not to use more than 3 shims to adjust. When adjusting, apply body sealer between the shim and the body.

3. Check the door fit and door lock hinges are adjusted correctly. Adjust the door lock striker by loosening the screws.

Sliding Side Door

REMOVAL & INSTALLATION

➡**Due to the weight and size of this door, it is recommended that you use a friend to help you with removal and installation.**

1. Remove the door trim panel as follows:
   a. Unscrew the door locking button.
   b. Remove the slide door open stopper.
   c. Remove the upper door trim.
   d. Remove the door trim panel.
2. Remove the service hole cover.
3. Remove the 3 center roller set bolts. Place a wooden block or equivalent under the door for protection and support it with a floor jack.
4. After removing the rail molding, remove the roller toward the rear.
5. Remove the door panel.
6. Remove the lower roller 3 set bolts. Place a wooden block or equivalent under the door for protection and support it with a floor jack.
7. Slide the door toward the rear side. Remove the upper roller from the cut-out part of the upper rail.
8. Remove the upper rail. To remove the center rail insert a prybar between the retainers and the door panel and pry it loose. After removing the set bolts, remove the center rail.
9. Carefully lower the jack and lower the door down to ground level and carefully remove it from the jack.
10. Installation is the reverse order of the removal procedure.

ADJUSTMENT

◆ **See Figures 10 thru 16**

1. To make the door rear vertical and horizontal adjustment use the following procedure:
   a. Adjust the door striker.
   b. With the door closed, adjust it so that the center roller is 0.04 in. (1mm) above the race.
   c. Adjust the center roller bracket. The center roller is installed parallel with the rail.
2. To make the door fore and aft adjustment use the following procedure:
Adjust by moving the center roller fore and aft. The center roller is installed parallel with the rail.
3. To make the front vertical adjustment, door fore and aft adjustment use the following procedure.
4. Adjust the slide door lock remote control as follows:
   a. Adjust the remote control so there is about 0.20 in. (5mm) play in the inside handle.

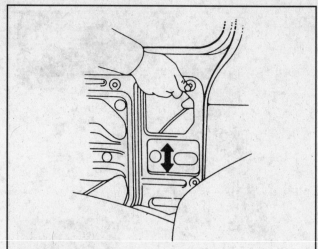

Fig. 10 When adjusting the sliding door on the Van, move the rollers vertically and horizontally

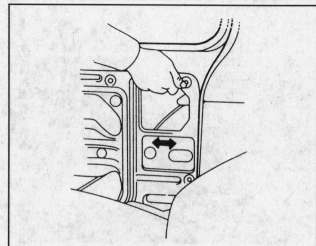

Fig. 11 Move the sliding door center roller fore and aft for adjustment

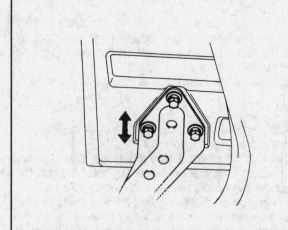

Fig. 12 Move the lower roller for the sliding doors front vertical adjustment

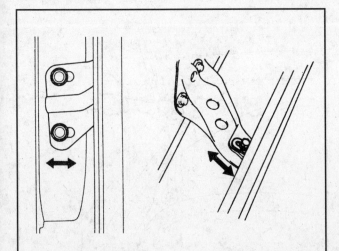

Fig. 13 Move the upper and lower rollers for the front horizontal adjustment . . .

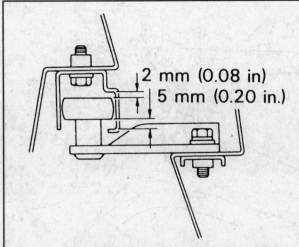

Fig. 14 . . . and make sure the clearance between the upper roller and rail is as indicated in the illustration throughout the entire stroke

2 mm (0.08 in)
5 mm (0.20 in.)

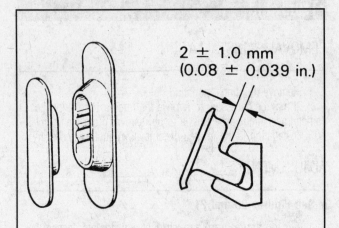

2 ± 1.0 mm
(0.08 ± 0.039 in.)

Fig. 15 Finger-tighten the male stopper on the body side. Close the door and determine its position, then adjust the lower male stopper

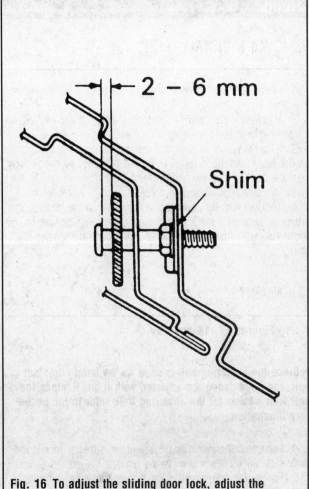

2 – 6 mm

Shim

Fig. 16 To adjust the sliding door lock, adjust the clearance between the striker and ratchet

b. Loosen the rear lock cable adjusting screw and lightly pull the cable until it is snug. Then return it about 0.04 in. (1mm) and tighten it down.

c. Loosen the remote control cable adjusting screw and lightly pull the cable until it is snug. Then return it about 0.04 in. (1mm).

➡Make the adjustment with the clamp for the cable and inner panel installed. Allow it to hang loose.

5. When operating the outside and inside handles, check that the front and rear locks release smoothly.

6. To make the door front horizontal adjustment use the following procedure:

Adjust the upper and lower the rollers. Be sure that the clearance between the upper roller and rail 0.08–0.20 in. (2–5mm) is good throughout the entire stroke.

7. Adjust the male stopper as follows:

a. Finger-tighten the male stopper on the body side, close the door and determine the door position.

b. Adjust the lower male stopper.

c. Check the door lock adjustment and adjust the clearance between the striker and the ratchet so as to obtain 0.08–0.24 in. (2–6mm).

Hood

REMOVAL & INSTALLATION

1. Protect the painted areas such as the fenders with a protective cover or equivalent.

2. Matchmark the hood hinges to the vehicle body. Loosen the hinge to vehicle body retaining bolts.

3. With the aid of an assistant remove the retaining bolts and lift the hood (with hood hinge assemblies attached to hood) away from the car. Remove the hood hinges (matchmark hinges to the hood for correct installation) if necessary.

4. Installation is the reverse of removal. Align the hood to the proper position. If a hinge is loosened or removed be sure to apply a suitable rust inhibitor under and around hinge after repairs.

ALIGNMENT

▶ **See Figures 17, 18 and 19**

➡**Since the centering bolt is used as the hood hinge set bolt, the hood cannot be adjusted with it on. Replace the bolt with washer for the centering bolt; refer to the necessary illustration.**

1. For forward/rearward and left/right adjustments, loosen the body side hinge bolts and move the hood to the desired position.

2. For vertical adjustment of the hoods front edge, turn the cushion.

3. For vertical adjustment of the rear end of the hood, increase or decrease the number of washers or shims.

4. Adjust the hood lock if necessary by loosening the bolts.

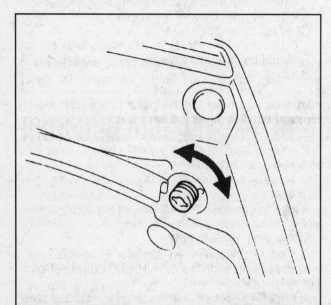

Fig. 17 When adjusting the hood height, turn the rubber adjuster in or out

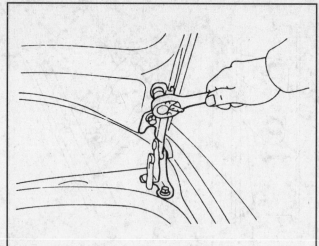

Fig. 18 Loosen the hood upper hinge to move the hood forward or rearward

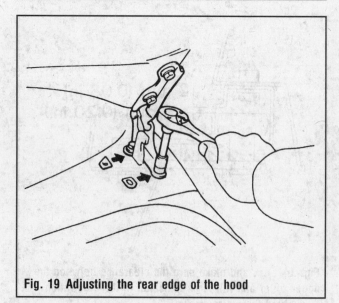

Fig. 19 Adjusting the rear edge of the hood

Trunk Lid

REMOVAL & INSTALLATION

1. Remove the hinge mounting bolts.

2. It may be necessary to remove the torsion bar if luggage compartment hinge assembly is to be removed from the vehicle.

3. Installation is the reverse of removal. Adjust as necessary.

ADJUSTMENT

▶ **See Figures 20 and 21**

1. For forward/rearward and left/right adjustments, loosen the bolts and move the luggage compartment lid the desired position.

2. For vertical adjustment of the front end of the lid, increase or decrease the number of washers (shims) between the hinge and compartment lid.

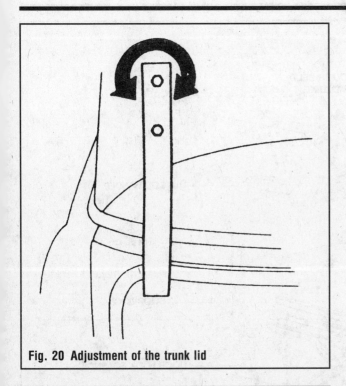

Fig. 20 Adjustment of the trunk lid

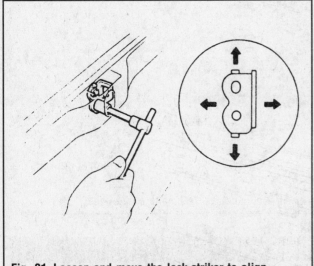

Fig. 21 Loosen and move the lock striker to align

3. To adjust the lock striker, loosen the mounting bolts and move the lock striker assembly in the correct position.

Outside Mirror

REMOVAL & INSTALLATION

♦ **See Figure 22**

1. Open the door and pry off the mirror cover which covers the 3 mirror retaining screws.
2. Roll down the window and hold onto the mirror assembly.
3. Remove the mirror retaining screws and remove the mirror from the door. If equipped with a power mirror, remove the electrical connector from the mirror.

➡ **On some models equipped with power mirrors, it may be necessary to remove the door panel in order to gain access to the electrical connector to the power mirror.**

4. Installation is the reverse order of the removal procedure.

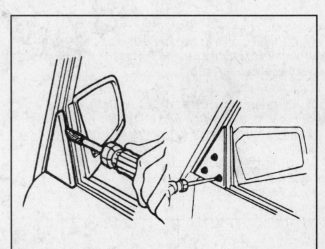

Fig. 22 When removing the outside mirror, carefully pry off the cover trim, then unscrew the mirror from the door

INTERIOR

Front Door

DISASSEMBLY AND ASSEMBLY

Cressida

1983–84 MODELS
♦ **See Figure 23**

1. Disconnect the negative battery cable. Remove the inside door handle bezel.

2. Remove the armrest and the courtesy light on the door.
3. Pry loose the outside mirror cover.
4. Insert a suitable prybar between the door panel retainers and the door panel and pry it loose. Unplug the 3 electrical connectors.
5. Remove the speaker assembly.
6. Disconnect the power mirror connector. Remove the 3 mirror set screws. Remove the wire clamp bolt and the clamp. Remove the mirror.
7. Pry loose the belt molding from the edge of the door panel and remove the molding.
8. Remove the inside door handle. Remove the service hole cover.

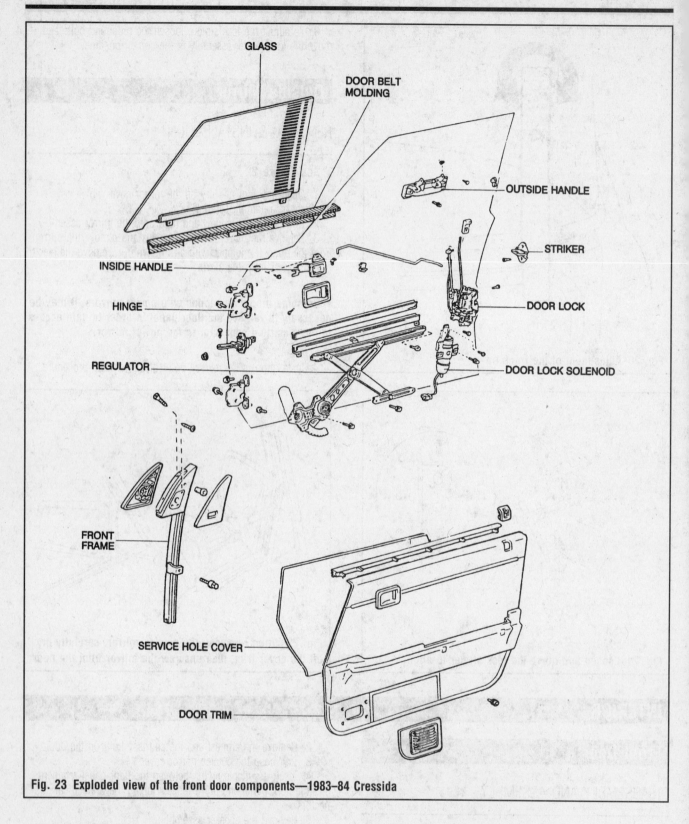

GLASS

DOOR BELT MOLDING

OUTSIDE HANDLE

STRIKER

INSIDE HANDLE

HINGE

DOOR LOCK

REGULATOR

DOOR LOCK SOLENOID

FRONT FRAME

SERVICE HOLE COVER

DOOR TRIM

Fig. 23 Exploded view of the front door components—1983–84 Cressida

9. Remove the 2 door glass channel mounting bolts and remove the door glass by pulling it upward.

10. Remove the door glass regulator mounting bolts. Remove the equalizer arm bracket mounting bolts. Remove the power window motor mounting bolts. Remove the door glass regulator through the service hole.

11. Remove the 2 front channel retaining screws under the weatherstripping. Remove the retaining bolt and screw and remove the front channel.

12. Disconnect the following linkages:
   a. Door open control
   b. Door lock control
   c. Door lock cylinder
   d. Outside control

13. Remove the outside handle, the door lock cylinder and remove the door lock.

14. To replace the door glass;

   a. Remove the glass channel assembly from the glass with a suitable pry tool.

   b. Apply soapy water to the inside of the weatherstrip.

   c. Install the door glass channel onto the new door glass by tapping it with a plastic hammer.

To assemble:

15. Place the door lock into the door cavity. Install the inside lock knob and install the door lock.

16. Install the outside handle. Install the door lock cylinder.

17. Connect the following linkages:

   a. Door open control link
   b. Door lock control link
   c. Door lock cylinder link
   d. Outside control link

18. Disconnect the control link. Raise the door handle approximately 0.020–0.039 in. (0.5–1.0mm) from the rest position. Fit the pin into the hole by turning the adjuster.

19. Check that the door fit and door lock linkages are adjusted correctly. Adjust the door striker by loosening the striker mounting screws.

20. Place the front channel into the door cavity. Install the one retaining bolt and 2 screws. Attach the glass run into the channel.

21. Install the door glass regulator through the service hole. Tighten the mounting bolts. Temporarily tighten the equalizer arm bracket mounting bolts.

22. Place the door glass into the door cavity. Install the glass to regulator with the 2 mounting bolts.

23. Install the door glass belt molding clips to the molding strip and tap the molding strip onto the upper panel by hand.

24. Install the outside mirror wire clamp and clamp bolts. Install the 3 set bolts and install the power motor connector.

25. Install the speaker assembly.

26. Seal the service hole cover with adhesive. Insert the lower edge of the service hole cover into the panel slit. Seal the panel slit with cotton tape. Do not block the trim clip seating with the tape.

27. Connect the inside handle control link and install the inside handle.

28. Install the trim. Install the outside mirror cover.

29. Install the armrest.

30. Install the inside door handle bezel and the courtesy door light. Be sure to adjust the door.

1985–88 MODELS
▶ **See Figure 24**

1. Disconnect the negative battery cable. Remove the inside door handle bezel.

2. Remove the 3 armrest retaining screws and the armrest. Unplug the 3 electrical connectors.

3. Pry loose the retainer cover for the outside mirror retaining screws.

4. Remove the door panel retaining screws and using a suitable pry tool, pry loose the door panel clips and remove the door panel.

5. Remove the 2 inside door handle screws. Partly tear off the service hole cover and disconnect the handle link from the door lock.

6. Remove the service hole cover.

7. Remove the power mirror harness from the door cavity and then disconnect it. Remove the 3 mirror retaining screws and remove the mirror.

8. Remove the 2 lower door glass retaining nuts. Remove the glass from the door glass regulator and lower the glass on the door cavity bottom. Remove the door belt molding set screws and remove the molding. Remove the door glass stopper retaining bolts and stoppers. Pull the door glass straight up and out of the door cavity.

9. Remove the door weather stripping. Remove all the door glass belt molding.

10. Remove the door glass runner. Remove the door glass runner clip. Remove the door frame molding.

11. Remove the 2 door frame set screws. Remove the 3 front channel retaining bolts and the front channel.

12. Remove the rear door frame.

13. Unplug the power window motor connector. Remove the door glass regulator mounting bolts. Remove the equalizer arm bracket mounting bolts and the door glass regulator through the service hole.

14. Disconnect the following linkages:

   a. Door open control link
   b. Door lock control link
   c. Door lock cylinder link
   d. Outside control link

15. Unplug the key cylinder light connector. Disconnect the link from the key cylinder. Remove the key cylinder retainer and key cylinder.

16. Unplug the outside door handle switch connector and remove the outside door handle bolts along with the handle.

17. Remove the door locking knob. Disconnect the door lock solenoid and switch. Remove the door lock solenoid mounting bolts. Remove the door lock with the door lock solenoid through the service hole. Remove the door lock solenoid from the door lock.

18. To replace the door glass:

   a. Remove the glass channel assembly from the glass with a suitable pry tool.

   b. Apply soapy water to the inside of the weather strip.

   c. Install the door glass channel onto the new door glass by tapping it with a plastic hammer.

To assemble:

19. Install the door lock solenoid to the door lock. Tighten the 2 screws after adjusting the switch so that there is no gap when the door is unlocked. Install the door switch with the 2 screws.

20. Install the door lock with the 3 screws. Install the door lock solenoid mounting bolt. Install the door locking knob. Attach the door lock solenoid and key lock unlock switch connectors.

21. Install the door lock switch to the outside door handle. Install the mounting nuts. Connect the link to the outside door handle.

22. Install the door lock cylinder with retainer. Connect the link to the door lock cylinder. Attach the key cylinder lock connector. Check the door lock and unlock operations and correct as necessary.

23. Place the door glass regulator through the service hole. Tighten the regulator mounting bolts. Temporarily tighten the equalizer arm bracket mounts bolts. Attach the power window connector.

24. Install the rear door frame assembly.

25. Place the front door frame assembly in the door cavity and install the 2 retaining bolts and 2 retaining screws.

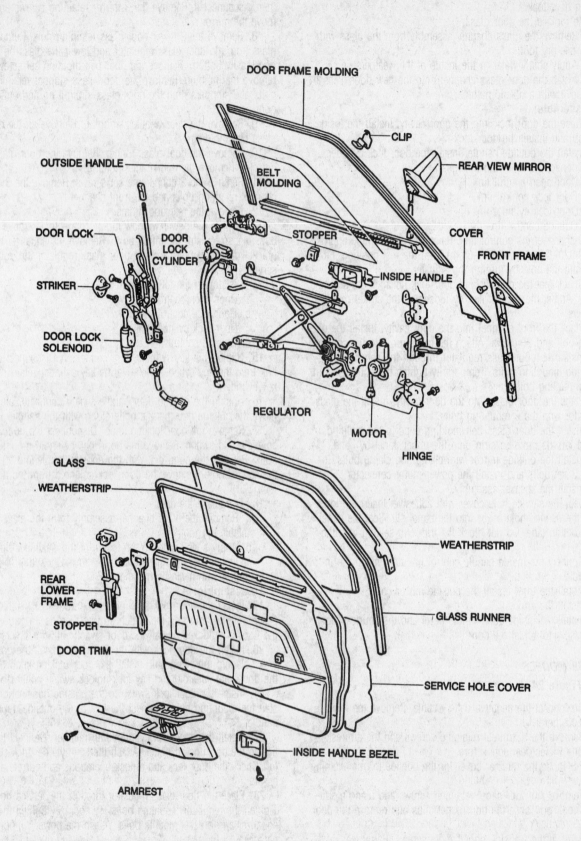

Fig. 24 Exploded view of the front door components—1985-88 Cressida

26. Install the door frame molding.
27. Install the door glass runner clips, runner and the weather stripping.
28. Place the door glass into the door cavity. Install the door belt molding. Install the door glass to the door glass regulator with the 2 mounting nuts.
29. With the door glass pushed against the rear frame side, install the 2 equalizer arm mounting bolts.
30. Install the door glass stoppers. Open the door glass 0.20 in. (5mm) from the fully closed position. With the stopper pushed against the lower side, tighten the mounting bolts. Check the door glass operation and alignment and correct as necessary.
31. Install the outside mirror and tighten the 3 set screws. Connect the power window motor harness and clamp it to the door panel.
32. Connect the inside handle linkage to the door lock. Install the service hole cover with adhesive. Insert the lower edge on the cover into the door panel slit. Seal the panel slit with cotton tape. Do not block the trim clip seating with the tape.
33. Install the inside door handle.
34. Install the door trim with clips to the door inside panel by tapping it lightly. Install the retaining screws. After pulling out the center portion to install the special clip to the door trim panel, press the head of the clip until it is flush with the surface of the door trim to lock it.
35. Install the door armrest and power window along with the door control switch set. Install the inside door handle bezel. Install the outside mirror retaining cover. Be sure to adjust the door as necessary.

1989–90 MODELS
▶ See Figure 25

1. Disconnect the negative battery cable. Remove the inside door handle bezel.
2. Remove the 3 armrest retaining screws and remove the armrest. Disconnect the 3 electrical wires.
3. Pry loose the retainer cover for the outside mirror retaining screws.
4. Remove the door panel retaining screws and using a suitable pry tool, pry loose the door panel clips and remove the door panel.
5. Remove the 2 inside door handle screws. Partly tear off the service hole cover and disconnect the handle link from the door lock.
6. Remove the service hole cover. Remove the 4 speaker retaining screws, unplug the speaker connections and remove the speaker.
7. Remove the power mirror connector from the door cavity and then disconnect it. Remove the 3 mirror retaining screws and remove the mirror.
8. Remove the retaining screw from the front edge of the door molding. Pry loose the clips from the edge of the panel and remove the front door belt molding.
9. Wind the door glass down into the door cavity. Remove the 2 lower door glass retaining nuts. Remove the glass from the door glass regulator and then lower the glass on the door cavity bottom.
10. Unplug the power window connectors. Remove the 4 door glass regulator mounting bolts. Remove the regulator through the service hole.
11. Remove the inside door lock link set screw. Disconnect the link from the door lock. Disconnect the opening control link from the door lock. Remove the 2 protector retaining screws and remove the protector.
12. Remove the bolt and the rear lower frame.
13. Disconnect the 2 door lock links from the door outside handle and door lock. Unplug the connector. Remove the 3 retaining screws and the door lock.
14. Remove the 2 door lock cylinder retaining bolts, and the lock cylinder with the link. Unplug the connector.
15. Unplug the connector. Remove the 2 outside door handle retaining bolts and remove the handle.
16. To replace the door glass;
   a. Remove the glass stopper, nut, stud bolt and washer and remove the glass assembly.
   b. Installation is the reverse order of the removal procedure.
To assemble:
17. Install the outside door handle along with the retaining bolts. Attach the connector.
18. Attach the door lock cylinder connector. Install the door lock cylinder with the 2 retaining bolts.
19. Install the door lock with the 3 retaining screws. Connect the connector. Connect the 2 links to the door outside handle and door lock.
20. Install the rear lower frame with bolt.
21. Install the protector along with the 2 retaining screws.
22. Connect the opening control link to the door lock.
23. Connect the inside locking link to the door lock and install the set screw.
24. Place the door glass regulator through the service hole. Temporarily tighten the equalizer arm bracket mounting bolts. Install the 4 regulator mounting bolts. Attach the connector.
25. Place the door glass into the door cavity. Install the glass to the regulator with the 2 glass mounting nuts. Install the door glass runner.
26. Adjust the equalizer arm up or down and tighten it when the glass is even and secure in the top of the door pillar. With the door glass fully closed, adjust the door glass stopper so it lightly makes contact with the glass plate.
27. Insert the claw of the clips on the door belt molding into the upper panel slit and push the molding onto the panel. Install the set screw to the molding.
28. Install the outside mirror with the 3 set screws and attach the connector.
29. Install the service hole cover with adhesive. Insert the lower edge on the cover into the door panel slit. Seal the panel slit with cotton tape. Do not block the trim clip seating with the tape.
30. Attach the speaker connections and install the speaker with the 4 retaining screws.
31. Connect the inside door handle links and install the handle with the 2 screws.
32. Attach the power accessory connectors. Install the door trim with clips to the inside door panel by tapping. Install the retaining screws and the hole cover. Attach the connector and install the armrest with the 3 retaining screws.
33. Install the outside mirror cover. Install the door inside handle bezel with screw. Be sure to adjust the door.

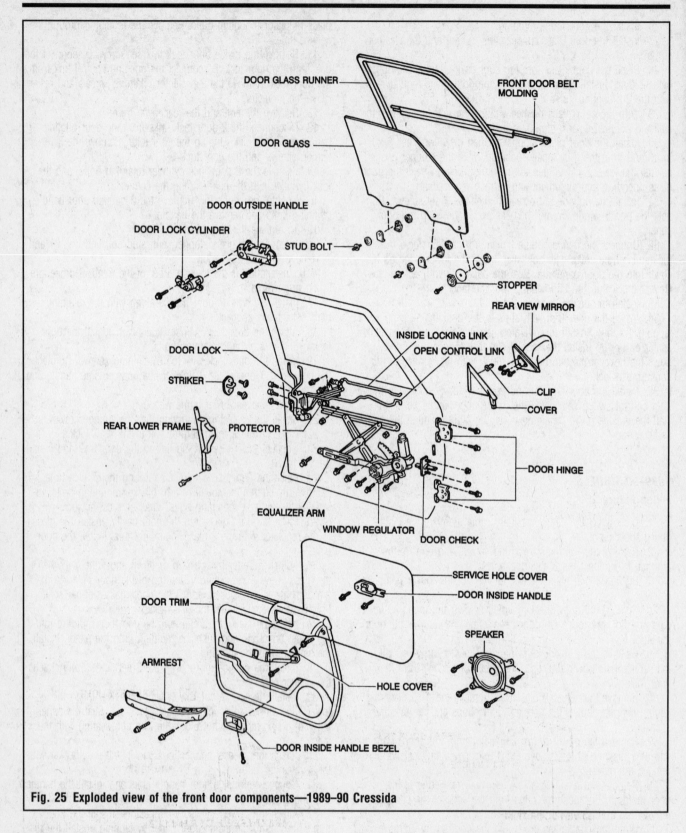

Fig. 25 Exploded view of the front door components—1989–90 Cressida

Van

▶ **See Figures 26 thru 49**

1. Disconnect the negative battery cable. Remove the inside door handle bezel.

2. Remove the armrest or pull handle.

3. If not equipped with power windows, remove the window regulator handle by pulling off the snapring with a cloth in between the window regulator handle and door panel.

4. Remove the courtesy light. Insert a pry tool between the retainers and the door panel. Unplug the wiring connector and remove the door trim panel.

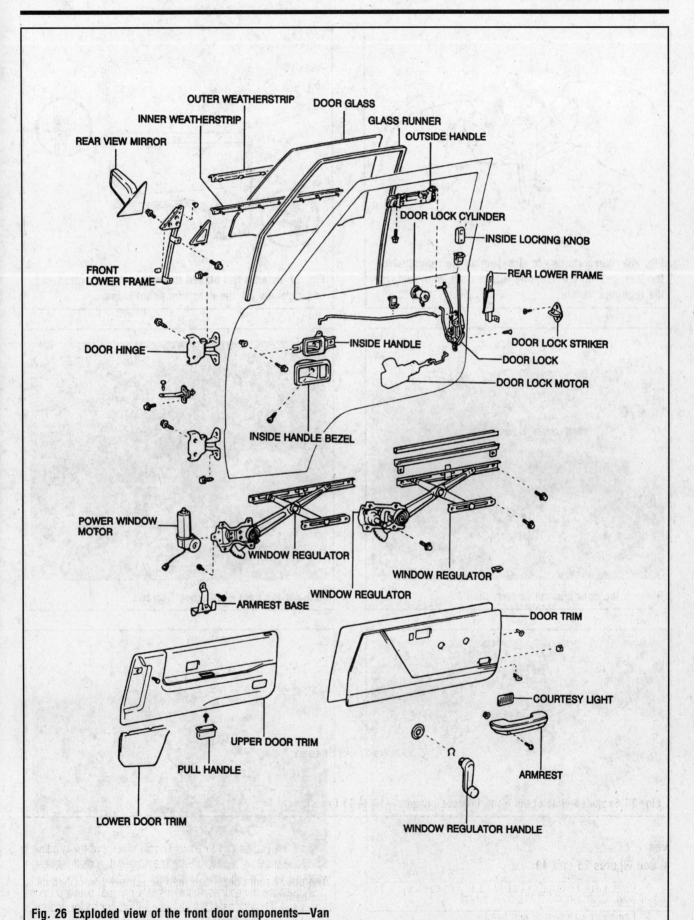

Fig. 26 Exploded view of the front door components—Van

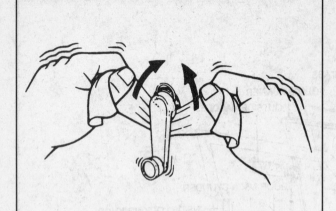

Fig. 26a When starting to disassemble the front door on the Van, pull off the snapring with a cloth, then remove the regulator handle

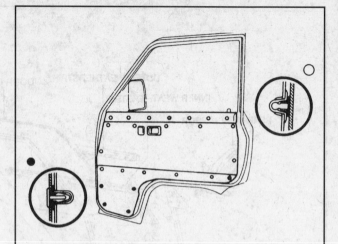

Fig. 27 Insert a flat bladed tool with a tape covered end and carefully pry the door trim panel loose

Remove the door armrest screws, then . . .

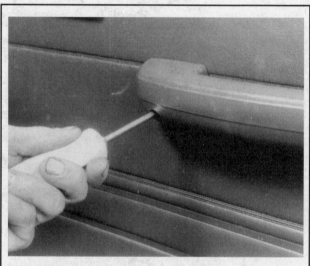

Remove the door handle bezel screws

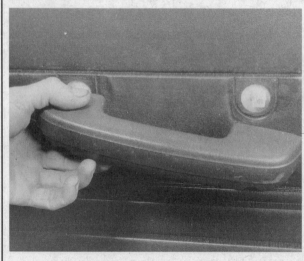

. . . pull the armrest off the door panel

The door handle bezel can then be removed from behind the handle

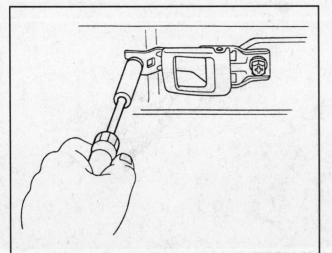

Fig. 28 Remove the two screws retaining the inside door handle—Van

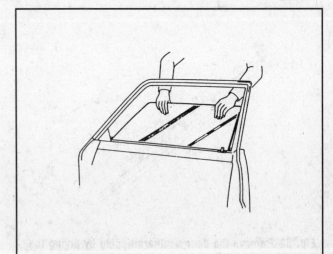

Fig. 31 Pull the door glass out of the door panel from the top as shown—Van

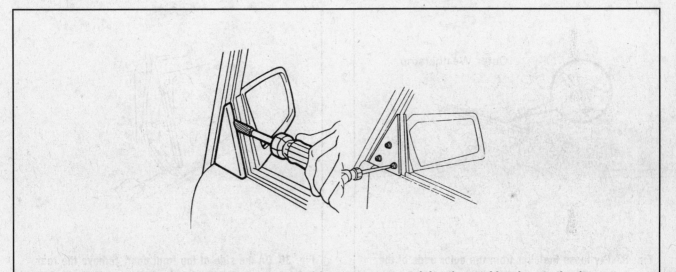

Fig. 29 Carefully pry off the cover trim, then remove the three setscrews retaining the outside mirror to the door

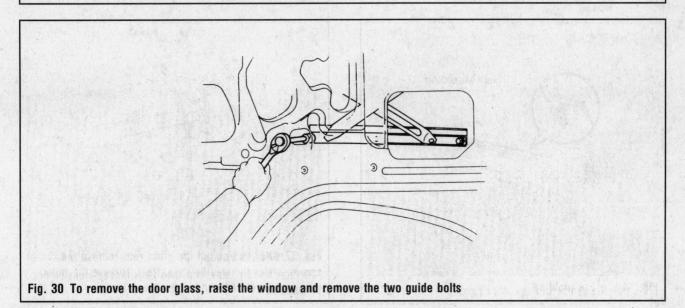

Fig. 30 To remove the door glass, raise the window and remove the two guide bolts

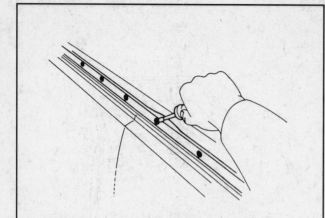

Fig. 32 Remove the door weatherstripping by prying the clips from the edge of the panel, then unfasten the upper door trim

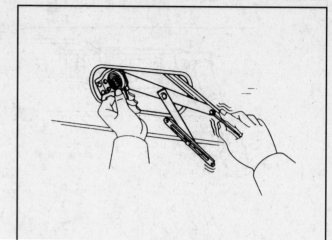

Fig. 35 Remove the window regulator mounting bolts and pull the unit through the service hole

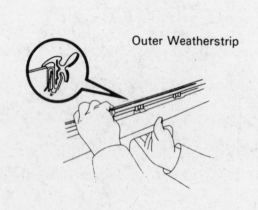

Outer Weatherstrip

Fig. 33 Pry loose the clips from the outer edge of the panel, then remove the weatherstrip . . .

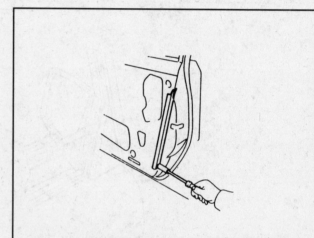

Fig. 36 On the side of the front door, remove the rear lower frame from the glass run—Van

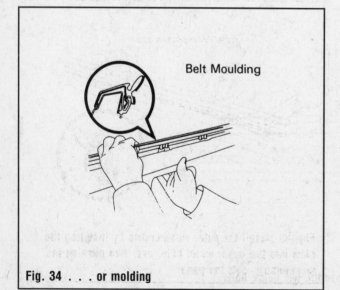

Belt Moulding

Fig. 34 . . . or molding

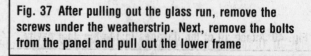

Fig. 37 After pulling out the glass run, remove the screws under the weatherstrip. Next, remove the bolts from the panel and pull out the lower frame

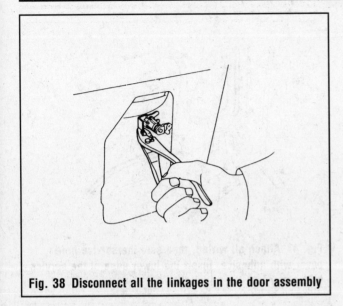

Fig. 38 Disconnect all the linkages in the door assembly

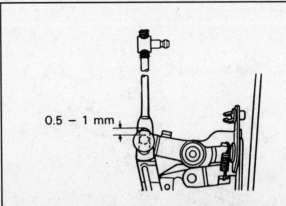

0.5 – 1 mm

Fig. 41 To adjust the outside door handle, disconnect the control link, then raise the handle from the rest position, and place the pin into the hole by turning the adjuster

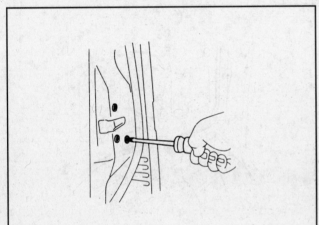

Fig. 39 When assembling the door, place the door lock into the cavity of the door and tighten the mounting screws

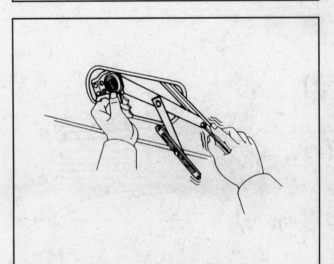

Fig. 42 Insert the window regulator into the door cavity—Van

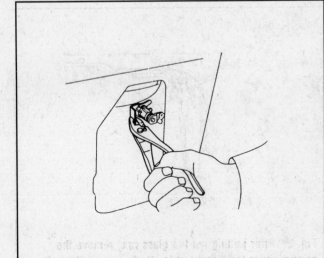

Fig. 40 Attach all of the linkages inside the door cavity

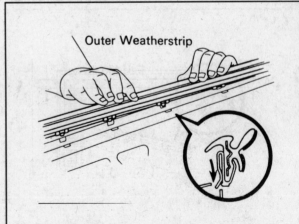

Outer Weatherstrip

Fig. 43 Install the outer weatherstrip by inserting the claw into the upper panel hole, and then pushing the weatherstrip onto the panel

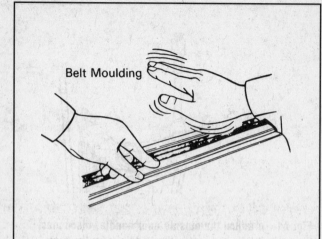

Fig. 44 To install the belt molding, tap it onto the upper panel by hand—Van

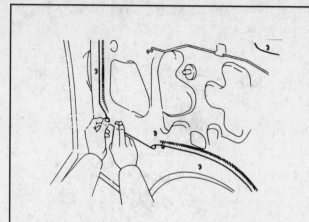

Fig. 47 Attach all wiring, then seal the service hole cover with adhesive. Insert the lower edge of the service hole cover into the panel slit

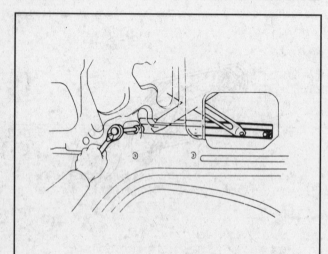

Fig. 45 Install the door glass into the door cavity and attach the regulator to the glass

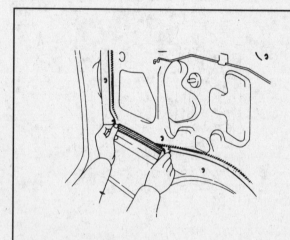

Fig. 48 Seal the panel slit with cotton tape, but do not block the trim clip seating

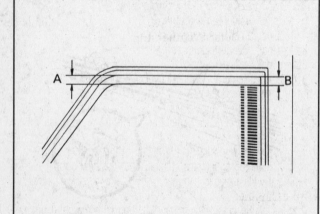

Fig. 46 Adjust the door glass equalizer arm up and down, and tighten it so that dimensions A and B are equal

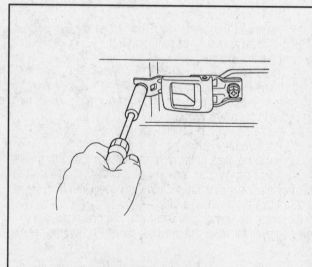

Fig. 49 Attach the inside door handle

5. Remove the armrest base. Remove the inside door handle retaining screws. Disconnect the control link from the handle and remove the handle.

6. Remove the service hole cover.

7. Pry loose the outside mirror retainer cover. Remove the 3 screws and the mirror. Unplug the electrical connectors from the mirror.

8. Raise the window slightly and remove the 2 door glass guide set bolts. Remove the door glass by pulling upward.

9. Remove the inner and outer weatherstripping moldings.

10. Unplug the power window electrical connectors. Remove the door glass regulator mounting bolts. Remove the regulator through the service hole.

11. Remove the rear lower frame from the glass runner.

12. Pull out the glass from the front lower frame. Remove the frame retaining screws located under the weatherstripping. Remove the frame retaining bolts and remove the frame.

13. Disconnect the following linkages:
   a. Door inside opening control link
   b. Door outslde opening control link
   c. Door outside locking control link

14. Remove the door lock cylinder.

15. Unplug the connector from the power door lock motor. Remove the door inside locking knob. Remove the 3 screws, 2 bolts and door lock. Remove the 3 screws, 2 bolts and door lock with the motor.

16. Remove the outside handle.

17. To replace the door glass:
   a. Remove the glass channel assembly from the glass with a suitable prytool.
   b. Apply soapy water to the inside of the weather strip.
   c. Install the door glass channel onto the new door glass by tapping it with a plastic hammer.

To assemble:

18. Install the door lock with the 3 screws and 2 bolts. Install the inside locking knob. Attach the connector to the power door lock motor.

19. Install the lock cylinder.

20. Connect the following linkages:
   a. Door inside opening control
   b. Door outside opening control
   c. Door outside locking control

21. Disconnect the control link. Raise the handle 0.079–0.098 in. (2.0–2.5mm) from the rest position. Fit the pin into the hole by turning the adjuster.

22. Install the front and rear lower frames.

23. Install the door glass regulator with the mounting bolts. Temporarily tighten the equalizer arm mounting bolts. Attach the connector to the power window motor.

24. Install the inner and outer weatherstripping moldings.

25. Place the door glass into the door cavity.

26. Install the glass to the regulator with the 2 mounting bolts.

27. Adjust the equalizer arm up and down and tighten it when the door glass sits flush on the top of the door pillar.

28. Attach the wire connectors.

29. Install the service hole cover with adhesive. Insert the lower edge on the cover into the door panel slit. Seal the panel slit with cotton tape. Do not block the trim clip seating with the tape.

30. Attach the wire connectors to the outside mirror. Install the mirror with the 3 screws. Install the cover.

31. Install the inside door handle. Attach the wiring connectors to the power windows. Install the door trim panel and courtesy light.

32. Install the armrest base.

33. With the door glass fully closed, install the window regulator handle and plate with the snapring. Install the armrest or pull handle.

34. Install the inside door handle bezel. Do not forget to adjust the door as necessary.

Rear Door

DISASSEMBLY AND ASSEMBLY

Cressida

1983–84 Models

▸ **See Figure 50**

1. Disconnect the negative battery cable. Remove the inside door handle bezel. Remove the armrest.

2. Pry loose the door trim panel.

3. Remove the door belt molding.

4. Remove the inside door handle. Disconnect the control link from the handle.

5. Remove the service hole cover.

6. Remove the upper set screw from the division bar. Remove the 2 set bolts from the panel. Pull out the glass runner from the division bar. Pull out the division bar from the door cavity.

7. Remove the quarter window together with the weather strip by pulling it forward.

8. Remove the door glass from the regulator roller. Pull the door glass upward to remove it.

9. Remove the door glass regulator mounting bolts. Remove the regulator through the service hole.

10. Remove the inside lock knob and link.

11. Disconnect the following linkages:
   a. Door inside opening control
   b. Door outside opening control
   c. Door outside locking control

12. Remove the door lock.

13. Remove the child protect cover and the outside handle with its 2 retaining bolts.

14. To replace the door glass;
   a. Remove the glass channel assembly from the glass with a suitable pry tool.
   b. Apply soapy water to the inside of the weather strip.
   c. Install the door glass channel onto the new door glass by taping it with a plastic hammer.

To assemble:

15. Install the outside door handle along with the child protector cover. Install the door lock.

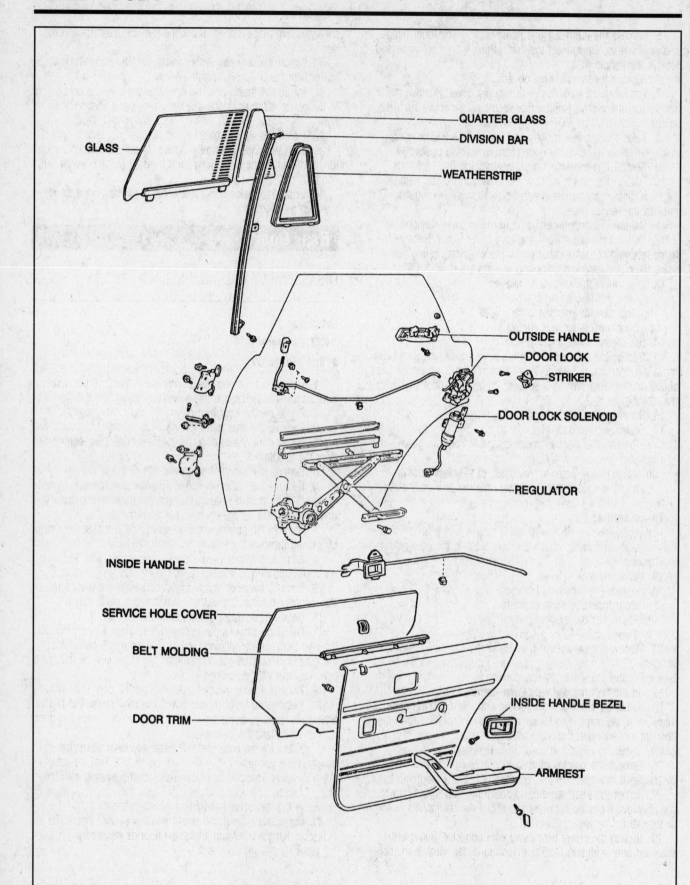

GLASS

QUARTER GLASS

DIVISION BAR

WEATHERSTRIP

OUTSIDE HANDLE

DOOR LOCK

STRIKER

DOOR LOCK SOLENOID

REGULATOR

INSIDE HANDLE

SERVICE HOLE COVER

BELT MOLDING

INSIDE HANDLE BEZEL

DOOR TRIM

ARMREST

Fig. 50 Exploded view of the rear door assembly—1983–84 Cressida

16. Connect the following linkages:
   a. Door inside opening control
   b. Door outside opening control
   c. Door outside locking control

17. Install door lock control link onto the door panel. Connect the linkage to the door lock. Disconnect the control link. Raise the handle 0.020–0.039 in. (0.5–1.0mm) from the rest position. Fit the pin into the hole by turning the adjuster.

18. Check that the door fit and door linkages are adjusted correctly. Adjust the striker by loosening the striker mounting screws.

19. Place the door glass regulator through the service hole. Tighten the mounting bolt.

20. Install the door glass in the door cavity. Install the door glass into the regulator roller.

21. Install the quarter glass.

22. Place the division bar in the door. Install one upper screw and 2 bolts. Install the glass run into the division bar. Apply soapy water to the glass runner.

23. Install the belt molding.

24. Install the service hole cover with adhesive. Insert the lower edge on the cover into the door panel slit. Seal the panel slit with cotton tape. Do not block the trim clip seating with the tape.

25. Connect the control link to the inside door handle and install the handle.

26. Install the door panel trim.

27. Adjust the equalizer arm up and down and tighten it when the door glass sits flush on the top of the door pillar.

28. Install the armrest and inside door handle bezel. Adjust the rear door.

1985–90 MODELS

♦ See Figures 51 and 52

1. Disconnect the negative battery cable. Remove the door handle bezel and armrest.

2. Pry loose the door trim panel.

3. Remove the door belt molding.

4. Remove the inside door handle. Disconnect the control link from the handle.

5. Remove the service hole cover. Remove the door glass stoppers.

6. Remove the 2 door glass mounting nuts. Lower the door glass into the bottom door cavity. Remove the weather stripping.

7. Remove the upper set screw from the division bar. Remove the 2 set bolts from the panel. Pull out the glass runner from the division bar. Pull out the division bar from the door cavity.

8. Remove the quarter window together with the weather strip by pulling it forward.

9. Remove the belt molding. Remove the door glass runner clip. Remove the door frame molding. Pull the door glass upward to remove it.

10. Unplug the power window motor connector. Remove the equalizer arm mounting bracket mounting bolts. Remove the door

glass regulator mounting bolts and remove the regulator through the service hole.

11. Disconnect the door lock control link and the outside control link.

12. Remove the inside lock knob and link.

13. Remove the door lock solenoid connector. Remove the door lock and door lock solenoid mounting bolts. Remove the door lock with the door lock solenoid through the service hole. Remove the door lock solenoid from the door lock.

14. Remove the outside door handle set bolts and handle.

15. To replace the door glass;
   a. Remove the glass channel assembly from the glass with a suitable prytool.
   b. Apply soapy water to the inside of the weather strip.
   c. Install the door glass channel onto the new door glass by taping it with a plastic hammer.
   d. To replace the door glass on the 1989–90 Cressida, remove the glass stopper, nut, stud bolt and washer and remove the glass assembly. Installation is the reverse order of the removal procedure.

To assemble:

16. Install the outside door handle.

17. Install the door lock solenoid to the door lock. Tighten the 2 screws after adjusting so that the gap becomes closed when unlocked.

18. Install the door lock with the 3 set screws. Install the door lock solenoid mounting bolt. Connect the door lock solenoid.

19. Install the inside lock knob and link. Connect the outside control link and inside lock link. Check the door lock and unlock operation and adjust as necessary.

20. Place the regulator through the service hole. Tighten the regulator mounting bolts. Temporarily tighten the equalizer arm bracket mounting bolts. Attach the power window motor connector.

21. Insert the door glass into the door cavity. Install the door frame molding. Install the glass run clip and install the bolt molding with the screw.

22. Install the quarter window glass with the weatherstrip.

23. Place the division bar in the door. Install the glass run into the division bar. Apply soapy water to the glass runner.

24. Install the weatherstripping molding.

25. Insert the glass to the front and rear glass runners. Install the door glass to the regulator with the 2 mounting bolts. With the door glass pushed up against the rear frame side, install the 2 equalizer arm mounting bolts.

26. Install the door glass stoppers. Open the door 0.20 in. (5mm) from the fully closed position. When the stopper is pushed against the lower side tighten the mounting bolts. Check the door glass operation and alignment.

27. Install the service hole cover with adhesive. Insert the lower edge on the cover into the door panel slit. Seal the panel slit with cotton tape. Do not block the trim clip seating with the tape.

28. Install the inside handle and door trim panel.

29. Install the armrest and power window switch. Install the inside door handle bezel and adjust the door as necessary.

Fig. 51 Exploded view of the rear door assembly—1985–91 Cressida

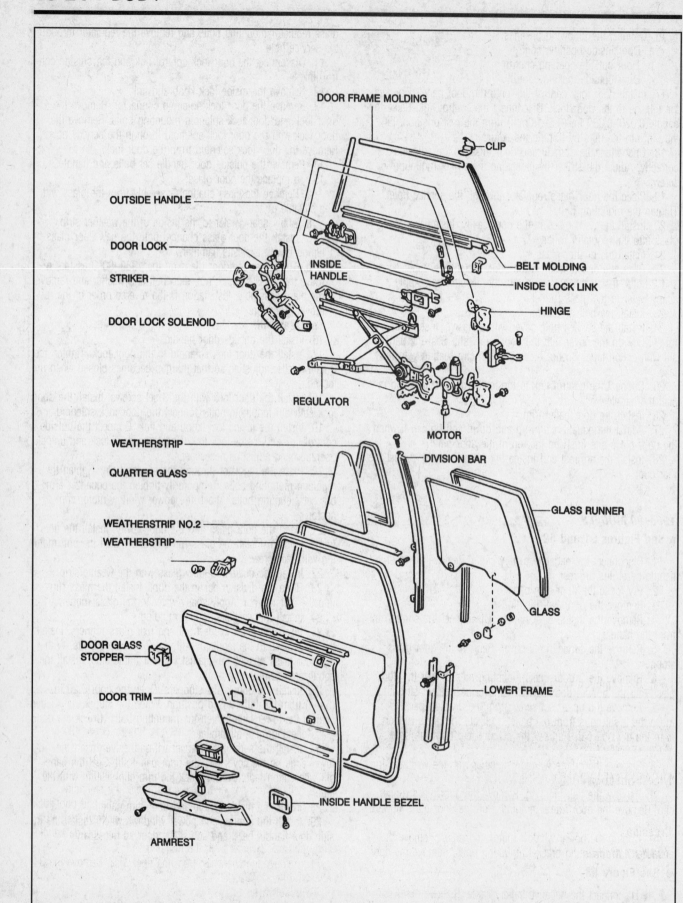

DOOR FRAME MOLDING

CLIP

OUTSIDE HANDLE

BELT MOLDING

DOOR LOCK

INSIDE HANDLE

INSIDE LOCK LINK

STRIKER

HINGE

DOOR LOCK SOLENOID

REGULATOR

MOTOR

WEATHERSTRIP

DIVISION BAR

QUARTER GLASS

GLASS RUNNER

WEATHERSTRIP NO.2

WEATHERSTRIP

GLASS

DOOR GLASS STOPPER

DOOR TRIM

LOWER FRAME

INSIDE HANDLE BEZEL

ARMREST

Fig. 51 Exploded view of the rear door assembly—1985–88 Cressida

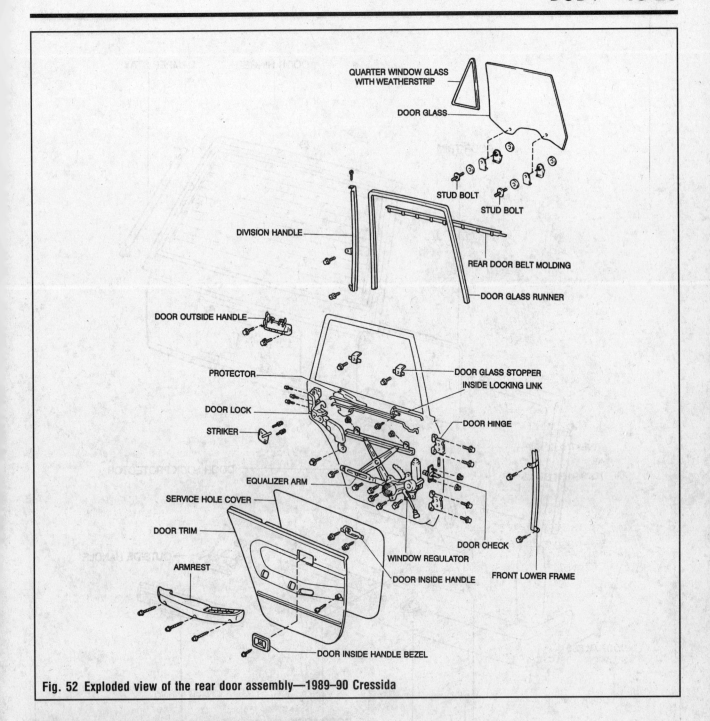

Fig. 52 Exploded view of the rear door assembly—1989–90 Cressida

QUARTER WINDOW GLASS WITH WEATHERSTRIP
DOOR GLASS
STUD BOLT
STUD BOLT
DIVISION HANDLE
REAR DOOR BELT MOLDING
DOOR GLASS RUNNER
DOOR OUTSIDE HANDLE
DOOR GLASS STOPPER
INSIDE LOCKING LINK
PROTECTOR
DOOR LOCK
DOOR HINGE
STRIKER
EQUALIZER ARM
SERVICE HOLE COVER
DOOR CHECK
DOOR TRIM
WINDOW REGULATOR
FRONT LOWER FRAME
ARMREST
DOOR INSIDE HANDLE
DOOR INSIDE HANDLE BEZEL

Tailgate

DISASSEMBLY AND ASSEMBLY

Cressida

1983–87 Models
♦ **See Figure 53**

1. Disconnect the negative battery cable. Remove the 6 door panel clips. Pry between the trim retainers and door panel to pry the door panel loose.

2. Remove the 3 lock protector retaining bolts and the protector.

3. Disconnect the control links from the door lock and door lock cylinder. Unplug the connector from the solenoid. Remove the 3 bolts, screw and door lock control with the solenoid.

4. Remove the 4 nuts from the outside handle and door lock cylinder. Unplug the connector from the door lock cylinder. Pull out the outside finish panel molding. Remove the outside handle and door lock cylinder from the molding.

5. Remove the connector from the door lock. Remove the 3 bolts and the door lock.

To assemble:

6. Install the door lock with the 3 bolts. Attach the connector to the door lock.

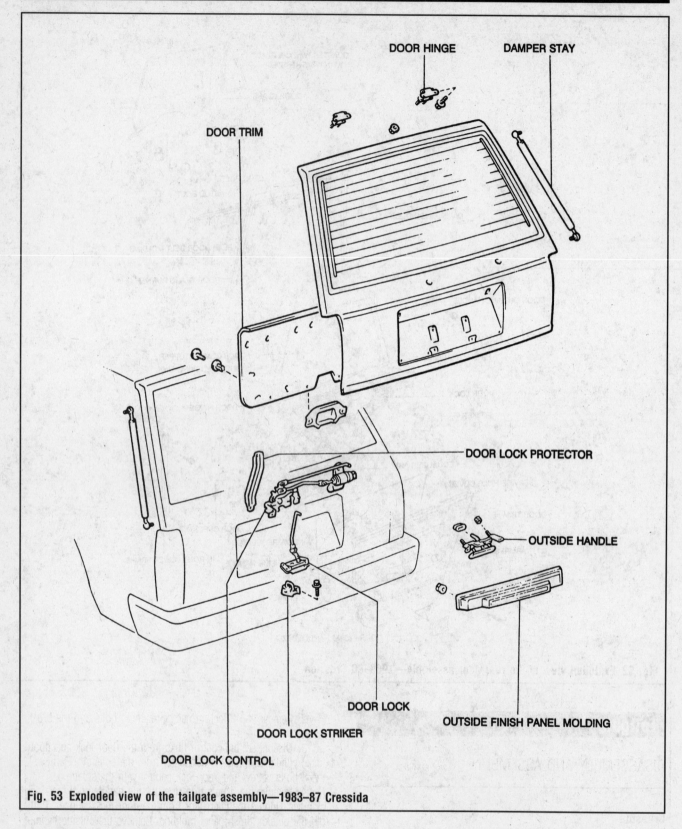

Fig. 53 Exploded view of the tailgate assembly—1983–87 Cressida

7. Install the outside handle and door lock cylinder to the outside finish panel molding.

8. Place the outside finish panel molding in position. Install the 4 nuts. Attach the connector to the door lock cylinder. Place the door lock control with the solenoid in position. Be careful of the outside handle lever position.

9. Tighten the 3 bolts and screw. Connect the links to the door lock and door lock cylinder. Attach the connector to the door lock solenoid.

10. Install the door lock protector and 3 bolts. Install the door trim with the clips inside the door panel by tapping. Be sure to adjust the back door.

Van

♦ **See Figures 54, 55, 56 and 57**

1. Remove the back door locking knob. Remove the back door inside handle. Remove the back door inside handle bezel.

2. Remove the door trim panel. Remove the service hole cover.

3. Disconnect the following linkages;
   a. The back door control motor
   b. The back door lock cylinder control

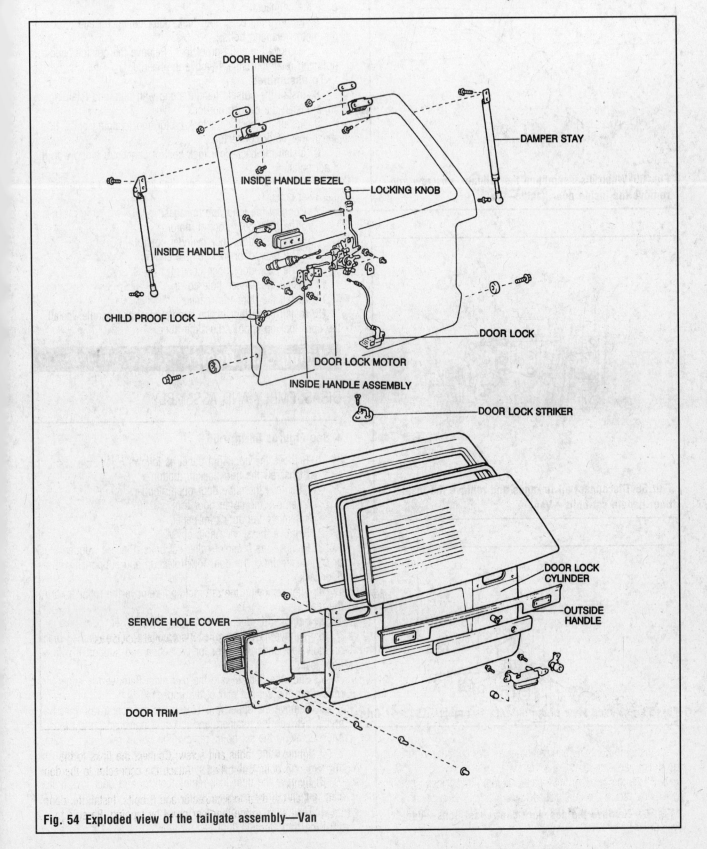

DOOR HINGE

INSIDE HANDLE BEZEL

LOCKING KNOB

DAMPER STAY

INSIDE HANDLE

CHILD PROOF LOCK

DOOR LOCK MOTOR

INSIDE HANDLE ASSEMBLY

DOOR LOCK

DOOR LOCK STRIKER

DOOR LOCK CYLINDER

OUTSIDE HANDLE

SERVICE HOLE COVER

DOOR TRIM

Fig. 54 Exploded view of the tailgate assembly—Van

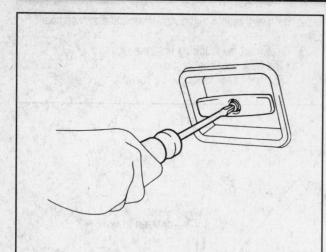

Fig. 55 When disassembling the tailgate, unscrew and remove the inside door handle—Van

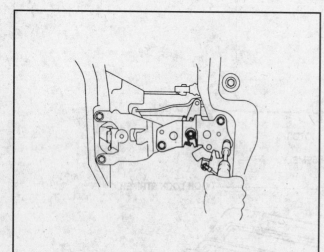

Fig. 56 Disconnect all linkages and remove the inside door handle set bolts—Van

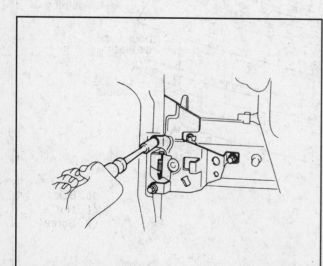

Fig. 57 Remove the door lock control set bolts—Van

c. The back door lock remote control
d. The back door open control

4. Remove the back door inside handle retaining bolts and remove the handle.

5. Remove the back door lock control set bolts and disengage the connector.

6. Remove the back door lock motor connector and remove the motor retaining bolts.

7. Remove the child proof lock. Remove the outside handle nuts and retaining clips. Remove the handle.

To assemble:

8. Install the outside handle along with nuts and retaining clips. Install the child proof lock.

9. Install the back door lock motor and retaining bolts. Reattach the motor connector.

10. Install the back door lock control connector along with the 3 set bolts.

11. Install the inside back door handle assembly along with the 3 set bolts.

12. Connect the following linkages;
    a. The back door control motor
    b. The back door lock cylinder control
    c. The back door lock remote control
    d. The back door open control

13. Install the service hole cover.

14. Install the door trim panel.

15. Install back door inside handle bezel and handle. Install the door locking knob. Adjust the door.

Sliding Side Door

DISASSEMBLY AND ASSEMBLY

◆ **See Figures 58 thru 66**

1. Remove the door trim panel as follows:
    a. Unscrew the door locking button.
    b. Remove the slide door open stopper.
    c. Remove the upper door trim.
    d. Remove the door trim panel.

2. Remove the service hole cover.

3. Remove the 3 center roller set bolts. Place a wooden block or equivalent under the door for protection and support it with a floor jack.

4. After removing the rail molding, remove the roller toward the rear.

5. Remove the door panel.

6. Remove the lower roller 3 set bolts. Place a wooden block or equivalent under the door for protection and support it with a floor jack.

7. Slide the door toward the rear side. Remove the upper roller from the cut-out part of the upper rail.

8. Remove the upper rail. To remove the center rail, insert a prybar between the retainers and the door panel and pry it loose. After removing the set bolts, remove the center rail.

9. Remove the upper roller from the door panel and remove the lower roller from the door rail.

10. Remove the door lock remote control and door lock motor after removing their retaining bolts.

11. Disconnect the following linkages:
    a. The rear slide door lock cylinder

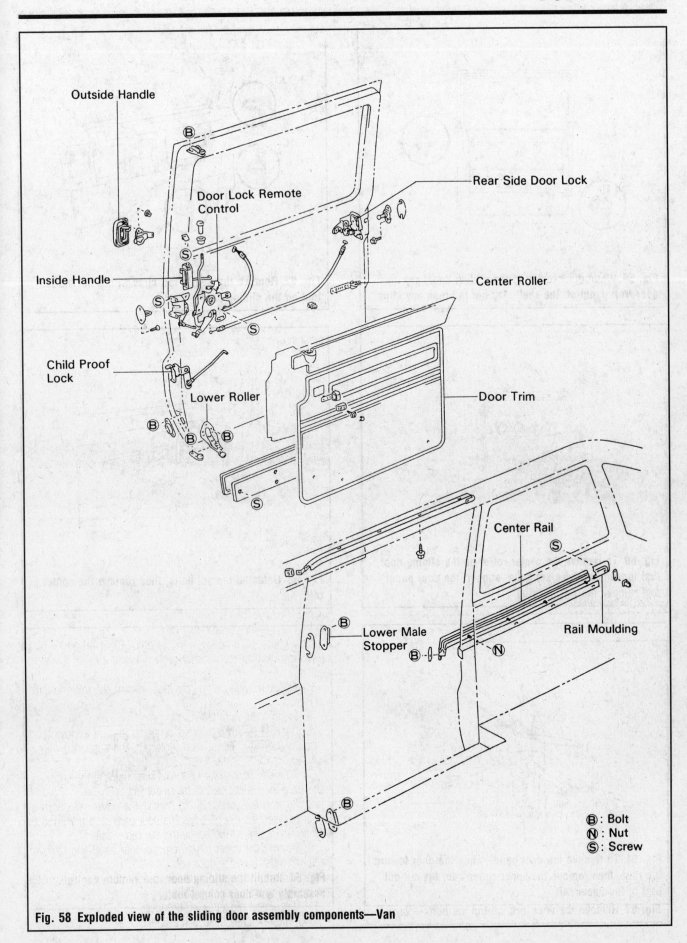

Outside Handle

Door Lock Remote
Control

Rear Side Door Lock

Inside Handle

Center Roller

Child Proof
Lock

Lower Roller

Door Trim

Center Rail

Lower Male
Stopper

Rail Moulding

Ⓑ : Bolt
Ⓝ : Nut
Ⓢ : Screw

Fig. 58 Exploded view of the sliding door assembly components—Van

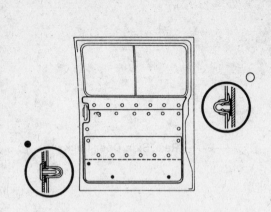

Fig. 59 When disassembling the sliding door, pry the door trim panel off the shell. Try not to break any clips

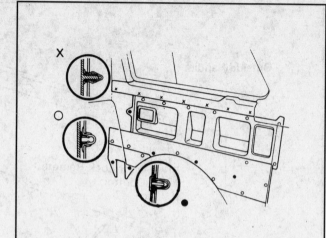

Fig. 62 Remove the center rail clips with a flat bladed tool on the sliding door—Van

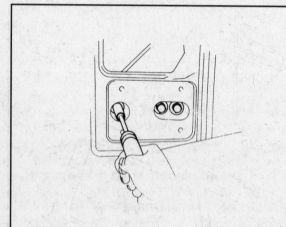

Fig. 60 To remove the center roller on the sliding door, first loosen the three set bolts, support the door panel and remove the rail molding

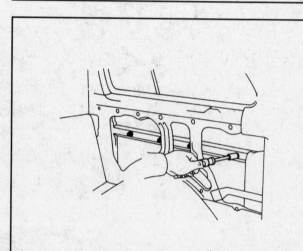

Fig. 63 Unfasten the set bolts, then remove the center rail

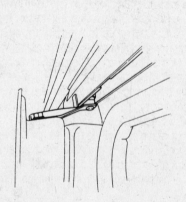

Fig. 61 To remove the door panel, slide the door toward the rear, then remove the upper roller from the cut-out part of the upper rail

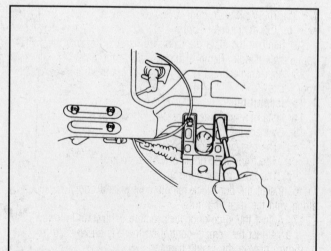

Fig. 64 Unbolt the sliding door lock remote control assembly and door control motor

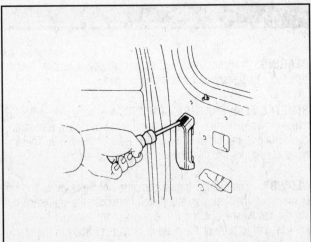

Fig. 65 Unscrew and remove the inside door handle— Van

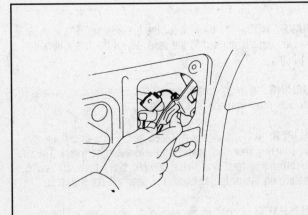

Fig. 66 Pull the sliding door lock assembly out of the door shell—Van

b. The front slide door lock open control

c. The door motor control

12. Remove the slide door outside handle. Remove the slide door inside handle. Remove the rear and front slide door locks.

13. After connecting the cable, install the front and rear slide door locks.

To assemble:

14. Install the slide door inside and outside handles.

15. Connect the following linkages:

a. The rear slide door lock cylinder

b. The front slide door lock open control

c. The door motor control

16. Install the door lock remote control and door lock motor along with the retaining nuts.

17. Adjust the slide door lock remote control as follows:

a. Adjust the remote control so there is about 0.20 in. (5mm) play in the inside handle.

b. Loosen the rear lock cable adjusting screw and lightly pull the cable until it is snug. Then return it about 0.04 in. (1mm) and tighten it down.

c. Loosen the remote control cable adjusting screw and

lightly pull the cable until it is snug. Then return it about 0.04 (1mm).

➡**Make the adjustment with the clamp for the cable and inner panel installed.**

18. When operating the outside and inside handles, check that the front and rear locks release smoothly.

19. Install the lower roller to the door rail and center roller to the door panel.

20. Install the center rail and the set bolts. Install the rear quarter trim. Install the upper rail.

21. Install the bolts of the lower roller. Install the upper roller from the cut-out part of the upper rail.

22. While pulling on the door panel, install the center roller parallel with rail.

23. Install the service hole cover.

24. Install the door trim and upper door trim and upper door trim. Install the slide door open stopper. Install the door locking button.

Inside Mirror

REMOVAL & INSTALLATION

1. Loosen the mirror assembly-to-mounting bracket set screw.

2. Remove the mirror assembly by sliding upward and away from the mounting bracket.

3. Install it by attaching the mirror assembly to the mounting bracket and tighten the set screw to 10–20 inch lbs.

➡**If the mirror bracket pad has to be removed from the windshield (or if it has fallen off), it will be necessary to use a suitable heat gun to heat the vinyl pad until vinyl softens. Peel the vinyl off the glass and discard. Install the new one as follows:**

To install:

a. Make sure glass, bracket and adhesive kit (rearview mirror adhesive or equivalent) are at least at room temperature 65–75°F (18–24°C).

b. Locate and mark the mirror mounting bracket location on the outside surface of the glass.

c. Thoroughly clean the bonding surfaces of the glass and bracket to remove old adhesive if reusing the old mirror bracket pad. Use a mild abrasive cleaner on the glass and fine sandpaper on the bracket to lightly roughen the surface. Wipe clean with a alcohol moistened cloth.

d. Crush the accelerator vial (part of the rearview mirror adhesive kit) and apply the accelerator to the bonding surface of bracket and windshield. Let it dry for 3 minutes.

e. Apply 2 drops of adhesive (part of the Rearview mirror adhesive kit) to the mounting surface of the bracket and windshield. Using a clean toothpick or a wooden match, quickly spread the adhesive evenly over the mounting surface of the bracket.

f. Quickly position the mounting bracket on the windshield. The ⅜ in. (9.5mm) circular depression in the bracket must be toward the inside of the passengers compartment. Press the bracket firmly against the windshield for one minute.

g. Allow the bond to set for five minutes. Remove any excess bonding material from windshield with an alcohol dampened cloth.

GLOSSARY

AIR/FUEL RATIO: The ratio of air-to-gasoline by weight in the fuel mixture drawn into the engine.

AIR INJECTION: One method of reducing harmful exhaust emissions by injecting air into each of the exhaust ports of an engine. The fresh air entering the hot exhaust manifold causes any remaining fuel to be burned before it can exit the tailpipe.

ALTERNATOR: A device used for converting mechanical energy into electrical energy.

AMMETER: An instrument, calibrated in amperes, used to measure the flow of an electrical current in a circuit. Ammeters are always connected in series with the circuit being tested.

AMPERE: The rate of flow of electrical current present when one volt of electrical pressure is applied against one ohm of electrical resistance.

ANALOG COMPUTER: Any microprocessor that uses similar (analogous) electrical signals to make its calculations.

ARMATURE: A laminated, soft iron core wrapped by a wire that converts electrical energy to mechanical energy as in a motor or relay. When rotated in a magnetic field, it changes mechanical energy into electrical energy as in a generator.

ATMOSPHERIC PRESSURE: The pressure on the Earth's surface caused by the weight of the air in the atmosphere. At sea level, this pressure is 14.7 psi at 32°F (101 kPa at 0°C).

ATOMIZATION: The breaking down of a liquid into a fine mist that can be suspended in air.

AXIAL PLAY: Movement parallel to a shaft or bearing bore.

BACKFIRE: The sudden combustion of gases in the intake or exhaust system that results in a loud explosion.

BACKLASH: The clearance or play between two parts, such as meshed gears.

BACKPRESSURE: Restrictions in the exhaust system that slow the exit of exhaust gases from the combustion chamber.

BAKELITE: A heat resistant, plastic insulator material commonly used in printed circuit boards and transistorized components.

BALL BEARING: A bearing made up of hardened inner and outer races between which hardened steel balls roll.

BALLAST RESISTOR: A resistor in the primary ignition circuit that lowers voltage after the engine is started to reduce wear on ignition components.

BEARING: A friction reducing, supportive device usually located between a stationary part and a moving part.

BIMETAL TEMPERATURE SENSOR: Any sensor or switch made of two dissimilar types of metal that bend when heated or cooled due to the different expansion rates of the alloys. These types of sensors usually function as an on/off switch.

BLOWBY: Combustion gases, composed of water vapor and unburned fuel, that leak past the piston rings into the crankcase during normal engine operation. These gases are removed by the PCV system to prevent the buildup of harmful acids in the crankcase.

BRAKE PAD: A brake shoe and lining assembly used with disc brakes.

BRAKE SHOE: The backing for the brake lining. The term is, however, usually applied to the assembly of the brake backing and lining.

BUSHING: A liner, usually removable, for a bearing; an anti-friction liner used in place of a bearing.

CALIPER: A hydraulically activated device in a disc brake system, which is mounted straddling the brake rotor (disc). The caliper contains at least one piston and two brake pads. Hydraulic pressure on the piston(s) forces the pads against the rotor.

CAMSHAFT: A shaft in the engine on which are the lobes (cams) which operate the valves. The camshaft is driven by the crankshaft, via a belt, chain or gears, at one half the crankshaft speed.

CAPACITOR: A device which stores an electrical charge.

CARBON MONOXIDE (CO): A colorless, odorless gas given off as a normal byproduct of combustion. It is poisonous and extremely dangerous in confined areas, building up slowly to toxic levels without warning if adequate ventilation is not available.

CARBURETOR: A device, usually mounted on the intake manifold of an engine, which mixes the air and fuel in the proper proportion to allow even combustion.

CATALYTIC CONVERTER: A device installed in the exhaust system, like a muffler, that converts harmful byproducts of combustion into carbon dioxide and water vapor by means of a heat-producing chemical reaction.

CENTRIFUGAL ADVANCE: A mechanical method of advancing the spark timing by using flyweights in the distributor that react to centrifugal force generated by the distributor shaft rotation.

CHECK VALVE: Any one-way valve installed to permit the flow of air, fuel or vacuum in one direction only.

CHOKE: A device, usually a moveable valve, placed in the intake path of a carburetor to restrict the flow of air.

CIRCUIT: Any unbroken path through which an electrical current can flow. Also used to describe fuel flow in some instances.

CIRCUIT BREAKER: A switch which protects an electrical circuit from overload by opening the circuit when the current flow exceeds a predetermined level. Some circuit breakers must be reset manually, while most reset automatically.

COIL (IGNITION): A transformer in the ignition circuit which steps up the voltage provided to the spark plugs.

COMBINATION MANIFOLD: An assembly which includes both the intake and exhaust manifolds in one casting.

COMBINATION VALVE: A device used in some fuel systems that routes fuel vapors to a charcoal storage canister instead of venting them into the atmosphere. The valve relieves fuel tank pressure and allows fresh air into the tank as the fuel level drops to prevent a vapor lock situation.

COMPRESSION RATIO: The comparison of the total volume of the cylinder and combustion chamber with the piston at BDC and the piston at TDC.

CONDENSER: 1. An electrical device which acts to store an electrical charge, preventing voltage surges. 2. A radiator-like device in the air conditioning system in which refrigerant gas condenses into a liquid, giving off heat.

CONDUCTOR: Any material through which an electrical current can be transmitted easily.

CONTINUITY: Continuous or complete circuit. Can be checked with an ohmmeter.

COUNTERSHAFT: An intermediate shaft which is rotated by a mainshaft and transmits, in turn, that rotation to a working part.

CRANKCASE: The lower part of an engine in which the crankshaft and related parts operate.

CRANKSHAFT: The main driving shaft of an engine which receives reciprocating motion from the pistons and converts it to rotary motion.

CYLINDER: In an engine, the round hole in the engine block in which the piston(s) ride.

CYLINDER BLOCK: The main structural member of an engine in which is found the cylinders, crankshaft and other principal parts.

CYLINDER HEAD: The detachable portion of the engine, usually fastened to the top of the cylinder block and containing all or most of the combustion chambers. On overhead valve engines, it contains the valves and their operating parts. On overhead cam engines, it contains the camshaft as well.

DEAD CENTER: The extreme top or bottom of the piston stroke.

DETONATION: An unwanted explosion of the air/fuel mixture in the combustion chamber caused by excess heat and compression, advanced timing, or an overly lean mixture. Also referred to as "ping".

DIAPHRAGM: A thin, flexible wall separating two cavities, such as in a vacuum advance unit.

DIESELING: A condition in which hot spots in the combustion chamber cause the engine to run on after the key is turned off.

DIFFERENTIAL: A geared assembly which allows the transmission of motion between drive axles, giving one axle the ability to turn faster than the other.

DIODE: An electrical device that will allow current to flow in one direction only.

DISC BRAKE: A hydraulic braking assembly consisting of a brake disc, or rotor, mounted on an axle, and a caliper assembly containing, usually two brake pads which are activated by hydraulic pressure. The pads are forced against the sides of the disc, creating friction which slows the vehicle.

DISTRIBUTOR: A mechanically driven device on an engine which is responsible for electrically firing the spark plug at a predetermined point of the piston stroke.

DOWEL PIN: A pin, inserted in mating holes in two different parts allowing those parts to maintain a fixed relationship.

DRUM BRAKE: A braking system which consists of two brake shoes and one or two wheel cylinders, mounted on a fixed backing plate, and a brake drum, mounted on an axle, which revolves around the assembly.

DWELL: The rate, measured in degrees of shaft rotation, at which an electrical circuit cycles on and off.

ELECTRONIC CONTROL UNIT (ECU): Ignition module, module, amplifier or igniter. See Module for definition.

ELECTRONIC IGNITION: A system in which the timing and firing of the spark plugs is controlled by an electronic control unit, usually called a module. These systems have no points or condenser.

END-PLAY: The measured amount of axial movement in a shaft.

ENGINE: A device that converts heat into mechanical energy.

EXHAUST MANIFOLD: A set of cast passages or pipes which conduct exhaust gases from the engine.

FEELER GAUGE: A blade, usually metal, of precisely predetermined thickness, used to measure the clearance between two parts.

FIRING ORDER: The order in which combustion occurs in the cylinders of an engine. Also the order in which spark is distributed to the plugs by the distributor.

FLOODING: The presence of too much fuel in the intake manifold and combustion chamber which prevents the air/fuel mixture from firing, thereby causing a no-start situation.

FLYWHEEL: A disc shaped part bolted to the rear end of the crankshaft. Around the outer perimeter is affixed the ring gear. The starter drive engages the ring gear, turning the flywheel, which rotates the crankshaft, imparting the initial starting motion to the engine.

FOOT POUND (ft. lbs. or sometimes, ft.lb.): The amount of energy or work needed to raise an item weighing one pound, a distance of one foot.

FUSE: A protective device in a circuit which prevents circuit overload by breaking the circuit when a specific amperage is present. The device is constructed around a strip or wire of a lower amperage rating than the circuit it is designed to protect. When an amperage higher than that stamped on the fuse is present in the circuit, the strip or wire melts, opening the circuit.

GEAR RATIO: The ratio between the number of teeth on meshing gears.

GENERATOR: A device which converts mechanical energy into electrical energy.

HEAT RANGE: The measure of a spark plug's ability to dissipate heat from its firing end. The higher the heat range, the hotter the plug fires.

HUB: The center part of a wheel or gear.

HYDROCARBON (HC): Any chemical compound made up of hydrogen and carbon. A major pollutant formed by the engine as a byproduct of combustion.

HYDROMETER: An instrument used to measure the specific gravity of a solution.

INCH POUND (inch lbs.; sometimes in.lb. or in. lbs.): One twelfth of a foot pound.

INDUCTION: A means of transferring electrical energy in the form of a magnetic field. Principle used in the ignition coil to increase voltage.

INJECTOR: A device which receives metered fuel under relatively low pressure and is activated to inject the fuel into the engine under relatively high pressure at a predetermined time.

INPUT SHAFT: The shaft to which torque is applied, usually carrying the driving gear or gears.

INTAKE MANIFOLD: A casting of passages or pipes used to conduct air or a fuel/air mixture to the cylinders.

JOURNAL: The bearing surface within which a shaft operates.

KEY: A small block usually fitted in a notch between a shaft and a hub to prevent slippage of the two parts.

MANIFOLD: A casting of passages or set of pipes which connect the cylinders to an inlet or outlet source.

MANIFOLD VACUUM: Low pressure in an engine intake manifold formed just below the throttle plates. Manifold vacuum is highest at idle and drops under acceleration.

MASTER CYLINDER: The primary fluid pressurizing device in a hydraulic system. In automotive use, it is found in brake and hydraulic clutch systems and is pedal activated, either directly or, in a power brake system, through the power booster.

MODULE: Electronic control unit, amplifier or igniter of solid state or integrated design which controls the current flow in the ignition primary circuit based on input from the pick-up coil. When the module opens the primary circuit, high secondary voltage is induced in the coil.

NEEDLE BEARING: A bearing which consists of a number (usually a large number) of long, thin rollers.

OHM: (Ω) The unit used to measure the resistance of conductor-to-electrical flow. One ohm is the amount of resistance that limits current flow to one ampere in a circuit with one volt of pressure.

OHMMETER: An instrument used for measuring the resistance, in ohms, in an electrical circuit.

OUTPUT SHAFT: The shaft which transmits torque from a device, such as a transmission.

OVERDRIVE: A gear assembly which produces more shaft revolutions than that transmitted to it.

OVERHEAD CAMSHAFT (OHC): An engine configuration in which the camshaft is mounted on top of the cylinder head and operates the valve either directly or by means of rocker arms.

OVERHEAD VALVE (OHV): An engine configuration in which all of the valves are located in the cylinder head and the camshaft is located in the cylinder block. The camshaft operates the valves via lifters and pushrods.

OXIDES OF NITROGEN (NOx): Chemical compounds of nitrogen produced as a byproduct of combustion. They combine with hydrocarbons to produce smog.

OXYGEN SENSOR: Used with the feedback system to sense the presence of oxygen in the exhaust gas and signal the computer which can reference the voltage signal to an air/fuel ratio.

PINION: The smaller of two meshing gears.

PISTON RING: An open-ended ring which fits into a groove on the outer diameter of the piston. Its chief function is to form a seal between the piston and cylinder wall. Most automotive pistons have three rings: two for compression sealing; one for oil sealing.

PRELOAD: A predetermined load placed on a bearing during assembly or by adjustment.

PRIMARY CIRCUIT: The low voltage side of the ignition system which consists of the ignition switch, ballast resistor or resistance wire, bypass, coil, electronic control unit and pick-up coil as well as the connecting wires and harnesses.

PRESS FIT: The mating of two parts under pressure, due to the inner diameter of one being smaller than the outer diameter of the other, or vice versa; an interference fit.

RACE: The surface on the inner or outer ring of a bearing on which the balls, needles or rollers move.

REGULATOR: A device which maintains the amperage and/or voltage levels of a circuit at predetermined values.

RELAY: A switch which automatically opens and/or closes a circuit.

RESISTANCE: The opposition to the flow of current through a circuit or electrical device, and is measured in ohms. Resistance is equal to the voltage divided by the amperage.

RESISTOR: A device, usually made of wire, which offers a preset amount of resistance in an electrical circuit.

RING GEAR: The name given to a ring-shaped gear attached to a differential case, or affixed to a flywheel or as part of a planetary gear set.

ROLLER BEARING: A bearing made up of hardened inner and outer races between which hardened steel rollers move.

ROTOR: 1. The disc-shaped part of a disc brake assembly, upon which the brake pads bear; also called, brake disc. 2. The device mounted atop the distributor shaft, which passes current to the distributor cap tower contacts.

SECONDARY CIRCUIT: The high voltage side of the ignition system, usually above 20,000 volts. The secondary includes the ignition coil, coil wire, distributor cap and rotor, spark plug wires and spark plugs.

SENDING UNIT: A mechanical, electrical, hydraulic or electro-magnetic device which transmits information to a gauge.

SENSOR: Any device designed to measure engine operating conditions or ambient pressures and temperatures. Usually electronic in nature and designed to send a voltage signal to an on-board computer, some sensors may operate as a simple on/off switch or they may provide a variable voltage signal (like a potentiometer) as conditions or measured parameters change.

SHIM: Spacers of precise, predetermined thickness used between parts to establish a proper working relationship.

SLAVE CYLINDER: In automotive use, a device in the hydraulic clutch system which is activated by hydraulic force, disengaging the clutch.

SOLENOID: A coil used to produce a magnetic field, the effect of which is to produce work.

SPARK PLUG: A device screwed into the combustion chamber of a spark ignition engine. The basic construction is a conductive core inside of a ceramic insulator, mounted in an outer conductive base. An electrical charge from the spark plug wire travels along the conductive core and jumps a preset air gap to a grounding point or points at the end of the conductive base. The resultant spark ignites the fuel/air mixture in the combustion chamber.

SPLINES: Ridges machined or cast onto the outer diameter of a shaft or inner diameter of a bore to enable parts to mate without rotation.

TACHOMETER: A device used to measure the rotary speed of an engine, shaft, gear, etc., usually in rotations per minute.

THERMOSTAT: A valve, located in the cooling system of an engine, which is closed when cold and opens gradually in response to engine heating, controlling the temperature of the coolant and rate of coolant flow.

TOP DEAD CENTER (TDC): The point at which the piston reaches the top of its travel on the compression stroke.

TORQUE: The twisting force applied to an object.

TORQUE CONVERTER: A turbine used to transmit power from a driving member to a driven member via hydraulic action, providing changes in drive ratio and torque. In automotive use, it links the driveplate at the rear of the engine to the automatic transmission.

TRANSDUCER: A device used to change a force into an electrical signal.

TRANSISTOR: A semi-conductor component which can be actuated by a small voltage to perform an electrical switching function.

TUNE-UP: A regular maintenance function, usually associated with the replacement and adjustment of parts and components in the electrical and fuel systems of a vehicle for the purpose of attaining optimum performance.

TURBOCHARGER: An exhaust driven pump which compresses intake air and forces it into the combustion chambers at higher than atmospheric pressures. The increased air pressure allows more fuel to be burned and results in increased horsepower being produced.

VACUUM ADVANCE: A device which advances the ignition timing in response to increased engine vacuum.

VACUUM GAUGE: An instrument used to measure the presence of vacuum in a chamber.

VALVE: A device which control the pressure, direction of flow or rate of flow of a liquid or gas.

VALVE CLEARANCE: The measured gap between the end of the valve stem and the rocker arm, cam lobe or follower that activates the valve.

VISCOSITY: The rating of a liquid's internal resistance to flow.

VOLTMETER: An instrument used for measuring electrical force in units called volts. Voltmeters are always connected parallel with the circuit being tested.

WHEEL CYLINDER: Found in the automotive drum brake assembly, it is a device, actuated by hydraulic pressure, which, through internal pistons, pushes the brake shoes outward against the drums.

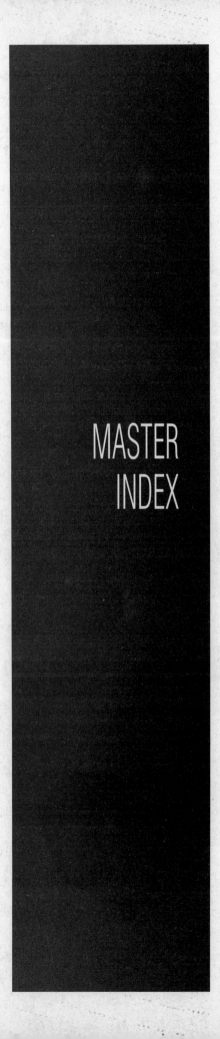

MASTER INDEX